INSIDERS' GUIDE® SERIES

D0733264

# INSIDERS' GUIDE® TO

# NORTH CAROLINA'S MOUNTAINS

## Including Asheville, Biltmore Estate, Cherokee, and the Blue Ridge Parkway

### TENTH EDITION

## CONSTANCE E. RICHARDS AND KENNETH L. RICHARDS

**INSIDERS'** GUIDE

GUILFORD, CONNECTICUT

AN IMPRINT OF GLOBE PEQUOT PRESS

All the information in this guidebook is subject to change. We recommend that you call ahead to obtain current information before traveling.

To buy books in quantity for corporate use
or incentives, call **(800) 962–0973**
or e-mail **premiums@GlobePequot.com.**

# INSIDERS' GUIDE ®

Copyright © 2010 by Morris Book Publishing, LLC

ALL RIGHTS RESERVED. No part of this book may be reproduced or transmitted in any form by any means, electronic or mechanical, including photocopying and recording, or by any information storage and retrieval system, except as may be expressly permitted in writing from the publisher. Requests for permission should be addressed to Globe Pequot Press, Attn: Rights and Permissions Department, P.O. Box 480, Guilford, CT 06437.

Insiders' Guide is a registered trademark of Morris Book Publishing, LLC.

Editor: Amy Lyons
Project editor: Lynn Zelem
Layout: Kevin Mak
Text Design: Sheryl Kober
Maps created by XNR Productions, Inc. © Morris Book Publishing, LLC

ISSN 1525-8076
ISBN 978-0-7627-5697-1

Printed in the United States of America
10 9 8 7 6 5 4 3 2 1

# CONTENTS

**Directory of Maps**

# ABOUT THE AUTHORS

**Constance E. Richards** is a journalist, travel writer, and editor based in Asheville, North Carolina. She grew up in Europe, where her American parents worked as educators for 25 years. A graduate of Georgetown University, Constance studied international relations and majored in Russian and German, with a concentration in Russian Area Studies.

This ultimately led her to move to Russia, after living in Berlin during a post-graduate internship. In Moscow she began her career working for ABC News, but moved into the field of print journalism, where she reported for *Time* magazine, *LIFE*, *People*, and Time-Life Books. As a foreign correspondent in Russia just shy of seven years, she also wrote for *Moscow* magazine, the *Moscow Times*, the *London Daily Telegraph*, *Sports Illustrated*, *Fortune*, and *Conde Nast Traveler*, among other publications.

Upon returning to the United States she continued to contribute to *Time*, *People*, and Reuters News Agency, and now writes for a number of national magazines, the *New York Times*, *Washington Flyer* magazine, *GO* magazine, and other airline publications, as well as authoring *Artful Asheville—Along the Urban Trail* (J. F. Enterprises, 2002), *Bloom's Literary Places: St. Petersburg* (Chelsea Publishing, 2005), *Creative Giftwraps* (Lark Books, 2000), and *Making Books and Journals* (Lark Books, 1998). She has been an arts columnist and restaurant reviewer, and is culinary editor for *WNC* magazine.

**Kenneth L. Richards** entered the Big Ivy Community of Buncombe County in Western North Carolina in the early 1960s. He and his wife, Irene Dillingham Richards, were married in Switzerland after first meeting in London. Irene is from Dillingham, North Carolina, in the Big Ivy Community.

For 25 years they were involved with international education in Europe. They have worked as school admininstrators, university teachers, authors, wine masters, conference organizers, and lecturers throughout Europe. They also published the journal *Education World*.

The Richardses conducted the first public wine-tasting in Asheville in 1963 in the former Battery Park Hotel. Since then, they have opened avenues in wine education as a historic venue at various universities. Their most recent publication is *The Family Named Dillingham: 375 Years in America*. It was coauthored with their colleague and cousin, Nancy Dillingham.

Ken has written about wine, food, and opera for numerous European and American publications. He was director of education at Biltmore Estate and is considered by the *Asheville Citizen-Times* entertainment editor Tony Kiss to be "Asheville's Bon Vivant." He is former North Carolina State Coordinator for Sister Cities International and is a popular lecturer and tour guide.

# ACKNOWLEDGMENTS

Thank you to the chambers of commerce and visitor centers of the areas we cover in these mountains for help in providing research information. Thank you to Dave Tomsky and Craig Distl, two consummate professionals, who always keep me "in the know" of what's happening around the mountains. A very special thank you and much love to my parents, Irene Dillingham Richards and Ken Richards, for instilling in me a love of travel at a very young age, as well as an understanding that all places can be delightful and interesting if you just look. And *spasibochka* to VB for keeping me company through many late-night deadlines and repeated trips through the winding roads and small towns of these *gori*.

—Constance E. Richards

There are many to thank: A man who knows these mountains like the back of his hand is my swimming partner, Jerry Arnold. He has provided good steerage. Frieda Husky, Eddie Swimmer, and Vice Chief of the Eastern Band of the Cherokee nation, Larry Blythe, have opened the world to us of the reality of our first Americans. Rick Lutovsky of the Asheville Area Chamber of Commerce and his staff, and Dianna Jackson Pearce of the Convention and Visitors Bureau, have provided insight in the hospitality field. Oscar Wong has always welcomed our inquiries concerning the microbreweries of the region. His Highland Brewing Company was among the first in the area.

Deb Bowman and her staff at Accents on Asheville and Donna Edmonds with Young Tours and her staff have provided touring opportunities and utilization of "insiders" in the strategies of tour planning for the thousands they host in Western North Carolina. A special thanks to the Asheville Historic Trolley Tours and to Greyline Trolley Tours of Asheville for inviting me to develop their touring programs. Benjamin Long IV and the folks at Montreat College, and the Chapel of the Prodigal, also need recognition and thanks for permitting me the opportunity to bring the multitudes to see the fresco art there. Penn Dameron, former executive director of the Blue Ridge National Heritage Area, and the committee supporting the Benjamin Long IV Fresco Trail of North Carolina have been most generous in permitting us to include that information in this book. Of further delight is to have a working relationship with the folks at Biltmore Estate who make this book available at their various points of sale.

I do wish to thank those at the Farmer's Market of Western North Carolina who welcome our guests and provide us with support in our endeavors. A special thanks to all those who have toured these mountains with me. Your comments have been enriching and helpful.

I must always be grateful to my coauthor, my daughter Constance, for sharing this opportunity. She has given me a "Father's Day" for life. And to my wife Irene, in addition to all you are, you opened the world and the people of these mountains to me. In proofing all I do, you live up to your legacy of . . . being my "refiner." I love you both.

To our readers, we wish you a good journey.

—Kenneth L. Richards

**North Carolina's Mountains**

**Northern Mountains**

**Central Mountains**

**Southern Mountains**

# PREFACE

We've covered a lot of ground since the first year this guide was published. High adventure unites with the serenity of the majestic Appalachian Mountains in North Carolina's high country. This might be reason enough to journey into the ancient land of the Cherokee, yet what draws people to these mountains again and again is manifold.

Nature, tradition, and culture merge in a beautiful display of mountain living in the westernmost part of the state. Diversity is a feature that has existed since early on, and continues as a catchphrase that rings true still today. The last decade has seen the greatest influx of new residents since the last turn of the century. And it's easy to see why.

Visiting great works of art, like Benjamin Long's frescoes, found throughout the area, is as popular as collecting clay pottery and hand-bound brooms. Asheville's tony downtown galleries and edgy River Arts District of over 40 artists' studios offers a juxtaposition of styles rarely found in a town of its size.

The mountains produce artisans—some self-taught, others with training from the respected Penland School of Arts and the John C. Campbell Folk School—of the highest caliber. Smaller schools and community colleges in the area do the same.

Dining in the North Carolina mountains also reaches the level of high artistry. From the best country cooking served up family style in old farmhouses or inns, to four-diamond restaurants in an urban setting, food plays an important role in these environs.

The scenic highways and byways wending through these parts make driving from point A to point B an adventure unto itself. Stately poplar trees rise from the valley floor, as do sourwoods, maples, oaks, gum trees, dogwoods, Fraser fir, and a dozen other species. Mountain laurel, rhododendron, azaleas, blue bells, and lady slippers are only some of the flora that dot mountain roads.

Apple orchards abound on the road from Hendersonville to Lake Lure and Chimney Rock. Great natural wonders such as the Linville Caverns, waterfalls throughout the mountains, and the "chimney" rock itself, can be as alluring as our great museums and manmade marvels, such as the grand chateau on the Biltmore Estate and St. Lawrence Basilica in Asheville.

There's nothing higher than Mount Mitchell in the eastern United States. The Great Smoky Mountains lie to the 6,684-foot peak's southwest. Northeast, sweeping into North Carolina, is the Blue Ridge of Virginia. The vistas offer views of numerous lakes in the valley below, and sometimes even a cloud or two.

The great elk that once populated the mountains have returned to the southern Appalachians via a conservation program in the Cataloochee area. More elusive, however, are the black bear that roam these parts, although some residents of Asheville and Black Mountain note nighttime visits to their trash barrels from time to time.

Clean industry has emerged as a growing entity within the agricultural and aquacultural fields here, turning tobacco crops into vinifera grape vineyards in support of the growing number of wineries in North Carolina. In Candler, Dick Jennings and his daughter develop trout farms for their Sunburst Trout Caviar, now a lead seller in New York and elsewhere. International and national companies exist here as well: Volvo of North America, Blue Ridge Paper Mill, Google, and others.

Institutions of higher education, such as the unique Warren Wilson College, Montreat College, Mars Hill College, Appalachian State University, Brevard College, Western Carolina University, and the University of North Carolina in Asheville, among others, continue to rank high on national lists.

A music camp swells with talented young musicians at Brevard Music Center all summer long, delighting crowds with concerts ranging from symphonic and opera to jazz and rock. The Swannanoa Gathering jives to a different tune—three weeks of classes and concerts for traditional mountain music, Bluegrass, and Old Time. The twice-yearly LEAF (Lake Eden Arts Festival) in Black Mountain introduces days of traditional and world music to the area.

And finally, as the song goes: "nothing could be finer than to be in Carolina . . ." whether traveling by car, bike, horse, kayak, or on foot in summer, spring, autumn, or winter. Once you're here, you'll want to stay—and increasingly, many have. With this the tenth edition of the Insiders' Guide to our mountains, we hope to lead you to all the right places and experiences for cherished memories for years to come.

# HOW TO USE THIS BOOK

You will often see us refer to this area as Western North Carolina. The WNC moniker refers to the mountains of North Carolina and is used interchangeably, actually more so, locally. Because the book covers such a large area, we have divided Western North Carolina into the following three sections in general: the Northern Mountains, Central Mountains, and Southern Mountains. While counties aren't usually important to travelers, they are a major *local* identifier, and where needed, we've listed the counties alphabetically. Under those county headings, we've again put most listings in alphabetical order. But in this latest edition we also highlight some of the larger towns as starting points for your journey.

A good place to begin this book is with the Area Overview and History chapter. From there you can go to regions or subjects that specifically interest you. That said, today there is so much information available on the Internet, and sometimes places change hands more quickly than we can update this book, so you'll find here a true guide with historical and practical information and entries of tried-and-true places, events, and activities that we recommend. We encourage you to consult local newspapers and magazines (noted in our Relocation chapter) for up-to-the-minute listings.

Speaking of relocation, are you moving to the Western North Carolina region or already live here? Be sure to check out the blue-tabbed pages at the back of the book, where you will find the **Living Here** appendix that offers chapters on relocation, retirement, health care and education.

We've included maps so you can orient yourself to each region. Be alert to the fact that place names can be confusing based on multiple spellings and multiple locations. One example is that of the *town* of Cherokee is on the Cherokee Indian "Reservation" (the Qualla Boundary, actually) in the northwestern part of the state in Jackson and Swain Counties, while the *county* of Cherokee is some miles away in the far reaches of southwest North Carolina (its county seat is Murphy). They are two entirely separate entities and areas.

Likewise, you will see the same name applied to wholly different locations or geographical formations. For example, in Clay County the name Tusquitee is given to a bald, a creek, a community, and a chain of mountains.

Native American names can also present a problem: On some maps you'll find a river in Jackson County spelled Tuckasegee. On other maps it is spelled Tuckaseigee. We've chosen the former version. Likewise, some maps list a Jackson County lake as Lake Glenville; others call it Lake Thorpe.

The Cherokee, descendants of those native inhabitants who developed a culture in these mountains over time, provide a rich heritage of legends and lore. We have included some of these materials throughout this book.

Listed in "Close-up" boxes throughout this Insiders' Guide are some of the classic scenic views. Have your camera ready and find your own. "Close-ups" also allow us to feature a place, an event, or a person in greater depth.

Scattered throughout the book are Insiders' tips, which offer quick insights and handy information.

With population movements, new roads and highways, relocating industries, and other factors of our modern world, change is evident everywhere. Nothing stays the same but the great and rugged peaks of this oldest mountain range in the world.

# AREA OVERVIEW AND HISTORY

Join us on a journey through mossy coves and hollows, over wildflower-studded pasture lands and dewy forest trails, past gurgling mountain streams and mellifluous waterfalls, into the green valleys and onto the misty blue ridges that comprise this glorious mountain range. Too much? Well you'll be waxing poetic as soon as you experience this nature in its fullest. Let your clock stand still for a moment and revel in the rejuvenating air, water, and earth of North Carolina's mountains.

Each county in Western North Carolina bears its own individual geographical features, history, and lifestyle. Each major town deserves a chapter, from cultural, educational, and medical centers like Asheville and Boone to the smaller pastoral settlements of Valle Crucis and Lake Lure.

In this chapter we offer "thumbnail sketches" of the area's counties and their largest population centers, as well as notable towns nearby. (We highlight the largest towns in parentheses.) After reading even more about each of the counties under their headings in the more specialized chapters that follow, we trust you will be sufficiently inspired to come out here to explore and discover these mountain enclaves for yourself.

## NORTHERN MOUNTAINS

### Alleghany County (Sparta)

Tucked up against the border of Virginia is rural Alleghany County, the northernmost of North Carolina's mountain counties. Only 230 square miles, Alleghany is one of the smallest counties in the state. It was once known as "the lost province," and for good reason, because it can only be reached by winding two-lane roads. Snow is not uncommon here, but the elevation, which ranges from 2,500 to 4,000 feet, does not sustain the winter sports more common in neighboring counties.

Indian hunters roamed this land thousands of years ago, but it was the ruggedly independent Scotch-Irish, English, and German pioneers who settled these hills and valleys in the late 1700s. The county was officially established in 1859 from parts of the surrounding counties of Ashe, Surry, and Wilkes. The name Alleghany is derived from the Indian word for "fine stream,"

which is fitting for an area nourished by the New River, one of the oldest rivers in the world. According to historians, this ancient river was named by surveyor Peter Jefferson, Thomas's father, who was surprised to find another "new" river behind the mountains.

The geographic remoteness of this county is more a blessing than a hindrance, for Alleghany County's natural isolation has preserved the rural America of more than 30 years ago. The pace is gentler in this small county of some 11,000 residents. Many in Alleghany County still live on family land that has been handed down for generations. And in tiny Sparta, the county seat with a population of only 2,000, Main Street is not just a location but an atmosphere.

Seven percent of the county's labor force works in agriculture-related businesses, such as tobacco, beef cattle, corn, and hay. Christmas tree production is the fastest growing farm industry in the county. Economic development is expected to continue in Alleghany County, especially with the improvement of the county's roads.

## Christmas Tree Country

Western North Carolina is Christmas tree country. Families have been farming Christmas trees here for generations. The Fraser fir is a dark green color and one of the most desirable trees on the market. Even heavy ornaments can be hung from its strong boughs. The silvery undersides of the soft needles are pleasant to the touch, and the tree retains them throughout the holiday season. The white pine is also an excellent Christmas tree. The White House has called upon North Carolina mountain tree farmers for its official tree at least nine times.

Just a few minutes to the east is the Blue Ridge Parkway, which had its historical beginning in 1935 at nearby Cumberland Knob and forms some 30 miles of the eastern boundary of the county. Then drive a little farther south on the parkway to Doughton Park, with its network of hiking trails and camping facilities. The easily accessible New River, well known among canoeing enthusiasts, provides easy and inexpensive opportunities for outdoor recreation.

For more information contact the Alleghany County Chamber of Commerce, P.O. Box 1237, Sparta 28675; (336) 372-5473, (800) 372-5473; www.sparta-nc.com.

## Ashe County (Jefferson)

Ashe County, the extreme northwestern mountain county bordered by Tennessee and Virginia, is marked by the curling length of the New River, one of this country's few north-flowing rivers. The New River's pervasive presence in Ashe is responsible for much of the unique character of this remote North Carolina county. Like its eastern neighbor Alleghany, Ashe County has enjoyed its isolation, allowing it to retain the more relaxed flavor of yesteryear.

Shawnee, Creek, and Cherokee hunters preceded European settlers, who arrived here in the 1750s, erecting their first permanent settlement in 1771 along Helton Creek. Ashe County's early settlers were part of the famous contingent of "overmountain men" who fought the decisive battle of King's Mountain during the Revolutionary War. By 1799 these lands were formally organized as a county and named for the Revolutionary patriot and North Carolina governor, Samuel Ashe.

The county seat was established at Jeffersonton in 1803. The town, named for Thomas Jefferson, is known today as Jefferson and lies 1 mile east of West Jefferson. The separately incorporated town of West Jefferson began as a lumber industry village when the railroad made its way here in 1914. Other villages sprang up along the path of the growing rail service. But the decline of the railroad in the decades after World War I had a detrimental effect on rural counties such as Ashe, and the ultimate termination of the county's rail service in 1927 served to isolate the area economically as well as physically.

The 1990s, however, proved to be a time of growth. A combination of Christmas tree farms, golf, and tourism began the revitalization. Ashe's pristine landscape and less-complicated lifestyle also attract new blood, particularly retirees. The county is actively seeking industrial growth, beckoning business with vastly improved and widened county roads.

The prominence of the New River in Ashe County and New River State Park make canoeing and camping popular activities in the area. Mount Jefferson, at an altitude of 4,683 feet, rises majestically out of a 474-acre state park, filled with easy-to-moderate hiking trails abundant with wildflowers. A cave near the top of the mountain is said to have sheltered runaway slaves during the Civil War. The Churches of the Frescoes in West Jefferson and Glendale Springs (see our Arts and Culture chapter) have gained national attention and brought visitors to the remote hilltops of Ashe County.

With only 10 percent of the county population of 24,400 living in the towns of Jefferson and West Jefferson, Ashe County is still largely rural. Villages cluster at crossroads, and individual farms crown the hillsides. Its proximity to bustling Boone, just 30 minutes away, makes Ashe County an appealing destination for the city person with a country heart.

For more information contact the Ashe County Chamber of Commerce, P.O. Box 31, West Jefferson 28694; (336) 246-9550; (888) 343-2743; www.ashechamber.com.

**i** You can see three states from Mount Jefferson in Ashe County. This vantage point is especially breathtaking at sunset. Take U.S. Highway 221 from Jefferson, turning onto SR 1152, and drive all the way to the top to the parking area. The Summit Trail is just a fraction of a mile from the highest point on Mount Jefferson.

## Avery County (Banner Elk)

Avery County, with a population of roughly 17,900 today, is a curious mix of peaceful rural life and sophisticated tourism. Settlement came slowly to this rugged place. Native Americans and mountain men alike hunted the land, yet few pioneers chose to make these peaks their home. One who did was the locally well-known settler William Linville, who came with his sons in 1766 only to be slain by hostile Indians near the spectacular waterfall and gorge that now bear his name.

This high mountain land is harsh in winter, but its clear air and cool summer temperatures attracted tourists as early as the 1870s. Boarding houses opened in Banner Elk to serve the seasonal visitors, and in 1891 the town of Linville was founded as a summer community for the wealthy. Roads continued to develop around the advancing railroad spurs that pushed through the area, opening remote ridges and valleys. Even so, the twists and turns of the topography left pockets of rural settlement untouched. It was not until 1911 that Avery County, named

for Revolutionary patriot Waightstill Avery, was officially formed, making it the newest and one of the smallest counties in North Carolina (only 247 square miles). Newland is the county seat.

Waightstill Avery was a lawyer in peacetime. In one heated debate with Andrew Jackson, these two combatants elected to settle their differences with a duel. A quirk of the law in North Carolina read that one could make a challenge, but the duel could not be fought within the boundaries of the state. So at sunrise on the selected morning, the men met on the field of valor in Jonesborough, Tennessee, just over the state line. Even stranger, neither wished to harm the other. Thus they fired their dueling pistols into the air, shook hands, and had a beaker of whiskey to celebrate their newborn friendship. Jackson even offered a gift to Avery. The whole problem had arisen from the so-called Bacon Law. Wrapped like a book, the package contained a slab of bacon.

Many visitors, now lowland residents, have returned for generations and maintain beautiful second homes in the exclusive areas of Grandfather Mountain, Elk River, and Linville Ridge. Banner Elk, home of Lees-McRae College and the famous Woolly Worm Festival, is also a popular skiing and golf resort community. Beech Mountain, the mile-high winter sport community, straddles Avery and neighboring Watauga Counties. These two communities are the more populated, tourism-driven parts of Avery County, while outlying areas of rural farmland continue much as they were early in the century.

Tiny Crossnore, in southern Avery County, was settled in 1833 and incorporated in 1925. Known for the Crossnore School established in 1911 to educate mountain children, this community is a pleasant reminder of early Western North Carolina town life. The county has a strong tradition in crafts, ranging from pottery and quilts to jewelry and furniture. Today Avery County also boasts the South's highest ski slopes, nine major golf resorts (public and private), and a number of natural landmarks.

The only notable changes in the rural landscape of Avery County are the geometric patterns of green that cover the hills around Linville, a sign of Avery County's successful Christmas tree industry, in which over 900 families are active.

For more information contact the Avery County Chamber of Commerce, 4501 Tyncastle Hwy, Unit #2, Banner Elk 28604, (800) 972-2183, www.averycounty.com; or the Beech Mountain Chamber of Commerce at (828) 387-9283, www.beechmtn.com.

---

## "Tar Heels"

The "Old North State" is self-descriptive. "Tar Heels" is another matter. Some versions have the term birthed during the Revolutionary War at the battle of King's Mountain. Others claim that it derives from the tar pits found in the eastern part of the state.

Those in Western North Carolina give credit to Zeb Vance, who claimed that his North Carolina troops had "stick-to-itiveness" during the War Between the States. He once chided Virginians of the Grand Army, saying that if they had had "Tar on your heels, you would have stuck yesterday in the fight, instead of running."

---

## Madison County (Mars Hill)

The rugged terrain of this western county, bisected by the powerful French Broad River, reflects the self-reliant spirit of the local folk and their industrious predecessors.

Madison County lies northwest of Buncombe County, bordered by Haywood and Yancey Counties and the state of Tennessee. Formed in 1851 from parts of Buncombe and Yancey Counties, Madison County is named for America's fourth president, James Madison. The county is largely rural and has a population of about 20,500, with 48 percent of that population living on farms (the

highest percentage in the state). Small towns in the area are Mars Hill, Hot Springs, and Marshall, the county seat.

Agriculture—wheat, cattle, corn, and tobacco farming—is still the primary source of income here, but some small manufacturing has also moved into the county. In the last 25 years, an increasing number of artisans and craftspeople have made Madison County home, finding the solitude of the county's heavily wooded mountains conducive to their work. After 11 years of planning and construction, I-26 opened a corridor through Madison County in 2003, connecting South Carolina to the Ohio Valley.

Mars Hill, the county's largest town, lies 20 minutes northwest of Asheville. As the home of Baptist-affiliated Mars Hill College, it is defined both by its scholastic roots and by the rugged individualism of Madison County's heritage. Attractive old brick storefronts face Main Street, a two-lane artery so narrow you could almost jump over it. Although the town remains pretty much as it was 50 years ago, the infusion of newcomers is increasing. Being a college town, the ubiquitous coffeehouse, pizza joint, and diner also compose the tidy downtown. Mars Hill is home to the Rural Life Museum and the Southern Appalachian Repertory Theater, and there is skiing nearby at Wolf Laurel. Still, this remains a charming old-fashioned hamlet that is kept dynamic by the presence of Mars Hill College.

Marshall, about 15 minutes west of Mars Hill, straddles the narrow hillsides cut by the French Broad River. Established around 1851, this town is much as it was at the turn of the 20th century. The river has seen to that. Its ebb and flow, and frequent overflows, seem to have suspended the city in time—this is Marshall's charm. Homes hug the hillsides surrounding the town. The cupola-topped courthouse, designed by Richard Sharp Smith of Biltmore Estate fame, commands a position at a crossroads within walking distance of the river. Marshall's arts community is also thriving, with artisans moving to the area and setting up home studios, often participating in downtown art markets at the Madison County Arts Council.

As early as the 1830s, Hot Springs was host to wealthy visitors in search of the healing powers of its springs. A number of hotels, taverns, and boardinghouses sprang up, only to fade away in later years. Today the town is experiencing a revival as travelers, day-trippers, retirees, and summer residents converge on the hills and settle into old hotels that are now quaint bed-and-breakfast inns. The Hot Springs Spa has also been reborn (see our Attractions chapter). Easy access to the French Broad River makes white-water rafting an important part of the town's tourist economy. And with the Appalachian Trail winding through town, Hot Springs is a popular respite for weary hikers.

For more information contact the Madison County Visitor Center, P.O. Box 1527, Mars Hill 28754; (828) 680-9031, (877) 262-3476; www .madisoncounty-nc.com; www.visitmadisoncounty .com.

## Mitchell County (Spruce Pine)

Mitchell County was formed in 1861 from portions of five counties: Yancey, Burke, Caldwell, McDowell, and Watauga. With a population of some 16,000 today, this county of only 220 square miles was named in honor of Dr. Elisha Mitchell, explorer of famed Mount Mitchell, the highest peak east of the Mississippi. The county is bordered by Tennessee and Avery, Yancey, and McDowell counties. Mining of quartz, feldspar, and mica are major industries here. In fact the Spruce Pine Mining District is recognized the world over for its ultrapure quartz, which is vital to the computer industry. Agricultural products such as tobacco, corn, apples, and more recently Christmas trees are also important in the county.

Spruce Pine is the largest town in the county with a population close to 3,000. Bakersville, the county seat, is surrounded by the long-established communities of Rock Creek, Cane Creek, Mine Creek, and Toe Cane. These tiny towns, nestled in the twisting mountain coves of Mitchell County, are home to generations of families. The origins of other delightfully named hamlets such as Loafer's Glory, Relief, Ledger, Bandana, and Altapass are worthy of note. Loafer's Glory, about 3 miles north of Bakersville on Highway 226, was christened by the wives of the community after they observed the unabashed loitering of their men on the front porch of the community store. Relief is named for a once-popular cure-all tonic, Dr. Hart's Relief, which was sold in the community at Squire Peterson's Store around 1870. No doubt the popularity of the tonic came from the large volume of alcohol it contained. The community of Ledger was named for the ledger book sent to Washington, D.C., by community residents who were trying to establish the amount of mail passing through the area and their need for a local post office. The railroad played a part in naming two Mitchell County hamlets: Bandana got its name from the bandana a railroad brakeman used to locate a proper site for a railroad station. The Clinchfield Railroad, passing over these mountains from Tennessee, reached its highest point at the aptly named community of Altapass before heading down the mountain.

The proliferation of gem mines in Mitchell County has long made this county popular with rock hounds. The North Carolina Museum of Minerals is just off the Blue Ridge Parkway (see our chapter on Rockhounding). Mitchell County is also home to the Penland School of Crafts. Sitting atop a mountain ridge, this internationally acclaimed school of the arts draws talented craftspeople and artists from all over the world (see our Mountain Crafts chapter).

For more information contact the Mitchell County Chamber of Commerce, Route 1, P.O. Box 796, Spruce Pine 28777; (828) 765-9483, (800) 227-3912; www.mitchell-county.com.

## Watauga County (Boone)

This county of 42,700 lies at the heart of North Carolina's high country. Formed in 1849, Watauga's 320 square miles are bordered by Tennessee and Avery, Ashe, Wilkes, and Caldwell counties. It was named for the Watauga River, which rises near Grandfather Mountain and flows north into Tennessee, where it converges with the Holston River. Watauga is an Indian word for "beautiful water."

An early emphasis on education led to the development of Watauga County as a center of higher education. The county was largely rural until 1899, when the Dougherty brothers founded the Watauga Academy in Boone, the forerunner of Appalachian State University. Part of the University of North Carolina system, ASU plays an important role in the growth of the area, with thriving Boone, the county seat, at its heart. Boone's permanent resident population of 13,330 doubles with the addition of the students and swells even more with the arrival of tourists throughout the year. The cultural base of the university and the town's tourist-geared entertainment offer something for everyone.

Boone has become a magnet for tourism and related industries. Its many restaurants, for example, have turned the city into a dining destination. The climate is suited for both winter and summer sports, with golf and skiing the prime diversions in the county. Resorts such as Hound Ears, Hawksnest, Seven Devils, and Ski Beech (partially in Avery County) offer a multitude of recreation options. And potters, weavers, painters, storytellers, traditional mountain musicians, actors, and artisans fill the area with creative energy.

Blowing Rock, 15 minutes south of Boone, is a picturesque mountain town perched on a ridge overlooking the John's River Gorge. The town takes its name from the rock formation over the gorge that creates an unusual current of air spiraling up from the valley below. The view from the Blowing Rock is breathtaking, as is the scenery from nearly every vantage point in town. Charming specialty stores and fine restaurants line Main Street, and excellent bed-and-breakfast inns are scattered along Blowing Rock's side streets, just a few steps from downtown. You can walk to almost everything here, including the town square, which is the scene of concerts and art shows in summer. Tourism is important to Blowing Rock, so the town leadership is working to retain its villagelike character.

Foscoe, on Highway 105 leading into Boone, has become known for its selection of craft and antiques shops. The community is blessed with a glorious view of Grandfather Mountain in nearby Avery County.

Valle Crucis, in central Watauga County, is also off Highway 105 at the junction of Dutch Creek and the Watauga River. Established as an Episcopal mission in 1842, it retains a largely rural character and has become a popular site for summer homes, unique restaurants, renowned inns, and unusual shopping.

Despite the busy pace of the tourist meccas, Watauga County offers plenty of quiet countryside. Heading toward Tennessee you can see some of the most scenic farmland in Western North Carolina. U.S. Highway 321 winds up, down, and around hillsides studded with craggy rocks and threaded with lazy, meandering creeks.

For more information contact the Boone Area Chamber of Commerce and Convention & Visitors Bureau, 208 Howard St., Boone 28607, (828) 264-2225, (800) 852-9506, www.visit boonenc.com; High Country Host, 1700 Blowing Rock Rd., Boone 28607, (828) 264-1299, (800) 438-7500, www.highcountryhost.com; or Blowing Rock Chamber of Commerce, P.O. Box 406, Blowing Rock 28605, (828) 295-7851, www.blowing rock.com.

## Yancey County (Burnsville)

Indians and mountaineers played vital parts in the development of Yancey County. The area was a thoroughfare for Cherokee Indians who roamed these rich hunting grounds. But the path of the Scotch-Irish settlers seeking a new country also led to these mountains and the fertile valleys, which are fed by Yancey's Cane and South Toe Rivers. Land grants for former Cherokee lands were awarded to hardy pioneers as early as 1777. In 1797 John Gray Blount was awarded a blanket charter for land that eventually became Yancey County. Traders, entrepreneurs, and new settlers began to arrive. The new county, formed in 1833, soon became one of the busiest and most prosperous in the region. Burnsville, also established in 1833, had long been a stage stop.

Prosperity blossomed until the Civil War left its mark both emotionally and economically. The Scotch-Irish settlers who dominated the area had no use for a war they viewed as based on slavery, a practice that was little heard of in the hard existence of most mountain families. And the heavy taxes and conscription imposed by the government to finance the war were burdens for Yancey's citizenry. The discord and hard times resulted in the formation of new counties: Madison, Mitchell, and the area that later became Avery County, leaving Yancey County with 311 square miles by the war's end.

The pioneer heritage of Yancey County has been preserved in Burnsville, a charming town that is a fine illustration of a bygone era. The county's largest community and county seat, Burnsville is anchored by a classic town square with a statue in honor of its namesake, Captain Otway Burns, a privateer during the War of 1812 and also a member of the North Carolina General Assembly. Life in the town still revolves around the square, and homes are nestled on the mountains rising on one side. A visit to coastal North Carolina in Beaufort will reveal many legends about Otway Burns; he is also buried there.

Agriculture—tobacco, corn, dairy products, and cultivated berries—still plays a vital part in the county's economy, as it did in pioneer times. Ornamental shrubs and Christmas tree production have also gained a hold. Mining has always been important here: The excavation of mica and feldspar and sand and gravel operations are found in the northern part of Yancey County, near Mitchell County.

Increasing numbers of retirees are settling here, and premier golf communities are springing up. The county has a population of roughly 18,000. The rich traditional local arts heritage has always drawn creative people, nurtured by the support of the dynamic Toe River Arts Council. The oldest summer stock playhouse in North Carolina—over 50 years old—is located in Burnsville.

Yancey County is blessed with seasonal changes and a topography that lends itself to outdoor recreation. The presence of the South Toe and Cane Rivers makes camping, tubing, canoeing, and kayaking easily accessible. The nearby Nolichucky River, flowing into Tennessee, is extremely popular with white-water enthusiasts. Hiking is favored due to the county's

network of some 100 miles of trails of varying degrees of difficulty. The Black Mountain Range in Yancey County features Mount Mitchell, at 6,684 feet the highest peak east of the Mississippi. You can reach this majestic peak from the Blue Ridge Parkway, which runs the length of Western North Carolina's mountains.

For more information contact the Yancey County Chamber of Commerce, 106 West Main, Burnsville 28714; (828) 682-7413, (800) 948-1632; www.yanceychamber.com.

**i** Mount Mitchell in Yancey County is the highest peak in the eastern United States at 6,684 feet. Take Highway 128, off the Blue Ridge Parkway at milepost 355.4. On a clear day the observation tower at the top of the mountain affords a 70-mile view.

# CENTRAL MOUNTAINS

## Buncombe County (Asheville)

Sitting high on a plateau surrounded by mountains, Buncombe County, population an estimated 229,000, has enjoyed a history of good fortune due to its position as a geographical crossroads. Today's appeal and growth of this city and its suburbs echoes the original boomtown era of the late 1880s. Development historically follows the path of primary water sources, and so it did here along the mighty French Broad River.

Trade with the Cherokee Indians was established as early as 1673 along the well-worn Indian paths that crossed at the site of present-day Asheville. The natural riches of the region and the flow of commerce soon drew large numbers of settlers. Samuel W. Davidson and his family were the first to settle in the region in 1784, along Christian Creek in the Swannanoa Valley. Trade continued to boom, and the county was officially formed in 1791. The business of government brought in scores of new settlers, traders, speculators, and adventurers. With this influx of new citizens, the well-traveled Indian paths soon became thoroughfares for traders and stock drovers from Kentucky and Tennessee moving through the French Broad Valley on their way to the open markets in South Carolina. The construction of the Buncombe Turnpike from 1824 to 1828 further secured this steady stream of trade.

From the early 1800s to 1880, Buncombe County settled into a period of bucolic bliss. Recovery from the Civil War was slow, and it was not until completion of the railroad in 1880 that the county came into its own. The railroads brought the moneyed class, which was attracted by the healthful climate, crisp mountain air, and sparkling social atmosphere. One young visitor, George Vanderbilt, vowed to return, and when he did he changed the county forever. After purchasing 125,000 acres, he set about building a castle. The construction of his Biltmore Estate in 1895 brought a legion of artists and craftspeople whose legacy remains as an influence on the area's architecture.

The 1920s were Buncombe County's boom time. The architectural character of Asheville, the county seat, was formed during these glory days, giving it the unique cosmopolitan flavor that continues to attract visitors as well as new residents. In particular, the demographic of young professionals and young families moving to the area has increased in the past decade. The city of roughly 78,000 and growing retains a small-town mountain charm wrapped in big-city sophistication that has not gone unnoticed by national and international travel media, which frequently include Asheville in top-ten listings and feature the town as a premier travel destination. The noted American novelist Thomas Wolfe was born here, bringing his native city unwelcome notoriety, according to Ashevillians, when he wrote of it in his coming-of-age novel, *Look Homeward, Angel.*

Downtown Asheville boasts the finest collection of art deco buildings this side of Miami Beach, and restoration of these old gems is booming. Pack Square, historically central to the city, and Haywood Street form the cultural and commercial heart of downtown.

The county is framed at all points of the compass with interesting communities. Just 15 minutes north of Asheville lies Weaverville, a town of roughly 3,000 with a charming Main Street. Many retirees choose to live in Weaverville, along with a growing number of young families seeking the slower pace of country life and an easing of property prices The completion of the I-19/23 connector to Tennessee, now titled I-26, has opened this area for nonstop traffic from Charleston, South Carolina, to Tennessee, Kentucky, and Ohio.

Ten more minutes north on the interstate will lead you to the area of Big Ivy, a pastoral mixture of bald hillsides, meadows, tobacco farmlands, and barns that connect the communities of Barnardsville and Dillingham. The pioneer Absalom Dillingham settled at the foot of the Great Craggies in the early 1800s, and his descendants continue to make it their home today. Several excellent examples of pre–Civil War and Civil War–era cabins remain in the area, with the Carson Cabin and schoolhouse restored to their former selves, and are located in the Big Ivy Historical Park.

Twenty miles east of Asheville, Black Mountain was established in 1893 as a quaint summer resort town known as Grey Eagle, attracting visitors looking for relief from the heat of the low country. Today much of its turn-of-the-20th-century charm is still intact. It is known for its wealth of antiques shops and cultural events. Avant-garde Black Mountain College operated nearby from 1933 to 1956, and a museum capturing the school's glory is located in downtown Asheville.

The French Broad River divides West Asheville from Asheville, giving West Asheville its distinct personality. Before being incorporated into the city of Asheville, West Asheville was very much its own town. Haywood Road, the main thoroughfare in West Asheville, is reminiscent of America in the 1950s or 1960s. A revitalization of the area today mingles new bakeries, organic markets, and coffee shops with second-hand shops, a pharmacy, gas stations, and old storefront offices. South Asheville is the county's fastest growing section of ready-made neighborhoods and planned community shopping commons. Finally, the French Broad River, Pisgah National Forest, and the Blue Ridge Parkway form the northern and eastern edges of the county, making outdoor activities just a short drive from the city center.

For more information contact the Asheville Area Chamber of Commerce and Convention & Visitors Bureau, 36 Montford Ave., Asheville 28801, (828) 258-6101, (800) 257-1300, www .ashevillechamber.org, www.exploreasheville .com; or the Black Mountain-Swannanoa Chamber of Commerce, (828) 669-2300, (800) 669-2301, www.blackmountain.org.

## Henderson County (Hendersonville)

From almost any place you happen to be in Henderson County, you can see mountains, yet much of the land consists of rolling hills. There are also marshes here similar to those in the lowlands, and some of the rich river valleys are surprisingly flat. That's because the county rests on a high plateau between the Blue Ridge and the Great Smoky Mountains. Elevations here range from 5,000 feet on Little Pisgah Mountain down to 1,400 feet at Bat Cave.

Hendersonville, the prosperous county seat, sits at an altitude of 2,200 feet, almost smackdab in the middle of the county. This bustling and ever-growing little city, with its pretty and very-much-alive downtown area, is just off I-26 and is actually closer to the Asheville Airport than Asheville is. It's long been one of Western North Carolina's most popular retirement areas. In 1838, when the 378-square-mile county was established out of a former section of Buncombe County, the Flat Rock community, just a few miles south of Hendersonville, was already a grand summer retreat for the wealthy citizens of Charleston, South Carolina.

In 1787 William Mills received one of the first land grants west of the Blue Ridge and left his mark in many of the names he gave to the area: Mills River, Mills Gap, Sugar Loaf Mountain, and Bald Top, to list a few. Mills was a Loyalist who was wounded and left for dead during the Revolutionary War's Battle of King's Mountain in 1781. The night after the battle, he made his escape in the darkness back to his home on the Green River

in what was then Rutherford County. Tories were frequently hanged during those volatile days (see Polk County), so he continued on up into the high country and hid in a cave in Sugar Loaf Mountain, which overlooked this rich plateau. He must have liked the land he saw stretched out below him, because he and his wife Eleanor eventually became the first white settlers in the area, and others soon followed.

More than 60 years later, in 1841, a vote was taken on whether to put Henderson County's seat of government in the little community of Horse Shoe (still a small and friendly place) or to situate it some 8 miles away near the Buncombe Turnpike close to the foot of Stoney Mountain. The voters chose the more centrally located turnpike site at what became Hendersonville. Charleston's Judge Mitchell King, who had a summer home in Flat Rock, gave the county a 50-acre tract on Mud Creek, known as Chinquapin Hill. Two other men donated an adjoining 29 acres. Streets were quickly laid out, and a courthouse was finished in 1842.

In the 20th century a number of well-known personalities have visited or established homes in Henderson County, including F. Scott Fitzgerald and Carl Sandburg. The Sandburg home in Flat Rock is now a National Historic Site open to the public. The lovable television legend "Howdy Doody" (a marionette) was in residence here until the death of his mentor, Buffalo Bob.

In the 1920s Florida's real estate boom reached up into Western North Carolina, as Sunshine State developers saw the potential for tourist dollars in all sorts of locales. Large hotels and resorts, some of them highly speculative, blossomed on ridges with grand mountain views. Many still dot the Western North Carolina mountains, but not all were so lasting. Nevertheless, many Floridians were introduced to Henderson County during this era, and the migration of residents from that state still occurs each spring, as they, like the Charlestonians more than 150 years ago, seek to escape the lowlands' heat and humidity and to "escape the vapors."

Such part-time residents almost double the population of this area each summer. Today

Henderson County has nearly 97,220 full-time residents. Hendersonville proper has a population of nearly 12,000, with approximately 30,000 in the Greater Hendersonville area. In the county you'll find the Flat Rock Playhouse (North Carolina's state theater), a number of amateur and semiprofessional theater groups, a symphony orchestra, and scores of talented writers, artists, musicians, and craftspeople.

Henderson County's economy is a diverse mix of light manufacturing, tourism, agriculture, and retirement. The county goes out of its way to fulfill the needs of its many senior citizens.

A number of small towns, such as Mountain Home and Fletcher, are beginning to merge into a nearly unbroken strip of businesses. Many of the small farms that stretched along U.S. Highway 64 West going toward Brevard are now broken up into large suburban plots or housing developments.

East of Hendersonville still remains "apple country," where approximately a million trees—a sight to behold during spring bloom—make the county the largest apple producer in the state and seventh in the nation. This glorious harvest is celebrated each Sept with a three-day Apple Festival, the largest and most popular of the many annual events held in Henderson County. The drive through apple country is dramatic for reasons other than spring apple blossoms and the fall harvest. Just down the road from the center of fruit production at Edneyville (about 8 miles from Hendersonville), you'll cross the crest of the Blue Ridge. Then, for the next 5 miles or so, the highway takes a precipitous dive through perpendicular peaks to Bat Cave and Hickory Nut Gorge. It's a quick reminder that Henderson is, indeed, very much in the mountains.

For more information contact the Hendersonville Visitors Information Center, 201 South Main St. or P.O. Box 721, Hendersonville 28793; (828) 693-9708, (800) 828-4244; www .historichendersonville.org, www.hendersonville chamber.org.

## Polk County (Tryon)

One might assume this county was named after the eleventh president of the United States, James Polk. This is not the case. Col. William Polk has been honored by the people of this region for his exemplary efforts in the Revolutionary War. He was wounded in 1775 and recovered in time to take his troops to join with George Washington in the Jerseys in Nov 1776. The rest is history. He later served as a trustee of the University of North Carolina. He often hosted his friends the Marquis de Lafayette and Andrew Jackson.

Most of Polk County's 234 square miles lie within the Blue Ridge foothills. The western edge, the area that's covered in this book, is mountainous. In this section we present an overview of the county's three municipalities: Saluda, Columbus, and Tryon.

Saluda, with a population of approximately 600, is on the county's western border at an elevation of 2,095 feet. It sits at the top of the steepest standard-gauge railroad grade in the eastern United States, known as the Saluda Grade. It's a small and winsome village that has long been a vacation and retirement spot and is home to quite a few artists and craftspeople. As in Henderson County, apples are the main source of farm income here.

Columbus and Tryon are "twin towns," separated by I-26, which goes northwest to Hendersonville and Asheville and southeast to Spartanburg and Charleston. It also connects at this point to U.S. Highway 74, which is a four-lane highway to Charlotte.

Columbus, sitting at an elevation of 1,131 feet, is the smaller of the two towns. Its population is only around 1,000. It is the county seat amidst the township, which has a population of 4,000. Columbus was named for Dr. Columbus Mills of Mills Spring, which is a small adjacent community that still retains its pristine character. Dr. Mills's ancestor, Col. Ambrose Mills, had been a Loyalist like his son William Mills, the man who first settled Henderson County. Unfortunately Ambrose was not as lucky as William. After the British lost the Battle of King's Mountain, William was left for dead and escaped; Ambrose was captured by Patriots and hanged.

The county was established in 1854. In 1855 the North Carolina legislature appointed a committee to locate a county seat within 2 miles of the center of the county. That done, a 100-acre tract of land was purchased for $1. By 1857 Columbus's imposing courthouse of handmade bricks was finished. The town is now a mix of late-19th-century homes, buildings, and churches, combined with condominiums, a modern hospital, a high school, and a college campus. The county population is now approaching 18,800.

Neighboring Tryon has a population of 1,800 full-time residents, more than half of whom moved here from some other part of the country. Tryon's original attraction was its climate, and for years the sick came here to improve their health. There's a well-publicized weather phenomenon in this area of the mountains known as the isothermal belt, or thermal belt, which provides a more equitable climate than other areas in the region. Caused by inversions of warm air, particularly in the spring and fall, this miniclimate enables apple growers in the region to produce abundant crops, and grapes and peaches thrive in the botanically rich Tryon area.

As settlers moved into this Cherokee land the relationship between the British and the Cherokee prospered. A peace treaty in 1730 resulted in a steady stream of British and American-born traders traveling up the old Blackstock Road from Charleston to exchange cooking utensils, cloth, and other items for furs and hides. Before too long, a sprinkling of trading posts and white families dotted the area.

The French and Indian War ended this "perpetual peace," and by 1756 forts were constructed in the face of the conflicts between the two cultures. The Block House, a fort near Tryon, still stands. Though it became a private home many years ago, the annual Block House Steeplechase was held there until the event became so popular that it was moved to the Foothills Equestrian Nature Center. (See our Recreation and Attractions chapters for more information on the event.)

The bloodshed was so heavy that, in 1767, Royal Governor William Tryon came in person to parley with the Cherokee. They established a boundary line that ran from a point near Green-ville, South Carolina, to the highest point on White Oak Mountain, which was renamed Tryon Peak by the settlers. The peak towers over the area and is particularly dominant when seen from I-26 and as you travel north toward Columbus and Tryon: The mountain comes into view dead ahead right at the North Carolina–South Carolina state line. The boundary, however, meant little to land-grabbing settlers, and it wasn't until the Battle of Round Mountain in the spring of 1776, which the Cherokee lost due to the defection of an Indian named Skyuka, that the Indians gave up their claim to this attractive territory.

By 1839 a post office, also named for Governor Tryon, stood at the foot of Tryon Peak. The community that grew up around it became a favorite resting place for drovers transporting livestock from Kentucky, Tennessee, and the higher mountains of North Carolina to ports on the coast. Though Tryon is now Polk County's largest town, it wasn't incorporated until 1885, primarily to accommodate the rail line that runs through the center of town.

Today the Tryon area is well known to horse lovers all over the nation for its large equestrian estates, steeplechases, fox hunts, and miles of bridle trails. In this storybook-like town, you'll find a number of charming antiques and gift shops and other family-owned businesses. The Tryon Theater on Trade Street was originally a 1920s vaudeville theater that now shows first-run movies and occasionally hosts theatrical performances.

Poet Sidney Lanier, who penned "Song of the Chattahoochee" and "The Marshes of Glynn," came to this area to try to cure the tuberculosis he contracted during five months in a Union prison camp during the Civil War. He had planned to stay in the Mimosa Inn in the little community of Lynn, but it was full, so he was given an upstairs room in the Lemuel Willcox house across the road, where he died on Sept 8, 1881. The Mimosa Inn is still in business (see our Bed-and-Breakfasts and Country Inns chapter). The Willcox house too still stands and is known as the Lanier House. Though the poet's stay in the area was brief, he has become a part of local lore. Nearby Lake Lanier was named for him, and Tryon's architecturally interesting and active public library is known as the Lanier Library.

As a point of clarification, the stately restored mansion of Royal Governor Tryon is not located here. It is on the eastern seaboard in New Bern, North Carolina, where the colonial government was established.

For more information contact the Carolina Foothills Chamber of Commerce, 2753 Lynn Rd., Suite A, Tryon 28782, (828) 859-6236; or Polk County Travel and Tourism at (800) 440-7848, www.polkchamber.org, www.nc-mountains.org, or www.polkguide.com.

## Transylvania County (Brevard)

This county, with a population of 30,200, has the distinction of being the only one in America called Transylvania. The name naturally leaves the residents open to some teasing about vampires and makes for wonderful T-shirt slogans and Halloween festivals. However, the name, which comes from the Latin for "across the mountains/ woodlands," is more than appropriate because 80 percent of this fair county's 378 square miles are covered by forests, almost half of which are managed by the U.S. Forest Service. Elevations in the county range from 1,020 feet at Horsepasture to 6,025 feet on Chestnut Ridge.

One of the most popular entrances to Pisgah National Forest, with all its beauty and recreational possibilities, is just outside Brevard, the county seat. From this entrance the two-lane U.S. Highway 276 climbs 16 miles to the Blue Ridge Parkway. Along that route you'll pass such alluring attractions as Looking Glass Falls, the Fish Hatchery, Sliding Rock (a natural water slide), and the Cradle of Forestry. (See our chapters on Waterfalls, Arts and Culture, and Forests and Parks.)

The county has more than 150 large waterfalls, hence its nickname, "The Land of Waterfalls." It could also be called "The Land of Music" because, in addition to the music of falling waters, rivers, and more than 200 miles of streams, it's the home of the international Brevard Music Festival

(see our Arts and Culture chapter). Also, Brevard College, a liberal arts institution within the town limits, is known for its fine music department, and the college hosts numerous events in all the arts. This creativity is contagious: Performing groups, artists, writers, and talented craftspeople contribute to the area's cultural milieu of art and music festivals, film festivals, craft shows, and other events that are an accepted part of daily life here.

For the Eastatoes, a band of the Cherokee that claimed this land until 1787, this area was mostly hunting grounds, where the Eastern buffalo was quite prevalent. At one time the Eastatoes had a small settlement near the present town of Rosman, where a hunting path crossed the headwaters of the French Broad River. Another well-used Indian trail came up from South Carolina near what is now Ceasar's Head State Park in South Carolina. It was this path, which came to be known as Douthit's Pass, that many settlers used when they migrated into the areas of Transylvania and Henderson counties. As the settlers pushed into the area, the peaceful Eastatoes retreated farther up into the mountains.

John Douthit Jr. grew up near the Moravian settlement of Old Salem and in 1790 bought 1,000 acres of land at Table Rock Mountain in South Carolina near the beginning of this path. His sister, Jose Douthit, married Robert Orr Jr. and lived in Brevard. John Douthit was an early pioneer who cut many trails through this rugged territory.

Civil War battles came no closer to Transylvania than Asheville, though a number of its citizens fought and died for the Confederate cause. Others, loyal to the Union, helped smuggle Union sympathizers through an "underground" from Georgia to Tennessee and on to the north.

There was even a private war called the Walton War that took place here in 1811, fought between Georgians and North Carolinians when both states laid claim to this area. The federal government, which had gotten the land through a treaty with the Cherokee, gave the property to Georgia, and its legislature named it Walton County in honor of George Walton, a signer of the Declaration of Independence. North Carolina claimed that the disputed area was a part of what was then Buncombe County. Hostilities arose, and in 1811 the North Carolina militia was sent in to throw the Georgians out. Skirmishes took place 2 miles southeast of Brevard. Some lives were lost, and a few prisoners were taken in the Walton War, but the two states finally agreed that the 35-degree line of latitude was the official boundary. The issue was finally settled in 1813 when surveyors proved that the land belonged to North Carolina.

Transylvania County itself wasn't established until May 20, 1861—the same day North Carolina seceded from the Union—when it was carved out of an eastern section of Henderson County and a western part of Jackson County. Brevard, Transylvania's county seat, was incorporated in 1868 with only 70 residents and seven registered voters. The town was named after Dr. Ephraim Brevard, a physician and the author of the Mecklenburg Declaration of Independence, which preceded the national Declaration of Independence by a year. (The Mecklenburg Declaration, which was drafted at the Mecklenburg Council of Safety in 1775, was sent to the Continental Congress in Philadelphia, but it never arrived.) Dr. Brevard died in 1780 at the age of 37 while in a British prison in Charleston, South Carolina; his statue now stands on Transylvania's courthouse lawn in Brevard.

Brevard's first post office was in the Red House, which is now a bed-and-breakfast inn. From those humble beginnings, Brevard, with a population of nearly 6,000 full-time residents, has blossomed into a lovely flower of a town with an attractiveness that is still growing. A five-lane connector to I-26 and the Asheville Airport, less than 20 miles away, is bringing new life to Brevard and to Transylvania's other small municipalities of Rosman and Lake Toxaway, the latter having some of the highest-priced real estate in the mountains.

For more information contact the Brevard Chamber of Commerce, 175 East Main St., Brevard 28712; (828) 883-3700, (800) 648-4523; www.brevardncchamber.org, www.visitwaterfalls.com.

# SOUTHERN MOUNTAINS

## Cherokee County (Murphy)

Cherokee County, the westernmost county in this region, is bordered by both Georgia and Tennessee, with Murphy, its county seat, only 20 minutes from either state and just two-hour drives from either Chattanooga or Atlanta. The 1996 Olympic white-water canoe event was held at the Ocoee Venue just 31 miles from the town of Murphy. It's a rural county of fertile river valleys lined with glorious mountain ridges. One of the most beautiful is the 10-mile-long, 2-mile-wide Valley River Valley, with the Snowbird Mountains soaring on one side and the Valley River Mountains on the other. Cherokee County's other small municipality, Andrews, lies near the head of this valley. Both it and Murphy are surrounded by the Nantahala National Forest, which takes up 92,363 acres of the county's 300,100 acres, offering facilities for all kinds of outdoor recreation, including off-road vehicle trails. (See our Forests and Parks and Recreation chapters for more on the Nantahala.) Another 37,000 acres are under the control of the Tennessee Valley Authority. This includes the 22-mile-long Lake Hiwassee and its connecting and much smaller Appalachia Lake, which together cut diagonally across the center of the county. They were created when the Hiwassee River was dammed in 1936 for both electricity and flood control, providing the county with a source of water-based recreation.

In 1549 Hernando de Soto and his men, who were in search of gold, were the first Europeans to pass through the area. They stopped for a time at the Cherokee town of Guasili near present-day Murphy. Later Spanish adventurers mined here, as evidenced by old tunnels, shafts, coin molds, and Spanish cannonballs found in the region. However it wasn't until the early 1700s that the first English-speaking explorers ventured into this corner of North Carolina. They described it as a "hilly land where the soil is deep and rich and rivers promise an easy route to the heart of the continent—or even beyond." Nearly another half-century passed before the Baptist Church established a mission school and church at the Old Natchez town on the Hiwassee River in 1820. The French had thrown the Natchez Indians out of Mississippi, and some ended up in this area, merging with the Cherokees. Ten years later, Col. A. R. S. Hunter built an Indian trading post at the present site of Murphy and called it Huntersville; in 1835, when a post office was established, he changed the name to Huntington and made himself the first postmaster.

In 1838 Fort Butler was built here as headquarters for the removal of the Cherokees, who were to be relocated to Oklahoma. Once that tragic task was accomplished, settlers flooded into the area. In 1839 Cherokee County was formed out of a portion of Macon County, and a year later it had a population of 3,427 residents. In 1851 Murphy was incorporated as its county seat. A decade later, when the county had little more than 9,000 citizens, it was asked to send 1,100 men to fight for the Confederate cause. The last battle of the Civil War took place at Hanging Dog Creek, about 4 miles northwest of Murphy, near the site of the Nantahala National Forest's popular Hanging Dog Recreation Area, which offers camping and access to Lake Hiwassee. Today, Murphy's population is estimated at 1,650; Andrews has 1,550 residents; the county as a whole tops out at around 27,800.

The first of Cherokee County's four ill-fated courthouses, a brick structure built in Murphy in 1844, was burned in a raid near the end of the Civil War. A second was torn down and replaced; two more burned. Understandably concerned citizens, and especially the local lawyers, urged that the next courthouse be "as totally fireproof as possible." So the fifth—a very beautiful structure—was built in 1927 of a regal blue marble found only in the Valley River Valley. You can visit the town of Marble (home of the blue marble) on Highway 141. The town prospered in the early part of the 20th century but is now a ghost of its former self.

In 1891 the Southern Railroad reached Murphy from Asheville, and a logging boom began. Not much remains from the pioneer and antebellum days of 1838 to 1870, but Cherokee County

has a substantial number of buildings and homes dating from the prosperous era that began in the 1880s. You can see examples of Greek Revival, Federal, Neoclassical, Victorian, and Queen Anne architecture here, and the residents have taken great pains to preserve this heritage. You'll also find an even larger slice of history preserved in the interesting Cherokee County Museum next to the courthouse. The cultural preservation and influence of the John C. Campbell Folk School at Brasstown on the line between Cherokee and Clay Counties can't be overestimated (see the Clay County listing following). Many festivals and fairs also take place in the region, including an old wagon train tradition, which is a highlight of the Fourth of July celebration in Andrews. Notoriously, this is also the area where Eric Robert Rudolph, one of the FBI's "Ten Most Wanted," hid out for five years and was subsequently apprehended in the town of Murphy, by rookie officer Jeff Postell, in 2003.

We think you'll love this rural and remote, but far from isolated, county. For more information contact the Cherokee County Chamber of Commerce, 805 Highway 64 West, Murphy 28906; (828) 837-2242; www.cherokeecountychamber .com.

## Clay County (Hayesville)

If you tend to look back with nostalgia to a simpler place and time, you'll want to travel to Clay County, Western North Carolina's smallest county in the southwesternmost corner of the state.

The county is as uncluttered and unpolluted a place as can exist on this planet today while being two hours, more or less, from Atlanta, Chattanooga, and Asheville. Stretched along its southern border, you'll find beautiful, mountain-encircled Lake Chatuge and its 132-mile shoreline. It's called the crown jewel of the Tennessee Valley Authority's (TVA's) many lakes because of its lovely setting. The lake, which North Carolina shares with Georgia, is not only pretty to look at, it's also a prime area for fishing and other water sports. The county, with a population of 9,760, has 65,650 acres of federal land, 43,400 of which make up part of the Nantahala National Forest, including the Fires Creek Bear Sanctuary in the high mountains of the northeastern corner of the county.

Much of Clay County is at an altitude of 1,900 feet, but peaks here can soar as high as 5,400 feet. In 1830, eight years before the Cherokee were forced out of the area, a single white settler, John C. Moore, moved here from Macon County with his wife and son. He grooved together a cabin of poplar logs in the Tusquitee section and cleared land for planting. After the Cherokee removal, people began to settle around Fort Hembree, a mile west of the present-day county seat of Hayesville, which had been built to enforce that removal. But even up into this century, Clay was an isolated area. It didn't become a county until 1861, when it was separated from Cherokee County. Its first industry, in fact, was a tanning company that sold its tanned deer hides at 12.5 cents per pound. Local folk used the hides to make shoes because there was no market where they could buy footwear.

Hayesville was named after state representative George Hayes, who had helped establish the new county. Within a few years Hayesville had a courthouse and a log jail that stood where the old brick jail now stands. It continues as a captivating structure housing history archives as the Clay County Historical Museum. The redbrick courthouse at the center of town was built in 1888 and is on the National Register of Historic Places. The Licklog Players, a regional theatrical group, makes its home at Hayesville's state-of-the-art Peacock Playhouse.

No place reflects the spirit of Clay County's magical preservation of some of the best aspects of the past better than the John C. Campbell Folk School at Brasstown. Both the school and Brasstown straddle the Cherokee-Clay county line and both counties claim it.

This homegrown, do-it-yourself spirit is obvious in other areas of life here, such as the Mountain Valley Farmers' Market, which takes place every Sat of the growing season from 7 to 11 a.m. on the square in Hayesville. Everything sold at this market is guaranteed to be homegrown or handmade, including vegetables, flowers, eggs, herbs, honey, ornamentals, baked goods, and crafts. It's also alive in the many festivals held on the town square. (See our chapter on Annual Festivals and Events.)

For more information contact the Clay County Chamber of Commerce, P.O. Box 88, Hayesville 28904; (828) 389-3704; www.ncmtnchamber.com.

## Graham County (Robbinsville)

There are sections of any county in Western North Carolina that can be called "rugged," but in 1872, when this area became a county, it was described by early explorers as "the most rugged, isolated, inaccessible land in all Eastern America." This 274-square-mile county is literally walled off by the Snowbird Mountains, the Cheoah Range, the Yellow Creek Mountains, and the western range of the Great Smoky Mountains, called the Unicoi. Elevations in the county range from 1,777 feet to approximately 5,560 feet at the western end of the county, which adjoins eastern Tennessee.

Graham County, with a population of 8,000, is at the southwestern boundary of the Great Smoky Mountains National Park. Approximately 60 percent of the county is in the Nantahala National Forest, including the 3,800-acre Joyce Kilmer Memorial Forest of virgin timber. Here you'll find trees that are hundreds of years old and grow 150 feet tall. Some are 20 feet in circumference at their bases. This memorial forest is a part of the 14,000-acre Joyce Kilmer–Slickrock Wilderness Area, which offers more than 60 miles of wilderness hiking trails. A 27-mile portion of the Appalachian Trail also crosses Graham County.

In addition to other wildlife, the woods here are famous for their "Rooshians," German wild boars that were mistakenly thought to be from Russia. An English company that planned to establish a high-priced hunting preserve in the mountains shipped them, along with other exotic game, to America. The preserve was a failure. The boars escaped, multiplied, and are still hunted here and in other sections of the mountains where they are notorious for rooting up the native habitat. Graham also contains more than 100 miles of clear mountain streams and 14,000 acres of lakes, including the fjordlike Calderwood and Cheoah Lakes, 2,800-acre Lake Santeetlah, and 30-mile-long Lake Fontana. On the last you'll find Fontana Village, a former town for the workers who built Fontana Dam in the early 1940s, now a large and lovely resort. (See our chapter on Resorts.)

Graham County was the home of Chief Junaluska, the Cherokee leader who saved Gen. Andrew Jackson's life in the Battle of Horseshoe Bend in the War of 1812. Ironically the same Andrew Jackson, as president of the United States, issued the order to round up and send the Cherokee to Oklahoma. Junaluska walked all the way back to North Carolina from that territory and was ultimately successful in his struggle to keep the remaining Cherokee people in the mountains, thus maintaining the Eastern Band of the Cherokee. He was more than 100 years old when he died. His grave is in Robbinsville (population 750), Graham's quaint county seat. The first road into Graham County was built in 1838 for the specific purpose of removing the Cherokee from their native land. Now a number of excellent highways enter the area from south, east, and north. Graham County's borders are 79 miles from Knoxville, Tennessee, and 88 miles from Asheville.

For more information contact Graham County Travel and Tourism Authority, 12 North Main St., Robbinsville 28771; (800) 479-3790. Or call the Chamber of Commerce at (828) 479-3790; www.grahamchamber.com or www.graham countytravel.com.

## Haywood County (Waynesville)

No one knows exactly when the first European settlers moved into the area that now makes up Haywood County, but some came more than 200 years ago, lending their names to many of the geographic points of interest here, such as Mary Gray Mountain. Others whose names stuck to the areas that they settled—Allens Creek, Francis Cove, Stamey Cove, and Ratcliffe Cove—have descendants whose names help fill the Haywood County phone book today.

In 1809 Haywood County was formed from a section of Buncombe and named for John Haywood, North Carolina's state treasurer from 1787 to 1827. Because the Cherokee moved west of the Tuckasegee River after the Revolutionary War, the new county was made up of 2,500 white residents. Land grants were given to numerous English, Scotch-Irish, German, and Dutch settlers.

Today Haywood County has approximately 56,500 residents and consists of 546 square miles of craggy mountains, rolling foothills, and deep valleys. The county is surrounded by the Great Smokies on the north, the Newfound Mountain Range on the east, the Pisgah Ridge on the south, and the Balsam Mountain Range on the west. Elevations range from 1,400 feet at Waterville on the Pigeon River to 6,621 feet on top of Mount Guyot. Nineteen peaks in the county are higher than 6,000 feet. The most noted is 6,030-foot Cold Mountain, the star of Charles Frazier's best-selling novel, Cold Mountain. Almost 40 percent of land is under the protection of the National Forest Service (Pisgah National Forest) and the National Park Service (24 miles of the Blue Ridge Parkway run through the county).

I-40 and a number of other highways, including U.S. Highway 19, U.S. Highway 23, and US 276, serve the county seat of Waynesville, 27 miles from Asheville. Haywood has three other incorporated towns: Canton, Clyde, and Maggie Valley. Waynesville is one of the county's oldest towns, established in 1809 as a voting precinct in an area that had been called Mount Prospect. When the county courthouse and jail were built here in 1810, the town's name was changed to Waynesville. A charming, arty town with its pretty Main Street, Waynesville is perched on top of a small plateau and has striking views in all directions. It has a population of nearly 10,000 full-time residents.

One of North Carolina's top 20 annual events is "Folkmoot," founded and hosted in Waynesville. This international extravaganza features the nations of the world every July with two weeks of street dances and performances conducted in Waynesville and throughout the mountains. (See our chapter on Annual Festivals and Events.)

Canton is the next largest town, with a population of 4,000. In 1861 there were only two houses where Canton now stands at the ford of the Pigeon River. After the Civil War, the hamlet known as Pigeon Ford grew to village size, and in 1881 the railroad track crept up into the Blue Ridge Mountains and stopped here, and the name was changed to Buford in honor of the railroad's president. In 1891 Buford was renamed Pigeon Ford, and in 1893 it was given the name it goes by today.

Neaby Lake Loganis is the site of the Boy Scouts of America Daniel Boone Council Camp, the Episcopal diocese, and the National Forest Service. Of the other two municipalities, Clyde, the home of the excellent Haywood Community College, has a population of 1,189; and Maggie Valley, named for the young daughter of its first postmaster, has just 354 people. However don't let Maggie Valley's small size fool you. This popular resort town 7 miles west of Waynesville draws thousands of visitors with its many attractions, music, and dancing at the Stompin' Ground and the Cataloochee Ski Area, North Carolina's oldest ski resort.

For more information contact the Haywood County Chamber of Commerce, 591 North Main St., Waynesville 28786, (828) 456-3021 or (800) 334-9036; and the Maggie Valley Chamber of Commerce, 623 Soco Rd. or P.O. Box 87, Maggie Valley 28751, (828) 926-1686, www.haywood-nc .com or www.visitncsmokies.com.

## Jackson County (Sylva)

Jackson County has a growing population of more than 34,600. Here the Blue Ridge Mountains, with their dramatically shattered and steep rock faces, roll in long, forested ridges toward the southwest. Elevations in the county range from 1,850 to 6,450 feet, with many 5,000-foot summits, and cool, high valleys that sit at 3,000 to 4,000 feet. Rainfall and waterfalls are abundant

in the region and lend, along with the 28,000 acres of national forests, a lush beauty to the landscape.

The prehistoric hieroglyphics made by ancient Native Americans who long predate the Cherokee on Judaculla Rock, between Cashiers and Cullowhee, give mute evidence that the area has attracted humans throughout the ages. (See our Attractions chapter.) However, it wasn't until 1828 that the first white settlers moved into the area. Yet by 1850 there were enough people in this broad depression between two mountain ranges drained by the Tuckasegee River to warrant a new county. Both Haywood and Macon Counties consented to part with some territory to form a new one.

The county stretches between the Balsam and Cowee Mountains and runs from the top of the Blue Ridge on the south to the Great Smoky Mountains in the north. The new county was named for Andrew Jackson, seventh president of the United States, and its first seat of government, Webster, for Daniel Webster, the American statesman and orator. Its settlements, strung along picturesque Tuckasegee River, grew into rustic towns. Three of them—Sylva, Dillsboro, and Webster—are incorporated and three others—Cashiers, Cullowhee, and Whittier—are not.

Sylva, at 2,039 feet in the northwestern section of the county, has more than 2,000 full-time residents. Most of the area's businesses and industries are here. The courthouse, which is reached by climbing 107 steps, was built in 1914 when the county seat was moved to Sylva. From its hilltop vantage point, the courthouse overlooks the river and the bustling town that stretches down two long streets. Sylva is the county seat.

A mile away, Dillsboro, founded in 1884, has a population of only 150, but its 50 or more shops have become home to the works of hundreds of artists and craftspeople. Thousands of visitors come here to ride the Great Smoky Mountains Railroad's excursion trains and to shop and spend time in this pretty and creative place. The famous old Jarrett House Inn is also here. (See our chapter on Bed-and-Breakfasts and Country Inns.)

Webster, the former county seat and the site of a number of historic homes, has a growing population of 452. The town was built on an Indian mound, and the surrounding area offers sweeping views of the Tuckasegee River.

Cullowhee, situated in the scenic Tuckasegee River basin and surrounded by mountains, forests, and streams, is the home of Western Carolina University. With a new performing arts and fine art museum and galleries, it is the center of arts and culture in the county. The university also has the Mountain Heritage Center, with its museum and programs that preserve and promote this region's unique heritage. The annual Mountain Heritage Day, a festival of traditional music, crafts, food, and fun that attracts thousands, is also held in Cullowhee.

Whittier lies at Jackson County's lowest elevation, 1,839 feet, in farming country on the border of Swain County. Dr. Clark Whittier of California, a relative of the Quaker poet John Greenleaf Whittier, established it. Nearby is the site of the Cherokee town of Stikohi or Stecoee, destroyed in 1776 in a preemptive strike after the Cherokee sided with the British at the beginning of the Revolutionary War. Later Col. William H. Thomas, white chief and friend of the Cherokee, established his home here and used treaty funds to buy land that became the Qualla Boundary, the home of the Eastern Band of Cherokee. (See our chapter on the Eastern Band of the Cherokee Nation.)

The deceptively small town of Cashiers actually has 1,250 residents, with several thousand more in the area surrounding it. The town sits high up in a mountain valley at an elevation of 3,478 feet, not far from spectacular Whiteside Mountain, whose sheer rock faces are the highest vertical drops in the east. Right outside town, you'll find the historic High Hampton Inn, which maintains its old traditions and a fine golf course. In the early 1900s several other inns were established in the area to serve Southern gentry escaping lowland heat and humidity. Many of these visitors ended up building summer homes, and the area has continued to attract vacationers and those who serve them. Nearby, for example, is Sapphire Valley, a huge community resort with all the amenities. Lake Glenville, right on the highway between Cashiers and Cullowhee—along with other small lakes in the Cashiers area—offers fishing, boating, canoeing, and other water sports.

For more information contact the Jackson County Chamber of Commerce, 116 Central St., Sylva 28779, (828) 586-2155 or (800) 962-1911, www.mountainlovers.com; and the Cashiers Area Chamber of Commerce, 1525 Highway 107 South or P.O. Box 238, Cashiers 28717, (828) 743-5191, www.cashiers-nc.com.

## Macon County (Franklin)

Somewhere back in time, American Indians built a mound known as Nik-wa-si along the banks of the Little Tennessee River. A town council house was built on its top, and the lodges of the city were spread up and down the valley. This site formed the government and spiritual center of the Middle Cherokee tribe. According to Cherokee tradition, the "Immortals" remain deep within the mound. They are the defenders of their people. A marker at the mound is now on East Main Street in Franklin, Macon's county seat.

It was here that Hernando de Soto came in search of gold in 1540; ironically his expedition totally overlooked the wealth of gemstones for which this area is now so famous. De Soto's visit, however, was relatively peaceful compared with what came later. In 1760 war broke out between the Cherokee and encroaching settlers, and the ancient town of Nik-wa-si was attacked by the British on several occasions and eventually destroyed. Finally, in the Treaty of 1815, the Cherokee gave up the land east of the Nantahala Mountains. Nantahala, meaning "land of the noonday sun," was so named by the Cherokee because only at midday does sunshine reach the bottom of the deep Nantahala Gorge.

This newly conquered territory became a part of Haywood County, and in 1817 Jacob Siler and William Britton journeyed from Buncombe County to set up a trading post, thus becoming the first white settlers in the area. They were not, however, the first to get to know it well. Botanist William Bartram had been hospitably received by the Cherokee during his stay at Nik-wa-si in 1777, and today's Bartram Trail, second in popularity only to the Appalachian Trail, actually passes through the city limits of Franklin. (See our chapter on Forests and Parks.)

Macon County was formed in 1828 and named after Nathaniel Macon, who served in the U.S. Congress for 36 years. The large territory that made up the original county was later broken up eventually to form all or parts of Cherokee, Jackson, Clay, Swain, and Graham Counties. Macon now covers 517 square miles and has a full-time population of about 32,100, though vacationers and second-home owners more than double that number every summer.

The town of Franklin, with a permanent population of around 3,600, was named after Jesse Franklin, one of the men who surveyed the town in 1820 and became governor of North Carolina within the year. The town was not incorporated until 1855. During the Civil War, Franklin was staunchly for states' rights and sent 1,000 of its 3,000 adult males to join the Confederate army. More than 50 percent of these men became casualties. As the war drew to a close, Col. George W. Kirk's Union regiment rode into Franklin and burned and looted the town.

Today Franklin sits at the convergence of three major highways—U.S. Highway 441, US 64, and Highway 28—at an elevation of 2,800 feet. Elevations in Macon County overall range from 1,900 feet in the Little Tennessee River basin to 5,500 feet at Standing Indian Mountain.

Macon County's other town is Highlands, which sits atop a mountain plateau at 4,118 feet, making it the highest incorporated town east of the Mississippi. Driving the narrow, curving stretch of US 64 along the Cullasaja Gorge that connects the two towns is an adventure in itself and offers some of the most-photographed waterfalls in the mountains, including Lower Cullasaja Falls, Bridal Veil Falls, and Dry Falls. Highlands was purposely created in 1875 by Samuel T. Kelsy and Clinton C. Hutchenson, who bought the land from the Dobson family of Horse Cove, a small community south of Highlands. A year later the two men sent flyers all over the country advertising the climate and altitude of the new "town," and by 1883 Highlands had 300 residents and was incorporated. Now its winter population hovers around 1,000, but that grows from 20,000 to 25,000 during the summer, not counting all the visitors who arrive to shop and take in the attractions of the surrounding area.

Where Franklin is rich in gemstones, Highlands is rich in botanical treasures. Macon County as a whole gets 50 inches of rain a year, but Highlands averages 70. This contributes to its unique plant life and led to the establishment of one of the oldest research centers in the country, the Highlands Biological Station, where scientists from all over the world study the area's flora and fauna. Highlands also has some of the most expensive real estate in the mountains. Summer residents support its fine shops, restaurants, and cultural events.

Macon County loves its visitors, and tourism is its leading industry, but the county is not solely dependent on it. Forestry products, farming, and ranching are still a large part of the local economy, and managers of new, nonpolluting industries are finding that this is an area where business and outdoor pleasure can be easily combined.

For more information contact the Franklin Area Chamber of Commerce, 425 Porter St., Franklin 28734, (828) 524-3161, www.franklin chamber.com; and the Highlands Area Chamber of Commerce, Fourth Street or P.O. Box 404, Highlands 28741, (828) 526-2112, www.highlands chamber.org.

## Swain County (Bryson City)

Swain County was created in 1871 out of parts of Jackson and Macon Counties and was named for David L. Swain, a former governor and president of the state university. The cabin in which he was born is in Asheville, incorporated in the Beaverdam Run condominium complex.

Eighty-five percent of the county's 553 square miles is federal land, which means it's mostly mountains, forests, streams, rivers, and wilderness. Yet this unspoiled, unhurried, unpolluted piece of paradise is just 60 miles from Asheville and 85 miles from Knoxville, Tennessee. The southern part of the Great Smoky Mountains National Park comprises 216,662 acres of the county; the Nantahala National Forest manages another 21,000 acres. And the Blue Ridge Parkway finally comes to an end—or originates, depending on which way you're traveling—in Swain County and takes up 709 acres of county land. In addition, 29,000 acres of the Cherokee Indian Reservation, including the town of Cherokee with its many diversions, is also within the county. The reservation is known as the "Qualla Boundary." The boundary begins in the north at Soco Gap, which connects into Maggie Valley. The town of Cherokee lies within that boundary. This includes the authentic Museum of the Cherokee and the Qualla Arts and Crafts Center. Leading from those centers are the directionals pointing the way to the outdoor theater where Unto These Hills drama is presented throughout the summer, and the 17th-century prototype of a living Cherokee village, Oconaluftee Village, stands.

The elevation at Bryson City, the county seat, is only about 1,800 feet, while just a dozen miles away, as the crow flies, the mountains soar to 6,643 feet at Clingmans Dome.

Some of the state's most scenic rivers—the Nantahala, Oconaluftee, and Tuckasegee—add their beauty and recreational possibilities to all the other attractions. The Nantahala River alone draws thousands of rafters and kayakers, and many white-water outfitters, including the well-known Nantahala Outdoor Center, are in or near Bryson City. Some great mountain biking trails in the area attract such events as Knobscorcher, one of the state's most popular series of mountain bike races. Fontana Lake stretches into the county just a few minutes west of Bryson City.

Bryson City, population 1,250, is a lively, attractive town on the banks of the Tuckasegee River, with parks both along the river and on its islands. It's a popular stop for passengers on the Great Smoky Mountains Railroad, which offers train excursions through the area. As if that weren't enough, annual riverfests, high-school band competitions, chili cook-offs, and other celebrations are held throughout the year. Needless to say, if you like the outdoors, you're going to love it here, because the 13,000 full-time Swain County residents have quick access to some of the largest expanses of wilderness areas in the eastern United States.

For more information contact the Swain County Chamber of Commerce, 210 Main St. or P.O. Box 509, Bryson City 28713; (828) 488-3681; www.greatsmokies.com.

# GETTING HERE, GETTING AROUND

A natural charm and mystery surrounds many parts of the North Carolina mountains, which are still considered to be wild and remote. Over time, the paths traveled by the bears, mountain lions, deer, and elk became hunting trails for Native Americans. These trails became the dusty and muddy roads used by early settlers. As time flows with the tides of progress, the roads became paved, curvy two-laners. Today, the magnificent highways of America bring travelers into these mountains on beautiful scenic drives. Not the least of these is the Blue Ridge Parkway. The Parkway winds its way southwest at an average elevation of 3,000 feet through the northern and central mountains, finally turning northwest in the southern mountains. It ends at Cherokee at the southern entrance to the Great Smoky Mountains National Park (see our Blue Ridge Parkway, Eastern Band of the Cherokee Nation, and Forests and Parks chapters). Yet there's still a wealth of wilderness to be found. And within this wilderness there is access to nature preserves, waterfalls, hiking trails, and the area's other attractions. Their lure continues to bring millions of visitors here each year.

National and state highways now crisscross this ancient land of the Cherokees. Two busy interstate highways—I-40 and I-26—intersect in Asheville, and just an hour or so south, I-26 crosses I-85 at Spartanburg, South Carolina, on that interstate's busy leg between Atlanta and Charlotte.

Getting to many of the best hiking trails, the prettiest waterfalls, and some of the most beautiful areas of the woods can involve taking Forest Service (FS) or unpaved secondary roads (SR). Many of these are steep, curvy, narrow, graveled, and often one lane with only small pull-outs to get around oncoming traffic. Passing is mostly impossible and certainly inadvisable. But, if your vehicle is in decent shape and its tank filled with gas, we encourage you to explore these adventuresome byways. Don't, however, be in a hurry, and watch out for logging trucks. It's also a good idea to stop by the closest ranger station (the numbers are listed in the Forests and Parks chapter) and ask about road conditions. Bad weather sometimes washes out whole sections of these roads or creates landslides.

The Asheville Regional Airport, adjacent to I-26 and strategically located between Asheville and Hendersonville, is connected to Brevard by a five-lane highway. The jetport located at the Asheville Regional Airport handles corporate and private air traffic. The more metropolitan central mountain area is also served by the ever-growing Greenville-Spartanburg International Jetport. The Charlotte-Douglas International Airport, one of the nation's busiest air hubs, is just two hours southeast.

When this wilderness first opened, few rail lines reached the region. Eventually the highest railroad point in the southeast was in North Carolina. Thomas Wolfe wrote of the nostalgia of hearing the train whistle at night. But alas, passenger trains into the mountains are now part of history. Today a number of railroads provide freight service to the mountains, and Amtrak serves nearby Greenville and Clemson, South Carolina, but rail passenger service in Western North Carolina is limited to a railroad excursion company, the Great Smoky Mountains Railroad. It is based in both Dillsboro and Bryson City, North Carolina (see our Attractions chapter).

# DRIVING IN THE MOUNTAINS

While airports and interstate highways make arriving in the North Carolina mountains extremely easy, you'll be taking other highways and byways in order to enjoy all the scenery and attractions this region offers. And that brings up the subject of patience. Driving in the mountains can require abundant patience, but it's usually not the kind demanded by bumper-to-bumper traffic jams. In many areas you'll have the roads mostly to yourself, yet you may need to allow double the time it would normally take to drive a set distance. The very nature of these steep-graded, twisting roads demands slower speeds. The top speed allowed on the Blue Ridge Parkway, for example, is 45 miles per hour, and some hairpin curves, even on major routes, require that you slow down to 15 miles per hour. In addition, sudden weather changes can bring blinding fog or downpours. In winter, unexpected ice, snow, and freezing rain can bring travel to a dangerous crawl.

Another thing that can—and probably should—cut into your traveling time is the incredible scenery you'll encounter along the way. Smoky mist curling out of a deep valley, a sunset turning a lake to rosy pink, a waterfall cascading down a mountainside, a highway pull-off offering a green-dappled vista that stretches for miles will tempt you to stop for a look. For those who enjoy the journey as well as the destination, the North Carolina Scenic Byways project covers 1,600 miles of picturesque North Carolina back roads, free of man-made eyesores. Each route was chosen for its particular attractions, based on historic significance or natural beauty, such as waterfalls, rivers, or land formations.

**i** The state maintains more than 77,000 miles of primary and secondary roads. North Carolina also has the largest state-maintained road system in the United States. North Carolina is commonly called the Good Roads State.

Here in the mountains of North Carolina, we are fortunate to have nine of these scenic byways, which cover 410 miles. You can identify the road you're traveling as a scenic byway from the distinctive white sign decorated with green mountains and blue waterways and the title NC SCENIC BYWAY emblazoned at the bottom.

The North Carolina Department of Transportation has issued a helpful, 91-page guide booklet for the entire state system of scenic byways. You can get a copy at most North Carolina welcome centers and DOT offices, or you can write to Scenic Byway Program, NC DOT, P.O. Box 25201, Raleigh 27611-5201. The publication is free, but in it you'll find an envelope that allows you to make a much-appreciated donation.

Pay attention and be ready to maneuver when driving through an area with falling rocks or rock-slide area signs (I-40 north of Asheville was closed for months in 1998 due to a huge landslide). It's possible to come around a curve and find a fair-size boulder in your path. Likewise, be prepared to share the roads with pedestrians, bicyclists, horseback riders, and a variety of wildlife. The last is particularly prevalent at night.

Here are a few other rules you should be aware of:

- A new resident must apply for a driver's license within 30 days of moving here. Bring your out-of-state license, proof of insurance, and proof of residency to a driver's license office of the North Carolina Department of Motor Vehicles; you'll have to pass a written exam and an eye exam. Each county has a DMV office. Most offices are open from 8 a.m. to 5 p.m.; some close for lunch from noon to 1 p.m.
- New residents also must register their vehicles and purchase license tags within 30 days. The title of the car or name of the lien holder, proof of insurance, and the odometer reading are required. Vehicles must also be inspected within 10 days of the registration date.
- The North Carolina Safe Roads Act forbids drivers to drink alcohol or to have an open container of an alcoholic beverage in the passenger area. All front seat passengers are required to wear seat belts. Children younger than four must ride in child safety seats. All

# Close-up

## The Interstate 26 Connector

After 11 years of planning and building, I-26 now connects Charleston, South Carolina, with the Ohio Valley, and what a road it is! In addition to underpasses for wildlife, there are run-off ramps for runaway trucks with special traps for containing hazardous waste spillage. An automated spray, triggered to de-ice the bridge approaching notorious Sam's Gap, which peaks at the North Carolina–Tennessee line, has been built as a winter safety feature. Even monarch butterflies have been given special consideration with the development of a special preserve filled with their favorite flowers and milkweeds high above the interstate.

A unique visitor center offers comfort and assistance as well as a gallery of traditional crafts native to the region. The center has vast picnic areas and offers great scenery. Photo opportunities abound all the way from Asheville north through Tennessee.

This corridor connects directly with I-81 at Johnson City and provides access to the culturally rich town of Abingdon, Virginia, with its grandiose Martha Washington Hotel and the Abingdon Theatre.

Along the way on I-26 West, one encounters the college town of Mars Hill. Heading east on U.S. Highway 19 just past Mars Hill, enter into Yancey County to the quaint town center of Burnsville, North Carolina. Located along US 19 are the historic Penland School of Craft, the town of Spruce Pine, and the Appalachian State University town of Boone.

These mountains were opened by the forerunners of the Cherokee Nation, the Paleo People, about 12,000 years ago. Their tracking of animal pathways became the thoroughfares of the Cherokee. In 1540 DeSoto and his Spanish conquistadors widened these paths in their search for wealth. French expeditions opened paths in their eastward explorations from the Mississippi, while the Scottish and English settlers widened the pathways to accommodate their westward movement from the Atlantic.

---

children younger than 12 must wear seat belts. There is no longer an exemption for vehicles registered outside the state. Children younger than 12 may not ride in the open beds of pickup trucks except when an adult is present to supervise the child, or the child is secured or restrained by an approved seat belt. Other exceptions are if an emergency situation exists, if the vehicle is operated in a parade with a valid permit or in an agricultural enterprise, or if the vehicle is being operated in a county that has no incorporated area with a population greater than 3,500. The state requires that headlights be on whenever windshield wipers are on. Motorcyclists are required to wear helmets and use their headlights at all times. It is illegal to send text messages on a cell phone while driving in North Carolina.

**i** If you're sightseeing at a leisurely pace, road etiquette asks that you pull over, when you can do so safely, and let those in a hurry pass by.

## COMMERCIAL AIRPORTS

### Central Mountains

**ASHEVILLE REGIONAL AIRPORT**
**61 Terminal Dr., Fletcher**
**(828) 684-2226**
**www.flyavl.com**
Western North Carolina's only commercial air service is centrally located on Highway 280, just 15 miles south of Asheville, and is easily accessed from I-26. The airport is tourist friendly and not far from all the most popular vacation destinations. Hendersonville is 8 miles from the Asheville airport; Brevard only 20; Waynesville,

36; Sylva, 57; Cashiers, 58; and Highlands, 69. This airport, the fourth largest in the state, is served by: Comair; USAirways; Atlantic Southeast Airlines (ASA), which is a Delta regional carrier; AirTran; Continental, Northwest Airlines; and USAirways Express carrying passengers to hubs in Raleigh, Charlotte, Atlanta, Pittsburgh, Detroit, Orlando, Dallas, and Newark.

The 900-acre airport has a wide primary runway, 8,001 feet long and 150 feet wide, capable of serving large aircraft. A full-service, fixed-base operator caters to all corporate, private, and charter needs. A shuttle service is provided by Airport Ground Transportation, which is available for long or short distances. Also on hand are four auto rental services: Hertz, Avis, Budget, and National. (Alternate airport transfer services are listed at the end of this chapter.)

Four boarding gates on two levels, increased parking (including 190 short-term and 590 long-term spaces), a cafeteria, sundries and newspaper/magazine shop, and lounge provide a pleasant seating area for those seeking sustenance. An attractive new art gallery features works of local artists. Across the hall "Books for Less"—used editions—can be purchased using the honor system. Just deposit the amount noted on the book into the lock box located on the shelf.

**i** A special photo exhibit of World War I and II airmen from Asheville is located at the Asheville Airport. Among the many photos one is of Kiffin Rockwell, ace of World War I. A character playing his role was in the early film *Layette Escadrille*. Also among the photos is that of Robert Morgan, World War II pilot of the B-17 Memphis Belle fame. The story of that plane and crew was featured in both a book and a movie.

#### ASHEVILLE REGIONAL AIRPORT GROUND TRANSPORTATION
**Airport Road, Fletcher**
**(828) 209-3660**
Transportation from the airport can be contracted at the facility located in the baggage claim area. There is no taxi stand at the Asheville Regional Airport, although taxis are available. Just check the yellow pages of the phone book. (Other transportation systems are listed at the end of this chapter.)

#### ODYSSEY AVIATION
**40 Lindbergh Lane, Asheville**
**(828) 684-6832**
**www.odysseyfsp.com**
This company shares the runway with the Asheville Regional Airport, offering 24-hour service for corporate and private aircraft. Tie-downs, fueling, flight instruction, and aircraft maintenance are available. The staff can arrange catering, car rentals, ground transportation, and hotel reservations. They offer complete services for the corporate and private flyer.

## GENERAL AVIATION

### Northern Mountains

#### ASHE COUNTY AIRPORT
**639 Airport Rd., Jefferson**
**(336) 982-3713, (336) 982-3899 after hours**
This public airport, which is off U.S. Highway 221, has a 4,300-foot paved and lighted runway. Tie-downs, fueling, flight instruction, and light aircraft maintenance are available. Rental cars are available from Ford and Chevrolet (336-246-8806) dealers in West Jefferson, 5 miles from the airport. The facility is open daily from 9 a.m. to 5 p.m.

**i** If you plan to fly your own plane, it would be a good idea to call the airports at which you intend to land and refuel. Smaller airports may not offer all the services to which you are accustomed.

#### AVERY COUNTY AIRPORT
**US 19 East, Spruce Pine**
**(828) 733-8200**
The elevation of this public airport is 2,750 feet. It has a 3,000-foot runway; fuel, flight instruction, and aircraft maintenance are provided. Its hours are 8 a.m. to 5 p.m. Mon through Sat and 1 to 5 p.m. Sun.

**BOONE AIRPORT**
346 Bamboo Rd., Boone
(828) 265-3598
This airfield, though privately owned, is open to all visitors to the Boone area in Watauga County. The field contains a 2,670-foot paved runway. Use is restricted to daylight hours only. Rental cars or taxis service the airport. Also available are maintenance, fuel, air tours, and flight instruction.

**ELK RIVER AIRPORT**
Hwy. 194, Banner Elk
(828) 898-9791
Use of this private airport, which is in Avery County and has a 4,600-foot paved runway, is restricted to members and guests of the Elk River Club. No fuel is available, and the runway is not maintained (snow clearing, etc.).

## Central Mountains

**HENDERSONVILLE AIRPORT**
1232 Shepherd St., Hendersonville
(828) 693-1897
www.hendersonvilleairport.com
This private airport, which began in a pasture in 1936, is open for public use. It has a 3,000-foot paved and lighted runway that can handle a wide range of aircraft. The facility also has hangar space, rents aircraft, provides fuel and maintenance, conducts flight training, and offers scenic flights, including rides in vintage aircraft provided by the nearby Western North Carolina Air Museum.

## Southern Mountains

**ANDREWS-MURPHY AIRPORT**
5840 Airport Rd., Andrews
(828) 321-5114, (888) 284-5114
www.smokymountainaero.com
Constructed in 1947, 2 miles from Andrews on U.S. Highways 19/129, this Cherokee County facility has a 5,000-foot lighted, asphalt runway and provides fuel and operational-level maintenance. It also offers hangars, tie-downs, plane rentals, charter flights throughout the country, air ambulance service, flight instruction, and sightseeing

flights, along with a pilot lounge. The airport is open from 8 a.m. to 6 p.m. seven days a week.

**JACKSON COUNTY AIRPORT**
626 Airport Rd., Cullowhee
(828) 586-0321
The Jackson County Airport sits just above Western Carolina University at Cullowhee about 2 miles northwest of town. The runway is 3,300 feet long. The elevation is 2,844 feet mean above sea level (MSL). The airport is operated under the Jackson County Airport Authority. It is currently unattended. Operating hours are from 9 a.m. to 6 p.m. seven days a week. It is equipped with pilot control lighting (PCL) and the fuel is on a self-serve basis 24 hours. They offer flight instruction, sightseeing flights, car rentals, and on-call mechanic service.

**MACON COUNTY AIRPORT**
1241 Airport Rd., Franklin
(828) 524-5529
The lighted runway of the Macon County Airport, called "the biggest little airport in North Carolina," has been extended from 3,800 feet to 4,400 feet. The facility, which is about 3 miles northwest of town off Highway 28, provides both 100LL-octane gas and jet-A fuel. On-site car rentals, flight instruction, sightseeing tours, and hangar space are other services. The airport can do maintenance work on most general aviation aircraft.

# BUS LINES

## Central Mountains

**APPLE COUNTRY TRANSIT**
526 7th Ave. E.
Hendersonville
(828) 698-8571
www.henderson.lib.nc.us/county/planning/
actransit/main.html
Transportation operates from Hendersonville to surrounding areas, including Asheville Airport, with nominal fees via subscription or dial-a-ride Mon through Fri. A monthly pass allows for unlimited rides.

## ASHEVILLE TRANSIT SYSTEM
**49 Coxe Ave., Asheville**
**(828) 253-5691**
The main terminal is beside the downtown post office on Coxe Avenue. One way to get there is to walk from the corner of Pritchard Park on Patton Avenue to the traffic light at the corner of Patton and Coxe. Turn left and walk 2 blocks to the terminal. Schedules for buses to many areas of town are available at the terminal and by calling the number above.

## GREYHOUND BUS LINE
**2 South Tunnel Rd., Asheville**
**(828) 253-5353, general information**
**(828) 253-8451, passenger agent**
**337 7th Ave. East, Hendersonville**
**(828) 693-1201**
**1880 Dellwood Rd., Waynesville**
**(828) 926-2327**
The Greyhound Bus Line is the only bus company providing long-range scheduled motor coach service from this area. The Buncombe County terminal is located east of the tunnel that connects downtown Asheville to Tunnel Road. The Waynesville terminal is located at the Red Barn convenience store, and the Hendersonville office is easily located in downtown Hendersonville.

These Greyhound facilities provide passenger and package service to all major U.S. destinations. The terminals open at 8 a.m., but closing times vary so call ahead. The toll-free number for Greyhound central reservations is (800) 231-2222; www.greyhound.com.

# TOURING COMPANIES

Whether you arrive by family vehicle, commercial jet, private jet, bike, kayak, canoe, or on foot, you can find opportunities for custom-made excursions through the following companies.

## ACCENTS ON ASHEVILLE
**(828) 251-9013, (800) 627-1185**
**www.accentsonasheville.com**

With offices on Sunset Mountain in the Grove Park Inn, Accents on Asheville provides guide and transportation services to local areas and beyond. Their services include transporting your group from your hotel and meeting you at airports throughout Western North Carolina, upstate South Carolina, and eastern Tennessee. They offer tours of historic Asheville, Cherokee (Qualla), Great Smoky Mountain Railroad, white-water rafting, artisans of the mountains studios, and the Biltmore Estate. Dine-around, providing a variety of dining experiences throughout the area, is another of their featured tours. Additional offerings are available through your personal request and contacts.

## ASHEVILLE GHOST TROLLEY
**Tour begins at 37 Montford Ave.**
**Across from the Asheville Chamber of Commerce**
**(888) 667-3600, (828) 681-8585**
Every Thurs, Fri, and Sat at 7:30 p.m., the author of *Haunted Asheville*, Joshua P. Warren, reveals the hidden secrets of ghosts in Asheville as the Asheville Historic Trolley Tour winds its way into the world of "Darkest Clouds in the Land of the Sky" for 90 minutes. Reservations are available at the numbers above, or pay at time of tour with cash, check, or credit cards.

## ASHEVILLE HISTORIC TROLLEY TOURS
**(828) 669-8046, (888) 667-3600**
**www.ashevilletrolleytours.com**
See all Asheville by riding the historic trolley with a 70-minute narrated tour. The trolley schedules are posted throughout Asheville and at the Asheville Area Chamber of Commerce, hotels, and other public venues. The route includes major attractions, the Thomas Wolfe Memorial, and Biltmore Village. Passengers may disembark at any stop along the way and reboard the trolley using the same ticket. A minimum of four trips are scheduled daily beginning from the Asheville Area Chamber of Commerce at 9:30 a.m. The trolley can be chartered for family reunions, weddings, and other special occasions.

## BREWS CRUISE
**Tours begin at Asheville Bewing Company,
77 Coxe Ave., Asheville**
**(828) 545-5181**
**www.brewscruise.com**
Experience a behind-the-scenes glimpse of the glory of beer with visits to three boutique breweries. It's a tasting and entertainment tour with stops at several of Asheville's microbreweries, making it easy to realize why Asheville was voted "Beer City USA." There are now ten microbreweries in this city.

## CAROLINA LIMOUSINE
**2019 Smoky Park Hwy., Asheville**
**(828) 258-2526**
This service offers a fleet of limousines in and around the Asheville area. The drivers are all professionally trained and their vehicles main complete bars and other amenities in the passenger area.

## DILLINGHAM-RICHARDS INTERNATIONAL, INC.
**Pearson Drive, Asheville**
**(828) 253-3943**
Custom-tailored tours are led by Western North Carolina's premier historian, lecturer, tour guide, and winemaster-cum-author, Insiders' Guide's own Ken Richards.

## ELITE LIMOUSINE
**3833 North Mills River Rd., Mills River**
**www.elite-limousine.com**
Services include a fleet of vehicles ranging from motor coaches to stretch limos, Hummers, and Lincoln Navigators, as well as Desotos and an Excalibur Empress for the bride and groom.

## GRAY LINE TROLLEY TOURS
**Depart from Asheville Visitor Center**
**36 Montford Ave., Asheville**
**(825) 251-8687, (866) 592-8687**
**www.graylineasheville.com**
Enjoy touring at your own pace. Stay on the trolley for a comprehensive 1.5 to 1.75 hour tour, or hop-off at any of Gray Line's seven trolley stops to shop, dine, and explore. You may reboard the next trolley to continue your tour. Tickets may be purchased on the trolley. Tickets may be purchased on the trolley or at the Asheville Visitors Center.

## LAZOOM TOURS
**Asheville Brewing Company, 77 Coxe Ave., Asheville**
**(828) 225-6932**
**www.lazoomtours.com**
The quirky 40-passenger art bus runs seven times a week through Asheville's downtown area, historic Montford, the River District Arts area, and more. The wild, fun, outrageous, historic comedy tour is not for the timid, and includes acting, storytelling, and even singing. The sometimes rowdy and completely idiosyncratic tours begin and end at Asheville Brewing Company.

> **i** Street parking in many small towns is often free, or else only a nominal fee of a few coins for a couple of hours is charged. Not so in Asheville. Parking at meters is strictly monitored, and if time runs out on the meter where you're parked, you'll be slapped with a ticket. Also, parking in private business lots around town means almost certain towing. So save yourself a lot of headaches and inconvenience and park in one of the three city garages centrally located downtown.

## PEGASUS TRANSPORTATION
**Asheville**
**(828) 281-4600, (800) 462-4062**
**www.pegasusairport.net**
Pegasus can be scheduled for airport pickups and customized touring. Additionally they feature transportation to dinner events, to Biltmore Estate, and Grove Park Inn. Their services range beyond the Asheville area to Charlotte/Douglas International Airport and to Greenville/Spartanburg Airport.

## RUNION TOURS AND CHARTERS
**319 Old Buckeye Cove Rd., Black Mountain**
**(828) 299-3733, (800) 770-2829**
This company offers air-conditioned luxury motor coaches for local, regional, and national touring.

## SPECIAL OCCASIONS LIMOUSINE
**Asheville**
**(828) 687-9918, (888) 288-9915**
**www.ashevillelimousine.com**
Their motto is "Anywhere, Any Time" and they offer 24-hour service. Their variety of premium class vehicles ranges from sedans to vans, Black Car Service (black stretch limousines) to luxury stretch limousines.

## WALKING TOURS OF HISTORIC ASHEVILLE
**(828) 777-1014**
**www.history-at-hand.com**
Explore the history of Asheville through its fascinating stories and architecture. There are three separate walking tours offered: Downtown Asheville, Historic Montford, Riverside Cemetery, and Family Store Tours. Learn about Asheville's vibrant Jewish community during the 1.5 hour Family Store Tour pointing out locations of some of the 400-plus Jewish businesses that supported the early economy of Asheville. All tours by appointment. Enhance your tour experience with a copy of *The Family Store: A History of Jewish Businesses in Downtown Asheville, 1880–1990*.

## YOUNG TOURS
**Riverside Drive, Asheville**
**(828) 258-0084**
**www.youngtransportation.com**
Through the creativity of Ralph Young Sr., this company became "people-movers" by bolting theater seats to a truck and transporting folks from Western North Carolina to the Chicago Exhibition in the 1930s, during the Great Depression when money was scarce. Again in 1982, with the World's Fair just down the road in Knoxville, Tennessee, the Young fleet was enlarged to provide transportation. Today they have a large fleet of mini-coaches and highway coaches with seating for 22 to 55 passengers.

They offer receptive tour services, shop services, and charter tours. Step-on guides are also available.

# CLIMATE

The Cherokee referred to their mountain home here as Sa-koh-na-gas, which means "blue," after the mountains' blue haze, which is created when sunshine and warm, humid air combine with the hydrocarbons produced by the region's thick forests. This single word was later elaborated into "the great blue hills of God" and "land of the blue mists."

The Great Smoky Mountains, on the other hand, were named for the fog that forms as a result of the temperature differences between the air and the mountains' many water sources. This cloudlike mist curls up from valleys and mountain peaks like smoke from a fire, particularly in the early morning, around sunset, and after rains.

This blue mist and curling "smoke" are integral parts of the landscape of both the Great Smokies and the Blue Ridge Mountains, as well as all the lesser-known cross ridges, such as the Graham, Nantahala, Snowbird, Balsam, and New Found Mountains.

The Land of the Sky, a more recent description, was culled from the title of an 1876 romantic novel set in this tranquil region.

## A PLACE FOR ALL SEASONS

Western North Carolina is also known as the Land of the Four Seasons for it is the long-lasting springs and autumns, plus mild winters and (increasingly hot!) summers, that have attracted tourists and new residents to the area for nearly two centuries.

Crocuses and daffodils start pushing up through the earth in late Feb, and the false spring that usually occurs around this time of the year can have you hiking or playing golf in your shirt sleeves. In March, tulip magnolias, yellow forsythia, and other early-spring flowers bravely brighten the landscape despite the real possibility of a late snowfall. By the end of April, dogwoods and silverbell trees are blooming everywhere. In May, mountainsides are afire with flame azaleas, and the dense thickets of several species of native rhododendrons begin their bloom bursts, a show that lasts right into July. May is also the time when a large portion of the mountains' spring wildflowers reaches its peak, including pink and white mountain laurels that coat the slopes and overhang roadways, rivers, and boulder-strewn creeks.

By June, summer greens up the region with all the lush, ferny beauty of a rain forest. Daytime temperatures are mostly in the 70s and 80s, but as summer plays out, a good month of heat and humidity requires air conditioners and electric fans, at least until a cooling thunderstorm comes along. Even then, by late evening the thermometer drops into the 70s, cooler still at higher elevations, and it's an extremely rare night when it could be considered too hot to sleep.

At any time you can find vast temperature differences by a quick change in elevation. For example, you can stretch the spring by several weeks if you follow the bloom from the valleys to the tops of the mountains, and in the fall the color changes begin at the top elevation and slowly work their way downward. The first hints of the colorful autumn to come are seen tinting some of the leaves at higher elevations as early as late Aug. In Oct, visitors by the thousands arrive to enjoy the brilliant red, yellow, and gold foliage display (see our sidebar on autumn leaves in the Blue Ridge Parkway chapter).

By mid-Nov, the barren branches of deciduous trees give mountain ridges a crew-cut look, and previously unknown lodgings peer from their wooded perches enjoying "winter views." But, while nights may bring freezing temperatures, days can be pleasantly warm. It's usually not until Christmas that the first frigid Alberta clipper roars south out of Canada. On those occasions temperatures can plummet to zero or below for a short period of time, and from then until well into spring, short spurts of bitterly cold weather, along with occasional snow or ice storms, alternate with surprisingly pleasant winter days. In most places the average snowfall in a typical year is around one foot, and even heavy snows usually disappear in a matter of days.

**i** Temperature changes are drastic in the mountains. Always take a sweater or jacket when driving from low altitudes to higher ones. We once experienced a sunny, warm day in downtown Asheville, which turned into a windy, icy hailstorm only 2,000 feet higher at a picnic area on the Blue Ridge Parkway.

Rain, on the other hand, is a year-round event. Slightly more falls in the summer than the winter. (Winter wet fronts, rising up from the Gulf of Mexico, actually warm things up.) In summer, rain often takes the form of sudden crashing late-afternoon and evening thunderstorms, sometimes with damaging winds and lightning. While such storms can spoil picnics and other outdoor activities, most residents enjoy these natural light-and-sounds shows, knowing the mountains offer protection from destructive tornadoes and hurricanes found elsewhere.

On the average, rainfall totals from 40 to 55 inches per year, depending on the location. But in the rain belt, which includes a large part of Transylvania County and the southern sections of Jackson and Macon Counties, 80 inches or more can fall in a typical year. All that water has to go somewhere, and much of it tumbles off cliffs and down mountainsides. Transylvania, which dubs itself the Land of Waterfalls, has more than 150 of these splendid water shows. Even so, the county hasn't cornered the waterfall market. Cascades and waterfalls, some of which plunge hundreds

of feet, can be found in abundance throughout the region. (See our Waterfalls chapter.) So can springs, creeks, rivers, ponds, and lakes. In fact, homes with such water sources are almost more the rule than the exception, and real estate ads touting "bold streams" are common, even inside the boundaries of some towns.

## A PEOPLE FOR ALL SEASONS

While the stamp of the Cherokee and the original Scotch-Irish settlers have made a deep mark on the area, later arrivals brought—and keep bringing—a wonderful array of cultural diversity and talent to the region. The hills still resound with the sounds of dulcimer and bagpipes, but you can hear rock 'n' roll and classical symphonies too. Here in the mountains, star-studded concerts and homegrown festivals are likely to attract the same enthusiastic crowds, and high-tech industries and nationally known holistic and spiritual centers thrive beside handmade crafts and old-time religion. The mix of Old World and contemporary lifestyles, played out against the dramatic backdrop of the mountains, makes this region irresistible to visitors and transplants alike.

### Hazy Days

Some days the mountain vistas don't go on forever. Smog and haze are a growing concern in the Blue Ridge Mountains. Not only are views sometimes obscured by smog, but the pollution also poses a threat to people with asthma and other health concerns. The local newspapers and broadcast media give a daily "air quality" report with a scale that ranges from green to red. Those with respiratory concerns, the very young, the elderly, and pregnant women should stick to lower elevations and/or stay inside when levels reach high orange and red.

# RESORTS

Resorts have been a part of this region for as long as some of the towns have been here. Which came first, then—resorts or towns? The town of Cashiers in the Southern Mountains developed around the High Hampton Inn. Another example is the Eseeola Lodge which was built first, followed by the development of the town of Linville around it.

Besides boarding houses or travelers' inns at the crossroads of mountain trails, hotels began cropping up for not just the weary traveler, but for the moneyed classes traveling via railroad from the north and the south, taking in the curatorial airs and water of the mountains.

The first resorts were nowhere near as elaborate or elegant as some of the vacation spots we have now, but, just like today's, they drew flocks of visitors seeking the relaxing and restorative beauty of the mountains.

## Price Code

Most of the accommodations in these chapters will accept major credit cards; we have noted those that accept none. Rates are based on double occupancy.

$.................. $80 to $100
$$ ............... $101 to $120
$$$ .............. $121 to $200
$$$$ ........... $201 and more

Amenities have changed with the times. Golf courses, swimming pools, Jacuzzis, and the like have been added, but such attractions can be found almost anywhere in the country. The unique allures of Western North Carolina's mountains as a resort area are the same as they have been for more than a century: a mild, healthful climate with four distinct and equally lovely seasons; botanical diversity unmatched in America; rock-strewn rivers and streams that'll sing you to sleep; mountains older than time stretching out to forever; more unspoiled wild areas than you could ever explore; and people who take the time to be polite.

## NORTHERN MOUNTAINS

### Avery County

**ESEEOLA LODGE** $$–$$$
**Linville Golf Club, 175 Linville Ave.**
**Linville**
**(800) 742-6717**
**www.eseeola.com**
Eseeola Lodge is noted as a Mobil Four Star resort for its tradition of excellence. It is "hunting-lodge" rustic on the outside, adorned with great barked slabs of mighty chestnut, and "English manor inn" comfort on the inside. Warm greetings are offered by the welcoming fireplace and the friendly staff. Directly behind the reception area is a great room with a fireplace and sections for lounging. One wing of the room houses the cozy, well-stocked library. Leading on through the double doors is a great hall, adorned with flags depicting the states and countries of those holding membership in the Eseeola Golf Club. Pristine white tableclothes grace the tables in the dining hall where the staff is attentive from start to finish. In order to enjoy the full range of the talented chef, one needs to book an extended stay as the menu changes daily.

The rooms are comfortable, with amenities ranging from a welcoming note from the general manager to posh bathrobes for lounging. Modern conveniences include private bathrooms, air-conditioning, telephones, hair dryers, and cable television. Brewing appliances are equipped with gourmet coffee and tea so you can enjoy a cup on your own private balcony. The *New York Times* and *Charlotte Observer* arrive at your door as well. Other available services include eight tennis courts, an outdoor heated swimming pool, croquet greensward, fully equipped exercise room, and, at this family-friendly resort, a children's playground and day camp.

For special pampering, schedule a session of massage therapy, either at the massage center or in your room. You can add your own touch of class to your getaway by ordering up a Grand Romance Package, Gourmet Picnic Baskets, and more.

The 18-hole championship golf course was designed by Donald Ross in 1924, and the Linville Golf Club has been recognized by *Golf* magazine as a Silver Medalist for Best Golf Resorts in America. Many golf legends have played on this award-winning course.

The course is open to members of the Linville Golf Club and to those staying at the Eseeola Lodge.

## Madison County

**WOLF LAUREL RESORT**  $$$–$$$$
**383 Wolf Laurel Rd., Marshall**
**(828) 680-9777, (800) 221-0409**
**www.wolflaurelresort.com**
Spread below 5,600-foot Big Bald Mountain, Wolf Laurel Resort is a 5,000-acre private resort community about 15 minutes north of Mars Hill. The resort is also open to mountain vacationers. Play 18 holes of golf on a challenging mountaintop course full of ridges, hills, and winding curves. The ski slopes of Ski the Wolf are just next door. (See our Golf and Skiing chapters.) Two tennis courts provide sport and recreation, as does hiking in the surrounding areas. A portion of the Appalachian Trail passes just a mile away. Fish in

a mountain stream, swim, or picnic in a wooded glade—this resort uses the surrounding environment to its great benefit.

## Watauga County

**CHETOLA RESORT**  $$–$$$$
**North Main Street, off U.S. Hwy 221,**
**Blowing Rock**
**(828) 295-5500, (800) 243-8652**
**www.chetola.com**
Chetola is the Cherokee word for "haven of rest." And as you approach the resort lodge down the country lane that winds around serene Chetola Lake, you will understand the inspiration for the name.

This fine resort just outside Blowing Rock (off the Highway 321 bypass) has a long history. The estate was first purchased by Lot Estes back in 1846 for a mere $5. He called it Silver Lake. The property changed hands and served the next 50 years primarily as a way station for coach traffic. Then at the turn of the 20th century, as roads improved, the inn became a fashionable accommodation for lowlanders escaping the oppressive heat of the Deep South. One such lowlander, Alabama lumberman W. W. Stringfellow, fell in love with the High Country, purchased the Silver Lake property, renamed it "Chetola," and built the fine manor house that remains today. The property was sold once again, in 1924, to J. Luther Snyder, known as the "Coca-Cola King of the Carolinas." Snyder bought additional adjoining property and continued to improve the estate. He built houses on the property for his children and their families and added a swimming pool and bowling alley.

The marvelous manor house is now home to the Manor House Restaurant, its ambience enhanced by the rich architectural character of the structure. Snyder's Soda Shoppe features sandwiches, burgers, and ice-cream specialties. It is located in the recreation center. A 42-room Chetola Lodge and Conference Center includes spacious suites and professional meeting and conference space.

The resort offers a wide variety of diversions: boating on seven-acre Chetola Lake, hiking on

## Close-up

## Crossnore makes history

The mountain town of Crossnore, North Carolina bears the name of its first postmaster. John Crossnore ran a general store where the post office was established. A name was needed for it and his was used.

This little town is located off U.S. Highway 221, 8 miles south of Grandfather Mountain. The Crossnore Weavers and Gallery is a working museum. Profits from sales are used to support the Crossnore School.

It was in the early 1900s that Dr. Mary Martin Sloop arrived in the mountains and began to carve a legacy of hope for an impoverished but proud people. She fought against child marriages and moonshining. She revitalized the almost forgotten art of handweaving. With some help, she built the Crossnore School, a beacon of light in caring for children, and then in 1951 she was named American Mother of the Year. Dr. Sloop died in 1962 and is buried in the cemetery adjoining the Crossnore Presbyterian Church.

This complex is worth a visit. In addition to the Weavers Gallery, the Sloop Chapel is a beautiful edifice comprised of wormy chestnut paneling on the interior housed by rocks from the Linville River.

Ben Long, world-renowned fresco artist, recently completed a piece in the Sloop Chapel. The title is "Suffer the Little Children," which personifies the mission of the Crossnore School. For more information, visit www.crossnoreschool.org.

the trails of Moses Cone Memorial Park just over the hill, cross-country skiing on the nearby Blue Ridge Parkway, and tennis on Chetola's five courts. Highlands Sports & Recreation Center at Chetola houses an indoor pool, a fitness center, whirlpool, sauna, massage therapy, body wraps, and regulation racquetball courts. Premier golf and skiing resorts are just minutes away in nearby Blowing Rock, Boone, and the Banner Elk area. You can fill your days and nights entirely with the luxury of Chetola. (See our Golf and Skiing chapters for more information.)

**HOUND EARS CLUB**      **$$$$**
**Hwy 105, between Boone and Blowing Rock**
**(828) 963-4321**
**www.houndears.com**
Cradled in a splendid valley of the magnificent northern mountains south of Boone off Highway 105 South is Hound Ears Club, which takes its curious name from a prominent rock formation on the ridge high above the club. You can reach the club on Highway 105, 6 miles from Boone. (A large sign will alert you).

A scenic, 18-hole golf course, complete with waterfalls, lakes, and streams, makes an interesting challenge for avid golfers. Tennis players can take to one of the six clay or two hard-surface courts here. Tennis instruction is available for all ages, or you can just enjoy a leisurely game with friends.

The swimming pool at Hound Ears is unique and secluded, tucked back into the mountain in a natural grotto. The huge rock grotto surrounding the pool and pavilion area creates a natural swimming spot with an important manmade comfort: The pool is heated to a constant 85 degrees.

If you like horseback riding, stables and bridle trails are just a few miles away at Moses Cone Memorial Park.

The long-range panoramic view from the balcony guest rooms in the Hound Ears lodge is incredible. Modified American Plan rates and special golf and tennis package rates are available at various times of the year.

## WESTGLOW SPA $$$$
**2845 US 221 South, Blowing Rock**
**(828) 295-4463, (800) 562-0807**
**www.westglow.com**

This is a year-round resort and European-style spa set in an elegant, historic plantation-style mansion that looms over the highway on its green hill. The object here is to pamper, rejuvenate, and reenergize yourself. The spa's program includes a variety of treatments—body sloughing, aromatherapy, herbal body wraps, Parisian body polish, facials, foot reflexology, and body massage. Fitness programs are also a large part of the schedule. Weekly weight management programs that include nutrition and diet assessment are also offered. The "resting room" has some of the best views in the High Country, awash in neutral colors, a glass-enclosed fireplace, and contemporary art.

But come simply to enjoy the lovely Greek-revival mansion that served as home to the artist and writer Elliott Daingerfield. Plush bedrooms and suites, luxurious Aqua di Parma bath accessories, the fabulous Rowland's dining experience, grand breakfasts, and charming evening wine and cheese meetings and music in the drawing room are among the many reasons to take respite here.

Choose from a day sampler to all-inclusive overnight stays. Rates vary according to the kind of treatment and length of stay.

## YONAHLOSSEE RESORT & CLUB $$$$
**226 Oakley Green, Boone**
**(828) 963-6400, (800) 962-1986**
**www.yonahlossee.com**

Yonahlossee is Cherokee for "trail of the bear." The emphasis here is on horseback riding and tennis. Both recreations are taken seriously, and this former girls' camp with its spectacularly lush, secluded 300 acres is the perfect setting for both.

The award-winning Racquet Club at Yonahlossee won the tennis industry's prestigious Court of the Year award in 1989. Six outdoor clay courts are surrounded by large viewing decks. Bad weather doesn't stall tennis enthusiasts here: Three indoor Deco-Turf courts with large climate-controlled viewing areas assure tennis play summer or winter, rain or shine.

Yonahlossee's Saddle Club continues over 60 years of tradition and accommodates the serious rider as well as the novice. A large 28-stall barn, spacious tack rooms, generously sized stalls, a lounge, and wash stalls provide all the necessary convenience any horse person (or horse!) could want. There are also miles of trails, an outdoor arena, and a cross-country jumping course. If you vacation with your horse, you can board him here while you visit. Year-round boarding is also available.

You can also take advantage of the outdoors at Yonahlossee's small lake, an ideal place for canoeing, fishing, and swimming. Or swim inside in the lovely 75-foot indoor swimming pool. Other golf and ski areas are about 20 minutes in either direction.

Accommodations include fully equipped, beautifully appointed cottage suites nestled in the woods of Yonahlossee. These casually elegant, rustic cabins have fireplaces and private decks. The resort also has two- and three-bedroom townhomes in contemporary designs of wood and glass, many with long-range views of the surrounding mountains.

The Gamekeeper Restaurant is on the resort grounds and has a tempting menu studded with exotic wild game dishes and other fine cuisine (see our Restaurants chapter).

# Yancey County

## CLEAR CREEK GUEST RANCH $$-$$$
**100 Clear Creek Dr., Burnsville**
**(828) 675-4510, (800) 651-4510**
**www.clearcreekranch.com**

The Clear Creek Guest Ranch is truly a resort for the entire family. Don't expect to be lounging around the pool with cocktails at this resort. Able to accommodate up to 50 people at a time in one- to three-bedroom units, the ranch welcomes families, couples, and groups, as well as individuals, because you won't be on your own here for long. You will have plenty of opportunities to join in group activities such as horseback riding, tubing, white-water rafting, hiking, barbe-cues, and other fun. The family-style seating in the dining room of the main lodge, a grand hall with a rustic adjacent living room area, ensures that you will get to know your neighbors over breakfast and other meals.

The atmosphere of Clear Creek is casual. At an elevation of 3,000 feet, the ranch perches at the foot of a mountain range and offers a splendid view of Mount Mitchell and the Pisgah National Forest environs. The guest units, built of rough-hewn log siding, are spacious and modern, with porches and rocking chairs outside each door. Air-conditioning and ceiling fans in each room are perfect for sultry summer nights, and large pine beds, covered with fluffy pillows and patchwork-quilt comforters keep you toasty warm on cooler evenings.

Most of your day will be spent on the trails, either riding (Western saddle) on the morning ride, afternoon ride, or all-day ride, led by expe-rienced wranglers (also students, many from a college specializing in equestrian studies); tubing down the South Toe River; white-water rafting with one of the local outfitters; golfing at the nearby Mount Mitchell Golf Course; hiking some of the many trails of the Pisgah National Forest; or sightseeing.

Counselors offer special activities for chil-dren between the ages of 5 and 12 during the summer. Ping-Pong, volleyball, pool, and video games are provided in a special building "just for kids."

The live-in chef and his helpers, usually col-lege students from all over the country, whip up three hearty meals a day for guests, including homemade soups, breads, pastries, and main dishes.

# CENTRAL MOUNTAINS

## Buncombe County

**GROVE PARK INN RESORT & SPA  $$$–$$$$**
**290 Macon Ave., Asheville**
**(828) 252-2711, (800) 438-5800**
**www.groveparkinn.com**

The Grove Park Inn is one of the premier land-marks of the city of Asheville. Kings, U.S. presi-dents, inventors, golf legends, famous actors, and writers (Eleanor Roosevelt, Franklin Roosevelt, Harry Houdini, George Bush, Henry Ford, Thomas Edison, and Mikhail Baryshnikov, to mention a few) have all passed through the massive stone portico of the Grove Park Inn.

The inn, built in 1913 from tremendous boul-ders blasted out of nearby Sunset Mountain, was an engineering marvel and the personal vision of dynamic entrepreneur E. W. Grove, who invented Grove's Chill Tonic, a drink claiming to have "medicinal" value for many aches and pains. He came to Asheville during the city's turn-of-the-20th-century boom period, attracted by the natu-ral beauty of the area and the city's possibilities. With the Grove Park Inn, E. W. Grove left not only an architectural legacy to the city of Asheville, but, by example, a spirit of business foresight and daring that continues to define the unique character of our small mountain city.

The inn has had continuous success through the years. The Sammons Corporation acquired the Grove Park Inn in the 1950s, and the result-ing growth and innovation spearheaded by this ownership continues in the Grove tradition. Two new wings, designed to maintain the archi-tectural integrity of the original structure, have been added. The Sammons Wing, built in 1984, also houses a gallery of specialty shops. In 1988 the Vanderbilt Wing was completed. It has 166 rooms, 28 of which comprise the private guest rooms and suites of the Club Floor. The original stone edifice is composed of 142 rooms.

The inn is furnished with antique pieces in the rich oak texture and artistic line of the Arts and Crafts style so popular in the early 1900s. The inn's Great Hall is dominated by fireplaces at either end. Measuring 6 feet deep, 6 feet high, and 12 feet wide, these hearths are truly room size in proportion. This majestic old inn with its distinctive red-shingled roof sits command-ingly on Sunset Mountain. With the lush golf lawn spread out before it, it makes a stunning visual impression on the approach from Kimberly Avenue.

Open year-round, the inn is alive with activity. Golf has always played a major role in the history of the Grove Park Inn. The 18-hole course, designed in the 1920s by renowned golf architect Donald Ross, has hosted many of golf's greats: Bobby Jones, Arnold Palmer, Jack Nicklaus, Ben Hogan, Sam Snead, Fuzzy Zoeller, and Doug Sanders, to name a few. A comprehensive golf program is administered by the inn's golf professional. There is also a well-stocked sports shop for your convenience.

Other recreation at the inn includes an indoor and an outdoor pool, racquetball and squash courts, and three indoor and six outdoor tennis courts, two of them clay. A tennis pro is on staff to give instruction and lessons. The inn also has a health club for aerobics, weight training, sauna, and whirlpool treatments and massage. In 2001 the inn added a world-class spa, built partially underground between the two residential wings.

Dining is an experience at the Grove Park Inn. The Blue Ridge Dining Room offers a breakfast, lunch, and dinner buffet, where tables groan with seasonal bounty.

Chops, the inn's elegant outdoor restaurant, needs no decor, only the colors of the evening sky. This eatery features all that is excellent in steak. Evening entertainment of jazz, pop, and classical music fills the air in the casual atmosphere of the terrace. For other fine dining, try Horizons at the Grove Park Inn. Reservations are required for Horizons and Chops.

## Henderson County

**HIGHLAND LAKE INN—A COUNTRY
RETREAT**                          **$$–$$$**
**Highland Lake Rd., Flat Rock
(828) 693-6812, (800) 762-1376
www.hlinn.com**
This country retreat offers an expanse of 180 wooded and pastured acres. Its award-winning restaurant offers breakfast, lunch, and dinner. Special events are offered monthly as well as a sought-after Sunday brunch. The *Wine Spectator*'s Award of Excellence is only one of the many accolades heaped upon the restaurant and the inn.

You can have your choice of accommodations. There are 20 rooms with private baths in the lodge, which has a spacious lobby with a large fireplace and an atmosphere that is modern and rustic at the same time. Each cabin duplex has one large room with a fireplace and one small room; each unit has its own entrance and private bath. The "inn" at Highland Lake has romantic rooms with fireplaces and whirlpools. There are also five cottages that range in size from two bedrooms and two baths to four bedrooms and two baths.

Just across the way, there's a nine-hole golf course; and—remember this is "Historic Flat Rock"—the Carl Sandburg Home, St. John in the Wilderness church, and the Flat Rock Playhouse are also just minutes away (see our Attractions and Arts and Culture chapters).

To get to the Highland Lake Inn—a perfect place for business conferences, group retreats, and family reunions as well as family or personal vacations—take U.S. Highway 25 South out of Hendersonville for about 5 miles and turn left onto Highlands Lake Road at the Pinecrest Presbyterian Church. The entrance to the inn is at the waterfall.

## Rutherford County

**THE CHALET CLUB**                 **$$$–$$$$**
**532 Washburn Rd., Lake Lure
(828) 625-9315, (800) 336-3309
www.chaletclub.com**
This secluded mountainside resort offers a lodge and seven spacious cottages. Fabulous views can be enjoyed from the large balconies. This family-owned and -operated resort pampers its guests with three meals a day of contemporary southern cooking. The meals are served buffet style in the dining room. Available activities are fishing, boating, water skiing, tennis, swimming, and hiking on 7 miles of private trails.

## Transylvania County

**EARTHSHINE**                      **$$$–$$$$**
**1600 Golden Rd., Lake Toxaway
(828) 862-4207
www.earthshinemtnlodge.com**

**Close-up**

## The Mystery of the Pink Lady

It's been said that there is a sad but gentle ghost residing within the gray granite walls of Asheville's historic Grove Park Inn, known as the Pink Lady. She has been seen, felt, and experienced by hotel employees and guests for more than a half-century. The mystery centers around Room 545 in the Main Inn, where employees, guests, and repair workers have seen or heard ghostly phenomena, including unexplained chills and rushes of cold air and the feeling of a presence of some type, prompting the hotel's engineering facilities manager in 1995 to write: "I was on my way back to check a recent bathtub resurfacing in Room 545. As I approached the room, my hair suddenly lifted from my scalp and stood on end on my arms. Simultaneously I felt a very uncomfortable cold rush across my whole body." His words echoed those of a painter who had worked in the hotel in the 1950s. Neither of these employees knew of the other's experiences.

Other employees as well as guests have mentioned that they have seen the luminous form of a lady dressed in pink party clothes, whisking around corners of the grand hotel. The legend dates back to senior employees' recollections of a young woman, dressed in pink, who fell to her death in the Palm Court Atrium around 1920, several stories below Room 545. The manager of the Grove Park Inn, who has seen the Pink Lady several times, explains: "It's like a real dense smoke—a pinkish pastel that just flows. It's a real gentle spirit, whatever it is."

The environmentally friendly simplicity makes Earthshine a wholly different kind of resort, but one that has gained national fame. Accounts of visits and articles on this unique destination frequently appear in the national media, and the L.L. Bean company has used Earthshine more than once as the setting for the photos in its famous catalog.

The cedar-log lodge, with its eight guest rooms and massive rock fireplace, was built by hand in 1988 by owners Marion Boatwright and Kim Mauer (with a little help from their friends) on the site of a 100-year-old homestead bordering Pisgah National Forest. Each room has a private bath and a "little house on the prairie loft" that makes it large enough for a family. Sunrise Cottage, a classic chalet, is also available for guests.

You can also learn homesteading skills, such as animal care and organic gardening. If you come in May, you can help shear sheep. Children can travel back through time 150 years when they work and play at Earthshine's pioneer homestead or its secret Cherokee hideout, where they'll learn ancient games, dances, work skills, and forest ways. They can also take a real wilderness trek—bushwhacking, creek hiking, and learning to build fires. On most Sunday nights kids can learn what it's like to camp out in a barn loft. Cowpokes who aren't quite ready for the trail can hone their skills taking ring rides.

In the evenings you can join in rousing sing-alongs, mountain dances, Cherokee ceremonies, games, and other entertainment. Or you can choose to simply relax in a hammock or rocking chair. Earthshine is also available for family reunions, weddings, training retreats, and seminars, and it operates a year-round outdoor education program for students in grade four and higher.

Rates include lodging and three mighty meals a day, prepared mostly from scratch (see our Restaurants chapter). There's an extra charge for horseback riding and the high ropes course.

**THE GREYSTONE INN** $$$$
Off US 64, Lake Toxaway
**(828) 966-4700, (800) 824-5766**
**www.greystoneinn.com**
Pampered comfort awaits you at Greystone. First, a little history: A hundred years ago, a group

called the Lake Toxaway Company built a 640-acre lake in the high mountains between Brevard and Cashiers that they called "America's Switzerland." There they created a five-story, 500-room hotel out of the finest woods and with the most modern conveniences, such as electric lights, bathrooms, elevators, steam heat, refrigeration, and long-distance telephone and telegraph service. They offered European cuisine, full orchestras for dancing and lavish balls, and all those outdoor sports we enjoy today: tennis, horseback riding, sailing, fishing, and more. The lake attracted Savannah native Lucy Armstrong Moltz. In 1915 she moved into her "small summer place" on the lake—a magnificent six-level, 16,000-square-foot Swiss chalet. However, weakened by a flood, the Toxaway dam broke in 1917. It took until 1960 to restore the dam and the lake. In 1985 the Moltz home, which is now on the National Register of Historic Places, was elegantly renovated and opened as the Greystone Inn.

Each of the 19 antique and period-reproduction bedrooms in the Mansion, as it's called, has its own unique character. The Lakeside Cottage, which was built in 1995, has two luxurious private suites with an adjoining door for families or couples traveling together.

Next door, the Hillmont Building (where 12 spacious, luxurious rooms have private balconies overlooking the lake) was built in 1988 in a manner that blends with the architectural style and furnishings of the Mansion. All these rooms have Jacuzzis, wet bars, sitting areas, and gas fireplaces.

The rates, which are on a Modified American Plan, include your room, an incredible High Country breakfast menu from which you can order anything you desire, and dinner with a varied menu. The rates include soft drinks and complimentary hors d'oeuvres; mid-afternoon tea, coffee, and cake served on a wicker-filled sunporch; a daily newspaper; water skiing, hydrosliding, and tubing with the boat, equipment, and driver provided; a daily champagne cruise on a canopied electric boat; use of a bass boat and fishing equipment; tennis court time; croquet, volleyball, and other outdoor sports; swimming in the pool or off the dock at the lake; and evening turndown service. A spa and sauna are on the grounds.

Maps are available to spectacular waterfalls and hiking trails on the Lake Toxaway property, and the inn has six mountain bikes for guests' use. On Wed, weather permitting, there's a mountaintop cheese and wine outing. Arrangements can be made for shopping excursions to Highlands, Cashiers, Brevard, and Asheville. The Greystone also owns memberships in the Lake Toxaway Country Club so that all their guests can make use of those facilities, including its 18-hole, par 71 championship golf course. During certain periods both green fees and golf carts are complimentary.

## Transylvania County: The Pretty Place

This is one of those spots known more by locals than by tourists. Well-attended Easter sunrise services are held here, as are many weddings. The waves-of-mountains vista is framed by an open-sided chapel, called Symmes Chapel, with steeply sloping tiers of seats fitted to the side of the mountain. The view is—we aren't exaggerating—truly breathtaking.

To find the Pretty Place, which is part of the facilities of Camp Greenville, a summer camp, take U.S. Highway 276 out of Brevard toward Greenville, South Carolina. Drive 12 miles until you see the turnoff at the YMCA Camp Greenville sign on the left. Follow the signs for about 4.5 miles, enter the camp, and drive to the chapel. It's a side trip well worth taking. However, no picnicking is allowed in the area.

# SOUTHERN MOUNTAINS

## Graham County

**HISTORIC FONTANA
VILLAGE RESORT**       **$–$$$$**
Hwy. 28, Fontana Dam
(828) 498-2211, (800) 849-2258
www.fontanavillage.com

Fontana is more than a resort. It's actually a small, secluded, self-contained town that's a fascinating part of our nation's history. In Dec 1941 the Japanese bombed Pearl Harbor, and the nation knew right away that it was going to need new sources of electrical energy to power the war effort. Twenty-four days later, on New Year's Day 1942, the Tennessee Valley Authority (TVA) got the assignment to build a 480-foot-tall dam, the highest in the eastern United States, across the Little Tennessee River. Overnight a village for workers and their families sprang up; the village included a school, a 50-bed hospital, churches, and space to play. Work on the dam went on around the clock, seven days a week. On Nov. 7, 1944, the project was complete; Fontana Lake's 10,600 acres filled with water, and electricity began to zip through the wires to Oak Ridge not far away over the mountains.

After the war there was power to spare for rural electrification, and the dam proved itself in flood control. Not long after that the village was transformed into a year-round resort and has been improving ever since. On the southern border of the Great Smoky Mountains National Park, Fontana Village offers guided hikes, arts and crafts shops, three swimming pools (one indoor), a giant waterslide, an exercise spa, horseback and bike riding, miniature golf, volleyball, basketball, softball, tennis, a playground, a trout pond, a church, a post office, a village store, an ice-cream parlor, the Village Grill for hamburgers and pizza, the Peppermill Buffet House, a small museum, and a host of activities, including traditional Smoky Mountain dances and other entertainment. It also operates the Fontana Marina on Fontana Lake, where you can take a lake cruise or rent all kinds of boats. The fishing is great in both the lake and nearby trout streams (see our Recreation chapter).

As for accommodations, you're almost sure to find something to fit your budget and group size. There are rooms at the inn (some with fireplaces), cottages with kitchenettes (some as large as three bedrooms and three baths with a fireplace and whirlpool), and campground sites.

In addition to the previously mentioned eating establishments, the village also has a fine restaurant at the inn, and the village store has provisions for meals in your cottage and for cookouts and picnics. Special weekend getaways are available in winter.

**i**   Graham County's Maple Spring Observation Point is the highlight of a 900-foot loop trail, designed for wheelchair use that includes a deck that opens to a sweeping view of mountain peaks and valleys. It is on Wagon Train Road (SR 1127) approximately 4.5 miles beyond the entrance road to the Joyce Kilmer Recreation Trail.

## Haywood County

**CATALOOCHEE RANCH**       **$$–$$$$**
119 Ranch Dr., Maggie Valley
(828) 926-1401, (800) 868-1401
www.cataloocheeranch.com

For more than 65 years Cataloochee Ranch has welcomed guests to its 1,000-acre resort that's a mile high in the Great Smoky Mountains. In 1934, when the area was still a pristine wilderness, Tom and "Miss Judy" Alexander acquired what had been a rugged sheep and cattle farm and turned it into this mountain legend. Today, family members still run the ranch, which borders the Great Smoky Mountains National Park.

The name Cataloochee comes from the Cherokee ga-da-lu-sti, which has been translated as "standing up in a row" or "wave upon wave," a reference, no doubt, to the range upon range of mountains—the Blue Ridge and the Smokies—that are visible here. The ranch itself has three major peaks: Fie Top, Moody Top, and Hemphill Bald, with elevations from 4,700 to 5,680 feet.

There are accommodations for 70 guests. You can stay in one of 16 cabins that sleep two to eight people (two of the cabins were originally pioneer log homes). Laurel and Wintergreen each have a living room, two bedrooms, two baths, and a fireplace. Azalea, Rhododendron, Sourwood, Chestnut, and Crabapple—one-bedroom, one-bath cabins—all have fireplaces. Four cabins—Pond House, Willow, Dogwood, and Sassafras—each have fireplaces and Jacuzzi tubs. They are great for couples. In the Silverbell Lodge, you have many options, including one- or two-bedroom suites or individual cabins with fireplaces.

The historic main Ranch House, once a large barn, also has guest rooms, a great room, and a dining hall. The furnishings throughout the resort feature colorful quilts and primitive or classic antiques that reflect the ranch's pioneer heritage. At this altitude air-conditioning is not needed. In early morning and during the evening, even in summer, a fire in the fireplace is usually more desirable.

Daily rates include breakfast and dinner. These are family-style feasts you'll never forget (see our Restaurants chapter). There are also frequent outdoor cookouts and a beer and wine service. Other amenities include a trout pond, a 20-foot heated swim-spa, horseshoe pits, Ping-Pong tables, a croquet court, and hiking paths.

But the real star here is horseback riding. The guided rides usually last two to three hours. Twice a year longer trips for experienced riders are offered. Call the ranch for more information.

Cataloochee Ranch is also the closest facility to the Cataloochee Ski Resort, just a mile over the hill, which has winter ski packages. Though no meals are served at the ranch at this time, stays here are very reasonably priced. Restaurant services are available at the ski lodge (see our Skiing chapter).

## MAGGIE VALLEY CLUB          $–$$$
**1819 Country Club Rd., Maggie Valley**
**(828) 926-1616, (800) 438-3861**
**www.maggievalleyresort.com**
The mountains, as is typical in this particular area, soar almost straight up around the valley where this resort is nestled. They also shelter it from extremes in temperature. In summer the greenness of its forested slopes and well-cared-for grounds and gardens is totally soothing to the soul. One of this resort's main attractions is its golf course. It has been the site of four North Carolina Open golf tournaments, and *Golfweek* rates it as one of America's best. There is also a driving range and practice area, a pro shop, locker room, and a professional staff that offers clinic and private instruction (see our Golf chapter for more information). Two hard-surface tennis courts are adjacent to the golf course. There's also an oversize swimming pool surrounded by trees, flower and herb gardens, and relaxing scenery.

The Valley Room, the resort's restaurant, serves breakfast, lunch, and dinner, including popular theme buffets. On some evenings there's live entertainment and dancing, including a clogging show on Thurs nights. A full-service lounge called the Pin High Club overlooks the golf course. Rates are reasonable here, and the resort also offers money-saving golf packages that include greens fees, use of the tennis courts and pool, full country breakfasts, and dinner at the Valley Room. In the winter you can get ski packages that include lift tickets at the nearby Cataloochee Ski Area and a full country breakfast.

Rooms in the guest lodges are spacious, and each has its own balcony, cable TV, and coffeemaker. Guest villas are on the golf course's back nine. Each villa has a living room, dining area, and furnished kitchen, and both one-bedroom, one-bath and two-bedroom, two-bath units are available. Ask about special vacation and golf packages.

**i** With so many fabulous dinners and snacks, resort guests find themselves putting on the pounds over a weekend. Be active and stroll the grounds before or after dinner and make use of the equipment or sports activities provided.

## WAYNESVILLE COUNTRY CLUB INN  $–$$$$
**176 Country Club Dr., Waynesville**
**(828) 452-2258, (800) 627-6250**
**www.wccinn.com**

This may be a contemporary resort, but it's kept one very old tradition of mountain inns: rocking-chair hospitality. French doors lead from the modern lodge to the 270-foot-long main terrace that overlooks the manicured acres of its golf course. As in the old days, it's lined with rocking chairs—just one hint of the southern hospitality you'll find here.

Nestled between the Blue Ridge and the western ridges of the Great Smokies, this resort offers 27 picturesque holes of golf with fairways winding like ribbons through the mountain valley (see our Golf chapter). Accommodations are gracious and varied. Rooms in the main lodge or its Woodcrest wing offer panoramic views of the first tee. The Brookside or the Fairway lodges have porches or balconies within putting distance of the golf course. For a more private setting, you can stay in the Senator or Governor cottages, or the two-bedroom Country Villa, which features a kitchen and dining area. All accommodations have cable TV and air-conditioning. There is also a swimming pool and two tennis courts near the main lodge.

For meals you have your choice of the main dining room or a light to lavish lunch at the Tap Room. (The Tap Room is also open at night.) Golfers can also grab a bite at the Creekside Pavilion. "Good food," the managers say, "is as important as good golf." In testament to this, all the bread is freshly baked on the premises.

The Tower Lounge is the place to go to quench your thirst. The resort's nine meeting rooms will seat from 10 to 300 people. Numerous golf, holiday getaway, and special winter packages are available.

## Jackson County

**FAIRFIELD SAPPHIRE VALLEY**     **$$–$$$$**
**70 Sapphire Valley Rd., Sapphire**
**(828) 743-3441, (800) 533-8268**
**www.fairfieldsapphirevalley.com**
It all began back in 1896 with the opening of Fairfield Inn on Fairfield Lake. Although the inn is gone, the pristine scenery and a distinctive way of life remain. Nestled in the south Blue Ridge Mountains, Fairfield Sapphire Valley has become a 5,700-acre, four-season resort community.

A wide variety of on-site amenities will please every member of the family. Sapphire Mountain Golf Club, a par 70 championship course, is highlighted by its signature waterfall hole. The tennis center features eight Har-Tru courts, two all-weather courts, and a complete pro shop with instruction. The newly renovated recreation center features one indoor pool, two outdoor pools, miniature golf, an exercise room, Jacuzzi and sauna facilities, and a game room. Scenic trail rides are the pride of the equestrian center. Leisurely canoe and paddleboat rides are available in season. Fishing is abundant in the streams and lakes on the property. The recreation department also offers daily excursions to area attractions, a nature program, and hiking. Kids Kamp makes summer an adventure for children ages 3 to 14. Winter sports include skiing and snowboarding.

Accommodations range from hotel rooms to three-bedroom condominiums. Three- and four-bedroom homes are also available.

There are two on-site restaurants that feature fine dining in a casual atmosphere. Mica's Restaurant and the Library Club are open for lunch and dinner to resort guests. O'Connell's Pub and the Library Lounge are available to members.

**HIGH HAMPTON INN AND**
**COUNTRY CLUB**     **$$–$$$$**
**Hwy. 107 South, Cashiers**
**(828) 743-2411, (800) 334-2551**
**www.highhamptoninn.com**
In the early 1800s Wade Hampton II, a South Carolina upcountry planter and owner of Millwood, a Columbia, South Carolina, plantation that was the social center of Southern aristocracy, bought 450 acres in Cashiers. The property served as a farm and hunting preserve and provided escape from heat, humidity, and malaria. Hampton's son, Wade Hampton III, spent a lot of time here before he went on to become a general in the Confederate army and, later, South Carolina's governor and a U.S. senator.

In the 1880s the Hampton Place in the mountains, which by now had a seven-bedroom

# Close-up

## The White Owl of High Hampton

As we mentioned in the listing for High Hampton Inn, Dr. and Mrs. Halsted, the second owners of the High Hampton property, gradually increased their holdings by buying out adjoining farms. In the process Dr. Halsted made an offer for a 50-acre homestead owned by Mr. Hannibal Heaton and his wife. He wanted to sell, but Mrs. Heaton adamantly refused.

"I'll kill myself if you sell our home," she supposedly told her husband.

But Dr. Halsted must have made an offer that Hannibal felt he shouldn't refuse, so off he went to close the deal. But when he returned home with the bill of sale, he found his wife hanging from an oak tree, and the story goes that there was a white owl flying around her head screeching like a crying woman. Some said it was the spirit of the woman herself.

Shortly after his wife's death, Hannibal Heaton disappeared from the Cashiers area and was never heard from again. Mrs. Heaton, a woman of her word, was buried in the Upper Zachary Cemetery, just a short distance from where the High Hampton Inn stands today. And it's still said by some that the owls heard at night around High Hampton are Mrs. Heaton, still crying over the home she loved and lost.

"cottage," a kitchen building, servants' quarters, and outbuildings, was sold to Dr. and Mrs. Halsted (she was Wade Hampton III's niece). Her husband had been the first professor of surgery at Johns Hopkins Hospital, and she had briefly served as head of nursing. They called the place High Hampton, from the title of his ancestral estate in England, known as High Halsted. The couple gradually increased the property to 2,200 acres (see "The White Owl of High Hampton" Close-up). They are responsible for many of the lovely trees and shrubs that are still seen on High Hampton's current 1,400 acres.

After the Halsteds' deaths in 1922, E. Lyndon McKee of Sylva, the father of the present owner, William D. McKee, purchased the estate. The present High Hampton Inn was completed in 1933, and to the pleasure of those who come year after year, time seems to stand still at this resort. "Nothing much changes here but the seasons," it's said. There are no televisions or telephones in the 120 rooms in the lodge and its cluster of cabins. And the accommodations are rustic rather than plush.

You can also rent two-, three-, and four-bedroom homes with fireplaces, kitchens, daily maid service, and resort privileges.

Very popular, but only one aspect of this venerable resort, is the 18-hole, par 71 golf course that offers a scenic vista with every swing of the club (see our Golf chapter). The late George W. Cobb, who designed the course, said, "I've yet to see a course designed by me or others with greater natural beauty or one more enjoyable to play." There are also five fast-dry clay tennis courts, a red-clay court, and a complete tennis shop with regularly scheduled clinics and private lessons.

Daily rates are on a Full American Plan, which includes three buffet-style meals a day. No gratuity or service charge will be added to your bill, and you are not expected to tip.

To reach High Hampton Inn, take US 64 to Cashiers and turn south on Highway 107. The resort will be on your left a short distance out of town.

# BED-AND-BREAKFASTS AND COUNTRY INNS

Everyone needs to get away from time to time to recharge and renew the spirit. Leave behind all the encumbrances of real life and get back to ourselves. Some of us like the anonymity of an obscure roadside motel, or the pure convenience of it, but then there are those times when a bit of real creature comfort and coddling wouldn't be too bad at all. In fact, for many, it's the only way to travel.

North Carolina's mountains are blessed not only with natural beauty but with scores of charming and graceful inns. These jewels can be found scattered all across the area and offer you pampering you probably don't even get at home. The memory of making new acquaintances, enjoying stimulating conversations, and experiencing gorgeous sights, sounds, and tastes will last long after the key has turned in your door back home.

Country inns abound in the Southeast United States. Bed-and-breakfasts hark back to the old English style of housing a traveler and fortifying him or her with a hot breakfast before the long ride onward. The establishments we recommend to you in this chapter are some of the finest examples of the bed-and-breakfast inns and country inns North Carolina's mountains have to offer. Some have lavish surroundings and interiors worthy of a museum estate, and some sport the more simple comforts of home. We've chosen each one—be it unique or traditional—because it offers the traveler a memorable stay. All are devoted to making your stay as pleasing as possible. We've given you the choice of large or small, elegant or rustic, in the heart of town or secluded in the countryside. Use this as a guide and strike out on your own to find out what's so special about Southern hospitality.

## Price Code

The average nightly rate for two adults at the facilities in this chapter is indicated by a dollar-sign ($) ranking in the following chart. Most businesses accept major credit cards for payment, but where no credit cards are accepted, we've noted that information.

| | |
|---|---|
| $ | $81 to $100 |
| $$ | $101 to $120 |
| $$$ | $121 to $180 |
| $$$$ | $181 and more |

These establishments have varying policies concerning children, pets, and cancellation; please inquire about these when you call to make reservations.

## NORTHERN MOUNTAINS

### Alleghany County

**BURGISS FARM BED AND BREAKFAST   $$$**
**294 Elk Knob Rd., off Hwy. 18**
**Laurel Springs**
**(336) 359-2995, (800) 233-1505**
**www.breakfastinn.com**
The Burgiss Farm Bed and Breakfast offers a rollicking good-time atmosphere and country hospitality, thanks to its genial innkeepers Tom and Nancy Burgiss.

A substantial addition to this 1897 farmhouse has created a house within a house. The addition, furnished with lodge-style comfort, has two guest rooms and a private bath, a massive great room with a stone fireplace rising the full height of the vaulted ceiling, a large Jacuzzi room, and even a mountain stream running through it. The complete privacy of these separate guest accommodations is very popular with honeymooners and families. Reservations are required and should be made as soon as you know your travel plans, as dates close out quickly. Also, an added goodie you might find in your room is complimentary wine from the small winery on the premises.

Room prices include your choice of breakfasts—served at the time you desire. Select items from Nancy's creative breakfast menu of such delights as Hawaiian pancakes, eggs Benedict, Canadian bacon, home fries, homemade breads, and baked fruit.

For lively entertainment check out the Burgiss Farm's Mountain Music Jamboree (see our Nightlife chapter). This bluegrass and old-timey mountain music community bash, which gets going every Sat night in the restyled barn, provides great fun. The Burgisses also keep mountain bikes around at no extra charge, for those who like to take a spin down the country roads. Tom and Nancy will recommend a good trail for guests, according to one's abilities.

### DOUGHTON HALL BED & BREAKFAST    $$$
**12668 Hwy. 18, Laurel Springs**
**(336) 359-2341**
**www.doughtonhall.com**
Less than a mile from the Blue Ridge Parkway's exit to rural Laurel Springs is Doughton Hall. Open year-round, this lovely Queen Anne–style home, built in the 1890s, was once home to former Congressman Robert L. Doughton, an influential figure in Congress during the 1940s. Doughton Hall, listed on the National Register of Historic Places, has been newly refurbished by innkeepers Pam and Ed Hall. We felt like part of the family the minute we stepped into the wonderful old entrance hall. The inn has marvelous woodwork, high ceilings, and old-fashioned sitting rooms. The Halls have furnished the home with antiques, some of them original to the house. Photos of Congressman Doughton during his term in Washington decorate the sitting room walls.

You have a choice of three guest rooms, two with private baths that include Jacuzzis. One room has a splendid queen-size brass bed. The buffet breakfast is generous enough to serve a crowd—eggs cooked to order, several kinds of fresh bread, country ham, sausage, bacon, croissants, and more—even if the house isn't full of guests.

You can fish from the creek at the end of the lawn, rock on the front porch, or have a cool drink in the gazebo.

## Ashe County

### RIVER HOUSE    $$$–$$$$
**1896 Old Field Creek Rd., off Hwy. 16 North, Grassy Creek**
**(336) 982-2109**
**www.riverhousenc.com**
The innkeepers have taken pains to re-create and maintain the gentler pace of a time past at River House, an elegant 1870 farmhouse that was once home to a local physician. The home has been meticulously restored and tastefully furnished with period antiques. River House sits near the Virginia border on 125 beautifully rolling acres, a mile of which hugs the New River. The inn, open year-round, offers two guest rooms upstairs in the main house, each with a private bath and a choice of queen- or king-size beds. These two front bedrooms have views of the lazy New River, one of the oldest in the world, and the mountains beyond.

You also have your choice of two cottages, one a former doctor's office, behind the main house. These offer guests a wonderful sense of privacy. Each of the four cottage rooms includes a sitting area and a whirlpool bath. Two rooms have private porches with views of the river or mountains or both!

River House is also home to an exceptional restaurant with a unique menu. (See our Restaurants chapter.)

## Avery County

### ARCHER'S MOUNTAIN INN    $$–$$$$
**2489 Beech Mountain Pkwy., Hwy. 184, Beech Mountain**
**(828) 898-9004, (888) 827-6155**
**www.archersinn.com**

Archer's Mountain Inn, nearly 5,000 feet above sea level, offers views of Sugar and Grandfather Mountains and acres of fresh mountain air, lush foliage, and surrounding flower and herb gardens. The inn has captivated a youthful, inspired audience. Guests enjoy the wood-paneled rooms with high cross-beamed ceilings, the personal fireplaces, the views of the opposing mountain ridge, the private porches with rocking chairs— somehow you just don't want to leave your room.

All rooms have fireplaces, private baths, real down comforters, and coffee- and tea makers. We love the Presidential Suite, a grand affair with 14-foot-high ceilings, a king-size four-poster bed, a large fireplace, a private balcony, and a glassed-in bathroom with a Jacuzzi. We sipped from the complimentary decanter of port until late in the evening, watching the lights twinkle in the valley below. When we opted for company, we sidled up to the bar in the inn's dining room where locals, the innkeepers, guests, and friends were watching the basketball play-offs. You won't be a stranger for long here.

The owners have built walking trails around the inn, which is perched on the edge of Beech Mountain, and a small waterfall flowing into the garden below the terrace, open for dining in the warm months. Breakfast for overnight guests includes a menu of omelettes, fluffy pancakes, French toast, fresh fruit, ham, sausage, bacon, and other offerings. Personal service, excellent food, and a homey but pampered atmosphere make it hard to leave Archer's Mountain Inn.

## THE AZALEA INN                $$$–$$$$
**149 Azalea Circle, Banner Elk**
**(828) 898-8195, (888) 898-2743**
**www.azalea-inn.com**
Originally owned by members of one of Banner Elk's founding families, the house has been restored with antiques, including Banner Elk's first claw-foot bathtub. From its elegantly furnished rooms to cozy porches, the seven-bedroom inn is a pleasing and restful escape.

In the heart of town, the inn is within walking distance of the village shops and many fine restaurants. A full breakfast completes your stay. Two vacation rental cottages are now in the back of the property.

## BANNER ELK INN BED & BREAKFAST                $$$–$$$$
**407 Main St. East, Banner Elk**
**(828) 898-6223**
**www.bannerelkinn.com**
This small, charming inn is convenient to Boone and the ski resorts of the northern mountains. The tasteful decor here has the flavor of both the Victorian era and Old World Europe. All five guest rooms have private baths. Ask about the third-floor Garrett Suite, which is perfect for honeymooners. It has a full bath with a tub for two, a view of the stone fountain in the English garden below, cable television, and a king-size bed.

Breakfasts including banana nut muffins, Parmesan omelette soufflé with cheddar cheese sauce, and pumpkin bread might be on the weekend menu. Weekday breakfasts are full service but a bit simpler. Enjoy gardens with a bubbling stone fountain in the spring and summer. Sugar Tree Cottage in back of the property is available for short-term rental.

## ESEEOLA LODGE                $$$$
**175 Linville Ave., Linville**
**(828) 733-4311, (800) 742-6717**
**www.eseeola.com**
This wonderful old inn is central to the history of Linville as well as to the development of the High Country as a tourist destination. The original Eseeola Lodge, destroyed by fire in 1936, had its beginnings at the turn of the 20th century with the advent of the railroad in these long-remote mountains. As a result of the railroad's coming, Eseeola Lodge and Linville soon became a fashionable watering place for the wealthy of the Southeast. Golf became a passion at the lodge, and a premier 18-hole course designed by renowned golf architect Donald Ross was added in the 1920s. In those early years Eseeola Lodge was the center of community activity and lively entertainment for the village of Linville. (See our Resorts chapter for more.)

ℹ️ Many bed-and-breakfasts and inns package their own coffee blends, jams, herbs, and other goodies. These small souvenirs make lovely gifts for friends, or the house sitter, back home . . . or for yourself as a reminder of a heavenly vacation.

## LINVILLE COTTAGE $-$$$
154 Ruffin St., Linville
(828) 733-6551, (877) 797-1885
www.linvillecottages.com
A whitewashed picket fence surrounds this restored, turn-of-the-20th-century Victorian farmhouse, with its English cottage perennial and herb gardens. The rooms are filled with antiques and collectibles. The charm of the cottage is accented by the eight-gable tin roof, plank floors, and featherbeds. A breakfast room overlooks Grandfather Mountain and the Blue Ridge Parkway. The accommodations allow comfortable lodging with enchanting rooms filled with simple country antiques and collectibles, but very, very casual. Delightful English country-cottage perennial and herb gardens surround the inn. The innkeepers serve a deluxe full continental breakfast of homemade breads and baked goods served with jellies and jams preserved from the gardens. The inn also houses a small shop out back filled with antiques and collectibles.

## Madison County

### BAIRD HOUSE $$$-$$$$
41 South Main St., Mars Hill
(828) 689-5722, (800) 297-1342
www.bairdhouse.com
This fine old house was once the home of Dr. John Hannibal Baird, a medical doctor of the late 1800s, who served the people living in the mountains around Mars Hill. In appreciation for his dedicated service, local residents built this home in the 1890s for Baird, his wife, and their nine children. It was considered one of the grandest homes in the area. Dr. Baird continued his medical practice until his death in the 1920s.

The home is furnished with 18th-century French, English, and American antiques, all chosen with a particular nod to history and many

with stories of their own, such as the Wellington chests used by British naval officers or the wood-framed fanlight .

Baird House contains five guest rooms, two with private baths. Two rooms have fireplaces. A full breakfast is served. Baird House is open year-round except Dec.

### THE DUCKETT HOUSE INN & FARM $$-$$$
433 Lanee Ave., Hot Springs
(828) 622-7621
www.ducketthouseinn.com
Hot Springs, once a fashionable destination for Victorians seeking the curative waters for which the town was named, continues to evoke that earlier charm. Always a popular stopover for hikers of the Appalachian Trail, which passes through town, Hot Springs is currently enjoying a renaissance of sorts, and the Duckett House Inn & Farm is part of that rebirth. With the inn as your base, you can enjoy white-water rafting, the Hot Springs Spa mineral baths, and hiking. This 1900 Victorian farmhouse has six guest rooms and a cottage that sleeps seven.

Room rates include a full vegetarian breakfast. Gourmet vegetarian dinners are available on weekends for an additional charge, made by the charming hosts and long-time Hot Springs residents Brian and Frank.

### MARSHALL HOUSE BED & BREAKFAST INN $-$$
150 Hill St., Marshall
(828) 649-9205
www.marshallhousebandb.com
Marshall House is nestled in the hillside above the town of Marshall, about 30 minutes northwest of Asheville. Noted society architect Richard Sharp Smith built this home in 1903 as the private residence of James H. White, a prominent Madison County community leader and political figure. The distinctive pebble-dash exterior is typical of the homes Smith built in the Asheville area and the cottages of Biltmore Village, commissioned by George Vanderbilt.

Marshall House fosters the serenity of that simpler time, characterized by the town of Marshall itself, just below on the banks of the French Broad River. Choice antiques decorate the house. Two rooms have private baths; the others have shared baths. A sumptuous breakfast of pancakes, French toast or waffles, eggs, and homemade breads or bagels is served to guests in the formal dining room. From the veranda you can see the spectacular French Broad River and the village that hugs its banks. A resident cat and dog share the house with you.

## MOUNTAIN MAGNOLIA INN & RETREAT $$$–$$$$
### 204 Lawson St., Hot Springs
### (828) 622-3543
### www.mountainmagnoliainn.com

The Rumboughs were the founding family of Hot Springs, which was originally called Warm Springs. The name emanated from the natural springs boiling from the ground. Confederate Col. James H. Rumbough built Rutland House in 1868 so that it had the space necessary to accommodate a family of 10. In the 1950s the last of the Rumboughs downsized Rutland by removing its tower and upper two floors. Pete and Karen Nagle of Charlotte, North Carolina, purchased the remains of this once-glorious estate in 1997, planning a minor renovation as their retirement home. But as the work got under way, they discovered that they had a mission to bring Rutland House back to its Victorian glory. They literally raised the roof, returning the upper floors and the tower to their former positions, and reclaimed the grounds from the overgrowth. Amidst this restored luxury, along with contemporary ventilation and heating, they offer individual guest rooms, three two-bedroom suites, and one three-bedroom house. The inn is open year-round except for Jan. The dining room and porch are open to the public for Sunday brunch and nightly dining. Nearby are the hot tubs for dipping and massages. The Appalachian Trail crosses nearby at Max Patch, and trails of lesser mileage also crisscross this mountain valley paradise.

## Mitchell County

### THE SWITZERLAND INN $$$–$$$$
### Mile 334, off the Blue Ridge Parkway, Little Switzerland
### (828) 765-2153, (800) 654-4026
### www.switzerlandinn.com

The Switzerland Inn is a landmark in the northern mountains. Perched high on a ridge, it straddles Mitchell and McDowell Counties and commands one of the most spectacular views in the region. In fact the view is so spectacular that the area derived its name from its resemblance to the equally beautiful mountain views of Switzerland, its European cousin. North Carolina State Supreme Court Judge Herriot Clarkson was the first to be inspired by the Swiss-like atmosphere of this knob, and he determined to make it his own, buying 1,100 acres in 1910. The charm of the place is its unchanging personality, remaining pretty much as it was almost 100 years ago.

The Blue Ridge Parkway exit at Little Switzerland is the only one on the parkway that leads to private land. The Jensen family, longtime seasonal residents who are now permanent mountaineers, purchased the inn in the 1980s. They have maintained the 55-room lodge and its surrounding grounds with the same devotion Judge Clarkson brought to Little Switzerland so long ago.

The Switzerland Inn is a veritable kingdom unto itself with quaint lodging, fine dining, and unusual specialty shopping. Guests mingle in the great hall, playing a friendly game of checkers, relaxing by the fire, listening to the charming strains of a Victorian-era music box, or just burrowing into the comfortable armchairs to watch the mists roll in over the mountain ridge. For summer fun the Switzerland Inn has an outdoor swimming pool and a tennis court.

Shopping along the little avenue of specialty stores adjacent to the Switzerland Inn is a bit like visiting Santa's Main Street. You can find anything from sinfully rich fudge and homemade candies to mountain crafts, unusual toys, ladies' fine accessories, and one-of-a-kind gift items.

If you stay a night at the Switzerland Inn, you'll want to stay a week. Book early for visits during mid-Oct, which is the peak of the leaf season in the North Carolina mountains. The inn is open May through Oct.

## Watauga County

### ALTA VISTA—GALLERY AND BED & BREAKFAST $$$–$$$$
2839 Broadstone Rd., Valle Crucis
(828) 963-5247
www.altavistagallery.com

This historic brick farmhouse in the heart of Valle Crucis cultivates more than just tasty breakfasts, gardens, and charming rooms—it also houses an art gallery on the first floor. With only three guest rooms, Alta Vista is a personable boutique bed-and-breakfast, much like any number of smaller pensions or guest houses in Germany or France. The rooms feature tasteful decor, antiques, queen-size beds, fresh flowers, and private tiled baths. The wonderful breakfasts here, set out on cafe tables in the spacious upstairs corridor, include a hearty breakfast quiche, cinnamon French toast, and home-baked muffins. The gracious hosts lay out homemade cookies on an antique sideboard each afternoon with cold or hot beverages. Alta Vista's perennial gardens deserve an after-breakfast stroll, and you might consider walking on to the Valle Crucis Community Park across the street. It borders the Watauga River.

Particularly engaging and unusual is the Alta Vista Gallery downstairs, which features more than 200 national and international artists. Originals as well as prints allow for an assortment of pricing. Owner Maria Santomasso-Hyde showcases her own impressionist oil paintings here, while you'll also find smaller items of glass, pottery, jewelry, and kaleidoscope crafts.

### GIDEON RIDGE INN $$$–$$$$
6148 Gideon Ridge Inn Rd., Blowing Rock
(828) 295-3644
www.gideonridge.com

Guests at Gideon Ridge are charmed by the magnificent family antiques throughout the house, the views from the rooms, the porches, and the gardens. Paths running through graduated banks dotted with rich yellow black-eyed Susans, rhododendrons, ivy, and a pergola make up the lush gardens. But the small touches will capture your heart here—afternoon tea was spread before us on the dining room island as we arrived. A pot of Earl Grey, which the innkeepers import from England, sat beside plates of light homemade shortbread and finger sandwiches.

Made of cedar and the red stone of Grandfather Mountain, the building itself hugs the ridge. The nephew of Moses Cone, a textile magnate who built mills in Greensboro with the money from his Cone Export & Commission Company in New York City, constructed the home as a mountain cottage in 1939. Carpets and Central Asian kilims lend the hall and dining room their natural earthen warmth. The walnut dining table, a fourth-generation family heirloom, is surrounded by high-back chairs. Four Russian impressionist paintings in muted hues decorate the walls. The artist was a friend of the innkeepers.

The butler's pantry is stocked for guests with cold juices and sodas, a kettle, and plenty of tea, coffee, and hot chocolate–making items. The 10 guest rooms are each unique—adorned with table and chair settings, a large bed, and decorative knickknacks. Seven of them have fireplaces. Think mahogany four-poster beds, marble sinks, and antique furniture in every room. Our favorite is the Sunrise View, set apart from the others with its own private entrance. The king-size bed, piled high with thick pillows and quilts, offers a view out the picture window of the sun rising over 90 miles of mountain peaks. Under the beamed cathedral ceiling is a Franklin iron stove, an open whirlpool tub surrounded by a stone wall, and a bathroom designed with an exposed stone wall in the shower. Each room has a private bath.

Breakfast, set at individual wooden tables in a glass-enclosed terrace above the gardens, can include stuffed French toast, cornmeal pancakes, muffins, waffles, sausage, and numerous other edibles, all attractively presented with fresh fruit.

ℹ️ Watch out for the leaf season, usually all of Oct and the latter part of Sept. This is when most bed-and-breakfasts and inns are completely booked, sometimes a year in advance. It's the perfect time to be in the mountains, but plan ahead for the most pleasurable and restful stay.

## THE INN AT RAGGED GARDENS    $$$–$$$$
**203 Sunset Dr., Blowing Rock**
**(828) 295-9703**
**www.ragged-gardens.com**

This grand old inn surrounded by a stone wall and lovely English cottage-style flower gardens is covered by the rustic chestnut bark siding frequently found on fine older homes in the High Country. Built as a seasonal summer "cottage," the estate has been remodeled to accept guests all year long in its 12 distinctive rooms. These rooms include five suites designed in the Arts and Crafts period style. Each has separate sitting areas, whirlpool baths for two, fireplaces, and balconies or patios looking into the formal rock-walled garden.

Our personal favorites are the Rock Garden Garret and the Evergreen Garret—soothing bedrooms under the eaves of the skylit roof. The Rock Garden is a suite with a king-size bed, a window seat, a whirlpool bath, and a giggling fountain in the reading nook. The Evergreen is resplendent with a unique handcrafted king-size bed, a corner fireplace, and a whirlpool bath with an old-fashioned dressing area—a lady's dream.

Another favorite is the Camelot Suite, a jewel-toned suite with soft ochre walls, a rock fireplace, wrought iron furnishings, and a Middle Eastern wall tapestry. The sitting room contains a twin bed and a love seat, separated from the bedroom by a pair of antique French doors. Other rooms—Monet's Garden, Moss and Lace, Blue Wisteria, and English Lavender—evoke floral garden visions as well.

The central focus of the Inn at Ragged Gardens is its magnificent stone staircase in the grand hall. Another excellent touch is the butler's pantry on the second floor, always furnished with sodas, juices, coffee, tea, mints, hot chocolate, and rich home-baked cookies presented under a glass dome. If the cookies haven't spoiled your breakfast appetite, pull close to the lace-covered table for eggs to order, fresh fruit cups, omelettes, pancakes, waffles, and sausage, only after you have helped yourself to the buffet of muffins, bagels, and breads. Candles glow on the mantel on misty cool mornings, while summer days allow for breakfast out on the porch overlooking the brilliant variety of flowers of the Ragged Gardens.

## LOVILL HOUSE INN                    $$$$
**404 Old Bristol Rd., Boone**
**(828) 264-4204, (800) 849-9466**
**www.lovillhouseinn.com**

This historic home, built in 1875, was the residence of Capt. Edward Francis Lovill, a decorated Confederate officer, North Carolina state senator, and a founding trustee of the Appalachian Training School, later Appalachian State University. In fact it was in the front parlor of Lovill House, the captain's occasional law office, where he and B. B. Daugherty drafted the papers establishing the university. The home continued as a Lovill family residence well into the 1970s.

You'll wake to the rich aroma of home-baked muffins and coffee outside your door. Enjoy a full gourmet breakfast, including seasonal fruit, home-baked breads, Belgian waffles, eggs Benedict, garden vegetable strata, and omelettes, accompanied by country ham, sausage, or bacon. The informal evening social hour is popular with guests of Lovill House. Groups gather outside by the stream, in the rockers on the front porch, or around the cozy front parlor fireplace.

You can hike the trails on the lovely grounds, or the innkeepers can recommend the best local restaurants. Restoration of the grounds and outbuildings continues, with plans for additional accommodations in the future.

The inn is furnished in a casually elegant country style, with a mix of antiques and quality reproductions. The wormy chestnut paneling was discovered during restoration and supplemented by matching refinished wood recovered from old, abandoned barns. The inn offers five guest rooms, each with a private bath, television (discreetly tucked away in a wooden cabinet), and telephone. Beds at the Lovill House are spread with down comforters. The innkeepers encourage you to let them know if you have special dietary requirements, if you'll be celebrating a special occasion, or if you require any other service to make your visit more enjoyable.

## MAPLE LODGE $$$–$$$$
**152 Sunset Dr., Blowing Rock**
**(828) 295-3331, (866) 795-3331**
**www.maplelodge.net**
This charming inn reflects the simplicity and grace of the 1930s and '40s. Named for the maple tree in the front yard, this pleasant two-story frame home was built as a boarding house for tourists. Staying at Maple Lodge reminds us of visiting the elegant, treasure-filled home of a favorite aunt, one who greets you warmly at the door, offers delectable goodies served on fine china and hot cider from her sunny kitchen out back, and ushers you to a more-than-perfect guest room. In short, you feel at home.

Maple Lodge has 11 guest rooms, each named for a garden flower. These rooms, with twin-, full-, queen-, or king-size beds, all have private baths. Some beds have lovely crocheted canopies.

A hearty buffet breakfast includes homemade muffins, breads, a variety of egg dishes, and fresh fruit.

Main Street in Blowing Rock is just a stone's throw from Maple Lodge, convenient to restaurants and shopping. Blowing Rock Stage Company performs just down the street in summer.

## MAST FARM INN $$$$
**SR 1112, off Highway 105, Valle Crucis**
**(828) 963-5857, (888) 963-5857**
**www.mastfarminn.com**
The Mast Farm Inn has been a landmark and vital part of the history of the High Country since 1885. It was operated as an inn by Finley Mast and his wife, Josephine, in the early 1900s. The Masts were known far and wide for their mountain hospitality, not to mention the bounty of their table.

In 1972 the Mast Farm Inn was included on the National Register of Historic Places. It remains one of the best examples of a self-contained mountain homestead in the state. The rambling 18-room Victorian farmhouse is the center of the inn and is open year-round. The main house has nine guest rooms, all with private baths. All rooms have queen- and king-size beds. Original outbuildings—the Blacksmith Shop, the Woodwork Shop, and the Loom House—have been converted to additional, comfortably furnished guest quarters.

The Raspberry Hill Cabin is the newest accommodation here. Built from white pine logs and featuring a cathedral ceiling, it is both rustic and spacious. Sit on the porch and rock for a while—you'll feel as though you own the valley. The cabin features two full bedrooms (one king, one queen), two bathrooms (one with a whirlpool tub), a loft with a double futon, a great room, and a fully equipped kitchen.

The Loom House, the log cabin originally built by David Mast in 1812, was Finley and Josephine Mast's first home. Here Josephine gloried in her weaving, at which she was expert. Some of her work has been featured in exhibits at the Smithsonian Institution. Today the Loom House is a special guest cottage with a kitchen, sleeping loft, and fireplace. The combination of period farmhouse antiques and modern conveniences at the Mast Farm Inn allows guests to easily enjoy the charm of turn-of-the-20th-century mountain life in North Carolina.

Rates include a bountiful breakfast. Breakfast offers something different on the menu every day, but it always features scrumptious homemade breads, fresh fruit, and jams, jellies, and preserves.

Dinner is served six nights a week from May through Oct and on weekends the rest of the year.

## TAYLOR HOUSE INN $$$$
**4584 Hwy. 194, Valle Crucis**
**(828) 963-5581, (800) 963-5581**
**www.taylorhouseinn.com**
This lovely, two-story farmhouse with double chimneys and a wraparound porch was built in

1911 for the family of C. D. Taylor. Today it has been transformed into a sophisticated European-style inn with farmhouse flair. Guests enjoy the inn's mountain escape for family reunions, wedding and anniversary celebrations, special luncheons or dinner parties, art shows, cooking classes, and flower shows.

Taylor House Inn is decorated with a mix of European and American country antiques, Oriental rugs, and original artwork. There are 10 spacious rooms in the inn, all offering private baths and goose-down comforters. Three of the rooms are suites, complemented by comfortable sitting rooms. A gourmet breakfast usually includes seasonal fruit, pancakes, fresh vegetables, and specially prepared egg dishes.

The inn's old milkhouse has been converted into a charming gift shop that offers unusual items, garden accessories, and specialty foods. A private massage parlor is located on the property, and a masseuse is on call for massages, manicures, and pedicures.

## Yancey County

### TERRELL HOUSE BED AND BREAKFAST                    $$–$$$
**109 Robertson St., Burnsville**
**(828) 682-4505, (888) 682-4505**
**www.terrellhousebandb.com**
A little off the beaten path in the friendly township of Burnsville, historic Terrell House is surrounded by mountains, offering its guests vistas of the Blue Ridge Mountains, the Bald and Unakas Ranges, and Seven Mile Ridge. The nearby Black Mountains are capped by the majestic Mount Mitchell. The inn is about 30 minutes from Asheville.

The 1900 Colonial-style home was built as a girls' dormitory for the Stanley McCormick School. You can choose from six lovely guest accommodations, each with its own personality and furnished with a queen- or full-size bed. Each room has a private bath with shower.

You will awake to the aroma of freshly brewed coffee, and a sumptuous breakfast is served in the dining room.

# CENTRAL MOUNTAINS

## Buncombe County

### ALBEMARLE INN                    $$$$
**86 Edgemont Rd., Asheville**
**(828) 255-0027, (800) 621-7435**
**www.albemarleinn.com**
This classic turn-of-the-20th-century Southern mansion once hosted Bela Bartok, during which time he wrote a symphony subtitled, "The Asheville Symphony." The inn offers classic comfort and a gourmet breakfast. It is only minutes from downtown Asheville.

### BLACK MOUNTAIN INN                    $$–$$$$
**718 Old Hwy. 70, Black Mountain**
**(828) 669-6528, (800) 735-6128**
**www.blackmountaininn.com**
Nestled in the forest, the inn was built originally as a stagecoach stop approximately 170 years ago. At the turn of the 20th century, the home was owned by Martha Mallory, who operated the inn as a tuberculosis sanitarium until her untimely death. She was killed on the railroad tracks on her way home from town. The house fell into ruin and became a squatter's camp, complete with cows stabled in the dining room! In the 1940s the house was refurbished and opened as the Oak Knoll Art Studio, which served primarily as a summer retreat. Ernest Hemingway, John Steinbeck, Norman Rockwell, and Helen Keller were among the guests attending the garden parties that were common events all summer long. In 1989 the house, badly in need of further restoration and updating, began its new life as the Black Mountain Inn.

With three acres of wooded property, it's an ideal location for guests who travel with pets. Seven comfortable guest rooms and one suite—the Artist Loft—are decorated in casual old-fashioned furnishings. Each room has its own private bath.

The Artist Loft is a restored art studio with more than 1,000 square feet of private sanctuary with wonderful views. Peter's Room rests among the trees. Throw open the seven windows and wake up with the birds. Fern's Room is one of the pet-friendly rooms. This large, first-floor room is capable of sleeping four and is perfect for families with young children. Emily's Room features a 7-foot, claw-foot tub.

Breakfast at the Black Mountain Inn is a sumptuous buffet featuring homemade granola. Fresh fruits, homemade breads or biscuits, and a main egg course, along with special blend coffee or tea, greet you each morning.

## BLACK WALNUT BED AND BREAKFAST INN $$–$$$$
288 Montford Ave., Asheville
(828) 254-3878
www.blackwalnut.com

Owners Peter and Lori White have operated specialty bakeries at Martha's Vineyard and in West Palm Beach, Florida. They provide many tantalizing breakfast moments for their guests. The Black Walnut Inn stands out significantly from its surroundings as a Shingle-style house built in 1899 by architect Richard Sharp Smith. The mayor of Asheville in the 1930's, Ottis Greene, made this his home. His former one -horse barn is now the updated and modernized "Cottage."
It was restored as a bed-and-breakfast in 1992.

Only a short walk from downtown, the inn is surrounded by a lushly landscaped garden of flowers, black walnut trees, conifers, ivy, perfectly trimmed shrubbery, and a burbling koi pond. Four guest rooms in the main house are filled with antiques, and the newlyrestored garden cottage is pet-friendly (do book this in advance). Plan to be greeted by Belle, a samoyan of high pedigree who welcomes guests with generous wags of her tail.

Enjoy cozying up to the fireplace in the graceful living room for afternoon tea, tidbits, and wine for those of age. A large front porch with rockers allows you to enjoy a balmy summer evening in this mountain town.

## CEDAR CREST $$$$
674 Biltmore Ave., Asheville
(828) 252-1389
www.cedarcrestvictorianinn.com

Less than a mile north of the entrance to Biltmore Estate sits another Victorian beauty. Rising from a flower-bedecked hill on lower Biltmore Avenue, Cedar Crest commands the ascent from Biltmore Village. The traffic scurries uphill toward downtown Asheville, but this exquisite bed-and-breakfast seems forever poised in the Gilded Age.

The opulent Queen Anne–style home was built in 1891 for prominent Asheville businessman William E. Breese. Breese played host to Asheville society, but as the century passed and the prosperous 1920s waned, Cedar Crest fell into disrepair. Through the years the home took on the guise of a sanitarium and, much later, a boardinghouse. Then the founding innkeepers answered an ad in *Preservation News* and came all the way from Wisconsin to rescue this lovely, faded lady. Careful restoration followed, much of it just removing decades of grime and ill-conceived decoration. What emerged was the amazing beauty of rich oak woodwork, intricately carved mantels, and solid Victorian construction. The inn has been lavished with period antiques: claw-foot tubs, delicate lace, brass beds, and Victorian collectibles.

Ten guest rooms are available at Cedar Crest, described by its innkeepers as "a passage to 1890." All rooms are air-conditioned and have telephones and private baths; some rooms have working fireplaces. The upper two floors also feature a sitting area, and guests can sit on the wide veranda. A separate guest cottage, built in 1915, adjoins the main house and is wonderful for vacationing families. The inn is open year-round, and its four acres are planted so that something is in bloom every season. (And there is even a croquet court.)

## CHESTNUT STREET INN $$–$$$$
176 East Chestnut St., Asheville
(828) 285-0705, (800) 894-2955
www.chestnutstreetinn.com

Enjoy a candlelit breakfast at Chestnut Street Inn in this historic district. Late afternoon tea and Fri evening social hour allow you to meet other guests in the antiques-filled parlors. Artworks by local artists provide extra interest. Large four-poster beds satisfy the need for downy comfort, as does the fluffy bathrobe provided for your stay. A chocolate on your pillow ends the day with the luxury in which you began it.

## THE GRAND BOHEMIAN HOTEL   $$$-$$$$
**11 Boston Way, Biltmore Village**
**(828) 505-2949**
**www.bohemianhotelasheville.com**

An unusual 104-room boutique hotel in Biltmore Village just outside the gates of the Biltmore Estate, the Grand Bohemian was built in a pebble-dash Tudor style that fits into its surroundings. The hotel is anything but usual on the inside—from a fireplace open on five sides in the lobby, to mosaic-covered check-in desks where guests are seated in leather chairs upon arrival—everything is a little different here. The privately owned Kessler Collection hotel has original artwork on every floor and a full-fledged art gallery with local and international art that holds artist receptions once a month. Piano music is played almost nightly in the bar, carved wood frames from Bali and India are placed in the ceilings and around doorways, sculptures dot the guest room hallways, and the Grand Ballroom on the top floor is filled with sparkling Swarovski crystal chandeliers. A spa and fitness center are in the main building, as well as the elegant Red Stag Grill (see Restaurants chapter) while an entire gallery annex is located in the smaller, but no less-charming, Manor House across the street.

## THE HAWK & IVY   $$$
**133 North Fork Rd., Barnardsville**
**(828) 626-3486, (888) 395-7254**
**www.hawkandivy.com**

Wake up gazing over a country meadow, take a morning walk to the fish pond or an afternoon stroll through the wildflowers, or even pick a bowl of berries for your breakfast with innkeeper Eve Davis at this country bed-and-breakfast retreat. Eve and her husband James, an ordained minister and licensed contractor, wear many hats at the Hawk & Ivy.

Set in 24 acres of wildflower fields, this farmhouse built in 1910 is only 20 minutes from Asheville but is completely in the country. You can choose between the main house bedroom or three bedrooms in the cottage across the way. The former has its own private bath and an heirloom four-poster bed covered in fine linens and a down comforter. Two bedrooms (one has a double bed, the other two twins), a large shared bath, full kitchen, and living room with fireplace, sofa, television, and phone compose the first floor of the guest cottage. Eve's flower arrangements embellish these charming quarters, as do the fine watercolors on the walls. A second-floor suite completes the cottage, taking up the entire light-filled loft space, and includes a full kitchen, bathroom, extra-long double bed, single bed, and queen-size pull-out sofa. The private deck overlooks a valley, mountain ridges, and the small lake. Both kitchens are supplied with fresh-ground coffee and tea, creamers, and condiments.

Guests dine at the long family table in the dining room, surrounded by early American Impressionist paintings. If weather permits, breakfast is served on the veranda. Breakfast might include a combination of several of the following: fresh baked goods, asparagus omelette, melons with strawberry puree, coffee cakes, baked vanilla French toast, or cheese grits casserole with jalapeños, all served on delicate family heirloom china.

The Davises encourage guests to stroll around the property and will recommend hikes close by. In the field above the farmhouse, a large festival "barn" is the setting for many a wedding, wedding reception, and family reunion. Two knolls have served as locations for nuptials, with live music and buffet tables elegantly arrayed in the rustic wooden structure. On occasion Eve teaches flower arranging and drying and herb preparation workshops out of the barn or in her art studio.

## THE INN AROUND THE CORNER   $$-$$$
**109 Church St., Black Mountain**
**(828) 669-6005, (800) 393-6005**
**www.innaroundthecorner.com**

The Inn Around the Corner features five lovely guest rooms in a restored 1915 Four Square

Victorian House. The upstairs porch, with porch swings and rockers, slows time to a standstill. All rooms have private baths. Quilts on the beds, soft colors, hand-stitched samplers, and floral arrangements mark Grandma's Room, while Beau's is decorated in muted country colors with a patriotic theme. Available only as a suite with Beau's room, Ashley's is a lovely old-fashioned room, located on the second floor with full-size canopied bed. The Spring Garden bears soft yellows, greens, and mauves, which carry out the botanical theme in this wicker-filled room with a full-size bed and single bed. A full-size bed is also available on the porch. A lovely view of the mountains awaits outside the private entrance to the second-story porch. A bountiful breakfast is served to guests in the dining room or on one of the porches, weather permitting. The innkeepers are amenable to special dietary requirements or requests, but be sure to tell them ahead of time.

The inn is close to Black Mountain's quaint downtown shopping area, with a variety of dining possibilities. The inn is also a short distance from a walking trail around Lake Tomahawk.

Hiking, kayaking, rafting, and fishing trips will gladly be arranged by the innkeepers for your enjoyment.

**THE INN ON MILL CREEK**          $$$
**1407 Mill Creek Rd., Ridgecrest**
**(828) 668-1115, (877) 735-2964**
**www.innonmillcreek.com**
Secluded among mountain laurel near the top of the Ridgecrest Pass, the inn's seven scenic acres are hidden in the Pisgah National Forest between the historic villages of Black Mountain and Old Fort.

The inn features four guest rooms or suites, each with private baths and many unique amenities. Also enjoy a two-story great room with a piano corner, a soapstone wood stove, and cozy riverbed-stone hearth. A library nook in the upstairs balcony for quiet reading is lit by a historic cathedral chandelier. The innkeepers provide two choices for your breakfast seating: a warm and open dining room with its own wood stove hearth and great view of the lake, or a

---

### Mount Pisgah

Mount Pisgah is the highest peak on the Asheville Plateau. Standing at 5,700 feet, this mountain overlooks western Buncombe County. Nudging it from the south is "The Sleeping Rat." On its face, after a fierce snow, one can see "The Bride and Groom."

Some folks believe Pisgah is a Cherokee word, but it is found in the Old Testament in Deuteronomy 34:1: "Then Moses went up from the plains of Moab to Mount Nebo, to the top of Pisgah . . . from there he saw the promised land." Assumedly the early settlers of this wilderness of Western North Carolina must have hoped they had reached the promised land after all the hardships they faced in carving trails and homes out of it. They were either Bible-believing people or as survivors became such—thus naming the symbol of their hope Mount Pisgah.

---

south-facing solarium overlooking the dam and waterfall. The solarium also provides a hot tub for evening stargazing or relaxing. Be sure to check out the creekside deck for sunning yourself as you listen to the waterfall or for enjoying a family cookout.

Enjoy the family fish lake, waterfall, and dam, which powers Andrews Geyser in the valley. A sunny deck overlooks the lake and the Long Branch of Mill Creek. The plentiful breakfasts are made with seasonal fruits and berries from the Carillons' own orchard.

**THE LION AND THE ROSE**          $$
**276 Montford Ave., Asheville**
**(828) 255-ROSE**
**www.lion-rose.com**

The Montford Historic District is home to some fine examples of Victorian architecture. The Lion and the Rose, one of these homes, is listed on the National Register of Historic Places. This handsome bed-and-breakfast inn is a simplified Queen Anne/Georgian-style residence, built in 1898, that celebrates the English style. And this stately mansion certainly seems "to the manor born."

The innkeepers Jim and Linda Palmer, have furnished all five faithfully restored guest rooms with period antiques and Oriental rugs. High embossed ceilings, oak woodwork, and leaded- and stained-glass windows are just a few of the architectural details that give distinction to the Lion and the Rose. Each room has a private bath. Jim, former school principal and Linda, former social worker, offer warm hospitality to all. Creatively they produce a breakfast encompassing a meritorial ray of sunshine in the luxuriously appointed dining room. Outdoor comfort is offered on the porch and in the adjoining garden.

## RED ROCKER INN                    $$$–$$$$
**136 North Dougherty St., Black Mountain**
**(828) 669-5991**
**www.redrockerinn.com**

The measured pace of the red rockers on the enormous porch overlooking the lovely gardens of this elegant inn gives you a feel for its relaxing atmosphere. Tucked away in a quiet residential neighborhood in the quaint village of Black Mountain, just 14 miles east of Asheville, the Red Rocker Inn is determinedly slow-paced.

The inn was a boardinghouse known as Dougherty Heights back in 1927. It became the Red Rocker Inn in 1964. The tranquility of the place is its hallmark, and the 17 exquisite guest rooms (each with private bath) reflect this search for inner peace. The warm fireplace and lovers' window seat in Elizabeth's Attic, the inspired stained glass of the Preacher's Room, and the white lace canopy bed in the romantic Anniversary Room are just a few of the thoughtful efforts to give visitors an island of calm. The inn is centrally heated and air-conditioned.

The dining room is a celebrated spot for guests as well as the community. With the generous bounty provided by the innkeepers, the dining room seems to be the only place where guests might exhibit a lack of self-restraint in this peaceful domain. The family-style meals, served on lace-clothed, candlelit tables, are robust and hearty Southern selections heaped on in generous proportions. The Red Rocker Inn is open almost year-round (Feb through Dec). Spectacular season's specials are offered during the winter, spring, and early fall.

## SOURWOOD INN                    $$$$
**810 Elk Mountain Scenic Hwy., Asheville**
**(828) 255-0690, (828) 253-2785**
**www.sourwoodinn.com**

Located just off the Blue Ridge Parkway on 100 acres, this is what a country inn is all about. Walking trails crisscross the forested land, but even just sitting in your room looking out over the mountain through the dense foliage below, you will know you have truly "gotten away from it all." Sourwood Inn is finely constructed of cedar trimmed with stone. The entire structure sits on hilly terrain at an elevation of 3,200 feet. Easily accessible to downtown Asheville, it is nonetheless in the countryside and can feel like wilderness, with densely growing trees and birdsong all around.

Each of the inn's 12 guest rooms has a private balcony overlooking the Reems Creek Valley, a woodburning fireplace, and a tub with a view! When you turn on your faucet to draw a bath, you will be amazed with the ensuing waterfall, thanks to Scandinavian faucetry. The French doors that open onto the guest room balconies let mountain breezes drift in at night. Decorated in muted forest and meadow colors, the rooms are as peaceful within as the idyllic countryside outside.

The inn also maintains numerous public areas—porches with rocking chairs, a lobby with plush chairs in front of a crackling fireplace, and a library stocked with books for your leisure time. There's also a game room downstairs with a billiard table. Susan and Jeff Curtis, who live on the premises, are innkeepers with Susan's parents Nat and Anne Burkhardt.

Sassafras Cabin is nestled in the woods 100 yards from the main inn. Complete with a screened-in porch, the cabin has two full baths, a fully equipped kitchen, a living/dining area, and a bedroom loft. There's a wonderful variety from which to choose at Sourwood Inn. You may never want to leave. Sink back into those chairs, admire the perfectly designed and built carpentry work and decorative touches, grab a good book from the library of Nat's favorites, kick up your feet in front of the fire, and plan a walk in the crisp fresh mountain air after dinner.

**TREE HAVEN BED & BREAKFAST**    **$$–$$$**
**1114 Montreat Rd., Black Mountain**
**(828) 669-3841, (888) 448-3841**
**www.treehavenbandb.com**
A gracious welcome brings you back to a more relaxed, timeless serenity in this 1908 restored home, surrounded by mature oaks, hickory, pine, hemlock, and chestnut trees. Centrally located just outside the gates of Montreat, only a mile from downtown Black Mountain, Tree Haven is ideally situated for both the casual stroller and the serious hiker. Return home to sit on the porch and watch the fireflies light up the night skies, or stroll the grounds bordered by a gently flowing creek. Innkeeper Carol Redmond has traveled the world as a delegate for the sport of synchronized swimming after being honored as a member of the Helms Swimming Hall of Fame. Previously from the West Coast, she has found Black Mountain to be a perfect place for rest and relaxation amidst nature's wonderland. International guests, especially, will find a helpful, if not bilingual, resource for local travel. Carol, an avid hiker herself, will help you find those hidden mountain trails when you can tear yourself away from the homey surroundings of the inn. Private baths, a whirlpool tub, air-conditioning, and a smoke-free environment ensure your comfort at Tree Haven. You can chose from rooms with king or queen beds. Vegetarian breakfasts are also available.

**WHITEGATE INN & COTTAGE**    **$$–$$$$**
**117 East Chestnut St., Asheville**
**(828) 253-2553**
**www.whitegate.net**

The first things you'll notice about this 1889 inn are the unique gardens and greenhouse that surround it. Deliciously landscaped with lush foliage, waterfalls, a koi pond, and a patio with a gas-log fire pit, the WhiteGate Inn makes it hard to want to come inside. But once you do, delight in the large rooms decorated with elegant antiques and Oriental rugs. Saunter down to breakfast, after reading the complimentary morning paper, to a three-course breakfast in the dining room. Monogrammed robes and down comforters have allowed you to revel in comfort the night before. A guest refrigerator remains stocked, and a library has a selection of DVDs, books, and CDs.

## Henderson County

**APPLE INN**    **$$–$$$$**
**1005 White Pine Dr., Hendersonville**
**(828) 693-0107, (800) 615-6611**
**www.appleinn.com**
Situated on three acres just 2 miles from downtown Hendersonville, this lovely home with its large wraparound porch was once the summer residence of a South Carolina lawyer and his family. Surrounded by dogwoods, azaleas, and 100-year-old oaks, poplars, and maples, it provides a quiet retreat conveniently close to all the many attractions of this popular area. Two fine restaurants and a number of interesting shops are within walking distance at the Laurel Park Shopping Center.

The inn, in one of the nation's largest apple-producing counties, offers five bright and comfortable rooms with private modern baths, each named after a different apple. They have been furnished charmingly with antiques and adorned with fresh flowers. In addition there is the Apple Branch, a two-bedroom, two-bath cottage that sleeps six. It has a full kitchen, dining area, and living room area, front porch, color cable TV, a private phone, and a private driveway. It's available by the week, month, or with a two-night minimum.

Each morning a delightful, home-cooked breakfast of fresh fruits, quiche, strudel, or French toast and tasty breads or muffins awaits you on the patio, accompanied by gourmet coffees and teas. Though relaxation is a favorite occupation at the inn, you can also choose a game of billiards, badminton, croquet, or numerous board games. The inn also has a corporate membership at Oak Hills Racquet Club, where you can swim or play tennis.

## THE CLADDAGH INN     $$$
**755 North Main St., Hendersonville**
**(828) 697-7778, (800) 225-4700**
**www.claddaghinn.com**
The regal old Claddagh Inn was Hendersonville's first bed-and-breakfast establishment. Built around the turn of the 20th century by an ex-mayor of Hendersonville, W. A. Smith, it was sold in 1906 and became the Charleston Boarding House, since it largely served Charlestonians escaping the heat of the coast for mountain coolness. In 1985 it was renamed the Claddagh (pronounced CLAW-da), a Gaelic symbol that represents love and friendship. The hospitality of its owners, Gerri and Augie Emanuele, lives up to the name.

Here you'll have a choice of 14 uniquely decorated, air-conditioned rooms, all with private baths, telephones, and televisions. Each has its own individual, old-fashioned, and charming flavor. The inn also offers a very large parlor and a cozy library with books, games, and a piano. Full—indeed, gigantic—breakfasts in the attractive dining room are included in the rates. The facilities are also available for small catered parties or meetings.

**i**   With so many bed-and-breakfasts in the area, we are hard pressed to mention them all. Therefore we urge you to explore on your own the member inns listed on the Asheville Bed & Breakfast Association Web site, www.ashevillebba.com. Or call (877) 262-6867 to order a variety of brochures before your visit.

## ECHO MOUNTAIN INN     $$–$$$$
**2849 Laurel Park Hwy., Hendersonville**
**(828) 693-9626, (800) ECHO-INN**
**www.echoinn.com**

This massive stone-and-frame inn 3 miles from Hendersonville was built in 1896 on a mountainside that overlooks the whole area—a spectacular view that's visible from many of the guest rooms and the dining room, which is open to the public for dinner. The view is particularly pretty at night with the city lights twinkling below. The inn's 23 rooms, many with fireplaces, are decorated with antiques and reproductions and have recently been remodeled. There is also one cottage and an annex with 10 suites, some with kitchenettes. All accommodations have cable television and telephones, and some have air-conditioning, although with an elevation of 3,100 feet, the last is seldom needed.

On the grounds you'll find shuffleboard courts and a swimming pool. Although the atmosphere at Echo Mountain is casual and leisurely in keeping with the nature of an authentic country inn, dinners here are quite exquisite and definitely gourmet.

To reach Echo Mountain Inn, drive west on Fifth Avenue in Hendersonville; this street will turn into the Laurel Park Highway.

## FLAT ROCK INN     $$$
**2810 Greenville Hwy., Flat Rock**
**(828) 696-3273, (800) 266-3996**
**www.flatrockbb.com**
The Flat Rock Inn is across U.S. Highway 25 from the Woodfield Inn and just as convenient to all local attractions. This elegant but homelike bed-and-breakfast was built in 1888 as a summer retreat by Charleston's R. Withers Memminger, a son of C. G. Memminger, the first secretary of the treasury for the Confederate states. Known locally as Five Oaks, the home was skillfully renovated in 1992, and its new owners, Dennis and Sandi Page (in their own words, "corporate dropouts from Dallas"), opened its doors to the public in 1993.

Currently the Flat Rock Inn offers four rooms with private baths, each elegantly Victorian but with beautifully different atmospheres. Two of the rooms have private, second-floor porches; a third offers a six-foot tub in an alcove behind lace curtains. Flat Rock Inn also offers splendid, family-style, Texas-size breakfasts with such gourmet items as eggs Benedict or cherry blintzes, as well as those country favorites: buttermilk biscuits topped with local jams and jellies.

Flat Rock Inn is open almost year-round, closing only during the first two weeks in Jan.

### MELANGE BED & BREAKFAST     $–$$$$
**1230 Fifth Ave. West, Hendersonville**
**(828) 697-5253, (800) 303-5253**
**www.melangebb.com**
"Luxuriously cosmopolitan" best describes this bed-and-breakfast, just a 15-minute walk from downtown Hendersonville. The mansion, complete with a pony barn and a dollhouse with six-foot ceilings, was designed and built by North Carolina's famous architect, Erle G. Stillwell, in 1920. In the 1960s its owner added marble mantels from Paris, crystal chandeliers from Vienna, and hand-painted porcelain accessories from Italy.

The old grandeur is still represented by the 11-foot, ornamented ceilings, the ornate mirrors, and marble fireplaces, now graced by contemporary comfort, fine tiles, Turkish rugs, books, candles, and flowers. Four guest rooms occupy the second floor, and a full-floor suite with two bedrooms is on the third. Each is named after its predominant color scheme: Rose, Pearl, Cinnamon, Green, and Red. And each has a private bath or Jacuzzi, hardwood floors, air-conditioning, a TV and VCR, and a private telephone. A large collection of video films and books is available for guests.

Depending on the season, a gourmet breakfast is served on the rose garden patio, on a Mediterranean porch, or in the formal dining room. It includes fresh fruits, an egg entree, coffee cakes, and thick, crusted bread served with self-prepared compound butters and delicious preserves. The yogurt here is homemade.

Special services are offered at an additional fee, such as fruit plates, champagne or special chocolates in your room, an elegant high tea, or a five-course candlelight dinner. You can also order a relaxation spa, a therapeutic massage, or a reflexology session from a certified therapist.

Hendersonville's Fifth Avenue is just 1 block over from US 64 West. Drive 0.8 mile from Main Street to Blythe Street. Turn left. On Fifth Avenue, Melange is on the left behind a hemlock hedge. The driveway is after the Melange sign.

### THE WAVERLY INN     $$$
**783 North Main St., Hendersonville**
**(828) 693-9193, (800) 537-8195**
**www.waverlyinn.com**
For a stay in pretty Historic Downtown Hendersonville, you can't find more handy accommodations than at the three-story Waverly, the oldest surviving inn in town, which is listed on the National Register of Historic Places. It's a 2-block walk from the Waverly to Hendersonville's dynamic downtown with its wonderful shops and restaurants and frequent art shows and festivals. Open year-round, the Waverly is a large and gracious inn, even though it now faces a street whose steady stream of traffic reflects the popularity of the town.

You'll get a good view of all this activity from the inn's long, wide veranda, which holds about 20 rocking chairs; there are almost that many on the upstairs porch, too. Polished wood, four-posters and turn-of-the-20th-century fittings fill the 14 guest rooms and one suite, all of which come with private baths, cable TV, and telephones. There are sitting rooms on all three floors.

In their rates innkeepers John and Diane Sheiry and Diane's sister Darla Olmstead include a hearty breakfast cooked to order—and that means all you can eat. There's also a social hour between 5 and 6 p.m. If hunger hits you anytime, we were told to just raid the cookie jar for one of Darla's famous delectables. That's a special delight for children, who are welcome at the inn. To find the Waverly turn north on Hendersonville's Main Street.

## Polk County
### THE MIMOSA INN     $$
**Mimosa Inn Dr., Tryon**
**(828) 859-7688, (877) MIMOSAINN**
**www.carolina-foothills.com**

This pretty, rambling bed-and-breakfast inn with its column-lined veranda has 200 years of history behind it. In the 1700s King George granted John Mills 90,000 acres of land in this area. He and his son operated Mill's Inn here along the trading trail that would become Howard Gap Road. After the Civil War, a Pennsylvania Presbyterian minister named Dr. Leland McAboy bought the inn, named it the McAboy House and, like the Millses, became known as a hospitable host. In 1903 Aaron French and David Sterns bought and modernized the property with innovations such as gaslight and hot and cold running water, added a casino/bowling alley, and renamed it the Mimosa Inn. Fire destroyed most of the building in 1916, sparing only the casino/ bowling alley, which was remodeled into the current Mimosa Inn.

The Mimosa Inn has 10 guest rooms, many with mountain views, and serves a hearty breakfast on the veranda or in the dining room.

**THE OAKS BED & BREAKFAST**             **$$$**
**339 Greenville St., Saluda**
**(828) 749-9613, (800) 893-6091**
**www.theoaksbedandbreakfast.com**
Built by a local banker as a private residence in 1894, this interesting, turreted house was a boarding home from 1905 until the 1940s. Tall trees set off the exterior, which features a wraparound porch with seasonal hanging baskets, wicker furniture, and a swing. Inside you'll discover an inviting library with a fireplace and a large, airy living room. The center of the house is the gracious dining room where delicious gourmet breakfasts are served family style.

Each of the inn's four distinctively decorated guest rooms has a private bath and cable TV. You have your choice of the Blue, Gold, Green, or Red Room, each of which contains a four-poster queen-size bed; an extra-long, full-size bed; or three single beds.

The property also has a separate and self-contained guest house, the Acorn, which boasts a nice view of the ivy-filled woods below.

The Oaks, which is open year-round, is just a short walk from the antiques, arts, crafts, and old-time stores of Saluda. To find this comfortable bed-and-breakfast, go to Saluda and take Greenville Street in the center of town. Drive a half-mile; the Oaks will be on your right. The Oaks is open Apr through mid-Dec.

---

## Polk County: White Oak Mountain

Polk County's topography varies from rolling foothills to level plains on one side and high timber-clad mountains on the other. You can see a great example of all this from what has been called "the greatest view east of the Rockies." Drive east on Highway 108 for just less than 5 miles to Houston Road (SR 1137). Turn left and drive a half-mile to a fork. Bear right for just more than a half-mile, turn left onto White Oak Mountain Road, and drive 2 miles to "The Brow," fronting the White Oak Condominiums near the top of Shunkawaken Falls. From this height of 3,000 feet on a clear day, you can see fields and farmlands stretching for 50 miles, and it's very pretty at night with all the lights twinkling below. Another great vista lies across the relatively flat mountaintop westward to the base of the last incline of Tryon Peak, which is the highest of a number of summits on the White Oak Mountain massif. It's called Sunset Rock, and it's a popular Polk County picnic spot with a view of rugged, steep mountain ranges flowing into each other.

---

**THE ORCHARD INN**             **$$$$**
**100 Orchard Inn Ln., Hwy. 176, Saluda**
**(828) 749-5471, (800) 581-3800**
**www.orchardinn.com**

This inn, sprawled with plantation-like elegance on a ridge, was built by the International Brotherhood of Railway Clerks and Engineers as a mountain getaway in the early 1900s, near the terminus of the steepest railway grade east of the Rockies. That engineering feat is a marvel even today, and a stay in this tranquil place is just as marvelous.

In addition to the nine guest rooms in the imposing main building, there are three remodeled cottages with fireplaces, whirlpool baths, and private decks. Each room and cottage has a personality of its own, from the delicate patterns on the wallpaper to its paintings, prints, stenciling, and quilts. The entire guest quarters are furnished with period pieces and antiques. Wide porches and a shaded deck hold swings, rockers, ferns, and blooming plants. You can relax on swings out on the grounds, too.

The Orchard Inn is a place of leisure, where a naturalist guides morning walks on nearby nature trails. The dining area is an airy, glassed-in porch that runs the length and along one end of the inn. From here a stunning view of the mountains stretches all the way into South Carolina. Full breakfasts and French Provincial dinners "with a country flair," say the hosts, are served, and dinner is open to the public by reservation. Complimentary hors d'oeuvres are offered prior to dinner. (See our Restaurants chapter.) You do need to keep in mind that Saluda is a "dry" town as far as alcoholic beverages go, but you may bring your own spirits. There's ice in the rooms.

**PINE CREST INN**                        $$–$$$
**5 Pine Crest Lane, Tryon**
**(828) 859-9135, (800) 633-3001**
**www.pinecrestinn.com**
In 1918 a hotel owner from Michigan, Carter P. Brown, created the charmingly rustic Pine Crest Inn. Later, in the 1920s, Brown played a leading role in establishing the Tryon Riding and Hunt Club that helped make Tryon the equestrian center it is today.

The Pine Crest Inn is still thriving. It's full of fireplaces, wide porches, tranquil gardens, bright lawns, and wooded grounds. The inn has 35 air-conditioned rooms, most with fireplaces and all

with telephones, televisions, and nice robes for guests. Rates include a full continental breakfast and complimentary sherry or port in the rooms. Both suites and cottages are available, along with a gourmet restaurant. (See our Restaurants chapter.)

The complex also has a lovely conference center available for retreats, seminars, or other gatherings. To get there turn off of Trade Street onto Market Street and follow the signs to the inn's entrance at the top of the hill.

**STONE HEDGE INN**                        $$$
**222 Stone Hedge Lane, Tryon**
**(828) 859-9114, (800) 859-1974**
**www.stone-hedge-inn.com**
The Stone Hedge Inn is on a 28-acre estate just 3 miles from Tryon town center. The inn property includes the main house, a guest house, and a poolside cottage, all surrounded by gardens, wooded walks, and rolling meadows. Each building is a unique fieldstone structure exhibiting the character of its 1930s vintage architecture. All six rooms are large with private baths, air-conditioning, cable television, and a telephone. Two rooms possess rich pine-paneled walls and ceilings, with a fireplace for a rustic feel, while those in the main house have highly decorative sculptured ceilings and antiques for a more formal ambience.

A full breakfast is served in the dining room, where large picture windows offer mountain views. The dining room, open to the public, serves dinner with an eclectic mix of contemporary specials and traditional favorites. (See our Restaurants chapter.)

## Rutherford County

**LAKE LURE INN**                        $$$$
**2771 Memorial Pkwy., US Hwys. 64/74,**
**Lake Lure**
**(828) 625-2525, (888) 434-4970**
**www.lakelureinn.com**
This stately inn overlooking beautiful Lake Lure has been a tradition in Hickory Nut Gorge since 1927. In its early days F. Scott Fitzgerald, President Franklin D. Roosevelt, and Emily Post came to Lake Lure Inn.

Today the inn, with 50 guest rooms, has been renovated and attracts scores of vacationers.

Guests may choose from a variety of chambers—standard rooms with two double beds or one queen, deluxe rooms with a king, or rooms with king- or queen-size bed and a pullout sofa in a large sitting area. There are also two suites, and all rooms are furnished with antique historic inn furniture. All rooms have color cable TV, phone, and a private bath. The spacious lobby runs the width of the hotel and is furnished with sofas, soft chairs, and area literature and newspapers to help plan your local sight-seeing. Fresh flowers and old photographs of famous former guests complement the decor. Cozy up to the fireplace in the main dining room for the complimentary continental breakfast, which includes cereal, breads, bagels, muffins fresh from the inn's kitchen, juices, coffee, and tea.

If you are lucky enough to be staying over for Sunday, a champagne brunch, served mid-Mar until mid-Nov, can be your meal of the day. This lavish buffet features a cutting station with prime rib and ham, omelette bar, waffle station, and a table of hot dishes and side dishes, including chicken, fish, and vegetables. Dessert selections often feature homemade cobblers and pies. The dining room also serves dinner Wed through Sat year-round; Tues dinner is added in peak season. (See our Restaurants chapter.)

The inn's outdoor pool has a sundeck, and a shaded veranda with benches and chairs allows you to look out over Lake Lure at the front of the inn.

## Transylvania County

**THE INN AT BREVARD**　　　　　　**$$-$$$**
**410 East Main St., Brevard**
**(828) 884-2105**
**www.theinnatbrevard.com**
This elegant, columned inn, listed on the National Register of Historic Places, is within easy walking distance of all the great shops and restaurants in downtown Brevard, and the Silvermont Mansion (see our Arts and Culture chapter) is just down the street. The inn has a distinguished history. It was built in 1885 as the private home of Mrs.

Woodbridge, a wealthy widow from Virginia who entertained the nobility of the Victorian era here, including her good friend, Lady Astor. Woodbridge bequeathed the house to her only daughter, Rebecca, who married William E. Breese, a prominent attorney and mayor of Brevard. In 1911 Breese hosted a reunion of the Confederate troops who served under Stonewall Jackson (Jackson's widow attended).

The house was sold in the 1940s and operated as the Colonial Inn for many years. There are five nonsmoking rooms in the main house, three with private baths. Ten cabin-style rooms with private baths are in the adjacent lodge. A full breakfast is included in the tariff.

**KEY FALLS INN**　　　　　　**$-$$**
**151 Everett Rd., Pisgah Forest**
**(828) 884-7559**
**www.keyfallsinn.com**
A quiet and restful stay can be yours in this large Victorian farmhouse built between 1868 and 1869. Formerly known as the Patton House after its original owner, John Patton, this bed-and-breakfast has four guest bedrooms and a two-room suite furnished with antiques. All have private baths. The house's porches are popular for reading, relaxing, and enjoying the view. A sumptuous breakfast is included in the price, and complimentary refreshments are served in the afternoon.

On the inn's grounds you'll find a tennis court with a view of Pisgah Ridge Mountains and a cookout and picnic area, where you may want to fry up some of the bass or bream you've caught from the inn's pond. Key Falls Trail begins on the grounds and climbs up to Key Falls, one of the many waterfalls in Transylvania County. The French Broad River borders one side of the property, which is just 2 miles from Brevard. Children 12 and older are welcome.

**THE RED HOUSE INN AND BED**
**AND BREAKFAST**　　　　　　**$-$$$**
**412 West Probart St., Brevard**
**(828) 884-9349**
**www.brevardbedandbreakfast.com**

## The White Squirrels of Brevard

In 1986 the Brevard City Council declared the city a squirrel sanctuary because some of the squirrels around here are super-special—they're white! We enjoy our gray squirrels, too, but the white variety, which you can see darting throughout the town, have become a symbol of Brevard. These squirrels are not albinos, as they have normal dark eyes and a dark stripe down their backs. The white squirrels have been migrating to the countryside around the town, probably because of Brevard's increased urbanization.

Four blocks from the center of town and on the road next to the Music Center, you'll find Brevard's oldest house. It was built as a trading post in 1851 after the first house, which was built in 1848, burned. The house survived years of neglect and several attempts to destroy it during the Civil War. It even managed to remain in the same family until some 20 years ago, when it was finally sold. The trading post closed in 1861, and the structure then became the W. P. Poor Tavern, which had four rooms for boarders. The street at that time was also called Poor Street, but the residents understandably didn't cotton to that! Hence the name was changed to Probart Street, after Poor's middle name, and so it remains today.

Since its days as a tavern, the building has been used as a residence, a railway station, the county's first courthouse, Brevard's first post office, a boardinghouse, a hotel, and briefly as a school. It's been added to and altered over the years, but the original foundation is still firm, and its four-corner chimneys are still functioning. The inn still has four guest rooms with private or shared baths, plus a small efficiency cottage

with a queen-size bed. Stay for a week and your seventh night is free.

And, yes, the house is painted red—the trim on its wide upstairs and downstairs porches is a bright contrast in white. The story goes that in the days when the streets had no numbers, the houses all had names. As the New England branch of the family had several homes, each called Red House, the family in Brevard decided to use that name too.

**THE SASSY GOOSE**     $$–$$$$
**1844 Reasonover Rd., Cedar Mountain**
**(828) 966-9493**
**www.sassygoose.com**

The Sassy Goose is really a miniature resort. The country-style lodge on a 50-acre site 10 miles from Brevard has three sunny guest rooms, each with a private bath and TV. Common space includes a library with a fireplace, a breakfast room, and a deck overlooking the lake. Two log-cabin suites with queen-size beds are tucked back in the woods. Each suite has a sitting room, a kitchenette, and a screened porch or a deck. There is a two-bedroom, two-bath cottage, complete with living room, kitchen, dining room, and sunporch, available as a weekly rental.

There are also a six-acre lake for swimming, fishing, and boating and a small par 2 golf course where you can practice your chip shot. Several regular golf courses are nearby. Bocce, croquet, horseshoes, and hiking are also available on-site.

The continental-plus breakfast consists of melon and berries, cereal, and a bread basket of good things to put in the toaster oven.

# SOUTHERN MOUNTAINS

## Cherokee County

**HAWKESDENE HOUSE**     $$$
**381 Phillips Creek Rd., Andrews**
**(828) 321-6027, (800) 447-9549**
**www.hawkbb.com**

Nestled on 20 acres in a mountain cove adjoining the Nantahala National Forest, Hawkesdene House combines the simple elegance of an English country house with the rustic beauty of the mountains. Children also love playing with the two resident dogs, Gigi and Tigger, and Smoky, the cat. For an extra cost, guests can venture out on llama treks with a packed lunch at dinner. Hiking treks with meals also take place.

## Graham County

### SNOWBIRD MOUNTAIN LODGE $$$$
**275 Santeetlah Rd., Robbinsville**
**(828) 479-3433, (800) 941-9290**
**www.snowbirdlodge.com**

The lodge, on the National Register of Historic Places, is built of native stone and chestnut logs—that wonderful tree that a foreign blight took from our forests. A massive stone fireplace dominates the main lodge room, which is paneled in butternut, and another warms up the dining room, paneled in cherry.

Thirty rooms—the lodge has a capacity for 50 guests—are paneled in a variety of native woods, with furniture to match. Handmade quilts, many in-room amenities, and private baths complete the comfort. None of the rooms have televisions or telephones.

From its spacious flagstone terrace, the inn offers a panoramic view of the Snowbird Mountain Range, and in the valley below are glimpses of Lake Santeetlah and the homes and fields of the Snowbird Indians. The lodge has an interesting 2,500-volume library. There are 2.5 miles of hiking trails on the property. You can swim in a mountain pool fed by a cool stream or spend the day fishing in any number of blue-ribbon trout streams nearby. Canoes and kayaks are available for rent at the lodge and are a great way to explore nearby Lake Santeetlah.

Evenings sometime include bluegrass music entertainment on the front porch or a slide presentation given by a resident botanist, herbologist, or wildflower expert.

The rates at Snowbird are on the Full American Plan, which includes a fine buffet-style breakfast, a hearty picnic lunch, and an exquisite full-menu dinner prepared by the staff with fresh, seasonal ingredients.

## Haywood County

### GRANDVIEW LODGE $$$
**466 Lickstone Rd., Waynesville**
**(828) 456-5212, (800) 255-7826**
**www.grandviewlodgenorthcarolina.com**

Grandview has nine year-round guest rooms and two two-room apartments available in the spring, summer, and fall. The rooms look out on two-plus rolling acres of landscaped grounds graced by apple orchards, grape arbors, and a rhubarb patch. Comfortable rockers line the porch.

All guest rooms have a king- or queen-size bed and a second bed, a private bath, color cable TV, and daily maid service. The three lodge rooms also have gas-burning fireplaces. A common room with a piano and other amenities will make you feel at home.

Full breakfast and dinner are included in the rates, and both are sumptuous meals planned around seasonal harvests of locally grown fruits, vegetables, and herbs. Meals are served family style, and special dietary needs can be accommodated. The public may dine here by making advance reservations.

### HERREN HOUSE $$–$$$$
**94 East St., Waynesville**
**(828) 452-7837, (800) 284-1932**
**www.herrenhouse.com**

Many bed-and-breakfasts are converted from private homes, but Herren House has been known for its hospitality since 1897, when it was a boarding house named "Savannah." (It takes its present name from its second owner, Mollie Herren, who owned the house early in the last century.) Six spacious guest rooms, one equipped for wheelchair accommodations, are full of vintage furnishings, complemented by modern amenities such as central air-conditioning. Each room has its own sitting area and private bath. There's even an octagon-shaped bedroom with a turn-of-the-20th-century, 48-pane window.

Breakfasts delight with seasonal fruit topped with orange-maple sauce, herb-baked eggs, gingery pancakes, apricot scones, and pineapple muffins, along with homemade chicken sausage.

Afternoon refreshments include chocolate delectables, homemade tea cakes, nut breads, cookies, a variety of teas, and freshly ground coffee.

Best of all, all this home comfort sits below soaring mountains on a quiet residential street just 1 block from Waynesville's captivating Main Street, full of irresistible shops and great places to eat. When you've worn yourself out enjoying Waynesville and all its nearby attractions, you can relax on Herren House's sprawling porches or in its fragrant garden.

## THE INN AT IRIS MEADOWS $$$$
**304 Love Lane, Waynesville**
**(828) 456-3877**
**www.irismeadows.com**
This fully restored turn-of-the-20th-century Greek Revival mansion sits on five acres of rolling meadows and iris gardens. It offers elegance for stately celebrations, honeymoons, relaxing escapes, and romantic getaways.

## MOUNTAIN CREEK BED & BREAKFAST $$
**146 Chestnut Walk Dr., Waynesville**
**(828) 456-5509, (800) 557-9766**
**www.mountaincreekbb.com**
Set on six acres at 3,500 feet, just 5 miles from the Blue Ridge Parkway and from downtown Waynesville and 15 minutes from Cataloochee's ski slopes, this year-round establishment offers four rooms and two suites. All four bedrooms in the main house have a private bath with a shower and two have a soaking tub. The interior walls are knotty pine and the closets are cedar-lined. The two upstairs rooms have their own private balconies overlooking a spectacular mountain view. Two suites are located in the original carriage house just next door. Each has its own private porch, queen-size bed, and Jacuzzi tub. The large common area features a huge fireplace along with 40 feet of floor-to-ceiling windows.

A full breakfast is served every morning, and guests can dine in or out on the 1,600-square-foot deck that wraps around the west side of the house with a view of the creek, trout pond, and mountains. Menus include such items as egg truffles, banana- or strawberry-stuffed French toast, or ham-and-cheese strudel.

## THE OLD STONE INN $$$$
**109 Dolan Rd., Waynesville**
**(828) 456-3333, (800) 432-8499**
**www.oldstoneinn.com**
Built in 1946 out of stone and poplar logs, the inn consists of a number of buildings. The main lodge houses two guest rooms and the cozy guest lounge and restaurant centered around a large stone fireplace. Wendell's Attic, on the second floor of the building, with its wood-burning stove, is a more intimate room for drinks and conversation. Several other structures surrounding the main lodge house the balance of the inn's 22 rooms. Most of these neat, clean, and rustic-feeling quarters have been restored and updated and have private baths, ceiling fans, cable TV, and porches with rockers.

This in-town, country lodge sits on a heavily wooded hillside thick with large rhododendrons and mountain laurels.

A full gourmet breakfast is included in your room rate. Dinner and light appetizers are available to both inn and outside guests. Hours vary by season. (See our Restaurants chapter.)

## THE SWAG $$$$
**2300 Swag Rd., Waynesville**
**(828) 926-0430, (800) 789-7672**
**www.theswag.com**
When the innkeepers at The Swag, which refers to a dip in a ridge, call theirs a mountaintop inn, they mean it! This inn sits on 250 acres at 5,000 feet on a private mountain with 50-mile views. Dan and Deener Matthews built what was to be a private family retreat using native stone and hand-hewn logs from old buildings, including a century-old church. They ended up turning the retreat into this highly praised inn.

The Swag's handmade quilts, woven rugs, and unique pieces of North Carolina art create an atmosphere of rustic elegance. Sixteen guest rooms all have private baths (some with whirlpools or steam showers, all with terry robes), and many feature balconies to bring that 50-mile view right indoors. Some rooms have fireplaces. There are also three cabins with separate sitting rooms and private porches and an extensive library to satisfy most literary tastes. One cabin has a billiard room and a hot tub. Outside a split-rail fence marks the boundary of the Great Smoky Mountains National Park with its many hiking trails, reached by The Swag's own private entrance. At the inn itself hammocks are handy places for a snooze, but for the more active, you can play racquetball on the indoor court, badminton and croquet outdoors, or swim in the secluded spring-fed pond.

A two-night minimum stay is required. The rates include three meals a day for two people, prepared by gourmet cooks and served atop 12-foot-long, handmade walnut tables (many of the inn's beds are also handmade and oversize). There are several private tables available, and a few outside reservations are accepted. Just remember that the inn is in a dry county, so bring your own spirits if desired. (See our Restaurants chapter.)

> **i** Maggie Valley Accredited Reservations (828-926-3786) is open year-round to help families and groups locate lodging. For more information write to P.O. Box 866, Maggie Valley 28751.

### THE YELLOW HOUSE                    $$$$
**89 Oakview Dr., Waynesville**
**(828) 452-0991, (800) 563-1236**
**www.theyellowhouse.com**
The Yellow House sits at 3,000 feet on top of a hill looking out to the ever-changing colors of the Blue Ridge Mountains. Located just a mile from Waynesville, it has been likened to a grand old duchess on a throne. One thing is for sure, when you arrive at this more than 100-year-old home, surrounded by three acres of lawn, garden, and ancient pines, prepare to be pampered. There are no televisions or other distractions in this quiet rural setting.

There are eight rooms total. All are charming and each has a fireplace, but our favorite is the E'staing Suite with both rooms opening on a private upstairs porch. From here, there's a pine-

framed view of the mountains and town, particularly fine at night when lights twinkle below and stars twinkle above. An adjacent cottage contains a French country kitchen. It offers two bedrooms, two baths, two fireplaces, and a view of the pond from every room.

The rates include your choice of a breakfast served in your quarters, in the dining room, or on the front veranda. Other amenities include appetizers and conversation in the evening and a refrigerator stocked with soft drinks. All rooms have coffee service, terry robes, and controlled music.

## Jackson County
### BALSAM MOUNTAIN INN                  $$$–$$$$
**68 Seven Springs Dr., Balsam**
**(828) 456-9498**
**www.balsaminn.com**
Gracing 26 acres, the three-story structure with its two-tier, 100-foot-long porches sits at 3,500 feet and is surrounded by 6,000-foot peaks. It was once the popular destination of passengers on the old Southern Railway, but in recent years the 50-room beauty had fallen into disrepair until Merrily Teasly bought it in 1990 and lovingly and authentically restored it. Today Sharon and Kim Shailer run the inn with ease and continue with a welcoming homey hospitality.

Today you'll have a choice of large rooms with private baths (including a few suites and bed/sitting rooms), graced with flowery prints, 10-foot wide hallways, a wicker- and plant-filled lobby, a fine library, a gift shop, a nature trail on the property, and easy access to Pisgah Forest hiking and the Blue Ridge Parkway. You'll also be very pleased with the inn's restaurant. Wonderful breakfasts are included in the rates, but you'll also want to enjoy the exceptional lunches and dinners offered to guests and by reservation to the public. (See our Restaurants chapter.)

### INNISFREE VICTORIAN INN              $$$$
**Highway 107, Glenville**
**(828) 743-2946**
**www.innisfreeinn.com**

As the name implies, this is a gabled Victorian. Wide porches run around two floors of this superb building overlooking Lake Glenville.

The nine guest rooms are named in keeping with its era, such as the Prince Albert Suite, with French doors leading to a private veranda; the sensuous Cambridge Room, which has a parking place next to its private entrance; the cheerful Canterbury Room, with a bay-windowed love seat that affords a view of flower gardens and mountains. Then there's Victoria's Grand Suite, which may be the most luxuriously romantic suite in the mountains. From its bay window you have a view of the lake and mountains that stretches for miles, and its elegant furnishings and art were gathered from around the world. A Jacuzzi is in the bathing chamber that also comes with a splendid view.

The Garden House, which follows the style of the main house, has two feminine boudoirs—the Elizabeth Barrett and Emily Brontë suites—each with a four-poster bed made up in French lace, a private veranda, and two fireplaces, one in the bathroom. There is also an ornate suite and a room with its own entrance. All the accommodations in the Garden House have wet bars, TVs, and private phones.

Rates include the candlelit breakfast in the Tower, a 5:30 p.m. hospitality hour with hors d'oeuvres served on the sweeping upper veranda, and Irish coffee and hot chocolate by the parlor fire each evening.

**i** There is a 3-mile, round-trip hike in Jackson County that takes you through a lovely mile-high meadow with superb views of the Pisgah National Forest. It is not a difficult hike. For part of the walk, you will be on sections of the Mountains-to-the-Sea Trail. Be sure to take a sharp left at the trail junction about 15 minutes from the start of your walk. To reach the trail, drive to the Bear Pen Gap parking overlook at milepost 427.6 on the Blue Ridge Parkway in Jackson County. The trail begins at the lower end of the parking lot.

## THE JARRETT HOUSE $
### 219 Haywood St., Dillsboro
### (828) 586-0265, (800) 972-5623
### www.jarretthouse.com

Not only is the Jarrett House one of the oldest inns in Western North Carolina, it's practically a tradition. William Allen Dills, founder of the town of Dillsboro, built it in 1882, just two years after the railroad came through. Because the train from Asheville stopped here at noon, the Mount Beulah Hotel, as the Jarrett House was called then, became the place for passengers and railroad employees to eat lunch. By 1894 the hotel was serving "comers and stayers" from great distances away, including two women from Edenton, North Carolina, who were the first females to be seen smoking cigarettes in these parts. As Mrs. Minnie Dills Gray, one of William Dill's daughters, recalls in her History of Dillsboro, the two smokers "set the countryside agog and gave zest to the neighborhood gossip."

Dill sold the hotel to R. Frank Jarrett of Franklin in 1894. Jarrett, capitalizing on a sulfur spring that bubbled up into a soapstone basin at the rear of the hotel, renamed the place the Jarrett Springs Hotel. However the busy owner left the running of the hotel mostly to his wife, Miss Sally. After his death in 1950, a hotel operator from Gainesville, Georgia, bought the hotel and renamed it the Jarrett House. It has changed hands a number of times since then but has never changed its policy of serving copious and delicious country cooking. (See our Restaurants chapter.)

The hotel, which is on the National Register of Historic Places, has 18 guest rooms with private baths and four with shared baths. While they're nothing fancy, they are loaded with atmosphere, and the whole place is like a step back to the turn of the 20th century. The Jarrett is open year-round. To find it, just go to Dillsboro—you can't miss it. No credit cards.

## Macon County
### 4-1/2 STREET INN $$$
### 22A 4½ St., Highlands
### (828) 526-4464, (888) 799-4464
### www.4andahalfstinn.com

This inn features 10 guest rooms, each with a private bath. Most rooms have king- or queen-size beds.

Rocking chairs await guests on the large wraparound porch. The innkeepers offer bikes, canteens, backpacks, trail maps, and advice. They know the trails and the best routes for the greatest views.

The inn is about a 0.5-mile stroll from Main Street through a pretty residential area, where the houses are hidden behind giant rhododendrons. In addition to the gourmet breakfast, the rates include afternoon refreshments in the parlor and the use of the outdoor hot tub. There's a two-night minimum on weekends and a 10 percent reduction for stays of five nights or longer, excluding holidays and Oct.

## BLAINE HOUSE $$$
661 Harrison Ave., Franklin
(828) 349-4230, (888) 349-4230
www.blainehouse.com

Here you'll find an elegant spacious room, Mildred's Suite, that offers a king-size bed, sitting area, and private bath/shower. Annie Mae's Suite is more romantic, with a queen-size bed and a spacious adjoining bath inviting you to relax in a 1925 pedestal foot tub. Minnie's Room offers a cozy country French motif with a gabled ceiling and pickled knotty pine walls, a king-size bed (or twins), dressing room, and private bath/shower. Charles' Room is a delightfully decorated provincial room with original knotty pine walls and offers a queen-size oak bed with an adjacent cozy reading room enticing you to relax and read a book after an adventurous day. This room has a private bath/shower. All rooms have cable TV and air-conditioning. Finally there's the two-story Blaine House Cottage, a fully furnished one-bedroom with a living/dining area, full kitchen, daily linen service, TV, air-conditioning, and a small balcony.

## THE CHALET INN $$$
285 Lone Oak Dr., Whittier
(828) 586-0251, (800) 789-8024
www.chaletinn.com

Nestled on 22 acres in a mountain cove, The Chalet provides gracious lodging and combines the traditions and congeniality of an Alpine *gasthaus* with rustic surroundings. A spring-fed brook curls around the inn on its way to the valley floor. The guest rooms have private balconies with carved wood railings festooned with flowers. European furnishings and German-Swiss windows continue the theme. From the Chalet's great room, you can view Doubletop Mountain, which dominates 19 miles of forested ridges.

The Chalet's four lovely rooms, one romantic suite, and one family suite offer comfortable lodging for couples looking to spend some time alone and for families with older children who are exploring the mountains. All rooms and suites have private baths and air-conditioning. The Romantic Suite has a sitting room with a fireplace and whirlpool tub, a private entrance, and a private patio. Guests at the Chalet Inn can enjoy its hiking trails, lawn games, and picnic area with a grill. A candlelit breakfast is served in the dining room or on the covered patio along the brook. It's a breakfast that satisfies all tastes: For the health conscious there's always plenty of fresh fruit, juices, and low-fat yogurt; for the world traveler with a hearty appetite longing for memories of the Alps, the German-style meats are fresh, and German whole-grain breads and Swiss muesli are imported. Also included are a variety of cheeses, fresh-baked *brotchen* (rolls), and soft-boiled eggs or an egg casserole.

## COLONIAL PINES INN $$$
541 Hickory St., Highlands
(828) 526-2060
www.colonialpinesinn.com

Large pillars framing a gigantic colonial American flag and a porch that stretches across the front of the house are a statement of eloquence and grace. This quiet country guest house was once home to several original Highlands families.

Within the inn is the warmth of knotty pine, antiques, and an eclectic mix of books, accessories, a playable grand piano, and a cozy fireside for chilly mountain evenings. The inn is surrounded by two acres of giant old rhododendron, hemlock, maple, and oak. Mountain views are spectacular from all rooms. There is also a guest house apartment on the property and a private cottage known as "Miss Rebecca's Cottage," which is a short distance away. The cottage is very special, sleeping two to six in three bedrooms, and it has two baths.

Breakfast for guests in the main inn is sumptuous. You will usually find freshly made jams from the berry bushes on the property.

### HERITAGE INN BED AND BREAKFAST                                    $$–$$$
43 Heritage Hollow Dr., Franklin
(828) 524-4150, (888) 524-4150
www.heritageinnbb.com

This bed-and-breakfast is in the Heritage Hollow, a private village within the town of Franklin, with restaurants, antiques, and mountain craft shops within walking distance. Each of its five immaculate bedrooms (two are available with kitchenettes) is decorated with antiques, collectibles, and quilts in a country-comfortable theme. For added privacy each room has its own entrance, porch, and shower bathroom. There is a Gathering Room with fireplace, cable TV, and phone, as well as a good selection of reading materials and videos. Most guests, though, end up in a rocking chair on the veranda enjoying the mountain scenery and serenity. Breakfast is hearty and homemade; early risers can have coffee on the veranda. Snacks and some refreshments are available throughout the day.

There is also a fully furnished, self-contained, one-bedroom apartment with a fireplace at the inn available for rent with a three-night minimum. (Breakfast is not provided with this rental.)

### THE MAIN STREET INN                                    $$$–$$$$
270 Main St., Highlands
(828) 526-2590, (800) 213-9142
www.mainstreet-inn.com

The Main Street Inn, built in the Federal Farmhouse style in 1885, has welcomed guests with Southern hospitality for more than a century. Formerly known as the Phelps House, it was restored to its original luster in 1998. The original hand-hewn beams in its adjacent Guest House were exposed through the addition of cathedral ceilings, and many of the original sand-forged windows were saved and reinstalled in the rooms as interior windows for the enjoyment of guests.

The inn, which is next door to all that wonderful Main Street shopping, features 20 cozy rooms, all with private baths, individual heating and air-conditioning, direct-dial telephones, and cable TV. Some rooms have sitting areas or balconies. Room rates include a hot country breakfast and afternoon tea.

### THE OLD EDWARDS INN AND SPA          $$$
Corner of 4th and Main Streets, Highlands
(828) 526-9319
www.oldedwardsinn.com

This gloriously-renovated hotel was established in 1876. The decor throughout has been carefully researched and restored in an elegant European country-manor style. Outstanding pieces of antique furniture and other decor add charm to every room  Have tea in the splendid wood-paneled library, or step into the spa to be truly transported away. Massage rooms sport crystal chandeliers, and a Roman-style mosaic-filled soaking room adjacent to the dry and wet saunas invite you to a long afternoon of relaxation.

The restaurant Madison's overlooks the courtyard gardens. Surrounded by a hedge that wards off traffic noise and passersby on Main Street, cascading waterfalls and a koi pond provide an idyllic atmosphere for relaxation and dining.

## Swain County

### CHARLESTON INN                                    $$–$$$
208 Arlington Ave., Bryson City
(828) 488-4644, (888) 285-1555
www.charlestoninn.com

This 1920s Victorian-influenced house has five rooms, each with private bath, while the inn next door has 14 rooms, each with a queen- or king-size bed and a porch or private balcony. An additional two-bedroom Gingerbread Cottage can accommodate couples, large groups, or families, though everyone retires to the parlor in the evenings to gather by the cozy fireplace. The TV room completes the lovely gardens with a gazebo and fountains. Your hosts serve a full breakfast in the dining room or outdoors on the veranda.

i For 35 years, an inn's inclusion in the Select Registry of Distinguished Inns of North America has assured the traveler of consistently high standards. It is comparable to the Relaise de Chateaux of Europe in expectations. Of the 400 member inns across the United States, 16 are found in North Carolina's mountains. All select registry inns are included in this chapter.

### FRYEMONT INN $–$$
245 Fryemont St., Bryson City
(828) 488-2159, (800) 845-4879
www.fryemontinn.com

Two generations of Browns have served as inn-keepers at this comfortable 37-room inn that sits on a mountain shelf overlooking the Great Smoky Mountains National Park. Everything about the inn, which has had a tradition in hospitality here since 1923, is "woodsy": its rustic exterior and lustrous hardwood floors; its chestnut-paneled bedrooms; the mountainous view from its tree-top rocking-chair porch; its lovely 80-degree swimming pool nestled in a grove of hemlock, dogwood, and poplar. The large lobby is more than matched by a giant stone fireplace that can hold logs 8 feet long. There is also a full-service lounge and a library.

All rooms have private baths, but no two are alike, except for their many-paned pocket windows that slide back to let in the mountain air. Adjacent to the main lodge are cottage suites, each with a living room, a bedroom with a king-size bed, a wet bar, and a working fireplace. Some suites have loft bedrooms; others have private decks.

Fryemont Inn's rates are reasonable and include both a hearty breakfast and dinner. The public can enjoy these wonderful meals by reservation. Fryemont Inn is open from Apr through Nov, but the cottage suites are open year-round.

### HEMLOCK INN $$$$
Galbraith Creek Rd., off US Hwy. 19,
Bryson City
(828) 488-2885
www.hemlockinn.com

This is an unpretentious place, but there's nothing unpretentious about the view. Hemlock Inn is built on a small mountain that overlooks three valleys, backed up by big mountains. Sitting on the front porch with a steaming cup of coffee in hand and watching the sunrise is something worth getting up early for! The inn opened in 1952 with nine rooms; its popularity grew, and the owners added 12 rooms and four cottages to meet the demand. The growth stopped there, because owner-innkeepers Elaine and Morris White and their guests like the informality and personal attention of a small inn.

The rooms and cottages (one very secluded and popular with honeymooners) are furnished in antiques and pieces made by mountain craftspeople. The rates include family-style breakfasts and dinners and all gratuities. Meals for the public are by reservation only. And, since the innkeepers always feature fresh foods native to the area, what good meals they are! (See our Restaurants chapter.)

# HOTELS AND MOTELS

In the preceding chapter we listed a number of inns and bed-and-breakfast establishments, and even at that, we barely scratched the surface of the area's many intimate and often historic establishments that have thrown open their doors to travelers. But such places are not for everyone—or not for everyone all the time. They certainly don't reflect all the accommodations we have in the mountains. There are dozens of reasonably priced, family-owned motels and cabins in and around our towns, and all the big chain hotels are represented throughout the region at locations very convenient to our attractions. Even in a small city like Hendersonville, there are more than 60 places to stay, with more opening all the time. Cherokee, a popular resort, has some motels and 110 cabins from which to choose, plus 27 campgrounds with more than 2,200 sites.

For this chapter we have chosen just a few of the larger, better-known establishments, plus some special smaller places you'll want to know about. But keep in mind that this is a guide, not a directory. For every listing we have here, there are many more similar types of accommodations in the same area. In short—except perhaps during the fall foliage season when the region is jam-packed with leaf-lookers—finding a great place to spend the night or an extended vacation is never a problem.

## Price Code

The average nightly rate for two adults at the facilities in this chapter is indicated by a dollar-sign ($) ranking in the following chart. Most businesses accept major credit cards for payment, but where no credit cards are accepted, we've noted that information.

| | |
|---|---|
| $ | $50 to $80 |
| $$ | $81 to $100 |
| $$$ | $101 to $120 |
| $$$$ | $121 and more |

These establishments have varying policies concerning children, pets, and cancellation; please inquire about these when you call to make reservations.

## NORTHERN MOUNTAINS

### Alleghany County

**ALLEGHANY INN**  $–$$
341 North Main St., Sparta
(336) 372-2501, (888) 372-2501
www.alleghanyinn.com
If you get off the Blue Ridge Parkway at milepost 217 at its junction with Highway 18 and drive about 15 minutes west to Sparta, you'll find the Alleghany Inn, a nice, reasonably priced family stopover. This 64-room, pleasantly furnished modern motel is open year-round. The inn offers cable TV, queen- and full-size beds, and king-size waterbeds. One efficiency is also available. There is also a conference center. Smoking is permitted.

### BLUFFS LODGE $$-$$$
**Mile 241, Blue Ridge Pkwy., Doughton Park**
**(336) 372-4499**

Bluffs Lodge sits on a broad hilltop on the Blue Ridge Parkway with expansive, long-range mountain views. Here, rangers provide interpretive talks around an outdoor fireplace in the patio area. The accommodations are comfortable, with lots of amenities like private baths and large closets in each room. The Bluffs Lodge Coffee Shop is just across the road.

## Ashe County

### BEST WESTERN ELDRETH INN $$-$$$
**829 East Main St., Jefferson**
**(336) 246-8845, (800) 221-8802**
**www.bestwestern.com**

Some people consider rocking chairs a way of getting fit. Others want something a little more heart pumping. This 48-room inn features both—rooms with a view of Mount Jefferson, complete with rocking chairs on the balconies, and a well-equipped fitness center. It also offers a range of room sizes with double-, queen-, and king-size beds. Nonsmoking rooms are available. The inn's restaurant serves home-style meals for breakfast, lunch, and dinner (except Sun night). Should you want to sample something different, Best Western Eldreth Inn is within walking distance of six restaurants. It is also next door to a shopping center and is only a short drive from the Ashe Country Frescoes (see our Arts and Culture chapter), canoeing on the New River, and local golfing.

### GREENFIELD RESORT $-$$
**1795 Mount Jefferson Rd., off U.S. Hwy. 221,**
**West Jefferson**
**(336) 246-9106, (336) 982-3381 (after hours)**
**www.5starcampsites.com/Greenfield-resorty**

Greenfield Resort is spread over approximately 100 rolling acres of pasture, originally part of the Rufus McNeil farm, ca. 1847, at the foot of Mount Jefferson. The McNeil homestead has been converted into a lively family-style restaurant. Greenfield also has a banquet room that

seats 300; a convenience store with crafts, ice, and produce; eight rustic rental cabins; camping facilities; three fishing ponds stocked with bass and bluegill; and miles of hiking trails that wind around Mount Jefferson. The cabins sit on a ridge opposite Greenfield restaurant at the base of spectacular Mount Jefferson. These units offer either one bedroom with a loft and shower or a two-bedroom efficiency with shower. There is also a large recreation room with cooking facilities. A bunkhouse-type cabin holding up to 22 people is also available.

The campground has 138 sites and can accommodate both RVs and primitive tent camping.

Greenfield features buggy rides, Civil War reenacts, and two rodeos a year, making the resort more than a tourist stop—it's a community gathering spot.

### JEFFERSON LANDING LODGE $$$-$$$$
**Hwys. 88 and 16, Jefferson**
**(336) 982-4149, (888) 292-2310**
**www.visitjeffersonlanding.com**

Jefferson Landing Lodge is a superb addition to this premier golf community. The tastefully decorated facility has 17 units and numerous amenities, including a full-service lounge. The lobby has a vaulted ceiling and large windows that offer a breathtaking view of the golf course. Jefferson Landing Lodge is open year-round, and townhome rentals and golf packages are also available. The Manor House has seven bedrooms.

### NATION'S INN $$
**107 Beaver Creek School Rd., West Jefferson**
**(336) 246-2080, (800) 801-3441**
**www.nationsinn.com**

This 52-room, two-story hotel is located near US 221. The rooms, all with outside entrances, feature king-size or double beds. Complimentary continental breakfast is served from 6:30 to 10:30 a.m. Nation's Inn also has a meeting room that accommodates 25. It also offers smoking and nonsmoking rooms.

## Avery County

**BEECH ALPEN INN** $$–$$$$
**700 Beech Mountain Pkwy., Beech Mountain**
**(828) 387-2252**
**www.beechalpen.com**
Beech Alpen Inn is a country inn under the same management as its neighbor, Top of the Beech, just down the road. The Beech Alpen Inn is open year-round, offering a cool retreat in the summer and ski opportunities in the winter. Some of the rooms in this rustic, European-style inn have fireplaces and balconies, and all rooms have exposed-beam ceilings as well as great views of the mountains and ski slopes at nearby Ski Beech. King- and queen-size beds are available. The Beech Alpen restaurant offers a menu of fine dining, featuring New York strip, filet mignon, superb crab cakes, and mountain trout prepared by their award-winning chef.

**i** Call ahead if you need a refrigerator in your room for picnic food or leftovers if you'll be staying a while. Not all hotels have them in every room.

**HOLIDAY INN OF BANNER ELK** $$–$$$
**1615 Tynecastle Hwy. 184, Banner Elk**
**(828) 898-4571, (800) HOLIDAY**
**www.holidayinn.com**
This classic Holiday Inn is less than a mile from the entrance to Sugar Mountain Ski Resort and only 6 miles from Ski Beech. The motel has 102 rooms (some nonsmoking), king-size beds, and cable TV with free HBO. Also enjoy use of the business center. Summer visitors can use the outdoor pool, volleyball court, horseshoe pits, and Ping-Pong tables.

You can dine at the Elk Cafe, the inn's full-service restaurant, which hosts buffets on the weekends. Meeting and banquet facilities are also available.

**HUMPBACK HOLLOW** $$$$
**Luther Franklin Lane, Newland**
**(828) 766-6555, (888) 263-3632**
**www.humpbackhollow.com**

Each of these unique cabins has a fully equipped kitchen, including microwave and charcoal grill. If you'd like to relax indoors after all-day hiking, there's a VCR and great selection of videos. All the cabins are decorated with antiques and country charm. Hosts Tom and Karen Acheson provide all linens, complimentary wood for the woodburning fireplace, and morning coffee. There are three cottages in all: The 200-year-old historic log cabin Sunalee offers all the modern conveniences, a deck and covered porch, two full baths, a large bedroom, and loft. The Conner Cottage has been built entirely of wormy chestnut and contains a gas-log fireplace and porch, two bedrooms, and one bath. Fiddlesticks is a log cabin with a gas-log fireplace and air-conditioning. With one bedroom and one bath, it's an ideal romantic getaway for couples. The large covered porch serves as a wonderful lounging area.

**PARKVIEW LODGE** $$–$$$
**US 221, off Blue Ridge Parkway at Mile 317,**
**Linville Falls**
**(828) 765-4787, (800) 849-4452**
**www.parkviewlodge.com**
This attractive lodge right off the Linville Falls exit of the Blue Ridge Parkway is a pleasant place with a friendly atmosphere. In addition to its 16 rooms, the complex has two cottages with kitchenettes and a suite on the picturesque grounds that back up to the parkway. You'll find plenty of wooded privacy and a swimming pool banked by cultivated wildflower beds. Parkview is popular with the parkway's hikers and campers, who occasionally stop in for a dose of civilization, especially hot showers. Parkview Lodge is open year-round and serves a complimentary continental breakfast. A craft shop and wine and beer shop are also on the premises.

**PINEOLA INN AND PINEOLA MOTEL** $–$$
**3085 Linville Falls Hwy., Pineola**
**(828) 733-4979**
**www.pineolainn.com**
Just at the head of the North Cove area on US 221 going up the mountain to Linville and Boone is the tiny crossroads of Pineola. The Pineola

Inn and the Pineola Motel, both owned by the same family, are very simple accommodations with reasonable rates. They're just a few minutes south of the major ski areas of Sugar Mountain, Ski Beech, and Hawksnest. The High Country Ski Shop and Pineola Country Store, also part of the complex, offer gifts, souvenirs, and ski gear. Ski equipment rentals and cross-country ski instruction are also available at the ski shop. You can ski cross-country on the nearby Blue Ridge Parkway. Ask the proprietor of the High Country Ski Shop about cross-country instruction and the best access to locations for this winter sport. Don't miss the Indian artifact museum at the rear of the Country Store. This amazing lifetime collection of Avery County's Dellinger family is one of the largest private collections of Native American artifacts in the area.

### SUGAR TOP $$$–$$$$
**303 Sugar Top Dr., Banner Elk**
**(828) 898-6211, (800) 764-2786**
**www.sugarmountainlodging.com**
If brilliant views, every modern amenity, and sleek contemporary decor top your list of must-haves at a vacation spot, then perhaps you should be staying at Sugar Top. Perched atop Sugar Mountain, this 10-story condominium resort offers arresting views from an elevation of 5,140 feet. The east side has a view of Grandfather Mountain, while the west side overlooks the Sugar Mountain ski slopes. All suites are approximately 1,100 square feet, with two bedrooms, two baths, dining area, living room with fireplace, private covered balcony, refrigerator, dishwasher, and wet bar. Amenities include an indoor pool, sauna, steam room, whirlpool, fitness center, 24-hour security, and front desk service.

## Madison County
### COMFORT INN—MARS HILL $$
**167 J. F. Robinson Lane, Mars Hill**
**(828) 689-9000**
**www.comfortinn.com**
This Comfort Inn has the good fortune of being close to Wolf Laurel ski slopes. There's also an outdoor pool for use, as well as cable TV and free HBO for guests. A free continental breakfast can be taken in the dining room with an exceptional view of the mountains.

## Mitchell County
### BIG LYNN LODGE $$$–$$$$
**10860 North Carolina 226 Alternate,**
**Little Switzerland**
**(828) 765-4257, (800) 654-5232**
**www.biglynnlodge.com**
Just off the Blue Ridge Parkway milepost 332.5 is delightful Big Lynn Lodge, a welcome sight after a long drive. This rustic inn is a combination of individual rooms and cottages in a woodland setting. Some rooms offer a spectacular view of the valley below. An exceptionally nice feature here is the complimentary inclusion of breakfast and dinner with all accommodations. There's an early-bird discount if you make reservations prior to the busy fall season. Enjoy a fireplace and player piano in the living room.

### PINEBRIDGE INN $$–$$$$
**101 Pinebridge Ave., Spruce Pine**
**(828) 765-5543, (800) 356-5059**
**www.pinebridgeinn.com**
The Pinebridge Inn has a history of hospitality. This school property, constructed in the early 1920s, was converted to the area's premier hotel and conference facility in 1985. The sturdy brick hotel houses 44 spacious rooms and suites, a deluxe apartment with Jacuzzi bath, and assembly and banquet space for small and large groups. Another accommodation on the grounds is a three-bedroom cottage with fireplace. The high ceilings and tall windows in these former classrooms provide a view of the beautifully landscaped courtyard. An extensive continental breakfast is served each morning. Pinebridge Inn is open year-round and offers group specials and discounts for area attractions.

Guests can also take advantage of Pinebridge Center, located just across the parking lot. This recreational and fitness center offers numerous recreational diversions including seasonal ice-skating in one of the South's largest rinks, indoor heated pool, whirlpool, sauna, steam room, and plenty of fitness equipment. A lighted 410-foot-long footbridge spans Riverside Park and connects the facilities to downtown Spruce Pine. This is a Three Diamond–rated AAA hotel.

## Watauga County

**THE ALPINE VILLAGE INN**          **$$–$$$**
**297 Sunset Dr., Blowing Rock**
**(828) 295-7206**
**www.alpine-village-inn.com**
The Alpine Village Inn is in the heart of Blowing Rock, within walking distance of Main Street and all the shops and restaurants. This attractive motel offers many of the detailed amenities of a bed-and-breakfast inn: 100 percent cotton towels, percale sheets, magazines and flowers in the rooms, individual heat and air-conditioning controls, cable TV, and complimentary newspapers and morning coffee. Antique furnishings and collectibles complement the homespun decor. Room refrigerators are available. The rocking chairs in the gazebo on the grounds are an invitation to take it easy. A room with a hot tub and fireplace is also available.

**THE BROYHILL INN &**
**CONFERENCE CENTER**          **$$$–$$$$**
**775 Bodenheimer Dr., Boone**
**(828) 262-2204, (800) 951-6048**
**www.broyhillinn.com**
This inn on the campus of Appalachian State University features seven suites and 76 guest rooms. There are 22 meeting rooms for small- to medium-size meetings and the Trillium Ballroom for as many as 850 guests. Support services for conferences and meetings include full catering service for meals and receptions, audiovisual equipment, and the services of professional technicians. The inn's dining room serves up a spectacular mountain view with every breakfast, lunch, and dinner. Duggins Lounge, a quiet and relaxing getaway, is open in the evenings.

**THE COTTAGES OF**
**GLOWING HEARTH**          **$$$$**
**171 Glowing Hearth Lane, Valle Crucis**
**(828) 963-8800, (800) 232-5080**
**www.glowinghearth.com**
The term "cottage" is a great misnomer here, because we are speaking of 1,500-square-foot houses with 18-foot white pine tongue-and-groove ceilings, 100-gallon double spas, king-size four-poster beds, imported Mexican terra-cotta tile flooring, a private driveway and a parking area for each domicile, and 25 windows per "cottage" so as not to miss any of the spectacular views.

A fully equipped kitchen, a 30-foot-long front porch, and a stone fireplace and hearth enable you to feel quite at home on your vacation. Of course it's not only the professionally designed interiors that make each of the Cottages of Glowing Hearth a dream vacation home but the small touches as well. Hand-painted ceramic tiles decorate the dining island, a video library with 500 titles can easily distract you, and a full concierge service for reservations, tee times, and other needs provides a near-perfect vacation experience.

**DAYS INN RESORT—BLOWING**
**ROCK**          **$$–$$$**
**8412 Valley Blvd., Blowing Rock**
**(828) 295-4422, (800) 329-7466**
**www.daysinn.com**
Here's a good bargain for families. Deluxe king and oversize rooms are among the 118 guest rooms available. An enclosed atrium has a heated swimming pool and hot tub. The coffee shop serves a full breakfast only. Days Inn has ski packages and discounts for senior citizens and tour groups.

**FALL CREEK CABINS**          **$$$–$$$$**
**176D Surber Road, Fleetwood**
**(336) 877-3131**
**www.fallcreekcabins.com**
Surrounded by miles of lush forest on all sides, a gurgling creek, and a small waterfall, Fall Creek Cabins seem far removed from civilization. But open the front door to your two-story cabin and you will soon realize that all your creature comforts have been taken care of. The cabins, built

from fragrant western red cedar, house two bedrooms, two baths, a living room, loft, and kitchen. The full kitchen, with dishes, blender, corkscrew, silverware, and washer and dryer, enables you to be completely self-sufficient once you've done your initial grocery shopping.

Stacks of newspaper for getting a good blaze started have thoughtfully been placed in a basket by the stone fireplace. An enormous stack of firewood sits just outside the cabin, and a gas grill on the front porch means grilling those steaks and sausages will be a snap, leaving more time for outdoor activities or a longer soak in the hot tub on the covered porch, whichever your inclination may be. You can find a VCR/DVD, videos, and board games for the whole family in each cabin. During the day be sure to explore the extensive hiking trails, streams, waterfalls, and a trout stream stocked by the state. You'll have to purchase a fishing license for about $10, which you can find at any hardware store, fishing and bait shop, or even large superstore.

## HEMLOCK INN AND SUITES $$
**134 Morris St., Blowing Rock**
**(828) 295-7987**
**www.hemlockinn.net**
For those of you who don't like to fool with the intimacy of a bed-and-breakfast, who prefer to be left to your own devices, or who prefer to spend your money on sightseeing, gifts, and food rather than your accommodations, the Hemlock Inn is for you. This motel-style inn is just off Blowing Rock's main street. It offers tidy rooms with double, queen-, or king-size beds, air-conditioning, private baths, and the added plus of a kitchenette in every room. A microwave, coffee pot, and refrigerator enable you to be quite independent in your travels here. Or if you plan on heavy-duty cooking, suites are available with fully equipped kitchens. You also have the choice of nonsmoking and nonallergenic rooms.

## HIGH COUNTRY INN $$–$$$
**1785 Hwy. 105 South, Boone**
**(828) 264-1000, (800) 334-5605**
**www.highcountryinn.com**

Built against the side of the mountain, High Country Inn takes advantage of its scenic wooded surroundings. This inn of native stone provides a variety of comfortable to luxurious accommodations.

All 120 rooms have been recently refurbished. You can indulge yourself in a suite, such as the deluxe Appalachian Room with a king-size bed, a whirlpool tub, and a cozy fireplace. This is a popular honeymoon destination, but it also draws skiers, golfers, and other groups interested in the High Country Inn's numerous discount packages. High Country Inn has facilities for conferences, receptions, and banquets.

Geno's Sports Restaurant is open daily for breakfast and dinner in season, while Geno's Sports Lounge is good for a drink and a nibble. Guests also can use the indoor/outdoor pool, hot tub, sauna, and fitness center.

## HILLWINDS INN $$–$$$
**315 Sunset Dr., Blowing Rock**
**(828) 295-7660, (800) 821-4908**
**www.thevillageinnsofblowingrock.com**
This delightful little motel-style inn offers a relaxing respite from a day of shopping and dining. Choose from a variety of rooms with two double beds, or queen- or king-size bed, private bath, and telephone and TV. No pretensions here—it's relaxed and close to shopping and restaurants in downtown Blowing Rock, so the inn is the choice for business travelers, as well as those who don't like a lot of fuss but do like privacy.

Flowers and benches decorate the exterior of the inn and maintain cozy seating in the lobby for sorting through the vast amount of information on the surrounding area, provided by the owners. A complimentary continental breakfast and wine and cheese reception are offered daily.

## HOLIDAY INN EXPRESS $$–$$$$
**1855 Blowing Rock Rd., US 321 East, Boone**
**(828) 264-2451, (800) SEE-MTNS**
**www.holidayinn.com**
The location is convenient—between Boone and Blowing Rock—and amenities are plentiful at this Holiday Inn Express. Recently renovated, this

motel features comfortable rooms plus free daily breakfast bar, free local calls, a fitness center, and an outdoor pool.

## THE MEADOWBROOK INN          $$–$$$
711 Main St., Blowing Rock
(828) 295-4300, (800) 456-5456
www.meadowbrook-inn.com

This gracious inn offers numerous amenities in elegant surroundings. Rooms and suites are furnished in a traditional decor, and deluxe accommodations include fireplaces and oversize whirlpool baths. A serene pond is bordered by landscaped grounds. The Meadowbrook Inn has an indoor heated pool and whirlpool and a fitness center. A glass-enclosed room adjacent to the pool area is used for meetings, conferences, and private dining. Ciao Bello!, offering casual Italian dining, overlooks the garden and pond.

## QUALITY INN APPALACHIAN          $$–$$$$
Conference Center, 949 Blowing Rock Rd., Boone
(828) 262-0020, (800) 228-5151

Only minutes away from Appalachian State's campus, area businesses, and recreation, this modern hotel offers big-city conveniences and amenities. Guests enjoy spacious suites, king and connecting rooms, an indoor/outdoor pool, a fitness center, a restaurant and lounge, and cable television. Full-service banquet facilities include catering, several meeting rooms, and a 3,750-square-foot ballroom. A complimentary morning paper is a nice touch. Smoke-free and wheelchair-accessible rooms are also available.

## SMOKETREE LODGE          $$–$$$$
11914 Hwy. 105 South, Foscoe
(828) 963-6505, (800) 422-1880 in NC
www.smoketree-lodge.com

The Smoketree Lodge is tucked away off Highway 105 leading directly into Boone, just a few minutes away. This hidden delight is sheltered by a canopy of trees that do much to give Smoketree its sense of privacy so near to bustling Boone. The lobby is graced by a massive fireplace that rises to the full height of the vaulted ceiling.

The Blowing Rock area has an array of small, clean, and cozy motels too numerous to mention here. If you prefer, take a drive through Main Street and its side streets. Most of these smaller motels are happy to take walk-ins if you are not quite sure of your travel plans beforehand.

The comfortable rooms at Smoketree each have kitchenettes, and laundry facilities are available on the first floor. The complex also includes a game room, an indoor pool, a hot tub, a sauna/exercise room, and gas and charcoal grills out back for picnic fun on the hill behind the lodge.

## SUPER 8 BOONE          $$–$$$
2419 Hwy. 105, Boone
(828) 264-4133, (800) 560-5942
www.graystonelodge.com

The gray stone exterior of this four-story inn links it to the Scottish influence of Linville, just south on the same highway. Built against the hillside, the inn's first two floors offer parking lot entrances.

The 100 rooms of the Super 8 have a number of comfortable variations that include luxury suites with king-size beds, parlors, and vaulted ceilings. Continental breakfast is free and served from 6:45 to 10 a.m. All rooms have cable TV. The inn also features an indoor heated pool. Special discounts are available.

## SWISS MOUNTAIN VILLAGE          $$–$$$$
2324 Flat Top Rd., Blowing Rock
(828) 295-3373, (888) 785-1188
www.swissmountain.com

The mountain cabins and chalets of Swiss Mountain Village offer the homey charm of a bed-and-breakfast with the privacy of your own home away from home. Set on lovely landscaped grounds, surrounded by a forest filled with native rhododendron and mountain laurel, Swiss Mountain Village has log cabins built from rough-hewn timbers. Each authentic Swiss-style chalet has a loft and stairway over a native-stone fireplace, and each comes furnished with everything you'll need to feel at home, right down to the towels, linens, stoneware, pots, and utensils. A washer and dryer are also included in each unit, so you could stay for days and only bring one suitcase. Hiking trails and a fishing pond are on the property for your outdoor recreation.

Studio and one-, two-, and three-bedroom units are available, each with queen-size beds and queen-size sleeper sofas. Some have extra twin beds or bunks, so bring a crowd.

### THE VILLAGE INN                                    $$
**7876 Valley Blvd., Blowing Rock**
**(828) 295-3380**
**www.thevillageinnsofblowingrock.com**
An intimate place with guest rooms, suites, and cottages, the Village Inn is situated on two landscaped acres with a brook, lake, gardens, and orchard. All rooms have private decks. A complimentary continental breakfast and wine and cheese reception are offered daily.

## Yancey County

### ALPINE VILLAGE                                    $$-$$$$
**200 Overlook Dr., Burnsville**
**(828) 675-4103, (866) 257-4638**
**www.alpine-village-resort.com**
Alpine Village is a unique animal. It has the individuality of a bed-and-breakfast, the serenity of a retreat, and the variety of a small resort. Yet it is highly affordable and a splendid alternative for large families or groups on the road for summer fun.

Set high back in the mountains in the shadow of spectacular Mount Mitchell, Alpine Village is a cluster of private one- and two-bedroom, chalet-style condominiums with all the amenities of home, each accommodating from four to six people. Most cabins are equipped with a kitchen, a dishwasher, a washer/dryer, a telephone, a whirlpool bath, linens, private decks, cable TV, and gas grills. A heated pool and a tennis court are on the grounds, and golf is available at a special discount to guests at nearby Mount Mitchell Golf Club (see our Golf chapter). You can rent these cabins by the night, week, or month. A two-night minimum stay is usually required.

# CENTRAL MOUNTAINS

## Buncombe County

### COMFORT SUITES                                    $$-$$$$
**890 Brevard Rd., Asheville**
**(828) 665-4000, (800) 228-5150**
**www.comfortsuites.com**
Comfort Suites caters to the corporate business traveler. The hotel contains 125 spacious rooms, each with a full- or queen-size bed, sleeper sofa, coffee pot, and refrigerator. Meeting space of 2,000 square feet can accommodate gatherings of up to 100 people. Complimentary deluxe continental breakfast, free airport shuttle, an exercise and hot-tub room, and an outdoor heated pool are some of the amenities provided by Comfort Suites. The hotel is next to the Biltmore Square Mall.

### CROWN PLAZA HOTEL AND
### RESORT                                            $$-$$$$
**1 Holiday Inn Dr., Asheville**
**(828) 254-3211, (800) 733-3211**
**www.ashevillecp.com**
This 120-acre resort caters to corporate and tourist groups. The individual traveler, however, will also find this an enjoyable resort conveniently located three minutes from downtown Asheville. An 18-hole golf course sprawls over rolling green hills and a fully stocked pro shop supplies all your sports needs. The resort's 10,000 square feet of meeting space accommodates a wide variety of functions, including ballroom banquets, sunset receptions, and boardroom meetings. All rooms feature balconies or patios and, of course, some fairly incredible views. Recreational amenities include tennis, a jogging trail, several swimming pools, an on-site exercise room, or a nearby full-service health club. Also available are children's programs and a game room so you can enjoy a peaceful meal while the kids play.

### DAYS INN ASHEVILLE MALL                           $$-$$$
**201 Tunnel Rd., Asheville**
**(828) 252-4000**
**www.daysinnashevillemall.com**

This Days Inn is a popular site for corporate groups, reunions, and senior citizen groups. It's an easy walk from here to the Asheville Mall and numerous restaurants along Tunnel Road. Guest rooms feature double and king-size beds, cable TV with free HBO and ESPN, and room service. The inn has an outdoor pool, and you can purchase tickets to Biltmore Estate here.

### THE DOUBLETREE BILTMORE HOTEL $$$–$$$$
115 Hendersonville Rd., Asheville
(828) 274-1800, (800) 228-5151
www.biltmoreinns.com

Since its construction several years ago, the Doubletree Biltmore Hotel in Asheville has become one of the prime fixtures in the southern end of town. The hotel's brick-and-stone exterior is a modern blend of the angles and lines and stately presence of the turn-of-the-last-century architectural opulence characterized by its neighbor, Biltmore Estate. The light wood-paneled interior and dramatic lighting of the hotel lobby complement the elegance of the lush furnishings.

The hotel has guest rooms and suites. All rooms have cable TV with HBO, valet and room service, and electronic door locks. A gift shop and fax machine are in the lobby. This hotel also caters to corporate business, with several flexible meeting rooms and on-site advance coordination of catering, audiovisual equipment, and entertainment.

### FOUR POINTS BY SHERATON $$–$$$
22 Woodfin St., Asheville
(828) 253-1851
www.starwoodhotels.com

Just off I-240, which loops around the city, Four Points by Sheraton is convenient to attractions at all points of the compass. This hotel has guest rooms, a swimming pool, meeting rooms, and a restaurant and lounge, with complimentary use of the YMCA across the street.

### HAMPTON INN—ASHEVILLE $$–$$$$
1 Rocky Ridge Rd., off I-26, Asheville
(828) 667-2022, (800) HAMPTON
www.ashevillehamptoninns.com

Southwest of the city, the Hampton Inn of Asheville has 121 nicely appointed guest rooms, a fully equipped fitness center, an indoor heated pool, a sauna, and a hot tub. Free airport transportation, nonsmoking rooms, and meeting facilities are also available. The Biltmore Square Mall, the Movies at Biltmore Square, and several fast-food restaurants are nearby. You can also ask them about their Tunnel Road Facility, which is close to Asheville Mall.

### HAYWOOD PARK HOTEL $$$–$$$$
1 Battery Park Ave., Asheville
(828) 252-2522, (800) 228-2522
www.haywoodpark.com

The Haywood Park Hotel was a prominent flagship in the resurgence of downtown Asheville. A full-service hotel in the heart of downtown was a risky business years ago, but the renovation of the historic Ivey's Department Store at the corner of Battery Park Avenue and Haywood Street into the sleek Haywood Park Hotel was backed by strong business commitment. The success of this undertaking brought a level of sophistication to the inner city that set the tone for the upscale mood and cultural renaissance enjoyed by downtown Asheville today.

The hotel renovation is an interesting use of space, opening up and reshaping the former boxy retail building. The adjoining atrium space, which houses shops, restaurants, and offices, brings the sky inside the heart of this city block with its vaulted ceiling, skylights, and gleaming glass elevator.

The Haywood Park Hotel has 33 exquisitely appointed guest rooms, some with great views of the architectural richness of downtown Asheville. Meeting rooms are also available, and the superb restaurant, the Flying Frog Café, a chic gathering place, makes the Haywood Park Hotel a popular dining spot for downtown business professionals and visitors alike. This fine hotel has also hosted a number of celebrities, whose photos line the lobby walls.

## HOLIDAY INN–ASHEVILLE $$–$$$
Biltmore West
**435 Smoky Park Hwy., at I-40 and US 19/23, Asheville**
**(828) 665-2161, (800) 228-2828**
**www.holidayinnbiltmorewest.com**
The six-story lobby atrium with a cozy fireplace is the focal point of this newly revamped hotel. The hotel has a restaurant and lounge, and local crafts are highlighted at a gift shop. Guests may use the hotel's health club, sauna, hot tub, and indoor-outdoor pool.

## RAMADA INN—RIVER RIDGE $$–$$$
**800 Fairview Rd., Asheville**
**(828) 298-9141, (800) 228-5150**
**www.ramadariverridge.com**
This hotel is in the eastern part of Asheville, off I-240 at the River Ridge Outlet Mall. Accommodations are moderately priced, and the hotel has 178 guest rooms, including a number of luxurious two-room suites with large whirlpool garden tubs, king-size beds, a living room, kitchen and dinette areas, and private balconies. A fax and a copier are in the lobby, and a continental breakfast is served by the fireplace in the large sitting area adjacent to the lobby. The Ramada Inn also has a pool, a playground, and volleyball and basketball courts. You can walk down the hill to the Outlet Mall.

## RENAISSANCE ASHEVILLE HOTEL $$$–$$$$
**Thomas Wolfe Plaza, Asheville**
**(828) 252-8211**
**www.ashevillerenaissance.com**
The 12-story Renaissance Asheville Hotel, a prominent feature on the skyline of downtown Asheville, provides guests with a breathtaking view of the city and the mountains beyond. This modern award-winning hotel has 275 guest rooms and seven suites, all decorated in an elegant style with all the amenities. Concierge service and health club privileges are available to guests, and there are nonsmoking floors.

The lobby contains a gift shop and a restaurant. The hotel also has 14 flexible meeting rooms with state-of-the-art conference planning and support. An 8,100-square-foot ballroom is also at your disposal.

The Renaissance is within walking distance of Pack Square, fine restaurants, shopping, and downtown galleries. It is a AAA Three Diamond hotel.

**i** **The Renaissance Hotel in Asheville is a stone's throw from the center of town. It's also right beside the Thomas Wolfe Memorial and the Urban Trail, and across from the YMCA with a great weight and workout room and two pools.**

## SLEEP INN—BILTMORE $$–$$$
**117 Hendersonville Rd., Asheville**
**(828) 277-1800, (800) 62-SLEEP**
**www.ashevillesleepinn.com**
This Sleep Inn across from Biltmore Village offers upscale quality accommodations at a reasonable price. Attractively furnished, this hotel offers a number of pleasing amenities: queen-size beds, smoking and nonsmoking rooms, connecting rooms, free continental breakfast, and free local calls. A fax and copier are also available for busy working travelers. The Biltmore Estate entrance is just a few blocks away.

## WILLOW WINDS $$$
**39 Stockwood Rd., Asheville**
**(828) 277-3948**
**www.willowwinds.com**
Only minutes from Biltmore Estate, these individual homes on 40 acres of land give you the full luxury experience of staying in a fully furnished domicile, including washers, dryers, equipped kitchen, televisions, VCR/DVD, and your own phone line. From one-bedroom homes to three-bedroom homes with two stories, these beautifully furnished residences also contain Jacuzzi tubs inside and hot tubs outdoors.

If you haven't bought your groceries yet, not to worry, you'll be supplied with a gift basket containing fresh fruit, cookies, coffee, and wine. A stocked pond on the property enables you to fish for your own dinner if you care to. Houses may be rented for as few as two nights in the off season and a minimum of five nights during high season.

## WINGATE INN $$–$$$
11 Rocky Ridge Rd., Asheville
(828) 665-4242, (800) 228-1000
www.wingateinnasheville.com

The Wingate Inn provides everything for the traveling businessperson. Free Internet access in every room means being truly connected while you're on the road. Guest rooms also feature a coffee maker, microwave, refrigerator, safe, hair dryer, and iron and ironing board. Meeting rooms are also available, and a fitness center lets you blow off steam at the end of the day. A complimentary expanded continental breakfast nourishes the hungry before it's time to hit the road.

## Henderson County

### HAMPTON INN $$
155 Sugarloaf Rd., Hendersonville
(828) 697-2333, (800) HAMPTON
www.hamptoninnhendersonville.com

Hampton Inn, right off the junction of I-26 and U.S. Highway 64 (take exit 18A going to Bat Cave), has 117 rooms and two suites. Amenities include cable television with HBO, free local phone calls, an outdoor swimming pool, health club privileges, senior discounts, and a free deluxe continental breakfast. Nonsmoking rooms are available, and third and fourth guests stay free of charge. From here, it's just a hop, skip, and a jump to Wal-Mart, the Blue Ridge Mall, and a number of familiar chain restaurants. A bit farther on is Hendersonville's historic Main Street, with its abundance of shops, restaurants, and galleries.

### THE QUALITY INN AND SUITES $$
201 Sugarloaf Rd., Hendersonville
(828) 692-7231, (800) 4-CHOICE
www.qualityinn-suiteshvl.com

This large facility is also at the junction of I-26 and US 64 (exit 18A). In addition to air-conditioned corporate, spa, and two-room suites, the inn has an excellent restaurant court and lounge overlooking an indoor, Olympic-size, heated swimming pool. The motel offers a full range of amenities, including a fitness room, sauna, free newspaper and local phone calls, banquet facilities, room service, a hot tub, and meeting rooms. All the sites of Main Street Hendersonville are nearby.

## Polk County

### DAYS INN $$
I-26 at exit 36, Columbus
(828) 894-3303, (800) 329-7466
www.daysinn.com

Situated between the twin towns of Tryon and Columbus, this facility offers many extras, such as an outdoor pool, suites with whirlpool baths, cable television with HBO, nonsmoking rooms, free continental breakfast, AARP discounts, mountain views, and 24-hour desk and wake-up services.

### PISGAH INN $$
Mile 408.6, Blue Ridge Parkway, Waynesville
(828) 235-8228
www.pisgahinn.com

The Pisgah Inn is a landmark on the Blue Ridge Parkway. From late Apr until early Nov, this inn's location, at 5,000 feet and just a hike down a trail from Mount Pisgah itself, offers you the opportunity to explore nature's unspoiled mountain seasons—and you barely have to step outside to do it. In addition to two double beds, a private bath, and color television, each room at Pisgah Inn has its own private porch or balcony directly overlooking Pisgah Ledge and the ever-changing play of lights and shadows on the mountain peaks below. A restaurant serves excellent food at very reasonable prices, and the view from the dining room is spectacular.

If you want to get out in all this beauty, you can hike on a number of trails—interconnecting with many other Pisgah Forest trails—that begin practically at the inn's door. This is a popular place so advance planning is important. You might simply be able to drop in and get a room,

i Winter weather of 2009 and early 2010 caused rock slides on many mountain roads. When traveling into the mountains be certain to check on road conditions before venturing forward. You might have to retrace your steps otherwise and find an alternative route.

but it's wiser to make reservations. During fall-foliage days, early reservations are essential.

## Rutherford County

**FAIRFIELD MOUNTAINS RESORT   $$$–$$$$**
**747 Buffalo Creek Rd., Lake Lure**
**(828) 625-9111, (800) 829-3149**
**www.fairfieldmountains.com**
This resort offers efficiencies, condominiums, rentals, and time-shares for travelers wishing to enjoy the scenery of Lake Lure and Chimney Rock and the recreation of two golf courses on the 2,400-acre Fairfield Mountains Resort property. Several of Fairfield's 100 units sit on the banks of the lake, opposite the town of Lake Lure. Others offer views of mountain ridges and foliage. Efficiencies include efficiency kitchens, telephones, TV, and air-conditioning. Larger two- and three-bedroom units also contain these amenities, but with a full kitchen.

Because many of the units are actually second homes that are rented out by the resort, you will find the interiors decorated to the individual tastes of the owners. This lends a delightfully homey and distinct atmosphere to each rental. Some homes maintain a two-day rental policy, but many allow for anywhere from a one-night's stay to several weeks or months.

If you don't feel like cooking, two restaurants located at the resort can provide pleasant dining. Legends Bar and Grill serves breakfast, lunch, and dinner, and Lakeview Restaurant serves dinner.

## Transylvania County

**BREVARD MOTOR LODGE                    $**
**US 64 and 750 N. Caldwell St., Brevard**
**(828) 884-3456**
While staying here, you'll be across the street from Brevard College's picturesque campus, within walking distance of downtown Brevard, and just minutes away from the Brevard Music Center. This small motel—all its rooms are on the ground floor—offers individual heating and air-conditioning, a small refrigerator in each room, a heated pool, and fax and copier service.

**HAMPTON INN                            $$**
**800 Forest Gate Center, Brevard**
**(828) 883-4800, (800) HAMPTON**
**www.hamptoninnbrevard.com**
This 81-room Hampton Inn is just off the main entrance to Pisgah Forest outside Brevard near the intersection of Highway 280 and US 64. The facility offers two conference rooms and continental breakfasts. There is no restaurant on the premises, but you'll be within walking distance of quite a few places to eat. Shopping, too, is at your front door in the Forest Gate Shopping Center.

**RAINBOW LAKE RESORT                    $$$**
**Rainbow Lake Dr., Brevard**
**(828) 862-5354**
**www.rainbowlake.com**
This serene mountain valley just across the road from the trout-filled headwaters of the French Broad River is perfect for those who want a quiet stay in the mountains. The 12 rustic cottages have front porches with porch swings and rockers. They are sprinkled throughout the woods overlooking a three-acre lake. Their simple board-and-batten exteriors belie the elegance within. The tastefully decorated interiors include original works of art, hardwood floors, fine furnishings, and fully equipped kitchens. Each has a private phone, cable TV, and air-conditioning. Some have fireplaces. You can choose from one, two, and three bedrooms. Here you'll find trails, boating, fishing, badminton, horseshoes, volleyball, streams, waterfalls, hammocks, quiet reading nooks, tranquility, and a summer symphony of crickets and frogs to sing you to sleep. Rainbow Lake is the perfect place for holding seminars and family reunions. Well-behaved, flealess pets are accepted with prior arrangements.

# SOUTHERN MOUNTAINS

## Cherokee County

**CHEROKEE HILLS GOLF AND**
**COUNTRY CLUB                   $$$–$$$$**
**Harshaw Road, Murphy**
**(828) 837-5853, (800) 334-3905**
**www.cherokeehillsgolfandcountryclub.com**

If you like to golf, this is the place to stay in Murphy (see our Golf chapter). The complex has 12 units available in the club's lodge that feature fully equipped efficiencies, including two queen-size beds, a bath with a tub and shower, kitchens, cable television, daily maid service, and air-conditioning. Spacious two-story town houses are available for rent at little more per night than you would pay at a fine hotel. Golf packages bring down the price even more. Rentals also include access to the pool, tennis courts, a restaurant, a golf course, a driving range, and a putting green.

**HOLIDAY INN EXPRESS HOTEL & SUITES  $$**
130 Holiday Inn Dr., Murphy
(828) 837-1111
www.hiexpress.com
A complimentary continental breakfast, indoor pool, and Jacuzzi are part of this newer hotel, and one of the fewer hotel/motels to stay in this far western portion of the state. Like most Holiday Inn Express hotels, this one contains a business center and pool.

## Clay County
**CHATUGE MOUNTAIN INN  $**
4238 US 64, Hayesville
(828) 389-9340, (800) 948-2755
www.chatugemountaininn.com
This facility is east of Hayesville on US 64 going toward Hiwassee, Georgia. It has clean, comfortable rooms, including one efficiency unit. All rooms have air-conditioning, cable television, and telephones. Although it's much like a typical 1960s style roadside motel, small creature comforts like rocking chairs in front of the rooms, a gas grill for cooking out, and suites available with full kitchens, make this a pleasant little respite.

## Haywood County
**BEST WESTERN  $$**
3811 Soco Rd., US 19, Maggie Valley
(828) 926-3962, (800) 528-1234
www.bestwestern.com
Best Western, formerly the Mountainbrook Inn, on the busy highway that cuts though the center of

this highly developed resort town, is within walking distance of many Maggie Valley attractions. Even so, you can relax on the rocking chairs here while you view mountains right from the front porch of your room. Or, during the summer season, you can unwind in a heated pool and large whirlpool spa. The grounds include a picnic area with grills. The large motel-type rooms contain two queen-size beds. There are full baths and showers, a couple of upholstered chairs with a small table, cable television with free HBO, and—probably best of all for the budget-conscious—a microwave, a refrigerator, and in-room coffee. There is no charge for children 17 and younger staying in the same room with a parent. Cribs are available at no cost. A continental breakfast is served each morning.

**BEST WESTERN SMOKY MOUNTAIN INN  $$**
330 Hyatt Creek Rd., Waynesville
(828) 456-4402, (800) 218-2121
www.bestwestern.com
At the Best Western Smoky Mountain Inn, you're within an hour's driving distance of some of our most famous attractions, including the Biltmore Estate, the Great Smoky Mountains Railroad, the Blue Ridge Parkway, the Cherokee Indian Reservation, and Ghost Town in Maggie Valley to name a few. The inn's modern, spacious, and comfortable rooms feature large picture windows revealing gorgeous mountain views. King-size, wheelchair-accessible, and nonsmoking rooms are available on request. Microwaves, minirefrigerators, and color TVs are standard. Complimentary continental breakfast is served each day. Daily newspapers, magazines, and reference books are available in the lobby. This inn is 5 miles north of the Blue Ridge Parkway on U.S. Highways 23/74.

**CHALET MOTEL AND APARTMENTS  $$**
48 Holland Dr., Maggie Valley
(828) 926-2811, (800) 371-8587
www.mvchalet.com
Nestled up and off US 19 in a secluded and quiet spot, Chalet Motel rents apartments, efficiencies, and rooms. These vary in the types of accommodations offered. One efficiency, for example, has a king-size bed and a kitchenette; another has a

queen-size bed and a full kitchen. The average apartment has a living-dining room combination, a bedroom with two double beds, and a separate full kitchen. They have heat and air-conditioning, cable television with HBO, AM/FM radio, and private patios with pretty mountain views. The lawn is flat and expansive and has shade trees, picnic tables and grills; there are trails and trout streams close by.

### TWINBROOK RESORT $$
**230 Twinbrook Lane, Maggie Valley**
**(828) 926-1388, (800) 305-8946**
**www.twinbrookresort.com**
Set on 20 acres, this four-season facility features 14 one-, two-, three-, and four-bedroom, individually crafted cottages with fireplaces, phones, and cable TV. The cottages are scattered among tall hemlocks. On site are an indoor pool, a hot tub, a game area, horseshoe pits, a volleyball court, and a playground.

## Jackson County

### COMFORT INN $$
**US 23/74, Mile 86, Sylva**
**(828) 586-3315, (800) 654-3315**
**www.comfortinn.com**
All rooms at Sylva's Comfort Inn have phones and cable television. The inn also has a swimming pool, serves a complimentary continental breakfast, and has other services and discounts you'd expect from a motel chain such as Comfort Inn. This one is near Sylva and Dillsboro on the highway to Waynesville.

### COTTAGE INN $$–$$$$
**Off US 64, Cashiers**
**(828) 743-3033**
Since 1932 the year-round Cottage Inn has been a mountain hideaway for quiet, lovely vacations. Each of the 14 air-conditioned cottages has a fireplace, kitchen, color TV, full bath, and deck and porch. In addition to the cottages is the Knolltop Lodge Bed-and-Breakfast with four guest rooms each with a private bath, air-conditioning, a common parlor with a TV and a fireplace, and a full breakfast daily.

The nine-acre complex also has an enclosed heated pool, a tennis court with a basketball hoop, a nature trail, a picnic pavilion, swings and hammocks, laundry facilities, and the Heathstone room for meetings.

### MOUNTAIN BROOK COTTAGES $$$
**208 Mountain Brook Rd., Sylva**
**(828) 586-4329**
**www.mountainbrook.com**
Midway between Sylva/Dillsboro and Franklin, these 12 brookside cottages offer fireplaces and equipped kitchens. Some have bubble tubs/saunas and king-size beds. There is also a spa/sauna bungalow. In addition Mountain Brook offers a game room, a stocked trout pond, and a nature trail. Wedding and honeymoon packages are available.

## Macon County

### HIGHLANDS SUITE HOTEL $$$$
**200 Main St., Highlands**
**(828) 526-4502, (877) 553-3761**
**www.highlandsuitehotel.com**
Just where the shopping stops on Main Street, you'll find the Highlands Suite Hotel, where all rooms are suites, each with individual climate control, whirlpool spa, two telephones, two 32-inch LCD cable TVs, VCR, microwave oven, wet bar, and refrigerator. In addition each living room has a queen-size convertible sofa bed, and each bedroom offers a choice of either one king-size or two extra-large twin beds. Many suites have gas-log fireplaces.

There are also complimentary continental breakfasts and evening wine and cheese, free parking in a covered garage, and free local phone calls. Nonsmoking rooms and walk-in closets are available options.

### SKYLINE LODGE $$$
**Flat Mountain Rd., Highlands**
**(828) 526-2121, (800) 575-9546**
**www.skyline-lodge.com**
At an altitude of more than 4,000 feet, Skyline is housed in a Frank Lloyd Wright–designed,

tastefully furnished building with 50 acres of grounds that have streams, lakes, waterfalls, and nature walks. Other attractions include a swimming pool, tennis courts, a gourmet restaurant, and a spa with a sauna, a steam room, and a whirlpool. The facility also offers facials, full-body massages, and foot- and hand-care sessions, along with guided fitness walks, aerobics, yoga, and seminars on healthful living (seminars are offered only to guests participating in the lodge's "Holiday Health" specials). Skyline Lodge is open year-round.

## Swain County

**BEST WESTERN GREAT SMOKIES INN**    **$$**
**U.S. Hwy. 441 at Acquoni Road, Cherokee**
**(828) 497-2020, (800) 258-1234**
**www.bestwesterninn.com**
Right across the street from the 8,000-square-foot Great Smokies Convention Center, this Best Western has 152 extra-large rooms with cable TV with a free movie channel; it also has a swimming pool. Myrtle's Table Restaurant at the facility serves breakfast, lunch, and dinner.

**HAMPTON INN OF CHEROKEE**    **$$**
**185 Tsagali Rd., US 19 South, Cherokee**
**(828) 497-3115, (800) HAMPTON**
**www.cherokeehampton.com**
The 67 rooms here each have an inside entrance, temperature controls, and cable TV with free movie channels. Half the rooms are designated nonsmoking. Children younger than 18 stay free in a parent's room. A free continental breakfast is available and a full-service restaurant is right next door.

**HARRAH'S CHEROKEE CASINO**
**AND HOTEL**    **$–$$$$**
**777 Casino Dr., Cherokee**
**(828) 497-7777, (800) 427-7247**
**www.harrahscherokee.com**
An enterprise of the Eastern Band of Cherokee Indians, this luxurious hotel has an indoor heated pool, whirlpool, fitness center, Selu Garden Café, Club Cappuccino, and a 10,000-square-foot con-

ference center. The 252 rooms include eight suites and a beautiful airy atrium includes natural stone pillars, carved wood elements and local Cherokee artwork.

**HOLIDAY INN CHEROKEE**    **$$**
**US 19 South, Cherokee**
**(828) 497-9181, (800) HOLIDAY**
**www.hicherokeenc.com**
Facilities here include 154 rooms with cable TV with a free movie channel, banquet facilities to accommodate up to 200, both indoor and outdoor pools, a whirlpool, and a sauna. The Chestnut Tree Restaurant serves breakfast and dinner.

**MOUNTAIN VIEW LOG CABIN**
**RENTALS**    **$$$$**
**Off US 441, Cherokee**
**(828) 497-9552, (800) 392-1003**
**www.mtnviewcabins.com**
Find peace and quiet within minutes of bustling downtown Cherokee and the recreational opportunities of the Great Smoky Mountains National Park. These cabins feature microwave-equipped kitchens, mountain-stone fireplaces, color cable TV, private indoor hot tubs, king-size beds, phones, all linens, and porches with rocking chairs and swings. The Mountain View Log Cabin office is at the Discount Souvenirs gift shop on US 441 North, about a mile from the entrance to the Great Smoky Mountains National Park.

**PIONEER MOTEL AND COTTAGES**    **$$**
**US 19 South, Cherokee**
**(828) 497-2435**
**www.pioneermotel.net**
Situated on 16 waterfront acres a half-mile from downtown Cherokee, Pioneer offers one-, two-, or three-bedroom cabins with full modern facilities overlooking the Oconaluftee River, or you can choose a spacious room in the motel. All rooms are air-conditioned and have cable TV. Other recreational amenities are fishing (with a tribal permit), basketball, horseshoes, a pool, and a picnic area on the premises.

# RESTAURANTS

**M**ountain cooking brings to mind visions of fluffy biscuits, thick gravy, corn bread, soup beans, buttery grits, soft-cooked vegetables like okra and squash, fried chicken, molasses-based barbecue, and deep-dish pies of all varieties, of course. Canning your own garden vegetables, wild berries, and fruits and making any dough from scratch are par for the course in the country kitchen. And you'll find plenty of family-style restaurants specializing in down-home cookin' throughout the region, but in contrast there are fine dining and ethnic restaurants as well.

As our area grows so, too, do the dining choices. You could easily plan a vacation around the culinary options in many of our towns and communities.

Our selections, which are featured by region, may vary greatly in style, from the smallest coffee shop with the best biscuits, burgers, and chocolate malts in the area to the most elegant haute cuisine from a French master chef. Variety is the spice of life, after all. There are also plenty of fast-food and franchise restaurants throughout the mountains. But we've tried to highlight places that give you a taste of the region and maintain a proven track record.

## Price Code

Most of these restaurants will accept major credit cards for payment; we've tried to note those that do not. While menu changes may certainly affect the pricing of some restaurants, we've provided a pricing guide for an idea of what you can expect on the check for a basic meal for two (without desserts and alcoholic beverages). This table does not reflect tax or gratuities. Enjoy!

| | |
|---|---|
| $ | Less than $20 |
| $$ | $20 to $35 |
| $$$ | $36 to $50 |
| $$$$ | More than $50 |

# NORTHERN MOUNTAINS

## Alleghany County

**STATION'S INN**      **$–$$**
14355 Hwy. 18, Laurel Springs
(336) 359-2888, (877) 528-7356
www.stationsinn.com
This country store, motel, and restaurant surrounds itself with everything motorcycle and car. Two dining rooms, porch seating, and a bar are decorated with gadgetry, signs, and items devoted to the all-American enjoyment of the open road. Burgers, hot dogs, pork tenderloin, ribs, and grilled chicken are the menu choices here. Live music arrives on the weekends.

## Ashe County

**GLENDALE SPRINGS INN AND
RESTAURANT**      **$–$$$**
7414 Hwy. 16, Glendale Springs
(336) 982-2103, (800) 287-1206
www.glendalespringsinn.com
Once a general merchandise store, a circuit courthouse, a post office, a chapel, a community center, and a boarding house, the inn features two wood-paneled dining rooms and one white and peach room, while side-porch dining by the garden is also available. (Read more about the inn in our Bed-and-Breakfasts and Country Inns chapter.) Lazy fans spin overhead in the main dining hall, where creaking wooden floors and an old piano evoke visions of Saturday night country jamborees. The ambience and cuisine are quite sophisticated here, with a seasonally changing menu.

Tables are covered in crisp linens, and the menu offers delicacies whipped up by the resident chef. Do call for evening reservations, but feel free to walk in for lunch.

**LOUISIANA PURCHASE**                           $$–$$$$
**397 Shawneehaw Ave., Banner Elk**
**(828) 963-5087, (866) 734-4124**
**www.louisianapurchasefoodandspirits.com**
If your heart belongs to the moss-draped avenues of New Orleans and the sultry tones of Bourbon Street, and your palate enjoys Cajun, Creole, or classic French cuisine, you'll want to try Louisiana Purchase in Banner Elk. The classy restaurant with the flavor of old New Orleans here in the High Country also specializes in classic French. Murals of the Big Easy lend atmosphere to this casually elegant restaurant, and live jazz on weekends adds to the New Orleans ambience of Louisiana Purchase. The restaurant has an extensive wine list, too. Reservations are suggested.

**MOUNTAIN AIRE SEAFOOD AND STEAK**
**HOUSE**                                        $–$$$
**Intersection of Hwys. 16 and 163,**
**West Jefferson**
**(336) 982-3060**
**www.mountainaireseafood.com**
This friendly restaurant is a welcome sight after working up an appetite traveling the winding two-lanes of Ashe County. (The restaurant is just minutes from Holy Trinity Church, up the road in Glendale Springs, where you can see the exquisite Ben Long fresco of the Last Supper.) The menu is noted for its extensive selection of fresh seafood, delivered several times a week from the coast. Fresh stuffed flounder, salt-and-pepper catfish, and stir-fried shrimp are customer favorites. You can also order a substantial filet mignon, chicken strips (grilled or fried), and even such delicacies as frogs' legs. Don't forget to try out the generous-size, homemade hush puppies—they're delicious.

Well-prepared, ample portions and excellent service have created a loyal clientele here.

**RIVER HOUSE**                                  $$–$$$$
**1896 Old Field Creek Rd., Grassy Creek**
**(336) 982-2109**
**www.riverhousenc.com**
The River House restaurant, part of a lovely 1870 farmhouse bed-and-breakfast inn, is a destination for diners from across the country and abroad. The fare at River House is an unusual mix of European haute cuisine and down-home American style. Unlike the petite-size servings you get in some restaurants, where presentation is the primary goal, generous portions are guaranteed at River House—and the presentation is impressive too. A four-course tasting menu follows the Salon Series entertainment on Sun afternoon.

**SHATLEY SPRINGS INN**                          $
**407 Shatley Springs Rd., Crumpler**
**(336) 982-2236**
**www.shatleysprings.com**
This rustic inn is known for its family-style country dining for breakfast, lunch, or dinner. The historic inn and cabins are also known for the natural mineral waters burbling nearby. Bring your own jug to take some home.

## Avery County

**ESEEOLA LODGE**                                $$–$$$
**175 Linville Ave., Linville**
**(828) 733-4311**
**www.eseeola.com**
This is a rare opportunity for elegant dining at an historic lodge (see our Resorts chapter). Experience a sumptuous breakfast, self-served from the buffet of fresh fruit, cereals, and breakfast breads, or a table service of heartier fare. Lunch and dinner are served at the club just across the road; there is a bar for sitting and sipping. Reservations for dinner are requested.

**FAMOUS LOUISE'S ROCK HOUSE**
**RESTAURANT**                                   $–$$
**10780 Linville Falls Hwy.,  Linville Falls**
**(828) 765-2702**
You can dine in three counties and never step outside the door of Famous Louise's Rock House

Restaurant, which is just 3 miles north of Linville Caverns. This quaint family-owned restaurant has the distinction of sitting directly on the spot where Burke, McDowell, and Avery Counties meet. Signs point the way to your dining location—and favorite county—or you can sit near the fireplace, the spot where all three counties come together! Your food will be cooked in Avery County, picked up by your waitress in Burke County, and very often served just over the line in McDowell County. Credit cards are not accepted.

**STONEWALLS** $$–$$$
**344 Shawneehaw Ave., Banner Elk**
**(828) 898-5550**
**www.stonewallsrestaurant.com**
This rustic stone building is home to a marvelous family restaurant that specializes in American cuisine, specifically well-turned steaks, luscious prime rib, and popular seafood dishes (the lobster is melt-in-your-mouth luscious). Stonewalls also has a superb salad bar. Stonewalls serves dinner only, seven days a week.

**TARTAN RESTAURANT** $–$$
**31 Coffey Rd., Linville**
**(828) 733-0779**
Here's a cozy, unassuming restaurant near Grandfather Mountain that serves a pleasing array of mountain favorites with Scottish flair. The menu offers breakfast, lunch, and dinner specialties, but the unique lunch sandwiches seem to be the place's calling card.

## Madison County
**THE LODGE AT WOLF RIDGE** $–$$
**US Hwy. 19-23N (I-26 West) exit 3,**
**Wolf Laurel**
**(828) 689-9400, (888) 689-1928**
**http://mountainflavor.com**
Soar with the eagles at the Lodge restaurant located at an elevation of 4,300 feet. The views fall off in all directions and can be admired from your table through the massive glass windows laced throughout the log structure.

Ribs, steaks, and such are served throughout the year. This family-friendly restaurant offers weekend mountain music and clogging by the best of the mountain dancers. The adventurous might want to order a 44-ounce steak, which is yours free if you clean your plate, including all sides as well. As if these views weren't enough—the staff will also host you on their ski lift for grander panoramas throughout the year.

The Lodge, with its blazing fireplace, is home to snow bunnies and serious skiers come wintertime. You can even rent a cabin on the adjacent slopes year-round. (See our chapters on Skiing, Golf, and Resorts.)

## Mitchell County
**CHALET RESTAURANT AT**
**SWITZERLAND INN** $$–$$$
**86 High Ridge Rd., Little Switzerland**
**(828) 765-2153, (800) 654-4026**
**www.switzerlandinn.com**
The views are phenomenal and the menu is varied with a good wine list in this cozy lodge-style locale. Menu items run the gamut from Cajun frogs' legs to New Zealand rack of lamb and plank salmon.

**KNIFE AND FORK** $–$$$
**61 Locust St., Spruce Pine**
**(828) 765-1511**
**www.knifeandforknc.com**
This little eatery on downtown Spruce Pine's lower street makes use of the best in locally grown produce and farm-raised fowl. With buttermilk-fried chicken that is juicier than juicy, grilled mountain trout stuffed with bacon, rabbit (yes, rabbit) paté, the perfect French onion soup, and other flights of fancy from a formerly L.A.-based couple is worth a visit. Seating is in front of big picture windows with the atmospheric view of trains passing on the tracks.

**UPPER STREET CAFÉ** $
**198 Oak Ave., Spruce Pine**
**(828) 765-0622**
This little boutique diner with mountain-friendly people closes at 2 p.m., but its 7 a.m. opening

# Close-up

## Caviar from Canton

Caviar from the mountains? It's not so unusual if you look at the early beginnings of fish farming: Dick Jennings founded Sunburst Trout Company in 1946 in the region of Pisgah National Forest. At first Dick supplied farm-raised trout, but then he began experimenting with smoked trout and trout pâté. In more recent years, working with his daughter, Sally Eason, who now heads the business, Dick has worked up the trout eggs, or roe, for eating. Eventually their caviar collection caught on in restaurants throughout the region. As in the case of the pungent mountain onion, the ramp, which found its way to the kitchens of New York chefs, so too has the rainbow trout caviar of the mountains of Western North Carolina caught on. Eason has even taken "coals to Newcastle" by traveling to Armenia, where sturgeon roe from the Caspian Sea reigns as king. She demonstrated to caviar collectors a better way to harvest the eggs. This caviar is best with poached trout or smoked trout, on salads, toasted bagels, or toast corners, and with cream cheese or butter.

time means early breakfasts Mon through Fri. This is traditional quick country dining in a tiny downtown.

## Watauga County

### BISTRO ROCA $$–$$$
**143 Wonderland Trail, Blowing Rock**
**(828) 295-4008**
**www.bistroroca.com**
A true insiders' locale for crispy-crust individual pizzas baked in the wood-fired brick oven, which is the centerpiece of this restaurant. Inspired porkchops, prosciutto-honey baked figs, robust burgers, pan-seared tuna, and other rustic dishes appeal to those locals who want to reconnect and relax in this cozy plaze tucked into a bend just past Blowing Rock's Mayview Lake. Sip on a digestif afterwards at Antler's Bar, where part of the decor features photos of patrons' dogs.

**i** To be clear: in the mountains, folks often refer to the noontime meal as dinner and the evening meal as supper.

### CRIPPEN'S $$$–$$$$
**239 Sunset Dr., Blowing Rock**
**(828) 295-3487**
**www.crippens.com**

Part of Crippen's Country Inn & Restaurant, this dining room has a strong tradition in the mountains for fine dining. Written up in national magazines and newspapers, Crippen's still aims to please each diner with specialties like Marinated and Grilled Breast of Chicken with Coconut-Ginger Sauce, Sweet Plantain Mash, and West Indian Pumpkin and Rosemary and Garlic Marinated Grilled Pork Tenderloin with Rosemary-Zinfandel Sauce, Sugar Snaps, and Goat Cheese-Chive Mash. The "chocolate" steak with a cocoa nib rub is quite interesting. A nice selection of fish entrees and specials are featured daily. This is a fairly formal dining affair, so plan ahead and make reservations. Creative cocktails at the bar are another specialty, and is the place where you will find locals congregating after work.

### DANIEL BOONE INN RESTAURANT $–$$
**130 Hardin St., Boone**
**(828) 264-8657**
**www.danlbooneinn.com**
Since 1959, this old-fashioned, family-style restaurant has been drawing locals and visitors for hearty dining in a historic structure that was Boone's first hospital. For a fixed price, big serving bowls and platters of food are brought to your table, including fried chicken, country-style steak,

biscuits, mashed potatoes, green beans, slaw, corn, fresh-stewed apples, dessert, and beverage.

In the summer, lunch and dinner are served each day. Winter hours are more limited. Children ages 4 to 11 receive discount meals, and meals are free for children 3 and younger. Reservations may be made for groups of 15 or more.

## THE GAMEKEEPER
### RESTAURANT                   $$$–$$$$
**3005 Shull's Mill Rd., Blowing Rock**
**(828) 963-7400**
**www.gamekeeper-nc.com**
The Gamekeeper is in a rustic lodge-style converted house built in 1926 near Yonahlossee Resort on Shull's Mill Road between Boone and Blowing Rock. This elegant restaurant, with starched linens, impeccable service, and unforgettable fare, accommodates guests in cozy private nooks warmed by a fireplace.

Dining here is a culinary experience: The menu is composed entirely of wild game—and not just venison either. Selections often include boar, antelope, and duck. The restaurant has a selection of fine wines to complement these exotic dishes.

## JACKALOPE'S VIEW              $$–$$$
**2489 Beech Mountain Pkwy., Banner Elk**
**(828) 898-9004**
**www.archersinn.com/jackalopes.htm**
Surrounded by lush flora, Jackalope's View faces the Grandfather Mountain ridge directly opposite. Open for dinner year-round, the restaurant and bar retain a familiar feel thanks to the individual attention of the proprietors. The hosts have created an eclectic menu of exquisitely crafted dishes, which changes seasonally. Wild game, including antelope steak, makes an appearance several times a year. Fresh herbs from the garden add bursts of flavor to the fresh brochette, thinly sliced toasted French bread with diced garlic, tomatoes, and fresh basil sprinkled over the top. Each entree, be it filet mignon, shrimp ziti, or tender crab cakes, shares the attractively presented dinner plate with fresh vegetables hand-picked from the local farmer's market by the chef.

Ceiling fans turn slowly overhead as the lights begin to twinkle in the valleys below, and the time for dessert and coffee pulls nigh. The fresh homemade desserts are impossible to resist, complemented with several different coffees and espressos made in the beautiful brass machine looming over the bar. A terrace provides for outdoor dining on warm summer evenings.

## MURPHY'S RESTAURANT & PUB      $–$$
**747 West King St., Boone**
**(828) 264-5117**
**www.murphysboone.com**
Murphy's, located in downtown Boone, has an imaginative menu, which attracts a lively crowd to its four dining venues. The traditional dining room is furnished with comfortable booths and live music entertains the masses. The sunny deck out back is an option until the end of Oct, when temperatures start to dip in the High Country. The bar area is a friendly place for a quick bite to eat, a little liquid refreshment, and a gander at a favorite sports channel on wide-screen TV, and an attached game room.

## OUR DAILY BREAD               $
**627 West King St., Boone**
**(828) 264-0173**
**www.ourdailybreadboone.com**
Our Daily Bread may become part of your daily routine after you try one of their sandwiches, homemade soups and chilis, and homemade pumpkin bread. The sandwiches are imaginative combinations, such as the Jamaican, a generous portion of turkey topped with pepper cheese and sweet relish on a roll; and the South of the Border, roast beef with pepper cheese and a spicy picante sauce. If you want a hot dog with a twist, you can order Our Daily Bread's Not Dog, a tofu-based vegetarian hot dog. But the most engaging items on the menu have to be the chilis (vegetarian chili is one choice) and homemade soups ladled into an edible bowl of scooped-out sourdough bread!

## THE RED ONION CAFE $$
227 Hardin St., Boone
(828) 264-5470
www.theredonioncafe.com

Walk into this chic establishment and you'll think you've found an art gallery, until the tempting aromas and solicitous waitstaff confirm that, indeed, you've found the Red Onion Cafe. Sitting in the heart of the university district, the restaurant serves creative soups, salads, sandwiches, quiche, pasta, and specialty items.

Prints, paintings, and sculpture by local and regional artists surround diners, and all of the art is for sale. The plant-draped piazza outdoors is also a popular dining spot, weather permitting.

## THE SPECKLED TROUT &
## OYSTER BAR $-$$
Main Street, Blowing Rock
(828) 295-9819
www.speckledtroutcafe.com

Since 1986, the Speckled Trout Cafe has been serving hearty breakfasts, lunches, and dinners that everyone seems to love. There's even trout for breakfast. The Big Daddy's Breakfast is panfried trout and two cheese-scrambled eggs, served with a biscuit or toast. Trout and oyster dishes dominate the dinner menu, which also includes a classic selection of steaks and interesting side dishes. Lunch is the tamer meal here, with standard sandwiches, soups, and salads.

## THE VILLAGE CAFE $$-$$$
Main Street, Blowing Rock
(828) 295-3769
www.thevillagecafe.com

It is a rare experience when a restaurant can transfer you to distant shores, evoke forgotten memories, or fulfill long-sought-after daydreams. Step off Main Street in Blowing Rock and down the path beside Kilwin's. At its end you'll find a tree-shaded courtyard and the Village Cafe. It could be an English garden in Britain's Lake District, it could be a flowered courtyard in Provence, but we only have to travel within our own mountains to find this jewel. The restaurant is tucked into the Randall Memorial Building, a quaint, white-frame cottage on the National Register of Historic Places that housed a mountain crafts co-op in 1907. Later the building served as the Blowing Rock Village Library.

Imagine the soft sweetness of Belgian waffles made to order, garnished with plump, fresh raspberries, blueberries, strawberries, and unbelievably light honey syrup. Most memorable are the variety of fresh soups daily: mushroom and hazelnut, sweet corn and green-pepper sauce, tomato, and smoked gouda. A cafe specialty is the marvelous homemade Argentine fugasa bread, which you may also pick up to take home. You may dine in the courtyard under the trees in fair weather. The Village Cafe is open seasonally, from late Apr to late Oct.

## WOODLANDS BARBECUE AND
## PICKIN' PARLOR $
8304 Valley Blvd., US Hwy. 321 Bypass,
Blowing Rock
(828) 295-3651
www.woodlandsbbq.com

Woodlands has been a favorite High Country dining landmark for several decades. The menu features chopped and sliced pork and beef, ribs, chicken, and home-style Mexican food. Woodlands caters, too. There's also live acoustic entertainment with no cover charge.

## Yancey County

### GARDEN DELI $-$$
107 Town Sq., Burnsville
(828) 682-3946
www.garden-deli.com

Ed Yuziuk is a transplanted mountaineer from New York City. This former owner and editor of the *Yancey Journal* couldn't find a real New York–style deli like the ones he remembered as a boy, so he opened his own. Satisfaction at last! Today his son and daughter-in-law operate the deli. All deli-lovers who happen upon this great little spot couldn't be more satisfied. During the summer season many customers prefer to eat on the spacious outside deck shaded by wisteria vines and willow trees.

### HILLTOP RESTAURANT $
109 West Main St., Burnsville
(828) 678-9123

A true 1950s-style diner with chili dogs, fried onion rings, burgers, and a chocolate shake so thick your straw will stand in it. Sit outside under sun umbrellas or inside at formica tables as locals catch up with each other.

### IN THE GARDEN CAFÉ & SHOPPE $
117 West Main St., Burnsville
(828) 682-1680

Sandwiches, wraps, and small salad plates made with organic and natural ingredients served in a garden atmosphere make this a nice spring or summer respite. Set back slightly from Main Street, it's the perfect place to take a book, have lunch and watch the world go by.

## CENTRAL MOUNTAINS

### Buncombe County

### BERLINER KINDL GERMAN RESTAURANT & DELI $$–$$$
121 Broadway, Black Mountain
(828) 669-5255

Hearty fare of sausages, schnitzel, sauerbraten (marinated pork), and other German delicacies makes its way to your table at this comfy restaurant. Beers are on tap and in bottles. German deli items and other wares are available at the check-out counter. The decor is adorable Bavarian kitsch.

### BISTRO 1896 $$–$$$
7 West Pack Sq., Asheville
(828) 251-1300
www.bistro1896.com

Situated in the main square of Asheville's downtown area, the bistro has copious outdoor seating and serves sandwiches, appetizers, and heartier fare. A stylish lounge off the dining area overlooking the square serves as the perfect people-watching perch, and vintage photographs of downtown Asheville add to the interior ambiance.

### BOUCHON $–$$$
62 North Lexington Ave., Asheville
(828) 350-1140
www.ashevillebouchon.com

Michel Baudouin brings another touch of internationalism to Asheville with his French bistro. He greets guests at the door and pops by your table during the course of your meal, adding a special welcome to this family-friendly establishment. The menu has a blended greeting of "Bon appetit, y'all." Textbook French tells us that *bouchon* is a cork; however, the concept behind the name here follows a tradition established in Lyon, France, of clustering neighborhood bistros offering French comfort food in a friendly atmosphere. Here you'll find a convivial atmosphere at the cozy bar and in the courtyard, as well as the brick-walled dining area. Hearty country French dishes are a delight and locals gather for all-you-can-eat mussels and frits night.

### CAFÉ POSANA $–$$
1 Biltmore Ave., Asheville
(828) 505-3969
www.posanacafe.com

Stylish and bright with contemporary lighting fixtures and local artwork, this anchor of Pack Square—Asheville's central square—serves breakfast, lunch, and dinner with a special nod to those with wheat and gluten allergies. Scrumptious pancakes and oatmeal brûlée with almonds and dried fruit give way to beet and nut-encrusted goat cheese salad for lunch, or grilled quail and mushroom risotto for dinner. Desserts read like a gourmet magazine. A cozy seating area with sofas and coffee tables encourages coffee or tea drinking in the afternoon.

### CITY BAKERY $
60 Biltmore Ave., Asheville
(828) 252-6063
www.citybakery.net

The aroma of fresh bread greets you at the door of City Bakery, housed in one of those grand old renovated storefronts on the revived Biltmore Avenue. You can pick up your daily loaf quota and dawdle for a casual lunch with friends at intimate little tables. (A sister store is located in the Grove Park neighborhood.)

## CLINGMAN CAFÉ     $-$$
**242 Clingman Ave., Asheville**
**(828) 253-2177**
**www.clingmancafe.com**
In the heart of Asheville's River Arts District, the café gathers an eclectic creative clientele for breakfast and lunch. Biscuits and wraps; a breakfast trifle of granola and yogurt; lunch sandwiches with turkey, relish, and cranberry sauce; hummus or lox bagels; salads; and more more are served inside or out, all surrounded by local art.

## THE CORNER KITCHEN     $-$$$
**3 Boston Way, Asheville**
**(828) 274-2439**
**www.thecornerkitchen.com**
In the heart of Biltmore Village, this charming restaurant offers dishes of distinction with new South flavor. Rotating exhibitions from local artists decorate the dining rooms. The charming cottage interior covers two floors and a lovely courtyard in one of Asheville's cutest neighborhoods.

## CUCINA 24     $$-$$$
**24 Wall St., Asheville**
**(828) 254-6170**
**www.cucina24restaurant.com**
Serving an array of innovative northern Italian dishes and wood-fired brick oven pizzas, this local is a favorite for those who like their Italian dishes in the usual courses of antipasti, primi, and secondi of seared sea scallops and fennel, duck scallopini, braised lamb shanks, and other fulfilling dishes. Enjoy a cheese course instead of dessert in the contemporary wood-and-black-toned dining room.

## EARLY GIRL EATERY     $-$$
**8 Wall St., Asheville**
**(828) 259-9292**
**www.earlygirleatery.com**
This little cutie serves up organic dishes and comfort food favorites. Homemade sausage and jams,

stuffed omelettes, and pancakes are dished up for breakfast. The light, airy design that overlooks the street is a winner for lunch and dinner dining also. Lunch features sandwiches and wraps, as well as salads with spring-fresh ingredients year-round. Dinner goes heavier, with duck breast over polenta and panfried chicken in addition to a menu of innovative specials. Sunday brunch finds a line forming at the door, so be sure to get there early, or be ready to wait. Lots of national exposure makes this a very popular place with in- and out-of-towners.

## FIG     $-$$$
**18 Brooke St., Asheville**
**(828) 277-0889**
**www.figbistro.com**
Somewhat off the beaten path, just outside Biltmore Village, this small bistro serves enlightened French-accented cuisine for lunch and dinncer. Outdoor seating in warm weather takes place in a charming shared courtyard.

## FLYING FROG CAFE AND
## FROG BAR     $-$$$$
**1 Battery Park Ave., Asheville**
**(828) 254-9411**
**www.flyingfrogcafe.com**
This exciting restaurant features creative interpretations of classical dishes by chef Vijay Shastri. This child prodigy had his own restaurant in this very spot when he was only 17 years old. Today, he and his father, Jay Shastri, have pooled the family's expertise to make this one of Asheville's most unusual—and excellent—restaurants. Vijay lends his special flair to the French Cajun, Indian, and Caribbean specialties.

The street-level Frog Bar features nightly drink specials and light meals or appetizers to be enjoyed at the see-and-be-seen outdoor cafe tables.

## JERUSALEM GARDEN CAFÉ     $
**78 Patton Ave., Asheville**
**(828) 254-0255**
**www.jerusalemgardenafe.com**
This Middle Eastern restaurant sits directly across from Pritchard Park in the city center. Stepping

# Close-up

## Asheville's Restaurant Row

Asheville now boasts its own literal restaurant row, thanks to an influx of eateries in the historic Grove Arcade. Located on the east side of the Arcade, restaurants spill out onto the sidewalk representing everything from California cuisine to Thai, Italian, South American, burgers, and hot dogs. Check out the interior and other side of the Arcade for Middle Eastern cuisine, unrivaled frozen custard, fresh produce, and snacks.

**Grove Arcade,** 1 Page Ave., Asheville, www.groveacade.com

**Carmel's Restaurant & Bar,** (828) 252-8730, www.carmelsofasheville.com; elegant California cuisine with a fine wine list

**Cats and Dawgs,** (828) 281-8100; Vienna beef hot dogs, catfish sandwiches, fries, soups, and salads

**Chorizo,** (828) 350-1332; scrumptious Latin fare, guacamole prepared tableside, great mojitos

**Modesto,** (828) 225-4133; Italian-influenced menu with wood-fired brick oven gourmet pizzas and savory specialties

**Santé,** (828) 254-8188; convivial European-style wine bar with wines by the glass or by the bottle, meat and cheese boards, and homemade dips for noshing; also retail bottle sales

**Thai Basil,** (828) 258-0036; roomy restaurant with fragrant Thai cuisine, Thai tea, and Thai coffee

**True Confections,** (828) 350-9480; soups, quiche, and biscuits for lunch, but cakes, pies, and coffees, well . . . take the cake

through the front door is like opening to a page from *The Arabian Nights* with tented ceiling, ornamental brass tables, and adorned cushions for seating, along with some chairs. The cuisine is a combination of Jordanian and Turkish delights, from falafel sandwiches to mezze plates and juicy kebabs. On weekends there is belly dancing in the tented party room and throughout the restaurant.

**THE LAUGHING SEED CAFE**      $–$$
40 Wall St., Asheville
(828) 252-3445
www.laughingseed.com
Tucked into charming Wall Street is the Laughing Seed Cafe, which specializes in international vegetarian cuisine. If you're not accustomed to an entirely vegetarian menu, you will be pleasantly surprised. Owners Joan and Joe Eckert are dedicated folks who strive to educate the dining public to the delicacies and flavors, not to mention the outright good health,that can be achieved with vegetarian cooking.

And this is not just rice and beans. We're talking about exotic and delicious dishes from Morocco to Thailand sharing the extensive menu with old favorites from closer to home.

Sunday brunch at the Laughing Seed is a real treat, too. (Downstairs Jack of the Wood Pub serves up microbrewed beer and enlightened pub grub.) Laughing Seed is closed on Tues.

**LIMONES** $$–$$$
13 Eagle St., Asheville
(828) 252-2327
www.limonesrestaurant.com

Part California, part Mexico, the menu here boasts all the freshness, innovation, and piquant flavors of both. A comfortable setting allows visitors to linger over blood orange or pomegranate margaritas and skirt steak with lime and fennel, a tangy ceviche, and many other inventive dishes.

**MAMACITAS** $
77 Biltmore Ave., Asheville
(828) 255-8080
http://mamacitasgrill.com

Walk down the line and point to what fresh ingredients you want in your burrito. It's that simple—your burrito will be made in front of you. Icy margaritas are great here, too. It's the perfect quick bite before a concert at clubs nearby.

**THE MARKET PLACE** $$–$$$$
20 Wall St., Asheville
(828) 252-4162
www.marketplace-restaurant.com

Ever since this restaurant opened in 1979 in downtown Asheville, breaking bread has been a celebratory ritual here. Over the last two decades plus, the Market Place has become a world-class restaurant, acclaimed by publications ranging from the *New York Times* and *Food & Wine* to *Bon Appétit*, *Southern Living*, and *Wine Spectator*. In the heart of Asheville's renovated downtown, a sophisticated, urban look provides a backdrop for classic culinary traditions infused with imaginative, contemporary twists. Featured are over 150 wines with more than 20 served by the glass. A recent change in ownership for the first time since its inception means a new vision for a new decade. Stay tuned. Reservations are suggested.

**MAYFEL'S** $–$$
22 College St., Asheville
(828) 252-8840
www.mayfels.com

A meat and three—that's the premise for this cute throwback to old blue-plate-special southern diners. Here, you'll find local art on the walls and, indeed, blue plate specials. But the sides are inspired: mac 'n cheese, crispy coleslaw with a twist, and other satisfying tastes. Weekends provide café au lait and beignets, early morning. In the warm seasons check out the late-night courtyard in back for cocktails.

**MELA** $–$$
70 Lexington Ave., Asheville
(828) 225-8880
www.melaasheville.com

This Indian restaurant represents all that is Lexington Avenue—urban chic with a little funkiness thrown in. Authentically prepared curry and tandoori meals are elegantly served in a large saffron-colored dining room with a wood-carved bar, which lends a decidedly big-city feel to this exotic establishment.

**NINE MILE** $–$$
233 Montford Ave., Asheville
(828) 505-3121
www.ninemileasheville.com

A great neighborhood locale, which features caribbean-inspired spicy pasta dishes, vegetarian plates, and micro-brew beers. Mango salsas and other garnishes are a great part of the cuisine.

**RED STAG GRILLE** $$–$$$$
22 Boston Way, Asheville
(828) 398-5600
www.bohemianhotelasheville.com

A unique dining experience awaits with a menu that reflects European comfort food with tinges of Austrian, Bavarian, and French influences. Game such as tender elk, duck, quail, and perfectly prepared trout, salmon, and other fish round out a menu that also includes a meatloaf that will be the best you've ever tried. The surroundings are of antlers, elk and deer mounts, twig chandeliers, a private dining room with a large square of onyx backlit by red lighting, and a bar top made of petrified wood.

## SALSA $–$$

6 Patton Ave., Asheville
(828) 252-9805
www.salsas-asheville.com

This sassy little downtown restaurant is short on space but big on taste and innovative cuisine. Salsa is the creation of Hector Diaz, who brought the wonderful culinary heritage of his native Puerto Rico to this popular eatery.

Expect innovative Caribbean fare with "mountain" touches, like wild mushrooms, goat cheese, pinto beans, greens, and other offerings. The menu may include herb chicken quesadillas and tacos made salsa style (fire-roasted pepper tacos and black bean and goat cheese tacos, both served with pico de gallo salsa, are two favorites). The Caribbean menu sparkles with unique ingredients, such as plantains with gazpacho salsa. Exotic root vegetables, unique to the Caribbean, as well as sweet potato and pumpkin are regular ingredients in the gigantic burritos and enchiladas. *Piñonos*, plantains stuffed with a variety of fresh herbs, meats, and vegetables, are always on the specials.

Salsa is a staple with locals, and since showing up in the *New York Times* and *Southern Living*, Salsa has gained a following with folks just visiting or passing through. Be prepared for a wait in the high season. Waiting diners mill around on the sidewalk in front talking about what they'll try this time. There is now outdoor seating in a cheerful alley adjacent to the cafe.

## STONEY KNOB CAFÉ $–$$$

337 Merrimon Ave., Weaverville
(828) 645-3309
www.stoneyknobcafe.com

Sit at the outdoor patio or by the fireplace in the wine bar addition—this former diner (in the family for over 40 years) serves up delightful Greek-inflected dishes in a cozy and creative atmosphere. Set off by itself on the road to Weaverville, Stoney Knob is a local favorite, whether for a platter of grilled chicken gyros, spicy grilled shrimp, or for blackberry brunch crepes.

## SUNNY POINT CAFÉ $

626 Haywood Rd., West Asheville
(828) 252-0055
www.sunnypointcafe.com

Bright and cheery with a sidewalk cafe, Sunny Point has been a beacon of change in West Asheville. Luscious brunches of organic produce, meats, homemade breads, and baked goods have achieved perfection at this adorable neighborhood joint. Open seven days and five nights. Come for the food, stay for the people-watching . . . lots of young families from the 'hood, local artists, and relaxed folk.

**i** West Asheville, a neighborhood divided by a bridge from downtown Asheville, has a Main Street quickly filling up with interesting restaurants, cafes, and boutiques. Check out more about them at www.onhaywood.com.

## TABLE $$–$$$

48 College St., Asheville
(828) 254-8980
www.tableasheville.com

Sparse and sleek design makes this dining room notable. Well-crafted dishes and favorites with a twist, such as pasta carbonara with fava beans and proscuitto, fish dishes, and other innovations attract regulars for a unique, urban experience. Desserts and old-fashioned cocktails also draw three stars here.

## TUPELO HONEY CAFÉ $–$$

12 College St., Asheville
(828) 255-4404
www.tupelohoneycafe.com

Indoors or out, this little cafe is a delight, from its French toast with mascarpone and sweet potato pancakes to the wholesome homemade tomato soup and choice-of-cheese grilled cheese sandwich. Oyster cocktails, spicy shrimp and grits, and grilled salmon over field greens allude to the Low Country sensibilities here. A basket of biscuits and corn muffins on the white linen–covered tables are a welcome touch.

i The Asheville Independent Restaurant Association (AIR) Web site breaks down eateries by cuisine, price point, and geographic location. Additionally, the site indicates special deals, discounts, and dining trends in the area. Visit www.airasheville.org.

### VERANDA CAFÉ & GIFTS $–$$
119 Cherry St., Black Mountain
(828) 669-8864
www.verandacafeandgifts.com
Wandering down Cherry Street is a delightful treat in Black Mountain. It is adjacent to the historic archives and galleries, where Cherry Street and State Street meet. Dining tables are set up throughout this charming little gift shop as well as on the back porch. The soups and sandwiches are unbeatable in creativity. Fluffy desserts grace the tea and coffee menu.

### ZAMBRA $–$$$
84 Walnut St., Asheville
(828) 232-1060
www.zambratapas.com
A Spanish/Moroccan–style bar and restaurant, Zambra offers Spanish-style tapas—a menagerie of small portions of delectable dishes to be shared by the whole table. Calamari are fried to crisp perfection and served with divine lemony salad greens, curried lamb and mushrooms nestle in a bed of garlic polenta, and dozens of other dishes are simply too tantalizing to skip. You may end up with a table covered in small dishes, if you're not careful. More alarming yet . . . you're sure to finish them off in one go! Spanish and French wines, sherries, and ports tickle the tongue, while the Moorish interior dazzles the eyes. Entree-size meals are also available. On the weekends Zambra invites musicians to make music in the bar area, sometimes even featuring a pale belly dancer or two.

## Henderson County

### CYPRESS CELLAR $–$$
321-C North Main St., Hendersonville
(828) 698-1005
www.cypresscellar.com
Cypress Cellar is a local favorite, with its homey atmosphere below-ground and a patio that sits at the bottom of the stairs from Hendersonville's Main Street. The fare is simple and casual Cajun-style, with perennials like gumbo, jambalaya, red beans and rice, and little po' boy sandwiches, as well as a selection of salads.

### FLIGHT $$–$$$
401 North Main St., Hendersonville
(828) 694-1030
www.flightwoodgrill.com
This restaurant in downtown Hendersonville maintains a modern wine bar and airy dining space on the first floor, with more seating upstairs. A grotto in back of the house offers wine tastings and appetizers certain times during the week. Look for the wood-fired brick oven pizzas and other delicacies. An *amuse bouche* and palate-cleansing sorbet are gracious house specialties.

### NEVER BLUE $–$$$
119 South Main St., Hendersonville
(828) 693-4646
www.theneverblue.com
Inventive cocktails here are colorful and fruity—particularly fun in the courtyard scene and the tiled interior of this happening Cuban-inspired restaurant. Roasted pork and grilled chicken with chopped salsas, plantain dishes, black beans and rice, grilled fish, and fresh and zesty accompaniments are the norm here.

### ONE LOVE $–$$
500 7th Ave. E., Hendersonville
(828) 551-8336
On a quiet street in an industrial section of town, this homey diner serves up true Jamaican dishes—like the curious ackee vegetable, beans and rice, plantains, curry goat, oxtail in a rich

brown sauce, buttery callaloo greens, yams, and saltfish (codfish), as well as fresh juices, Jamaican soda pop, and teas.

## SEASONS AT HIGHLAND LAKE INN $$$–$$$$
86 Lillypad Lane, Flat Rock
(828) 693-6812
www.hlinn.com

With much of the food grown right on the premises in organic gardens and greenhouses, which you're welcome to tour, you can be assured that the food here is some of the freshest you'll find anywhere and in a very picturesque setting. Besides a seasonally changing a la carte menu, Seasons is known for excellent themed buffet meals. Reservations are recommended. Also see the inn's entry in our Resorts chapter.)

## SINBAD RESTAURANT $$–$$$
202 South Washington St., Hendersonville
(828) 696-2039
www.sinbadrestaurant.com

If you like well-prepared Middle Eastern cuisine and seafood—or even if you think you don't—you should try the dishes here. They are superb and served amid authentic Lebanese ambience. You can order Middle Eastern classics such as kabobs, curry, grape leaves, kebbeh, tabouleh, hummus, baba, and falafel, or select from delicately prepared seafood, Sinbad's own creations, daily specials, or vegetarian dishes.

For those of you who are less adventurous, local dishes are prepared with a European flair. The bread alone would be worth coming for. Downstairs, a bar with a fireplace is an ideal place for small, private parties.

Sinbad's is open for lunch and dinner Tues through Sat. The restaurant also serves beer, wine, and cocktails.

## UMI $–$$$
633 North Main St., Hendersonville
(828) 698-8048
www.umisushinc.com

A fantastic addition to this town's dining scene—Umi offers an array of gorgeous and tasty sushi platters, all in an elegant and sleek two-dining room space. Belly right up to the sushi bar itself to see the magic happen.

## WEST FIRST PIZZA $–$$
101B 1st Ave. West
Hendersonville, NC 28731
(828) 693-1080

A vast contemporary space with a beautiful wood-fired oven as its centerpiece, West First has created a huge following of crisp-crust pizza lovers. Goat cheese, gorgonzola, pesto, and artichokes, are only a few of the toppings that up the ante here from a regular tomato-pie joint. European-style bread is also baked here; sandwiches and house-made desserts are also spot-on.

## Polk County

### THE ORCHARD INN $$$$
100 Orchard Inn Lane, Saluda
(828) 749-5471, (800) 581-3800
www.orchardinn.com

This lovely, plantation-type inn with its beautiful view of the Warrior Mountains has an elegant glassed-in dining area that stretches across the back and around one corner of its main building. The chef will carefully prepare your four-course dinner according to the seasonal food available, Thurs through Sat.

### PINE CREST INN $$$$
200 Pine Crest Lane, Tryon
(828) 633-3001
www.pinecrestinn.com

The dining room at Pine Crest, with its hunter green, burgundy, and deep blue decor, is reminiscent of an elegant English tavern. Both breakfast and dinner are served to the public here by reservation only, and the menu changes every day. If you're lucky, they might be serving cornmeal crusted catfish with citrus-horseradish reduction. All entrees are perfectly matched with fresh vegetable and various starches, such as chive mashed potatoes or creamed barley on mushroom risotto. The Pine Crest Inn's dining room is open Mon through Sat.

**STONE HEDGE INN** $$$
222 Stone Hedge Lane, Tryon
(828) 859-9114
www.stone-hedge-inn.com

A meal at this stately stone manor is an equally stately pleasure. Big picture windows cover one wall, so no matter where you sit in the dining room you have a stunning mountain view. The eclectic menu offers contemporary cuisine as evening specials, along with traditional favorites such as broiled North Carolina mountain trout, Black Angus beef filet, veal piccata, and shrimp scampi. Entrees include homemade soup or salad, rice or potato or pasta, and rolls. A delectable selection of homemade desserts includes the Chocolate Amaretto Passion Cake, rum cake, seasonal pies, cheesecake, and locally made ice cream.

## Rutherford County

**LAKE LURE INN VERANDA
RESTAURANT** $-$$$
2771 Memorial Hwy., Lake Lure
(828) 625-2525, (800) 277-5873

This stately inn overlooking beautiful Lake Lure has been a tradition in Hickory Nut Gorge since 1927. The dining room is an elegant setting for such gourmet offerings as roasted vegetable and herb cheese terrine, lobster ravioli with lobster sauce, Rendang shrimp and scallops, or veal medallion au poivre vert. For the little ones who might have trouble pronouncing these fancy dishes, Lake Lure Inn offers chicken finger and hamburger platters (and cheese tortellini in tomato sauce for discriminating pint-size palates).

**LARKIN'S ON THE LAKE** $$-$$$$
1020 Memorial Hwy., Lake Lure
(828) 625-4075
www.larkinsonthelake.com

Gorgeous views of Lake Lure only add to the atmosphere of a relaxing place that offers fresh mountain trout, hand-cut steaks and tender ribs, in addition to elegant dishes and a good wine list. For a casual take on some of the dishes, plus sandwiches, burgers, and peel and eat shrimp, try

the Bayfront Bar and Grill, under the same venue's tutelage.

## Transylvania County

**BROWN TROUT MOUNTAIN GRILLE** $$$
502 Blue Ridge Rd., Lake Toxaway
(828) 877-3474
www.browntroutgrille.com

On entering the grille, you truly walk into a cave-like atmosphere because the Brown Trout is cut back into the mountain. Soft music creates a pleasant background and is served up live throughout the evening.

Menu items range from thrown pizza crust to sauces so light they need to be eaten quickly so they won't float off the plate. One specialty produced by Chef Daniel is shrimp and grits with a cream sauce laced with ham strips. The grits are highly refined at a local stone gristmill. Another is saddle of venison with a white almond-based sauce, which almost defies earthly description. Native mountain trout is a must on the menu. The trout, and other seafood, is served in a variety of elaborate ways.

Reservations are important as many people have discovered this hideaway.

**EARTHSHINE** $$$
1600 Golden Rd., Lake Toxaway
(828) 862-4207
www.earthshinemtnlodge.com

This unusual resort takes pride in offering healthful, delicious foods prepared from scratch—"or pretty darn close"—and has opened its almost-red-meat-free, buffet-style lunches and dinners to the public. Though each meal is limited to a one-entree menu, these change frequently. You might, for example, be served a lunch consisting of everything you ever wanted for building your own Mexican creation: flour tortillas, refried beans, seasoned taco meat, sautéed chicken strips with onions and peppers, and Spanish rice—and that's just the hot stuff! Or you could be served chicken cordon bleu, Earthshine-style. You can be sure that lunch will include homemade bread and a fresh salad bar. Now you can go there for breakfast too.

**THE FALLS LANDING RESTAURANT**     **$$**
**18 East Main St., Brevard**
**(828) 884-2835**
**www.thefallslanding,com**
When it comes to fresh seafood with a Caribbean touch, the owners of the Falls Landing, former longtime residents of the Virgin Islands, know how to do it right! Their Cajun mahi-mahi is done to a turn, too. When you come here, it's essential that you try the famous conch fritters (we bet you can't eat just one!).

Fresh nightly specials include lots of fresh seafood, steaks, pasta, and chicken. Fri night is lobster night. If you're lucky, you might be there when superb cheese soup is on the menu. The bar also mixes some excellent drinks. Lunch is served at the Falls Landing, located just across from the courthouse on Main Street, every day; it's open for dinner from Tues through Sun.

**ROCKY'S SODA SHOP & GRILL**     **$**
**36 South Broad St., Brevard**
**(828) 877-5375**
Rocky's offers another trip into "the old days" with its ice-cream concoctions, great shakes, real old-time hamburgers, and other treats hot off the grill. It's a nice complement to D. D. Bullwinkel's general store right next door. You can get breakfast, lunch, and dinner at Rocky's Mon through Sat. It's also open on Sun for lunch.

**THE SQUARE ROOT**     **$-$$$**
**33 Times Arcade, Brevard**
**(828) 884-6171**
**www.squarerootrestaurant.com**
Set off the main street in a small alley, the Square Root's outdoor terrace leads to the sublime bar area. A polished slab of oak that still resembles the tree comprises the counter. More interesting woodwork on the floor, brick walls, and artwork make for a delightfully warm interior. A pecan sweet-brie appetizer is a signature dish, and solid dinner fare makes for enjoyable evenings.

**i**   Dining in can be a real treat when ingredients are made up of fresh, homegrown produce. During the growing season, most small towns here have farmers' markets once or twice a week where local gardeners and farmers come to sell what they've harvested that morning. You can often find homemade jams, jellies, relishes, and the like here, too. Just ask.

**THE TAVERN BY THE FALLS**     **$-$$**
**9 Toxaway Falls Dr., Lake Toxaway**
**(828) 966-9226**
**www.thetavernbythefalls.com**
The setting of the Tavern is a view of the Toxaway Falls pouring over a great granite dome. You can sit out on a wide, enclosed deck that overlooks the falls while you enjoy a variety of dishes from fabulous fried trout to enormous platters of crispy fried chicken. If the weather isn't conducive to outdoor dining, you'll find the dining room, with its gas-log fireplace, cozy and friendly. The menu is eclectic and well executed, with cobblers for dessert.

# SOUTHERN MOUNTAINS

## Cherokee County

**DOYLE'S CEDAR HILL**     **$$-$$$**
**925 Andrews Rd., Murphy**
**(828) 837-3400**
**www.doylescedarhill.com**
Touting itself as "casual-formal," Doyle's does indeed offer a little something for everyone. Lunch and dinner are served indoors or out on the patio, with a separate menu for each. There is live music most nights.

**SHOEBOOTIES**     **$-$$**
**25 Peachtree St., Murphy**
**(828) 837-4589**
**www.shoebootiescafe.com**
A longtime local favorite, Shoebooties maintains a hometown feel with plenty of booth seating and hearty appetizers, good soups, and pleasant entrees with vegetable sides.

## Haywood County

**CATALOOCHEE RANCH** $$
119 Ranch Dr., Maggie Valley
(828) 926-1401, (800) 868-1401
www.cataloocheeranch.com

Cataloochee Ranch has endured and prospered in the same family for more than a half-century for many reasons, including its lovely location high on a mountain overlooking Maggie Valley. The food it serves has also played a big part in its popularity. These are family-style meals to which the public is invited by reservations only. The Cataloochee Ranch is open year-round, but meals are served in the winter by special arrangement only (for more information, see our Resorts chapter).

**LOMO GRILL** $$–$$$$
44 Church St., Waynesville
(828) 452-5222
www.lomogrill.com

Brick walls, hardwood floors, a quiet elegance, and the sweet smell of the wood-burning Argentine grill enfold you when you enter the Lomo Grill. This is the place to come when you're in the mood for a relaxed, leisurely dinner.

In the true Italian and Mediterranean tradition, each selection is cooked to order with the finest natural ingredients available. You could, for example, start with an appetizer of Lomo Involtini de Melanzane, which is grilled eggplant, French goat cheese, sun-dried tomatoes, Parmesan cheese shavings, fresh basil, tomato sauce, and cumin yogurt sauce. Follow that with a Lomo Caesar salad, and then choose from an extensive menu of entrees that include pastas, fish, poultry, veal, or beef.

**THE OLD STONE INN** $$$–$$$$
109 Dolan Rd., Waynesville
(828) 456-3333, (800) 432-8499
www.oldstoneinn.com

The rich warmth of wood envelops you in the Old Stone Inn's guest lounge and dining room, and dinner here is a hearty affair. Entrees include such choices as beef tenderloin in puff pastry, Muscovy duck with apricot glas, and cedar-planked salmon trout fillet. Your entree is accompanied by several vegetables, including fantastic vegetable casseroles, and freshly baked bread. Desserts include Grand Marnier Crème Caramel, and such ice-cream delights as the Smoky Mountain Brown Bear Ice-Cream Coupe for Two.

Dinner is available here by reservation (for more information, see our Bed-and-Breakfasts and Country Inns chapter).

**THE SWAG** $$$$
2300 Swag Rd., Waynesville
(828) 926-0430, (800) 789-7672
www.theswag.com

The Swag, an exclusive inn 5,000 feet up in the Smoky Mountains with 50-mile views, takes a limited number of outside guests by reservation only for its lunches Mon through Sat, its sensational dinners seven days a week, and its unforgettable Sunday brunches. The chef-chosen dinners feature four-course meals.

The Swag is open from mid-May through Oct (see our Bed-and-Breakfasts and Country Inns chapter for more information). Reservations required.

## Jackson County

**BALSAM MOUNTAIN INN** $$$
68 Seven Springs Dr.ff US 74/23, Balsam
(828) 456-9498

Many people come to dine at the Balsam Mountain Inn for the older-era atmosphere captured by this turn-of-the-century inn, only to come back again and again for the great food. Dine on entrees like fresh-caught mountain trout, prime rib, ham with brown sugar–citrus glaze, or chicken in an artichoke, mushroom, and white wine sauce, with hearty sides of wild rice or rich potatoes gratin. (For more information on Balsam Mountain Inn, see our Bed-and-Breakfasts and Country Inns chapter.)

**HIGH HAMPTON INN** $$–$$$$
U.S. Hwy. 107, Cashiers
(828) 743-2411, (800) 334-2551
www.highhamptoninn.com

The High Hampton Inn believes in tradition, right down to the food it serves. Many dishes you'll eat—served buffet style at the inn—are the same favorites you'd have found here 50 years ago: fried chicken, fresh local trout, and prime rib; a memorable cream of peanut soup; a cranberry Waldorf salad; Southern-style vegetables such as stewed corn; homemade bread, including sausage cornbread; and peppermint ice cream with chocolate syrup. (For more information, see our Resorts chapter.)

**THE JARRETT HOUSE** $$
**219 Haywood Dr., Dillsboro**
**(828) 586-0265, (800) 972-5623**
**www.jarretthouse.com**
When R. Frank Jarrett owned this inn from 1894 until his death in 1950, he let his wife, "Miss Sallie," run the place. However, he cured the hams that were served, and the great platters of fried ham, red-eye gravy, hot buttermilk biscuits, and North Carolina's famous sourwood honey were said to make strong men weep because they were too full to eat as much as they wanted.

Great platters of food—which still include ham, gravy, and biscuit—load down the tables in the Jarrett House. An aging dining room might put off some, but you'll find longtime favorites, such as fried chicken and mountain trout, along with all the fixins' to be true and authentic country-style.

No reservations are required except for groups of 10 or more (for more information on the Jarrett House, see our Bed-and-Breakfasts and Country Inns chapter). Credit cards are not accepted.

**LULU'S CAFE** $$
**612 West Main St., Sylva**
**(828) 586-8989**
**www.lulusonmain.com**
Dining at Lulu's is a lovely adventure in eating. You can choose from a menu that includes really good vegetarian, Greek, Italian, Caribbean, Indonesian, and American food. The restaurant's unusual decor has a fresh look. It consists of mulberry walls, moss green chairs, and floral table-cloths; black accents and burgundy ceiling fans set off colorfully matted black-and-white photos. Lulu's is open year-round for lunch and dinner Mon through Sat.

## Macon County

**THE GAZEBO CREEKSIDE CAFE** $
**44 Heritage Hollow Dr., Franklin**
**(828) 524-8783**
**www.gazebocreeksidecafe.com**
This award-winning cafe is the perfect place to relax and unwind. Built around an old gazebo, the beautiful outdoor setting allows for creekside seating while you enjoy the abundant North Carolina bird life. Open for lunch only, the homemade fare includes soups, salads, deli sandwiches, desserts, gourmet coffees, and ice-cream delights. The Gazebo is open from Apr through Oct. Credit cards are not accepted.

**ON THE VERANDAH** $$$
**1536 Franklin Rd., Lake Sequoyah, Highlands**
**(828) 526-2338**
**www.ontheverandah.com**
The scenic dining setting overlooking Lake Sequoyah sets the tone for the exquisite menu at this restaurant, to which *Wine Spectator* magazine has given its Award of Excellence yearly since 1987. The food is prepared with fresh ingredients and is cooked to order.

For starters you can order roasted eggplant with fresh tomatoes, herbs, and goat cheese or flame-roasted shrimp with citrus soy dressing, followed by a Thai roasted-peanut salad with romaine lettuce, scallions, shredded carrots, and alfalfa sprouts. For an entree you could have, among other things, stir-fried scallops on angel-hair pasta with a peppered ginger-scallion sauce or sautéed lamb chops with a honey-roasted pecan and ancho chili crust, mint aioli, and lemon walnut couscous. Daily fresh fish and seafood specials are paired with complementary wines.

This family-owned restaurant offers a library of bottles of hot sauces from everywhere. They even bottle their own special recipe. It is offered as a take home sale item in a three pack.

In addition to dinner, On the Verandah offers a Sunday champagne brunch with soup, a salad bar, Mimosa cocktails or Kir Royale, and such entrees as poached eggs on crab cakes topped with fresh lime Hollandaise sauce.

## RISTORANTE PAOLETTI $$$
**440 Main St., Highlands**
**(828) 526-4906**
**www.paoletti-nc.com**

Arthur Paoletti and his family have made their restaurant a definite destination. Even Chef Wolfgang Green (see Wolfgang's on Main) brings his guests here for dinner when he chooses not to cook. Because practice makes perfect, it might be said that the family "practiced" serving fine cuisine for 20 years at Delray Beach in Coral Gables, Florida. They've gotten it down really well now. They specialize in the freshest coast fish and seafood dishes. Their homemade pastas, breads, and desserts sing out, "Il Italiano." Veal chops with champagne cream, roasted rack of lamb, and dry aged Angus sirloin strip steak are just a few of the extensive offerings on their menu.

Their 20-page wine list provides a trip around the world without leaving the table. Their wine cellar has been designated by the *Wine Spectator* for an Award of Excellence.

## WOLFGANG'S ON MAIN $$$
**474 Main St., Highlands**
**(828) 526-3807**
**www.wolfgangs.net**

Wolfgang's is located in one of the oldest houses in Highlands, built in 1880. Whether dining inside by a fireplace on a handmade rhododendron table, outside on the awning-covered deck, or in the garden pavilion, you're in for a dining treat.

Wolfgang and Mindy Green are legends in their own time and in Highlands. Working the front of the house, Mindy is certain to offer a warm welcome, exuding a sense of hospitality.

Chef Wolfgang, former executive chef for the Brennan's Family Commander's Palace in New Orleans, is internationally acclaimed, having won numerous awards, including chef of the year in both Jamaica and Texas. His background brings a freshness and variety to a menu that's so attractive, it's really difficult to decide what to order.

New Orleans specialties include Wolfgang's Signature Soup, a shrimp and lobster bisque; crawfish étouffée; Maryland blue crab cakes served on a lobster cream sauce with pecan-crusted shrimp; Veal Medallions Wolfgang on a cabernet sauce topped with crawfish and béarnaise sauce; as well as many other selections.

Some favorites with locals are Chef Wolfgang's fresh mountain trout with pine nuts, Trout Cote D'Azur, and Trout Admiral.

Wolfgang's is one of three restaurants in Highlands to have received the prestigious *Wine Spectator* Award of Excellence, beginning in 1999.

Wolfgang's is open for lunch and dinner every day except Wed.

## Swain County

### HEMLOCK INN $–$$
**Galbraith Creek Rd., Bryson City**
**(828) 488-2885**
**www.hemlockinn.com**

The food at the Hemlock Inn, set on 65 wooded acres, 3 miles from the Great Smoky Mountains National Park, is so good that, at their guests' insistence, the inn put many of its recipes into a cookbook called *Recipes from Our Front Porch*. If you are not a guest here (see our Bed-and-Breakfasts and Country Inns chapter), you can still make a reservation for dinner Mon through Sat. You'll be seated at a lazy-Susan table laden with native foods, including fruits and vegetables provided by the Hemlock's neighbors' gardens (in the summer, you may be offered corn on the cob picked just a few minutes before it's cooked and served). Entrees might include country ham and fried chicken, accompanied by homemade yeast rolls and biscuits with mountain honey. The delicious desserts are all made from scratch too.

The Hemlock Inn is open May to Nov. While you're here, make time to sit in a rocking chair out front and enjoy the view. Credit cards are not accepted.

# NIGHTLIFE

In many of our mountain communities, the appeal of life is the love of the land and the opportunity to control the pace of life, so you won't find too many dusk-to-dawn party venues here. Instead, the emphasis is on music—traditional, old-time, alternative, folk, singer-songwriter, country, Latin, reggae . . . and a whole lot more.

Additionally, our urban centers have an excellent reputation for post-theater or concert cocktails and dessert. Asheville, for one, is a beacon for sophisticated diners, theatergoers, and art aficionados. Live music is so popular here, you'll find a variety any night of the week, in several different venues, such as the nationally known Orange Peel and its new private club, Pulp. There is a thriving downtown, both day and night. The people who live downtown, in the vast lofts with wooden floors and beamed garrets, grab their morning coffee and newspaper at the corner coffee shop, walk to Sunday brunch at several cafes with such offerings, and spend their summer evenings chatting over a glass of wine at the outdoor Italian trattoria.

Join them in sampling nightlife into the wee hours, dancing at a club, or listening to jazz in the intimate atmosphere of a New Orleans–type jazz bar. In several mountain towns, boutique cinemas feature first-run foreign films and award-winning American movies. Poetry slams and original plays, evening exhibition openings at art galleries, and several excellent venues for daily live music and dance propel this area into the forefront of local entertainment. A number of even smaller cities in the North Carolina mountains maintain brewpubs, manufacturing their own special flavors and types of beer and housing a dartboard or two, or possibly even a pool table.

Mainstream nightlife here is generally found in the restaurant/bars in larger mountain cities (see our Restaurants chapter). Not only can you enjoy a night out with friends over a great meal, you can also find first-rate musical entertainment. This ranges from piano mood music to mellow acoustic guitar, honky-tonk country to hot jazz, and pulse-blasting rock. The fine restaurants and cafes in Blowing Rock, Hendersonville, Boone, and other communities often offer live music.

Colleges and universities in the region contribute much to mountain nightlife (see our Arts and Culture chapter). We've got your typical raucous college pubs and bars found in any campus town, if that's what you crave. On the flip side, however, you can also find mellow, laid-back coffeehouses, featuring singer-songwriters, poetry evenings, authors' readings, or even games of checkers and backgammon.

Major concert arenas are still out of our region, as far away as Atlanta, Charlotte, or Greenville, South Carolina, but the Asheville Civic Center and the more intimate Orange Peel Social Aid and Pleasure Club get their quota of big-name performers as well.

In this chapter we present a number of representative nighttime entertainment listings in the mountains, including some of the restaurants that offer exceptional entertainment as part of the dining experience. Because of the trendy nature of nightlife, nightspots lend themselves to frequent openings and closings and changing of hands. Therefore we have noted the more established and highly recommended locales and urge you to check local newspapers for up-to-the-minute entertainment listings.

# NORTHERN MOUNTAINS

## Alleghany County

### ALLEGHANY JUBILEE
25 North Main St., Sparta
(336) 372-4591
www.sparta-nc.com

Start stompin' your foot and tappin' your toes—this is old-time music. Housed in the old 1930s-era movie theater on Main Street in Sparta, the Alleghany Jubilee provides a weekly stage for local country talent, old-time music, and lively square dancing. Other than high school football, the Alleghany Jubilee is Sparta's main attraction on the weekend.

The Jubilee square dance is held every Fri night from 8 to 11 p.m. The Jubilee old-time music livens up Sat again from 8 to 11 p.m. or whenever the music stops. This is family entertainment, folks.

Admission is usually around $5 for adults, and children get in free.

### MOUNTAIN MUSIC JAMBOREE
9331 Hwy. 16, Glendale Springs
(336) 384-4079, (800) 803-4079
www.mountainmusicjamboree.com

Once held in the old barn at the Burgiss Farm Bed-and-Breakfast in southern Alleghany County, the Mountain Music Jamboree has a home all its own in a 7,200 square food dance hall that also serves up a fantastic country buffet. This regular weekend party is dedicated to the preservation of traditional mountain music and dance, and generally held on Sat nights.

Two different bands play each week, spotlighting the creative talents of mommies and daddies, aunts and uncles.

**i** Be aware that some counties in North Carolina are dry. That means you won't get a drink there. Some restaurants will allow "brown bagging" and might charge a small corkage fee.

## Avery County

### BEECH MOUNTAIN STREET DANCES
Beech Mountain Hwy., Banner Elk
(800) 468-5506

In summer check out these lively monthly street dances in mile-high Beech Mountain. This unique recreational community offers fun every season of the year. Dates and times vary, so call ahead of time.

### LOUISIANA PURCHASE
Hwy. 184, 397 Shawneehaw Ave., Banner Elk
(828) 898-5656
www.louisianapurchasefoodandspirits.com

The Purchase draws young and old alike to live jazz and their wine bar on Fri and Sat nights. Local jazz duo Culpepper and Dulin are often featured Thurs night. The wine list has been recognized by *Wine Spectator* as one of the best in the country.

## Watauga County

### CONTRA DANCING AND TRADITIONAL AMERICAN FOLK DANCING
165 Morris St., Blowing Rock
Hwy. 194, Apple Barn, Valle Crucis
(828) 297-1393
www.blowingrock.com

Enjoy the resurgence of these art forms of traditional folk dances. In winter dancers gather from 7 to 10 p.m. the second Sat of the month at Blowing Rock Elementary. The summer schedule is the same, but groups meet at the Apple Barn at Valle Crucis. Newcomers are welcome!

### KLONDIKE CAFE
441 Blowing Rock Rd., Boone
(828) 262-5065

The Klondike Cafe is a diamond in the rough. This gutsy bar serves deli sandwiches, gourmet burgers, Mexican dishes, and imported and premium domestic beers. But the grub is not the attraction. Outside, the patrons claim spots at the long tables running the length of the building. Sitting like birds on a wire, Klondike's clientele, mostly college students, but also locals and hardy tourists, hang out and watch Boone go by on U.S.

Highway 321, the Blowing Rock Road. Inside, live entertainment keeps the place rockin', and sports on wide-screen TVs and weekly dart tournaments add to the mix. The place opens at 11 a.m. and closes when everyone goes home. You kind of figured that, didn't you?

## MURPHY'S RESTAURANT & PUB
**747 West King St., Boone**
**(828) 264-5117**
**www.murphysboone.com**
Murphy's has been a landmark in Boone for more than 10 years. The drawing card at this busy place is its imaginative menu, which attracts a lively crowd to its four dining areas. Two bars offer a friendly place for a quick bite to eat, a little liquid refreshment, and a gander at a favorite sports channel on one of three wide-screen TVs. (See our Restaurants chapter for more information on Murphy's.)

## WOODLANDS BARBECUE AND PICKIN' PARLOR
**8304 Valley Blvd., Blowing Rock**
**(828) 295-3651**
**www.woodlandsbbq.com**
Woodlands features live entertainment nightly with no cover in a down-home casual atmosphere. Woodlands holds all ABC permits, so you can enjoy your favorite cocktail or beer while enjoying some of the best music our region has to offer.

# CENTRAL MOUNTAINS

## Buncombe County

### BARLEY'S TAPROOM
**42 Biltmore Ave., Asheville**
**(828) 255-0504**
**www.barleystaproom.com**
Drawing on a grand mixture of the young professional crowd, visitors, good ol' boys, couples, rugby players, alternative types, and just about everyone else who lives in Asheville, Barley's offers 40 beers on tap. On certain nights, jazz,

acoustic guitar, and blues resonate over the convivial din. There is no cover charge.

Regional microbrewed beers are on tap from Highland Brewing Company, Asheville's first microbrewery, which is downstairs at Barley's.

The friendly staff, a combination of students, artists, actors, and jolly bartenders, will make you feel like a regular your first time there. This is the place where everyone comes before and after barhopping! But upstairs, Barley's has created another bar. This loft, where smoking is allowed, contains red pool tables, dartboards, and lots of young vivacious people. No food may be taken to this upstairs bar, so eat downstairs first before you go up to play.

### BOBO GALLERY
**28 Lexington Ave., Asheville**
**www.bobogallery.com**
Two San Franciscans opened this late-night bar and gallery where DJs spin dance music and alternative jams late into the night. Open Wed through Sat after 4 p.m. The wine bar also houses local artwork.

### CLUB HAIRSPRAY
**38 North French Broad Ave., Asheville**
**(828) 258-2027**
**www.clubhairsray.com**
This club complex actually includes two more venues: Patio Cabaret, with a cabaret drag show on Sunday, and Hairspray Cafe, with a long bar and pool tables. Though it is billed as a gay club, it's not exclusive. It's adjacent to a dance venue that has undergone several ownership changes over the past few years. Today the dance portion is called Cub 828. So no matter what your proclivity, if you're dying for a night of shaking your booty with a fun crowd, look no further. Musically themed evenings feature techno, industrial, jungle, garage, goth, and others.

### FINE ARTS THEATER
**36 Biltmore Ave., Asheville**
**(828) 232-1536**
**www.fineartstheater.com**

Asheville's only downtown cinema is an ode to resplendent movie houses of the past. The Fine Arts Theater maintains a grand hall with art deco sconces, mauve stucco walls, and plush seats in the high-ceilinged main theater. Upstairs, another more intimate theater runs an alternate film offering. Fine foreign films, independents, and less-commercial American films are featured here.

Besides the usual sweets and popcorn, beer and hard ciders, coffee, and biscotti are also sold. This cinema, a drama theater at its inception and later an X-rated movie theater during a period of downtown Asheville decay, has been fully reconstructed and restored to lavish splendor. Go for the quality films, go for the atmosphere, go for the history!

**GREY EAGLE**
**185 Clingman Ave., Asheville**
**(828) 232-5800**
**www.greyeaglemusic.com**
Located in the artsy River District, with working studios just a stone's throw away, Grey Eagle has a devoted audience. The club highlights singer-songwriters, regional bands, and top national acts like Arlo Guthrie, Doc Watson, Leo Kottke, and others. The bar serves local brews, and a Cajun kitchen satisfies the hungry. It's the ultimate laid-back, quality music scene. If you're lucky, you can catch one of the occasional Latin dance evenings.

 A summer secret in Asheville is the adorable Mayfel's Courtyard. The College Street eatery filters into the courtyard on summer nights with a tikki bar, refreshing "Mayfelaide" cocktails (like lemonade but with ginger and alcohol!), twinkle lights, little gurgling fountains, and a magical atmosphere all on cobblestones with cafe chairs and tables. Mayfel's, 22 College St., Asheville, (828) 252-8840, www.mayfels.com.

**JACK OF THE WOOD**
**95 Patton Ave., Asheville**
**(828) 252-5445**
**www.jackofthewood.com**
This English-style pub, which features darts, long wooden tables and benches, and a small raised stage, is a great drop-by nightspot for any season. Celtic music jams have people bringing their own instruments on certain nights of the week, while regular groups, ranging from folk to Celtic, to balladeers, to bluegrass and alterna-grass take the stage on the weekends. Bring your Greenman Ale (made by Jack of the Wood's own brewers) outside to the benches, and you'll be sure to hear the tales of all sorts of interesting folks. Mon night is quizzo game night.

**i** Bars in North Carolina have a 2 a.m. last call, so night owls, start early!

**MAGNOLIA'S**
**26 Walnut St., Asheville**
**(828) 251-5211**
**www.magnoliasasheville.com**
This raw bar and grille turns into one big party when the sun goes down on the weekends. Sometimes Asheville blues legend Kat Williams takes the stage, or other bands play rousing cover tunes, while patrons push away tables and chairs on the enclosed patio to dance into the night.

**THE ORANGE PEEL SOCIAL AID**
**AND PLEASURE CLUB**
**101 Biltmore Ave., Asheville**
**(828) 225-5851**
**www.theorangepeel.net**
This is the music hall that Asheville has long been waiting for. A nonsmoking venue that can hold up to 1,000, it now pulls in national and international musicians but also has a steady stream of famed local and regional performers on any given day of the week. A grand stage, plenty of dancing room, and a long chrome bar are home to benefits, parties, and concerts alike. Pulp, the venue's new private club downstairs is smaller, and it is possible to gain entry for one night for an additional fee.

ℹ Due to the erratic nature of night-clubs and bars, and their often quick turnover, we have listed the mainstays of various towns. Be sure to check the local papers of each town for an up-to-date listing. In Asheville the *Mountain Xpress* newspaper runs an excellent listing of concerts, locales, and movies; look for Take Five, the daily newspaper's weekend section on Fri.

### STELLA BLUE
**31 Patton Ave., Asheville**
**(828) 236-2424**
**www.stellabluelive.com**
This spunky club has come a long way. Although the decor is fluorescent paint against black with pool tables in the back, this music hall catches some great bands. The dance floor is adequate, though you practically have to walk through it to reach the bar on entering the club. Well-known regional bands play here, as well as eclectic groups from all over. Nationally known hip dance bands like Mandorico and Los Straitjackets seem to perform on a fairly regular basis.

### TRESSA'S DOWNTOWN JAZZ & BLUES
**28 Broadway, Asheville**
**(828) 254-7072**
**www.tressasdowntownjazzandblues.com**
The New Orleans–style jazz bar, a private club that welcomes guests for a nominal fee, has all the ambience, musical variety, and spectacular patrons of a venue in a major cosmopolitan center. Nut brown walls, a long oak bar, original pressed-tin ceiling, and linen-covered individual tables, including two window tables, make up the foundation of Tressa's, located in a 1913 building. The fully stocked bar, mirrored and framed with columns, offers exquisite martinis, spicy Bloody Marys, wines, champagnes, and many other cocktails.

Music ranges from blues and jazz to Latin groove, with a brigade of live bands every week. Co-owners Tressa and Terry stir up liquid concoctions while dressed in elegant evening garb. But you'll be sweating away on the crowded dance floor or straining to hear your date over the cheerful din. Call ahead for the music schedule and for information concerning membership if you'll be around for a while. The VIP Lounge with its Breathe oxygen bar at Tressa's upstairs is an elegant addition to this place. First, it's nonsmoking; second, it's much quieter and less populated than the party downstairs. There's also plenty of seating either by the windows, overlooking Broadway, by the nifty fireplace, at the chic bar, or past the oxygen bar with intimate tables. Enjoy an oxygen boost with "flavored" mixtures for 10- to 20-minute intervals. Upstairs is open Wed through Sat and definitely worth a visit. This is one place where you will want to toss on a silk scarf, a bevy of beads, or a dress shirt—all without pretension, but for the fun of it.

ℹ Often bars or dance venues will advertise themselves as "private clubs." Generally a member can sign you in as a guest, or you might be charged a nominal fee for "membership" at the door.

## Rutherford County
### LAKE LURE TOURS
**2975 Memorial Hwy., Lake Lure**
**(828) 625-1373**
**www.lakelure.com**
Lake Lure Tours offers twilight and dinner cruises May through Oct, weather permitting. Reservations are required to get aboard. Sip on champagne as you cruise the coves of lake Lure.

## Transylvania County
### EARTHSHINE
**1600 Golden Rd., Lake Toxaway**
**(828) 862-4207**
**www.earthshinelodge.com**
When you have dinner at this resort, you get entertainment that alternates from folk sing-alongs and folk dance to interactive Cherokee programs and campfire tales (see our Resorts chapter). Reservations are required.

# SOUTHERN MOUNTAINS

## Cherokee County/Clay County

**CHEROKEE INDIAN RESERVATION
HARRAH'S CHEROKEE CASINO**
777 Casino Dr., Cherokee
(800) HARRAHS
www.harrahscherokee.com
Open seven days a week, 24 hours a day, this popular casino—three football fields big—has 2,300 video gaming machines, three restaurants, a gift shop, a child-care facility, and a 1,500-seat theater with big-name, live entertainment. Tribal Bingo is also available in Cherokee. (See our Attractions chapter for details.)

**JOHN C. CAMPBELL SCHOOL DANCE EVENTS**
1 Folk School Rd., Brasstown
(828) 837-2775, (800) FOLK-SCH
www.folkschool.org
Square and contra dances, clogging, and circle dances with live musicians and callers are held here both on weekends and during the week. You also can learn English country dances and Balkan and other folk dances. A free introduction to contra, square, and circle dances with recorded music is held every Tues night from 7 to 8 p.m. for folk school students and interested local residents. Community contra and square dances with live music are held twice a month, usually on the first and third Sat from 8 to 11 p.m. Call for details.

## Haywood County

**BOGART'S RESTAURANT AND TAVERN**
222 South Main St., Waynesville
(828) 452-1313
www.bogartswaynesville.com
No matter what type of music you like, you'll eventually hear it if you drop into Bogart's for a couple of Fri or Sat nights. A little bit of everything—folk, country, rock, and blues—is played here, though not every week. It's a fun watering hole, with a cozy upstairs loft area.

## A Leap of Love

The view from Henderson County's Jump Off Rock stretches across the high plateau of Henderson and Transylvania Counties to the ascending peaks of Pisgah Forest. Jump Off Rock got its name more than 300 years ago when a young Cherokee chieftain and the woman he loved used to meet here. When he was called away to tribal wars, she would climb to this overlook to watch for his return, often singing an Indian love call—but there was never an answer. Finally, returning warriors brought news of her lover's death in battle.

At twilight, it's said, she climbed to the rock, sang a few notes, and jumped off. Lore has it that on some moonlit nights you can still hear her song. To reach the rock from Hendersonville, drive out Fifth Avenue West, which turns into Laurel Park Drive, and follow the road until it ends at Jump Off Rock.

**CAROLINA NIGHTS**
3732 Soco Rd., Maggie Valley
(828) 926-8822, (888) 622-7469
www.maggievalleyusa.com
Full-scale productions of country music, gospel, and pop, along with magicians and comedians, can be enjoyed here every night from spring until fall and on weekends in the winter. Closed on Sun. Tickets may be purchased for the dinner and show, or just the show.

**DIAMOND K DANCE RANCH**
1 Playhouse Dr., Maggie Valley
(828) 926-7735
www.thediamondkdanceranch.com

Here you can enjoy country music and dancing on the fabulous 2,000-square-foot dance floor. Dancing lessons are offered on Fri evenings. Diamond K is open on Fri and Sat evenings. Admission is under $10 for adults and no charge for children under 12. A snack bar is available, and no alcohol is served.

## MAGGIE VALLEY OPRY HOUSE
3605 Soco Rd., Maggie Valley
(828) 926-9336
www.raymondfairchild.com

From May through Oct, bluegrass, mountain music, and dancing take place beginning at 8 p.m. nightly. Maggie Valley is the home of Raymond Fairchild, five-time world champion banjo picker. He and his special guest performers are always dropping in to keep everyone's toes tapping.

## THE STOMPIN' GROUND
3113 Soco Rd., U.S. Hwy. 19, Maggie Valley
(828) 926-1288
www.stompingroundpresents.com

From spring through fall every Fri and Sat from 8 to 11 p.m., the Stompin' Ground, going strong since 1982, offers music and dancing in "the mountain clogging capital of the world." No alcohol is served at this 100-seat music hall, so it's fun for the whole family. Just come in and stomp!

# ARTS AND CULTURE

Long known for a rich craft heritage, the North Carolina mountains have now become prime breeding ground for impressive and innovative fine art and cultural events. The arts are flourishing here due to home-grown talent, as well as an influx of professional artists generating just the right mix of creativity and commerce.

Asheville can be considered the hub of arts in the region, continuously making the top-ten lists of great arts destinations in the country.

Artists' studios can be found in every hollow and each back road, side street, and suburban neighborhood in Western North Carolina. Contemporary crafts with novel material or new techniques have made their mark on the area. Professional painters and sculptors have infused new energy into the contemporary art scene in the mountains. Community art leagues and artists' guilds nurture the growth of emerging artists in nearly every county and town, be it culture-rich Asheville, with art galleries on every street, or quiet West Jefferson, with artists' studios and boutique galleries slowly changing the landscape of small-town America. While changes have been progressive for the most part, the downturn in the economy has not gone unnoticed in the art world here. A number of galleries have folded, and continue to do so at an alarming rate.

Over 45 theater groups are registered in the area, many showcasing equity actors and featuring experimental works, along with classic favorites.

Music, too, echoes a mountain heritage, derived in part from the historically isolated life of our early settlers. These mountaineers culled their music from the soul of the hills and from the melodies carried on the wind. Born of the first front-porch sing-alongs, with "banjo pickin' and guitar playin'" at sundown and the bittersweet ballads rising out of the mountain coves, the musical legacy found in North Carolina's mountains continues to thrive. More interesting is that it flourishes alongside the strains of a classical symphony, delicate chamber music, inspirational choral music, fervent black gospel, lively barbershop harmony, jazz, swing, and contemporary folk music.

The mountains also have numerous groups for ballet, contemporary dance theater, traditional mountain clogging, international folk dance and Old World contra dance, and even country-and-western line dancing.

Museums document the history of these mountains. Some are more academic museums devoted to departmental disciplines and regional displays of traditional mountain life, while others are restored farmhouses, grand old homes, and vast estates that stand as tributes to the virtues and careers of pioneering citizens. Best of all, these museums are not of the stodgy, cement-building stock. These home museums transport you into the past with the scent of aged wood, slightly musty attics, and wildflower-filled surroundings. They welcome you to step onto the back porch and drink in the deep valley views just as the mountain settlers of yore did.

This chapter gives you a glimpse into the melting pot of artistic interests that mirrors the quality of life here—and helps define it. The abundance of arts and crafts in this region and their many similarities often make it hard to characterize what is an "art" and what is a "craft." Here we have tried to differentiate between arts and craft galleries or artisans' studios (these studios are described in the Mountain Crafts chapter). Consult both chapters closely, as you may well find part of what you are looking for in each.

# ART GALLERIES

## Northern Mountains

### Ashe County

**THE ACORN GALLERY**
103 Long St., West Jefferson
(336) 246-3388
www.acorngallery.com
This gallery features original paintings in oil or watercolor, and prints from realist painter Raney Rogers. Visit the gallery and adjoining garden center for perennials and ornamental evergreens.

**RIVER ROCK GALLERY**
101 North Jefferson Ave., West Jefferson
(336) 219-0089
www.riverrockgallery.com
Fine art and handcrafted works from over a dozen cooperative members mark this gallery's repertoire. The gallery's long-term objective is to provide and promote art education and appreciation in Ashe County. A number of projects are in the works to assist artists, aspiring artists, and the community at large. With over 1,000 square feet and high ceilings, track lighting, and wood floors, this gallery leads the way in West Jefferson's growing arts community. The gallery features paintings, drawings, sculpture, pottery, woodturnings, woodworking, jewelry, stained glass, pressed flowers, woodblock prints, music, weaving, and more.

**TIN ROOF GALLERY & STUDIO**
103 North Jefferson Ave., West Jefferson
(336) 246-3337
www.tinroofstudio.com
Fine art, mixed media paintings, original hand-pulled prints, and handmade enameled jewelry can be found at this little showroom.

### Avery County

**THE ART CELLAR**
920 Shawneshaw Ave., Banner Elk
(828) 898-5175
www.theartcellaronline.com

Along with a wonderful selection of fine art representing the work of local artists, the Art Cellar in Banner Elk features animation art and "outsider art." It's folk art created by those outside the art world's mainstream.

**CARLTON GALLERY**
10360 NC Hwy. 105 South, Banner Elk
(828) 963-4288
www.carltonartgallery.com
Carlton Gallery celebrates close to three decades as the largest, most established gallery in the High Country. Fine art and upscale handmade crafts from over 300 artisans are showcased here. The gallery is situated under the gaze of Grandfather Mountain between Boone and Banner Elk on Highway 105.

> **i** If old cemeteries fascinate you, check out the large one at Old Mother Church on Fort Hill, overlooking the town of Robbinsville in Graham County. Its exact founding date is unknown, but it probably dates back to the 1840s. The present building at the site, constructed around 1875, has served as a one-room school, a court of justice, and a place of worship.

**CLARK GALLERY**
393 Shawnehaw Ave., next to
Louisiana Purchase, Banner Elk
(828) 898-2095
www.clarkgallerync.com
The owner of this gallery is a master of painting the landscapes and seascapes of the American continent and the islands of the Caribbean. His paintings of the entertainment world of New Orleans are especially favored by those who collect his works. James Kerr's paintings are exhibited in many prominent galleries throughout the country and are in hundreds of private and corporate collections throughout the United States, Canada, Europe, and the West Indies. Hours vary, so call for an appointment.

## Mitchell County

### ENERGY XCHANGE
**66 Energy Xchange Dr., off Hwy 80 North, Burnsville**
**(828) 675-5541**
**www.energyxchange.org**
A fascinating area of studios that utilize landfill gas as an energy source for small enterprise in craft and horticulture, and to meet local energy needs. The Craft Gallery includes the work of four potters and two glassblowers who work as residents in the project.

### PENLAND SCHOOL OF CRAFTS
**Visitors Center, Penland Road, off U.S. Hwy. 19 East, Penland**
**(828) 765-6211**
**www.penland.org**
We discuss this wonderfully unique, historic school in greater detail in our Mountain Crafts chapter, but it bears repeating that this facility and staff play a crucial role in preserving North Carolina's mountain heritage of arts and handcrafts. You can visit the school's gallery, which has a collection of the works of students and former students. Blown glass, handcrafted jewelry, wood sculpture, weaving, watercolors, and works in oil are all artfully displayed and available for purchase.

### SEDBERRY POTTERY
**Mine Creek Road, off U.S. Hwy. 226, Bakersville**
**(828) 688-3386**
**www.sedberrypottery.com**
Trained at the Rhode Island School of Design, Ken Sedberry works in clay, drawing from his artistic intuition and a wealth of experience as an instructor in Helena, Montana, at the Archie Bray Foundation, and the Catholic University in Washington, D.C. Today he fills his studio, near Loafer's Glory, with marvelously imaginative decorative pottery as well as wood-fired, functional tableware, all illuminated with a brilliant palette of color.

### TWISTED LAUREL GALLERY
**221 Locust St. (Lower St.), Spruce Pine**
**(828) 765-1532**
This downtown gallery represents more than 140 artists in all media from the tri-county area: Mitchell, Yancey, and Avery counties. You'll find exquisite handblown glass as well as colorful stained-glass work. Functional and decorative pottery, fiber art, handmade jewelry, watercolor, oil paintings, and glass are featured here.

## Watauga County

### ALTA VISTA GALLERY
**2839 Broadstone Rd., Valle Crucis**
**(828) 693-5247**
**www.altavistagallery.com**
Located on the first floor of a charming bed-and-breakfast, this gallery features mostly two-dimensional art of the surrounding mountain scenery from area artists. Some jewelry and woodwork are also represented.

### DOE RIDGE POTTERY
**149 West King St., Boone**
**(828) 264-1127**
**www.doeridgepottery.homestead.com**
Doe Ridge showcases pottery in all its forms in downtown Boone. You can find both functional stoneware like French butter jars and vegetable steamers, as well as decorative works and handmade Christmas ornaments. Commissions for promotional logos are also a great feature here.

### GALLERY 9
**10244 Hwy. 105 South, Foscoe**
**(828) 963-6068**
**www.gallery9.com**
This elegant gallery features contemporary and traditional painting, indoor and outdoor sculpture, wearable art jewelry, photography, vibrant glassworks, clay, wood turnings, raku, and original pastels by nationally and internationally known artists.

### HANDS GALLERY
**543 West King St., Boone**
**(828) 262-1970**
**handsgallery.org**

This gallery has been a part of the Boone arts scene for more than 30 years. A consistently fine selection of wearable fiber art, wood sculpture, and imaginative, functional, and decorative pottery is featured here.

## IAGO
**1165 Main St., Blowing Rock**
**(828) 295-0033**
**www.iagoblowingrock.com**
A beautifully appointed space for inspired handcrafts. IAGO specializes in jewelry, art, glass, fine art, sculpture, home decor accents, copperware, pottery, woodcrafts, metal crafts, and stained glass.

## MAIN STREET GALLERY & CO-OP
**960 Main St., Blowing Rock**
**(828) 295-7839**
**www.blowingrockfinecrafts.com**
This cooperative gallery features a variety of glass, prints, photography, stained glass, functional and decorative pottery, woven pieces, leather work, and wearable art. Special exhibits are on display each season.

## MORNING STAR GALLERY
**915 Main St., Blowing Rock**
**(828) 295-6991**
**www.morningstartgalleryusa.com**
Established in 1985, Morning Star Gallery shows primarily handcrafted treasures: paintings and sculptures, pottery and jewelry, glass, wood, etchings, and garden accessories and small whimsies.

## PARKWAY CRAFT CENTER
**Mile 294, Blue Ridge Parkway, Blowing Rock**
**(828) 295-7938**
**www.southernhighlandcraftguild.org**
In the splendid Victorian-era home known as Flat Top Manor, this distinctive craft center offers room after room of traditional and contemporary crafts of the finest quality. Since 1951 the center has come alive every May through Oct with demonstrations and displays by members of the prestigious Southern Highland Craft Guild of works in clay, fiber, wood, fabric, metal, and materials native to the mountains. Be sure to save some time to sit on a rocking chair on the expansive front porch and take in one of the most inspiring views in the mountains.

## Yancey County
### BLUE ROCK STUDIO AND GALLERY
**2250 US Hwy. 80 South, Burnsville**
**(828) 675-9058**
**www.bluerockstudio-nc.com**
This light-filled space features wood, fiber arts, sculpture, photography, and paintings, but specializes in clay and glass.

### THE DESIGN GALLERY
**7 South Main St., Burnsville**
**(828) 678-9869**
**www.the-design-gallery.com**
A mother/daughter team has amassed the work of more than 100 local artisans. The selection includes original paintings, etchings, art glass, pottery, woodwork, furniture, textiles, sculpture, metals, book art, and jewelry. A new feature is Mayland Court Furniture, which is a full line of furniture, handcrafted and handpainted to the buyers' specifications.

### SILENT POETRY
**120 West Main St., Burnsville**
**(828) 682-7998**
**www.silentpoetry.com**
A downtown Burnsville gallery with five showrooms filled with locally made pottery, handblown glass, wreaths, stained glass, serigraphs, etchings, oils, and watercolors.

### TOE RIVER CRAFTS
**4590 US 80 South, Burnsville**
**(828) 682-7215**
**www.toeriverarts.org**
Six miles south of tiny Micaville, on US 80 South, is Toe River Crafts. This rustic crafts cooperative gallery represents the work of several nationally known Yancey County artists and craftspeople, many whose work has been shown across the country. You will find finely crafted, one-of-a-kind works at Toe River Crafts, from prints to metals, fiber arts, paper, wood works, photography, pottery, and watercolor.

## Central Mountains
### Buncombe County
**16 PATTON**
**16 Patton Ave., Asheville**
**(828) 236-2889**
**www.16patton.com**
Two floors feature the works of regional and local artists. Monthly themed exhibitions introduce new artists throughout the year. High quality landscapes and some figurative work are the norm.

**AMERICAN FOLK ART & FRAMING**
**64 Biltmore Ave., Asheville**
**(828) 281-2134**
**www.amerifolk.com**
This shop features cheerful and intriguing outsider art, as well as contemporary crafts such as pottery and wood sculpture. Also a frame shop, American Folk Art features a vast array of frames from elegant to barnwood styles.

**ASHEVILLE GALLERY OF ART**
**16 College St., Asheville**
**(828) 251-5796**
**www.ashevillegallery-of-art.com**
One of Asheville's oldest galleries, this downtown art space represents a fine assortment of area artists, such as popular local watercolor artist Ann Vasilik. The gallery is a co-op, where the artists run the gallery themselves.

**THE BENDER GALLERY**
**57 Haywood St., Asheville**
**(828) 225-6625**
**www.thebendergallery.com**
Beautiful glass art in every form, from vessels to stained glass, wall hangings, and sculptures by leading national glass artists, grace this airy two-level space.

**BLACK MOUNTAIN COLLEGE MUSEUM & ART CENTER**
**56 Broadway St., Asheville**
**(828) 350-8484**
**www.blackmountaincollege.org**
This gallery space showcases the works of former students and teachers of the experimental college that drew luminaries to Asheville, such as Robert Rauschenberg, John Cage, and others. Multimedia exhibitions are also held here in conjunction with themes based on the former college.

**BLUE SPIRAL 1**
**38 Biltmore Ave., Asheville**
**(828) 251-0202**
**www.bluespiral1.com**
The elegant and luminous gallery space of Blue Spiral 1 in downtown Asheville is a masterfully planned multilevel showcase for painting, sculpture, and fine crafts. Changing exhibits cover the expansive 15,000-square-foot space. A separate wing includes pull-out display "walls" on wheels for more exhibition space. This is a true state-of-the-art gallery.

The Blue Spiral 1 is also home to the largest collection of paintings by Will Henry Stevens (1881–1949). Stevens was a renowned regionalist and modernist who worked in oils, watercolor, pastels, and mixed media.

**FINE ARTS LEAGUE OF THE CAROLINAS**
**362 Depot St., Asheville**
**(828) 252-5050**
**www.fineartsleague.org**
This nonprofit art instruction studio is dedicated to the development of the realist artist. The league offers seminars and workshops with visiting artists, art historians, and related experts in the field of fine art. Intensive classes cover such themes as anatomy, craftsmanship, color theory, perspective, and composition. A gallery in the league's space features guest artists as well as student works. Salon Fridays take place on the last Fri of the month—they feature teacher/student exhibitions and receptions.

**GALLERY MINERVA**
**8 Biltmore Ave., Asheville**
**(828) 255-8850**
**www.galleryminerva.com**
Minerva features emerging local artists and work from artists around the United States in various

## The North Carolina Fresco Trail

Remote Ashe County, in the far northwest corner of North Carolina's mountains, seems an unlikely place for a collection of religious frescoes, but this is where the trail starts . . . or ends, depending on which way you're approaching.

Noted American artist Ben Long, born in Statesville, found his niche as an artist who keeps alive the ancient art of the fresco. Fresco painting is a tenuous art, based as it is on the immediate application of pigment to wet plaster. So quickly does the bonding of the two take place that great skill and meticulous planning must be maintained in order to achieve beautiful results.

In 2005 a Benjamin F. Long Fresco Trail Consortium, which included representatives from Burke, Buncombe, Iredell, and Wilkes counties, created the Fresco Trail, growing into Ashe, Mecklenburg, and most recently, Avery Counties.

A grant from the Blue Ridge National Heritage Area (covering 25 counties in Western North Carolina) has provided the consortium to create a Web site, print brochures with trail locations, and create educational materials to be used in schools, colleges, and universities. (www .benlongfrescotrail.org).

In two picturesque Episcopal churches, St. Mary's in West Jefferson, on Highway 194, off U.S. Highway 221, and Holy Trinity, just off Highway 16 at Glendale Springs, are housed a collection of wonderful religious frescoes created by Long and his students, spanning a period of years from the mid-1970s to the mid-1980s. The marvelous beauty of the work and the powerful subjects have drawn thousands of visitors from all over the country to witness firsthand the evocative frescoes that decorate the walls of these tiny churches.

Over the last 30 years Benjamin Franklin Long IV has established an international reputation as a portrait painter and rare contemporary master of the ancient art of "true fresco," painting directly on wet plaster walls. Born in Texas, Long is the grandson of McKendree Robbins Long (1888–1976), a revivalist preacher and visionary painter whose early art training had grounded him firmly in the Western classical tradition. Benjamin F. Long IV grew up in Statesville, North Carolina, and studied at the University of North Carolina at Chapel Hill and the Art Students League in New York. Traveling to New York City, Long became a member of the Art Students League and began studying with Robert Beverly Hale and Frank Mason. In 1967 he interrupted his art studies to enlist in the Marine Corps, serving two years in Vietnam, initially as an infantry officer and later as a combat artist.

Upon leaving Vietnam, Long traveled to Italy to apprentice himself to Pietro Annigoni. Long committed himself to Annigoni for almost eight years, working beside him in fresco work and teaching himself to paint in oil.

After completing several frescoes in Italy, including the only painting by a non-Italian at the Abbey of Montecassino, Long brought his fresco talent to America. Since 1978, Long has completed 13 frescoes in North Carolina, including a dome at the TransAmerica building in Charlotte.

Besides his major fresco work, Long has had works in the Royal Academy as well as the Royal Portrait Society. He has exhibited in Florence, London, Paris, Atlanta, San Francisco, and North Carolina, and is represented in major collections in Europe and North and South America. He has lived and worked in Europe for over 30 years and now divides his time between Europe and Asheville, North Carolina. He recently founded the Fine Arts League of the Carolinas, a school designed for the needs of the classically trained artist.

mediums, usually more contemporary subject matter. The owner Anna Parker-Barnett also offers art consulting.

## GALLERY OF THE MOUNTAINS
**Grove Park Inn, 290 Macon Ave., Asheville**
**(828) 254-2068**
**www.galleryofthemountains.com**
Treasure hunting—that's what a visit to this gallery is all about. Here, amidst the grand setting of the historic Grove Park Inn (see our Resorts chapter), you can find a treasure at every turn, including charming handcrafted wearables, jewelry, pottery, Arts and Craft movement lamps, and accessories.

## GRAND BOHEMIAN GALLERY
**11 Boston Way, Biltmore Village**
**(828) 398-5555**
**www.grandbohemiangallery.com**
Inside the new Grand Bohemian Hotel this state-of-the-art gallery features international, national, and local artists, with monthly receptions that spill out into into the grand lobby. The exhibition continues on each floor of the hotel with artwork on every available wall space. A private viewing room in the gallery allows collectors to consider artwork under different lighting conditions. Unique, one-of-a-kind jewelry is also very popular here.

## THE HAEN GALLERY
**52 Biltmore Ave., Asheville**
**(828) 254-8577**
**www.thehaengallery.com**
A spacious gallery with a minimalist atmosphere—artwork is not crowded in here—Haen showcases landscape painting, graphic art, and sleek sculpture from a variety of local, regional and southeastern artists.

## HOFMAN STUDIOS
**11 Roberts St., Asheville**
**(828) 232-1401**
**www.hofmanstudios.com**
Founded by internationally known artists Ian and Jo Lydia Craven, and now reinvented by artisan Michael Hofman, the gallery features elegant

dinnerware, orchid pots, bowls, and sculptures that have been imprinted by antique lace and finished with an array of luminous glazes.

## JEWELS THAT DANCE
**63 Haywood St., Asheville**
**(828) 254-5088**
**www.jewelsthatdance.com**
The imaginatively conceived jewelry pieces of Jewels that Dance gallery are works of art wrought in gold and silver. Rings, pins, and necklaces sport unusual features that will catch your fancy. The gallery is next door to Asheville's Pack Library, downtown.

## NEW MORNING GALLERY
**7 Boston Way, Biltmore Village, Asheville**
**(828) 274-2831**
**www.newmorninggallerync.com**
Started in 1972 as a modest crafts gallery, the New Morning Gallery is one of the best showcases of fine handcrafts in the region. Owner John Cram describes New Morning Gallery as "art for living." You can enjoy browsing the newly expanded shop filled with lovely sculptural pottery, handmade jewelry, fine art glass, and unusual furniture.

## SEVEN SISTERS GALLERY
**117 Cherry St., Black Mountain**
**(828) 669-5107**
**www.sevensistersgallery.com**
The wonderfully rustic brick interior, original pressed-tin ceiling, hardwood floors, and antique furniture—all serving as display space for gallery work—set the mood for this relaxed gallery that is an integral part of Black Mountain. Seven Sisters Gallery is an anchor for the Cherry Street Historic District in this quaint old resort town.

## VADIM BORA GALLERY & STUDIO
**30½ Battery Park Ave., Asheville**
**(828) 254-7959**
**www.vadimborastudio.com**
This bright upstairs gallery features sculpture, paintings, and graphics from professional artists from around the world, as well as the works

of master sculptor and painter Vadim Bora. A regional sculpture exhibition takes place here annually. Bora's own studio is adjacent.

## WOOLWORTH WALK
**25 Haywood St., Asheville**
**(828) 254-9234**
**www.woolworthwalk.com**
An egalitarian art bazaar, the walk maintains individual artisans' booths that feature everything from jewelry to photography, clothing, pottery, and much more.

## Henderson County
**THE ARTS COUNCIL OF HENDERSON COUNTY, INC.**
**538-A North Main St., Hendersonville**
**(828) 693-8504**
**www.acofhc.org**
A leader in advocating and promoting the arts in this county, the Council manages the county's only public art gallery and produces an annual schedule of diverse exhibitions that have featured local, regional and national artists. Art on Main and the Open Studio Tour are annual events that bring artisans and the public together.

## SILVER FOX GALLERY
**508 Main St., Hendersonville**
**(828)698-0601**
**www.silverfoxonline.com**
The Silver Fox maintains an interesting collection of utilitarian works like collectible salt-shakers, artisan lighting, indoor and outdoor furniture, as well as paintings, and sculpture. A collection of Judaic arts and jewelry is also unique here.

## WICKWIRE
**330 North Main St., Hendersonville**
**(828) 692-6222**
**www.wickwireartgallery.com**
Wickwire, a fine art/folk art gallery, "seeks the bread that sustains the heart." It goes out of its way to display the visions of emerging local artists. At the same time the gallery also represents some very well established names, including three Smithsonian artisans and two "North Caro-

lina Living Treasures." The addition of decor items like hand-crafted furniture by local and regional artisans, has gained the gallery a new audience.

## Polk County
**HEARTWOOD CONTEMPORARY CRAFTS GALLERY**
**21 Main St., Saluda**
**(828) 749-9365**
**www.heartwoodsaluda.com**
With a focus on a more contemporary collection, this gallery is the perfect place for anyone who not only enjoys fine crafts, but also likes to bask in the small-town atmosphere that makes Saluda special. Regional and national craftspeople of the highest caliber display their wares here, such as delicate porcelain sculpture, pottery (one of the finest collections in the region), jewelry in all its forms, wood items, garden sculpture, and original prints and paintings.

**i** When visiting Saluda Mountain Crafts in Saluda, take the time to visit the old-fashioned ice-cream parlor right next door. Fudge Mountain Ice Cream makes its own ice cream and fudge and serves it up in an authentic atmosphere, created with antique items from old ice-cream parlors, old RKO movie theater marquees, and cabinets made from the lockers of the Virginia Senate Building.

## TRYON PAINTERS AND SCULPTORS
**Tryon Fine Arts Center**
**34 Melrose Ave., Tryon**
**(828) 859-3822**
**www.tryonpaintersandsculptors.com**
Composed of 160 amateur and professional artists, some of whom are nationally known, this organization presents 10 art show openings a year, including artists from all over the United States. The group's shows are held both at the Tryon Fine Arts Center and at the Gallery Too in the Farwell Annex next door. Workshops and regular art and sculpture classes are held in the studio, which also contains a retail store featuring members' creations.

## UPSTAIRS ARTSPACE
**49 North Trade St., Tryon**
**(828) 859-2828**
**www.upstairsartspace.org**
The Upstairs Artspace got its name from former upper-floor locations, the first being an artist's upstairs bedroom when the gallery was founded in 1978. Now, more than 30 years later, though definitely in a downstairs space, the name has stuck. It is a well-known contemporary art gallery that features fine arts and crafts, children's art, literary readings, musical performances (including a monthly Pickin' Parlor), art education, and other events.

## *Transylvania County*
### BREVARD COLLEGE VISUAL ARTS
**1 Brevard College Dr., Brevard**
**(828) 883-8292**
**www.brevard.edu**
Exhibitions of visual art at the college can be found in two locations: the Mezzazine Gallery in the Paul Porter Center for Performing Arts and the Spiers Gallery in Sims Art Center. In addition to displays of art produced by the faculty and students, visitors may enjoy the talents of regionally and nationally known artists. Exhibitions include work that spans the spectrum of the visual arts, including ceramics, painting, sculpture, photography, and installations.

## GALLERY ON MAIN
**53 East Main St., Brevard**
**(828) 885-7299**
**www.galleryonmainnet**
You'll find originals and limited-edition prints by artists such as Bob Timberlake and wildlife artist Bob Travers, as well as Civil War art. A full-service framing department can help get those on your wall.

## RED WOLF GALLERY
**8 East Main St., Brevard**
**(828) 862-8620**
**www.redwolfgallerync.com**
This is a small and astute space with vibrant landscapes, woodwork, and copper sculptures that is owned by the Dergara family. Itdisplays works of the family artistans as well as local and regional artists. The building in which the gallery is housed underwent restorations to recreate a marvelous façade.

## TRANSYLVANIA COMMUNITY ARTS CENTER AND GALLERY
**349 South Caldwell St., Brevard**
**(828) 884-2787**
**www.tcarts.com**
This gallery highlights local and regional artists with ten themed exhibitions a year. Nov brings the annual Art Mart, a sale of fine arts and crafts at significantly discounted prices.

# Southern Mountains
## *Haywood County*
### BLUE OWL STUDIO AND GALLERY, INC.
**11 North Main St., Waynesville**
**(828) 456-5050**
**www.blueowlnc.com**
If you wonder how the cities and landscapes of the mountains appeared in yesteryear, you can relive some of those days in this gallery. Filled with antique graphics of the past, the artists at Blue Owl bring them to life in brilliant hand-painted colors. Animal paintings on wood are predominant here—particularly black bears, wolves, raccoons, and other creatures indigenous to this area.

**i** Many arts councils in various towns hold "gallery hops" or "gallery crawls" every few months. During these events galleries and studios throw their doors open wide to the public, sometimes offering light hors d'oeuvres and wine, while visitors stroll from gallery to gallery for some art appreciation and a bit of socializing. Often the artists are on hand to discuss their works. Check local newspaper listings or consult individual art councils.

**EARTHWORK'S ENVIRONMENTAL GALLERY**
21 North Main St., Waynesville
(828) 452-9500
www.earthworksgalleries.com
This large gallery covers Southwestern arts and crafts and Native American wildlife themes. You'll find rugs, pillows, and runners from the Zapotec Indians of Mexico; woodturnings by local artists; gourd art; stone carvings from Africa; and captivating paintings and prints by Native American artists.

**T. PENNINGTON ART GALLERY**
15 North Main St., Waynesville
(828) 452-4582
www.tpennington.com
You'll be amazed by the excellent colored-pencil drawings of Western North Carolina created by Teresa Pennington. In addition to original works, the gallery also carries limited-edition prints of local mountain scenes.

**TWIGS & LEAVES**
98 North Main St., Waynesville
(828) 456-1940
www.twigsandleaves.com
A downtown gallery with ceramics, paintings, intriguing hand-made decorative pieces, and jewelry is a big draw on Main Street. The gallery is packed full, but be sure to peruse the cases of jewelry for one-of-a-kind hand-wrought works by both professionals and emerging artists.

## Jackson County

**CITY LIGHTS BOOKSTORE**
3 East Jackson St., Sylva
(828) 586-9499
www.citylightsnc.com
In addition to offering new and used books, City Lights has a small gallery of rotating exhibitions from local artisans, and sells book accessories such as place-holders and reading pillows.

**FINE ART MUSEUM**
Fine and Performing Arts Center
Western Carolina University
Hwy. 107, Cullowhee
(828) 227-3591
www.wcu.edu

This gallery on the university's campus in the new Fine and Performing Arts Center offers art exhibits by local, regional, and national artists on a year-round basis. The Fine Art Museum includes nearly 10,000 feet of exhibit space featuring a growing permanent collection and interdisciplinary programs.

i Waynesville's Mast General Store (63 North Main St.) makes for interesting browsing anytime (see our Shopping chapter). Now its Mast Store Crafter Series demonstrations make it the home of a real learning experience. Several times a month, talented craftspeople show off their skills in such things as doll making, jewelry design, raku masks, and stenciling. Call (828) 452-2101 for more information about the series.

**OAKS GALLERY**
Hwy. 441, Dillsboro
(828) 586-6542
www.oaksgallery.com
The talents that flower in these mountains are beautifully expressed in this gallery with the works of over 100 local artisans. Located at the Riverwood Shops, the Oaks Gallery maintains ceramics, wood arts, jewelry, glass and other gifts from area artists.

**TREE HOUSE POTTERY**
148 Front Street, Dillsboro
(828) 631-5100
www.treehousepotterync.com
At Tree House Pottery you can see pottery being made in an open studio by artisans Travis Berning and Joe Frank McGee. Other artists' ceramic works are carried here also.

**RIVERWOOD PEWTER SHOP**
Hwy. 411, Dillsboro
(828) 586-6996, (800) 530-2547
www.riverwoodpewter.com
The Riverwood Shops developed around a hand-hammered pewter business established in 1930. The Riverwood Pewter Shop is still here making

hand-hammered pewter on the premises and via mail order.

## Macon County

### THE BASCOM
323 Franklin, Highlands
(828) 526-4949
www.thebascom.org
The Bascom is a nonprofit center for the visual arts in Highlands, and has a beautiful new home as of May 2009: a six-acre, "green," architect-designed pastoral campus where it serves people through high-quality rotating exhibitions, classes and educational presentations. The campus features historic buildings, a covered bridge, a nature trail, a 27,500 square-foot main building for two-dimensional adult and children's art, a separate reconstructed Studio Barn for three-dimensional art, a café, a shop, and a terrace for venue rentals.

### BRYANT ART GLASS STUDIO
260 Franklin Rd, Hwy. 64, Highlands
(828) 526-4095
www.bryantartglass.com
Dwight Bryant has rediscovered the secrets of the pharaohs. Dipping into antiquity for the process of handmade fused-glass plates, bowls, and platters, as perfected by the ancient Egyptians, Bryant has brought this to life with colorful designs of pink dogwood, purple iris, pansies, and orange and yellow sunflowers. He has also infused numerous other designs, including birds and other fauna and flora.

### MUSEUM OF AMERICAN CUT AND ENGRAVED GLASS
472 Chestnut St., Highlands
(828) 526-3427
The brilliance of cut glass illuminates the interior of the log house in which it is exhibited. Curators and collectors George and Bonnie Siek share their love of this medium. The American Brilliant Period, acknowledged to have started with the 1876 Centennial Exhibition in Philadelphia, ended in 1916 with the onset of the First World War. This museum opens up a dazzling new world to many; it is as overwhelming as the

myriad patterns of frost on a windowpane or a waterfall glistening in the sun.

### SUMMERHOUSE GALLERY
Hwy. 106 South, Highlands
(828) 526-5577
Tiger Mountain Summerhouse Gallery is the showroom for woodworks. This shop sells hand-crafted furnishings, including custom lodge furniture and country reproductions of beds, tables, dressers, and other items for the entire house.

### THE UPTOWN GALLERY
30 East Main St., Franklin
(828) 349-6708
www.mcaauptowngallery.org
Members of the Macon County Art Association (see Art Organizations) display their oils, pastels, watercolors, acrylics, mixed media, and sculpture here on a year-round basis.

## MUSEUMS

### Northern Mountains

## Watauga County

### APPALACHIAN CULTURAL MUSEUM
University Hall Drive, Boone
(828) 262-3117
www.museum.appstate.edu
You must visit this fine museum of Appalachian cultural heritage. Located in University Hall in Boone just off the campus of Appalachian State University, it has a fascinating collection of artifacts spanning eons—from prehistoric times to the present. You can view special exhibits depicting highlights of life in our mountain region. Groups can take advantage of the specially guided tours led by museum staff (call for a reservation). These personalized illuminations of history focus on all aspects of living in the mountains, now and in the past. University Hall also houses the Appalachian Collection, a wonderfully varied assortment of music, books, and documents pertinent to the region. The offices of the Appalachian Consortium and the Center for Appalachian Studies are also here.

## HICKORY RIDGE HOMESTEAD
**591 Horn in the West Dr., Boone**
**(828) 264-2120**
**www.horinthewest/museum.htm**
This living history museum, sponsored by the Southern Appalachian Historical Association, is composed of a series of log structures, a main log cabin, a weaving room, and a smokehouse, all depicting the period of the late 18th century in the Appalachian mountains. The homestead reflects the same period covered by the outdoor drama *Horn in the West*, also on the site. The Olde Christmas Celebration and the Hickory Ridge Homestead Apple Festival in Oct are two special events celebrated here.

# Central Mountains
## *Buncombe County*
### THE ASHEVILLE ART MUSEUM
**2 South Pack Square, Asheville**
**(828) 253-3227**
**www.ashevilleart.org**
Founded in 1948, this first-rate museum maintains a fine permanent collection of 20th-century American art, including the work of such renowned artists as Romare Bearden, Jacob Lawrence, and George Inness; the sculpture of Louise Nevelson; and contemporary abstracts of Asheville natives Kenneth Noland and Donald Sultan. Permanent works are rotated every few months to bring new interest to the museum's collection, and significant traveling exhibitions are curated several times a year. A new expansion of the museum is planned for 2010–2011.

### BILTMORE ESTATE
**1 Approach Rd., Asheville**
**(828) 225-1333, (800) 411-3812**
**www.biltmore.com**
Don't miss the spectacular private working estate established in 1895 by railroad heir George Vanderbilt. Vanderbilt chose his original 125,000 acres well and created a lavish 250-room mansion styled after his favorite chateau in France's Loire River Valley, and it's filled with antiques and artifacts (for much more information, see our chapter on the Biltmore Estate).

### BILTMORE HOMESPUN MUSEUM
**111 Grovewood Rd., Asheville**
**(828) 253-7651**
**www.grovewood.com**
Built in 1917, the English-style pebble-dash cottage housing the museum was one of the original Biltmore Homespun Shop buildings. Photos and artifacts preserve the old weaving operation begun a century ago under the auspices of Edith Stuyvesant Vanderbilt, wife of railroad heir George Vanderbilt of Biltmore Estate. Artifacts such as bolts of cloth, antique handmade looms, and an original, old-time clock bring back the flavor of the Biltmore Industries and Biltmore Homespun Shops of days gone by. During the week there are weaving demonstrations throughout the day. There's no entrance fee.

### ESTES-WINN ANTIQUE AUTOMOBILE MUSEUM
**111 Grovewood Rd., Asheville**
**(828) 253-7651**
**www.grovewood.com**
Next door to Grovewood Gallery, in the massive original weaving shed that once housed 40 looms for the old Biltmore Industries, is the Estes-Winn Antique Automobile Museum. This delightful collection is a veritable history of how America took to the highway, from the first Model T to shiny post–World War II roadsters. You can fantasize about grand old autos such as a 1926 Cadillac and a 1927 La Salle convertible. There's even a 1922 La France fire engine on display that once was used by the Asheville Fire Department. They just don't make 'em like they used to!

### PACK PLACE EDUCATION ARTS AND SCIENCE CENTER
**2 South Pack Square, Asheville**
**(828) 257-4500**
**www.packplace.org**
This spectacular, 92,000-square-foot complex is a monument to the determination of such leading Asheville citizens as the late Roger McGuire,

whose vision was to realize the potential of downtown Asheville. The success of Pack Place has finally become reality, and visitors and citizens alike are discovering the delights of this diverse cultural center. Pack Place is the union, adaptation, and renovation of several historic structures and is home to the Asheville Art Museum, the Colburn Gem and Mineral Museum, the Health Adventure, Diana Wortham Theatre, and the YMI Cultural Center.

The Colburn Gem and Mineral Museum is an exploration of the geological world around us. The museum, founded in 1960, highlights gems and minerals of all shapes and sizes from around the world, as well as those specific garnets, rubies, emeralds, and gold deposits that make North Carolina a rock hound's delight (see our chapter on Rockhounding).

The Health Adventure, founded in 1968, is a marvelous hands-on learning center, providing children and adults special insights into the human physical condition and related applied sciences. Two theaters accommodate school groups for educator-led programs. Thoughtfully planned, hands-on exhibits such as Brain Storm, Body Works, Miracle of Life, and the Creative Play Space (for children younger than 8) invite young curiosity.

The Diana Wortham Theatre is a gem of a performance space for audiences, performers, and technicians. The 500-seat theater is an intimate, sophisticated setting with a full-size stage, exquisitely detailed woodwork, impeccable acoustics, and accessibility for people with disabilities. Diana Wortham Theatre presents, produces, and hosts performing arts events that range from Shakespeare to Mamet, classical ballet to modern dance, lectures to performance poetry, symphonies to Brubeck, and world-renowned storytellers to local school pageants.

The YMI Cultural Center, also a part of the Pack Place complex, is on the corner of Market and Eagle streets, southeast of Pack Square, in an architecturally rich, century-old structure commissioned by George Vanderbilt. This museum is the home of changing exhibits and a permanent collection of artifacts that focus on the local, national, and international African-American heritage.

The Adventure Place is an imaginatively stocked gift shop designed to complement the various museums found at Pack Place. A fascinating lobby exhibit entitled "Here is the Square . . ." traces three centuries of Asheville history and the evolution of Pack Square itself.

Tickets are required for admission to each of the museums.

## SMITH-MCDOWELL HOUSE
**283 Victoria Rd., Asheville**
**(828) 253-9231**
**www.wnchistory.org**
This fine old Asheville residence is on the campus of Asheville-Buncombe Technical Community College. The stately, early Victorian-era home, built around 1840, is Asheville's oldest brick residence, furnished with period antiques. You'll enjoy the marvelous architectural details and appointments of this palatial beauty. Personalized tours are available. There is a nominal admission fee.

## SWANNANOA VALLEY MUSEUM
**223 West State St., Black Mountain**
**(828) 669-9566**
**www.swannanoavalleymuseum.org**
The Swannanoa Valley Museum, open seasonally from Apr through Oct, is the guardian of a remarkable collection of artifacts of everyday life in Western North Carolina, from pioneer times to recent years. Local residents donated many of the items here. This unique museum is also home to an exhibit honoring Rafael Guastavino, architect and designer of the century-old Basilica of St. Lawrence in Asheville; displays spotlighting Billy Graham's crusades; the U.S. Navy artifacts of Rear Adm. G. C. Crawford; and an extensive collection of wildflower photography. The museum is open Tues through Sat 10 a.m. to 5 p.m. and Sun 2 to 5 p.m.

## THOMAS WOLFE MEMORIAL
**52 North Market St., Asheville**
**(828) 253-8304**
**www.wolfememorial.com**
Asheville's native son, noted author of the classic coming-of-age novel *Look Homeward, Angel*,

spent his boyhood here in his mother's rambling old boardinghouse on Spruce Street, just off legendary Pack Square. This old house figured prominently in Wolfe's work and is important for its ability to convey the forces that helped shape this remarkable American writer. The Thomas Wolfe Welcome Center adjacent to the house offers information about the house and the author.

**ZEBULON B. VANCE BIRTHPLACE**
**Reems Creek Road off Old U.S. Hwys. 19/23, Weaverville**
**(828) 645-6706**
**www.nchistoricsites.org/vance/vance.htm**
This charming mountain homestead was home to one of North Carolina's most prominent political figures. Zeb Vance began his career as a lawyer, assuming public office by the young age of 24. He was elected governor of North Carolina three times, most notably during the Civil War. He also served three terms as a U.S. senator. At his death in 1894, this most capable public servant was admired by colleagues and beloved by his constituency. His life and career are profiled in an exhibit in the adjoining visitor center.

The two-story cabin and outbuildings are reconstructions, built from hewn yellow pine logs around the original chimney with its two massive fireplaces. The furnishings and household items depict the period from 1790 to 1840 and include a few pieces original to the Vance family.

## Henderson County
**CARL SANDBURG HOME**
**1928 Little River Rd., Flat Rock**
**(828) 693-4178**
**www.nps.gov/carl**
Carl Sandburg—poet, author, lecturer, musician, onetime political activist, social thinker, and winner of two Pulitzer Prizes for his four-volume *Abraham Lincoln: The War Years* and his *Complete Poems*—spent the last 22 years of his life at Connemara, a 240-acre farm 3 miles south of Hendersonville. The main house was built in 1838 as a summer home for Charleston's Christopher Gustave Memminger, who served as secretary

---

# A Hillside in Highland Park

A bright star among the Montgomery, Alabama, Southern belles, Zelda Fitzgerald left a path of broken hearts behind her. An accomplished painter, she also wrote. The dark shadows of her mind eventually brought her to Highland Psychiatric Hospital in Asheville, founded in 1904 by Dr. Robert Carroll. In 1939 Dr. Carroll gave 100 percent interest in the hospital to Duke University. Zelda, who earlier had been diagnosed in Europe with schizophrenia, frequented the sanitarium from the 1930s until her death in an all-consuming hospital fire in 1948. Meanwhile, her husband, author F. Scott, resided at the Grove Park Inn during his visits with her.

The former hospital grounds are now known as Highland Park. Amid this landscape Zelda once painted; you will find a plaque dedicated to her.

---

of the treasury for the Confederacy from 1861 to 1864. Like many mountain residents today, Memminger wanted to escape the heat and humidity of the coast, while Sandburg sought relief from cold northern winters.

Sandburg moved here in 1945 with his wife, three daughters, grandchildren, and his wife's prize-winning Chikaming goats—a herd that grew as large as 200; the milk was turned into a successful dairy operation. The Sandburgs spent happy and productive years in a lovely setting of rolling pastures, ponds, lakes, and wooded mountains. Sandburg died in 1967, and Connemara became a National Historic Site the following year. It's open daily except on Dec 25.

To reach the site drive south on U.S. Highway 25 and turn onto Little River Road at the Flat Rock Playhouse. Park at the Visitors Information Center and, after viewing the exhibits there, take the lovely walk past a small lake up to the main house for a guided tour. (Access assistance for wheelchairs is provided.) Later, stroll about the farm and pet the goats and other farm animals if you don't mind risking an occasional bite, peck, or kick. Hike the 2.6-mile round-trip trail up to Glassy Mountain, one of Sandburg's favorite walks, for a mountain ridge and valley view.

In midsummer there are free dramatic renditions of some of Sandburg's writings offered by the Apprentice Company of the Flat Rock Playhouse in the outdoor theater (call for performance times). Connemara is particularly festive during the Christmas season, which is celebrated in "Sandburg style" on Sat evenings from Thanksgiving until Christmas. The park is closed only on Dec 25.

## THE HISTORIC HENDERSONVILLE DEPOT AND MODEL RAILROAD
**Seventh Avenue and Maple Street, Hendersonville**
**(828) 693-0605**
**www.avmrc.com**

Hendersonville got its first train depot in 1879, which was replaced in 1902 by the present structure. Now the quaint building has undergone restoration. Dressed up in its original colors, it houses an operating 420-square-foot model railroad in its old baggage room. The model features the Hendersonville, Asheville, Brevard, and Saluda stations, including the Saluda Grade (the steepest grade in the country), plus mountains, waterfalls, lakes, towns, and industries. The train runs over 500 feet of track and has more than 100 switches. It's open to the public free of charge year-round (donations are appreciated) from noon to 3 p.m. on Wed and 9 a.m. until noon on Sat.

## THE HISTORIC JOHNSON FARM
**3346 Haywood Rd., Hwy.191, Hendersonville**
**(828) 891-6585**
**www.historicjohnsonfarm.org**

Located 4 miles north of Hendersonville on Highway 191, this late-19th-century, 15-acre tobacco farm became a popular summer tourist retreat in the 1920s. Today, owned by the Henderson County Public Schools, an 1870s brick farmhouse, 1920 boarding house, barn-loft museum, 10 historic buildings, and two nature trails are operated as a heritage education center and farm museum. Guided tours are available at 10:30 a.m. and 1:30 p.m. Tues through Sat from May through Oct, and Wed through Sat from Nov through Apr. A small admission is charged for guided tours.

## WESTERN NORTH CAROLINA AIR MUSEUM
**1340 Gilbert St., Hendersonville**
**(828) 693-9708, (800) 828-4244**
**www.wncairmuseum.com**

It's appropriate that this air museum, in the state where flight was born, is located at the Hendersonville Airport. That also enables it to feature spring and fall air shows. Award-winning, beautifully restored airplanes as well as restored replica antique and vintage planes are on display here. They range from a 1917 Nieuport 11 (Bebe) replica to a 1950s Ercoup and a Corbin Ace. You can even view a 1510 ornithopter designed by Leonardo da Vinci. The museum is open each Wed, Sat, and Sun from noon until 6 p.m. Admission is free, but donations are welcomed. Gifts and souvenirs are available. Museum memberships and lifetime memberships are also available.

## Polk County
### POLK COUNTY HISTORICAL ASSOCIATION & MUSEUM
**1 Depot St., Tryon**
**(828) 859-2287**
**www.polkcountyhistoricalsociety.com**

Housed in the old but charmingly renovated Tryon railroad depot, the association exhibits household, agricultural, and historical artifacts used by the early settlers and Indians in this area. There is also a collection of folklore, old maps, records, and pictures, including important items in American history such as "the cannonball that started the Civil War," said to have been picked up at Fort Sumter by a young Union officer,

Abner Doubleday. Monthly historical meetings are held, and the public is invited. The museum is open on Tues and Thurs from 10 a.m. until noon and by appointment. Admission is free, but donations are appreciated.

## Gift of the Magi

William Sidney Porter claimed to his final day that it was only a coincidence that both he and a large sum of money were missing from the Texas bank where he was a teller in 1894. Eventually Porter found his way to Asheville and as both a widower and as the noted author, O. Henry, married a local girl, Sara Lindsey Coleman. He obviously became familiar with many of the mountain folks, as he used mountain names and the circumstances of folks from this region in "The Gift of the Magi." To commemorate this tale, the Urban Trail of Asheville displays a plaque with items from the story (cast in bronze) surrounding it. It is located on Patton Avenue close to Pack Square. Meanwhile, in death, O. Henry remains in our area noted by a simple grave marker in Riverside Cemetery, William Sidney Porter.

### Transylvania County
**ALLISON-DEAVER HISTORICAL HOUSE**
**Hwy. 280, Pisgah Forest**
**(828) 884-5137**
**www.preservingourpast.org**
Just two days before it was scheduled to be demolished, Western North Carolina's oldest frame house west of the Blue Ridge Mountains was saved by the Transylvania County Historical Society. Built in Quaker or Federal architectural style in the early 1800s by Benjamin Allison, it

housed his family of 11 children. In 1830 he sold the house and its 420 acres to William Deaver, who, in the early 1840s, remodeled the six-room, 1,100-square-foot structure into a Greek Revival house and expanded it. Then in the 1860s, the roof was raised to make room for second- and third-floor Charleston-, or Low Country–style porches. This "house-restoration museum" is open for tours from Apr through Oct from 10 a.m. to 4 p.m. on Fri and Sat and on Sun from 1 to 4 p.m. There is no admission charge, but donations for this ongoing project are appreciated.

### CRADLE OF FORESTRY
**US 276, Pisgah National Forest**
**(828) 877-3130**
**www.cradleofforestry.com**
There is an old story, though probably not true, that claims someone told George Vanderbilt that if he was going to build a baronial estate (Biltmore House and Gardens certainly qualifies), he should have a baronial forest—and that's how scientific forestry got started in America. True or not, in the late 1800s George Vanderbilt hired Gifford Pinchot to restore and manage the forest on the 8,000 acres surrounding his famous estate. His holdings were later expanded to 125,000 acres that, after his death, became part of Pisgah National Forest.

In 1895 Dr. Carl Schenck, a brilliant German forester, succeeded Pinchot and was a magnet for young men wishing to learn the new sustainable forest methods. As a result, in 1898 Schenck started the Biltmore Forest School, the first forestry school in America. For his campus he utilized an old schoolhouse and abandoned farm buildings in a 3,200-foot-high valley that was named the Pink Beds, after its lush bloom of flowers. In 1964, 6,500 acres in this area were established as a National Historic Site and became known as the Cradle of Forestry.

Special interpretive programs and guided tours are offered here, and you can view an excellent 18-minute movie depicting the relationship between Vanderbilt, Pinchot, Schenck, and the Forest School students. The Forest Discovery Center has a Biltmore Forest School exhibit with a collection of artifacts as well as "Schenck's Office," where you'll find period furniture and artifacts and can look through the windows and listen to a conversation between Dr. Schenck and a student. (See The Cradle Keeps Rocking Close-up in our Forests and Parks chapter.)

There are two beautiful, mile-long paved trails, each with guided tours that will tell you of the Cradle's history and teach you a lot about the plants and trees along the way. The Forest Festival Trail has many forest demonstration projects, an old sawmill, the first little fish hatchery in Pisgah, and a old Climax logging train on display—children love to climb on it and ring the bell. The Biltmore Campus Trail winds through the school's old campus of original and reconstructed buildings. In addition to the schoolhouse, there's a general store, a two-story frame house built in 1884, another farmhouse that was used as student quarters, a blacksmith shop, an old barn that Schenck converted to an office, two former ranger houses designed by Schenck (known as the Black Forest Lodge and the Cantrell Creek Lodge), an old-time vegetable garden, and more.

## JIM BOB TINSLEY MUSEUM AND RESEARCH CENTER
### 20 West Jordan St., Brevard
### (828) 884-2347
### www.jimbobtinsleymuseum.org

Transylvania County may seem an unlikely place to find a cowboy museum, but this is a great one. It houses the extensive collection of art, memorabilia, and research records of Jim Bob Tinsley, a Brevard native and famous author, educator, and musicologist. He performed with Gene Autry in the late 1940s and has received many awards for his work, including one from the National Cowboy Hall of Fame for his book (one of 10) *He Was Singing This Song*, a compilation of traditional American cowboy songs.

Here you'll find original art, lithographs, photographs, and bronze statues by famous sculptors of the caliber of Frederick Remington. There is also, as you might expect, a lot about country-and-western music, including a large collection of records, tapes, and CDs. There are reels and TV tapes of western movies and old television programs played during office hours. And there are all those other things connected to cowboys: saddles, spurs, branding irons from famous ranches, Florida Cracker cowboy whips, and an original Zane Grey 30-foot riata, to name a few items.

But Tinsley's interests go far beyond cowboys. The museum contains his historic Transylvania County memorabilia, including one of only six known Gillespie rifles. The gun dates from the early 1880s and was manufactured at the Gillespie rifle factory in nearby South Mills River. You'll also find art and literature concerning two of his other passions: pumas and sailfish.

## SILVERMONT MANSION
### 364 East Main St., Brevard
### (828) 884-3156

John Silversteen and his wife, Elizabeth, moved to Transylvania County in 1902. He opened the Toxaway Tanning Company, around which the town of Rosman grew, and later established the Gloucester Lumber Company. His enterprises, the largest in the county, provided work for several hundred people until the 1950s. He was active in and generous to the community, building the first brick elementary school in Rosman and donating the land for that town's high school.

But he's most remembered for Silvermont, the 1917, 33-room, Colonial Revival house that still stands on its spacious grounds on East Main Street. Here the Silversteens raised their three daughters—two went into business with their father; one became a noted singer who performed with the likes of Arturo Toscanini and Leopold Stokowski under the name of Adelaide van Wey.

Silvermont was willed to the county when the last daughter died in 1972. It was placed on the National Register of Historic Places in 1981. Full of interesting furniture and Silversteen memorabilia, its first floor is used for community club meetings, by private groups, and as a senior meal and recreation center. The eight-acre grounds have tennis and shuffleboard courts, a basketball court, a playground, and a picnic area. On summer evenings square dancing takes place on Tues, ballroom dancing on Wed, and mountain music "on the porch" on Thurs. Christmas at Silvermont features decorations by the Transylvania Council of Garden Clubs, usually involving musical performances.

The mansion is available for weddings, receptions, family reunions, class reunions, and other special events, but is closed when not in use.

## Southern Mountains
### Clay County
**HISTORICAL ARTS MUSEUM**
**21 Davis Loop, Hayesville**
**(828) 389-6814**
**www.clayhistoryarts.org**
The museum, housed in the town's old jail, is devoted to local history and is sponsored by the Clay County Historical and Art Council. Here you'll see a cross-section of memorabilia—the first telephone switchboard and a kitchen from the 19th century—from earlier times. Receptions and showings of local artists are also held here. It is open from June through Sept.

### Cherokee County
**CHEROKEE COUNTY HISTORICAL MUSEUM**
**87 Peachtree St., Murphy**
**(828) 837-6792**
This museum is housed in the former Carnegie Library building, right next to the even grander county courthouse. Its largest collection is devoted to the life of the Cherokee during their many centuries in the mountains and their removal to Oklahoma. Murphy itself was established near the site of the ancient Cherokee village of Guasili (pronounced "gau-ax-u-le"), visited by de Soto in 1540, and was also the site of Fort Butler, the largest of the forts built in the area for the Cherokees' removal via "The Trail of Tears."

In the museum are leftover weapons from Spanish explorers and another large collection of tools, housewares, and other items from the early pioneer days in the region. Some of the most interesting things among the mineral and rock collections are "fairy crosses" (see our Close-up, Little People and Fairy Crosses). These naturally occurring little stone crosses, called staurlite (pronounced "starlight") crystals, are supposed to bring the finder good luck. Some can be as large as 3 inches across. They still turn up around Hyatt Creek southeast of Marble and around Fishermare Branch, Almond Creek, between Parsons Branch and Burnt Branch, and around the Brasstown area.

The museum also houses a collection of more than 700 priceless dolls donated by Louise S. Kilgore. They include, among other things, representations of famous personalities (including Elvis and Princess Diana) and unique older dolls made in prefactory days. The collection takes up about one-fourth of the space on the museum's top floor. The museum is open Mon through Fri from 9 a.m. until 5 p.m. Admission is free.

### Haywood County
**CANTON AREA HISTORICAL MUSEUM AND VISITOR CENTER**
**36 Park St., Canton**
**(828) 646-3412**
With its library of old family histories and historical documents, this city-run museum, housed in the town's old library building, is an excellent place to research local history. Displays include artifacts, records, heritage handicrafts, and pictures from the past, all of which combine to tell the story of the settling of Canton and the Pigeon River area, Haywood County, and Western North Carolina (in that order of importance). The artifacts include everything from Indian arrowheads and tools to butter molds, quilts, glassware, and pottery.

**THE SHELTON HOUSE MUSEUM OF NORTH CAROLINA HANDICRAFTS**
**307 Shelton St., Waynesville**
**(828) 452-1551**
The Shelton House, built in 1875 and listed on the National Register of Historic Places, is the setting for these comprehensive exhibits of 19th-century crafts. It also has an interesting exhibit of handicrafts made by artisans who have participated in the educational demonstration of heritage crafts in the North Carolina State Fair's Village of Yesteryear since 1951 (see our Mountain Crafts chapter for more information). Exhibits include

# Close-up

## Little People and Fairy Crosses

Those of us steeped in Western culture know all about the Old World's fairies, elves, gnomes, trolls, and the like, but few of us are acquainted with the Little People who reside in these mountains, though some folks of European descent have encountered them over the years. James Mooney, in his classic work, *History, Myths, and Sacred Formulas of the Cherokees,* first published in 1900 by the Bureau of American Ethnology, identifies a whole pantheon of spirit folk, some of whom are mentioned in other legends in our book.

The Cherokee's name for Little People is *yunwi tsunsdi.* They usually live in rock caves on mountainsides, though one group, called *yunwi amaiyinehi,* lives in water (they are the ones fishing enthusiasts should try to please). When full grown, *yunwi tsunsdi* are only as tall as a man's knee, but they are well formed and handsome, with long hair down to their heels. They love music and spend a lot of time singing and dancing.

They are also powerful workers of wonders. Generally speaking, they are kind and helpful (particularly to children or people lost in the woods) but not always. If you hear their drumming in the distance, don't follow the sound: If disturbed in their homes, Little People will cast a spell that will make you lose your way. Even if you are found, you may spend the rest of your life in a daze. If you find an object, such as a knife or other item in the woods, you must say, "Little People, I want to take this," because if you don't and it belongs to them, they will throw stones at you on your way home.

Like the busy elves in Western lore, they will sometimes come near a human house at night and, before morning, finish a great task like clearing a field that would require the efforts of a huge workforce. However, if you hear them at work, don't go out to see them, or you'll die.

Many little footprints were seen, and a number of encounters with these little folk were described in accounts by both Indians and whites (mainly hunters) at the end of the 19th century. Some of these took place near or at the head of the Oconaluftee River, which flows through the present-day Cherokee Indian Reservation. There is also a certain spot in what is now the Great Smoky Mountains National Park where *yunsi tsunsdi* came to the Cherokee during summer solstices to tell them, among other things, tales of the Cherokee nation's history.

One day, the Little People were near Brasstown, doing their favorite things—singing and dancing—when a foreign "messenger" arrived and told them the sad tale of Christ's death on a cross. They were so moved, they cried. As their tears fell, they turned into little stone crosses that can still be found today. A wonderful collection of these Fairy Crosses can be seen in Murphy's Cherokee County Historical Museum (which is described in this chapter).

a working Pioneer Village and a collection of railroad memorabilia. The museum is open from 10 a.m. to 4 p.m. Tues through Fri, May through Oct. There is an admission charge.

### Jackson County

**MOUNTAIN HERITAGE CENTER**
Western Carolina University,
Administration Building
U.S. Hwy. 107, Cullowhee
(828) 227-7211
www.wcu.edu

If you're of Scotch-Irish ancestry, this museum is a must! Even if you're not, it's a very special place for learning about the land, culture, and people of the Appalachian region. A large permanent exhibit, "Migration of the Scotch-Irish People," relates the saga of this group's departure from their native Scotland to settle in Northern Ireland, and in a later generation, its journey from Ulster to the New World. It also highlights the homes and culture that developed here in the coves and hollows of Western North Carolina. Murals and a life-size, 18th-century Irish cottage make the story come alive. Other exhibits illustrate the mountains' natural history and society, both past and present.

This section also preserves objects of historical significance, including the heirlooms of hundreds of families who lived here. There are exhibits on cornshuck handcrafts and the traditions of milling, tilling, and stilling corn. A good place to start your tour is in the museum movie theater, where nine-projector, multi-image shows complement the thematic exhibits. The center also publishes books and other materials on mountain culture. All these—the exhibits, the shows, and the literature—are based on thorough and extensive research.

The Mountain Heritage Center is also the focus for Mountain Heritage Day, held in Sept, which attracts more than 35,000 visitors (see our Annual Festivals and Events chapter). There is no admission charge.

### Macon County
**MACON COUNTY HISTORICAL SOCIETY MUSEUM**
**36 West Main St., Franklin**
**(828) 524-9758**
**www.maconhistorical.org**
This museum, supported by the Macon County Historical Society, preserves the area's heritage through displays of artifacts, documents, and photographs that illustrate the social, cultural, and historical background of the county.

**SCOTTISH TARTANS MUSEUM AND HERITAGE CENTER**
**86 East Main St., Franklin**
**(828) 524-7472**
**www.scottishtartans.org**
If you can't get to Scotland this year, this museum, recognized and authorized by the Scottish Tartans Society (the official registry of all publicly known tartans), is the next best thing. Opened in 1994, the 3,200-square-foot facility includes exhibits of tartan and Highland dress from 1700 to the present and shows the evolution of the kilt and the weaving of tartan. It also traces the

influence of the Scots and other settlers on Appalachian and Cherokee culture and the history of North Carolina. Those of Scottish ancestry can investigate the tartan research library and find their family's tartan in the Tartan Room. There is also a great gift shop full of Celtic and Scottish treasures. All tartan items are imported from Scotland and come in 100 percent new wool. You'll also find scarves, shawls, sashes, tams, men's ties, caps, and children's items. Immediate delivery can be had on books, music, clan videos, jewelry, Highland dress items, dirks, skean dubbs, and Scottish weaponry. The museum is open year-round from 10 a.m. to 5 p.m. Mon through Sat. Admission is $2 for adults and $1 for children.

# MUSIC

## Northern Mountains
### Ashe County
**ASHE COUNTY CHORAL SOCIETY**
**First Baptist Church, West Jefferson**
**(336) 246-ARTS**
This group of community singers works each year to stage both a holiday and a spring concert. The holiday concert in Dec features religious and secular music, while the spring concert consists of a blend of contemporary pops and religious music.

### Watauga County
**MUSIC IN THE MOUNTAINS WITH JOE SHANNON**
**Various venues, Boone**
**(828) 264-8118**
**www.mountainhomemusic.com**
This lively concert series is also a weekly television show taped every Fri evening at 8 p.m. in Boone. Remarkably entertaining, it's part traditional mountain shindig, part Appalachian cultural history lesson.

Every week a musical guest takes the stage, setting the tone for the evening's entertainment. Guests have provided gospel, bluegrass, banjo, fiddle, old-time string band music, and even songs of the Civil War, accompanied by traditional instruments. The program is highlighted by a one-on-one interview with one of the "old masters" of our Appalachian musical and cultural heritage. The shows are taped and aired on local Boone radio.

In the summer the concert series takes place at various venues. During the fall all shows take place at the Blowing Rock Arts Center on Sunset Drive.

### SCHOOL OF MUSIC FACULTY
### RECITAL SERIES
**Appalachian State University, Boone**
**(828) 262-4046, (800) 841-ARTS**
**www.appstate.edu**
The Appalachian State University School of Music Faculty Recital Series is an eagerly anticipated series of concert events in the High Country. These performances are scheduled monthly during the academic year and are also open to the public.

## Central Mountains
### *Buncombe County*
### ASHEVILLE BRAVO CONCERTS
**(828) 252-6777**
**www.ashevillebravoconcerts.org**
This venerable cultural arts membership organization is responsible for bringing the finest in national and international ballet, jazz, choral groups, and classical orchestral music to Asheville. The Diana Wortham Theatre in Pack Place is the location for all performances. Season membership as well as individual tickets are available.

### ASHEVILLE CHAMBER MUSIC SERIES
**Unitarian Universalist Church**
**1 Edwin Place, Asheville**
**(828) 253-2579**
This organization sponsors five concerts a year featuring nationally renowned artists of chamber music. The concerts are presented in the Unitarian Universalist Church, 1 Edwin Place, off Charlotte Street in north Asheville. Season or individual tickets are available. Students are admitted free.

### ASHEVILLE CHORAL SOCIETY
**Beverly Hills Baptist Church**
**777 Tunnel Rd., Asheville**
**(828) 299-9063**
**www.ashevillechoralsociety.org**
Founded in 1977, the Asheville Choral Society has a membership of about 60 to 85 amateur and professional singers. The group performs concerts that include classical and contemporary masterpieces of choral literature. The Asheville Choral Society has appeared with both the Asheville Symphony and the North Carolina Symphony Orchestras.

### ASHEVILLE LYRIC OPERA
**Pack Place, Asheville**
**(828) 236-0670**
**www.ashevillelyric.org**
David Craig Starkey brought his talents from New York and the Metropolitan Opera Company to Asheville, as founder and general and artistic director of the Asheville Lyric Opera. World-class artists, brought from the fine opera houses of New York, Vienna, and from across the United States, grace the Asheville stage. Together with local talent, they've brought the stage of the Diana Wortham Theatre at Pack Place alive with the fun of Gilbert and Sullivan's *The Pirates of Penzance*, the tragedy of *I Pagliacci* and *Madama Butterfly*, and the poignancy of *La Bohème* and *Amahl and the Night Visitors*.

### THE ASHEVILLE SYMPHONY ORCHESTRA
**Asheville Civic Center, Asheville**
**(828) 254-7046**
**www.ashevillesymphony.org**
The distinguished Asheville Symphony Orchestra is led by maestro Daniel Meyer, the city's first Gen-X conductor. This community orchestra consistently provides exceptional concerts and continues to set new challenges for itself each season. The popular Masterworks Series, composed of six concerts, features distinguished, internationally known guest artists. In addition the orchestra performs its annual Children's Concert in Oct, a holiday pops concert in Dec, and a spring pops concert in May.

## Henderson County
**BLUE RIDGE COMMUNITY COLLEGE CONCERTS**
**Blue Ridge College, College Drive, Flat Rock**
**(828) 692-3572, ext. 306**
**www.brcc.edu**
On Mon nights in a season stretching from Sept to Apr, the college's Division of Community Services sponsors eight classical music concerts in the 150-seat auditorium of the Patton Building. Many of the performers have national reputations, and about half the concerts feature outstanding students from the North Carolina School of the Arts in Winston-Salem. One concert is reserved to display the talents of a local professional. In addition around three times a year, special benefit performances are given to help support the college's music department. Call for ticket prices.

**THE HENDERSONVILLE CHORALE**
**(828) 692-3211**
**www.hendersonvillechorale.com**
This group was founded in 1974 and was incorporated as a nonprofit organization in 1979. Ever since, it has enriched the lives of the residents here, both singers and listeners, by presenting two concerts a year of quality chorale literature of all historical periods. Eighty-five to 100 voices strong, these volunteers (it's a nonaudition group; no one is turned away) perform in Dec and May at the acoustically fine First Baptist Church. Call for ticket prices.

**HENDERSONVILLE SYMPHONY ORCHESTRA**
**538 North Main St., Hendersonville**
**(828) 697-5884**
**www.hendersonvillesymphony.org**
Talented guest artists from around the nation are delighted to perform with this jewel of an orchestra. Totally community supported, it's made up of 60 to 70 music professionals, talented retirees, and students and is conducted by Dr. Thomas Joiner. This results in six vibrant concerts a year of a quality normally found in large cities. The group also gives pops and children's concerts and an occasional special benefit. Since 1978 it has been the mentor to a string of educational programs in the Henderson County Public Schools. The symphony supports a coaching program for youth ensembles, adult ensembles, a full youth orchestra, a young artist competition, and a one-week summer string camp.

## Polk County
**TRYON COMMUNITY CHORUS**
**P.O. Box 54, Tryon**
**(828) 259-6092**
The Tryon Community Chorus is an all-volunteer group of people from the foothills. Two concerts are given each year: one during the Christmas season and another in the spring. Participation is open to all singers. Rehearsals are held on Mon at Tryon Congregational Church, beginning approximately 10 weeks prior to performances. These are presented in the Polk County High School auditorium on a Fri night and Sun afternoon. Proceeds from the concerts go toward scholarships sponsored by the Tryon Rotary Club.

**TRYON CONCERT ASSOCIATION**
**Tryon Fine Arts Center**
**34 Melrose Ave., Tryon**
**(828) 859-8322, (828) 859-9050**
This association sponsors a series of quality musical programs featuring artists of note from Oct through May at the Tryon Fine Arts Center. Membership is by subscription and open to anyone who enjoys a wide variety of musical presentations. Volunteers manage all aspects of the concerts.

## Transylvania County
**BREVARD CHAMBER ORCHESTRA**
**P.O. Box 1547, Brevard**
**(828) 884-2823**
**www.tryonarts.org**
Established in 1978, this 55-piece orchestra of paid professionals from the Carolinas and Georgia has been conducted since 1980 by Virginia Tillotson, head of the Music Department at Brevard College. The five-concert season has performances scheduled in Sept, Nov, Dec, Feb,

and Apr. Two programs feature the full orchestra, while two showcase smaller, more intimate ensembles. Each concert highlights critically acclaimed guest artists. The fifth concert is a festive Christmas program featuring the orchestra and the choirs of Brevard. A benefit concert, always something special in the way of guest artists and themes, is held once a year, usually in March. The BCO is Orchestra in Residence at the Paul Porter Center for Performing Arts at Brevard College. Season tickets are available. Individual tickets for specific concerts are available in advance only at the Porter Center box office. That number is (828) 884-8330.

## BREVARD COLLEGE
### 400 North Broad St., Brevard
### (828) 883-8292
### www.brevardcc.edu

Long known for its outstanding music curriculum, the college schedules a number of cultural events throughout the school year. These have been greatly enhanced by the Paul Porter Center for Performing Arts. The public is invited to enjoy recitals, musicals, choral groups, and instrumental ensembles as well as dance and drama that involve students and teachers.

Through its Life and Culture Program, Brevard also sponsors lectures, concerts, and writers and poetry series and has sponsored musical performances by such renowned groups as the Russian Folk Ensemble, the Audubon String Quartet, the Dutch vocal ensemble Quince, the National Opera, and the Preservation Hall Jazz Band.

## BREVARD MUSIC CENTER
### 349 Andante Lane, Brevard
### (828) 884-2011, (888) 384-8682
### www.brevardmusic.org

Held on 140 beautiful acres just on the outskirts of town, the Brevard Music Festival had its beginning in 1936. Today it presents more than 70 different concert events from mid-June through mid-Aug in the center's 1,800-seat, open-sided auditorium. Lawn tickets are available after all house seats have been sold. Performances include symphony orchestra, opera, jazz, Broadway musicals, pops, and those of internationally acclaimed guest artists. Included in the past seasons' appearances were Kathleen Battle of the Met, composer/entertainer Marvin Hamlisch, harpist Deborah Henson-Conant, pianist Garrick Ohlsson, Rhythm & Brass, the U.S. Army Orchestra, and staged productions of Gilbert and Sullivan's *The Mikado*, Puccini's *La Bohème*, Massenet's *Manon*, and Herbert's *Naughty Marietta*.

More than half of the events are free to the public. Among these have been *Peter and the Wolf* and *Beauty and the Beast*, special young persons' concerts, free for kids on Sat. Bach's Lunch and BYOP (bring your own picnic) are lunchtime favorites. Have lunch with the students as they perform delightful music.

## TRANSYLVANIA CHORAL SOCIETY
### Brevard
### (828) 884-2645

This is a nonauditioned group of about 45 singers. Formed by Ruth Hunter about 20 years ago to offer church choir members in the community a forum for singing major sacred works, it's now open to anyone who loves to sing. It meets at Brevard-Davidson River Presbyterian Church weekly except during the summer. Concerts of classical choral music are offered twice a year, in the spring and at Christmas. The concerts are usually at the Presbyterian Church.

# Southern Mountains
## *Cherokee/Clay Counties*
### THE BRASSTOWN CONCERT ASSOCIATION
### P.O. Box 105, Brasstown
### (828) 837-8822
### www.mapaa.org/html/bca.html

Since 1927 this association has brought artists from the outside world to what, until a few decades ago, was a beautiful but remote area of the mountains. Today it presents six concerts, three in the spring and three in the fall, that vary from flute to harp to string quartets to brass quintets to fabulous performers of ethnic music from around the world. These concerts, which take place at 3 p.m. on Sun afternoons, can be enjoyed at the John C. Campbell Folk School. (See our chapter on Mountain Crafts.)

### JOHN C. CAMPBELL FOLK SCHOOL CONCERTS
1 Folk School Rd., Brasstown
(828) 837-2775, (800) FOLK-SCH
www.folkschool.org

Free Folk School Concerts are held most Fridays at 7:30 p.m. at the school's historic Keith House Community Room on Brasstown Road. During late spring and summer, weather permitting, the event moves to the Festival Barn. (Bring a lawn chair and follow the signs from the Keith House parking area.) These concerts range from traditional gospel and bluegrass to music for handbells to western song and cowboy poetry.

## Macon County

### HIGHLANDS CHAMBER MUSIC FESTIVAL
P.O. Box 1702, Highlands
(828) 526-9060
www.h-cmusicfestival.org

Since 1981 the Highlands Chamber Music Festival has presented a stunning month-long series of chamber music. The July-Aug season features about 15 concerts held at the Episcopal Church of the Incarnation and the Highlands United Methodist Church. Visit the Web site for current information on performers and ticket prices.

# THEATER

## Northern Mountains

## Ashe County

### ASHE COUNTY LITTLE THEATER
Various venues, West Jefferson
(336) 246-ARTS
www.ashecivic.com

Ashe County is well represented by this amateur theatrical group, which features local actors of all ages in an energetic annual program of popular Broadway productions. Past productions have included *Oliver!*, *The King and I*, and *The Sound of Music*.

## Avery County

### LEES-MCRAE COLLEGE
191 Main Street, Hwy. 194, Banner Elk
(828) 898-5241
www.lmc.edu

Mile-high Banner Elk is the lovely location for this dynamic little college (see our Education chapter). The college is innovative both academically and culturally and promotes a yearlong calendar of cultural arts events that is amazingly diverse for a school its size. The Lees-McRae College Summer Theater, established as a semiprofessional theater in 1984, is one of the foremost theatrical attractions in the High Country.

Past productions have included *Fiddler on the Roof*, *Man of La Mancha*, and *Guys and Dolls*. The Performing Arts Series, sponsored by the college's Performing Arts Department, offers consistently interesting dramatic productions, one-act plays, traditional mountain dance performances (clogging), and other concerts throughout the academic year. All are open to the public.

## Watauga County

### APPALACHIAN STATE UNIVERSITY
287 Rivers St., Boone
(800) 841-ARTS
www.pas.appstate.edu

Boone's community-minded university offers a series of cultural events throughout the year. The Department of Theater and Dance at ASU presents a wide array of one-act plays, full dramatic productions, and dance performances, all of which are open to the public. The ASU Forum Series is the university's formal lecture series that has featured national speakers addressing topics of national and international importance.

During the summer the community is treated to An Appalachian Summer Festival, offering the best in music, dance, theater, visual arts, and symposia. The Performing Arts Series also brings national and international performers to the campus. These events are also open to the public. (See the Music section in this chapter for information on recitals and concerts; see also our Education chapter.)

## BLOWING ROCK STAGE COMPANY
**Blowing Rock Arts Center**
**Sunset Drive, Blowing Rock**
**(828) 295-9627**
**www.blowingrockstage.com**
The Blowing Rock Stage Company is the High Country's resident professional theater, drawing the services of professional Actor's Equity players every summer. The artistic home of the theater company is the Blowing Rock Arts Center, adjacent to Blowing Rock Elementary School. Local and summer residents of the High Country, as well as scores of tourists, fill every performance of this fine theatrical company mid-June through mid-Aug.

## BLUE RIDGE COMMUNITY THEATER
**Various venues, Boone**
**(828) 297-3155**
**www.blueridgecommunitytheater.com**
For over 30 years Blue Ridge Community Theater (BRCT) has brought the best in amateur theatrical production to the High Country. The 200 local actors who regularly participate in BRCT stage two yearly productions: a fall drama and a spring musical.

### *Yancey County*
## PARKWAY PLAYHOUSE
**202 Green Mountain Dr., Burnsville**
**(828) 682-4285**
**www.parkwayplayhouse.com**
The Parkway Playhouse opened its doors in 1947 as the Burnsville Playhouse. Eventually it was housed in a former school gymnasium, which was moved up the South Toe River to its present location. As the oldest continuously producing summer stock theater in North Carolina, The Parkway Playhouse is a "teaching theater" that utilizes a small corps of professional actors, pre-professional college students, as well as people from the WNC community who have a passion for theater. Performances begin in June and end in Sept, with a typical variety of three musicals and two to three plays per year. It also includes a Youth Theater Institute. Collaborative relationships have been established with Mayland Com-

munity College, the Toe River Arts Council, and the Southern Appalachian Repertory Theatre.

## Central Mountains
### *Buncombe County*
## ASHEVILLE COMMUNITY THEATRE
**35 Walnut St., Asheville**
**(828) 254-1320**
**www.ashevilletheatre.org**
This award-winning theater is ranked one of the best in the Southeast, consistently providing the Asheville area with the best in live theater since its inception in 1946. This long tradition of excellence has a colorful heritage that includes an association with the late motion picture actor Charlton Heston. Heston was codirector of ACT in the 1947 season, making it his springboard to stardom the following year when he returned to New York.

The Asheville Community Theatre produces a six-show season that includes the best of Broadway musicals, comedies, and classics. An edgier program of plays is held at the blackbox theater within ACT, called 35 Below. During intermission visitors can enjoy rotating exhibitions in the lobby gallery space.

## MONTFORD PARK PLAYERS
**Montford Park Recreational Facility**
**Montford Avenue and Pearson Drive, Asheville**
**(828) 254-5146**
**www.montfordparkplayers.org**
This legendary Asheville theater company grew out of one woman's fascination with the English Bard. Founder Hazel Robinson created the Montford Park Players on a financial shoestring back in 1973, bringing the works of Shakespeare to the public. The plays in those days were performed in the natural, grassy amphitheater of old Montford Park, with costumes and props scavenged by Ms. Robinson and her loyal thespian followers. As the Great Man said, "The play's the thing." And so it was.

The performances are free, but in the true tradition of early Shakespearean troupes, a hat is passed at intermission. You can find the Montford Park Players at the outdoor amphitheater of Montford Recreation Center, 1 block off Montford Avenue at the intersection of Montford Avenue and Pearson Drive.

A highlight of the Christmas season is the Montford Park Players' production of *A Christmas Carol*. This energetic production has been performed at the auditorium of Asheville High School and also at Diana Wortham Theatre at Pack Place.

### NORTH CAROLINA STAGE COMPANY
**15 Stage Lane, Asheville**
**(828) 350-9090**
**www.ncstage.com**

One of the most energetic and interesting professional theater companies to set up shop in the mountains, NC Stage Company consistently pushes the envelope with bold directing and contemporary pieces by both national and local playwrights. The intimate blackbox theater also adjoins an art gallery/reception hall.

## Henderson County

**FLAT ROCK PLAYHOUSE, THE STATE THEATRE OF NORTH CAROLINA**
**2661 Greenville Hwy., Flat Rock**
**(828) 693-0731**
**www.flatrockplayhouse.com**

Flat Rock Playhouse, the State Theatre of North Carolina, is a professional theater operating under a contract with the Actors' Equity Association, the national union of professional actors and stage managers. Founded in 1937, the playhouse entertains more than 65,000 guests each season. Eight productions are offered between late May and mid-Oct annually. A variety of comedies, musicals, and dramas, which range from world premieres to the latest from Broadway and London to the classics, compose the summer/fall series.

The Playhouse's dual mission of producing and providing education in the performing arts includes a ten-show professional series; a summer and fall college apprentice and intern program; performances and cabaret series by the YouTheatre; year-round classes and workshops for students from kindergarten through adults.

### HENDERSONVILLE LITTLE THEATRE
**The Barn on State Street**
**1025 State St. Hendersonville**
**(828) 692-1082**
**www.hendersonvillelittletheatre.org**

This all-volunteer group of players has entertained the town since 1966, putting on four shows in a refurbished barn from Sept to May. These shows usually include a couple of comedies, a mystery, and sometimes a serious drama. There are more than 400 members in this organization, and a large number of them actively work on each production.

## Polk County

**TRYON LITTLE THEATER**
**Tryon Fine Arts Center**
**516 S. Trade St., (performances at 34 Melrose Ave.), Tryon**
**(828) 859-2466, (828) 859-3545 (info. line)**
**www.tltinfo.org**

Since 1969 this organization has produced more than 100 plays and musicals. The nearly 800 members create six productions a year at the Tryon Fine Arts Center, including at least one musical each season. There are more than 150 individuals participating in some facet of every production. Tryon Little Theater also holds acting workshops and play-reading groups. It has sponsored various theatrical events, premiered original productions, and won a North Carolina Theater Award.

## Transylvania County

**BREVARD LITTLE THEATRE**
**P.O. Box 544, Brevard**
**(828) 884-2587**
**www.brevardlittletheatre.org**

This theatrical group is the official theater company of the city and county. It's also the Resident Community Theater Company at Brevard College. The Barn Theater, overlooking scenic King's Creek on the Brevard College campus, was renovated and refurbished for the 1999 season.

The group produces four plays for a season that runs from Oct through Aug. It also puts on children's plays, including the very popular *The Nutcracker* in Dec. In addition, there's a very active "BLT to Go" group that provides benefit performances for community and charitable organizations.

Certain productions are also staged at the larger Dunham Auditorium on the college campus.

## Southern Mountains
### Cherokee County
**THE VALLEYTOWN ARTS CENTER**
**Third and Chestnut Streets, Andrews**
**(828) 321-3453**
**www.andrewsvalley.com**
This center, originally the First Baptist Church, has been renovated with the purpose of providing a facility for the community to stage performing and visual arts. It houses both the Community Youth Players, an ensemble of young local talent that has been active since 1986 and that performs a Christmas play in early Dec and another performance in the spring, and the Andrews Community Theater, which offers plays throughout the year. Concerts and other events are also staged here. Call for information.

### Clay County
**LICKLOG PLAYERS**
**301 Church St., Peacock Playhouse,**
**Hayesville**
**(828) 389-8632**
**www.licklogplayers.org**
This volunteer organization was started as a small community theater in 1977. In searching for a name that reflected this area, the founders thought of the Davis family, early settlers who felled trees and cut notches in the logs to hold salt for their cattle. This area became known as Licklog, and so the name was adopted.

Today, Licklog Players has grown into a regional theatrical group with talent drawn from several surrounding states. It's housed in the 250-seat, air-conditioned Peacock Playhouse with state-of-the-art facilities. The players offer productions year-round, including comedies, farces, mysteries, dramas, musicals, and children's performances.

### Haywood County
**HAYWOOD ARTS REPERTORY THEATRE**
**250 Pigeon St., U.S. Hwy. 276 South,**
**Waynesville**
**(828) 456-6322**
**www.harttheatre.com**
HART is the region's most active theater company, producing seven main stage productions each year and up to six "studio" shows, including major musicals, classics, and new plays. In recent years the theater has hosted a production direct from off-Broadway, sent a production to New York, and staged a new play in its studio that won honors at the John F. Kennedy Center. The Performing Arts Center, where HART is at home in a summer stock barn-style facility, sits in the middle of an eight-acre National Historic Site shared with the Museum of North Carolina Handicrafts. It includes a 250-seat auditorium, a visual arts gallery, and a 75-seat studio theater.

### Jackson County
**KUDZU PLAYERS**
**P.O. Box 834, Sylva**
**(828) 586-8133**
The Kudzu Players, a community theater group of around 50 people, offers popular plays on a regular basis in the former courtroom of the historic Old Jackson County Courthouse and alternately at Western Carolina University. Call for information and ticket prices.

### Macon County
**HIGHLANDS PLAYHOUSE**
**362 Oak St., Highlands**
**(828) 526-2695 (tickets), (828) 526-9443 (information)**
**www.highlandsplayhouse.org**
This community theater has been operating since 1938. The playhouse stages four productions in a season that runs from June into Aug. It combines professional talent with outside equity guest stars.

## Swain County

**SMOKY MOUNTAIN COMMUNITY THEATRE**
**30 Main St., Bryson City**
**(828) 488-3030**
**www.smctheatre.com**
The Smoky Mountain Community Theater presents four plays a year in an old movie theater on Main Street. The group itself refurbished the more-than-50-year-old structure, installing a sophisticated lighting system, building dressing rooms, and more than doubling the size of the stage. Members are undaunted by large-scale productions.

# DANCE

## Central Mountains

### Buncombe County

**ASHEVILLE BALLET/ FLETCHER SCHOOL OF DANCE**
**4 Weaverville Rd., Asheville**
**(828) 252-4761**
**www.ashevilleballet.com**
This distinguished school of dance, started more than 50 years ago by the late Beale Fletcher, is an institution in Asheville. The school's performing arm, the Asheville Ballet, annually produces a polished, well-received version of *The Nutcracker* for holiday audiences and regularly trains dancers who enter major troupes around the country.

**ASHEVILLE CONTEMPORARY DANCE THEATRE AND THE NEW STUDIO OF DANCE**
**20 Commerce St., Asheville**
**(828) 254-2621**
**www.acdt.org**
This fascinating, experimental dance/theater company presents lavishly produced original works adapted from ancient legends of different world cultures—particularly the richly imaginative Aztec and Mayan legends, such as the story of the feathered serpent Quetzalcoatl. Meticulous research, typically taking as long as eight months, incorporates experimental movement, puppets, sword play, mime, traditional music, and interpretive costuming (including some interesting ones of sculpted foam) for each production. The

6- to 15-member company has performed across the Southeast, in France, and in Cuba, and offers artistic exchanges with international dance theater companies.

**TERPSICORPS**
**Diana Wortham Theatre, Pack Place, Asheville**
**(828) 252-6342**
**www.terpsicorps.com**
Still one of Asheville's newer dance companies, Terpsicorps brings in professional dancers from various troupes around the country to perform at Diana Wortham Theatre in modern dance pieces choreographed by the young founder of this troupe. Often the works are narrative in nature, in addition to minimalist modern dance.

### Polk County

**TRYON DANCE GUILD**
**P.O. Box 638, Columbus**
**(828) 894-3051**
Twice a year, in the spring and fall, this guild, under the auspices of the Polk County Community Schools, presents performances by renowned national dance groups. Shows are held in the 700-seat Polk County High School Auditorium. Free performances are presented to students throughout the county.

# LITERARY ARTS

Many bookstores in all the mountain areas offer a fine schedule of literary readings. Poets and authors from all parts enjoy a turn in the mountains and read from their best-sellers, offering a question-and-answer session afterward. Check local listings in the *Mountain Xpress*, daily papers, and free weekly entertainment papers.

## Central Mountains

### Buncombe County

**POETRY ALIVE!**
**20 Battery Park Ave., Asheville**
**(828) 255-7636, (800) 476-8172**
**www.poetryalive.com**
Interaction is the life's blood of this arts organization, which was formed back in 1984 with

the express purpose of popularizing poetry and making it more accessible to the general public, children in particular. The prime focus of Poetry Alive! is making poetry, education, and fun synonymous, a feat accomplished over and over again by this innovative organization.

About five to nine teams of poets/performers travel the nation, bringing the richly illustrative world of poetry to all who will listen and watch. Transfixed audiences from kindergartners to college students watch as the words leap off the page, and all manner of poetry—epic poems, sonnets, classics from world culture, doggerel, and humor—come to life before their eyes.

### THE WRITERS' WORKSHOP
**387 Beaucatcher Rd., Asheville**
**(828) 254-8111**
**www.twwoa.com**
This busy organization is geared to writers—amateurs, professionals, and youthful budding scribes—of all ages. For over two decades this membership group has been dedicated to the promotion of all things literary.

The Writers' Workshop offers support, evaluation, competition, and valuable workshops designed to enhance the spark of inspiration and help it grow. A quarterly newsletter and regular literary competitions are yearly highlights. Nationally known professional writers are judges for these contests and participate in an annual professional writers' forum in Asheville, sponsored by the Writers' Workshop. This special series is open to the public. Past participants have included such literary greats as Eudora Welty, Alex Haley, John Le Carre, E. L. Doctorow, Kurt Vonnegut, and Peter Matthiessen.

### Transylvania County
**TRANSYLVANIA WRITERS' ALLIANCE**
**c/o Sandy Jones**
**150 W. Southwood Dr., Brevard**
**(828) 884-44429**
Both professional and amateur writers meet to share and critique their works and hear tips from successful authors. In addition to monthly meet-

ings, there are weekly critique sessions. These sessions, for both poetry and prose, are held on separate days. There are also occasional workshops with professional leaders.

## ART ORGANIZATIONS

### Northern Mountains

### Alleghany County
**ALLEGHANY COUNTY ARTS COUNCIL**
**Grayson and Cherry Streets, Sparta**
**(336) 372-2578**
The Alleghany County Arts Council, housed in a charming historic house in Crouse Park in downtown Sparta, is a young organization that sponsors local artists in yearly exhibits held in the local public library. The council also puts on the annual Blue Ridge Mountain Craft Fair on the last Sat in June at the Justin Higgins Agricultural Center and Fairgrounds on U.S. Highway 21 in Sparta. (See our Annual Festivals and Events chapter for information about county fairs.)

### Ashe County
**ASHE COUNTY ARTS COUNCIL**
**303 School Ave., West Jefferson**
**(336) 246-2787**
**www.ashecountyarts.org**
This organization is headquartered in a lovely old stone building known as the Ashe Arts Center. This structure, constructed as a community center during the Great Depression, was a Works Progress Administration project. The Ashe County Arts Council is an active organization that sponsors 32 in-school arts programs, numerous arts residencies in the school system, and eight community concerts. The group also sponsors continuously changing exhibits of the work of local artists in its Ashe Arts Center gallery.

### Avery County
**AVERY COUNTY ARTS COUNCIL**
**P.O. Box 2505, Banner Elk**
**(828) 898-8755**
**www.averyartscouncil.org**
The Avery County Arts Council coordinates myriad cultural activities for county residents. The

group sponsors numerous arts festivals during the year, such as a Christmas Craft Show and the Very Special Arts Festival in the spring. It also creates opportunities for arts through education and programming.

## Watauga County

**WATAUGA COUNTY ARTS COUNCIL**
**604 West King St., Boone**
**(828) 264-1789**
**www.wataugaart.org**
This county arts council is housed in the Jones Community Center in downtown Boone, a building that's also home to two art exhibition galleries. The council is a vital part of the community, sponsoring a number of events during the year and promoting education in the arts with fund raising for the support of art scholarships. The council office is open Wed through Sat.

## Yancey County

**TOE RIVER ARTS COUNCIL**
**Town Square, Burnsville**
**(828) 682-7215**
**www.toeriverarts.org**
This incredibly busy arts council serves two counties (Yancey and neighboring Mitchell) with an inordinate number of artists and craftspeople—in part due to the presence of the revered Penland School of Crafts in Mitchell County (see our entry in this chapter and our Mountain Crafts chapter).

Services provided by the Toe River Arts Council include a winter arts program and a symphony program. The group also sponsors art and music festivals each summer, along with summer art workshops. The group has developed a map outlining the location of the numerous studios of Yancey County artists and craftspeople and a free directory listing all the cultural offerings in the two-county area served by the council.

## Central Mountains

## Buncombe County

**ASHEVILLE AREA ARTS COUNCIL**
**11 Biltmore Ave., Asheville**
**(828) 258-0710**
**www.ashevillearts.com**

This nonprofit organization has been dedicated to the support and perpetuation of the cultural arts in the Asheville/Buncombe County area for more than 50 years. The group provides technical support, management assistance, and allocation of grants and other funding to emerging artists and area cultural activities and organizations. The Arts in Education program brings art into the schools. The arts council works closely with the community in an effort to identify these needs. Regular exhibitions are displayed in the gallery space, and an annual ball raises funds for the arts. The Front Gallery features work by local artists.

**SOUTHERN HIGHLAND CRAFT GUILD**
**Mile 382, Blue Ridge Parkway**
**Off U.S. Hwy. 70 East, Asheville**
**(828) 298-7928**
**www.southernhighlandguild.com**
The Southern Highland Craft Guild was founded in 1930 as an educational, nonprofit organization to provide economic support for the many talented craftspeople in the Southern Appalachian region. Today the guild is composed of more than 700 members in a nine-state Southeast region. Members submit applications and are selected by a board, based on the merit of their work. The Allanstand Craft Shop in the Folk Art Center (milepost 382), east of Asheville, and the gift gallery of the Moses H. Cone Memorial and Visitors Center (828-295-7938; milepost 293) near Blowing Rock in Watauga County, serve as retail outlets for members' works.

(See our Blue Ridge Parkway and Attractions chapters for more about the Folk Art Center and the Moses H. Cone Memorial.)

## Henderson County

**THE ARTS CENTER OF HENDERSON COUNTY, INC.**
**538 North Main St., Hendersonville**
**(828) 693-8504**
**www.acofhc.org**
This center offers openings of art collections and juried competitions. One such opening featured a gala evening with a jazz band in support of the Outside/Folk Art Exhibition—The Blackwell

Collection. A silent auction was held in conjunction. Another event was the juried competition entitled "The Human Figure." An educational program is offered as well.

## THE HENDERSON COUNTY ART LEAGUE
**Opportunity House**
**1411 Asheville Hwy., Hendersonville**
**(828) 692-0575**
**www.artleague.net**
The Art League was established in 1958 and is a tax-exempt, not-for-profit corporation. Its purpose is the promotion, development, and enjoyment of the visual arts. Currently over 220 members represent all levels of artistic achievement from professional to beginner. The league meets at the Opportunity House on the third Wed of each month at 1:45 p.m. Each month it offers a new exhibit of its members' work and a demonstration of techniques or methods by qualified artists. On the first Sun of each month, the league holds a reception and exhibit for a guest artist. All of these events are open to the public. The Sidewalk Art Show has been held on Main Street in downtown Hendersonville for over 40 years.

## HENDERSON COUNTY ARTS COUNCIL, INC.
**401 North Main St., Hendersonville**
**(828) 697-9278**
**www.hendersonarts.org**
Henderson County Arts Council, a superactive organization, sponsors special art events throughout the year, including the spring Jubilee Arts Festival and a performance of Folkmoot, the International Dance Festival. In cooperation with the North Carolina Museum of Art, the council promotes art education through its Art Appreciation School Slide Program in Henderson County schools. It's also responsible for the Mountain Arts Program, the Regional Arts Project Grant Program, and the distribution of public and grant monies for the arts in the county.

## WESTERN NORTH CAROLINA QUILTERS GUILD
**P.O. Box 3121, Hendersonville, NC 28793**
**www.westernncquilters.org**
This guild was founded in 1982 to promote the art of quilting and provide an opportunity for area quilters to get together—a modern-day version of the old "quilting bee." Meetings are held on the third Thurs of each month at the Trinity Presbyterian Church, 900 Blythe St. The guild features lectures, workshops, and quilt shows. An extensive lending library filled with current books, patterns, magazines, and videos is available to all members, who also receive an informative newsletter called *Grainlines*.

## Polk County
### CAROLINA CAMERA CLUB
**Tryon Fine Arts Center**
**34 Melrose Ave., Tryon**
**(828) 859-8322**
Photography buffs in this group get to share their mutual interests and improve their skills at monthly meetings and through other programs. The club is affiliated with the Photographic Society of America and is one of more than 30 camera clubs in six states that form the Southeastern Council of Camera Clubs. A monthly newsletter is available, and there is an annual contest for members' photographs. Award-winning images are exhibited in the Tryon Fine Arts Center lobby in Jan and Feb. Anyone interested in photography may become a member, and visitors are always welcome.

## TRYON FINE ARTS CENTER
**34 Melrose Ave., Tryon**
**(828) 859-8322**
**www.tryonarts.org**
A nonprofit organization, Tryon Crafts, located in the Tryon Fine Arts Center, sponsors classes that include weaving, silversmithing, enameling on copper, rug hooking, crewel and needlepoint, macramé, wood carving, knitting, chair caning, stained glass, lampshade making, and oshibana. Tryon Crafts also has a weaving cottage on Tryon Fine Arts Center property called the Cate-Hall Weaving Center. Member shows are held each year at Christmas and in spring, and a shop is open next to the Tryon Crafts office on the lower level of the TFAC building.

The arts center for the town is 100 percent privately funded. Built in 1969, the center contains a 345-seat theater with a hearing-impaired system, an exhibition room called Gallery I, a Mural Room for meetings and receptions, art studios, a crafts room for classes, and an outdoor garden. In addition to all the activities of its affiliates, TFAC offers musical performances by local and professional artists, recounting of personal travel experiences, benefits, lectures, slide shows, Christmas song fests, summer socials, North Carolina Shakespeare Festival performances, jazz bands, contemporary subject seminars, and more.

### TRYON YOUTH CENTER
**Hwy. 176, Tryon**
**(828) 859-5371**
This organization provides social, artistic, recreational, educational, and cultural experiences for the young people of the area. Each year the center puts on a Youth Center Summer Musical in the Tryon Fine Arts Center auditorium, but most of its activities are centered in a 5,300-square-foot building on Highway 176 that's also available for rent by other community organizations and individuals.

### Transylvania County
**PAUL PORTER CENTER FOR PERFORMING ARTS**
**400 North Broad St., Brevard**
**(828) 884-8330**
An elegant and stately structure, the center features the Concert Hall with superb acoustics, the Morrison Theater, and the Institute for Sacred Music. Events range from orchestral, chamber, and folk concerts to theatrical productions, art exhibitions, and seminars. The activities are planned to match this distinctive milieu tastefully and to reflect the rich cultural diversity found in Western North Carolina.

### TRANSYLVANIA COUNTY ARTS COUNCIL
**321 South Caldwell St., Brevard**
**(828) 884-2787**
**www.tcarts.org**

This Community Arts Center in an old church houses the arts council, an exhibition/performance hall (where exhibits change monthly), and an educational wing where classes are held throughout the year.

In its effort to provide inspiration and support to local artists, art groups, and school children, TC Arts oversees 30 art programs and services, including Grassroots Arts and Regional Artist Project grant programs. TC Arts also joins Brevard College in presenting the Performing Arts Series for the community. The council holds a fall and a spring gala fund-raising event each year. The annual Holiday Tour of Homes and Studios is held the second Sat in Dec.

This organization sponsors a summer Festival of the Arts, a weeklong celebration of the visual and performing arts, usually held the second week in July. TC Arts also sponsors a juried show of regional artists from six Western North Carolina counties at the Transylvania Fine Arts and Crafts Exhibition, held at Brevard College's Spiers Gallery in July.

## Southern Mountains
### Haywood County
**HAYWOOD COUNTY ARTS COUNCIL**
**86 North Main St., Waynesville**
**(828) 452-0593**
**www.haywoodarts.org**
Ensconced in a new office on Waynesville's charming Main Street, the HCAC sponsors International Festival Day—a day of dance, music, food, and a juried crafts show—each July in association with Folkmoot, the International Dance Festival. HCAC also is involved in Haywood's own production of *The Nutcracker* and the annual Holiday Tour of Homes.

The council brings the Atlanta Ballet to Waynesville for its two-week annual residency in late summer. In addition to open rehearsals, the ballet holds workshops for area youth.

Gallery 86, the Arts Council's first-floor space, holds thoughtful exhibitions of local and regional artists.

## Jackson County

**JACKSON COUNTY ARTS COUNCIL**
**P.O. Box 755, Cullowhee**
**(828) 293-5458**
Whether it's dance, literature, drama, or the visual arts, this council lends its support to dozens of activities and performances each year, including lectures, concerts, and exhibitions.

**JACKSON COUNTY VISUAL ARTS**
**ASSOCIATION**
**640 W. Main St., Sylva**
**(828) 293-3407**
The approximately 60 member-artists of this group meet monthly and sponsor monthly exhibits (featuring mostly local artists) at Gallery One in Sylva. The association provides art classes for adults and especially for youth and children.

**WESTERN CAROLINA UNIVERSITY FINE AND**
**PERFORMING ARTS CENTER**
**Hwy. 107, Cullowhee**
**(828) 227-7211**
**www.wcu.edu/fapac**
Western Carolina University provides a year-round showcase for artistic performances, featuring WCU students and faculty and entertainers of national renown, particularly with its arts center. The $30 million Fine and Performing Arts Center at Western Carolina University is an exciting cultural arts and art education destination for Western North Carolina and the surrounding region. The university's Lectures, Concerts, and Exhibitions Series brings music, dance, and theatrical productions to campus each year, and the department of communications and theater arts stages its own high-quality plays. The Fine Art Museum includes nearly 10,000 feet of exhibit space, featuring a growing permanent collection, an exciting schedule of contemporary art and fine craft, and related interdisciplinary education programs.

## Macon County

**ARTS COUNCIL OF MACON COUNTY**
**3 East Main St., Franklin**
**(828) 524-7683**
**www.artscouncilofmacon.org**

Macon County's Arts Council, which is dedicated to getting people actively involved in the arts, describes itself as "extremely volunteer driven." Here you'll find ongoing, year-round programs and performances, including concerts, lectures, and other presentations.

**THE ARTS LEAGUE OF HIGHLANDS**
**P.O. Box 2133, Highlands 28741**
**(706) 746-2556**
The Arts League of Highlands, founded in 1980, is a nonprofit association of artists and supporters of visual arts and serves the Western Carolina/ North Georgia mountain areas. The group meets every fourth Wed at the Performing Arts Center. The league, with over 100 members, sponsors several shows a year, supports and helps publicize visual arts in the area, and takes field trips to galleries, art shows, and other places of interest.

**MACON COUNTY ART ASSOCIATION**
**30 East Main St., Franklin**
**(828) 349-4607**
One of the oldest art associations in Franklin (1962) continues to grow and flourish. Members are artists of oil, pastel, watercolor, acrylics, mixed media, and sculpture. These members run the Uptown Gallery for displaying and selling their artwork. Many of these originals depict the surrounding Appalachian Mountains, in addition to genres of all subjects.

## Swain County

**SWAIN COUNTY CENTER FOR THE ARTS**
**1415 Fontana Rd., Bryson City**
**(828) 488-7843**
Because only a small group of people makes up this council, it concentrates its efforts as a funds and grants distributing agency for supporting existing groups instead of sponsoring any special events itself. One exception is its cosponsorship of some of the town's festivals, and its work with the local recreation department on a number of activities. One of the council's main areas of support is a countywide program that brings special teachers of arts, crafts, and music into the schools.

**Close-up**

## Reel to Reel: Films Made in the Mountains

The mountains of North Carolina form a dynamic backdrop for the big screen. While exploring this area, make note of sites for some of the films listed below.

This first listing is of those made at Biltmore Estate. Grace Kelly graced *The Swan* along with Louis Jordan and Alec Guinness. Peter Sellers emulated a gardener rescued by Shirley MacLaine in *Being There*. Tim Conway and Don Knotts survived the mystery of *Private Eyes*. *Forrest Gump's* run across America included the roadways of Biltmore Estate. The little wealthy kid, *Richie Rich*, luxuriated in Biltmore House. Hannibal, in the film "Hannibal" dined in his own inimitable style with Biltmore sharing billing with scenes in Italy. *Patch Adams* was shot on the back 40, at the Princess Anne Hotel in Asheville, and in the mountains of Madison County, while the King's courier in *The Last of the Mohicans* drove an ornate carriage across the brick bridge at the Bass Pond on Biltmore Estate. *Thunder Road,* starring Robert Mitchum, had some scenes at Biltmore and along the rivers and mountains of Western North Carolina. Gracing Biltmore in *Mr. Destiny* were Michael Caine and Sir Laurence Olivier.

Meanwhile, Harrison Ford was escaping his pursuers in *The Fugitive* in Dillsboro and along the Tuckasegee and Oconaluftee Rivers. This featured the expenditure of an engine from the Smoky Mountains Railroad crashing into the Illinois State Prison Bus. Also down in the southern mountains Jodie Foster, as *Nell,* portrayed a taste of mountain living of years ago. *Song Catcher* depicted another portrayal of mountain living and mountain music of an earlier century. That was filmed around the hamlet of Dillingham.

Filmdom presidents Jack Lemmon and James Garner in *My Fellow Americans* were on the run through Marshall, marched in a parade in Asheville, rode the Great Smoky Mountains train, landed a helicopter at Lake Lure, and continued their adventure to the Lagoon at Biltmore, where the White House was standing in an adjacent field. Some years earlier Patrick Swayze and Jennifer Grey did their famous lifts from Lake Lure in *Dirty Dancing*.

Baseball reigned at Asheville's McCormick Field with the filming of *Bull Durham*. Meanwhile just up Biltmore Avenue at Pack Square, many of the scenes were shot for the early silent film *Conquest of Canaan*. Some of the old-timers of Asheville were extras in the Civil War film *Tap Roots* featuring Susan Hayward and Van Heflin. According to these fellows, it was such a low-budget film that they donned Yankee blues, proceeding to fire across the French Broad River at the Rebels. Cameras stopped rolling as they changed into Confederate grey and crossed the river to return fire.

Daniel Day-Lewis and company were all over these mountains in *The Last of the Mohicans*. The film company had offices on Pack Square. They rented a warehouse for costuming across from the Ritz restaurant in "The Block" on South Market Street, taking many of their meals there. The Red Coats marched from Grove Park Inn to the English Manor Inn on Charlotte Street. Waterfalls at Linville were featured as a hiding place, but to no avail. Lake James was the scene of the fallen Fort William Henry. And Chingachgook made his stand as the last Mohican at Chimney Rock as Hawkeye raced up the mountain firing his muskets, dispersing the enemy, in a desperate run to assist his adopted father.

Here for a drying-out period in *28 Days* was Sandra Bullock with the main scenes taking place at the Blue Ridge YMCA Conference Center, standing in as the Sanatorium, and the Black Walnut Bed and Breakfast in Historic Montford providing the domestic ambience for the kitchen scene of ranting, raving, and smashing dishes. And most recently Robert Redford used the former grounds of old Camp Sequoya up Reems Creek just past the Zebulon Vance birthplace outside Weaverville for the film *The Clearing*.

# OTHER CULTURAL EVENTS, ORGANIZATIONS, AND INFORMATION

## Northern Mountains

### Madison County

MARS HILL COLLEGE
100 Athletic St., Mars Hill
(828) 689-1217
www.mhc.edu

Mars Hill College is a fundamental source for a variety of cultural activities in the Madison County area. The celebrated theater, art, history, and music departments continually provide excellence in each of those disciplines.

The Southern Appalachian Repertory Theatre (SART) at Mars Hill College grew out of the exceptional talent of the college drama department and has, for more than 30 summers, perpetuated the best in classic and popular theater. SART has also served as the premiere stage for a number of emerging playwrights. The college's Department of Art maintains gallery space and features the exceptional talent of both students and faculty members.

The Department of Music at Mars Hill is well known for the talent that continues to emerge from its academic program. Concerts and recitals by students and faculty are open to the general public. This department, in cooperation with the Student Activities Department, has been instrumental in bringing the finest in musical concerts and dance performance (such as the Joffrey Ballet, among others) to the campus.

Mountain heritage is a vital focus of this college. To that end Mars Hill's Rural Life Museum is devoted to the presentation and preservation of the history of the unique lifestyle of our pioneer forebears. The museum is also home to the William A. Barnhill Collection, a personal photographic legacy illustrating mountain life in Western North Carolina in 1914, seen through the eye of the young roving photographer. The college also features a series of public service forums and a variety of speakers during the year, addressing current national and international issues.

### Watauga County

AN APPALACHIAN SUMMER FESTIVAL
229 Rivers St., Boone
(828) 262-6084, (800) 841-ARTS
www.appsummer.org

For one glorious month each summer, Boone comes alive with an intense, exciting celebration of the arts. This July explosion of theater, music, dance, and art is Appalachian State University's annual arts blowout, drawing visitors from across the Southeast. Now in its 24th season, An Appalachian Summer Festival is an interactive arts festival, with workshops, art competitions, concerts, and exhibits designed to please the entire family.

Children can participate in their own special art and creative writing workshops. All tastes are satisfied during Appalachian Summer. Music ranges from the classic strains of the North Carolina Symphony to New Orleans jazz and traditional bluegrass, and from well-known singer-storytellers to the country/folk stylings of musical artists. The Atlanta Ballet, the Parsons Dance Company, international folk dancers, and mountain cloggers and buck dancers all perform during that one month in Boone. The excitement is contagious.

## Central Mountains

### Buncombe County

FINE ARTS THEATER
36 Biltmore Ave., Asheville
(828) 232-1536
www.fineartstheatre.com

This restored movie theater (a triple-X cinema in the 1970s) screens award-winning independent and foreign films. The main theater is an ode to the finer days of cinema, with dimmed brass sconces, plush seats, a high ceiling, and finely draped stage. The smaller upstairs cinema is as cozy as the main hall is elegant. More than just your regular Milk Duds and Goobers, the snacks at the Fine Arts range from beer to biscotti. Catch the excellent first-run films shown here, because it's the only place in town you can!

# Close-up

## The Asheville Urban Trail

The Urban Trail in downtown Asheville, a meandering 1.7-mile walk through Asheville's history via plaques and sculptures, was created by volunteers and community donors over a period of 10 years. It initially began as a way to attract people to a sparsely populated downtown and ended up as a contributor to one of the largest collections of public art in the state.

Thirty "stations," in the form of sculptures or sidewalk plaques, take you through numerous eras, starting with the pioneering age when the mountains were first developed by settlers (on what was Cherokee land), through the industrial era, to the period of blossoming art deco architecture in the city, and onwards. Locally based and national artists were commissioned to create sculptures and bas-reliefs that would echo this history.

A bronze sow and her piglets, turkeys, and other creatures' footprints in concrete symbolize the drovers taking their livestock to market over these very crossroads in the station of the same name, for example. A little bronze girl bending over for a drink from a fountain symbolizes the innocence of childhood. A giant iron in front of the Flat Iron Building recalls an old Asheville laundry that was once part of the neighborhood.

The trail has, in fact, become such a success that other cities in North Carolina and elsewhere are trying to emulate it. Now, of course, the downtown is abuzz with activity, thanks, in part, to the Urban Trail. The Asheville Area Arts Council offers maps of the Urban Trail and conducts walking tours. *Artful Asheville—Along the Urban Trail*, by one of the authors of this book, supplies a more in-depth examination of each aspect of the trail, along with walking maps, history, and a guide to art venues in the city.

**UNIVERSITY OF NORTH CAROLINA ASHEVILLE**
**One University Heights, Asheville**
**(828) 251-6600**
**www.unca.edu**
This exceptional liberal arts university (see our Education chapter) provides the city of Asheville and surrounding area with a diverse and continuously entertaining array of cultural arts offerings.

The in-house cultural arts departments of music, drama, and art offer an equally impressive schedule of events: first-rate theater productions, Tanglewood Children's Theater, university gallery shows for both students and faculty, and community-based organizations such as the UNCA Community Chorus, the UNCA Community Concert Band, and the UNCA Community Jazz Band. These are open by audition to any musically trained or inclined citizens of any age in the Asheville area. The groups present various public concerts during the year.

One of the best-received UNCA cultural events is the summer Concerts on the Quad Series. These free performances on the grassy stage of the university quad in the center of the campus happen every Mon from 7 to 8:30 p.m. during June and July and are always well attended by area residents as well as UNCA students.

**WCQS-FM**
**73 Broadway St., Asheville**
**(828) 253-6875**
**www.wcqs.org**
This is the Asheville area's exceptional public radio station. The community-based FM station began back in the 1970s on the campus of the University of North Carolina at Asheville and moved to its present location in 1984. Programming features classical, jazz, folk, and traditional music; in-depth local news and information; and National Public Radio. It's available on several frequencies in the Western North Carolina area.

# SHOPPING

Each of the three geographical regions identified in this book is anchored by a major shopping location or group of locations: Boone in the Northern Mountains; Asheville, Hendersonville, and Brevard in the Central Mountains; and Waynesville, Highlands, and Dillsboro in the Southern Mountains. Fanning out from these cities are towns and country crossroads that add to your shopping options. You'll find quite a bit of sophisticated shopping in many of these areas—from art and antiques to jewelry and unique home decor. Don't forget our "general stores" that sell just about anything, and we have the big malls and outlet shopping, too.

Don't miss the buys waiting for you out in the countryside, where a turn down a back road can put you at the door of a charming country store. Once the backbone of our rural economy, these simple shops are often treasure troves of Americana. If you are an antiques aficionado, you may be amazed at the great buys you can find in the middle of nowhere. What looks like an old farmhouse with junk out on the front porch may actually be an "antique barn," where you can find fascinating old farm tools, cupboards, tables, dishes, and the like.

Because shops do tend to open and close so quickly, we'll describe the best shopping areas here, and several notable merchants who continue to make their mark. But take some time to discover all the little places down alleys and off in the countryside. These are often the greatest of treasure troves.

## NORTHERN MOUNTAINS

### Ashe County

#### Glendale Springs

In the beautiful and remote countryside of Glendale Springs in Ashe County, you won't find scads of shops or a mall. There's not a chain store in sight, but you will hit upon a few choice gift shops.

**GREENHOUSE CRAFTS**
**248 J. W. Luke Rd.**
**(336) 982-2618**
**www.greenhousecrafts.com**
Greenhouse Crafts is located across the road from the Holy Trinity Episcopal Church, where noted North Carolina artist Ben Long completed his fresco of "The Last Supper" in the early 1980s. (The other of the two Churches of the Frescoes is St. Mary's Episcopal, about 12 miles away near West Jefferson, off U.S. Highway 221). Greenhouse Crafts has tastefully complemented the frescoes'

religious theme with angel statuary, inspirational art, literature, and an array of music. The shop also has traditional mountain crafts, collectible figurines, and unusual functional and whimsical pottery, such as a playful set that depicts Noah's Ark. Handmade jewelry, including silver rings and bracelets made in the area, can be found here, along with stained-glass lamps, gorgeous wooden dulcimers, and other smaller gift items.

#### Jefferson

Jefferson and West Jefferson, only a few miles apart, are towns so small and ubiquitously 1950s America that they could well be part of a Hollywood movie set. Secondhand shops, galleries, and a coffee shop or two enliven these quiet main streets.

#### West Jefferson

**ORIGINALS ONLY GALLERY**
**3-B North Jefferson Ave.**
**(336) 846-1636**
**www.originalsonlygallery.com**

This comely gallery features paintings of American artists who have spent a great deal of their lives abroad. Lenore Depree, who lived in the Middle East, offers most fascinating lithographs and even a commissioning service of original Persian storybook art.

## SALLY MAE'S EMPORIUM
**10 South Jefferson Ave.**
**(336) 846-9069**
**www.sallymaesemporium.com**
Browse the vendors in this spacious shopping arcade, where you can find antiques, glass work, soaps, pottery, and even a gourmet foods section. During warm seasons one can even buy bouquets of fresh flowers here.

## Todd
**TODD GENERAL STORE**
**Highway 194**
**(336) 877-1067**
**www.toddgeneralstore.com**
As you wend your way along scenic Highway 194 in Ashe County, you'll come upon the charming crossroads community of Todd, originally named Elkland, that's halfway between Boone and West Jefferson. This was a thriving lumber town when the railroad was king, but once the region was lumbered out, the community seemed to heave a great sigh and disappear.

Where once there were two hotels, a bank, a post office, a buzzing mill, nine stores, and doctor and dentist offices that served mill workers and railroad men, there is now only tough little Todd General Store, on the banks of the New River. The store is the heart of the tiny community and a reminder of its glory days.

Its interior has been restored, but in a leisurely way. The collectibles and genuine antiques that cover the two stories seem like they've always been there. Folks still gather on stools and straight-back chairs around the potbellied stove, which is fired up in cold weather. Simple wooden shelves hold groceries, staples for a community that would rather come here to shop than drive north to Jefferson or south to Boone. And you can still buy home-baked goods here, prepared by the women of the valley. Penny candies (well, close to a penny) are crammed beneath vintage glass-front store cases.

A lunch counter is also open at the General Store, where you can get a hearty barbecue sandwich and monstrous pickles—no skimping on portions either. The store sells gift items, antiques, collectibles, and souvenirs of your ramble here.

## Avery County
**ALMOST RODEO DRIVE**
**Suite 101, Hwy. 184**
**(828) 898-4553**
This is a boutique for ladies' and children's clothing (there is another location on Main Street in Blowing Rock). The pieces are fairly unique and of natural fabrics. Ladies' sparkly party wear and designer names are a big draw.

### Banner Elk

The Shoppes of Tynecastle is an attractive grouping of specialty shops at the junction of Highways 105 and 184. Sports shops, galleries, home furnishings stores, nail salons, and kitchen and wine stores are anchored by a distinctive stone tower that makes this destination easy to spot.

Head north on Highway 184 to the town of Banner Elk and its attractive upscale shopping complex called the Village at Banner Elk.

## Beech Mountain
Beech Mountain is primarily a ski resort community, but there is a hardy contingent that lives here year-round. We've included a few of the places where year-rounders shop.

**FRED'S GENERAL MERCANTILE COMPANY**
**501 Beech Mountain Pkwy.**
**(828) 387-4838**
**www.fredsgeneral.com**

This store has stepped in to fill the void for the brave few who live here year-round, as well as for the legion of tourists who continually make the pilgrimage to mile-high Beech Mountain. Fred Pfohl and his colorful, old-fashioned store anchor the community. Among Fred's inventory are groceries, ski accessories, warm clothing, crafts, toys, even hardware and toothbrushes.

Stay and have lunch at Fred's Backside Deli (828-387-9331) at the rear of the store. And you can't miss, nor would you want to, Wildbird Supply (828-389-4838), also inside Fred's General Mercantile Company. The company's motto is, "Wildbird's supplies everything but the birds," and that includes seed, feeders, books, and nature guides. In back of this store you can watch birds, squirrels, and chipmunks romp and munch on the feed left in the landscaped forest-garden plot. Fred's motto reads, "If we don't have it, you don't need it."

## Watauga County
### Blowing Rock

This quaint mountain village about 15 minutes from Boone has a walkable Main Street, which is an easy stroll from almost every accommodation in town, so you don't have to worry about parking. Irresistible specialty and antiques shops line this main thoroughfare, and truth be told, it seems like there are new shops with every visit. We've mentioned some favorites here, but keep your eyes peeled for fabulous home decor, gift, and jewelry shops in this downtown that's easily covered in a day.

### APPALACHIAN RUSTIC FURNISHINGS
**1085 North Main St.**
**(828) 295-9554**
This shop displays incredible handmade furnishings and objects for home, lodge, camp, and cabins. We fell in love with the birch-bark lamps and picture frames. Mirrors made of wood and moss brought out our primal instincts for house and home, and who wouldn't want a handmade rocking chair or table from the finest wood in the Blue Ridge?

Fitch's workshop is a few miles down the road in the countryside, so you won't get to see any on-site working, but he does maintain photographs around the shop of various pieces being handcrafted.

### BOB TIMBERLAKE GALLERY
**946 Main St.**
**(828) 295-0008**
On the corner of Main Street and US 221, Bob Timberlake Gallery carries a collection of popular furniture lines and original artwork, prints, books, and home decor by this Salsbury, NC artist, who also maintains a home in Blowing Rock. The Bob Timberlake Inn, decorated in said furnishings and art is located at Cheetola Resort.

### CABIN FEVER
**915 Main St.**
**(828) 295-0520**
Cabin Fever offers a complete collection of log cabin and vacation home furnishings. Choose from unique and distinctive furniture, lighting, kitchen items, bed-and-bath decor, hardware, gifts, and more. Cabin Fever is a family-owned business with its largest store located in downtown Blowing Rock.

### CROSSTRADE INTERNATIONAL
**1087-2 Main St.**
**(828) 295-8691**
**www.crosstrade.org**
This shop, filled with hand made crafts from Brazil (for the most part), is owned by a couple who has adopted several Brazilian children. The proceeds from the crafts they bring back from their travels—etched glass, clay cooking pottery, textiles and baskets—go to the craftsmen and their communities to help them sustain themselves off their art.

### DE PROVENCE ET D'AILLEURS
**131-8 Morris St.**
**(828) 295-9989**
This elegant shop features gifts and accessories imported directly from France, particularly from the area of Provence. Collectibles include Quim-

per Faience, blown and bubbled glasswork from Biot, and many "one of a kind" items straight from the French markets. Household accessories include Provence linens, pottery, natural soaps, lamps, and other fine casual tabletop items. You'll also find hand-crafted furniture and original French artwork.

### HANNA'S ORIENTAL RUGS & GIFTS
**1123 Main St.**
**(828) 295-7073**
Another fine shop on Main Street, Hanna's sells imported items of exceptional quality, including Oriental and Central Asian rugs, exquisite Austrian Swarovski crystal, Lladro porcelain figurines, and cloisonné, jade, and ivory pieces from around the world.

### MARTIN HOUSE
**1098 Main St.**
The Shoppes of Martin House is an assortment of shops all in one place. This former residence, built on Main Street in the late 1800s, and adjoining cottages showcase all kinds of pretty and practical things: clothing, candy, toys, gourmet coffees, gems, candles, vintage reproduction photographs, and Victorian floral arrangements.

Some of the fine shops in the area include the Chicory Suite Martin House (828-295-4231), a quaint cottage off the Martin House courtyard in back that sells gourmet coffees and kitchen items. It smells wonderful too! G. Whiliker's & Co. Martin House (828-295-9549) has a jumble of whimsical toys, games, puzzles, and books to tickle any child's fancy. Follow your sweet tooth to Sweet Rosie's Martin House (828-295-9318), where you can fill a brown bag with old-fashioned candies and nuts (you can also buy gourmet pet treats here).

### NEACO
**1081 Main St.**
**(828) 295-0709**
**www.neaco.com**
This is an eclectic shop that features a variety of "sophisticated-cool" items such as cocktail napkins with funny sayings, lounge and jazz CDs, contemporary lighting fixtures, invitations and cards, sassy parlor games, and other chic novelties. It's the place to pick up unusual decorative welcome mats, serving utensils with rhinestones, and other such lovelies.

### PLEASANT PAPERS
**105 The Village Shoppes, South Main St.**
**(828) 295-7236**
One of our favorite shops tucked back into an alcove on South Main Street is Pleasant Papers. Here you can find any number of beautifully embossed notecards, cards with elegant floral and gold borders, or even with Southwestern and Impressionist motifs—anything for wedding invitations, baby showers, New Year's party invites, and the list goes on. You can also order writing paper specially engraved with your own logo or initials, and certainly you will find the perfect pen here for your correspondences. Writing the folks back home has never been so thrilling!

### SERVES YOU RIGHT!
**SouthMark on Main Street**
**(828) 295-GIFT**
Serves You Right! by Karyn Kennedy Herterich, a Blowing Rock seasonal resident from Florida, is dedicated to offering unique gifts and essentials for the kitchen, dining room, and bar, with particular emphasis on tableware, party, and entertainment accessories. Key vendors in this 1,000-square-foot store are Bernardaud/Limoges, Faberge, Battersea, Herend Porcelains, Lynn Chase Designs, Mariposa, Penzo of Africa, Royal Worcester, Vietri, and other quality lines. The shop also maintains a variety of whimsical gifts, such as Extendible Forks, which allow you to eat off others' plates, and other fun gift items. Styles and designs for trays, placemats, serving accessories, and paper goods number in the hundreds in this charming store.

### POPPY'S BY DESIGN
**1128 Main St.**
**(828) 414-9300**
**www.poppysofblowingrock.com**
A fun shop filled with flirty clothing and decor for the home, too. (The owners often decorate

homes at Chetola Resort and elsewhere in the area. You can see some of the same elegant silk floral arrangements here.

## SOUTHMARK
### 1179 Main St.
### (828) 295-3700

SouthMark was the first new shopping development on Main Street in over 50 years when the landscaped shopping center opened in 1992. Inspired by Blowing Rock's turn-of-the-20th-century thriving resorts, the distinctive Victorian-influenced structures of towers and gables serve as a gateway to the south entrance of town. English gardens display summer topiaries of swans, lions, and rabbits, making SouthMark a unique place to shop. Eight of the area's most upscale shops are located here, with an additional six all-weather seasonal pavilions, which open in May. Shoppers may find Herend and Faberge china here—or even paint their own pottery next door. Ladies' and children's apparel have a home in two shops here, as do high-end crafts, a sports collectibles shop, and a bookstore. The seasonal pavilions offer additional merchandise from wellness products, flowering baskets, and plants to pizzas and salads.

## WINDWOOD ANTIQUES
### 1152 South Main St.
### (828) 295-9260

For English country pine and the cottage look, visit this shop across from Blowing Rock Realty. You can also find reproduction pieces, such as those popular antique armoires that have been converted into entertainment centers.

## Boone

Boone and the nearby towns of Blowing Rock, Foscoe, Banner Elk, and Valle Crucis create a beehive of tourist shopping activity. Specialty shops, outlet sites, crafts and fine art galleries, and antiques shops abound here.

## DOWNTOWN BOONE

Shopping in downtown Boone gives you a chance to see the town's revived main thoroughfare, King Street. To find this historic street from Highway 105 as you enter the city, turn left at the intersection of U.S. Highway 321, and wind your way through the university district. The shops on West King Street sell quality clothing, jewelry, gifts, fine art, and pottery—a bit of everything in one place. With so many students around, you can count on funky clothing and accessories shops, along with lots of music and dorm-decor stores. It does seem that there's a fair amount of turnover, but some faithful standbys are listed here.

If you're looking for an unusual card or book, need a pen or sketchbook, have a sweet tooth, want to find a special toy or game to keep your young backseat driver busy, or would like to buy a CD with music as inspiring as the mountains, Boone's downtown shops can accommodate you.

## ART WALK
### 611 West King St.
### (828) 264-9998
### www.artwalkboone.com

A wonderful combination of the area's artisans meet here on three floors. Find everything from paintings and jewelry to ceramic pottery, photographs, ornaments and hand-crafted decor for the home. It is situated in 9,500 square-feet of a beautifully renovated building in downtown Boone.

## CANDY BARREL
### 624 West King St.
### (828) 268-0666

You'll be sorry if you pass up the decadently rich fudge and handmade candies in this 19th-century-style sweet shop. It carries more than 500 varieties of candy.

## DANCING MOON EARTHWAY BOOKSTORE
### 553 West King St.
### (828) 264-7242

This tiny shop offers those unique books, cards, and posters you can't find at a chain store. It also carries incense, candles, and other items. (See our Close-up on Bookstores.)

## FOOTSLOGGERS
**139 South Depot St.**
**(828) 262-5111**

Footsloggers carries all the stylishly rugged, top-quality clothing and footwear for those who like the outdoors or just the outdoorsy look. This is also the place to go in Boone for all kinds of camping, hiking, and outdoor gear (see the Outfitters section of our Recreation chapter for more information).

## GRAPEVINE MUSIC
**641 West King St.**
**(828) 264-7168**

Celtic tunes and New Age music seem to be appropriate anthems for the mountains, and Grapevine Music has sounds that soothe the spirit. You can find mountain bluegrass on the rack, too.

## LORETTA'S VENDETTA
**681 West King St.**
**(828) 268-9830**

This little locale speaks to the cool cats of yore and those who relish mid-century modern from afar. This emporium of 1950s to '70s cocktail paraphernalia features bubble chairs and atom-shaped coffee tables.

## MAST GENERAL STORE
**630 King St.**
**(828) 262-0000**

If you're looking for wool socks and flannel, down-filled outerwear, and general mountain attire, this is the place. Just like its sister stores in Valle Crucis and other spots in this area, Mast General Store in Boone stocks quality leisure clothing, hats, belts, and other leather accessories.

We like the seasonal sale bins! The Boone store is a two-story, turn-of-the-20th-century-style department store in the restored 1913 Boone Mercantile at the corner of King and Depot Streets. Boone's Mast Store also carries shoes, housewares, and gifts and has departments for children and maternity needs (see the Mast entry under Valle Crucis).

The candy shop adjacent to the clothing section is one step over the threshold into sugar heaven. Sold by the pound, the candy is stocked in barrels. Just carry your little basket around and start filling it up with old-fashioned horehound candy, peppermints, taffy, imported hard coffee candies, mints, and other tooth-rotting goodness!

## OLD BOONE ANTIQUE MALL
**631 West King St.**
**(828) 262-0521**

This is a storehouse of American and European antiques spread over three floors and 27,000 square feet. Here you'll find antique jewelry, furniture, linens, decorative items, prints, and family china from more than 75 dealers. Take your time browsing. Each vendor has set up almost an entire store within the allotted space.

## PURVEYORS OF ART AND DESIGN MATERIALS
**499 West King St.**
**(828) 265-0209**
**www.artpurveyors.com**

This is where you can stock up on art materials, instruction books, and frames—the expert staff will dole out free advice. The shop carries popular brands of oil paint, canvases, pastels, and other art supplies for pros and hobbyists alike.

## THE SHOPPES AT FARMER'S HARDWARE
**661 West King St.**
**(828) 264-8801**

This decades-old landmark formerly known as the Farmer's Hardware and Supply Company is replete with creaking wood floors, back open stairways, and large picture windows on two floors. Some 35 individual merchants fill the many booths of the 12,000-square-foot space with everything ranging from farm antiques to gems and handmade jewelry, housewares, sweets, artwork and photography, clothing, and much more in the basement.

## US 321

This busy highway serves as the primary link between Boone and Blowing Rock and it is here that you might fulfill a great deal of your shopping needs if you take the time to stop.

## THE INCREDIBLE TOY COMPANY
**3411 US 321 South**
**(828) 264-1422**

Toys, toys, toys! The kids will see this one before you do, so you might as well be prepared to stop and enjoy this fun place between Boone and Tweetsie Railroad. It offers a large selection of educational toys, games, books, puzzles, science kits, and the well-known Brio and Playmobil sets.

## THE MUSTARD SEED MARKET
**5589 US 321**
**(828) 295-4585**

You might miss this little stand if you blink. This unassuming roadside market on US 321 at Aho Road, 2 miles north of Blowing Rock, is open daily and is much more than a produce stand. English garden statuary, unusual perennial flowers, honey, herb vinegars, hand-painted gifts, and custom-made flags share the space with the fresh fruits and vegetables.

## TANGER SHOPPES ON THE PARKWAY
**279 US 321**
**(828) 295-4444, (800) 720-6728**

This well-landscaped outlet center provides a delightful shopping experience while you're visiting the area. The center features 32 name brand outlets—some the best known in the industry—such as Gap, Nautica, Polo Ralph Lauren, Coach, Bass, Izod, Royal Doulton, Jones New York, Kaspar, Jockey, Big Dog, and Geoffrey Beene. Cooks will especially enjoy Corning Revere and Kitchen Collection, which feature every gadget a cook needs. The center also features a full-service restaurant, Parkway Cafe, and well-known Kilwins, serving locally made gourmet ice cream, candy, and fudge. Relax in the courtyard and enjoy a meal or a treat. Since being purchased by the national outlet industry giant Tanger Factory Outlets, the center has added amenities such as wheelchairs and strollers, as well as a centrally located office that sells gift certificates and disperses information about Tanger's 33 centers.

## TANNER FACTORY STORE
**US 321 Bypass**
**(828) 295-7031**

This shop sells quality Doncaster fashions at attractive outlet prices. A second store is located near the entrance to Sugar Mountain in Avery County (828-898-6734).

## Foscoe

Where Highway 105 passes through Foscoe, south of Boone, you'll find a corridor known for antiques shops. Classic English, French, and American 18th- and 19th-century pieces are displayed by the community's many professional antiques dealers. The Foscoe area is a hot destination for Western North Carolina innkeepers and bed-and-breakfast proprietors.

Going hand in hand with the sale of antiques in Foscoe are galleries of fine art, traditional crafts, and unique specialty shops along Highway 105.

## DEWOOLFSON DOWN
**9452 Hwy. 105**
**(828) 963-4144, (800) 833-3696**

Did you ever wonder where innkeepers get those sumptuous down comforters for your nightly lodging at some of the Boone area's best bed-and-breakfast inns? Well, the secret's out . . . it's DeWoolfson Down, 9 miles south of Boone on Highway 105.

But there is so much more here: down pillows hand-stuffed to your order, silk comforters from China, Egyptian cotton sheets designed in France, crisp damasks from Germany, and silky Jacquard sheets from Italy—with up to 590 threads per inch. Clear out the trunk of your car before you come because you won't go home empty-handed.

## STAFFORDSHIRE ANTIQUES
**8599 Hwy. 105**
**(828) 963-4274**
**www.englishantiqueimports.com**

Anglophiles, take note! This is one of two shops on Highway 105 that imports directly from the British Isles. Eight miles south of Boone, this shop concentrates on 18th- and 19th-century antique furniture imports. Two red English phone booths stand outside the shop. You can't miss them.

## Valle Crucis

**THE HAM SHOPPE**
**124 Broadstone Rd.**
**(828) 963-6310**
**www.thehammeshopandmore.com**
Up Highway 105, just as you turn toward scenic Valle Crucis, is the Ham Shoppe. This is a store for jams, jellies, homemade breads, pies, dry pasta, and other staples for your kitchen. Even better though, are its made-to-order takeouts. Touted as "Ham Sweet Hams," the mouthwatering honey-glazed, spiral-cut baked hams are the obvious house specialty. But there is so much more to feast on here: strawberry-rhubarb pie, ham spread, cinnamon buns, preserves, and fresh-baked sourdough bread. Use the Ham Shoppe as your special corner grocer or as a deli—it serves this dual purpose well.

**MAST GENERAL STORE**
**Highway 194**
**(828) 963-6511**
**www.mastgeneralstore.com**
The ultimate shopping destination once you reach Valle Crucis is the historic Mast General Store on Highway 194. Built in 1882 by Henry Taylor, the store was sold around the turn of the 20th century to W. W. Mast. Over the next 70 years, the Mast family business established a tradition in the region for offering "everything from cradles to caskets." The interior of the store remains very much the same as it was a century ago. The old post office, still in service, is at one end, and the store's classic potbellied stove, an asset in these snow-prone hills, is still a central element.

You'll delight in a ramble around this old-time mercantile. Sit out on in the porch swings or rockers on the back porch. This is where you should be sipping your ice-cold A & W or hot-and-spicy ginger ale. It certainly revved us up after lunch for more sight-seeing. This place has quality seasonal apparel, camping and fly-fishing gear, as well as sun hats, shoes, hiking boots and sandals. The candy store offers barrels of taffy, jawbreakers, horehound candy, licorice, and about a hundred other sweets sold by weight. Just take your basket around and fill it up.

## Yancey County

### Burnsville

The small-town charm here adds to the fun, especially if you're looking for a break from malls and megamarts.

**DK PUTTYROOT AND THE**
**ORCHID TEAROOM**
**132 West Main St.**
**(828) 678-9588**
**www.dkputtyroom.burnsville-nc.com**
Stationery, hand-bound journals, imported papers, inkwells, ink, writing implements, and teas make this a treasure trove for the letter writer and the crafter. Owned by two sisters, the two-story shop maintains several cozy, themed tearooms upstairs.

**NEEDLE ME THIS**
**112 West Main St.**
**(828) 682-9462**
**www.needle-me-this.com**
The region is famous for its fine handcrafts, so you will not want to miss the display of finished quilts at this little shop. You can order a custom-made quilt here, too. For do-it-yourselfers, the shop carries fabrics and notions and offers sewing and quilting classes.

**SOMETHING SPECIAL**
**102 West Main St.**
**(828) 682-9101**
This is a place where the country crafts and gifts are abundant and unique. The shop carries pottery, wooden shelving, prints, and home-decorating items.

# CENTRAL MOUNTAINS

## Buncombe County

### Downtown Asheville

The renaissance of Asheville's inner city as a shopping destination is well-known and has been touted in magazine and newspaper articles nationally. What is particularly pleasing to Asheville's visitors and residents alike is that the downtown is

# Close-up

## Grovewood Studios and Gardens

Directly across from the Grove Park Inn is the Grovewood Gallery, Gardens, Homespun Museum, Car Museum, Artist Studios and Grovewood Café. These pebble-dash buildings take one back to the days when Fred Seely, Grove Park Inn manager and son-in-law of the inn owner E.W. Grove, bought the Biltmore Estate Homespun Industries from Edith Stuyvesant Dresser Vanderbilt, the widow of George Vanderbilt. He moved the business from Biltmore Village and into these buildings. Eventually, local philanthropist Harry Bloomberg would purchase the buildings and the Biltmore Homespun Industries from Fred Seely Jr. He continued the homespun clothing industry over the next several years, but eventually closed it.

The late Bloomberg, once a leader in the automotive industry in Asheville, replaced 45 looms with historic antique motor cars, trucks, and a fire engine. There is no admission fee to view these beauties of an earlier era; however, donations can be placed in a wishing well, which supports the American Cancer Society.

In addition to fine dining at the Grovewood Café, or visiting the museums, observing artisans plying their trade, or shopping in the gallery, one can enjoy a picnic among the outdoor sculptures with the majestic Grove Park Inn at one shoulder and a glorious panorama of the mountains once owned by George Washington Vanderbilt.

a very pedestrian-friendly place. There are several municipal parking garages downtown. If you're an energetic shopper, you'll want to make a day of it, with lunch at one of Asheville's charming downtown restaurants and bistros. The visual appeal of the city's architecture is an added bonus, with prime examples of art deco design throughout.

You can start with the so-called Renaissance Corridor of Biltmore Avenue near Pack Square. What was once a decaying, questionable area lined with blank storefronts is now a thriving avenue of upscale shops and art galleries.

Wall Street, Haywood Street, and Battery Park Avenue, anchored by the historic and architecturally interesting Flat Iron Building, constructed during Asheville's boom period in the 1920s, is also a good area for shopping for unique clothing, jewelry, fine art, music, handmade chocolates, and the like.

Funky shops on Lexington Avenue, Walnut Street, and Broadway sell vintage clothing, antiques, unique lighting, imported home furnishings, flowers, and so much more. A weekend may just be enough time to explore all the shopping possibilities in downtown Asheville.

### AD-LIB
### 23 Haywood St.
### (828) 285-8838

This store features women's clothing that emphasizes natural fabrics and colors. A collection of hats hangs on one wall, and one section of the shop is devoted to unique leather shoe styles. Comfort and quality are of the utmost importance here. Sweaters, jumpers, dresses, shirts, skirts, and pants in silks, linens, cottons, and wools in an array of magnificent natural colors set this clothing store apart from others. Ad-Lib also sells artistic jewelry, candleholders, and one-of-a-kind picture frames.

### ASHEVILLE WINE MARKET
### 65 Biltmore Ave.
### (828) 253-0060

You can take home an exquisite sampling of the grape from the Wine Market. Winemaster Eberhard Heide is the proprietor and will assist you in your choice of premium international wines and beers. The array is staggering, so you might be wise in choosing Eberhard's famous Wine Samplers, six international vintage wines specially priced and

# Close-up

## Bookstores

When you're on the road, bookstores are almost as important as gas stations. They offer you a connection to the community through books on local legends, maps of trails and tours, and cards of nearby places of beauty. Many include works by local authors who wax poetic about the mountains, drawing inspiration from the region. Asheville has branches of well-known bookstores, including Barnes & Noble, B. Dalton Bookseller, Books-A-Million, and Waldenbooks (which also has stores in Boone, and Hendersonville). The following is a list of some of the region's other bookstores.

### ASHEVILLE

**Battery Park Book Exchange** (1 Battle Square; 828-252-0020; www.batteryparkbookexchange.com). Visit this unique venue where gently-used tomes, crisp new art books, and leather-bound classics share space with petit syrahs and cavas by the glass or bottle. These are served at the marble bar or in cozy reading corners with elegant sofas and easy chairs.

**Blue Ridge Parkway Bookstore** (Folk Art Center; Mile 382, Blue Ridge Parkway; 828-298-0495). Small but well stocked, this bookstore offers the best selection in nature books, trail maps, books on regional culture, and beautiful wildlife cards.

**Book Rack** (485 Hendersonville Rd.; 828-274-5050). Book Rack has a great selection of half-price used paperbacks that are sold and traded in a fresh and friendly environment.

**Captain's Bookshelf** (31 Page Ave.; 828-253-6631; www.captainsbookshelf.com). Secondhand and rare books, as well as signed tomes, find their way here from various collections. Since 1976 the store has held occasional readings, author signings, and photo and art exhibitions.

**Downtown Books and News** (67 Lexington Ave.; 828-253-8654). You can usually buy hard-to-find newspapers, periodicals, and obscure books at this excellent and interesting combination newsstand/used-book store. Subjects include foreign, obscure fashion, computers, food, art, photography, and alternative living.

**Malaprop's Bookstore/Café** (55 Haywood St.; 828-254-6734; www.malaprops.com). Malaprop's is simply an Asheville institution. We remember sipping our hazelnut coffee in the cafe, hunched over our high school homework, dreaming of literary travels, while ethereal music provided the background sounds for this haven of learned tranquility.

Owner Emoke Bracz, a writer, poet, and translator of Hungarian poetry and literature, fine-tuned the art of the book trade in the more-than-20-year life span of this once-small bookstore and cafe. Now two doors down from its original cramped-but-cozy space, Malaprop's boasts shelves of fascinating fiction, alternative nonfiction, prose, and poetry, as well as a large section with works of local authors and books on the region. Coffee table gift books, stationery, cards, journals, and artistic calendars make this one-stop shopping for all your literary gift needs. And then there's the cafe! Author signings, prose readings, poetry readings, and singer-songwriter evenings gather hoards of literati of all types into the spacious adjoining cafe.

**Montford Books & More** (31 Montford Ave.; 828-285-8805; www.montfordbooks.com). This new shop at the entrance to the historic Montford neighborhood sells "gently-used" books, new CDs and locally crafted gift items like jewelry, bookmarks, notecards, and more. Free Wi-Fi access and hot coffee are available.

**Once Upon a Time** (7 All Souls Crescent; 828-274-8788). This is more than a bookstore. It offers the area's largest selection of children's fiction and nonfiction, books, games, tapes, and even children's clothing.

## BLOWING ROCK

**Pleasant Papers** (105 The Village Shoppes, South Main St.; 828-295-7236). More than a bookstore, this fine shop also includes quality papers, greeting cards, and specialized gifts.

## BOONE

**Dancing Moon Earthway Bookstore** (553 West King St.; 828-264-7242; www.the dancingmoon.com). Dancing Moon specializes in books and magazines of the healing and spiritual arts. This small shop also carries unique travel books, cards and posters, music CDs, candles, and even incense and oils.

## BREVARD

**The Book Nook** (15 South Broad St.; 828-883-9745). The Book Nook has new and used books, that, as its proprietor proclaims, "contain only natural ingredients: sex, murder, adultery, joy, sorrow, passion, and mayhem." If you don't see what you're looking for, they'll be happy to conduct book searches for you.

**Cradle of Forestry in America Interpretive Association** (100 South Broad St.; 828-884-5713). This nice store is stocked with nature-related books, gifts, prints, forest maps, literature, and national forest information. This nonprofit organization puts the money it makes right back into our area's magnificent national forests. It oversees another bookstore in the Cradle of Forestry itself in Pisgah Forest.

**Highland Books** (409 North Broad St.; 828-884-2424). Highland carries the latest in new paperbacks and hardbacks in fiction and nonfiction and a wonderful, large selection of greeting cards and gifts. The staff welcomes browsers. It has extensive gardening and children's sections and travel and regional books, including nature books, field guides, and maps. There's a comfortable reading area where you can peruse a book or preview some of the videos of local interest.

## CASHIERS

**Chapter 2** (Ingles Shopping Center; US 64 East; 828-743-5015). Chapter 2 carries new and used books and has a large selection of cookbooks, books of regional interest, and children's books. Its real forte, however, is fiction.

## DILLSBORO

**Time Capsule** (Riverwood Oaks Gallery; Highway 441; 828-586-1026). This shop, with more than 10,000 volumes, specializes in used, rare, and out-of-print books, but it also has a good selection of hiking, flower, and other regional nature books. It's across the railroad tracks from Front Street.

## HIGHLANDS

**Cyrano's Bookshop** (390 Main St.; 828-526-5488). Cyrano's describes itself as "cozy but complete." It's also defined by customer service, and the staff promises to track down hard-to-find titles.

## SYLVA

**City Lights Bookstore & Cafe** (3 East Jackson St.; 828-586-9499; www.citylightsnc .com). City Lights offers new and used books, including great regional and children's sections, as well as cards and calendars. Enjoy your book purchase with a specialty coffee, soup, sandwich, salad, and/or dessert either in the store or at the outside seating area. On Fri and Sat evenings, acoustic and folk musicians provide live entertainment.

## WAYNESVILLE

**Blue Ridge Osondu Books and Cafe** (152 South Main St.; 828-456-6000; www .brbooks-news.com). Blue Ridge Books and former Osondu Booksellers merged into this modern bookstore and cafe that features international magazines, sundry genres of books, and accessories. The cafe has Wi-Fi, a pleasant seating area, and a counter for muffins, cookies, scones, and coffee and tea beverages.

packaged. You can also buy specialty items for the wine connoisseur at the Asheville Wine Market.

### BLOOMIN' ART
**60 Haywood St.**
**(828) 254-6447**

This is more than just a florist. Besides fragrant bouquets, baskets, and unusual items of floral artistry, you'll find plant holders and flowerpots.

### DOWNTOWN BOOKS AND NEWS
**67 Lexington Ave.**
**(828) 253-8654**

Toward the funkier north end of Lexington Avenue, you'll find this excellent book and magazine store. (See the Close-up on Bookstores in this chapter for more details).

**i** Souvenirs for friends, family, or the house sitter back home can be as simple and delightful as a jar of local jam or honey. Check out the Western Carolina Farmer's Market in Asheville or any number of small tailgate markets on Saturday mornings.

### EARTH GUILD
**33 Haywood St.**
**(828) 255-7818**

Its gorgeous storefront is a good indication of the quality of handcrafts you'll find inside. Weaving, pottery, handmade jewelry, and other lovely wares are all visible behind large streetfront windows. You can also find supplies for making your own crafts.

### A FAR AWAY PLACE
**11 Wall St.**
**(828) 252-1891**

This is more than a store: Part gallery, part shop, it's a total experience. The talents of artisans from more than 40 native cultures are represented in this gallery/shop. Exquisite ancient artifacts hang alongside the work of present-day artists. An excellent array of music native to faraway lands is also on display. You'll find jewelry, clothing, hats, bags, stationery, and books here, devoted to lands beyond our hemisphere.

### GROVE ARCADE
**1 Page Ave.**
**(828) 252-7799**
**www.grovearcade.com**

One of America's shopping arcade jewels, the Grove Arcade reopened in 2002 after years of renovation after the previous tenants, the National Climactic Data Center, moved out with the construction of the new Federal Building. The arcade houses an open market, individual shops, and antiques stores. Cafes, delis, and restaurants also fill the venerable space that was lovingly brought back to its original splendor by experts around the country. You must see the interior as well as the exterior to appreciate all the shops the arcade has to offer. Not all of them are visible from the streetside.

**i** Wait until dark, when the lights of Asheville begin to twinkle, and drive along Town Mountain Road up the crest of the mountain. Start at Old Toll Road, which winds along behind Grove Park Inn and through residential areas and runs into Town Mountain Road. As you climb higher, you'll be able to see the lights of Asheville below, the view widening as you ascend the ridge. Soon the other side of the ridge will open up so that the lights of Marion appear in the distance.

### KRESS EMPORIUM
**19–21 Patton Ave.**
**(828) 281-2252**
**www.thekressemporium.com**

An architectural landmark, the Kress building in downtown Asheville was built in 1918 as a five-and-dime. Constructed of rich ceramic tile, the Kress building is only one of the many brilliant examples of art deco in the city. For years the building fell into disrepair and its first floor was used for various flea markets. Today this restored space is a showcase for over 80 artists, artisans, sculptors, hatmakers, jewelry designers, and many others devoted to artistic endeavors. Artists rent booths, decorate the walls, and add their works, so you are essentially strolling through 80 galleries under one roof.

Everything from Turkish kilims, heirloom stitched children's clothes, handmade dolls, and shimmery velvet hats to paintings, hand-carved furniture, antique tools, black-and-white art photos, glass sculptures, and much, much more is on display in this high-ceilinged bright hall.

## THE L.O.F.T.
### 53 Broadway
### (828) 259-9303

This eclectically funky shop, filled with a menagerie of distressed furniture, paper lamps, candles, natural soaps, stationery, frames, handmade journals, and other gift and decorative items, is truly a local favorite. Handmade paper, beeswax soaps, picture frames, mirrors, sketchbooks, plush furniture, flowerpots, and so much more grace this home designer's dream of a shop. "L.O.F.T." stands for Lost Objects, Found Treasures.

## MALAPROP'S BOOKSTORE/CAFÉ
### 55 Haywood St.
### (828) 254-6734
### www.malaprops.com

Fascinating books, gifts, gourmet coffee, and stimulating conversation mingle at Malaprop's new location, just a few doors down from the old one. This bookstore is one of the mainstays of downtown Asheville and a popular stop for visitors and locals. Visiting authors, special events, poetry readings, and the spacious coffeehouse make Malaprop's much more than just a place to buy books. (See our Close-up on Bookstores.)

## MOBILIA
### 42 Haywood St.
### (828) 252-8322
### www.mobilianc.com

A very groovy furniture and home design store shows design classics as well as rare and hard-to-find pieces by the furniture industry's most visionary manufacturers and upstart designers. Some local comtemporary artwork can be found here, though the shop's new owners are trending toward more organic, earth tones and materials.

## MOUNTAIN LIGHTS
### 30 North Lexington Ave.
### (828) 253-0080

This beautiful shop maintains a glowing inventory of unique lamps, candles, twinkle lights, and any accessories having to do with lighting your home sumptuously. Moroccan goatskin lamps, paper lanterns, beaded chandeliers, candles, copper sconces, and other beautiful options make this a real treasure hunt for the home.

## TOPS FOR SHOES
### 27 North Lexington Ave.
### (828) 254-6721

This is another of those gutsy establishments that survived the decay of downtown and persistently worked to make the area a viable business district again. Since the 1970s, Tops has been known for quality footwear for the whole family, and the shop has a reputation for its service and large inventory. If you're shopping at Tops, parking is free at the city parking deck on Rankin Avenue.

> **i** As in many other parts of the country, you can usually find any item you're looking for at about one-tenth the retail price by traveling around to garage sales. There are hundreds happening here every week. Pick up a local paper to find out where they are.

## WOOLWORTH WALK
### 25 Haywood St.
### (828) 254-9234
### www.woolworthwalk.com

This former Woolworth's, originally constructed in the 1920s, was brought back to life after renovation and the infusion of booths and wall spaces featuring the work of local and regional artists and crafters. Decorative art, jewelry, glass, pottery, textiles, painting, metal sculpture, photography, and other imaginative art and crafts make this a lively emporium of gifts. Several artists maintain working studios on the lower level.

## Biltmore Village

Moving along to the south end of Asheville, near the entrance of Biltmore Estate, reached by taking Biltmore Avenue or McDowell Street south, you will find Biltmore Village. Geographically in Asheville, this junction of cobblestone streets and old buildings is an "incorporated town" (see our Area Overviews chapter). Therefore we're discussing the village separately.

When George Vanderbilt constructed his mansion in 1895, it was obvious that such a grand place would need a town at its gate to supply it. Vanderbilt didn't have to start from scratch; he merely purchased the existing village of Best, a good distance from the mansion on the outskirts of Asheville. Construction of suitable lodging for his craftspeople gave the new village a distinctively English-hamlet look that it has retained. The original cottages, which have the pebble-dash exterior used in some Asheville homes of the period, today form a cluster of specialty shops, restaurants, and galleries. The creative spirit, it seems, has survived the century. Mr. Vanderbilt would be pleased.

Biltmore Village's cobbled sidewalks along such streets as Angle, Swan, and All Souls will lead you past a delightful assortment of shops.

### BELLAGIO
**5 Biltmore Plaza**
**(828) 277-8100**
**www.bellagioarttowear.com**
This is a most unusual shop devoted to wearable art. Richly colored, sensually textured fabrics are transformed into exquisite garments and then complemented by handcrafted jewelry. Unique handbags, shoes, and jewelry make this spot well worth a stop.

### NEW MORNING GALLERY
**7 Boston Way**
**(828) 274-2831**
**www.newmorninggallerync.com**
This gallery and shop occupies two stories and is surrounded by urban landscaping. This is one of the South's premier arts and crafts shops, displaying the work of some of America's finest artists

and craftspeople for more than 30 years. The lavish show space for handcrafted furniture is a place to dream.

### ONCE UPON A TIME
**7 All Souls Crescent**
**(828) 274-8788**
This is a splendid bookshop that will please your child with its thousands of books, toys, children's music, story tapes, artwork, and more. (See our Close-up on Bookstores.)

## Black Mountain

Only 15 minutes east of Asheville is Black Mountain, a picturesque village that is an antiques lover's delight. In the historic district anchored by Cherry Street, near the town's old train depot, is a cluster of shops that have fine antiques and collectibles. Black Mountain is an extremely walkable shopping town where everything from handcrafts to artwork, collectibles, and antiques is available within a few tiny blocks. State Street is Black Mountain's main artery.

### BLACK MOUNTAIN ANTIQUE MALL
**105 Sutton Ave.**
**(828) 669-6218**
The BMAM has Southern primitives, folk art, and vintage linens and displays an antique quilt collection. It is one of the older, more-established antique malls here, and it offers many cases of small items for browsing as well.

### THE CHERRY STREET ANTIQUE MALL
**139 Cherry St.**
**(828) 669-7942**
This antiques mall sells items from many dealers. It's a great place to spend time browsing. Two floors house the wares of 18 dealers, with items as small as jewelry trinkets or as large as pieces of furniture. The mall also sells antique craft pottery.

### HOWARD'S ANTIQUES
**121 Cherry St.**
**(828) 669-6494**
This shop sells hot collectible antique toys and sturdy oak furniture. Especially fun are the inven-

tive toys (compare these unique pieces with modern action figures and the other plastic stuff in malls today!).

## SONG OF THE WOOD
**203 West State St.**
**(828) 669-7675**
Follow your heartstrings to the melodies of Song of the Wood. The talented musicians here play lively tunes on handcrafted hammered and mountain dulcimers and other traditional musical instruments. Selling instruments and tapes and CDs of their own music is a side business.

## Asheville Malls and Shopping Centers
The Asheville area has long been known for its tradition of crafting talent and resourcefulness. Entrepreneurship is alive and well here also, and it's been aided by an influx of newcomers in the last 20 years who have added fresh ideas and culturally diverse backgrounds to an already interesting mix of creative people. The tourism-based economy here has spawned new growth and the revitalization of Asheville's downtown.

There are two large malls in the area: the **Asheville Mall,** 3 South Tunnel Rd., (828) 298-5080, and **Biltmore Square Mall,** 800 Brevard Rd., (828) 667-2210. And a recent spate of development has brought major retail stores to all corners of the area.

Don't overlook the shops along the main streets of the area's small towns for some quaint alternatives. Some nearby towns have developed their own shopping districts that draw outside visitors. One of these is the village of Black Mountain, 15 minutes east of Asheville, which has become known as a haven for antiques (see details in the Black Mountain section in this chapter). And if you look, you're apt to find a favorite shop out in the county that's noted for its special wares, personal service, or both.

Another not-to-be-missed shopping experience is the **Western North Carolina Farmers Market,** 570 Brevard Rd., southeast of Asheville (see our Attractions chapter). Its 36 acres offer fresh produce, quality plants and garden supplies, crafts, and just about everything you'd expect to find at an old market square.

## Henderson County
### Flat Rock
**HAND IN HAND GALLERY**
**2713 Greenville Hwy.**
**(828) 697-7719**
Located in the historic Flat Rock area, the shop offers works of porcelain artist Avid Voorhees and jeweler Molly Sharp. Works of other artists in a variety of media range from handmade glass-bead jewelry to hand-forged wrought iron work. It is just past the Carl Sandburg house on U.S. Highway 25, which is also known as the Greenville Highway.

**SECRET GARDEN**
**2720 Greenville Hwy.**
**(828) 697-1331**
It's worth the short drive down the Greenville Highway (US 25 South) in order to pay a visit to this special shop—particularly if you or a loved one loves gardening and garden themes. In addition to flowers and plants, the shop is filled with small, decorative garden sculptures and plaques, small fountains, garden flags, garden books, small framed flower prints, T-shirts, hats and tote bags with garden themes, and flowery doormats, just to name a few items found here.

For children there are stuffed critters like raccoons, turtles, and insects found in the garden. Then there's a whole selection of floral scents, soaps, and candles. Make sure, too, that you don't miss the downstairs shop. Besides a flower-bedecked patio, there's a "kitchen/dining" area with floral- and fruit-painted china, unique wine racks, canisters, and so on. Another room holds tapestries, plant stands, and fabulous rayon-chenille throws.

The next driveway south of the shop takes you to a cutting garden where you can select and cut fresh flowers and pay by the stem.

## Hendersonville
Over two decades ago, when main streets in most small towns were dying due to competition from big malls and discount stores, Hendersonville, which didn't even have a mall at the time, was taking steps to keep its downtown vital. The facades of historic buildings were exposed

and refurbished, and Hendersonville's wide Main Street became a serpentine drive lined with trees and blooming plants. Park benches, too, became a permanent part of the Main Street scene. They are fine spots for resting tired feet, chatting with a friend, or eating takeout in the sunshine while you watch the world go by. Few weeks pass without a downtown festival, art show, or other event taking place here.

If there's any problem with downtown, it's that the very popularity of the area sometimes makes finding a parking spot difficult. But if you don't mind walking a block or two, that problem can usually be solved by going to one of the large metered parking lots on Church or King Streets, which run parallel to Main Street, 1 block away in either direction. There are also parking areas on Fifth and Sixth avenues between Main and King. Though there are no meters on Main Street or its side streets, watch your 15-minute or two-hour limit if you want to avoid a ticket, because, again, due to the downtown's popularity, the limit is strictly enforced. That's a pity, in a way, because a couple of hours is never enough time to browse through all the places you'll want to visit, much less shop and enjoy lunch in one of the area's good restaurants.

Here's just a sampling of some of the places you might find interesting in Hendersonville.

## 508 MAIN STREET
**508 Main St.**
**(828) 692-8506**
The diverse items you'll find inside this shop are as elegant as its green-and-gold exterior. These include, among many other things, seasonal florals and silk flowers, gold and sterling silver jewelry, decorative garden items, home-decor flags, pen-and-ink drawings, stationery, a locally made card line, and locally made chocolates. The shop also carries the Aromatique home fragrance line and Maralyce Ferree's line of Berber and fleece coats and drizzle-wear.

Bunny, the shop's owner, also creates gift baskets of local foods and fragrance that are delivered anywhere in Henderson County and shipped nationwide.

## ASSEMBLY REQUIRED
**Village Square on Hwy. 191**
**(828) 692-9677, (800) 486-2592**
This full-service brew shop has all the equipment, books, kits, and ingredients that you need for making your own beer, wine, liquors, cheese, vinegars, and sodas. If you also need advice, owners Jack and Marilyn Bradt can provide plenty of that, too.

## BANANA MOON
**338 North Main St.**
**(828) 697-1941**
This is by far our favorite clothing store on Main Street, and one of our favorite sections is the selection of outfits made of flax. In addition to all the dresses, sweaters, hats, and handbags, there's everything wonderful for the bath and oodles of charming jewelry. Be prepared to buy.

## BARBARA'S ANTIQUES
**421 North Main St.**
**(828) 697-1550, (877) 793-7476**
Antiques and fine china exquisitely displayed is a hallmark of this lovely shop. China, in fact, is owner Barbara McCoy's specialty. Here you'll find beautiful examples of Wedgwood, Bavarian, Prussian, English, and other fine china fit for the most elegant dining room.

## BEEHIVE RESALE SHOP
**451 North Main St.**
**(828) 692-8882**
For more than two decades the popular Beehive Resale Shop has provided top-quality women's clothing at affordable prices. It carries some terrific brand-name women's fashions and accessories at a fraction of the regular retail price, and the inventory changes daily.

## BLUE RIDGE MALL
**1800 Four Seasons Blvd.**
**(828) 697-1745**
Anchored by Belk, JCPenney, and Kmart, this mall is full of boutiques and specialty shops and is the site of a number of special events, such as craft shows put on by the Henderson County Crafters Association.

## THE CONSIGNMENT GALLERY
**411 North Main St.**
**(828) 697-7712**

By visiting these two North Main Street shops, owned by Tippy and Arthur D'Amato, you could furnish and decorate an entire home with quality antiques and still be able to adorn yourself or a loved one with some incredible estate jewelry.

Past-'N-Present is the place to go for a single piece or for whole sets of furniture. Although the shop specializes in mahogany and oak, you also can find Victorian couches, marble-top chests, player pianos, antique telephones, mirrors, clocks, and lamps. You can also buy excellent wall decorations. In addition to paintings, there are prints, including those by Salvador Dalí and second-edition Audubon prints.

The Antique Consignment Gallery has some furniture pieces but concentrates more on china, glass, and collectibles. Here you'll find modern and antique jewelry, china by top names, sterling silver plates, figurines by Lladro, Hummel, and Armani, and much more. And Arthur, who writes a column on antiques for a local paper, will be happy to give you some tips on distinguishing the real antique from the fake.

**i** Many towns around the mountains show their hospitality by providing visitors with centrally located public restrooms. In Hendersonville, you'll find them in Iron Gate Marketplace at 318 North Main St. between Third and Fourth streets and at Henderson County Travel & Tourism, 20 South Main St. located between Barnwell Street and Allen Street.

## THE CURB MARKET
**221 North Church St.**
**(828) 692-8012**

The Curb Market started out on Main Street in 1924 with eight merchants selling their wares beneath umbrellas. It has mushroomed to 137 selling spaces, many staffed by third- and fourth-generation sellers. Merchants here are required to be Henderson County residents and to make or grow all items they sell. Among these are fresh vegetables, fruits, flowers, dairy products, baked goods, jams, jellies, pickles, relishes, and handmade gifts of all kinds, including afghans, aprons, booties, dolls, folk toys, pillows, quilts, rag rugs, table linens, walking sticks, woodwork items, and wreaths.

## DANCING BEAR TOYS, LTD.
**418 North Main St.**
**(828) 693-4500**

In addition to almost every toy currently popular with children today, Dancing Bear carries a good selection of delightful puppets, costumes, puzzles, and educational toys and books.

## A DAY IN THE COUNTRY
**130 Sugarloaf Rd.**
**(828) 692-7914**

This store, just off I-26 at the Hendersonville exit, has one of the area's largest selections of unique and unusual gifts, including afghans, collectibles, gourmet foods, tapestries, antique and French country furniture, silk floral arrangements, and more.

## DAYS GONE BY GIFTS AND COLLECTIBLES
**303 North Main St.**
**(828) 693-9056**

Until a few years ago, this was the location of downtown's oldest business, Justus Pharmacy, established in 1882. Retaining all its old-time flavor, it's now a place where you can find drugstore/soda-fountain collectibles. Afterward sit down for an old-time ice-cream soda or sundae at the Old-Fashioned Soda Parlor.

## THE GOLDSMITH BY RUDI, LTD.
**324 North Main St.**
**(828) 693-1030**

Rudi Haug has been doing business in Hendersonville since 1975 and is now helped by his son and daughter. This large, full-service jewelry store is so popular for new purchases, custom designs, and jewelry repairs that there are five full-time jewelers working to fill the orders. The store does mounting, engraving, and restyling.

At Rudi's, in addition to the finest in all kinds of jewelry, you can buy clocks, fine Swiss watches, a great line of pen sets, and silver picture frames. There's also a fabulous array of gold and silver charms, including a popular Hendersonville charm that comes in three sizes in gold or silver.

## HONEYSUCKLE HOLLOW
**512 North Main St.**
**(828) 697-2197**
Romance and nostalgia fill the air at Honeysuckle Hollow. Vintage clothing, linens, lace, scarves, fragrances, glassware, candles, antiques, and jewelry turn this shop into an exciting treasure hunt. It's the place to go, too, for wonderful cards and relaxing contemporary, classical, and traditional tapes and CDs.

## JANE ASHER'S FOURTH AND MAIN ANTIQUE MALL
**344 Main St.**
**(828) 693-0018**
The antiques and collectible lover will find 5,000 square feet of friendly, one-floor shopping here put together by 25 dealers. Though this is certainly the place to come if you like European clocks (you can get your clock repaired here, too), this store also carries a tempting array of fine china, glassware, art glass, dolls, Victorian quilts, toys, beaded Victorian bags, religious artifacts, costume and fine estate jewelry, old-fashioned sewing tools, and lots and lots of buttons. Prices on the whole are moderate, but you can find the rare and expensive piece here, too.

## MAST GENERAL STORE
**527 North Main St.**
**(828) 696-1883**
True to its atmosphere, this beautifully restored 1905 emporium is chock full of old-time mercantile items, but you can also find quality outdoor gear, footwear, and traditional clothing for all four of our seasons. The original Mast General Store opened in Valle Crucis in 1883.

## MEHRI & COMPANY
**501 North Main St.**
**(828) 693-0887**

*Opulence* describes this unique store. Mehri & Company carries estate and antique jewelry, unique gifts, custom silk arrangements, and antique furniture, tapestries, and collectibles. You'll also find wonderful table linens, plushy pillows, and unique picture frames. If it's not of high quality, you won't find it here.

## PURPLE SAGE
**416 North Main St.**
**(828) 693-9555**
This is the place to go if you're a gourmet cook, know one, or would like to become one. You'll find pots, pans, knives, kitchen gadgets, coffee, cookbooks, gifts, and imported and domestic wines. There's a wine cellar downstairs, and Purple Sage also holds periodic wine tastings and cooking classes. The award-winning chef/owner of Expressions Restaurant has added Purple Sage to his library of culinary enterprises.

## SOMEWHERE IN TIME
**514 North Main St.**
**(828) 693-5900**
You lose track of time in this shop's vast array of Victorian and country collectibles and antiques. It's the perfect place to browse and browse and, of course, buy. Be sure to check out the items on the half-price table.

## SWEET MEMORIES
**430 North Main St.**
**(828) 692-8401**
The focus here is on regional fine crafts, including a distinctive selection of Southeastern art glass, functional and decorative pottery, jewelry, wood, fiber, metalwork, china painting, and handcrafted gifts.

## TOUCHSTONE GALLERY
**318 North Main St.**
**(828) 692-2191**
We never go to Hendersonville without dropping in to see what beautiful art and whimsical creations are displayed at this gallery, which specializes in contemporary American art and exceptional craft items. We seldom leave without being creatively inspired ourselves.

**VILLAGE GREEN ANTIQUE MALL**
**424 North Main St.**
**(828) 692-9057**
It will take you a while to see all the quality antiques and collectibles here. The mall contains 12,000 square feet full of inventory brought in by 35 dealers from six states. Shipping and delivery services are available.

**WICKWIRE**
**330 North Main St.**
**(828) 692-6222**
This fine art/folk gallery displays both established and emerging artists. (See the Art Galleries section of our Arts and Culture chapter.)

## Naples
**CRYSTAL VISIONS**
**5920 Asheville Hwy., exit 13**
**(828) 687-1193**
This unique shop is a bookstore, and much more. Its product line offers all things for spiritual growth resources. Among these items are fountains, crystals, candles, chimes, angels, music, prisms, fairies, jewelry, pyramids, and aromatherapy.

## Rutherford County
### Chimney Rock/Lake Lure
Most folks visit the Chimney Rock/Lake Lure area to see the Chimney or to boat and swim in Lake Lure. Another good reason to visit this thermal belt is for the rest and relaxation afforded by the many lodges, motels, cabins, and RV sites. There are those who make it a destination for fine dining as well.

Esmeralda Inn even offers a chef's table that takes you beyond the already extraordinary dining experience in their dining room. The chef's table is a glassed-in air-conditioned area situated directly in the kitchen. The room can accommodate up to eight persons. You participate in the meal by observing the chef prepare your four courses. He interacts with you as he brings the meal to your table.

Shopping at Chimney Rock Park Sky Lounge takes you back to the days of penny arcades and yesteryear in America, when everyone brought home souvenirs of salt water taffy, items embossed with the name of the town or site visited, spoons, postcards, and other memorabilia. In addition you can find walking sticks, T-shirts, caps, and copies of *The Last of the Mohicans*, which was filmed in the area.

The road going through Chimney Rock/Lake Lure was once a main route from Asheville to Charlotte, North Carolina, via Rutherfordton. This two-lane road is known by at least three names: Highway 64/74-A, Lone Star Memorial Highway, and Andrew Jackson Highway. Just prior to entering the town of Chimney Rock from the west, you have crossed the eastern Continental Divide, leaving Henderson County and entering Rutherford County. The shops lining the road are self-explanatory as tourist destinations. You can find novelties, sandwiches, fudge, and ice-cream cones. Pick and choose based on your interest. Permit us to suggest two that we have found of special interest.

**EDIE'S GOOD THINGS**
**Highway 64/74-A**
**Chimney Rock Village**
**(828) 625-0111**
Edie offers fine crafts, most of which are handmade by artisans of the mountains. Pottery from the Barking Spider of Penland area is available. Jewelry by the four-generation-old firm of Stuart Nye of Asheville can be found here. An entire section is metalwork of menorahs and other religious symbols. Wood, glass, and clay have been sculpted and turned into objects of art. Although small, the shop does have a first and second floor, and a roof with spectacular views. Edie is certain to invite the shopper to go up on the roof for a grand view of Chimney Rock. If you are looking for fine crafts, this is the place.

**JULIE'S GOURMET MARKET**
**AND SPECIALTIES**
**2402 Memorial Hwy. (64/74-A)**
**(828) 625-2990**
Julie's is a half-mile east of the lake and has been an oasis since 1996. She offers something special

for the discerning palate with her large selection of wine and cheese. For the camper who wants a quick meal already prepared, Julie can supply it. These range from smoked salmon pâté to pasta and other Italian specialties. She even carries prime steaks, poultry, fresh fruits, and vegetables. If you need a gift basket for someone back home, Julie can assist you in selecting the items and then ship it for you. These quality items are reasonably priced.

## Transylvania County
### Brevard

A few years ago the heart of downtown Brevard was struggling to find itself. Many people predicted doom for downtown commerce after Kmart and Wal-Mart opened in separate shopping centers at about the same time and took Belk and other downtown businesses with them. Quite the opposite has happened. Brevard's central district is vitally alive as the heart of Transylvania County's social life.

Shopping here is more attractive than ever. Brevard is perched on top of a high hill and is graced by an old, redbrick courthouse where Main and Broad streets meet. Lovely views of the mountains of Pisgah National Forest rise in the west. Here you have a choice of festivals, art shows, and entertainment all year long. On summer weekends there's nearly always music on the courthouse lawn, including programs by musicians from the Brevard Music Center. And an array of shops and restaurants, both new and old, have turned this into a delightful place to roam and enjoy.

Businesses stretch up and down Main and Broad and spill over onto all the side streets. Merchants and restaurateurs have even moved into some of Brevard's interesting old houses, transforming them into enticing shops and eateries. We've included a sampling of stores you can find in downtown Brevard. It's best to simply follow your nose in and out of all the pretty and fun shops. Stop in, too, at the **Transylvania County Arts Co-op,** 7 East Main St., across from the courthouse, to view original works by local artists.

Down the street the **Chamber of Commerce,** 35 West Main St., (828) 883-3700, is loaded with visitor information, and it has an art gallery too.

## BREVARD ANTIQUE MALL
**57 East Main St.**
**(828) 885-2744**

Brevard's largest antiques shop has 20,000 square feet of quality antiques and collectibles, featuring 60 booths on three floors. There are always really beautiful pieces here with enough room to display them properly.

## CELESTIAL MOUNTAIN MUSIC AND FOLK ART
**16 West Main St.**
**(828) 884-3575**

You're likely to find people making music when you walk into this store, and you're sure to encounter a fascinating array of musical instruments, such as handcrafted mountain dulcimers, Celtic harps, guitars, dobros, mandolins, autoharps, and crystal flutes—and you can schedule lessons to learn how to play them. The shop also records traditional music and makes instrument repairs.

## D. D. BULLWINKLE'S
**38 South Broad St.**
**(828) 862-4700**

This unique shop, which specializes in Southern products, is practically impossible to describe—you'll have to see it for yourself. The shop sells dozens of kinds of penny candy, gourmet coffee, gifts, books, beautiful handmade furniture, jams, jellies, relishes, T-shirts (some with local logos), and—our favorite—very funny horse swings made from old tires.

Adjoining the shop is Rocky's Soda Shop, where you can enjoy an old-fashioned milkshake, meal, or snack (see our Restaurant chapter for more information on Rocky's).

## THE FOREST PLACE
**100 South Broad St.**
**(828) 884-5713**

This shop is a real find. It brings the forest into the city. Educational manipulatives, books, CDs, and all sorts of nature-oriented items are available. Maps, compasses, backpacks, water bottles, and sweats are on the shelves. This is just one of the many outlets across the United States that serve as a retail conduit for our forest system. All profits go to the support of environmental and forestry programs.

### THE FRAME-UP
**4 West Main St.**
**(828) 883-2385**
This is the place to go for fantastic archival framing. The store also carries one-of-a-kind jewelry, wood turnings, handmade furniture, and beautiful (framed, of course) prints, as well as blown glass, porcelain, and pottery.

i Not only do our local thrift stores support excellent local charities, they can dress you in style. Four like-new silk blouses were a steal for 25 cents each at a sale in Brevard's Humane Society Thrift Shop on East Main Street.

### HERITAGE ANTIQUE MALL
**15 West Main St.**
**(828) 883-4323**
Fifteen or so carefully chosen dealers bring everything from the finest antique furniture to vintage comic books, all beautifully displayed. Here's the place to look for a rare book. If you've been looking for a special, specific something, put your desire on file with owners Greg and Sandy Wagner; they'll try to locate it for you. The mall specializes in antique fishing gear.

### JEANIE'S BOUTIQUE
**112 South Broad St.**
**(828) 884-9573**
For superfeminine fashions at prices so low you won't believe the tags, go to Jeanie's. The shop sells stunning Indian clothing at a cost that's often less than you'd pay at discount dress stores. Stay a while and chat with the shop's interesting owner.

### MAIN STREET LTD.
**224 East Main St.**
**(828) 884-4974**

Housed in a grand, two-story white house, this shop is filled with exquisite surprises, including gift baskets, home accessories, and camp care packages for the many children who attend summer camps in the area. The store's unique gift wrapping turns any purchase into a celebration.

### O. P. TAYLOR'S
**2 South Broad St.**
**(828) 883-2309**
This store is a world unto itself. The main attractions are the toys that fill its two floors and flow down the stairs, sometimes right out on the sidewalk. One entire room is devoted to toy trains. Handmade wooden toys and educational games are here, too.

### THE PROPER POT
**44 East Main St.**
**(828) 877-5000**
You'll find just the thing for the cook in your life. In addition to kitchenware, the Proper Pot sells linens, gift baskets, and gourmet teas and coffees.

### THE WHITE SQUIRREL SHOPPE
**2 West Main St.**
**(828) 877-3530, (888) 729-7329**
This wonderful shop's jam-packed with collectibles; odds and ends of small, wonderful pieces of furniture; lamps; statues; and gifts and crafts. There are also a number of its namesake white squirrels in all sizes and shapes. These make great souvenirs of the area because there really are white squirrels in Brevard (see the White Squirrels of Brevard sidebar in our Bed-and-Breakfasts and Country Inns chapter).

## SOUTHERN MOUNTAINS

### Haywood County

#### Waynesville
Where downtown Brevard is built on a hill, Haywood's county seat sits on a high plateau. This affords mountain views in all directions. And like Hendersonville, Waynesville, with its turn-of-the-20th-century buildings, brick sidewalks,

park benches, and plants, has made its charming downtown one of the most popular shopping spots in the county. There's an interesting mix of more than 50 stores here: boutiques, galleries, specialty shops, family and service stores, and restaurants. An influx of elegant home furnishing shops and galleries brings shoppers from larger cities and Tennessee for weekend trips.

We've never had a problem finding a parking spot on Main Street, but if you do, there's free parking on Montgomery and Wall streets, both of which run parallel to Main Street, 1 block in either direction. From Wall Street, a couple of walkways lead right down to Main. While you're here, take time to visit the Shelton House (828-452-1551), just off Main Street, home to the Museum of North Carolina Handicrafts (see our Mountain Crafts chapter).

If you don't shop yourself out in Waynesville, you should travel another 10 or 15 minutes to Maggie Valley. Here, along a 3-mile stretch of U.S. Highway 19, you'll find a bonanza of craft and souvenir stores. There is lodging, RV parks, camping, restaurants, and other attractions (see our Attractions, and Nightlife chapters).

## BLUE OWL STUDIO AND GALLERY, INC.
### 11 North Main St.
### (828) 456-5050
Hand-painted antique graphics of North Carolina's mountains are the mainstay of this gallery, but you'll find other interesting items here, too. (See Art Galleries in our Arts and Culture chapter.)

## CANDY BARREL
### 55 North Main St.
### (828) 452-0075
Its name explains it all. Barrels and baskets brimming with candies line the walls and run in a great aisle down the center, assailing you with scents of sweetness. Anything you find here sells for under $6 a pound, so you can mix the flavors to your taste buds' content. If that wasn't enough, there's a soda fountain in the rear, and you can enjoy its treats there or at the tables on the store's "front porch." There are various kinds of homemade fudge, too.

## CHLOE & CO.
### 117 North Main St.
### (828) 452-7792
Housed in a small stone building that was Waynesville's first library, the selection at this upscale boutique is not large, but the items here are ever so tempting! There are stylish ladies' fashions and accessories and a number of excellent pieces of fine antique furniture.

## EARTHWORK'S ENVIRONMENTAL GALLERY
### 21 North Main St.
### (828) 452-9500
Earthwork's brings together arts and crafts of this county and Mexico's Native Americans. Africa is also represented. (See Art Galleries in our Arts and Culture chapter.) The Earthwork's Frame Gallery (828-456-3666) is at 152 South Main St.

## GATEKEEPERS
### 4 North Main St.
### (828) 698-5466
Excellent taste is reflected in the home accessories, gifts, and furniture found here. And the old building with its squeaky wooden floors and tin ceiling is almost as interesting. There's a fine garden shop in the rear.

## HOME-TECH: THE KITCHEN SHOP
### 5 North Main St.
### (828) 452-7672
The items here can make cooking an adventure. This kitchen shop offers all that is necessary to make a cook a chef. In addition to cookbooks, it has fine German-made cookware, small appliances, Burton burners and stove-top grills, gourmet coffees and all the items needed to brew them, handmade cutting boards and butcher-block tables, gift baskets made to order, and much more.

## MAST GENERAL STORE
### 63 North Main St.
### (828) 452-2101
In addition to selling outdoor clothing and gear, this store also serves as a ticket office for local cultural events. The original fixtures of this early 20th-century store are still in place, including

rocking chairs for its customers. Old-time housewares and other unusual items are stocked on the mezzanine. Periodic demonstrations by well-known regional craftspeople are also held here.

### RIDGE RUNNER NATURALS
**33 North Main St.**
**(828) 456-3003, (800) 525-3009**
Ridge Runner carries nature-inspired gifts for all ages: birdfeeders, wind chimes, nature puzzles, T-shirts, books, games, walking sticks, maps, and much more.

### T. PENNINGTON ART GALLERY
**15 North Main St.**
**(828) 452-4582**
To see Teresa Pennington's amazing skills at reproducing mountain scenes with colored pencils is worth the trip to this gallery. (See Art Galleries in our Arts and Culture chapter.)

### TWIGS & LEAVES
**98 North Main St.**
**(828) 456-1940**
David Erickson and his wife, potter Kaaren Stoner, whose studio is in this craft gallery, call their shop "an adventure into the art of Nature," and it certainly is! Kaaren's leaf-enhanced pottery, arches and outdoor seatings made of twigs and branches, nature photos and handmade fountains, meditation pools and organic plant vessels, whimsical lizards, and many, many other artists' nature-related items, plus reasonable prices, make it nearly impossible to leave this shop without making a purchase.

### WHITMAN'S BAKERY & SANDWICH SHOP
**18 North Main St.**
**(828) 456-8271**
Whitman's is one of the busiest stores in town. The wonderful smells wafting out the door tend to lure you right in. And believe us, the sandwiches layered between freshly baked bread are hard to beat! It's another great place for sweet tooths, too.

## Jackson County
### *Dillsboro*
Sylva is the county seat of Jackson County, and it's a bustling town stretched out along two busy one-way streets graced with a number of very nice shops and restaurants. But it's the tiny, doll-like town of Dillsboro, just a mile down Business U.S. Highways 19/23, that's the real shopping mecca for tourists and area residents alike. It's also one of the stops made by excursion trains of the Great Smoky Mountains Railroad, which brings even more visitors to Dillsboro.

With a shopping area approximately 2 blocks long and two streets wide (plus the railway that runs through the middle of town), you wouldn't think there could be so much to see, but there is. The following are only a few of nearly 50 shops and restaurants you'll find in this village. Most are open Mar through Dec, giving many of the crafters who supply and often own the shops here time to craft and restock during the winter months.

Dillsboro is a delight in any season, but the fantasy finish to the Dillsboro shopping season takes place on the first two Fridays and Saturdays in Dec when the Christmas Luminaries is held. Thousands of candles light the way to extended evenings of musical entertainment and complimentary refreshments.

Here's just a brief sampling of the treats in Dillsboro.

**i** If you are shopping for something unique or for certain types of products, save yourselves some time by calling the local chamber of commerce or visitors centers (listed in the Area Overview chapter) for stores that might carry the items on your list.

### BRADLEY'S GENERAL STORE
**52 Front St.**
**(828) 586-3891**
When you've visited all the stores listed here and a great many others, you'll find respite at Bradley's General Store, which has country gifts,

home furnishings, and—best of all—an antique, but working, soda fountain.

### DOGWOOD CRAFTERS
**90 Webster St.**
**(828) 586-2248**

Housed in a large, renovated log building around the corner from Front Street, this is one of our favorite stores in Dillsboro. We are particularly taken with the lovely, artistic cornhusk dolls, but there also are hundreds of contemporary and traditional handicrafts on display, including pottery, pillows, art, and toys.

### ENLOE MARKET PLACE
**78 Front St.**
**(828) 586-3603**

Housed in an historic old home, Enloe carries fine gifts, prints, and home accessories and offers a children's corner full of items to delight the kids. Want to impress your friends? Pick up a few bars of monogrammed soap.

### FRONT STREET COMPANY/YARN CORNER
**64 Front St.**
**(828) 586-0089**

Needleworkers will love the variety they'll find at this shop. Gifts, fine yarns, handpainted needlepoint, and cross-stitch supplies are sold here. You can also take a class or receive assistance on your latest project. And for a respite before more shopping, you can dine at the Front Street Cafe or out in the courtyard. Front Street Company is a great place to purchase delectable gourmet items like teas and coffees, plus jams and jellies, which make great gifts or personal indulgences.

### GALLERY Z
**134 Front St.**
**(828) 586-3383**

The mountains are becoming world famous for studio glass, and at Gallery Z you can see some samples of it in the form of candleholders, lamps, vases, and perfume bottles.

### MOUNTAIN POTTERY
**152 Front St.**
**(828) 586-9183**

At Mountain Pottery you can see pottery being made in an open studio. It's also got the town's largest selection of handmade porcelain, stoneware, and raku. The pottery is supplied by more than 75 craftspeople from the region.

### THE NATURE CONNECTION
**Front Street**
**(828) 586-0686**

This is a delightful store for both adults and children. It's full of home and garden accessories: fountains, metal sculpture, clocks, blown glass, and birdhouses and feeders. Nature themes are also found in the books, guides, T-shirts, music, educational items, and toys. And this list doesn't begin to cover what you'll find here.

### RIVERWOOD PEWTER SHOP
**Highway 441**
**(828) 586-6996, (800) 580-2547**

The Riverwood Shops developed around a hand-hammered pewter business established in 1930. The Riverwood Pewter Shop is still here making hand-hammered pewter on the premises. You'll find the shop 1 mile south of U.S. Highways 74/23.

### RIVERWOOD'S OAKS GALLERY
**Highway 441**
**(828) 586-6542**

Right next door to the Riverwood Pewter Shop, this cooperative of more than 80 Appalachian craftspeople is a showcase of weaving, jewelry, glass, wood, wearables, and pottery.

### VILLAGE STUDIO
**130 Front St.**
**(828) 586-4060**

The talents that flower in these mountains are beautifully showcased in this gallery. It's filled with paintings and prints by area artists, handmade dulcimers, gifts, and cards. The gallery-style shop also displays decorative accessories for home and office. The studio also does professional framing.

## Macon County

### Highlands

"There's just no place like Highlands," is a comment heard frequently. It's true, and the town has gone out of its way with rules and regulations to make sure that its small but busy downtown stays as nice as it is now. Highlands is also well named. Its elevation of 4,118 feet provides pleasant summertime temperatures for roaming its Main Street and surrounding shopping areas. If you've never been to Highlands before, you might want your first stop to be at the **Visitor Information Center,** 386 Oak St., (828) 526-2112, just above Town Hall on US 64. Not only will the staff give you the scoop on the whole area and a shopping guide that includes a map, but there are also public restrooms here.

On Main Street you can spend hours roaming in and out of the shops, where you'll find a wide variety of clothing, jewelry, art, gifts, handicrafts, toys, bird and bat houses, food, furniture, flowers, and so on. If there's one overriding theme, it's quality. The residents who occupy some of the most expensive real estate in the mountains expect it, and if the droves of shoppers who come here from other areas are any indication—the friendly merchants of Highlands aim to please.

Any first-time Highlands' shopper will be immediately drawn to Main Street's diverse shops. But don't stop with Main Street. Highlands has a number of distinctive shopping areas, including quite a few of its side streets. One example is Fourth Street: Shops here are referred to as "on the hill." Other small Highlands shopping centers (all within walking distance of downtown) include Wright Square, Oak Square, and Mountain Brook Square. There are also some great shops on the main roads leading into town.

Just keep in mind when contemplating a Highlands' shopping spree that some of these stores close after Oct or Dec or are open only on weekends. At this high an elevation, where winters can be bitter cold, a lot of residents and some storeowners spend the colder months in warmer climes.

**ACORNS**
**465 Main St.**
**(828) 787-1877**
This shop features European and American antiques, gifts, glass, unique lighting, and elegant accessories. It is part of the beautiful Old Edwards Inn complex.

**BRYANT ART GLASS STUDIO**
**260 Franklin Rd., US 64**
**(828) 526-4095**
Everything glass is made here by fusing together pieces of glass at 1,500 degrees in a kiln. Ground enamels are used for colors and crochet doilies or stencils for the designs. Awarded commissions include the cobalt and clear-glass plates designed for the Charlotte Mint Museum of Craft and Design. (See our chapter on Arts and Culture.)

**HOUSE OF LORD**
**341 Main St.**
**(828) 526-9147**
Long an elegant fixture on Main Street, House of Lord is the place to go for fine jewelry and art. The lines carried here are by internationally known designers.

**JULIANA'S**
**366 Main St.**
**(828) 526-4306**
Antiques and decorative accessories are featured in this shop. You will find specialties such as majolica, Victorian silver plate, and other gift items.

**MCCULLEY'S CASHMERE**
**242 South Fourth St.**
**(828) 526-4407**
McCulley's, with another shop in Aspen, Colorado, specializes in Scottish cashmere knitwear for women and men. There is also jewelry and accessories from which to choose.

**MIRROR LAKE ANTIQUES**
**215 South Fourth St.**
**(828) 526-2080**

This full-service antiques store has a large selection of estate jewelry. It's the place to look for semiprecious stones, mineral specimens, gold jewelry, jewelry design, and remodeling.

### STONE LANTERN
### 395 Main St.
### (828) 526-2769

This is one of our favorite shops in Highlands. It's not just the beautiful, well-chosen items from Asia found here. It's the wonderful way in which they're displayed. Expect some high prices, but the quality is worth the cost.

### TIGER MOUNTAIN WOODWORKS
### 2089 Hwy. 106 South
### (828) 526-5577
### www.summerhousehighlands.com

Shopping for a rustic look? This shop sells handcrafted furnishings, including custom lodge furniture and country reproductions, such as beds, tables, dressers, and other items for the entire house.

### THE TOY STORE
### 364 Main St.
### (828) 526-9415

We never go to Highlands without dropping in at the Toy Store to see the latest in toys and games. Here you'll find old and new favorites, plus stuffed animals, dolls, and so much more.

### WHISKERS
### Main and Third Streets
### (828) 526-3612

Whiskers specializes in gifts for pets and their people. You'll find collars, catnip toys, biscuits, decorative leashes, bones, bowls, T-shirts, and all manner of things pet lovers can't do without.

## Cherokee County

If you go any farther west in North Carolina than Cherokee County, you'll be in Tennessee. If you go south from there, then welcome to Georgia. So with just about 20 miles within the North Carolina state line, you can still have your "last cup of coffee" before leaving the state. The Daily Grind and Wine coffee shop and wine bar (46 Valley River Ave., (828) 835-7322) in Murphy advertises just that idea. You can find quaint, old-timey Southern town centers in Murphy and in Andrews. There is also the opportunity to pick up a big chunk of folklore while you are here.

The Mountains to the Sea Trail begins in this corner of North Carolina. By following a meandering line you can make it to the sea by crossing over Mount Mitchell, the Appalachian Trail, the Blue Ridge Parkway, and plenty of cities and towns all the way to Manteo, North Carolina, and the Atlantic Ocean. The highway distance is about 550 miles. The meandering footpath is about twice that.

So tuck into a bed-and-breakfast or tie-down your RV and enjoy the ambience of this special corner of North Carolina.

# RECREATION

Leisure time reigns supreme here in the mountains. The quality and diversity of recreational opportunities are unparalleled. After you've been swept along in a white-water raft, gone aloft in a hot-air balloon, come close to nature on a scenic hiking trail, and reeled in a trophy trout on a mountain lake, you're still not finished. Whether you prefer the tamer environs of a city park or the wild river adventure just over the ridge, you'll find just what you're looking for in these hills. The suggestions that follow are just a few of the recreation possibilities.

This chapter highlights the various city and county park areas and their accompanying recreation programs. We also give you an overview of the Lakes, White-water Rafting and Kayaking, the Rivers, Canoeing, Fishing, Hunting, Mountain Biking, Rock Climbing, Hiking, Camping and Campgrounds, Horseback Riding, Off-Road Vehicle Trails, and Other Recreation (like hot-air ballooning and bowling). Listings of a few of the region's guides and outfitters are at the chapter's end. For a list of contact information for ranger stations and National Park Service visitor centers, see our Forests and Parks chapter.

## OUTDOOR SAFETY

Beware the unprepared hiker. Remember that nature, as spectacular as it can be, is also a powerful force and should be respected as such. There are basics of common sense and courtesy that are important to remember whenever you venture into the national parks and forests, as well as other wilderness areas. Be aware when you enter a primitive environment that you will be faced with the challenge of being entirely self-sufficient for whatever time you remain there, and for a lost hiker that could run into days. Invariably, every year a hiker or two is lost in the mountains, requiring rescue teams to scour the area. Often there will be no shelters, campgrounds, water spigots, or restrooms, and wilderness trails are maintained to the most primitive standard. There will be few blazes or signs, so a compass and topographic map and knowledge of how to use them are essential.

Park officers are empowered to enforce the federal regulations on which these rules are based. You can look over a copy of these at park offices throughout the region (see the listings in our Forests and Parks chapter).

## Driving

When traveling by car on the Blue Ridge Parkway or the back roads of the national forests, make sure you observe all traffic regulations and drive a vehicle that's in good working order. Breaking down in some of the remote regions can spell disaster (or at least great inconvenience). Have enough gasoline to take you to your destination and back again, because gas stations are few and far between on the parkway and can seem a world away when you're sitting by the wayside on a dusty back road. Bring along necessary auto tools and a good spare tire, and make sure your brakes and headlights are in good working order. (These mountains often have steep grades to negotiate, and the Blue Ridge Parkway's 27 tunnels require the use of headlights.)

When packing the car for the trip, include the following items: a first-aid kit, flashlight, blanket, light jacket or sweater, and a change of clothing in case the weather changes (see our chapter on Climate). In case of a total breakdown, there's always AAA. For emergency road service, call (800) 222-4222; in Asheville you can call (828) 253-5376. This is also the number of the local AAA travel office. (Nonmembers will be charged, but they will be helped in an emergency.)

## What to Pack

For any extended hiking or camping activity that will be longer than just a stroll to a waterfall, always have these essentials with you: a map, a compass, a flashlight/headlamp with extra batteries and bulbs, extra food, bottled water, extra clothing, sunglasses, first-aid supplies, matches in a waterproof container, and fire starter.

When taking off into the woods, don't forget to take along a respect for the land and your own personal safety. Before you step foot on the trail, study a map of the area. (Maps are often available at visitor centers and ranger stations or posted on a bulletin board near park entrances.) Know where you're going and don't stray from the trails, many of which are clearly marked. It's easy to become disoriented in deep woods, and steep drop-offs covered by foliage can mean sudden disaster. If you get lost, stay put; you're easier to find that way. It's good to have a pocket whistle when hiking. Use three blasts on the whistle to alert those in search of you. If you get lost near a stream or creek, follow the water downstream; it will most likely lead to a community.

Dress properly for the season, and wear sturdy worn-in shoes with thick, absorbent socks to prevent blistering. This helps in terms of comfort as well as navigation of rough terrain. Changes in elevation make for unpredictable weather. Be aware of the potential for change and be prepared.

When hiking or camping, never go alone. Always tell someone your route (you are required to sign in with a park ranger for overnight hikes in national parks). And always make your whereabouts and intentions known to others. Carry plenty of water. Streams may look sparkling and your thirst may be great, but, unfortunately, the water can be contaminated.

Carry along a fully charged cell phone, but do be aware that you may not find a signal everywhere in these mountains.

## Trails

Trails are rated by difficulty level, steepness, how obvious the trail is to follow, and the roughness of the tread. Markers indicating difficulty are provided by the forest service and are usually at the beginning of the trail. The easiest trails have obvious routes and easy grades, with some pitches up to 20 percent maximum and a relatively smooth tread. They are indicated by a green mark with a slight curve. More difficult trails are marked with a curving blue line and have routes that are usually recognizable but are somewhat challenging with moderate grades, with some pitches up to 30 percent maximum and a smooth to rough tread. A most difficult trail may not be recognizable, requiring a high degree of skill, and may have a steep grade with some pitches greater than 30 percent and rough tread. The hardest trails will have markers with a black zigzag on them.

You should not leave any trail unless you have the equipment and survival skills to meet any condition of terrain, climate, or exertion. Mechanical forms of transportation are not allowed in some wilderness areas. Although most trails are open only to hikers, some are designated for horse use in the Southern Nantahala and Shining Rock Wildernesses. Mountain bikes are not permitted, and you may not hike with a group of more than 10 people. Check in at the ranger station before your hike.

## Food and Cooking

It's a good idea to bring a camp stove if you have one (or can borrow or rent one). They have improved in size and utility. If you must have a fire, make sure you control it. Use existing fire rings when possible. Make sure the fire is dead before leaving, using sand or water to douse the smoldering embers thoroughly. Fires are prohibited in the Shining Rock Wilderness and Middle Prong Wilderness Areas; therefore you must carry a backpack stove if you wish to cook in this area. Bring plenty of energy-rich, protein-packed edibles. You'll be exerting a great deal of energy while hiking, swimming in mountain pools, or rafting and kayaking. Any type of "bar"—be it granola, fruit, oatmeal—packs easily and staves off hunger on the trail. Homemade trail mix with raisins, dried fruits, nuts, a few carob or chocolate chips, and sunflower seeds is fairly free of additives and added sugars. A handful can keep you going on those uphill climbs.

Carry plenty of water (squeeze bottles are the most easily accessible) and drink often, even when not thirsty. You may become dehydrated before you feel the urge to quench your thirst.

## What to Do with Waste

Remember the rule of seasoned campers and hikers: "Pack it in—pack it out." Leave no sign of your time in the woods, not only for the sake of future generations but also for the benefit of the true residents of the woods—the wildlife. Use thoughtful methods of sanitation. Bury all human waste and toilet paper in a hole 6 inches deep and at least 100 feet away from any water source. Tampons and pads should be carried back out with you in sealed containers—the scent of blood could attract bears or other wild animals. Do use biodegradable soap and a wash pan; scatter your wash water away from creek banks. Obviously you should take all trash back out with you. Carry resealable bags that can be shut almost airtight for your food waste.

## Wild Animals

Be aware of your intrusion into the animals' woodland home. Leave all wild animals alone. Bears come out occasionally in the mountain park lands, particularly in the southern mountains near the Great Smoky Mountains National Park. Do not approach bears. They may look cuddly, but they can be dangerous. If one approaches your car, stay inside with the windows rolled up. Make noise on the trail or at your campsite—bears won't be interested in investigating foreign clamor. Before you sleep, take all food out of your tent. Seal your edibles as securely as possible in a backpack and hang it from a tree several yards from your sleeping area.

Snakes seldom bite unless disturbed or teased, but be aware of them and be able to identify poisonous snakes. Rattlesnakes and copperheads thrive in these parts. Dry conditions tend to bring snakes to water sources. Take note: Rattlesnakes do not always rattle their tails before striking and can strike from any position, in any direction. If you are struck by a poisonous snake and have no suctioning kit, seek help immediately. Immobilize the limb and keep the wound below heart level at all times. Try to identify the markings on the snake, so medical personnel will know which antivenin to administer. Not every bite will require antivenin, but every bite does need medical evaluation.

Rabies can be carried by the common raccoon, another cute, cuddly looking creature you don't want to approach. Rabies affecting even squirrels and domestic kittens has been reported from time to time. A rabid animal will generally foam at the mouth, act aggressively, and have wild eyes, often rolling back into the head. Stay far away from such animals. If bitten, seek medical treatment immediately.

## Insects

Ticks can be a problem in the warmer months. Infected ticks can cause Lyme disease. (Should a tick bite you, leaving a red spot that takes on the looks of a bull's-eye, itches, and is accompanied by a fever, see a doctor as soon as possible. These are the indications of Lyme.) Check yourself after being in the woods and follow these tips: Wear light-colored clothing so you can quickly spot ticks on you, tuck pant legs into socks; use insect repellent with DEET, and do not remove ticks with your fingers. Use pointed tweezers or splinter pickers. Lightly grasping the body of the insect, gently and slowly pull the body straight out, so as not to leave the head behind. Do not squeeze the tick, as this could push its bacteria directly into the victim's bloodstream. You should save the tick and take it with you when you seek medical help, enabling the physician to analyze it and prescribe prophylactic antibiotics if necessary.

Mosquitoes can flourish in the damp woods, so bring plenty of repellent. West Nile virus has arrived in the mountains and has claimed its first human victim. So be particularly vigilant about protecting yourself from mosquitoes: Use insect repellent even over clothing, and wear long pants, socks, and long sleeves in heavily infested areas. Mosquitoes are most active from dusk to dawn, so consider avoiding outdoor activities during the early morning or evening hours.

According to the Centers for Disease Control, most people who are infected with the West Nile virus will not have any type of illness. It is estimated that 20 percent of the people who become infected will develop West Nile fever: mild symptoms, including fever, headache, and body aches, occasionally with a skin rash on the trunk of the body and swollen lymph glands.

The symptoms of severe infection (West Nile encephalitis or meningitis) include headache, high fever, neck stiffness, stupor, disorientation, coma, tremors, convulsions, muscle weakness, and paralysis. It is estimated that one in 150 persons infected with the West Nile virus will develop a more severe form of disease.

### Plant Life

Foliage is abundant on the trails. One of these plants, poison ivy, a common bush, causes an itchy rash and more severe reactions in those allergic to it. It grows as a vine or short shrub with three glossy light-green leaves per stalk. Avoid it. If you feel you have been in poison ivy, wash your skin thoroughly with soap and warm water after contact. The oily sap this plant emits, known as urushiol, can cling to pets' fur, clothing, shoelaces, even gardening tools for an extended period and plague you months afterward. Wash everything that may have come into contact with the plant. Don't burn green plants—some may be poison ivy, which rendered a Waynesville singer voiceless for months after inhaling the noxious smoke.

### Hunting

Also, be aware of hunting season. If you hike trails during hunting season, always wear bright "hunter orange" for your protection. Deer season runs from early to mid-Oct and again from late Nov to mid-Dec. Bear season runs from mid-Oct to early Nov and again from mid-Dec to early Jan. These are very general time frames. Be sure to call for specific dates each year.

You can call the 24-hour phone line at the North Carolina Wildlife Resources Commission (919-662-4381 or 800-662-7137), for information on hunting and fishing seasons and regulations in this region of North Carolina.

### Waterfalls

Waterfalls are another deceptively beautiful lure of nature here in the mountains. They have a magnetic quality, but they can be deadly. Each year someone thinks the view must be better from the top of the falls—a fatal mistake. There have been numerous deaths in the past few years due to slipping and falling from the tops or even sides of waterfalls. The rocks in any of our mountain streams are moss-covered and slippery, and the water rushing over the falls is swift and cold. One misstep can be the last. View these wonderful waterfalls at the proper distance and from the bottom, looking up. Do not attempt to climb them. Use that zoom lens to get a closer look.

### Hypothermia

Hypothermia, the condition that causes a potentially fatal drop in body temperature, is a term you need to know. And contrary to popular belief, you don't have to be stranded in a snowstorm to experience this life-threatening condition. Whenever cold, moisture, and fatigue persist, it takes only a few hours to bring on the fatal results of hypothermia. Poor food intake, improper clothing, and alcohol can contribute to the problem.

Symptoms of hypothermia include exhaustion, uncontrolled shivering, confusion, loss of motor coordination, slurred speech, irrational behavior (like trying to disrobe in the cold), and unconsciousness. A victim of severe hypothermia, which occurs when the body core temperature falls below 92 degrees Fahrenheit, shivers in waves, cannot walk, curls into a fetal position to find the last remnants of warmth in the body, and has rigid muscles. All forms of hypothermia must be treated immediately by drying and warming the victim.

For mild hypothermia add more layers of clothing, put on dry clothes, increase physical activity, and seek shelter.

For moderate hypothermia add food and fluids, heat the victim with body contact, and get the victim in a sleeping bag with another person who is wearing light clothing (to transfer body heat).

For severe hypothermia create a shell of total insulation around the victim and surround the victim with dry clothing, blankets, and multiple sleeping bags. Wrap all of the above in plastic to prevent heat loss as the core temperature rises and pushes warmer blood toward the extremities. Feed the victim warm sugar water a bit at a time.

Urinating will help conserve heat by emptying the bladder and concentrating body heat on the contracted inner organs. Do not expose the hypothermic victim to extremes of heat. Extremes of heat will burn the victim or can shock the heart. Remember that even a 50-degree day can bring on hypothermia if conditions are wet and windy. Keep your head covered in this kind of weather. Body heat may quickly be lost without a hat.

All victims of hypothermia should get medical attention.

### Heat Exhaustion and Heat Stroke

In warm weather the sun can be intense at these higher elevations, especially in the summer months. And it's getting hotter. Local weather announcers say we're breaking records every month with record highs. Bring along enough sunblock for all exposed skin. We also recommend sunglasses to cut the glare, and a sun hat. Bring plenty of fluids along and drink them, whether you're thirsty or not. You may become dehydrated even before you feel the urge to quench your thirst. Heat exhaustion, which can lead to heat stroke, must be taken care of immediately. A major increase in the body core temperature can kill a victim within minutes.

Signs to watch out for are sweating, increased pulse, weakness, dizziness, nausea, and thirst. Signs of heat stroke are hot skin, either very pale skin or very flushed skin, decreased urine output, increased temperature, and a change in mental status—disorientation and incapacity to reason or make judgments. Try to help relieve these symptoms immediately.

For heat exhaustion, rest in the shade, replace fluid loss with a water-and-salt solution (a teaspoon of salt per quart of water), remove all but the most necessary articles of clothing, and refrain from further physical activity for the day.

For heat stroke move the victim to a cool spot. Remove the victim's clothing and pour water on the extremities. Then fan him or her, increasing air circulation and evaporation, or cover the victim with cool, wet cloths and fan him or her. You can also immerse the victim in cool (but not cold) water. Do not allow the heat-stroke sufferer to become cold or the body will begin shivering to produce more heat. Also make sure the person refrains from all physical activity; then seek medical help.

### Final Thoughts

Nature can be formidable, but it can also inspire. Don't be afraid of challenging yourself, but do enter into your outdoor endeavors armed with knowledge, preparation, and training. If you're a wilderness novice, read outdoor magazines before your trip. If we remember to respect the natural environment, our visits to these wood and park lands will be memorable for all the right reasons.

## COUNTY AND CITY PROGRAMS AND AREAS

When time allows, we mountain folk tend to head for the fabulous recreation offered by the 1.5 million acres of public lands in our area (see our Forests and Parks chapter), often overlooking the many recreational opportunities right in our cities and towns. In this section we describe some of those recreational possibilities. And we haven't even attempted to include the ever-so-many private clubs and spas that abound in the region.

### Northern Mountains
### Alleghany County
**CROUSE PARK**
**Grayson and Cherry Streets, Sparta**
This city park provides a playground and covered picnic areas on the grounds of the Crouse House, the former home of one of Sparta's leading citizens. Basketball, volleyball, and horseshoes are also popular here.

## *Ashe County*

### ASHE PARK
### Off Old Highway 16, Jefferson

Centered in a lush green valley, Ashe Park is well equipped for fun with two tennis courts, two baseball fields, two covered picnic areas, a barn-like covered building that can house groups up to 75, four bathrooms, plenty of parking, and a breathtaking view of Mount Jefferson. It's also home to the county's Old Time Fiddler's Convention celebrated each year.

### WEST JEFFERSON PARK
### Church Avenue West, Jefferson

West Jefferson's city park is a pleasant, grassy expanse on the rolling hills behind Main Street. Picnic tables are scattered by the creekside, and a basketball court crowns the hill.

## *Avery County*

### BANNER ELK TOWN PARK
### Highway 194, Banner Elk

This city park is behind Nations Bank, just north of the stoplight in Banner Elk. A few benches, flowers, and a walkway add pleasant touches to this small city park.

### SUNSET PARK
### Beech Mountain Parkway, Banner Elk

This intimate little memorial park on a half-acre gives visitors a lovely place to stop and reflect on the incredible natural beauty of mile-high Beech Mountain.

## *Watauga County*

### BLOWING ROCK MEMORIAL PARK
### Main Street, Blowing Rock

Picnic tables, a children's playground, and tennis courts fill this picturesque public park in the center of tiny Blowing Rock. Just off the main street, the park lends itself to outdoor lunches and ice-cream cone breaks. The park is also the center of village cultural events.

### BOONE GREENWAY PEDESTRIAN WALKING AND BIKING TRAIL
### Boone

The access point for this ambling trail is adjacent to the university parking lot on Dale Street and the Watauga County Parks and Recreation Complex on Complex Drive.

### BROYHILL PARK
### Off Main Street, Blowing Rock

This serene, beautifully landscaped city park, highlighted by a small, placid lake, is just behind Main Street in Blowing Rock. A walking path, beautiful gazebo, and ducks gliding across the water make this pleasant little park a favorite of local residents and visitors alike. A hiking path actually calls for some hearty climbing on the way back, during which you will pass leafy rhododendrons, a little waterfall, and forestation.

### WATAUGA COUNTY PARKS AND RECREATION DEPARTMENT
### 1012 State Farm Rd., Boone
### (828) 264-9511

The county parks and recreation department oversees a number of this area's recreational attractions. Countywide schools are home to a number of park facilities, such as lighted tennis courts, lighted athletic fields for football and soccer, outdoor basketball and volleyball courts, and numerous children's play areas.

The Watauga County Swimming Complex on Complex Drive (828-264-0270) is a popular High Country recreation spot. In an area where winter can bring a definite chill, the indoor, heated 25-meter pool, diving pool, and adjoining children's pool are welcome entertainment. It is open daily, year-round, and the public is welcome. Modest fees vary according to age. Season passes are available. A changing schedule of Red Cross swimming instruction, aquacise, senior exercise, and scuba classes is available on request.

Tot Lot Park, in front of the Watauga County Swimming Complex, is a play area for all children. A picnic shelter, volleyball court, and restrooms are nearby.

An outdoor county pool with a capacity for 60 swimmers is open seasonally from Memorial Day through Labor Day at Green Valley School off Highway 194 East. Hours are noon to 6 p.m. Tues through Sat and 1 to 6 p.m. on Sun.

Howard's Knob Park, open from Apr 1 to Oct 31, is at the highest elevation in the city of Boone. To get to this pleasant little park, head west on King Street, turn right across from the Daniel Boone Inn, and proceed to the top of the hill. You'll find picnic tables, wildflowers, and a great view of Boone at this five-acre park.

## Central Mountains

### Buncombe County

#### ASHEVILLE PARKS AND RECREATION

**Asheville City Hall**

**(828) 259-5800**

Asheville's parks and recreation facilities are scattered throughout the city and provide a multitude of recreational activities and cultural programs for all ages. Many of these are play areas, some with picnic tables and other amenities. The sites are open daily from 6 a.m. to 10 p.m. and can be used free of charge. Maps of park locations are available from the office of city parks and recreation.

Outdoor public swimming pools are found in Malvern Hills (Sulphur Springs Road) and also on Walton Street. They are open June through Aug and charge a moderate admission. The pools offer Red Cross Learn to Swim classes, fitness, and lifeguard certification training. Approximately 20 public tennis courts dot the city for year-round use on a first-come, first-served basis. Some of these hard-surface courts are lighted for evening play.

#### BUNCOMBE COUNTY PARKS AND RECREATION

**49 Mount Carmel Rd., Asheville**

**(828) 250-4260**

This comprehensive county recreation program includes a multitude of services and recreation sites throughout Buncombe County. Athletics are a big part of the program. Softball, soccer, and tennis are available through a number of leagues, teams, and associations in cooperation with or sponsored by the department.

The Aston Park Tennis Center on Hilliard Street (828-255-5193) offers memberships, clinics, private lessons, and regular tournament play. The court facility is free to use and is open beginning in Apr Mon through Thurs from 9 a.m. to 9 p.m. and Fri through Sun from 9 a.m. to 7 p.m. After Thanksgiving, the center is open Sat, Sun, Tues, Wed, and Thurs from 10 a.m. to 6 p.m.

Lake Julian District Park off Long Shoals Road is a thermal lake, used as a cooling agent for the CP&L electric facility on its shore. The lake, south of Asheville in the Skyland area, is a family recreation park open year-round for fishing, canoeing, paddleboating, and outdoor games. A children's play area and picnic shelters are also available. Fishing is allowed from shore or by boat for a rental fee. Patrons must provide their own electric motor—gas motors are not allowed. North Carolina fishing laws are enforced, and a local lake permit is required. Hours are 8 a.m. to 6 p.m. Oct to Mar, in Apr from 8 a.m. to 8 p.m., from May through Aug 8 a.m. to 9 p.m., and in Sept from 8 a.m. to 8 p.m.

The Buncombe County Parks and Recreation Department operates a variety of recreational park sites along the French Broad River and at numerous other points in the county. There are also many athletic fields, community centers, and public pools.

The parks and rec department also sponsors a variety of county-wide enrichment classes in the arts and Red Cross swimming instruction. Call the main number provided earlier for more information.

#### FRENCH BROAD RIVER PARK

**Amboy Road and Riverview Drive, Asheville**

One of Asheville's most beautiful parks, the park meanders alongside the tranquil French Broad River and features an area of open green space with old trees, a wildflower garden, a paved trail, a gazebo, picnic tables and grills, an observation deck, and a small playground. The Dog Park features a large fenced-in area so that dogs may run leash-free.

## LAKE LOUISE
### Lake Louise Drive, Weaverville

Just under a mile from Main Street in this small town north of Asheville is Lake Louise, a human-made lake developed in 1911. The park once sported a dance pavilion on an island in the middle of the lake. Back then, a daily trolley line from the big city of Asheville brought dapper gentlemen and ruffle-skirted young ladies to Lake Louise for evening dance socials.

Today, Lake Louise, with its central 40-foot-high fountain, is enjoying a new generation of visitors of all ages. Walkers on the popular lake path can observe an assortment of tree species cultivated by the Tree Board of the Town of Weaverville. You can identify more than 34 kinds, including sycamores, river birch, Japanese maples, flowering cherry, sugar maples, weeping willow, sweet gum, redbud, and Virginia Pine. This place is popular with local school groups with junior botanists in tow.

Lake Louise also offers a children's playground, an outdoor exercise facility, public restrooms, and picnic shelters for visitors. Hours are 7 a.m. to 11 p.m. daily year-round.

## LAKE TOMAHAWK PARK
### South Laurel Circle Drive, Black Mountain
### (828) 669-2052

This lovely little lake and 20-acre park in a residential area of picturesque Black Mountain was a WPA Depression–era project. Visitors can enjoy the scenic water view, well-trod walking path, landscaping, and resident waterfowl. A community center, public pool, and play areas are part of Lake Tomahawk Park. The park opens around 5 a.m. and closes around midnight.

## Henderson County
### BOYD PARK
### Main Street, Hendersonville
### (828) 697-3079

This city park is within walking distance of downtown. It has a miniature golf course and an activity building used for meetings and events, such as local cat shows. There are also two tennis courts that are open until 11 p.m. year-round.

## YMCA
### 810 Sixth Ave. West, Hendersonville
### (828) 692-5774

Just a few blocks from downtown, this complex is one of the more popular places in Hendersonville. It includes a gymnasium, four lighted tennis courts (two are Har-Tru composition courts), and a weight-training/wellness center with free weights and Nautilus and aerobic equipment. There is also a five-lane, 25-meter, heated indoor swimming pool as well as a whirlpool and sauna. The Y offers classes and activities for both children and adults.

## Polk County
### POLK COUNTY RECREATION DEPARTMENT
### Park Street, Columbus
### (828) 894-8199

The Polk County Recreation Department, which is dedicated to serving citizens of all ages, offers programs in aerobics, youth basketball, youth volleyball, line dancing, men's basketball, and stretch-and-strengthen exercises at Stearns Gym on Walker Street. Gibson Park on Park Street boasts a baseball field and swimming pool. The pool, open from June through Aug, offers family passes, swimming lessons, and water aerobics.

## Transylvania County
### BREVARD COLLEGE
### 400 North Broad St., Brevard
### (828) 883-8292

Many of the recreation facilities at Brevard College, including the indoor swimming pool, are open to the public through inexpensive continuing education classes that include aerobics, water aerobics, beginning rock climbing, and even golf. The campus is also a popular place for runners and walkers.

## SILVERMONT PARK
### East Main Street, Brevard

Open seven days a week from 8:30 a.m. until 10 p.m., Silvermont has two lighted basketball courts, three tennis courts, a playground, a picnic shelter, and a walking path located on the grounds of a historic mansion. Mountain Music Night with a live local artist is free of charge every

Thurs from 7:30 until 10 p.m. (See our Arts and Culture chapter for more on Silvermont Mansion.)

## SOUTH BROAD PARK
**South Broad Street, Brevard**
The small picnic area found at this arboretum is a lovely place to bring a lunch. It's right next to a large multipurpose playing field.

# Southern Mountains
## *Cherokee County*
### ANDREWS RECREATION PARK
**Andrews**
**(828) 321-2135**
Andrews Recreation Park has a beach volleyball court, basketball and tennis courts, a softball field, playground equipment, and an area for horseshoe games. In addition there is a Little League baseball field, picnic areas, swimming pools, and the Andrews Community Center, which contains a large room with a stage, a smaller meeting room, and kitchen and restroom facilities. The park is wheelchair accessible.

### HALL MEMORIAL PARK
**First Street, Andrews**
**(828) 321-2135**
Right next to the Andrews Chamber of Commerce, this park and its gazebo play host to summertime country and gospel concerts and many other events. The Valleytown Cultural Arts Center built the park.

### HIWASSEE RIVER PARK
**Murphy**
**(828) 837-6617**
The colorful displays of flowers, bushes, and trees were planted and are maintained by volunteers with Cherokee County CARE. The park features a walking path, benches, and picnic tables.

### KONEHETE PARK
**103 Konehete St., Murphy**
**(828) 837-6617**
This large city park offers a swimming pool, four lighted tennis courts, and four baseball/softball fields (three with lights). There are also areas for fishing, volleyball, two soccer fields, and outdoor basketball courts.

Organized activities include swim teams, football, basketball, baseball, softball, and soccer leagues for children, youth, and adults. Wrestling, gymnastics, aerobics, line dancing, basketball, and other events are held in the park's Old Rock Gym. Runners and walkers can use the trail or sidewalks throughout Konehete Park or use the running track at the Murphy High School.

## *Clay County*
### CLAY COUNTY RECREATION PARK
**Hwy. 175, Hayesville**
**(828) 389-3532**
This popular public park, not far from the 140-foot-high Chatuge Dam, is on Highway 175 on Lake Chatuge (see our information on this lake in the Lakes section of this chapter). The park has 25 campsites, picnic and swimming areas, a boat launch, and a ballpark.

## *Graham County*
### GRAHAM COUNTY RECREATION COMPLEX
**Knight Street, Robbinsville**
**(828) 479-7983**
The county has a large complex formed by the elementary and middle schools, the public library, and the community and senior citizens center. All the buildings are located in the same area.

This complex also contains tennis courts and a swimming pool. The pool is open from June through Aug; there is a small admission fee.

## *Haywood County*
### TOWN OF CANTON RECREATION PARK
**Penland Street, Canton**
**(828) 646-3411**
This city park, roughly 17 acres in size, contains three picnic sheds and numerous outside picnic tables, two outdoor basketball courts, four lighted tennis courts, play equipment both for small children and teenagers, and two Little League baseball fields. The park's swimming pool and wading pool are open from the middle of May until the first of Sept.

Canton also has an entertainment shelter and bandstand where summer programs are held. Around the park is a 1-mile walking and jogging trail along the banks of the Pigeon River. The parks department uses the sports fields at area public schools for team sports.

## TOWN OF WAYNESVILLE RECREATION PARK
**128 West Marshall St., Waynesville**
**(828) 456-9541, (828) 456-8577**
There's plenty of action at this park, which consists of six hard-surface tennis counts, two outdoor basketball courts, a swimming pool, two picnic areas with shelters, a playground, three softball/baseball fields, two sand volleyball courts, a modified golf driving range, soccer fields, shuffleboard, a quarter-mile track and fitness trail, a horse-show ring, and a recreation building. The City Parks and Recreation Department, which runs the complex, also sponsors all kinds of youth and adult team sports and special events that include an open tennis championship, a trout fishing festival, an Easter egg hunt, and judo and bridge tournaments. For senior citizens there are craft and exercise classes, trips, health programs, and meals. There's a full complement of fitness, hobby, and education classes for other adults and children, too.

## *Jackson County*
The Jackson County Parks and Recreation Department (828-586-6333) operates eight facilities. With 12 full-time staff members and an annual budget of around $250,000, it is able to offer lots of activities year-round. Use the central phone number to get more information on the following areas:

## DILLSBORO RIVER PARK
**Dillsboro**
Canoers and kayakers can access the Tuckasegee River through this one-acre park. The park has picnic tables.

## RALPH J. ANDREWS COUNTY PARK
**Pine Creek Road, Glenville**
**(828) 743-3923**
Built on land near the Glenville dam donated to the county by the Nantahala Power Company, this 78-acre park offers full RV hookups, tent camping, picnicking, hot showers, and boat ramp access to Lake Glenville. To reach it go about 1.5 miles north of the Glenville Post Office until you come to Pine Creek Road on the left. Follow the signs to the park entrance, approximately 2 miles down the road.

## WESTERN CAROLINA UNIVERSITY
**Hwy. 107, Cullowhee**
**(828) 227-7317**
Recreation facilities at the university include the Reid Health and Physical Education Building, Breese Gymnasium, A. K. Hinds University Center, and Ramsey Regional Activity Center. Among the indoor and outdoor sports available here are tennis, volleyball, basketball, swimming, bowling, handball, racquetball, softball, badminton, table tennis, and archery. The university also promotes extensive student intramural and athletic programs and offers Tiny Tot and Youth Swim programs in the summer. The swim program is open to the public. Also open to the public are continuing education courses in yoga, t'ai chi ch'uan, hydrorobics, and other fitness classes.

## *Macon County*
## HIGHLANDS RECREATION PARK
**US 64, Highlands**
**(828) 526-3556**
The recreation center here is open to the public from 8 a.m. to 10 p.m. Mon through Sat and noon to 6 p.m. on Sun. It offers swimming, a Nautilus room, tennis courts, and aerobics—all for a small fee. You can join a cardiovascular program or play softball, baseball, volleyball, basketball, bridge, and duplicate bridge here. Classes are taught in tumbling, rappelling, and wrestling. There is a picnic shelter with a playground nearby. The parks department also sponsors a Fourth of July Celebration, complete with a parade and fireworks, as well as a summer playground program, various bazaars, and a craft festival.

# Close-up

## Finding Cold Mountain

Ever since Charles Frazier's *Cold Mountain,* a novel about a Civil War soldier's walk home to his beloved Ada, became a best-seller and its 2003 cinematic version was a box office hit, people have been wanting to know how to find this 6,030-foot peak, located in Haywood County. There is a trail to the top, but only very experienced hikers should take it. It's steep, poorly marked, and according to how you go, 14 to 16 miles round-trip.

Those not so footworthy can take U.S. Highway 276 from the Blue Ridge Parkway toward Waynesville. This roughly follows along Wagon Road Gap along the east side of the mountain. Near Cruso turn onto U.S. Highway 215, which will run along the western side of the peak. This 50-mile circle will take you past many of the coves, creeks, and churches mentioned in the book and bring you back to the Blue Ridge Parkway not very far south of where you left it.

If you haven't time for this wonderful tour, just stop at the parkway's milepost 420. The massive peak in the distance is Cold Mountain.

---

**MACON COUNTY RECREATION PARK**
**US Hwy. 441 South, Franklin**
**(828) 349-2090**
The many attractions at this large and well-maintained park include softball fields, indoor and outdoor basketball courts, shuffleboard and tennis courts, horseshoes, a children's playground, a loop walking trail, a gymnasium, a swimming pool, two outdoor picnic shelters, and four conference/party rooms. The community building here is open from 8 a.m. to 5 p.m. daily.

**i** As viewed from the Macon County Osage overlook, the mountains seem to go on forever in shifting hues of blue and green. At certain times during the year, the mountains are totally shrouded in blue, which gives both the mountains and the Blue Valley Overlook their names. For a view you won't forget, drive 5.5 miles south of Highlands on Highway 106. Just a bit farther down this same highway, you'll come to the Osage Overlook with another great view of the Blue Valley.

### Swain County
**ALARKA COMMUNITY PARK**
**Alarka Road, Alarka**

Years ago, when an old school building burned in this community west of Bryson City, the town used the land as the site for a fire department and a park with a playground, a picnic area, a nice jogging trail, and a pavilion.

**THE BRYSON CITY ISLAND PARK**
**Access on Island Street, Bryson City**
As early as 1890 the editor of the *Swain County Herald,* the county's first newspaper, urged the county commissioners to strike a bargain for Island Park, as he called the seven-acre island in the Tuckasegee River, "where citizens may find a pleasant rendezvous far from the noise and bustle of city life." However it wasn't until 1986, almost a century later, that Bryson City's downtown island, reached by a swinging bridge, finally became a park.

A lot of history has happened here. It's said, for example, that one of Jesse James's gang members lived on the island for a while (see Iron Foot Island Close-up).

A lighted trail circles the island and tags identify many of the native plants and wildflowers along the trail. Boy Scouts who used the island for a camping site and headquarters in the 1930s and 1940s built the interpretive center. Island Park has a launching site for canoes and kayaks and areas for picnicking and fishing.

### RIVER FRONT PARK
**Island Street, Bryson City**

This half-acre park that runs along the Tuckasegee is the site of the town's Riverfest. It also has a picnic area, including a covered pavilion and a walking trail. Another of Bryson City's parks, the small Ela River Park, also on the Tuckasegee, is used mostly for picnicking and fishing.

### SWAIN COUNTY RECREATION PARK
**West Deep Creek Road, Bryson City**
**(828) 488-6159**

This attractive 34-acre park has a lighted field for baseball and softball, four lighted tennis courts, a basketball court, two playgrounds, shuffleboard and volleyball courts, horseshoe pits, a pavilion and picnic area, and a jogging trail. There is also an outdoor swim complex with an Olympic-size pool, an intermediate pool, and a kiddie pool. The pools are open June through Aug for a small admission price. Season tickets are available.

The list of organized activities includes several softball leagues, volleyball, soccer, aerobics, line dancing, tennis, and swimming lessons. Youth programs feature karate, winter ski instruction, ball programs, and a billiards league. The parks department also sponsors events such as the Christmas Extravaganza.

# THE LAKES

Most of our mountain lakes are found in the central and southern mountains. Some of the smaller ones are private or in residential resort communities. Here we've listed some of the more popular lakes that have public access areas.

## Central Mountains
### *Buncombe County*
**LAKE JULIAN**
**Overlook Road extension access off**
**Highway 146**
**(828) 684-0376**

Lake Julian is a thermal lake used as a cooling agent for Carolina Power and Light. Therefore the lake is deliciously warm, often reaching a scorching 95 degrees in summer! You might find the power plant that looms over one side of the lake a bit disconcerting, but the water never goes below 50 degrees in winter—the best time for fishing here is between Oct and Mar.

Several covered picnic areas make this a favorite spot for family reunions and company gatherings. Picnic shelters range in size from 4 to 10 picnic tables and can be rented for about $20 and $35 for Buncombe County residents. Nonresidents pay roughly $35 and $45. A children's playground, volleyball court, and horseshoe pit provide some free landlubber entertainment. Paddleboats, fishing boats, or canoes can be rented for under $10 an hour if you are a county resident. If not, then expect to pay about double. If you bring your own boat, there is a launch fee of under $5 per day. When there's room, a boathouse and dock can hold your sailboat for approximately $120 (residents) and $180 (nonresidents) per year. The lake is well stocked with bass, crappie, catfish, brim, and talapia, and the price for fishing is nominal.

Lake Julian Park is open from 8 a.m. to 9 p.m. Apr through Aug, 8 a.m. to 8 p.m. in Sept, and 8 a.m. to 6 p.m. Oct through Mar. It is closed on Thanksgiving, Christmas, and New Year's Day.

### LAKE POWHATAN RECREATION AREA
**FR 3484**
**(800) 280-CAMP**

Lake Powhatan is a popular destination with a lot to offer besides the pretty little lake for fishing (it also has a swimming beach and a lifeguard on duty). There are 96 sites for tents and trailers (no hookups), a trailer dump station, picnic tables with grills, restrooms with flush toilets, hiking trails, information hosts, and a central supply of drinking water. The campground is open from mid-Apr through Oct, and the Forest Service provides numerous activities during the summer season. (See the Camping section in this chapter.)

Powhatan is in the Bent Creek Experimental Forest with a system of hiking trails that can get confusing, so pick up a map from the campground office at the entrance to the area. The Western North Carolina Arboretum with its 10 state champion big trees is near Lake Powhatan.

## Rutherford County
### LAKE LURE
### U.S. Highway 74

This sparkling jewel is one of the most picturesque lakes you'll find anywhere—Chimney Rock Park and other spectacular mountains tower over it, and its 1,500 acres include 27 miles of shoreline. You'll find a number of marinas here, but before you haul your boat to the lake, you should be aware that launch fees have been set high to lessen lake congestion. Also, because of its beauty, the shoreline here is quite developed. Still, you'll find a protected, sandy beach area for public use. It is in the center of the Lake Lure Recreation Area, across from Lake Lure Inn.

Lake Lure Fun Center is filled with opportunities. It is located directly on the public beach. There is an admission charge that provides access to the swimming area. Within the Fun Center are climbing areas for kids, slides into the lake, and many other activities. You can rent a snappy little scooter from Hickory Nut Cycles and explore the roads of Lake Lure/Chimney Rock area. Helmets are required and supplied. You must have a valid driver's license.

A water shuttle service operates between the Resort Marina and the Lake Lure Marina. From the Lake Lure Marina, you can easily walk to the Fun Center and the beach. Exploratory boat excursions of Lake Lure are available through Lake Lure Tours. Their toll free number is (877) FUN-4ALL.

# Southern Mountains
## Cherokee County
### CHEROKEE LAKE
### Access off Highway 294

Operated by the Tennessee Valley Authority, this small lake, about a mile in circumference, is fed by the backwaters of Lake Hiwassee. Its pier is a great place to take children fishing, and the pier is designed for easy access for individuals with disabilities.

### LAKE HIWASSEE
### Access off US 64

Built in 1935, the TVA's 307-foot-high, 1,376-foot-long Hiwassee Dam is the highest overspill dam in the United States. It blocks the Hiwassee River to form the center of recreation and fishing in Cherokee County—the 22-mile-long, 6,090-acre Lake Hiwassee. Its 163-mile shoreline is almost completely surrounded by the Nantahala National Forest. In 1955 a second generating unit was added to the dam, along with the world's largest electric motor and reversible pump-turbine, which enable water from the dam to be used to generate electricity during peak hours. During off-hours, the water is then pumped 205 feet back into the Hiwassee reservoir for reuse.

The lake is known for its smallmouth bass and walleyes, but fishermen will also find largemouth bass, bluegill, and crappie here.

The Hanging Dog Recreation Area is less than 4 miles northwest of Murphy off US 64. The area features a 26-site campground, a picnic area, hiking trails, and a boat launch ramp. (See Camping section for more information.) There are also a couple of marinas in the area.

## Clay County
### CHATUGE LAKE
### Access off US 64

Stretching from Clay County into Georgia, Chatuge Lake, with its gradual 132-mile shoreline, backed up by high mountain peaks, reminds us of a Swiss alpine lake. It provides endless hours of water sports and fishing and presents some of the most beautiful views in the county. Thirty-two species of fish have been caught here; smallmouth and largemouth bass, spotted bass, and sunfish are the important sport catches. Striped/white bass hybrids are also stocked annually to control the gizzard shad population, and threadfin shad are stocked periodically to augment the prey bass.

Built in 1941 by the Tennessee Valley Authority, Chatuge has been called the crown jewel of the TVA system because of its picturesque setting. It is also one of the most developed of those lakes, with more than 76 miles of shoreline in private hands. There are three commercial marinas in the area.

The popular Clay County Recreation Park, not far from the 144-foot-high Chatuge Dam, sits on

# Close-up

## Iron Foot Island

Iron Foot Island, Bryson city's seven-acre island park, is just downstream from the Cherokee's Old Mother Town of Kituhawa. Several Cherokee battles with other tribes and whites were fought in the island's immediate vicinity.

The most famous battle occurred in the 1700s and involved the Shawano, a tribe the Cherokee had fought for many years. A noted Shawano leader, Tawa-li-ukwanun, led a raid on the town of Tikwalitsi, near the present site of Bryson City. A Cherokee conjurer named Dead-wood-lighter forecast that the raiders would set an ambush on the island. Some of the Cherokee warriors took his advice and forded the river above the island, entering the site from the rear. But some didn't listen and went straight up the north bank of the river, where they were taken "like fish in a trap." After several bloody encounters, the Shawano were driven up Deep Creek and over the Smokies at Clingmans Dome.

The island was named for Ralph Clark, alias "Iron Foot." While riding with Jesse James, tradition has it, one foot had been shot off during a train robbery. To equalize his gait an iron stirrup was attached to the limb with the missing foot. Clark lived on the island as a hermit.

the reservoir 6.2 miles from Hayesville on US 64 (turn right onto Highway 175). Here you'll find 25 campsites, picnic shelters, a ballfield, a swimming area, and a boat launch ramp.

Another good facility on the lake, this one in the Tusquitee Ranger District of the Nantahala Forest, is the Jackrabbit Mountain Recreation Area. It is on a pine-wooded peninsula that has three camping loops with 103 campsites, a swimming beach with shower facilities, hiking trails, two picnic areas, and a boat launch ramp. To get to the Jackrabbit Mountain Recreation Area, drive 2.5 miles down Highway 175 from US 64; turn right on SR 1155.

### Graham County
#### CHEOAH LAKE
#### Access along Highway 28
This long and narrow Graham County lake is just a few miles west of Fontana Lake. Lying tranquilly between steep green hills, it is reminiscent of a Scandinavian fjord. The water is so clear, you can usually see right down to the bottom. A turn onto U.S. Highway 129 from Highway 28 will bring you to the 225-foot Cheoah Dam, which was built between 1917 and 1919 on the Little Tennessee River. In 1930 the Calderwood Dam farther down-

river in Tennessee formed Calderwood Lake, which is contiguous to its twin, Cheoah.

#### SANTEETLAH LAKE
#### Access off US 129 North
This emerald-green lake in the center of Graham County is popular with both motorboaters and canoeists. Santeetlah has a reputation as one of the best bass-fishing lakes in the area, and pike and crappie are also plentiful. Three public boat ramps are located along its shores. A popular one is at Cheoah Point off US 129 North, just outside Robbinsville near the ranger station (see the list of ranger stations in our Forests and Parks chapter). Cheoah Point also has a campground with 26 campsites, water, flush toilets, a picnic area, and a boat ramp. It is open from Apr 15 until Oc 31. (See Camping in this chapter.) To get to Cheoah Point, take US 129 North for 7 miles, turn left at the sign, and go 0.8 mile.

### Jackson County
#### LAKE GLENVILLE
#### Highway 107
Lake Glenville Dam, 4 miles north of Cashiers, was built on the Tuckasegee River in Jackson County in 1941. It was renamed Lake Thorpe in 1951 after

Nantahala Power's first president, J. E. S. Thorpe. Today it's marked as Lake Thorpe on many, but not all, maps, but it's still Lake Glenville to most people in this area. The 6-mile-long lake covers 1,462 acres and offers 26 miles of shoreline. At an elevation of nearly 3,500 feet, it's the highest major lake in the eastern United States. Lake Glenville is a great place to cruise, canoe, swim, ski, and fish. Mountain trout, walleye, brim, pike, and largemouth and smallmouth bass are the fish you can expect to catch here.

Three marinas in the Glenville community rent pontoon, fishing, and ski boats. These are well marked by signs on Highway 107. The Ralph J. Andrews County Park also provides boat access to the lake. This reservoir is the source of water for a hydroelectric plant at the 1,200-foot level, said to be one of the highest facilities in the East. To visit it, turn off of Highway 107 onto Pine Creek Road and drive about 2 miles past the Ralph J. Andrews County Park to the power plant. The beach area near the dam is a favorite spot for swimming and sunbathing.

## Macon County
### CLIFFSIDE LAKE RECREATION AREA AND VANHOOK GLADE CAMPGROUND
### Access off US 64 West

Cliffside—a pretty and popular little lake in the Nantahala National Forest—is a great place to picnic, swim (the water is cold!), boat, hike, and fish (mostly for rainbow and brook trout). Here you'll find 17 picnic tables, two picnic shelters, a bathhouse with cold-water showers and flush toilets, and the Clifftop Vista Shelter.

There are numerous hiking trails in the area, including an interpretive loop around the lake. Cliffside Vista trail climbs 3 miles to an overlook of the lake. Tent camping used to be allowed here, but all camping has now been moved to the nearby Vanhook Glade Campground, though campers may use Cliffside Lake and showers. (See our Camping section in this chapter for more information on the Vanhook Glade campground.) There is a day-use parking fee at Cliffside from May 1 through Oct 31.

### NANTAHALA LAKE
### Access off Wayah Road

This large lake, which provides electricity for the Nantahala Power and Light Company, is in a remote area of Macon County, reached by the paved-but-very-windswept, two-lane Wayah Road (SR 1310). The regular releases of water that supply the fast rides for rafters and kayakers on the Nantahala River cause the lake's water level to vary widely. Nevertheless fishing is good here. In fact Nantahala Lake is the only lake in the state that contains Kokanee salmon, a freshwater hybrid of the sockeye salmon. There are two public access sites: Rocky Branch, on the east side of the lake just off Wayah Road; and in the Choga area on the lake's western arm, off FR 440. There's a school and a volunteer fire department in the nearby Nantahala Community but no stores to speak of, so stock up ahead of time with what you need for an outing here.

## Swain County
### FONTANA LAKE
### US 129

At an elevation of 1,710 feet, this deepwater lake reaches 30 beautiful miles into the mountains, covering 10,530 acres when full. Much longer than it is wide (it has a 240-mile shoreline), Fontana runs east and west with the Great Smoky Mountains National Park on the north and the Nantahala National Forest on the south.

The lake was created in the 1940s by the Tennessee Valley Authority's Fontana Dam (see the Fontana Dam listing in our Attractions chapter). You'll find public boat launches on Fontana's south shore. There are also boat docks at the Fontana Village Resort (see our Resorts chapter), along with sight-seeing cruises and boat rentals, including Wave Runners, bass boats, houseboats, pontoon boats, and ski boats. The lake is home to abundant smallmouth and largemouth bass, native trout, and walleye. You'll also find white bass, muskie (some 4 feet or more in length), and a number of panfish.

# WHITE-WATER RAFTING AND KAYAKING

Western North Carolina and its adjoining states have some of the country's most thrilling white water. We've described some of the most popular rivers for rafting and kayaking in this section, listing them in alphabetical order.

Trips on all these rivers can be booked though any number of white-water rafting companies that provide guides and instruction. Children must weigh at least 60 pounds before being permitted to raft (because that's how big they've got to be to fit into a life jacket safely). Some companies also rent rafts, canoes, and kayaks and offer canoe and kayak clinics. The following are just a few of the white-water runners in the region. Some run trips in other states and other countries.

**CAROLINA OUTFITTERS RAFTING**
12121 US Hwy. 19 West, Bryson City
(828) 488-6345, (800) 468-7238
www.carolinaoutfitters.com

**NANTAHALA OUTDOOR CENTER**
11044 US 19 West, Bryson City
(828) 488-2175, (800) 232-7238
www.noc.com

**WAHOO'S ADVENTURES**
3385 US Highway 321, Boone
(828) 262-5774, (800) 444-RAFT
www.wahoosadventures.com

## THE RIVERS

### The Chattooga River

The Chattooga, made famous by the movie *Deliverance*, can produce some of the best white water in the Southeast and is one of our personal rafting favorites. Designated as a Wild and Scenic River by Congress in 1974, the Chattooga has its headwaters in the North Carolina mountains and flows south to form the boundary between South Carolina's Sumter National Forest and Georgia's Chattahoochee National Forest. There is a 6-mile "floating section" from an access point on South Carolina Highway 28 about 1.5 miles from its border with Georgia. This stretch is also open to canoers and tubers, and while it can be a real challenge, it's great for family rafting trips with children or for youth groups.

One section of the Chattooga has been designated as Section IV. It provides a really exciting raft ride. You'll get great wilderness scenery, steep and technical rapids, and frequent ledges and waterfalls, such as the super-rush of Five Falls. Check with the guide companies for more information. Enjoy the outdoors, but don't venture beyond your capabilities.

> **i** When white-water rafting for the first time, pay attention to everything your guide says. Always remember the most important thing—if you fall in, keep your feet up and float. Do not try to stand—you may get caught in the rocks and drown in as little as three feet of water, under the rushing force of the current.

### The French Broad River

The French Broad is one of the world's oldest rivers, and you seem to keep running into it or one of its many forks—including the North Fork, the East Fork, the West Fork, and the Middle Fork—almost anywhere you travel in the valleys of the central mountains. It was not named, as some think, after a Parisian lady. The French Broad got its name in the 17th century when explorers realized that unlike the area's other rivers, this one flowed to the west toward the land claimed by the French. To the Cherokee, it was the "Long Man," and its many forks were called "Chattering Children."

Longer, warmer, and wider than many mountain rivers, the French Broad offers rapids that range from class II to class V. Class II offers slow moving waters good for floating and drifting. The river becomes more active as the nomenclature increases. Class V rapids, therefore, require more expertise in the fast moving water.

How challenging the river is depends on the amount of rainfall and the season. High water and big waves occur most often in the spring and early summer; in midsummer and fall it's usually a more gentle river that's better for canoeing and family outings.

## The Nantahala River

Because the Nantahala River is a controlled-release river from the Nantahala Dam upstream, it has usually consistent white water from spring until fall. Its clear and quite cold waters rush the rider for 9 miles through the spectacular Nantahala Gorge in the Nantahala Forest. This is one of the most heavily used white-water rivers in the region, with a constant flow of rafters and kayakers who are fun to watch even if you don't care to join in the sport. Typical raft trips include class III rapids at Nantahala Falls.

## The New River

The New River is one of the few north-flowing rivers in America. This river runs through the geographically remote Alleghany and Ashe Counties. Though one of the oldest rivers in the world, the New River was named by surveyor Peter Jefferson (Thomas's father) who was surprised to find this "new" river behind the mountains. The North and South Forks of the river flow over 100 miles through forested mountains and valleys. They join just south of the Virginia state line, and the river continues through Virginia. Because of its scenic beauty and recreational value, a 26-mile stretch of the South Fork has been designated a National Scenic River.

The headwaters are shallow with a few mild rapids, allowing for easy paddling. This river is ideal for family fun—for large groups and less-experienced canoers and kayakers. Tubing is great on this river; it allows you to meander downstream at a relaxed pace. Children love tubing, and many outfitters can supply you with dual tubes, allowing Mom or Dad to share the tube with a smaller child. Fishing and swimming are also excellent in this river.

## The Nolichucky River

The Nolichucky River that runs through a gorge in the Pisgah National Forest in North Carolina and the Cherokee National Forest in Tennessee has few rivals in the East during the high waters of early spring. Calm pools along the way allow you to catch your breath from some of the adrenaline-pumping rapids you'll have come through. The rafting season here is from Mar through Oct.

## The Pigeon River

The Pigeon River in the heart of the Smokies near Gatlinburg and Pigeon Forge, Tennessee, has been considered a "dead" river for nearly 40 years, due to pollution and electric power generation. Now new regulations are restoring its health and requiring the power company to pump 1,200 cubic feet of water per second through the gorge. The upper part of the Pigeon offers exciting class III and class IV rapids; the lower section is better suited to the inexperienced and to families with children.

**i** White-water rafting, canoeing, mountain biking, or horseback riding can all be so much fun that you keep at it a little too long. When aching muscles or sunburns act up, check out the Health Care chapter for medical facilities to help you get back to normal. First aid can often be obtained from your outfitter or guide, but don't count on them having much more than the basics.

## CANOEING

Mountain lakes, including most of those mentioned earlier, are excellent places to go canoeing. Experienced canoeists also like to paddle "white-water rafting and kayaking" rivers. (No canoeing is allowed, however, on the Chattooga River until it crosses the Georgia–South Carolina line.) The New, Davidson, and Green Rivers are also popular, but the French Broad, along with its many tributaries, is probably the favorite and has been designated as a canoe trail by the state. This river forms near Rosman, where the North, West, Middle, and East Forks of the French Broad meet; then it gathers force and below Asheville becomes a wide, sweeping waterway that at times can demand some solid canoeing experience.

If you are inexperienced or simply want assistance with your trip, several companies in the area are outfitters specifically for canoeing.

## French Broad River Access Areas

### BLANTYRE RIVER PARK
### Old Blantyre Road

This four-acre park on the western boundary of Henderson and Transylvania Counties off US 64 has river access and a canoe landing ramp.

### BUNCOMBE COUNTY RIVER PARKS

There are several river parks in Buncombe County. South of Asheville, three parks—Hominy Creek River Park, Bent Creek River Park, and Glen Bridge River Park—hug the French Broad River along Highway 191 and offer easy access. The Ledge River Park is north of town off Highway 251. Water picks up speed here.

### CHAMPION PARK
### US 64

You can put your canoe in at this park or access the river just west of Rosman, where US 64 West crosses the North Fork of the French Broad. These accesses put you in the quieter stretch of the French Broad as it meanders through woods and farms.

### HAP SIMPSON PARK
### U.S. Highway 276

From Island Ford it's 13 miles to this park, just south of Brevard. It's a small, pleasant park with picnic tables and river access. A 15-mile paddle from here will take you to the Blantyre River Park, mentioned earlier.

### ISLAND FORD ACCESS AREA
### Off US 64 West

To reach this area 13 miles downstream from Champion Park, turn off US 64 West onto Island Ford Road just a short distance outside Brevard. There's a large sign marking the site at the bridge across the river on Island Ford.

### TRACKING STATION
### Off Highway 215

During the spring and after a rain, sections of the North Fork of the French Broad are runnable, but only by the very experienced canoeist. Cutting through a gorge on the eastern edge of the Nantahala National Forest, the trip is 7.2 miles from the access point by the bridge at the old tracking station just off Highway 215 (SR 1326) to the access point on US 64 at Island Ford Road near Brevard mentioned in the Island Ford description earlier. In that distance the river drops 390 feet with a difficulty factor generally of 4 to 5 (two areas rate a 6). Before you attempt this run, make sure that the river gauge on the south side of the bridge at US 64 is at least 3 inches above 0. You need that much water for a reasonably safe journey on the North Fork.

### WESTFIELD RIVER PARK
### Fanning Bridge Road

This 19-acre park has river access, a canoe landing camp, and a recreation area. Fanning Bridge Road is off Highway 280 at the northern boundary of Henderson and Buncombe Counties.

ℹ️ Even if you didn't bring along your bike or your canoe, there are many recreational equipment rentals available in North Carolina's mountains.

## FISHING

No matter where you are in the Western North Carolina Mountains, you're never more than a few miles from a fishing lake, a trout pond, or one of our hundreds of miles of trout streams. However, with the exceptions noted below, North Carolina State fishing licenses and permits are required for all residents and nonresidents older than 16 who want to fish. Anyone younger than 16 may use a parent's or guardian's license. Licenses and permits are available at most discount stores, such as

Wal-Mart and Kmart. The cost will range from $20 to $40 depending on the duration of the license and whether or not you are a state resident.

## Fishing in National Forests

Fishing in national forest lakes is allowed year-round, but fishing in the forests' rivers and streams is regulated and sometimes restricted. To fish in state-designated trout waters, anglers will need a North Carolina fishing license and trout permit. Streams located on game lands require a special-use permit as well.

Brook, brown, and rainbow are the dominant species of freshwater trout in the area, and for management purposes public mountain trout streams are designated as Wild Trout Waters (high-quality waters that sustain trout populations by natural reproduction) and Hatchery Supported Waters (waters that must be stocked periodically to sustain fishing and are usually closed in Mar). These are further classified as Catch and Release/Artificial Lures Only, Catch and Release/Artificial Flies Only, and Delayed Harvest Waters. These designations are marked with specifically colored signs along the watercourses, but these colors can vary from area to area, so acquaint yourself with them.

Because regulations, including catch limits, change according to where you're fishing, it's up to you to know the rules. So before baiting a hook, contact the North Carolina Wildlife Resources Commission (919-662-4373) for full information or pick up a copy of *N.C. Inland Fishing, Hunting, and Trapping Digest* where licenses are sold.

## The Cherokee Indian Reservation

The Cherokee Indian Reservation has 30 miles of regularly stocked streams. State records for a brown trout (15 pounds, 8 ounces) and a brook trout (7 pounds, 7 ounces) were caught in these waters. To fish in tribal water, you need no state license, North Carolina or otherwise. All you need is a Tribal Fishing Permit, available at nearly two dozen reservation businesses.

The permit sells for a nominal fee and is valid for one day, with a creel limit of 10 fish. Permits

for longer periods, such as three or five days, are also available. Children younger than 12 don't need a permit as long as they are with someone with the proper permit. Fishing is permitted on the reservation from a half-hour before sunrise to a half-hour after sunset. Most of Mar is closed to fishing, with the annual season opening the last Sat of Mar and continuing until the last day of Feb the following year.

Over 400,000 rainbow, brook, and brown trout are added to the existing fish population each year, so some streams are closed on Tues and Wed for stocking. The reservation's "Fish and Game Management" brochure, which is readily available almost everywhere, gives the schedule for which streams are closed for stocking. If you'd prefer pond fishing, you'll find three well-stocked trout ponds on Big Cove Road in front of the KOA campground. A tribal permit is required to fish in ponds and streams.

## The Great Smoky Mountains National Park

The Great Smoky Mountains National Park has more than 600 miles of streams full of rainbow and brown trout. Some of the more popular ones include Deep Creek, Noland Creek, and the Oconaluftee River and its tributaries. Remote Forney, Hazel, and Eagle creeks, all very good fly-fishing streams, can only be reached by boat over Lake Fontana, by horseback, or by long treks through the park. In the park you must have either a valid North Carolina or Tennessee fishing license; fishing stamps are unnecessary. Make sure you check park regulations at a ranger station or visitor center before you fish.

Possession of any native brook trout is prohibited. That's because that fish's range in the Smokies has declined by 70 percent since 1900 due to unsound logging practices before the park was established and from competition with the rainbow and brown trout that were introduced into the waters.

## Trout Ponds

Other places where you don't need a state fishing license are the more than 35 trout farms scattered throughout the region. You can contact the North Carolina Agricultural Department (919-733-0635) or a local North Carolina Cooperative Extension Service for a trout farm brochure that lists the names, addresses, and phone numbers of members of the North Carolina Trout Growers Association and includes a map to help you find the farms. Recreational trout fishing in these ponds requires no elaborate equipment, and there are no limits to the catch. Many places will clean your fish free of charge.

Rates at trout farms vary. You might pay $2 or $3 per pound or perhaps $10 per day with a catch limit.

## HUNTING

Among the species of game available to hunters in North Carolina's mountains are deer, turkey, bear, squirrel, grouse, raccoon, wild boar, red and gray fox, rabbit, dove, and waterfowl. The North Carolina Wildlife Resources Commission (919-733-0635) schedules such seasons as deer (bow and arrow),

### Beware: Deer Hunting Season

The Sierra Club reminds its members that deer gun season (which usually runs from Nov to Dec) is the most dangerous part of the hunting season. Therefore it's wise to stay out of both public and private game lands during such times. The game lands include the Pisgah and Nantahala National Forests and the Shining Rock, Middle Prong, Linville Gorge, and Southern Nantahala Wilderness Areas. The club's advice: "Go to the Great Smoky Mountains National Park, where there is no legal hunting allowed. If you must go into the woods, wear blaze orange that is visible from all directions."

deer (gun), deer (muzzle loading), black bear, squirrel, grouse, quail, wild boar, and wild turkey.

To hunt in national forest game lands, you must have a hunting license and a game-lands use permit. A big-game license is required for hunting deer, turkey, bear, and wild boar. Hunters entering game lands from the Blue Ridge Parkway must have a hunter parking and crossing permit, which is good for a one-year period and obtained in person from a park ranger (see the list of ranger stations in the Forests and Parks chapter). However, you must have a hunting license to get a parking and crossing permit.

Licenses and permits can be purchased at most discount stores, such as Wal-Mart; and at other sports-oriented places, such as gun shops or camping supply stores. To help you with regulations, pick up a copy of *N.C. Inland Fishing, Hunting, and Trapping Digest* where licenses are sold.

## MOUNTAIN BIKING

Rugged root-covered forest floors, gradual but devastating hillside climbs, lush trails near rushing creek beds—this is the biking environment you will encounter in this region. Mountain biking is one of the fastest-growing sports in the mountains, and while the Nantahala National Forest and the Great Smoky Mountains National Park have their share of great riding trails, Pisgah Forest is gaining a reputation as the place to go for this sport. There are more than 400 miles of marked trails in Pisgah Forest alone, and the rugged and often difficult terrain on many of these paths makes them a sporting challenge even for the experienced biker. Not all trails, however, are that bad (or good, depending on how tough a biker you are!).

Some of the trails on our public lands are gated forest service roads that are closed to motor traffic and have good riding surfaces. Some are single-track forest trails with a great variety of rigorous turf. However, because such trails are shared with hikers, some of the more popular hiking trails, such as the Pink Beds Loop in Pisgah Forest, are only open to bikers from Oct 16 to Apr 14, when there are fewer hikers.

Ski resorts are taking advantage of their slopes in the warmer months by opening them up to mountain bikers. Check out the Skiing chapter for Web sites of ski areas that potentially offer summer recreation, too.

## ROCK CLIMBING

Rock climbing is not for the faint of heart, but for those intrepid few who have taken to this sport, the rewards can be exhilarating. North Carolina's mountains offer some spectacular granite outcrops, sheer cliffs, and steep gorges that make for rock-climbers' heaven. Some of the experts even practice ice climbing in the region.

This high-risk sport requires knowledge, practice, and focus. Bouldering, a good first start, allows you to apply climbing moves just a few feet off the ground. Anything more advanced should be done in the company of an expert rock climber.

The staff at a number of outdoor outfitters will lead rock-climbing expeditions to favorite climbing spots here in the North Carolina mountains (see the Outfitters section at the end of this chapter). Below we have listed several rock climbing spots favored for their ease (or difficulty, depending upon your experience). Obviously there will be many more throughout the mountain region, so ask around, especially at the outfitter shops.

### Northern Mountains
#### Shiprock Mountain
Just outside Blowing Rock and behind Grandfather Mountain, Shiprock Mountain can be accessed off the Blue Ridge Parkway at milepost 303, Rough Ridge parking area (do not park along the side of the parkway). It offers a range of climbing for all levels and is a more traditional crack climbing area that does not require bolts.

#### Table Rock
There are four access sites at Table Rock. To get there from Asheville, take U.S. Highway 221 North to Linville Falls. At the Rock House Restaurant, turn right onto Highway 183, which turns into Highway 181. Follow the signs to Table Rock parking and picnic area. Paths will lead you down to the rock area. Another path from the parking/picnic area leads to three popular climbing faces: North Carolina Wall, the Amphitheater, and the Chimneys. Don't try to climb around the waterfall, though; it's forbidden and dangerous.

### Central Mountains
#### Snake Den
Snake Den is north of Asheville in Barnardsville. Take U.S. Highways 19/23 North to the Barnardsville exit. Drive several more miles to town, where you take the Dillingham Road to the right. At the end of Dillingham Road, take a left. The pavement ends within 2 miles. Continue on a twisting, winding road that is a Forest Service road. Go about 5 more miles on this Forest Service road until you reach the rock face on your left, within 2 feet of the road. You can't miss it.

## HIKING

Here in the North Carolina Mountains, we are blessed with an amazing array of beautiful places to explore on foot. There's the spectacular Blue Ridge Parkway that runs almost the entire length of Western North Carolina, and our proximity to major national forests such as Pisgah and the Great Smokies brings hiking possibilities virtually to our back doors. The Appalachian Trail runs right through our mountains. Numerous state and memorial parks in the region also have marked hiking trails. But be alert: The blazes on some trails are becoming faded and more difficult to see.

Be prepared with appropriate clothing and walking shoes or boots suited to the terrain and take water and food along if you'll be traveling any distance into a remote area. Be aware of the sudden weather changes that can occur in these mountains. It's a good idea to carry a small flashlight and a whistle in case you get lost. If you do get lost, stay put. Three periodic short bursts on your whistle will help alert others to your location (see our section on Outdoor Safety in this chapter).

In this section we point out just a few of the top hiking destinations, but you can find your own favorites by just heading toward the horizon or along a dusty country road that runs through a forgotten wood. Numerous excellent books on the subject are available, including: *Hiking North Carolina (Second Edition)*, *Hiking the Blue Ridge Parkway (Second Edition)* and *Best Easy Day Hikes Blue Ridge Parkway*, all by Randy Johnson; *Scavenger Hike Adventures: Great Smoky Mountains National Park* by Kat and John LaFevre; and *Walking the Blue Ridge (Third Edition)* by Leonard M. Adkins. And be sure and take advantage of another valuable resource: ranger stations in your area. (See our Forests and Parks chapter for a listing.)

**i** If you're hiking alone, let friends know where you are going, which trails you might be taking, and how long you will be gone. A cell phone is often a lifesaver in unusual circumstances, but be aware that reception can be weak or nonexistent in many areas.

## Northern Mountains

Hiking in the northern mountains is centered around the Blue Ridge Parkway and the popular trails of Cumberland Knob, the 30-mile trail system of Doughton Park, the mist-shrouded trails of Mount Mitchell (see our chapter on Forests and Parks), or the family-outing trails of Moses Cone and Julian Price Memorial Parks (see our chapter on the Blue Ridge Parkway).

Grandfather Mountain, near Linville, is another popular hiking area; a permit and fee are required (see our Attractions chapter). The 3,000-acre preserve is laced with nine trails designated by the National Park Service as National Recreation Trails that vary in length and levels of endurance.

Glen Burney Trail skirts the cascading New Year's Creek in Blowing Rock, as the stream falls into the John's River Gorge south of town. The 1.5-mile foot trail is steep—it descends some 800 feet below Blowing Rock—and provides breathtaking vistas of two substantial waterfalls: the 45-foot Glen Burney and the 55-foot Glen Mary. Take Laurel Lane off Main Street to the Annie Cannon Park parking area where a wooden trail map marks the trailhead.

## Central and Southern Mountains

Even in the more urban central mountain region surrounding Asheville, there are plenty of easy-to-get-to hiking opportunities. Head out on the Blue Ridge Parkway where many trails intersect with parking and overlook areas or stroll along the paths that follow the Swannanoa River on the Warren Wilson College campus just east of Asheville. The North Carolina Arboretum also features many miles of wildflower-rich, wooded trails in its 426-acre park.

US 276 from the Blue Ridge Parkway down to Pisgah National Forest is a hiker's paradise. Some of the favorite trails originating off this highway include North Cove, Pilot Mountain, Art Loeb, Coon Tree, Looking Glass Rock, Cedar Rock, and Black Mountain Trails. Stop by the ranger station/visitor center just a mile inside the forest's boundary for maps and information. There is also a 0.6-mile Pisgah Ecology Trail behind the center. (For other great hiking trails, see Three Famous Trails Close-up in the chapter.)

# CAMPING AND CAMPGROUNDS

You can pitch a tent in the woods, down a creek prong of a wilderness area, or within a designated forest campground here in the mountains of North Carolina.

## Blue Ridge Parkway

**CRABTREE MEADOWS**
**Mile 339.5**
**(828) 675-5444**
Seventy-one tent sites and 22 RV sites lie close to large grassy clearings. The lawn of wildflowers runs up to the forest edge, with mountains visible in the distance.

The campground has the requisite picnic tables, grills, and tent pads, but no showers. Water fountains and hand water pumps are centrally located.

# Close-up

## Three Famous Trails

### THE APPALACHIAN NATIONAL SCENIC TRAIL

This legendary trail runs through 14 eastern states from Mount Katahdin in Maine to Springer Mountain in Georgia and takes an average of four to five months to hike. More than 9,000 people have made this journey, but thousands of others have enjoyed shorter sections of it.

Almost 302 miles of the Appalachian Trail pass through our mountains. The trail crosses the Georgia–North Carolina line near Bly Gap in Georgia, runs through the Nantahala National Forest, crosses into the Great Smoky Mountains National Park at the Fontana Dam, cuts diagonally across the length of the park, and weaves its way along the North Carolina–Tennessee border, exiting our state near Elk Park. It is blazed with white rectangles and a chain of shelters are spaced 8 to 12 miles apart throughout the entire trail.

You can access this famous trail at many points throughout its journey through North Carolina. Any good trail map of the region will show you where. You can also get detailed guidebooks at district offices or from the Appalachian Trail Conference, P.O. Box 807, Harpers Ferry, WV 25425-0807. For more information, call toll-free (888) 287-8673 or visit www.appalachiantrail.org.

### THE MOUNTAINS-TO-THE-SEA TRAIL

The trail, which was begun in 1985, will eventually run from Clingmans Dome, the highest point in the Great Smoky Mountains National Park, to the state's lowest elevation on the Outer Banks at Nags Head. This will be a travelway with various sections open to hiking, mountain biking, horseback riding, and/or canoeing. It will cover more than 900 miles and is scheduled to be completed in the year 2020. However, 216 miles already cross our mountains from Blowing Rock on the Blue Ridge Parkway south to Balsam Gap, where the parkway crosses US 19 north of Sylva.

This trail will take you through just about every ecosystem found in the Southern Appalachian Mountains, from high-elevation grass balds to cove hardwood forests and from mountain ridges to thickets of rhododendrons. It is generally blazed with three-inch white dots, except in areas such as the Middle Prong Wilderness, where routed wood signs point the way.

### THE BARTRAM TRAIL

From 1773 until 1777, William Bartram, a Philadelphia naturalist, traveled throughout the Southeast, writing exact and vivid descriptions of the plants and animals he saw and of the Native Americans he encountered. He published the writings in 1791 as *The Travels of William Bartram,* and they are still wonderful to read today.

Now a memorial trail follows as closely as possible his original route across South Carolina, Georgia, and the Nantahala National Forest of North Carolina. The trail enters the state just south of Highlands, near Rabun Bald, curves in a north-to-west direction through Western North Carolina, and will eventually link up with the John Muir Trail in Tennessee. Currently it climbs from the Georgia line to the crest of the Blue Ridge Mountains before descending to the Little Tennessee River Valley south of Franklin. Here a canoe trail down the Little Tennessee River to Franklin is under consideration. At Franklin it turns west and ascends the Nantahala Mountains to Wayah Bald, which at 5,385 feet is the highest point on the trail. It joins the Appalachian Trail briefly and descends to Nantahala Lake. Continuing mainly on private lands, it reaches Appletree Campground in the upper Nantahala Gorge then climbs up and over Rattlesnake Knob before reaching the "put in" on the Nantahala River. From the river it ascends Tulula Gap and continues along the crests of the Snowbird Mountains. The trail has been constructed as far as Porterfield Gap, south of the Joyce Kilmer Memorial Forest.

To learn more about this trail, order maps, or to become a member of the society that is establishing the trail, write to the North Carolina Bartram Trail Society, Route 3, P.O. Box 406, Sylva 28779. Maps are also available from the NFS.

This is a quiet, peaceful area awash with rhododendrons and hardwood trees and a good base camp for hiking in the Pisgah National Forest; trails lead to scenic falls on Crabtree Creek. Crabtree Falls Trail, a strenuous 2.5-mile loop, begins near the campground entrance. A camp store, gas station, and restaurant/gift shop are also nearby.

## DOUGHTON PARK
**Mile 239.0**

No reservations are needed here. It's first come, first served; about $10 per adult, $5 for Golden Age Passport holders, and youths younger than 18 stay for free. There are 110 tent sites, including tent pads, picnic tables, grills, and lantern posts scattered in wooded areas and around a grassy hillside. A smaller area with 25 RV sites lies across the road, though none of the sites have hookups.

Restrooms and water spigots are available but no showers. This is camping as it was meant to be! The park itself covers approximately 6,000 acres in Alleghany and Wilkes Counties and is the largest park on the parkway. It was named after Robert Lee Doughton, a U.S. representative who served from 1911 to 1953 and who was an advocate for the construction of the parkway.

## JULIAN PRICE
**Mile 297.0**
**(828) 963-5911**

Reservations aren't required for Julian Price. Like Doughton Park, it's first come, first served; about $10 per adult, $5 for Golden Age Passport holders, youths younger than 18 free. This campground sprawls across both sides of the parkway near Price Lake. One hundred twenty-nine tent sites lie fairly close together, divided by blossoming rhododendron bushes. Sixty-eight RV sites are also available, though with no plug-ins. Tent pads, picnic tables, grills, and spigots provide adequate comforts.

There are restrooms but no showers; firewood can be purchased nearby. The park is marked by mild terrain, covered by a dense hardwood forest. Poplars, chestnut trees, and maples make a pleasant canopy for hikers and campers.

Canoes may be rented at the lake, and hiking trails nearby lead to two smaller lakes and creeks.

## LINVILLE FALLS
**Mile 316.3**
**(828) 765-7818**

Fifty-five tent sites and 20 RV sites are available in the campground of this 440-acre wooded park. Tent site 15 is the most secluded. The surrounding forest seems almost primordial with moss-covered trees and waterfalls that plunge through the granite walls of Linville Gorge. Fishing in the nearby Linville River is allowed, and a visitor center and bookstore provides campers with plenty of area information.

## MOUNT PISGAH
**Mile 408.6**
**(828) 235-9109**

The entrance to Mount Pisgah Campground with its 70 tent sites and 70 RV sites lies directly across from Pisgah Inn on the parkway. Small sites, close together, are arranged in three landscaped loops. A dense forest adds privacy. There are no showers, but central hand water pumps and individual picnic tables, grills, and lantern posts are provided. Maps of the area, including hiking trails, are available at the camp. A picnic area lies in a meadow bordered by rhododendron.

## Great Smoky Mountains National Park

Of the 10 developed campsites in this national park, five are in Tennessee and five are in North Carolina. All have tent sites, picnic tables, fireplace grills, and bathrooms with cold water and flush toilets but no showers. There are a limited number of trailer sites but none of them have hookups. Sewage disposal stations are located at the Smokemont, Cades Cove, Deep Creek, and Cosby Campgrounds and across the road from the Sugarland Visitors Center about 5 miles south of Gatlinburg, Tennessee on US 441. The stations aren't available for use in winter.

Three of the campgrounds—Elkmont and Cades Cove on the Tennessee side and Smokemont on the North Carolina side—take reservations from May 15 through Oct 31, which can be made by calling (800) 365-2267 up to five months in advance. All other campgrounds are on a first-come, first-served basis.

No more than six people may occupy a site (two tents or one RV and one tent). Group camping sites are available at Big Creek, Cades Cove, Cataloochee, Cosby, Deep Creek, Elkmont, and Smokemont. Reservations at group camps are required and can be made by calling (800) 365-2267 or (423) 436-1266.

There is a seven-day limit at any campground between May 15 and Oct 31 and a 14-day limit between Nov 1 and May 14. Pets are allowed in the campground as long as they are on a leash or otherwise confined.

The following list of camping areas shows the number of campsites, fees per night, open/close dates, and maximum RV lengths. To locate these camps, pick up a map or ask for directions at any of the park visitor centers listed in our Forests and Parks chapter, which also contains additional information on the Great Smoky Mountains National Park. Most sites have overnight fees.

## ABRAMS CREEK
### Abrams Creek Road
There are 16 camping sites at the Abrams Creek campground on the northwestern edge of the park. It is reached from US 129 as it circles the eastern end of the scenic Chilhowee Reservoir in Tennessee. Some sites will take RVs up to 12 feet long and are open from Mar 21 to Nov 3.

## BALSAM MOUNTAIN
### Balsam Mountain Road
When you camp here be sure to have a sweater handy even in the summer, because at 5,310 feet it's the highest and coolest of the park's developed campgrounds. To reach it, turn off the Blue Ridge Parkway onto Balsam Mountain Road. Here you'll find 46 sites (some will take 30-foot RVs) and a 1-mile, self-guided nature trail through alpine woods. Balsam Mountain is open from May 23 though Sept 29.

## BIG CREEK
### Big Creek Park Road
This campground, which costs $10 a night, is just 2 miles off I-40. It has a ranger station and 12 campsites, and is open from May 21 through Nov 3. A very narrow, graveled, one-lane road leads from this area to the Cataloochee campground some 15 miles away, but should the Cosby campground be full, don't attempt this road with trailers or RVs or in the dark. In fact no RVs are allowed at Big Creek.

## CADES COVE
### Campground Road
One hundred fifty-nine sites capable of handling 35-foot RVs are available at this popular campground in Cades Cove, home to 700 people in the last century. (See our Forests and Parks chapter.) A few of these early buildings are still preserved, and the areas they originally cleared for farming are wonderful places to spot all kinds of wildlife, particularly in the early morning and late evening. This campground is open year-round.

## CATALOOCHEE
### Cove Creek Road
This is another campground in the area of two pioneer communities, Little Cataloochee and Big Cataloochee. With a combined population of 1,200 people, it was the largest settlement in the Smokies. Some buildings are still there (see our Forests and Parks chapter), and this area, too, is a good place to see wild turkey and deer.

The pretty campground, tucked into tall evergreens, has 27 sites and will take some 31-foot RVs. To reach it take partly paved/mostly graveled Cove Creek Road off of US 276 for nearly 12 miles. We think you'll find the rather rough trip and sharp curves worth it. Cataloochee is open from Mar 21 through Nov 3.

## COSBY
### Cosby Park Road
Even if you don't want to camp, this is a good place to go to hike. In addition to a self-guiding nature trail, there are trails that will take you through lovely woods and to waterfalls. (Ask folks at the camp office for some suggestions.)

If you do want to camp, you are likely to find room at one of the 175 campsites here when other campgrounds are full. You can reach Cosby campground by taking US 321 and cutting south on Tennessee Highway 32. Turn onto Cosby Park Road. The campsites will take 25-foot RVs. Cosby is open Mar 21 through Nov 3.

## DEEP CREEK
### Deep Creek Road

The Deep Creek campground, just outside Bryson City, rests on the site of yet another pioneer community and is a great place to go even if you don't want to camp here. It's only a short walk from the campground to Toms Branch, Juneywhank, and Indian Creek Falls. In addition Deep Creek is a popular place to go tubing.

The campground has 189 sites, some of which are suitable for 26-foot RVs. In the summer programs that are advertised on the camp's bulletin board are offered at the camp's amphitheater. The campground is open from Apr 11 through Nov 3, but is open to picnickers and hikers year-round.

## ELKMONT
### Elkmont Road

The Elkmont campground lies 1 mile off Little River Road, one of the easiest (except for the traffic) and most popular drives in the park. Early in this century Elkmont itself was a summer resort with dozens of cottages. Today it has 120 campsites, some suitable for 32-foot RVs.

There is a self-guiding nature trail here, and park rangers offer programs for campers and noncampers alike. Elkmont is open from Mar 21 through Dec 1.

## LOOK ROCK
### Foothills Parkway

Look Rock, named for Look Rock Mountain, is a campground just off the Foothills Parkway. This is an 18-mile drive that follows the crest of Chilhowee Mountain between US 321 and US 129 on the western side of the park.

Look Rock has 92 sites, some of which will take 35-foot RVs. It is open May 23 through Nov 3.

## SMOKEMONT
### Newfound Gap Road

The site of this popular campground was once a small pioneer settlement and then a booming logging village. It was operated by Champion Fibre, which owned 93,000 acres of timber here prior to 1931. Today, second-growth timber has hidden old lumbering scars, but a stroll from the parking area will bring you to Mingus Mill, where corn has been ground into meal since 1886.

There is a short, self-guided nature trail along the stream in the campground that contains 140 sites, some suitable for 27-foot RVs. Smokemont is open year-round.

## Backcountry Camping

A free backcountry permit is required for all persons spending the night in the park's backcountry. (Day-hikers are not required to register or to obtain permits.) Backcountry permits are available at most park campgrounds, ranger stations, and at the Sugarlands and Oconaluftee visitor centers. Registration areas at ranger stations and campgrounds are accessible 24 hours a day. Visitor center registration stations are open from 9 a.m. to 5 p.m.

Camping is permitted only at designated sites and shelters. The few backcountry campsites and all shelters require advance reservations. A Great Smoky Mountains Trail map for backcountry campsite locations and information is available at visitor centers for $1. To make a reservation call (423) 436-1231 from 8 a.m. to 6 p.m. seven days a week.

(For more information on the Great Smoky Mountains National Park, see our Forests and Parks chapter.)

## National Forest Camping

Most national forest campgrounds have no hookups, but all developed campgrounds have at least one 25-foot parking spur, and many campgrounds have one or more campsites that can accommodate a large motor home or trailer that's 35 feet long or longer. Some sites provide pull-through drives. Primitive camps that are scattered all over the forests, including the wilderness areas, are for tents only. A few of those that offer some amenities, like drinking water, are listed below.

In addition to these listed campgrounds, there are also 10 group camps designed for organized groups of from 25 to 100 people: Rattler Ford in the Cheoah District; Apple Tree and Kemsey Creek in the Wayah District; Kuykendall, Cove Creek, and White Pines in the Pisgah District; Silvermine and Harmon Den Horse Camp in the Appalachian French Broad District; Briar Bottom in the Appalachian Toecane District; and Boone Fork in the Grandfather District. Group camps are available only by reservation through the district office where the site is located. (See our list of district offices in the Forests and Parks chapter.) The exceptions are the campgrounds located in the Pisgah District. Call toll-free (877) 444-6777 at least 10 days but no more than 360 days in advance for group camping and no more than 240 days in advance for family camping.

## Nantahala National Forest Camping
### CABLE COVE
**FR 520 off Hwy. 28 East**
**Cheoah District**
**(828) 479-6431**
Near Fontana Lake, this camping area that's open from Apr 15 through Oct 31 offers 26 sites, restrooms with flush toilets, a picnic area, water, fishing, trails, and a boat ramp.

### CHEOAH POINT
**Off US 129 North, Cheoah District**
**(828) 479-6431**
At this area on Santeelah Lake, you'll find 26 sites, restrooms with flush toilets, water, a picnic area, a boat ramp, swimming, fishing, and trails. It is open from Apr 15 through Oct 31.

### HANGING DOG
**Hwy. 1326 West**
**Tusquitee District**
**(828) 837-5152**

A popular camping area on Lake Hiwasee, Hanging Dog has 67 sites, a picnic area, flush and vault toilets, water, a boat ramp, fishing, and trails. It is open from Apr 15 through Oct 31.

### HORSE COVE
**FR 415**
**Cheoah District**
**(828) 479-6431**
Located almost 17 miles from Robbinsville and open from Apr 15 through Oct 31, Horse Cove has 18 sites, water, flush and vault toilets, fishing, and trails. There are also five sites open in winter at no fee, but there is no water available at that time.

### HURRICANE CREEK
**FR 67, Wayah District**
**(828) 524-6441**
This is a primitive camp with undesignated sites and no drinking water. However it offers vault toilets, fishing, and horse and hiking trails. It is open from Mar 15 through Jan 1, depending on the weather.

### JACKRABBIT MOUNTAIN
**SR 1155, Tusquitee District**
**(828) 837-5152**
Open from May 1 through Oct 31, this large camping area on Chatuge Lake has 103 sites and provides a dump station, a picnic area, flush toilets, amphitheater, showers, drinking water, swimming, a boat ramp, fishing, and hiking trails. There are evening programs in season.

### STANDING INDIAN
**Old US 64, Wayah District**
**(828) 524-6441**
There are 84 campsites at this campground located on the Nantahala River, along with a picnic area, restrooms, an amphitheater, shows, drinking water, and hiking trails. Standing Indian is open from Mar 31 through Dec 1. There is a small fee per car for day use.

# Close-up

## The Legend of Standing Indian Mountain

Many years ago, say the Cherokee, a great winged monster swooped down and carried off a child playing near the village and took him to a cave high in the cliffs of a nearby mountain. Frightened people from all around came together and prayed to the Great Spirit for help in getting rid of the huge beast. After days and nights of prayer, a dazzling lightning bolt and a booming thunderclap came out of a clear sky and shattered the mountain, killing the creature and its offspring.

The lightning was so powerful, though, that it destroyed all the trees on the mountain's summit, producing the bald top that it has to this day. It also turned a warrior, who was posted on the mountain to keep an eye on the beast, to stone. Some said it was his punishment for being a poor sentry. Over the hundreds of years since this event occurred, this standing Indian has been worn away to a pillar of stone with an ill-defined head on top. In fact you may even have some trouble distinguishing the stone pillar from the jumble of rock that surrounds it, but you will be able to see the cliffs that were torn asunder by the Great Spirit's lightning bolt.

### TSALI
**FR 521, Cheoah District**
**(828) 479-6431**
Made up of 42 campsites on Fontana Lake, Tsali has a picnic area, flush toilets, showers, drinking water, a boat ramp, fishing, hiking, biking, and horse trails. There is a trail-use fee in this popular area. It is open from Apr 15 through Oct 31.

### VANHOOK GLADE
**Off US 64, Highlands District**
**(828) 526-3765**
Since Vanhook Glade is located just off picturesque and popular US 64 near Highlands and all its attractions, you might have to be a little lucky to get one of the 20 sites in this campground in high season. It has flush toilets, drinking water, and hiking trails. Campers also have access to adjoining Cliffside Lake and can use the showers there. Vanhook is open from May 1 through Oct 31.

### *Pisgah National Forest Campgrounds*
**BLACK MOUNTAIN**

**FR 472, Appalachian District, Tocane Station**
**(828) 682-6146**
This very attractive campground on the South Toe River has 46 sites, flush toilets, drinking water, an amphitheater, fishing, and hiking trails. It's open from Apr 14 through Nov 1. The fee includes guided activities in season.

### BOONE FORK
**FR 2055, Grandfather District**
**(828) 652-2144**
On Boone Fork this 15-site campground has a picnic area, restrooms, drinking water, and hiking trails. Open from Apr 1 through Dec 31.

### CAROLINA HEMLOCKS
**Hwy. 80, Appalachian District, Tocane Station**
**(828) 682-6146**
Here you'll find flush toilets, drinking water, swimming, fishing, hiking trails, and 32 campsites. There is also a picnic shelter that is available by reservation. The area is open from Apr 14 through Nov 1.

### CURTIS CREEK
**FR 482, Grandfather District**
**(828) 652-2144**
This tents-only campground has no-charge, primitive, undesignated sites. There are, however, drinking water, vault toilets, a picnic area, fishing, and hiking trails. It is open from Apr 1 through Dec 31.

## DAVIDSON RIVER
**US 276, Pisgah District**
**(828) 877-3350**

One of the most popular campgrounds in North Carolina's mountains, Davidson River (situated along the beautiful river of the same name) has 161 campsites and is just 1.3 miles inside the Brevard entrance to Pisgah National Forest. It offers a dump station, flush toilets, an amphitheater, showers, drinking water, fishing, and hiking trails. There are also guided activities in season. It's open all year. Reservations are available—and advisable—by calling toll-free (877) 444-6777.

## LAKE POWHATAN
**FR 806, Pisgah District**
**(828) 877-3350**

This is another extremely popular campground on Lake Powhatan; it's less than 8 miles from Asheville and has 98 sites, a dump station, a picnic area, flush toilets, showers, drinking water, swimming, fishing, and hiking trails. A lifeguard and guided activities are offered in season. Lake Powhatan is open from Apr 7 through Nov 1. You can also make reservations at this campground by calling (877) 444-6777.

## MORTIMER
**Hwy. 90, Grandfather District**
**(828) 652-2144**

Mortimer has 23 sites, a picnic area, vault toilets, drinking water, hiking trails, and fishing for a fee. In winter there is no fee, but there is also no drinking water.

## NORTH MILLS RIVER
**SR 1345, Pisgah District**
**(828) 877-3350**

Located on North Mills River, this campground has 28 sites, a dump station, a picnic area, flush and vault toilets, drinking water, hiking trails, and fishing. It is open from Apr 1 through Nov 15, and there is a 50 percent reduction in the fees during the off-season.

## ROCKY BLUFF
**Hwy. 209 South, Appalachian District, French Broad Station**
**(828) 622-3202**

This campground on Spring Creek has 30 sites, a picnic area, flush toilets, drinking water, an amphitheater, hiking trails, and fishing. It's open from May 1 through Oct 31.

## SUNBURST
**Hwy. 215, Pisgah District**
**(828) 877-3350**

Based at the site of an old logging town, Sunburst has 14 sites, a picnic area, flush toilets, and drinking water. It's open from Apr 1 through Dec 30.

# HORSEBACK RIDING

This is true "horse country." Beautiful horse farms—many specializing in Arabians, Appaloosas, Tennessee Walkers, or other breeds—beautify our mountain landscapes. Riding stables and riding schools are scattered throughout. Many children have horses for pets instead of dogs or cats, and two horses in a pasture seem almost as common as two cars in a garage. WATCH FOR HORSES signs dot the secondary roads, and somewhere in the region nearly every weekend, a horse show takes place.

## Where to Ride

Part of the reason for the popularity of horses here is that there are so many places to ride. In addition to private trails, fields, and pastures, there are many quiet dirt and paved roads that are used for horseback riding. There are also designated riding trails in the Pisgah and Nantahala National Forests and in the Great Smoky Mountains National Park. These are clearly marked with a horse sign, and you're not allowed on any other trails, though horses are permitted on many Forest Service roads.

The Tsali Recreation Area in the Nantahala National Forest (see our earlier Fontana Lake entry) is one of the premier riding areas in the Southeast. There is a trail fee charged. There is access to more than 18 miles of bridle trails, but

---

# Off-Road Vehicle Trails

The late 1980s locked the Forest Service in conflict with the owners of off-road vehicles. Jeeps, four-wheelers, motorcycles, and other all-terrain gadabouts were racing through the forests, creating erosion that polluted streams and endangered some trophy-trout waters, including the Lower Tellico.

Today, the Forest Service, off-road vehicle (ORV) owners, environmentalists, and landowners whose property was being harmed have worked out a plan that sanctions areas for the sport and establishes rules and regulations to govern it. At this time an individual does not need a permit to use an area set aside for ORVs (or ATVs, all-terrain vehicles), but that could change. A fee is charged for groups or commercial events. You don't even have to have a valid driver's license, but minors who operate these vehicles must be under the direct supervision of adults.

Trails in these areas range from a 15 percent pitch to a 50 percent pitch. You must know your vehicle and have good driving skills, and you should wear a sturdy helmet to lessen your chance of head injuries. Other tips for riders: Protect against erosion and stay on the road or trail, don't cut across switchbacks, and avoid wheel spin and wet trails. The following ORV areas are marked with symbols that show what kind of vehicles are allowed. Some old routes are badly eroded and have been closed to heal—don't ride on them.

## Brown Mountain

Brown Mountain has one four-wheel-drive trail in this area west of Lenoir. The other trails are open to ATVs and dirt bikes. There is no user fee.

## Roy A. Taylor ATV Trail System

This trail, in the Wayhutta section, east of Sylva, is open only to ATVs and dirt bikes. Trucks and jeeps are not allowed. User fee is $3; a season pass costs $20.

## Upper Tellico

North of Murphy, Upper Tellico is open to all ATVs, dirt bikes, and four-wheel-drive vehicles.

---

be forewarned: Mountain bikes are also allowed here, and although hikers and bikers should yield to horses, riders should always yield to motorized vehicles. Meandering through pine and hardwood forests, the trails cover terrain as varied as wide-packed dirt paths and rocky ones that overlook the lake.

In the Pisgah Forest two of the longer trails are the 12-mile South Mills River Trail in the Pisgah District and the rugged 18.4-mile Buncombe Horse Range Trail in the Appalachian Toecane District. The latter trail is suitable for overnight rides; on Community Hill, at 5,782 feet, you'll find a trail shelter with 10 wire bunks, a picnic shed, a horse corral, and a nearby spring.

Although most horse trails in the Pisgah District are for day rides or for primitive camping along the trails only, there is more developed camping at the South White Pines group campsite and the Harmon Den Horse Camp (tents only, open year-round). For more information contact the Pisgah District office at (877) 444-6777 or see National Forest Camping in this chapter.

## Rider Etiquette

To lessen the impact on trails, the park service staff asks that horseback riders travel in groups of six or fewer and that they stay on designated pathways, because cutting across switchbacks tramples plants and can cause severe erosion. Try to avoid tying your horse to a tree, but if this becomes necessary, use a rope or a tree-saver hitch to avoid damage. It's better to picket or hobble your horse and move stock periodically to reduce trampling and prevent overgrazing.

To protect water quality keep horses at least 200 feet from water sources and carry a water bucket and weed-free feed with you. Scatter manure and fill in pawed holes, especially when breaking camp. Horseback riders are required to yield to motorized vehicles, but bikers and hikers are supposed to yield to horses. Because trails are often narrow and some horses are skittish, it helps if you tell hikers where to wait while you pass.

**i** When horseback riding, always wear long pants and boots with a separation between shoe sole and heel. Wearing shorts on a leather saddle will chap and blister your thighs in no time. Shoes without any type of heel may cause your entire foot to slip through the stirrup, and you could be dragged under the horse if thrown.

## Riding Stables

Perhaps your involvement with horses only goes as far as wanting to take a trail ride. You can do that easily enough. There are many places in the mountains that rent horses and most also provide a guide.

Most riding stables are open from mid-Apr until the end of Oct. Most have age requirements for children.

We've described a few of the stables in our mountain area.

### Northern Mountains
**ARROWMONT STABLE AND CABINS**
**1157 Pine Creek Rd., Glenville**
**(828) 743-2762, (800) 682-1092**
**www.arrowmont.com**
Arabians, Appaloosas, and Tennessee Walkers are featured here. There are five trails that offer a range of views, from mountaintops to picturesque valleys and streams. Lessons and a guide are included in the cost. The stables are closed on Sun.

**BLOWING ROCK STABLES**
**1500 Laurel Lane U.S. Hwy. 221, Blowing Rock**
**(828) 295-7847**
Blowing Rock Stables and Blowing Rock Equestrian Preserve is almost a mile outside the town of Blowing Rock. Guided trail rides pass near Bass Lake and around the Manor House at beautiful Moses Cone Memorial Park. You can ride daily from Apr through Dec for an hourly fee. Boarding is offered at $300 per month seasonally and $250 a month yearly. Prices are subject to change.

### Central Mountains
**EARTHSHINE LODGE**
**1600 Golden Rd., Lake Toxaway**
**(828) 862-4207**
**www.earthshinemtnlodge.com**
Earthshine specializes in two- and three-hour Western-style horseback and mule rides. There's a two-rider minimum, a five-rider maximum, and a minimum age of 12, and reservations are required.

Free corral kiddie rides are offered at scheduled times for guests.

**PISGAH FOREST STABLES**
**476 Pisgah Dr., Brevard, Pisgah National Forest**
**(828) 883-8258**
Explore the forest on half-day or full-day trail rides or excursions that last three days and two nights (four-person minimum). For rides of more than an hour, there is a two-person minimum. Reservations are required two days in advance. Children must be 6 years old to ride alone.

Pisgah Forest Stables offers a three-hour waterfall ride.

### PISGAH VIEW RANCH
**70 Pisgah Ranch Rd., Candler**
**(828) 667-9100**
**www.pisgahviewranch.net**
Set in the shadow of Mount Pisgah, this ranch offers breathtaking views and 2,000 acres of fields and forests. Horseback riding across this picturesque acreage is under $30, with one low rate for ranch guests. The ranch is open May 1 through Nov 1 and features delicious home-cooked meals in a large old-fashioned dining room. Reservations are required. Watch for the signs.

## Southern Mountains
### CATALOOCHEE RANCH
**Route 1, P.O. Box 500**
**Maggie Valley 28751**
**(828) 926-1401**
**www.cataloochee-ranch.com**
Two-hour and all-day accompanied rides are available on the 1,000-acre "mountain-top paradise" for adults and children older than 6. Reservations are required.

### CHUNKY GAL STABLES
**10981 US 64 East, Hayesville**
**(828) 389-4175**
This stable offers horseback riding, horse training, riding instruction, and long- and short-term boarding. You can choose between one-, two-, and four-hour rides. Arena riding is also offered for children and beginners. Chunky Gal is located 11 miles east of Hayesville. Trail rides are also available.

### FONTANA RIDING STABLES
**Hwy. 28, Fontana Dam**
**(828) 498-2211, (800) 849-2258**
Horseback rides can be around the village (one hour), up a trail with lake views (one hour), or a journey to waterfalls (two hours).

### HEMPHILL MOUNTAIN CAMPGROUND
**Off Maggie Valley Road, Waynesville**
**(828) 926-0331**

Here you can get hourly or day rides, including trips into the Great Smoky Mountains National Park. There are also pony rides for children.

### UTAH MOUNTAIN RIDING STABLES
**1200 Utah Mountain Rd., Waynesville**
**(828) 926-1143**
Explore hundreds of acres of trails on one- to three-hour rides. Children must be older than 5 to ride. Younger ones may ride double with an adult.

## Clubs, Sites, and Events
Although horses are a part of the lifestyle in all areas of the Western North Carolina, the heart of horse country is in the Central Mountains, particularly in Polk County around Tryon. In fact it's the top area in the state for steeplechases and other equestrian activities. Below are just a few horse-lover activities. (Check out our chapter on Annual Festivals and Events for others.)

## Central Mountains
### BILTMORE ESTATE EQUESTRIAN CENTER
**Biltmore Estate**
**(828) 225-1454**
**www.biltmore.com**
Guests can expect to find guided trail rides on some 100 miles of trail throughout the Biltmore Estate. The Equestrian Center offers riding for children and adults as well.

### FOOTHILLS EQUESTRIAN NATURE CENTER
**3381 Hunting Country Rd., Tryon**
**(828) 859-9021**
**www.fence.org**
The Foothills Equestrian Nature Center, or FENCE, presents more than 18 various equestrian events during the year and provides interpretive nature study for adults and children (see the FENCE listing in our Attractions chapter). The 330-acre preserve has equestrian facilities with stabling, a steeplechase course, three show rings, a cross-country course, and access to the Foothills Equestrian Trails Association (FETA) trail system.

**TRYON RIDING AND HUNT CLUB**
**P.O. Box 1095, Tryon 28782**
**(828) 859-6109, (800) 438-3681**
**www.trhcevents.com**
For more than 60 years the Tryon Riding and Hunt Club has hosted the Spring Block House Steeplechase held on the next-to-last Sat in Apr, and the Tryon Horse Trials, where horses perform dressage, stadium jumping, and cross-country, held in Oct.

**THE WESTERN NORTH CAROLINA**
**AGRICULTURAL CENTER**
**1301 Fanning Bridge Rd., Fletcher**
**(828) 687-1414**
There's a horse show here nearly every weekend, and most are free. The free shows start at 8 or 9 a.m. and finish around 9 p.m. There is a charge for the occasional rodeo and gaited horse shows, which start at 6 or 7 p.m. Admission for gaited shows is usually under $10.

## OUTFITTERS

The North Carolina mountains are home to many outstanding recreation outfitters who provide services for outdoor enthusiasts. These services can be as comprehensive or specialized as you want, depending on the outfitter and what you want to do. Recreational clothing, customized adventures, specialty bike parts, and canoeing supplies—these are some of the stock in trade at the region's outfitters, which are divided into two basic types: retail and full-service.

In most North Carolina mountain counties, you'll find retail outdoor outfitters that supply the fundamentals for fun but not guide services. The shops can clothe you in sturdy foot gear, jackets, pants, and vests to protect you from the elements, and they carry packs, from overnight frame backpacks to roomy day packs. Retail outfitters can provide hiking and camping food supplies, including a dehydrated five-course meal and the packable Sterno stove on which to cook it. And they have maps—detailed USGS topographical maps or basic day-hike trail maps—

plus compasses and safety gear to get you there and back. Don't hesitate to ask questions. These people make a business of supplying recreation needs and can put you in touch with professional guides or just recommend a local day hike, fishing spot, or swimming hole.

# Other Recreation

There are other things to do with your leisure time in the mountains, including some activities that could be considered a bit unusual.

## Hot-Air Ballooning

**Mount Pisgah Balloons**
1410 Pisgah Hwy., Candler
(828) 667-9943
This operation began more than 15 years ago when ballooning was just catching on. Mount Pisgah Balloons, 30 minutes from Asheville, conducts pleasure tours over the mountains for around $110 per person. The company has found that hot-air travel attracts all ages: Its oldest balloonist was a local man in his 90s whose ride was a birthday gift from his children.

## Bowling

**Tarheel Lanes**
3275 Asheville Hwy., Hendersonville
(828) 253-2695, (828) 692-5039
Western North Carolina's largest bowling center, featuring 32 lanes, is 2 miles north of downtown Hendersonville. It's a modern facility that also has a billiard and video game room, a pro shop, and a snack bar. Tarheel Lanes hosts local, state, and regional bowling tournaments.

The popularity of mountain biking and river canoeing has created a demand for superior service and products for these two sports, and specialty shops have sprung up in some mountain counties to fill the void. These places concentrate on service and repair, but the owners, more often than not, know their merchandise from longtime experience. Rentals are usually also available, as are tours. A full-service outfitter does it all, supplying everything from gear to guided treks.

The primary focus with adventure services is group adventure, often including the entire family in the white-knuckle thrills of white-water rafting, canoeing, caving, or rock climbing, depending on the outfitter. Safety is given paramount consideration and detail. Gear is available as a sideline, or you can rent it for the trip.

Below, we've listed some of the well-known outfitters and adventure services here in North Carolina's mountains.

## Northern Mountains

### APPALACHIAN ADVENTURES
**Grade Road off Hwy. 194, Todd**
**(336) 877-8800**
**www.appalachianadventures.com**
This company outfits for canoeing, kayaking, tubing, and mountain biking on and along the New River. It is also a retail outlet for wilderness kayaks. Appalachian Adventures is based at an old train depot built in 1888. The landmark structure brims with a variety of gifts from the arts and crafts arena.

In spring, mid-Apr through mid-May, the outfitters are open weekends only. Beginning mid-May it's open seven days a week. All reservations require a 50 percent deposit. Call for a range of prices. Biking adventures take you through the back roads of Historic Todd and into green pastures, past old farms, and by the New River. The outfitters provide premapped routes, ranging from flat easy-to-ride pavement to more advanced rugged gravel and hilly terrain.

### BOONE BIKE AND TOURING
**899 Blowing Rock Rd., Boone**
**(828) 262-5750**

This full-service bike shop near Appalachian State University offers high-quality models, accessories, repair service, and rentals.

### EDGE OF THE WORLD SNOWBOARD SHOP AND WHITEWATER RAFTING
**Hwy. 184, Banner Elk**
**(828) 898-9550, (800) 789-EDGE**
**www.edgeoworld.com**
Edge of the World guides rafting and canoeing tours on a portion of the Watauga River in the northwest part of the county. They also supply caving and rock-climbing equipment. But here in the High Country of Watauga County, where skiing is king, no other outfitter covers the snowboarding scene as well as Edge of the World. The best quality equipment and advice are at your disposal here. You can also shop online from their Web site.

### FOOTSLOGGERS
**139 South Depot St., Boone**
**(828) 262-5111**
**www.footsloggers.com**
This upscale outdoor retailer in downtown Boone is popular with both students and tourists in the High Country of the northern mountains. It carries a full array of high-quality outdoor clothing, hiking boots, rock-climbing and hiking equipment, and camping gear (see our Shopping chapter for more details).

### HIGH MOUNTAIN EXPEDITIONS
**915 Main St., Blowing Rock**
**(828) 295-4200, (800) 262-9036**
**www.highmountainexpeditions.com**
For information and guide service for overnight camping, caving, trips, family float trips, and whitewater rafting on the Nolichuckey and Watauga Rivers and Wilson Creek Gorge, High Mountain Expeditions is one of the best places to go. When you stop for lunch, you will enjoy a gourmet feast by the river. All meals are prepared fresh daily by the Speckled Trout Cafe in Blowing Rock. They also outfit other popular mountain sports and offer kayak clinics, packages, and specialty trips.

## MAGIC CYCLES
**140 South Depot St. #2, Boone**
**(828) 265-2211**
**www.magiccycles.com**
Magic Cycles is a specialty bicycle shop that also carries a large line of accessories. The staff repairs all types of bikes; rentals are also available.

## NEW RIVER OUTFITTERS & GENERAL STORE
**10725 US 221 North, Jefferson**
**(336) 982-9193**
The historic New River General Store in Ashe County is the site of this well-known river outfitter, a seasonal adventure operation focusing on family tubing and canoeing along the New River. Camping and fishing areas are nearby.

## RIVERSIDE CANOE AND TUBE RENTALS
**2966 Garvey Bridge Rd., Chestnut Hill**
**(336) 982-9439**
**www.riversidecanoeing.com**
Riverside offers canoe trips by the hour, day, or weekend. Prices include paddles, life jackets, and shuttle service. Inner tubes of all sizes are also available. At the facility itself, enjoy other recreation, including basketball, volleyball, and horseshoes.

## ROCK & ROLL SPORTS
**280 East King St., Boone**
**(828) 264-0765, (800) 977-ROCK**
Rock & Roll is a full-service bike and rock-climbing shop, offering sales, service, rentals, and tours. They also offer equipment for ice climbing.

## WAHOO'S OUTDOOR ADVENTURES AND CANOE OUTFITTERS
**3385 US 321, Boone**
**(828) 262-5774, (800) 444-RAFT**
**www.wahoosadventures.com**
Wahoo's—you can almost feel the white-water spray in your face—is an apt name for this adventure-trek outfitter that emphasizes white-water rafting. During the summertime Wahoo's conducts rafting adventures down the Nolichucky River in nearby eastern Tennessee, several sections of the Watauga River, the French Broad and

Pigeon Rivers near Asheville, and the Ocoee in southeastern Tennessee, which was the site of the '96 Olympic Games canoe and kayak competition.

## ZALOO'S CANOES
**3874 Hwy. 16 South, West Jefferson**
**(336) 246-3066, (800) 535-4027**
**www.zaloos.com**
Zaloo's is one of the oldest adventure operations in the High Country, guiding canoeists along the pastoral turns of the New River, one of the world's oldest and one of the few north-flowing rivers in America. These people know the New River like the back of their hand. Canoe season runs from mid-Mar to late Oct. Individual canoes and tubing rentals are also available.

# Central Mountains
## BLACK DOME MOUNTAIN SPORTS
**140 Tunnel Rd., Asheville**
**(828) 251-2001, (800) 678-BDMS**
**www.blackdome.com**
Black Dome is one of those shops that does it all. In operation since 1993, this outfitter store has an expert staff and nationally known brands of gear and outdoor clothing for mountain sports as well as bikes and kayaks. You can also make your purchases through the shop's mail-order service.

Black Dome's local mountaineering guide service offers an array of adventure trips throughout Western North Carolina. Rock climbing is a specialty here, and the company's special-use permits allow excursions into Pisgah National Forest, not only for climbing, but also for caving, backpacking, and day hiking. Linville Gorge, Table Rock, and Wiseman's View are featured destinations. Also offered are guided flatwater trips for those who want to canoe.

## CLIMBMAX MOUNTAIN GUIDES
**43 Wall St., Asheville**
**(828) 252-9996**
**www.climbmaxnc.com**
Obviously this outfitter's specialty is climbing. Experienced guides offer craggy rockface climbs to chilly ice cliffs. Climbing is taught in an indoor

facility at the downtown Asheville location. Educational clinics and classes are continued in the field for those who want to move beyond bouldering.

ClimbMax offers customized guided backpacking, hiking, and rock-climbing trips to various destinations around Western North Carolina. This outfitter reaches even beyond our borders, with trips to the American Northwest and volcano climbing in Mexico.

### DAVIDSON RIVER OUTFITTERS
**26 Pisgah Forest Hwy., Pisgah Forest**
**(828) 877-4181**
Specializing in fly-fishing, this outfitter can supply all the clothing and equipment you'll want for this sport. They also have fly-tying material, rent fly rods and reels, and offer fly-fishing lessons and instructional trips.

### HEADWATERS OUTFITTERS INC.
**Intersection of US 64 and Hwy. 215, Rosman**
**(828) 877-3106**
**www.headwatersoutfitters.com**
Headwaters provides canoeing, kayaking, and tubing adventures. It specializes in trips on the French Broad River but will also provide canoeing on other rivers by appointment. Trips range from 10 to 20 miles. Expect a 10-mile trip to take three to four hours and a 20-mile trip to last six or seven hours. A favorite place to go tubing is on the North Fork of the French Broad. Headwaters provides a drop-off, and the lively mountain waters will take you right back to their shop. The company also offers a full-day "sea" kayak adventure on Lake Jocassee with an instructor/guide, transportation, and a very nice lunch as another option. It can also arrange fishing trips, waterfall tours, and other outdoor excursions. Headwaters is open from Apr through Oct.

### HEARN'S CYCLING & FITNESS
**34 Broadway, Asheville**
**(828) 253-4800**
Hearn's is a tradition in downtown Asheville. Since 1896 the name Hearn has been synonymous here with bicycles. From the turn-of-the-20th-century elegance of bicycle touring to the mad dash and rugged individualism of mountain biking of 100 years later, Hearn's has seen it all. This versatile shop has a wide variety of bikes, parts, and accessories. They offer custom design and complete repair.

### LOOKING GLASS OUTFITTERS
**90 New Hendersonville Hwy., Pisgah Forest**
**(828) 884-5854, (866) 351-2176**
**www.lookingglassoutfitters.com**
This store offers clothing, footwear, and equipment for rock climbing, backpacking, and hiking. It is a retail store, but also offers some canoeing trips and hiking tours.

## Southern Mountains

### NANTAHALA OUTDOOR CENTER
**13077 US 19, Bryson City**
**(828) 488-2175, (800) 232-7238**
**www.noc.com**
NOC, a long-established, employee-owned company, deserves its good reputation. The center can arrange food and lodging, and provide canoe and kayak instruction, white-water rafting, custom-designed programs, bicycle tours and rentals, and foreign and domestic adventure travel. It also has an outfitters store.

### SLICKROCK EXPEDITIONS INC.
**P.O. Box 1214, Cullowhee, NC 28723**
**(828) 293-3999**
**www.slickrockexpeditions.com**
Slickrock specializes in recreational and educational backpacking, camping, and canoeing trips in the southern wilds. The company's trips in the southern Appalachians include North Carolina's Joyce Kilmer/Slickrock Wilderness, Big Snowbird Wilderness, Bonas Defeat Gorge, and Panthertown Valley. Slickrock also runs a number of themed canoeing trips throughout the United States, including on the Big South Fork National River in Tennessee. The latest offerings are canoe trips on the Rio Grande Wild and Scenic River in Texas. Trips are completely outfitted and led by a professional wilderness guide.

# SKIING

Western North Carolina's first ski resort began at Cataloochee around 1961 in the Maggie Valley area of Haywood County when a farmer wanted to use his high-altitude land in the winter. Cataloochee is the oldest of the ski resorts in North Carolina and it adjoins the Great Smoky Mountains National Park.

Beech Mountain Ski Resort (now Ski Beech), which opened in 1969, creating a new type of larger ski operation that would incorporate an Alpine village atmosphere. Skiing in the mountains had finally arrived.

Thanks to the latest advances in snowmaking technology and some cold winters, ski season, which generally runs from late Nov through Mar, can be enjoyed this far south, too. Recent warm winters, however, have shortened the season.

Lift tickets for area resorts usually run under $40 on weekends, depending on the resort, and drop by as much as $10 during the week. Ski rentals and lessons will add to that cost. Resorts have also learned to diversify, offering a wide variety of package deals, attractions, discounts, and one-stop vacation planning. They also cater to snowboarding. Some resorts have incorporated snowboard parks to accommodate these slope surfers. Tubing, or sliding down a hill on a large inner tube, akin to sledding, has also been introduced by several resorts. This is a great activity for the kids and folks who want to come along for the trip but don't necessarily want to ski this time.

Cross-country skiing, another popular slant on the sport, is enjoyed along country roads and forest trails with every heavy snowfall. It's found mostly, however, in the High Country of the northern mountains, usually on restricted routes along Blue Ridge Parkway areas, such as Roan Mountain (along the Tennessee and North Carolina border), Doughton Park (on the parkway just outside the town of Sparta), and other parkway links. There's also some cross-country skiing on private trails at Ski Beech. For more information on cross-country skiing, call the rangers' office of the Blue Ridge Parkway (828-295-7591). For a complete overview of skiing in the mountains of North Carolina pull up Web site www.skinorthcarolina.com. And remember: Be safe. Check out the Outdoor Safety section in our Recreation chapter.

## NORTHERN MOUNTAINS

### Avery County

**HAWKSNEST GOLF AND SKI RESORT**
**1800 Skyland Dr., Banner Elk**
**(828) 963-6561, (888) HAWKSNEST**
**(828) 963-6563 (snow report)**
**www.hawksnest-resort.com**

This resort maintains 12 slopes: three beginner, six intermediate, and three advanced, with a peak elevation of 4,819 feet. The vertical drop is 619 feet. Their newest slope, Top Gun, a.k.a. Ski Challenge of the South, is reported to be the best new slope in the Southeast. Two double-chair lifts and two surface lifts get you to the top. The facility offers a restaurant and lounge, cafeteria, lockers, equipment and clothing rentals, ski lessons, and a snowboard park. Kiddy Hawk is a great program available for children ages 5 to 12. Nighthawk, however, is way past their bedtime; this program gives avid skiers the opportunity to ski under the stars on Fri and Sat until 2 a.m. On these evenings live music entertains guests in the Nest lounge. Discount rates are available for groups of 20 or more.

## SUGAR MOUNTAIN SKI RESORT
**1009 Sugar Mountain Dr., Banner Elk**
**(828) 898-4521, (800) SUGARMT (after Nov)**
**www.skisugar.com**

Sugar Mountain Ski Resort sits at 5,300 feet above sea level. Among the 20 slopes at Sugar are 7 beginner, 10 intermediate, and 3 expert runs. The vertical drop is 1,200 feet. The mountain is serviced by five chairlifts and three surface lifts. Sugar Bears is Sugar Mountain's ski program for children. The resort also offers equipment rentals, ski lessons, a tubing run, lockers, a nursery, game room, two cafeterias, lounge restaurant, deck grill, and club called the Last Run Lounge. The resort offers discounts for groups of 15 or more.

## Madison County
### WOLF RIDGE RESORT
**578 Valley View Circle, Mars Hill**
**(828) 689-4111, (800) 817-4111 (after Nov 1)**
**www.skiwolfridgenc.com**

Wolf Ridge is just north of Asheville, a drive of about 40 minutes via U.S. Highways 19/23. The highways split about 20 miles from Asheville; follow US 23 north and watch for signs that lead to the Route 3 (Wolf Laurel) turn-off.

This resort is the newest of Western North Carolina's ski areas. Students from nearby Mars Hill College find it a convenient alternative to the resorts farther north, as do a number of Asheville's city dwellers.

The Wolf offers 54 acres of skiable terrain, in the form of 20 slopes for beginners as well as more advanced skiers. Elevation is 4,600 feet, with a vertical drop of 650 feet. Four lifts and one high-speed, quad chairlift service the mountain. Ski lessons are offered hourly every day until 7 p.m. The lodge provides a ski shop, clothing and equipment rentals, and a grill. Snow-tubing has taken the Wolf by storm, and its new Snow-Tubing Park allows for all-day and evening tubing. Even better, tubers don't have to hike back up the hill, but rather they can hook their tubes up to a lift and ride their tubes back to the top, while enjoying the view. Lessons, season passes, discount packages, night skiing, and a children's

Wolf Cub program (for children 5 to 7) are also offered at Wolf Ridge.

Accommodations are available at Scenic Wolf Resort (see www.scenicwolfresort.com), within walking distance of the slopes. Special packages and group rates are available.

## Watauga County
### APPALACHIAN SKI MOUNTAIN
**940 Ski Mountain Rd., Blowing Rock**
**(828) 295-7828, (800) 322-2373 (snow report)**
**www.appskimtn.com**

This family-owned ski resort, begun in 1962, continues to be a popular destination for vacationers. Appalachian Ski Mountain offers 10 slopes—two beginner, three intermediate, three advanced, and two freestyle terrain—with a peak elevation of 4,000 feet. The vertical drop is 365 feet. You can get up the hill on two quad chairlifts, one double chairlift, one rope tow, and one handle-pull tow.

A Bavarian-style 45,000-square-foot lodge with a giant fireplace overlooks the slopes, housing a cafeteria, ski shop, and gift shop. A 200-foot observation deck allows for generous views. Lockers and clothing and equipment rentals are available, as are adult lessons and a SKIwee instruction program for youngsters 4 to 12.

The second weekend in Dec marks Appalachian Ski Mountain's anniversary, which is always celebrated with 1962-vintage ski rates—a bargain in anybody's book. Appalachian is also the home of the French-Swiss Ski College, one of the finest ski schools in the country.

Another fun celebration at Ski Mountain is the New Year's Eve fireworks display against the backdrop of a snow-covered slope. An outdoor ice-skating rink allows for skating under the stars.

The only in-season closing times for the slopes are Christmas Eve night and all day on Christmas. The ice-skating arena is open from Thanksgiving until the end of the ski season, including Christmas. And on Valentine's night, after skiing, a grand fireworks display takes place. Group rates for 15 or more people are available on request. The reservations department can book skiing and lodging for you.

## SKI BEECH
**1007 Beech Mountain Parkway,**
**Beech Mountain**
**(828) 387-2011, (800) 438-2093**
**www.skibeech.com**
At 5,505 feet above sea level, Ski Beech is the highest ski area in eastern North America. Established in 1969, the ski resort provides the complete winter sport experience from A to Z. Central to the resort is Beech Tree Village, a complex of facilities designed to anticipate the skier's every need. Its shops and services include equipment and clothing rentals, several gift shops, ski schools, a variety of restaurants, a nursery, video game facility, ski lessons, ski patrol, and even an outdoor ice-skating rink.

Ski Beech has 15 slopes, offering terrain for the beginner all the way to the seasoned expert. The vertical drop measures 830 feet. The mountain is serviced by a total of 10 lifts. A half-pipe run is available for snowboarders, along with snowboard rentals for those who just want to try it out. Ski Beech also features a skating rink.

Through the resort rental offices, a variety of accommodations are available, including 650 privately owned townhomes and chalets, four inns, and a B&B. You can come for your vacation and never have to leave the resort. Multiday packages and group rates are available.

# SOUTHERN MOUNTAINS

## Haywood County

### CATALOOCHEE SKI AREA
**1080 Ski Lodge Rd., Maggie Valley**
**(828) 926-0285, (800) 768-0285**
**(800) 768-3588 (snow report)**
**www.cataloochee.com**
Cataloochee, North Carolina's first ski resort, has long been one of the region's favorites. Its mile-high location provides fine conditions for making and keeping snow. Omigosh, the area's longest advanced slope, plummets 2,200 feet from the very top of 5,400-foot-tall Moody Top Mountain and joins up with the 1,800-foot Lower Omigosh, an intermediate slope. These along with seven

other advanced, intermediate, and beginner runs offer skiers plenty of options to match their skills. There are two double chairlifts and one surface lift, and night skiing is offered from Tues through Sat. Snowboading began at Cataloochee in 1984. There are now nine trails, and snowboard clinics are offered seven days a week, five times a day.

You can contact Cataloochee for discounted stay-and-ski packages with accommodations in the Maggie Valley area. After you work up an appetite on the slopes, the lodge provides hot, home-cooked meals, or you can enjoy a toddy around the circular fireplace or on the deck.

## Jackson County

### SAPPHIRE VALLEY SKI AREA
**4350 Hwy. 64 West, Cashiers**
**(828) 743-1164**
**www.skisapphire.com**
Sapphire Valley Resort, which bills itself as "a resort for all seasons," has its own ski area for its property owners and resort guests, in addition to such outdoor sports as golf (see our Golf chapter), tennis, horseback riding, canoeing, fishing, swimming, and hiking. The ski area is composed of a novice hill with a rope tow and intermediate and advanced slopes served by a chairlift. There's a base lodge that contains a ski shop and rental shop; a ski school is housed in a separate building. Night skiing is available but cross-country skiing is not. Snowboarding came to Sapphire in 1995 with two trails and clinics available. After a workout on the slopes, skiers can relax at the resort's health club with its indoor pool, Jacuzzi, and sauna.

### SCALY MOUNTAIN OUTDOOR CENTER
**7420 Dillard Rd., Scaly Mountain**
**(828) 526-3737**
**www.scalymountain.com**
From winter to summer, this center is fun for the whole family. Snowtubing and ice-skating, trout fishing and summer tubing on artificial turf—there's never a dull moment at Scaly Mountain. Parents can relax on the terrace while the kids are busy playing, then all gather at the Lodge BBQ and Trout House for a well-deserved lunch.

# GOLF

ool summers and mild winters divided by long rejuvenating springs and lingering, colorful autumns make "mountain golf," as it's commonly called here, a year-round pleasure. During the dog days of summer, you can head for one of the higher-altitude courses—up at 3,000 feet or more—for a decided drop in degrees. Or later in the year, if a particular day seems too chilly for a game, you can play one of the courses in the warmer "thermal belt" down around Tryon in Polk County, where the elevation is only 1,100 feet.

Wherever you play, you'll be surrounded by beauty and challenged by courses sculpted around undulating hills, deep mountain valleys, rivers, lakes, waterfalls, and majestic rock formations, all kept lusciously green by some 50 inches of rainfall spread relatively evenly throughout the year. Because of the hilly nature of many of the courses, golf carts are popular. Some courses require them.

There are dozens of public, semipublic, resort, and private courses scattered around the region. Some resort courses are open only to guests, but many offer reasonably priced golf packages that include accommodations and, often, meals. Others are open to the general public, but most require advance reservations. Here we give you a taste of the variety offered at our favorite courses that allow some public play.

Contact the Great Smoky Mountains Golf Association, P.O. Box 18556, Asheville 28801, or the chambers of commerce of individual Western North Carolina counties for more detailed information.

## NORTHERN MOUNTAINS

### Alleghany County

**NEW RIVER GOLF AND COUNTRY CLUB**
**611 Golf Course Rd., Sparta**
**(336) 372-4869**
New River Golf and Country Club is an 18-hole, par 71 rolling terrain course featuring front and back nines as different as night and day. The front nine is like a flatland course, whereas the back nine is a true mountain course, with many hills. Yardages are 5,601 and 5,741 (women's and men's tees). The club is open to the public daily, and greens fees run under $30. To get here, turn at the sign after Twin Oaks General Store on U.S. Highway 221 South.

### Ashe County

**MOUNTAIN AIRE GOLF CLUB**
**1104 Golf Course Rd., West Jefferson**
**(336) 877-4716**
**www.mountainaire.com**
This well-established public course offers 18 holes on well-maintained fairways complemented by the natural, rugged beauty of the Appalachian Mountains. Greens fees are under $40 per person including cart. Amenities include carts, club rentals, and a driving range. Lessons and seasonal memberships are available, as are group rates. The club pro is Mark Hagel. The developers here also offer home sites in an adjacent golf course community called Fairway Ridge.

## Avery County

**BLUE RIDGE COUNTRY CLUB**
**US 221 North, Linville Falls**
**(828) 756-7001**
**www.blueridgecc.com**
This relatively new semiprivate championship golf course sits in a beautiful valley with wonderful mountain views. Four tee boxes allow for various skill levels and playing options. Yardage for this challenging mountain course ranges from 4,800 to 6,900. The course features subtle elevation changes, gentle terrain, and mountain vistas. Ongoing development is enhancing the course's lovely North Cove Valley location. Fees include carts.

Memberships are available. The Lodge at Blue Ridge operates as a 12-suite facility with all rooms including a private riverfront deck and a stone fireplace. Conference rooms are also available.

**HAWKSNEST GOLF AND SKI RESORT**
**2058 Skyland Dr., Banner Elk**
**(828) 963-6561, (888) 429-5763**
**www.hawksnest-resort.com**
Located off Highway 105, Hawksnest Golf Course is nestled high in the Blue Ridge Mountains. This par 72 course with large bentgrass greens offers the challenge of a true mountain course to golfers of all abilities. The thrill of playing this championship course is surpassed only by the majestic views from every hole (and the cool High Country weather). Facilities also include a well-stocked golf shop and full-service snack bar. Yardage is 4,799 and 5,953.

## Madison County

**WOLF LAUREL RESORT**
**383 Wolf Laurel Rd., Mars Hill**
**(828) 680-9772, (800) 221-0409**
**www.wolflaurelresort.com**
Wolf Laurel Resort offers an 18-hole championship course adjacent to "Ski the Wolf." Just 35 minutes north of Asheville, it offers many extras: a clubhouse and conference facility, pool, tennis, dining, putting greens, and a croquet lawn. The course offers magnificent views. Golf and ski packages are available.

## McDowell County

**OLD FORT GOLF COURSE**
**1001 Golf Course Rd. Off I-40, Old Fort**
**(828) 668-4256**
This nine-hole, semiprivate course, established in 1962, lies southeast of Old Fort and is easily accessed off I-40. This rolling course has a small lake, a few streams, and a difficult dogleg on the third hole. The facility contains a driving range, pro shop, and snack bar. Individual yearly memberships are available.

## Mitchell County

**GRASSY CREEK GOLF CLUB**
**2360 Swiss Pine Lake Dr., Spruce Pine**
**(828) 765-7436**
**www.grassycreek.com**
This public championship 18-hole, par 72 course is just 4 miles from the Blue Ridge Parkway. An 8,000-square-foot clubhouse includes a restaurant, meeting space, and pro shop. There is also a driving range on site. Greens fees are $35 weekdays and $42 weekends and include carts. Yardage is 6,277 and 5,744.

## Watauga County

**BOONE GOLF CLUB**
**Fairway Drive off U.S. Hwy. 321, Boone**
**(828) 264-8760**
**www.boonegolfclub.com**
This 18-hole course designed by Ellis Maples is a par 71. Level and gently rolling fairways and large bentgrass greens are features. Yardage is 6,400. The club is open daily to the public and features electric carts and a restaurant.

**WILLOW CREEK GOLF COURSE**
**354 Bairds Creek Rd., Vilas**
**(828) 963-6865**
This challenging nine-hole, par 27 course is set in a valley. The course features a great deal of variety and offers senior citizens and student discounts during weekdays. Yardage is 1,351 and 1,574. The golf course is 3 miles outside Boone, coming from Banner Elk on Highway 105.

## Yancey County

**MOUNT MITCHELL GOLF CLUB**
**7590 Hwy. 80 South, Burnsville**
**(828) 675-5454, (828) 675-4923 (rentals)**
**www.mountmitchellgolfresort.com**
This perfect vacation course is cradled in the valley below Mount Mitchell, the highest peak east of the Mississippi. Vacation rentals—privately owned houses and town houses—are available around the perimeter of the course. It is a lovely, scenic location. Yardage ranges from 5,500 to 6,500.

# CENTRAL MOUNTAINS

## Buncombe County

**BLACK MOUNTAIN GOLF COURSE**
**18 Ross Dr., Black Mountain**
**(828) 669-2710**
This public par 72 course, operated by the town of Black Mountain, about 20 minutes east of Asheville, boasts one of the country's longest par 6 holes at 747 yards. The course offers not only challenging fairways but marvelous views of the surrounding mountains. The quaint town of Black Mountain, noted for its antiques shops, restaurants, and musical tradition, is nearby.

This friendly, community golf course offers a multitude of discounts for senior citizens, Black Mountain residents, junior golfers (18 and younger whose parents are not members), and families. A pro shop and snack bar are also available.

## Henderson County

**CROOKED CREEK GOLF COURSE**
**764 Crooked Creek Rd., Hendersonville**
**(828) 692-2011**
This 18-hole, 6,636-yard, par 72 championship course, situated just 1.5 miles from Hendersonville, is close enough for residents to take off for a quick game on a long lunch hour. Open to the public year-round, the course has a wide-open feel with Bermuda grass fairways and bentgrass greens. There's a practice green, range, snack bar, and pro shop. Crooked Creek provides both riding and push carts as well as lessons from a pro.

> **i** Tiger Woods is developing a new course at the Cliffs of Fairview, outside of Asheville.

**CUMMINGS COVE GOLF AND COUNTRY CLUB**
**3000 Cummings Rd., Hendersonville**
**(828) 891-9412**
**www.cummingscove.com**
Designed by Robert E. Cupp, former on-site golf architect of Nicklaus Design Company, this Scottish-style course has been rated as one of the top 50 in North Carolina by *GolfWeek* magazine. Embankments flank many of the greens of this challenging 5,288-yard, par 71 course, and woods border the entire course. Amenities include a modern clubhouse, pro shop, tennis courts, and pool.

Cummings Cove is 8 miles from Hendersonville off U.S. Highway 64 West and is semiprivate. Tee times are required.

> **i** Due to frequent Carolina showers, it's wise to get a covered cart and stick an umbrella in your golf bag.

**ETOWAH VALLEY COUNTRY CLUB AND GOLF LODGE**
**470 Brickyard Rd. Etowah**
**(828) 891-7141, (800) 451-8174**
**www.etowahvalley.com**
Conveniently situated halfway between Hendersonville and Brevard in the small community of Etowah, this semiprivate, 18-hole championship course, designed by Edmund Ault and beautified by horticulturist Jean-Claude Linossi, has bentgrass greens measuring up to 9,000 square feet. Its three 9-hole courses and four tee positions allow for a variety of 18-hole combinations. For example, the rather flat south course plays from 2,822 to 3,507 yards (par 36); the west course, with its large greens and bunkers, from 2,800 to 3,601 yards (par 36); and the open, rolling north course from 2,615 to 3,404 yards (par 37).

Other amenities include modern lodges, lighted putting greens, a driving range, heated swimming pool, clubhouse, bathhouse, fitness center, pro shop, restaurant, lounge, and meeting and banquet facilities for groups of up to 200.

For a different sort of challenge—or for non-golfing family members—Etowah provides a full-size, bentgrass greensward for croquet players and offers croquet packages along with a variety of golf packages. For example, a spring-through-fall, three-night weekend getaway golf package includes lodging, breakfast, dinner, club storage, and unlimited greens fees.

### ORCHARD TRACE GOLF CLUB
**942 Sugarloaf Rd., Hendersonville**
**(828) 685-1006**
Night doesn't bring an end to golfing at this 18-hole, par 54, 2,139-yard public course nestled in the heart of Henderson County's apple country. Seventy-two floodlights illuminate its entire 34 acres, making it the first fully lighted links in Western North Carolina. The course is made up of bluegrass fairways and bentgrass greens meandering around a small pond and two winding creeks. Hole distances vary from 81 to 212 yards. The clubhouse features a snack bar and a pro shop. (Seniors rate offers a $2 discount until 5 p.m. Mon through Fri.)

## Polk County
### RED FOX COUNTRY CLUB
**2 Club Dr., Tryon**
**(828) 894-8251**
**www.redfoxcc.com**
The Red Fox Country Club, designed by architect Ellis Maples and opened in 1966, was quickly recognized as one of the top 100 championship courses in the country. Situated less than 2 miles from I-26, its 18 holes are serenely set amid mountain streams that wind to a 30-acre lake. Here you'll find wide fairways; large, sloping greens; a practice green and range; locker room; snack bar; rental clubs; and pro shop.

For many years Red Fox was operated as a private club, but it became semiprivate in the mid-1980s. Memberships range in price from $1,000 to $4,000 per year, but the public is also permitted to play Mon through Fri. Golfers who

enjoy competition can sign up for Red Fox's mailing list and will be invited to play in its open golf outings held throughout the year.

## Rutherford County
### CLEGHORN PLANTATION GOLF & COUNTRY CLUB
**183 Golf Circle, Rutherfordton**
**(828) 286-9117**
**www.cleghornplantation.com**
This 18-hole George Cobb-designed  course is in the foothills of the mountains. The course measures 6,819 yards with a course rating of 73.0 and slope of 132. There are elevated tee boxes, heavily bunkered greens, and rolling fairways that make each round of golf at Cleghorn unique. All fees include the cart.

### LAKE LURE GOLF & BEACH RESORT AT FAIRFIELD MOUNTAIN
**112 Mountain Blvd., Lake Lure**
**(828) 625-3016, (800) 260-1040**
**www.laleluregolf.com**
A 27-mile shoreline of Lake Lure and the surrounding mountains create an idyllic experience on this 18-hole course. Additionally there are three restaurants, a fitness center, a marina, tennis courts, and three pools. To add even more interest, the movie *Dirty Dancing* was filmed at this site. Contact the resort for fees and other inquiries.

### MEADOWBROOK GOLF CLUB
**1211 Meadowbrook Rd., Rutherfordton**
**(828) 863-2690, (866) 863-2690**
This 6,400-yard course was built on the historic Deck family farm. It continues to be family owned. The 18-hole course runs up hills and down, through meadows, and along two creeks, creating challenges on both nines. All rates include carts.

## Transylvania County
### GLEN CANNON COUNTRY CLUB
**337 Glen Cannon Dr., , Pisgah Forest**
**(828) 883-8175**
**www.glenncannoncc.com**

Glen Cannon, a semiprivate course, is just 3 miles from downtown Brevard. This is one of the more established golf courses in the area, having been here for several decades. Beautiful scenery surrounds this club, which offers a well-maintained 6,270-yard, 18-hole championship course that's open year-round. There's even a picture-perfect waterfall on no. 2. Amenities include tennis courts, a clubhouse, and swimming pool.

Though it is a semiprivate course, area visitors who live outside a 50-mile radius of Brevard may play on a per-day basis.

## SHERWOOD FOREST GOLF CLUB
**Hwy. 276 South, Cedar Mountain**
**(828) 884-7825**
**www.sherwoodgolfclub.com**
Sherwood Forest, a 1,000-acre community resort, sits on a high plateau in the Blue Ridge Mountains, 8 miles south of Brevard on Highway 276. Its 18-hole, par 54 golf course, open to the public, has Pencross bentgrass greens and stream-caressed fairways, bordered with the area's marvelous rhododendrons and mountain laurel. A river runs through the course, whose relative flatness makes it one of the few mountain courses where you don't have to ride. The front nine is heavily wooded, and the back nine is wide open. Water hazards are on eight holes.

> **i** Does your golf game improve in the mountains? Some players swear their shots travel higher and farther here due to the thinner atmosphere.

# SOUTHERN MOUNTAINS

## Cherokee County

**CHEROKEE HILLS GOLF AND COUNTRY CLUB**
**Harshaw Road, Murphy**
**(828) 837-5853, (800) 334-3905**
**www.cherokeehillsgolfandcountryclub.com**
Semiprivate Cherokee Hills, with its 18-hole championship golf course, lies in a picturesque mountain valley 3 miles east of Murphy. In addi-

tion to a 12-unit lodge, this community resort offers town houses for rent or for sale, along with home sites, tennis courts, a pool, restaurant, and complete pro shop. Golf packages start at $75 per night, per person, double occupancy and include lodging and golf with a cart.

## Clay County

**CHATUGE SHORES GOLF COURSE**
**260 Golf Course Rd., Hayesville**
**(828) 389-8940**
**www.chatugeshoresgolf.com**
This very attractive 18-hole, par 72 course serves the residents of several surrounding counties including Clay, Cherokee, and Graham. Yardage is 6,687. For residents of this area, annual family memberships are around $350. Membership includes the use of the swimming pool and tennis courts. There is a small charge for non-members to use the pool.

## Haywood County

**LAKE JUNALUSKA GOLF COURSE**
**756 Golf Course Rd., Waynesville**
**(828) 456-5777**
This attractive golf course is directly across the highway from the Lake Junaluska Conference Center. Several holes provide panoramic views of the 200-acre lake and surrounding mountains.

**MAGGIE VALLEY CLUB**
**1819 Country Club Dr., Maggie Valley**
**(828) 926-1616, (800) 438-3861**
**www.maggievalleyresort.com**
This nationally acclaimed, 18-hole, par 72 course has been the site of four North Carolina Open Golf Tournaments and numerous other tournaments. *GolfWeek* rates Maggie Valley as one of America's best, and its bentgrass greens have been ranked among the top 15 in the nation. It's diverse and challenging: The first nine holes run through the rolling terrain of the valley, while the back nine wind through the mountains.

Accommodations include cozy guest rooms and mountainside villas surrounded by more than 35,000 square feet of well-tended gardens.

There is a heated pool, a restaurant, and a pub that offers resort-style nightlife. Call for special package rates.

## SPRINGDALE COUNTRY CLUB AND RESORT
**200 Golfwatch Rd., Canton**
**(828) 235-8451, (800) 553-3027**
Springdale is another community resort centered around its excellent golf course. Eleven miles from Canton, not far from its entrance to the Blue Ridge Parkway, and surrounded by the grandeur of the Great Smoky Mountains, the course measures a challenging 6,812 yards from the championship tees. The 429-yard, par 4 no. 4, for example, has you punching your second shot through a narrow opening up to a trap-protected green. On the flatter and shorter back nine, the 417-yard, par 4 no. 15 doglegs left and calls for a second shot across a pond.

But, while the golf may be exciting, this family-owned resort is casual and relaxed. Because golf is the name of the game here, you won't find pools, spas, tennis courts, or fancy dress codes. You'll find family-style, home-cooked meals served overlooking the 18th green and cozy cottages with rocking chairs, a view, and television. Other amenities include a practice green, range, chipping green, two restaurants, rental clubs, and pro shop. Package tours include accommodations, breakfast, dinner, unlimited golf cart, and unlimited golf. For permanent stays one- and three-acre home sites and town houses are for sale.

## WAYNESVILLE COUNTRY CLUB INN
**176 Country Club Dr., Waynesville**
**(828) 456-3551, (800) 627-6250**
**www.wccinn.com**
Here 27 holes of golf blend with mountain streams, ponds, and the ever-present mountain views. The links, made up of lush fairways and picture-perfect bentgrass greens, consist of three separate and distinct par 35, nine-hole courses that start and finish at the clubhouse. Each hole offers four sets of tees, thus ensuring a pleasurable experience for golfers at all levels of play.

Guests can choose from lodge rooms, cottages, or villas, and several restaurants. You'll also find tennis courts, a pool, and a pro shop. Be sure to ask about Waynesville's special Getaway Holiday Packages as well as daily golf packages that start as low as $35 per person, double occupancy, during the uncrowded winter season.

# Jackson County

## HIGH HAMPTON INN AND COUNTRY CLUB
**Hwy. 107 South, Cashiers**
**(828) 743-2450, (800) 334-2551**
**www.highhamptoninn.com**
Sitting at 3,600 feet, this 1,400-acre estate with its private 35-acre lake surrounds a historic country inn and its nearby cottages. All of these are just steps from the 18-hole, 6,012-yard, par 71 golf course designed by George W. Cobb that provides a scenic mountain view. The cost, including a cart, is $55 (subject to change), $48 if you are a guest at the resort. In addition to the course, there are two putting greens and an excellent practice range with the tee area covered for protection against rain. High Hampton also offers a series of three- and four-day golf schools from Apr through Oct designed for beginners, intermediates, and more advanced players. Each year there are two tournaments, one in June and one in Sept, for seniors (age 50 to 64) and superseniors (age 65 and older).

Facilities include tennis courts, a play area, an archery field, and sports fields. An excellent children's activity program is offered from June 1 through Labor Day. There is also a well-equipped exercise room. The lake is popular for swimming, sailing, canoeing, rowing, and pedaling boats. You'll also find an exercise trail and several walking trails, with guided walks weekly. All meals are served buffet style, and High Hampton's famous afternoon tea is offered from 4 to 5 p.m. (See our Resorts chapter for more information.)

## SAPPHIRE MOUNTAIN GOLF CLUB
**50 Slicer's Ave., Sapphire**
**(828) 743-1174, (800) 533-8268**
This challenging 6,147-yard golf course, with water hazards on 9 holes, plus a waterfall hole, is a part of the 5,000-acre, all-season Sapphire Val-

ley resort that grew around the old Fairfield Inn, built in the late 1890s. This is the perfect place to go with nongolf-playing family members, because while you're out on the links, they can entertain themselves with horseback and canoe rides, fishing, swimming, hiking, and tennis and join in supervised programs for children. A recreation complex offers a heated indoor pool with sauna and whirlpool, an exercise/weight room, table tennis and pool tables, game machines, and minigolf. (See our Resorts chapter for more information on Fairfield Sapphire Valley.)

**i** The top of Whiteside Mountain in Jackson County offers a fantastic view of Cashiers Valley, the upper Chattooga River watershed, and the surrounding Blue Ridge Mountain peaks. A fairly easy 1.5-mile loop circles the summit with a 0.5-mile side trail to Devil's Courthouse. From Cashiers, take U.S. Highway 64 West for 5 miles to Whiteside Mountain Road (SR 1690). Turn left onto this road and continue for about a mile until you reach the Whiteside Mountain parking area on your left. There is a $2 per vehicle parking fee (see our Forests and Parks chapter).

## Macon County

### MILL CREEK COUNTRY CLUB
341 Country Club Dr., Franklin
(828) 524-4653, (800) 533-3916
www.millcreekcountryclub.com

Bordered on three sides by the incredible natural beauty of the Nantahala National Forest, the main attraction at this 380-acre community resort is still the 18-hole championship golf course. Rolling terrain, rippling creeks, and thick stands of pine and willow trees interweave with the lush fairways and carefully manicured greens. As interesting as it is beautiful, this course can challenge players of any skill level. Half- and three-quarter-acre home sites and single-family homes are for sale. Two-day, weekly, and monthly rentals of deluxe villas also are available. Prices vary with the season. Golf packages are available. Please call for rates.

## Swain County

### SMOKY MOUNTAIN COUNTRY CLUB
1300 Conley Creek Rd., Whittier
(828) 497-2772, (800) 474-0070
www.smokymountaincc.com

In 1996 Swain County finally got a golf course that proved worth the wait. Since then the county-owned course, set in the beauty of the Smoky Mountains, has gone through several cosmetic changes to increase both its attractiveness and playability. The course was designed by J. Porter Gibson and modified by Brassie Gold Corporation. Each designer used the natural mountain terrain to develop a challenging place to play, and the resulting par 70, 6,500-yard championship course, with its change in elevation approaching 1,000 feet, gives each hole a different and delightful view of the mountains. Each hole also offers unique challenges. From the par 3s to the par 5s, no player is likely to get bored.

You'll find this fine golf experience a little more than a mile from the Smoky Mountains Expressway (U.S. Highway 74) and 7 miles from both downtown Bryson City and Cherokee. There are a number of pricing options that allow anyone to play at a reasonable rate. Many local hotels offer golf packages and a multiplay package can be purchased at the golf course clubhouse. Yearly memberships are also available.

**i** For a stunning view of the town of Highlands in Macon County, drive to the nature center on Horse Cove Road just outside town. It's a 20-minute, moderate hike from there to the Sunset Rocks Overlook. In addition to Highlands, you'll be able to see the whole of historic Horse Cove. A sign, RAVENEL PARK, marks the trailhead.

# FORESTS AND PARKS

Western North Carolina is home to more than half of the Great Smoky Mountains National Park and two huge national forests. The Pisgah National Forest and the Nantahala National Forest combined cover more than a million acres scattered over several tracts. In addition the National Park Service oversees the large section of the Blue Ridge Parkway that crosses this region of the state (see our Blue Ridge Parkway chapter). There are also three very diverse state parks to be enjoyed: New River, Mount Jefferson, and Mount Mitchell, plus two state forests: DuPont State Forest and Holmes Educational State Forest. Ten thousand rugged acres make up the Green River Game Lands.

In this chapter you will find a number of hiking and recreational possibilities, but there are many other suggestions in our Blue Ridge Parkway, Recreation, and Waterfalls chapters for getting out and about in our parks and forests. Detailed camping information can be found in our Recreation chapter. As a handy reference, we have included here a special section that lists all ranger stations, their locations, and phone numbers. They are a great source of information on forest trails, camping, plant life, wildlife, etc. And before you head out, check out the Outdoor Safety section in the Recreation chapter.

## THE GREAT SMOKY MOUNTAINS NATIONAL PARK

This national park, with 276,063 acres in North Carolina and 244,345 acres in Tennessee, hosts nine million visitors annually, making it the most heavily used national park in the country. Congress authorized it in 1926, but because the land was difficult to acquire from both individuals and timber companies, it wasn't dedicated by Franklin Roosevelt until 1940—and just in time, too! During the latter part of the 19th century, and even more so in the early part of the 20th, loggers were stripping these mountains bare, taking, at first, the most easily accessible trees from land that was later included in the park.

Lucky for us the loggers hadn't gotten around to some of the steeper and more remote areas. As a result we still have approximately 110,000 acres of old-growth forest within the 520,408-acre park. Some of these trees, such as poplar and spruce, are over 400 years old. However, in the more than half a century since cutting stopped, second-growth trees have made such a good comeback that most of us can't tell which areas are old growth and which are second growth.

As important as the park's trees are—and there are more than 130 species here—they are only one part of the area's unique ecosystems, which contain 1,500 varieties of flowering plants, 300 kinds of mosses, and 2,000 different fungi. Among the wildlife that makes its home here are 200 species of birds, 60 species of fur-bearing animals, 48 different kinds of fish, and 38 species of reptiles. Of the last, the only two poisonous species are the timber rattlesnake and northern copperhead, the venoms of which are seldom lethal. Of the 27 species of salamanders that make the Smokies the salamander capital of the world, two of the most notable include Jordan's salamander, a subspecies found only here, and the hellbender, which can grow up to 2½ feet long. Reintroduction efforts are bringing back the red wolf and river otter. Eastern elk have been returned to the park as part of a research project and are flourishing. The American bison that once roamed these mountains can only be found on farms today in Western North Carolina.

The most famous inhabitant here is, of course, the black bear. Around 1,700 make these mountains their home, giving it one of the country's highest bear densities. It's likely, therefore, that if you spend much time in the area, you'll come across a bear or two. To help make such an encounter fortunate instead of frightening, read *Bear Aware* (Third Edition) by Bill Schneider.

Except for some fishing it's against the park rules to disturb any of the plants and animals in this wildlife sanctuary.

The Great Smoky Mountains National Park has 17 peaks more than 6,000 feet high. The highest in the park is 6,642-foot Clingmans Dome, which is accessible by trail and by car. Some 250 million years ago, these mountains, some of the oldest on earth, stood more than 15,000 feet tall, but time and erosion have worn them down to the beautiful and often-dramatic forms they take today. The park is also enhanced by 700 miles of fishing streams. Many provide rainbow and brown trout all year long, but possession of any brook trout, our native trout, is prohibited. A Tennessee or North Carolina fishing license is required, but trout stamps are not. Check out the regulations at a ranger station or visitor center before you fish (see our Recreation chapter for more on fishing regulations).

For general information on the park, call (865) 436-1200. You can call or write to get a free catalog of books, maps, hiking guides, and videos that you can purchase. Park headquarters is at 107 Park Headquarters Rd., Gatlinburg, TN 37738.

**i** Because Great Smoky Mountains National Park is next to Cherokee, Pisgah, and Nantahala National Forests, visitors need to pay attention to where they are. A perfectly legal activity in a forest may get you cited before a court of law if you do the same thing in a park.

## Getting Around by Vehicle

One hundred and seventy miles of paved roads and one hundred miles of gravel roads penetrate the park, some of them built by settlers in the 1800s, but there are no gasoline or automobile services, and speed limits are 45 mph or slower. US 441, which is closed to commercial vehicles, is the only highway that goes completely through the park. There are numerous scenic pullouts all along this route through Newfound Gap, and a 7-mile spur road (closed in winter) goes out to Clingmans Dome. Efforts are made to keep the highway open all year, but always check at the nearest visitor center for winter road conditions. Sometimes the road is closed due to snow or ice, and sometimes only vehicles with chains are allowed. Although snow is fairly uncommon in the valleys, Newfound Gap receives an average of more than 5 feet a year.

Under normal weather and traffic conditions, it should take about an hour to cross the park on US 441 if you don't make any stops, but during the peak visitor season from May until Oct or in bad weather, it can take much longer. There are other spur roads, some of them unpaved and some of which are closed in winter, that lead to special areas of interest or campgrounds in the park. These "back roads" offer access to less visited areas and are often scenic in their own right. Most are one way and can accommodate two-wheel-drive vehicles. Check on the conditions of these roads, however, before attempting them. A flash flood or mudslide sometimes makes them impassible.

Most park roads are open to bicycles. No off-road vehicles of any kind are allowed anywhere in the park.

## Getting Around by Foot

The park's vast area is crisscrossed by over 850 miles of hiking trails, more than half of which are in North Carolina. Many of these trails were converted from old logging railroad grades or old logging roads. There are 51 official hiking trails and 11 self-guiding nature trails. You can pick up a leaflet about each nature trail as you enter it. For visitors just passing through, there are several trails right off of US 441 that are marked by signs.

A relatively level trail in this area, the Kephart Prong Trail, is 9 miles north of Cherokee. It begins by crossing the Oconaluftee River on a footbridge and will take you 4 miles to the Kephart Prong shelter and back, passing the remains of a 1930s Civilian Conservation Corps camp along the way. The longest trail in the park is the 69 miles of the Appalachian Trail between Fontana Dam and Davenport Gap. (You must obtain a free backcountry overnight permit to camp at shelters along the Appalachian Trail, but no permits are necessary on those sections of the trail outside the park boundaries.) The second-longest trail is the 43-mile Lakeshore Trail on the north shore of the Fontana Dam.

If US 441 is open, you can cross-country ski on the Clingmans Dome Road as well as on other roads that are closed in winter. Horseback riding is permitted on designated trails. Saddle horses are available from about Apr 1 to Oct 31, near the park's headquarters at the Gatlinburg entrance to the park.

Pets, on leashes or otherwise contained, are permitted in the park but are not permitted on trails or cross-country hikes. There are two exceptions: the Gatlinburg Trail and the Oconaluftee River Trail.

## Places to Stay

Aside from the hundreds of motels, inns, cabins, bed-and-breakfasts, RV parks, and campgrounds that offer accommodations just outside the park (some can be found in our Hotels and Motels, Bed-and- Breakfasts and Country Inns, and Recreation chapters), there are 10 developed campgrounds within the park itself. Five of them are on the North Carolina side (see our Recreation chapter). From mid-May through Oct nature walks and evening programs are offered at most developed campgrounds.

To camp in the backcountry, you need a permit. You can pick one up free of charge from any park ranger station, campground, or at the Oconaluftee and Sugarlands Visitor Centers. However some backcountry campsites and shelters are so heavily used that they require reservations. Call the Backcountry Reservation Office (865-436-1231), open 8 a.m. to 6 p.m. daily,

a month in advance if possible. You can only stay one night in a shelter and three nights in a backcountry campground.

LeConte Lodge, on 6,593-foot Mount LeConte, is the only lodge in the park. It's open from mid-Mar to mid-Nov and is accessible only by trail. The shortest trail to the lodge is nearly 5 miles one way, and reservations are required over a year in advance due to its popularity. Call or write LeConte Lodge, Gatlinburg, TN 37738, (865) 429-5704.

**i** There are over 270 miles of road in the Smokies. Most are paved, and even the gravel roads are maintained in suitable condition for standard two-wheel-drive automobiles. Travel times on most roads will average 30 miles per hour or slower.

## Some Points of Interest
### Clingmans Dome

At 6,642 feet, this is the park's highest peak, the third highest in eastern America, and the highest point on the Appalachian Trail. It can be reached by a 7-mile-long spur road off US 441 at Newfound Gap. From the parking lot a fairly steep half-mile trail takes you to an observation platform, which offers an incredible panoramic view.

In addition to the Appalachian Trail, there are other nearby trails you can pick up at Clingmans Dome. One easy trail for a family hike is the 2.2-mile (4.4 miles round-trip) Andrews Bald Trail. Look for the marked hiking trail at the west end of the parking lot. After about 1,000 feet the trail will fork. The right fork goes to Silers Bald. The left fork to Andrews Bald will take you downslope through a spruce fir forest to a grassy bald with excellent views to the south toward Fontana Lake. It's especially nice when the flame azaleas bloom in late June or early July. This trailhead is not accessible by car from Dec 1 through Apr 1.

### Cades Cove

When these mountains were turned into a park, many of the people on small farms and in the communities had to leave. Restored log cabins

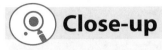

# Close-up

## Reintroducing the Elk

Great elk once roamed the region of the Great Smokies and much of North Carolina's mountains but were rendered nearly extinct by overhunting and loss of habitat. The last elk in North Carolina was believed to have been killed in the late 1700s. In Tennessee, the last elk was killed in the mid-1800s. By 1900, the population of elk in North America had dropped to the point that hunting groups and other conservation organizations became concerned the species was headed for extinction.

An experimental release of elk into Great Smoky Mountains National Park began in February 2001 with the importation of two dozen elk from the Land Between the Lakes National Recreation Area along the Tennessee–Kentucky border. In 2002 and 2003 the Park Service imported more of the animals from Canada to astounding success – so much so, that park rangers found themselves sometimes rounding up elk who had strayed away from the Park and onto farmers' land

All initial elk were radio collared and monitored during the five-year experimental phase of the project. Project partners include the Rocky Mountain Elk Foundation, Parks Canada, Great Smoky Mountains Natural History Association, Friends of the Smokies, the U.S.G.S. Biological Resources Division, and the University of Tennessee. Numerous elk calves have been born and survived.

The majestic elk do appear in the park to graze in the early morning hours and late evening.

and barns in a number of areas remind us of these hardy settlers. Few places, however, are as beautiful and well preserved as Cades Cove, which contains more pioneer structures than any other location in the park. Pastures, old buildings, and open vistas are a photographer's dream. And if you are in Cades Cove very early in the morning, you'll likely see deer and other wildlife feeding in the cove. There's an 11-mile, one-way loop that circles this scenic mountain valley and many of its historic buildings. Numerous ranger-led walks and lectures on a variety of subjects are held in Cades Cove every day of the week during the summer season.

There are also numerous hiking trails in the area, many leading to lovely waterfalls. (Because many of these are in Tennessee, they are not included in our Waterfalls chapter.) One, Abrams Trail, begins in the back of Cades Cove loop road and is a moderate 5-mile, round-trip hike. Abrams Falls has the largest water volume of any of the park's falls and is among the most photogenic. The 2-mile Cades Cove Nature Trail is great for

families wanting an hour's outing. Pick up a brochure explaining the cove's cultural and natural history before you take this hike. Surprisingly few people use this convenient trail.

To reach Cades Cove take the Little River Road, a winding but relatively flat road that follows the Little River, from the Sugarlands Visitor Center on US 441 near Gatlinburg. (See our listing of ranger stations in this chapter.)

### Cataloochee Valley

The most rugged peaks in the southeastern United States surround this 29-square-mile secluded valley, many of which are over 6,000 feet tall. The valley was once the largest and most prosperous settlement in what is now the park with a population of about 1,200 residents. The churches, a school, and several houses and barns remain. Once known for its farms and orchards, today it's famous for its dense wildlife.

Cataloochee Valley is definitely off the beaten track and requires a 10-mile drive on a winding, narrow, mostly gravel, relatively well-maintained road that seems much longer than it is. To reach it take U.S. Highway 276 toward I-40. Just before it dead-ends into the interstate, turn left onto Cove Creek Road and follow the COVE CREEK MISSIONARY BAPTIST CHURCH signs. There is a ranger station in the valley where you can get more information on the area. There is also a campground with 27 sites that is open from Apr to Nov. (See our Recreation chapter for more information on camping.)

## Mingus Mill

Mingus Mill is ½ mile north of the Mountain Farm Museum on the Newfound Gap Road. Built in the early 1800s, it's an excellent example of a water-powered gristmill, and it's still grinding corn. Hours vary, but the mill is usually open daily in the summer and on spring and fall weekends.

## Mountain Farm Museum

From May through Oct you can walk through a collection of southern Appalachian farm buildings, located at the park's southern entrance at Cherokee, with park interpreters who explain life as it existed here generations ago. These buildings, including a chestnut-log farmhouse, barn, apple house, springhouse, and blacksmith shop, were built in the 19th century and assembled for various locations throughout the park in the 1950s. Admission is free.

### Roaring Fork Motor Nature Trail

Three miles from Gatlinburg, you can take this 5-mile, one-way loop through rich hardwood forests and past historic buildings and rushing mountain streams. To get to it turn onto Airport Road in Gatlinburg. Enter the park and follow the Cherokee Orchard Road to the Roaring Fork Motor Nature Trail. No RVs, trailers, or bicycles are allowed on this route.

## NATIONAL FORESTS

As we mentioned earlier, the Nantahala and Pisgah National Forests cover more than a million acres in the North Carolina mountains, including a number of wilderness areas. These vast forest lands of rivers, lakes, waterfalls, spectacular views, wildlife, and the richest plant life in the country can be accessed by federal and state highways, forest roads, and trails. You'll find that they can easily be explored by car, on foot, by kayak or canoe, and in designated areas, by horseback, mountain bikes, and off-highway vehicles. (See our Recreation chapter for more information on some of these outdoor sports and camping.)

**i** Driving in the mountains presents new challenges for many drivers. When going downhill, shift to a lower gear to conserve your brakes and avoid brake failure. For cars with automatic transmission, use L or 2. Keep extra distance between you and the vehicle in front of you, and watch for sudden stops or slow-downs.

### Nantahala National Forest

This national forest, in the southwestern part of our mountains between Waynesville and Murphy, contains more than 516,000 acres, sometimes taking in huge chunks of land and sometimes consisting of relatively small plots. When you travel in this part of Western North Carolina, you're constantly entering and leaving

## Friends of the Smokies

Over 60 years ago a group of people joined together to establish a national park here to preserve and protect the natural wonders of the region. This organization, based at 160 South Main St. in Waynesville, is still dedicated to fund-raising and to restoring, preserving, and enhancing the park. For an extra fee, a special license plate for North Carolina may be purchased to support the Smokies. For more information and an application call (828) 452-0720 or visit their Web site at www.friendsof thesmokies.org.

the forest. Although this might not make managing these public lands easy, it certainly makes for a lot of diversity.

Elevations in the forest range from a high 5,800 feet at Lone Bald in Jackson County to a low 1,200 feet in Cherokee County along the Tusquitee River below the Appalachian Lake Dam.

To get a better handle on this vast area, which is the largest of the four national forests in North Carolina, it's best to break it down into its four districts.

## CHEOAH RANGER DISTRICT
**US Hwy. 129 North, Robbinsville**
**(828) 479-6431**

The Cheoah Ranger District is made up of 120,000 acres in Graham and Swain Counties that adjoin four large reservoirs (Lake Fontana, Lake Santeetlah, Lake Cheoah, and Calderwood Lake) and offer a network of 225 miles of hiking trails, including a 27-mile section of the Appalachian Trail. The Cheoah Ranger Station, adjacent to Lake Santeetlah on SR 1116 and 2 miles north of Robbinsville, is built on the site of a Civilian Conservation Corps campsite and contains an interpretive trail and a fine overlook of the lake. Here you can get forest information and maps.

Sitting to the southwest of the Great Smoky Mountains National Park, this part of the Nantahala Forest is often overlooked by visitors, but the slightly off-the-beaten-track district provides some incredibly beautiful places. First off, there is the 3,800-acre Joyce Kilmer Memorial Forest, which, maintained in a primitive state, has one of the nation's most impressive remnants of old-growth forest. The Gennott Lumber Company, which started timber operations in the area in 1890, once owned the timber here, but—lucky for us—these trees were never cut. Now this memorial forest is a part of the 14,000-acre Joyce Kilmer–Slickrock Wilderness Area and contains magnificent examples of more than 100 species of trees, including yellow poplar, hemlock, sycamore, basswood, dogwood, beech, and several species of oaks. Many of them are hundreds of years old, and some are more than 20 feet in circumference and more than 100 feet high.

The area was set aside in 1936 as a memorial to Joyce Kilmer, the soldier-poet and author of the poem "Trees," who was killed in France during World War I.

The Joyce Kilmer National Recreation Trail is an easy 2-mile loop that takes you past some of these great giants, many felled by age or lightning. In some areas the tree canopy is so thick that sunlight never reaches the ground. You'll also find a picnic area here and an outstanding variety of vines, ferns, and early-spring wildflowers and shrubs, such as mountain laurels, rhododendrons, and flame azaleas. No plants, living or dead, may be removed from this area. Wildlife is abundant in this undisturbed forest. The adjoining Slickrock Wilderness Area, with 13,100 acres in North Carolina, contains 60 miles of hiking trails that meander along streams and climb high ridges. It's home to bears, bobcats, and nonnative, environment-uprooting wild boars and has a number of dispersed, primitive, no-fee campsites.

For those who want more comforts, such as picnic tables, restrooms, and water taps, there are two campgrounds, not very far from the memorial forest. Horse Cove Campground, which charges $8 a night, has 18 units, and is by a rushing mountain stream called Little Santeetlah Creek. Rattler Ford campground nearby is reserved for groups.

To get to the Joyce Kilmer Memorial Forest, take US 129 out of Robbinsville to SR 1127 and follow the signs. Both the Horse Cove and Rattler Ford campgrounds are off SR 1127.

There are two forest recreation areas near Lake Fontana. The Tsali Recreation Area has 41 camping units with showers and flushing toilets, a boat-launching area, and 38 miles of biking and horseback-riding trails. The popular trail network here now charges a nominal fee for horses and bikes. The Cable Cove Recreation Area also offers camping and hiking, with boating access on Fontana Lake. It's 4 miles from Fontana Dam, the Appalachian Trail, and the entrance to the Great Smoky Mountains National Park. The area also has a mile-long nature loop trail marked with placards that will help you identify the plants and trees growing along it as well as some historical features. There is a small camping fee. On Lake Santeetlah, the Cheoah Point Recreation Area has developed camping, picnicking, fishing, and boating facilities. There is an $8 camping fee but no charge for day use. Nearby the Wauchecha Bald Trail provides access to the Appalachian Trail (see our Recreation chapter for more information on all these recreation areas).

Of all the outstanding wild places in the Cheoah District, two great favorites with anglers, hunters, and primitive camping enthusiasts are the Big Santeetlah Creek area and the 10,000 or so acres that encompass the headwaters of Big Snowbird Creek. The latter was one of the last areas to be settled by whites in North Carolina, and it was here in 1836 that a number of Cherokee Indians fled to escape exile in Oklahoma. For more information on these two areas, contact the Cheoah Ranger Station.

### HIGHLANDS RANGER DISTRICT
**2010 Flat Mountain Rd., Highlands**
**(828) 526-3765**

The Highlands Ranger District covers more than 105,000 acres in Macon, Jackson, and Transylvania Counties. Within it you'll find the 39,000-acre Roy Taylor Forest, which has some off-road vehicle trails (see our Recreation chapter) and Jackson County's rugged Tuckasegee Gorge.

The Highlands District also contains two national and wild scenic rivers, the Chattooga and the Horsepasture. The Chattooga, on which the movie *Deliverance* was filmed, is very popular with white-water rafters, but only after it passes the South Carolina/Georgia border (see our Recreation chapter). No canoeing is permitted on either river within the district. The Horsepasture River is noted for its five waterfalls. Other famous waterfalls in this district include Whitewater Falls, Glen Falls, Dry Falls, and Cullasaja Falls.

One of the most famous mountains in the Nantahala Forest is Whiteside Mountain, between Highlands and Cashiers off U.S. Highway 64 on the eastern Continental Divide. Said to be one of the oldest mountains on earth, it rises more than 2,100 feet from the valley floor to an elevation of 4,930 feet. Its spectacular north and south faces

---

## Cherohala Skyway

For a beautiful perspective on our lovely mountains, travel the 51-mile Cherohala Skyway that connects the Tellico Plains in southeast Tennessee to Robbinsville, North Carolina. (In Tennessee, take Tennessee Highway 165 and in North Carolina take North Carolina Highway 143.) Called a mini-Blue Ridge Parkway, it travels through some of the best scenery of the Cherokee and Nantahala National Forests, thus the name which is a combination of Cherokee and Nantahala.

Much of the two-lane blacktop in North Carolina looks down on the Snowbird, Slickrock, and Joyce Kilmer Forests. On clear, unhazy days you can see into the Great Smoky Mountains National Park. Restrooms, picnic areas, and scenic overlooks are constructed along the way. Spirit Ridge, a lookout just east of Hooper Bald, is wheelchair accessible and offers one of the most expansive views along the route.

---

contain sheer cliffs ranging from 400 to 750 feet in height. They were formed of metamorphic rock commonly called Whiteside granite, gneiss containing a high content of feldspar, quartz, and mica, along with such minerals as pyrite and rare monazite. The white streaks seen on its south face are feldspar and quartz. These don't show up on the north face due to lichens and mosses that cover the stone.

A 2-mile loop trail, designated as a National Recreation Trail, runs on the top of the mountain. It offers unparalleled views of the east, south, and west, where you will see at least 27 other peaks, the Cashiers Valley and the upper Chattooga

River watershed. To reach the mountain drive 6.9 miles from the main Highlands intersection on US 64 going toward Cashiers and turn onto White-side Mountain Road (SR 1600). From Cashiers the turn is just past the Jackson-Macon county line. After about a mile, you'll arrive at the mountain's parking area and the trail that follows the edge of the cliffs. Use extreme caution here with pets and children. This is a popular place for rock climbing, but it's only suitable for experts. The rock face is closed to climbers from Feb 15 through July 15 to protect nesting peregrine falcons.

Cliffside Lake and the Van Hook Glade Recreation Areas, off US 64 between Highlands and Franklin, form one of the district's most popular camping, swimming, and fishing areas. Camping here is $10 a night, and day use is $3 per car. This popular area fills up quickly, but there are also a number of primitive camping areas in the district. You can get information and maps at the district office off US 64 just outside of Highlands or at the Highland Visitor Center in downtown Highlands. The visitor center is open daily from May through Oct; the office is open year-round from Mon through Fri.

## TUSQUITEE RANGER DISTRICT
**201 Woodland Dr., Murphy**
**(828) 837-5152**
Elevations in the 158,579-acre Tusquitee Ranger District range from 1,200 feet to 5,499 feet at Standing Indian Mountain. It's most famous for its "chain of lakes"—Appalachia Lake, Hiwassee Lake, and Chatuge Lake—which offer opportunities to boat, water ski, fish, and swim. You can stay right on Hiwassee Lake at the forest's Hanging Dog Recreation Area, which has a large campground, a picnic area, hiking trails, and a boat launching ramp. At Chatuge Lake, the Jackrabbit Mountain Recreation Area has 103 camping sites, a swimming beach with shower facilities, hiking trails, picnic areas, and a boat launching ramp.

Just to the north of Chatuge Lake, you'll find the Fires Creek Bear Sanctuary, a 14,000-acre block of land that's been set aside as a haven for black bears. This area offers excellent trout fishing, picnicking, hiking, and camping. The most famous hiking trail in the area is the 25-mile-long Rim Trail, which follows the ridge around Fires Creek over several high-elevation balds that provide super-scenic vistas. There are several primitive camping areas here that include Huskins Branch, Hunter Camp, and Bristol Fields.

The Leatherwood Falls Picnic Area provides picnic sites near Leatherwood Falls, plus a wheelchair-accessible trail for wheelchair fishing along Fires Creek (see Leatherwood Falls in our Waterfalls chapter for more information). Another interesting place to visit in this district is the Beech Creek Seed Orchard west of Murphy off FR 307. This nursery supplies the southern Appalachian forests with genetically improved seeds of white, shortleaf, and Virginia pines for reforestation. The orchard also has extensive hardwood clone banks of black cherry, oak, and yellow poplar. You can get district information and maps at the district office off US 64 east of Murphy.

## WAYAH RANGER DISTRICT
**90 Sloan Rd., Franklin**
**(828) 524-6441**
The Wayah District (*wayah* means "wolf" in Cherokee) is centrally located in the Nantahala National Forest. Its 134,000 acres are adjacent to the Cherokee Indian Reservation in the north and extend all the way down to the Georgia border in the south. Within these boundaries you'll find the Nantahala River Gorge, with opportunities for white-water rafting and kayaking; two famous national trails, the Appalachian Trail and the Bartram Trail, which meet on Wayah Bald (see the Three Famous Trails Close-up in our Recreation chapter); the Standing Indian Basin; and the Southern Nantahala Wilderness Area.

The 25,515-acre Southern Nantahala Wilderness Area, created in 1984, is managed by the Nantahala National Forest (10,900 acres are in North Carolina) and by the Chattahoochee National Forest in Georgia (where the remaining acreage is located). Elevations here range from 2,400 feet to 5,499 feet on Standing Indian Mountain, with numerous peaks higher than 4,000 feet. The terrain, cut by streams, is steep and rugged. The forests are often dense, but there are grass-

# Ranger Stations

The offices of the National Forests in North Carolina are at 160-A Zillicoa St., Asheville, (828) 257-4200. To reach them, take the UNCA exit off U.S. Highways 19/23. You can contact the U.S. Forest Service for help and information in the following areas:

## Nantahala National Forest

### Cheoah Ranger District
U.S. Highway 129 North, Robbinsville
(828) 479-6431

### Highlands Ranger District
2010 Flat Mountain Rd., Highlands
(828) 526-3765

### Tusquitee Ranger District
201 Woodland Dr., off U.S. Highway 64 East, Murphy
(828) 837-5152

### Wayah Ranger District
90 Sloan Rd., Franklin
(828) 524-6441

## Pisgah National Forest

### Appalachian Ranger District, French Broad Station
U.S. Highways 25/70, 88 Bridge St., Hot Springs
(828) 622-3202

### Appalachian Ranger District, Tocane Station
U.S. Highway 19 East Bypass, Burnsville
(828) 682-6146

### Grandfather Ranger District
Route 1, exit 90 (Nebo/Lake James exit) Off I-40, 9 miles east of Marion
(828) 652-2144

### Pisgah Ranger District
1001 Pisgah Hwy., U.S. Highway 276, north of Brevard
(828) 877-3265

heath balds along many of the high ridges. All of the developed trails within this wilderness are rated "more difficult" to "most difficult." The Georgia portion of the wilderness has no developed trails. However, old roadbeds, which have been closed to vehicles, are suitable for hiking. Many of these old roads connect with trails in North Carolina. Several trails are open to horse travel. These are clearly marked by horse-with-rider signs.

Standing Indian Basin is a horseshoe-shaped drainage basin for the Nantahala and Blue Ridge Mountains. It's rimmed by several peaks that are more than 5,000 feet in elevation: Albert Mountain, Big Butt, Little Bald, and Standing Indian Mountain. There is an abundance of wildlife and recreational opportunities here, particularly hiking. The nicely landscaped Standing Indian Campground, which is open from Mar 31 to Dec 1, has 84 camping sites, picnic areas, water, and sanitary facilities for a fee of $10 a night. The Nantahala River, which flows right through the campground, offers fine trout fishing. No reservations are required.

Hikers and backpackers will find a special parking area at the Backcountry Information Center on FR 67, less than a half-mile from the campground and picnic area gate. The Appalachian Trail curves around the south and east ridge of the basin with various trails ascending off it. Trailheads can also be found all along FR 67, including the John Wasilik Memorial Poplar Trail that takes you to the second-largest yellow poplar in the United States.

The Big Indian Loop is a good horseback-riding trail—also shared with hikers, hunters, and fishers. It begins at a wildlife field off FR 67 about 4 miles beyond the Backcountry Information Station and meanders through extensive rhododendron and birch thickets with good views of Big Indian Creek. Just follow the orange blazes. And while you're here, you'll probably want to climb Standing Indian Mountain. To do so take the Kimsey Creek Trail that begins at the Backcountry Information Center off FR 67, where there's a bulletin board containing information about the area's many trails, then follow the blue blazes to the road bridge in the campground. Immediately after crossing the bridge, take the Park Creek Trail to the first blue-blazed trail leading to the left. This is the Kimsey Creek Trail, a moderately difficult trail that follows Kimsey Creek upstream, crossing it several times. Along the way you'll go through three wildlife fields where you may see deer, grouse, or other wildlife. When it ends at Deep Gap, you can turn left on the Appalachian Trail and continue a little more than 2 miles to Standing Indian Mountain. Backtrack (about a 7.5-mile round-trip) or return downhill on the rather strenuous Lower Ridge Trail, another popular but steeper trail that's also used to get to Standing Indian Mountain (about a 10-mile hike). You can also drive to Deep Gap on FR 71, thereby cutting the hiking distance to the summit to just more than 2 miles—a 4-mile round trip.

## Mountains-to-the-Sea Trail

Allen de Hart founded Friends of the Mountains-to-the-Sea Trail in 1997. He and Alan Householder were the first to hike the entire 934 miles from Clingmans Dome in the mountains of Western North Carolina to the Outer Banks at the Atlantic Ocean in that same year. In Oct 2002, 23-year-old Jason Pass of Waynesville, North Carolina, was the third person to complete the entire walk and the first to do it solo. His trek began at Clingmans Dome in the Great Smoky Mountains National Park on Sept 2, ending Oct 20 at Jockey's Ridge State Park on the Outer Banks. Scores of people continue this tradition every season.

## Pisgah National Forest

In 1886 George Vanderbilt came to this area and bought several thousand acres of abused farmland near Asheville. Here he built his famous Biltmore Estate, which still belongs to his family but is open to the public (see our Biltmore Estate chapter). To reclaim this used-up land, he hired Gifford Pinchot, a young American who had gotten his degree in scientific forestry in France. America had no schools of forestry at that time, so the studies could only be pursued in Europe.

When the opportunity arose, Vanderbilt also began to buy up acreage in what is now Pisgah Forest. His dream, and that of Pinchot, was to create a vast estate where forest resources could be conserved for a continual supply of goods. Eventually he owned 125,000 acres and named this vast tract after Pisgah National Mountain, a prominent peak on his land. (In the Bible, Pisgah was the mountain from which God showed Moses the Promised Land. The Asheville area's 5,721-foot mountain is thought to have been named by Rev. James Hall, a chaplain who accompanied Gen. Griffith Rutherford on his punitive strike against the Cherokee in 1776.)

Pinchot left Biltmore Estate at the request of Theodore Roosevelt to establish what would become the United States Forest Service. Vanderbilt replaced him with a German forester, Dr. Carl A. Schenck, who eventually started America's first school of forestry in the Pink Beds, a 20,000-acre parcel known for its lovely mountain laurels and other flowering plants. The area where the school stood is now a National Historic Site called the Cradle of Forestry. It still retains many of the school's structures, some of which were former buildings of the settlers who lived in the Pink Beds. The Cradle also offers guided trail walks and a great visitor center with a wealth of exhibits (for more specific information see our Close-up, The Cradle Keeps Rocking).

In 1914 George Vanderbilt died at the age of 52 of complications from appendicitis. Shortly after that, his widow, Edith, wrote a letter to the secretary of agriculture that began, "Sir: I now confront the question of what disposal I shall make of Pisgah Forest, which, under the terms of my late husband's will, has passed to me without qualifications or condition." What she did was pass on 80,000 acres of the land to the Forest

Service that her husband's former employee, Gifford Pinchot, now headed.

Over the years other tracts have been added to this glorious forest so that it now contains 495,979 acres, which is more or less split across the middle by the Blue Ridge Parkway. It contains three wilderness areas: Shining Rock, Linville Gorge, and Middle Prong. The Appalachian Trail runs along its border with Tennessee, and the relatively new Mountains-to-the-Sea Trail crosses through the forest (see the Three Famous Trails Close-up in our Recreation chapter). There are many other popular attractions here, such as the Fish Hatchery, the Pisgah Center for Wildlife Education, Roan Mountain Gardens, and Sliding Rock. (There are small parking fees at both Roan Mountain and Sliding Rock, with season passes also available.)

Pisgah Forest surrounds the East's tallest mountain, 6,684-foot Mount Mitchell, a state park unto itself. Pisgah has some 40 recreational areas that offer fishing, camping, hiking, and so on. Some have developed campgrounds, but some provide only primitive camping in order to protect the environment, because this forest is a botanical wonderland. For example, the whole state has 55 species of orchids, and 39 of them are found in Pisgah. More than 200 species of plants grow on Roan Mountain alone. Pisgah is more of a whole piece than the Nantahala National Forest, but it still has some scattered boundaries and is divided into four districts. The most used, with more than five million visitors a year, is the Pisgah District, heavily composed of the land that was originally owned by the Vanderbilts.

## APPALACHIAN RANGER DISTRICT, FRENCH BROAD STATION
## US 25/70, Hot Springs
## (828) 622-3202

This is an area of Pisgah National Forest that can almost guarantee you solitude. Mostly in Madison County with a little bit of the northeast section of Haywood thrown in, it contains 79,292 acres of some of the Appalachians' most isolated and craggy terrain. Many peaks here are more

than 4,000 feet, the highest being Camp Creek Bald at 4,844 feet. This area is rich in botanical surprises, including a number of threatened or endangered species.

The district's only developed campground is the Rocky Bluff Campground and Picnic Area, on a tree-covered ridge a little more than 3 miles south of Hot Springs on Highway 209 South. There is also a primitive campground at Harmon Den, and there are picnic areas at Murray Branch and Big Creek.

The district includes some 25 trails covering 127 miles, including 3 horse trails. Nearly 85 miles of the Appalachian Trail travels the mountain ridge forming the North Carolina–Tennessee state line. The famous trail can be accessed in many places, including on Max Patch Mountain (4,629 feet), where there are extraordinary views from its grassy summit. To reach Max Patch by car, drive south from Hot Springs on Highway 209 South for 7.3 miles. Turn south on SR 1175 and drive 5.3 miles to SR 1181. Three miles on this gravel road will take you within a half-mile of the top. There you can take a 1.4-mile loop trail across its summit or a 2.4-mile trail around the top for great views from all sides.

## APPALACHIAN RANGER DISTRICT, TOCANE STATION
## US 19 East Bypass, Burnsville
## (828) 682-6146

The 74,458-acre Tocane Station is full of history. Even the name dates back to the Cherokees, because it comes from the Toe and Cane Rivers that are in this area. According to legend, Toe was the nickname of an Indian princess, Estatoe, who wanted to marry a young brave from another tribe. Her people not only rejected the marriage proposal, but they killed the young man, after which the princess drowned herself in the river that came to be called Toe.

In 1913 the National Forest Service purchased the first 25,000 acres that make up this district on the slopes of the Black Mountains. More than 55 miles of the Appalachian Trail meander in and out of North Carolina and Tennessee along a ridgeline to the north. The Craggy Mountain Scenic Area (not to be confused with Craggy Gardens on the Blue Ridge Parkway) is in the southwestern section of the district, where you'll find Douglas Falls (listed in our Waterfalls chapter).

One of the most renowned spots in this district is Roan Mountain Gardens, or simply "The Roan," as it's called around here. This 6,286-foot bald summit is the highest point of the Unaka Mountains, a range that forms a high barrier between eastern Tennessee and Western North Carolina. Even when it was nearly inaccessible, Roan Mountain was famous for its scenic beauty. In 1877 Gen. Thomas Wilder built a 28-room log inn on its summit and replaced that in 1885 with the 166-room Cloudland Hotel. His ads read: "Come up out of the sultry plains to the 'land of sky,' magnificent view above the clouds where rivers are born, a most extended prospect of 50,000 square miles in six different states, 100 mountain tops over 4,000 feet high in sight."

The hotel was abandoned after 1900 and burned just before World War I. After that the old stands of spruce and balsam fir trees were cut, and the rootstock of the lovely purple rhododendrons that grew here was sold to nurseries, leaving only a few straggling bushes. But nature prevailed, and the flowering shrubs came back in neat clumps rather than in dense thickets, though some of these bushes grow from 15 to 20 feet tall and produce up to 800 blooms each. Today, like the guests of the Cloudland Hotel, you can enjoy the far vistas, stunning sunrises and sunsets, and full-circle rainbows, plus 600 acres of rhododendron gardens and 850 acres of Fraser fir. The deep magenta-pink flowers are usually in full bloom during the last two weeks of June. You can learn much more about these and Roan Mountain's other wonderful plants on a self-guided trail through the gardens.

The name of the mountain is a mystery. Some say it came from a roan horse left on the summit by Daniel Boone. It may be from the red-berried "roan tree" that grows on its crest. Another mystery is the strange "music" heard there from time to time that sounds like the humming of thousands of bees. Scientists think that electrically charged air currents swirling by each other near the peak might cause it.

The gardens are on Highway 261, 13 miles north of Bakersville. The road to the gardens is open from approximately May 1 through Oct 31, depending on the weather. There is a $3 parking fee.

There are two family campgrounds in the Tocane District: the Carolina Hemlocks Recreation Area and the Black Mountain Recreation Area (see our Recreation chapter for more information). There are areas for picnicking, fishing, swimming, and hiking. A mile-long Hemlock Nature Trail begins at the swimming beach. Two others, Colbert Ridge Trail and the Buncombe Horse Range Trail, start nearby.

Three miles on up Highway 80, turn right on FR 472 and drive 3 miles to reach the Black Mountain Recreation Area. The Briar Bottom Group Camp (reservation required) is in the same area. From the group camp's gate, the 1-mile Briar Bottom Trail loops the campground, crossing two footbridges in the process. Both hikers and bikers use it. Another short trail goes up Setrock Creek to a waterfall. Both the Mount Mitchell and Lost Cove Ridge Trails are accessible from the campground. (See our Recreation chapter.)

## GRANDFATHER RANGER DISTRICT
**Route 1, exit 90 (Nebo/Lake James exit)**
**Off I-40, 9 miles east of Marion**
**(828) 652-2144**

This very scenic district's 186,735 acres cover parts of Avery, Burke, Caldwell, and McDowell counties. Very near its center is the 10,975-acre Linville Gorge Wilderness Area, where you can still find virgin forests in deep coves and four different species of rhododendrons.

There are two campground/picnic areas in the district: the primitive, tents-only Curtis Creek Campground and the Mortimer Campground. The area also has two primitive camps in the Wilson Creek area at Chestnut and Kawana, and there are other picnic sites at Barkhouse on Highway 181 and at Mulberry, north of Lenoir. (See our Recreation chapter for more information.)

The Linville Gorge Wilderness Area offers a well-worth-it challenge to hikers and rock climbers. Here the Linville River drops 2,000 feet in a 14-mile series of cascades between steep escarpments. Camping in the gorge is limited to three days and two nights. To control the numbers, a free camping permit that you can get from the Forest Service (828-257-4203) is required on weekends and holidays from May 1 through Oct 31. You can get permits at the ranger's office off I-40, 9 miles east of Marion or at the Linville Falls Visitor Center (828-765-1045; milepost 316 at Linville) on Kistler Memorial Highway, which is open from 9 a.m. to 5 p.m. from Apr through Nov.

Famous Linville Falls is not a part of the Linville Gorge Wilderness Area. Just off the Blue Ridge Parkway, it's under the management of the National Park Service (see our Blue Ridge Parkway and Waterfalls chapters).

The Grandfather District has around 70 hiking trails, but many are not blazed or well maintained, so be sure to get information and good maps of the area before setting out. The one exception is the Mountains-to-the-Sea Trail, 46.5 miles of which run through this forest.

**i** Any time you visit the Cradle of Forestry, take the camera for spectacular views of Looking Glass Falls on U.S. Highway 276; take bathing suits or shorts for riding down Sliding Rock.

## PISGAH RANGER DISTRICT
**1001 Pisgah Hwy., US 276**
**(828) 877-3265**
This district's 156,103 acres take in parts of Buncombe, Haywood, Henderson, and Transylvania counties. It contains more than 275 miles of hiking trails that range from easy to very strenuous as well as horse trails and trails open to mountain bikes. The most challenging and the longest trails are the 31.7 miles of the Mountains-to-the-Sea Trail that runs through the district and the heavily used 30-mile Art Loeb Trail. The Pisgah District also has four campgrounds, plus three group campgrounds. Among the most popular are the Davidson River Campground right on the beautiful Davidson River, just 1.5 miles from the Brevard entrance to the forest on US 276, and

Lake Powhatan (see our Recreation chapter) on FR 3884 about 13 miles south of Asheville.

Definitely the most popular and used part of Pisgah National Forest is the 16-mile stretch of US 276 from the Brevard entrance to the Blue Ridge Parkway. This route brings you to the Davidson River Campground, the Pisgah District Ranger Station, the Fish Hatchery, the Pisgah Center for Wildlife Education, famous Looking Glass Falls and Sliding Rock, a natural waterslide (see our Waterfalls chapter), and the Cradle of Forestry next door to the Pink Beds picnic area. All along this route, you'll find picnicking spots by the

## Deep Gap Trail

One of our favorite hikes, which includes places where you pull yourself up by rocks and tree roots, is Mount Mitchell's Deep Gap Trail. This excellent but strenuous 8-mile round-trip hike covers four knobs on Mount Mitchell, the highest peak on the eastern seaboard at 6,684 feet. You'll see incredible wildflowers and coniferous forests, as well as ferns and lush mosses. To reach the trail entrance in this state park on Highway 128, off the Blue Ridge Parkway at milepost 355.4, leave your car in the picnic area parking lot. Walk directly through the picnic area until you reach a gravel trail with marker DEEP GAP TRAIL. This is a rough hike that will bring on a quick sweat with its straight uphill climbs: pack plenty of water and a snack. It gets very chilly (so bring a jacket) in this high elevation, and much of the trail is the solid granite of the mountain. A walking stick and dependable shoes are a good idea. This is one of the most challenging hikes of the area.

Davidson River and numerous hiking trails. One very popular one is Looking Glass Rock Trail, a strenuous 6.2-mile round-trip hike to the top of a huge granite dome, which dominates the area and is very popular with rock climbers. Also try Moore's Cove, a 1.4-mile easy hike that ends at a lovely waterfall that you can walk behind (see our Waterfalls chapter).

Two of Pisgah Forest's three wilderness areas are also in the Pisgah Ranger District: the 18,500-acre Shining Rock Wilderness and the 7,900-acre Middle Prong Wilderness.

## STATE PARKS

### GORGES STATE PARK
**Located on the NC–SC state line**
**Access off US 64 just east of Hwy. 281 South, Sapphire**
**(828) 966-9099**
This newest of state parks in North Carolina offers a primeval experience. It can be reached from Sapphire off Highway 281. Bring your own water and sandwiches. There are no facilities. You will find the splendor of plunging waterfalls, rugged river gorges, sheer rock walls, and one of the greatest concentrations of rare and unique species in the eastern United States. The surrounding forest is a virtual rain forest collecting more than 80 inches of rain per year with an elevation that rises some 2,000 feet in only 3 to 5 miles. Put this all together and it spells a bounty of waterfalls.

There are numerous trails that follow the Horsepasture River (National Wild and Scenic River), Toxaway River, Bearwallow Creek, and Windy Falls. Some of the mountains to be hiked are Chestnut, Grindstone, and Misery Mountain.

Backpack camping is permitted at traditional sites along the Foothills Trail. Horses and mountain bikes are permitted on Auger Hole Road from Frozen Creek Road to Turkey Pen Gap on the western boundary of the park. Unlicensed ATVs are prohibited by state regulations throughout the state park system. Licensed four-wheel-drive vehicles are permitted on Auger Hole Road for access to WRC gamelands during hunting season.

A parking area with restrooms and picnic table is planned for Highway 281 South and also in the Frozen Creek Road access area. Boat access to Lake Jocassee is currently available through Devil's Fork State Park in South Carolina.

## A Bass of a Fish Tale

Lake Jocassee, just inside South Carolina, is not only one access to North Carolina's newest park, Gorges State Park, but it has also produced the fourth-largest small-mouth bass ever caught in the entire United States. And at nine pounds and seven ounces, it beat the old South Carolina record as the largest ever taken from Lake Jocassee.

It all happened on a dark and calm night when Rosman, North Carolina, resident Terry Dodson took his rod and reel to the lake to gather a supply for the Old Toxaway Baptist church fish fry. He knew that something big had hit when the pole bent and the line started running. Claiming that it wasn't that much of a fight, he landed the big fellow and by the next morning of May 3, 2001, the South Carolina state biologist confirmed that this was a record-breaking catch.

This lake, sitting plumb on the state line, offers canoe and boating opportunities in addition to fishing.

### MOUNT JEFFERSON STATE PARK
**Jefferson County access: SR 1149**
**From Hwy. 163 to SR 1152**
**(336) 246-9653**
Mount Jefferson sparked interest as a park area in the 1930s when the Works Progress Administration constructed a rough 2-mile road to the summit of the mountain. It took another 20 years of

local interest and persistence to reach state park status, which Mount Jefferson achieved in 1956.

Mount Jefferson is positioned geographically between the north and south forks of the New River and was once part of a broad plateau that formed much of the region. The drainage line formed by these two water sources played an important part in the formation of the mountain itself. Eons of weathering and erosion ultimately created Mount Jefferson, the majestic promontory that rises 1,600 feet from the rolling meadows and valleys below.

The drive up the mountain provides spectacular views, particularly at sunset, and you can see three states from the top (Tennessee is to the west and Virginia to the north). There are overlooks along the way and two moderately difficult trails at the top. The Summit Trail is just a fraction of a mile from the highest point on Mount Jefferson, and the 1.1-mile Rhododendron Trail that begins at the terminus of the Summit Trail is a delightful, self-guided, moderately difficult trek through the forest with stops at numbered stations. The lush beauty of the purple Catawba rhododendron makes this trail a delight in early June. This trail also passes by a rock outcrop called Luther Rock, made up of a volcanic amphibolite rock that gives Mount Jefferson its dark cast. The trail circles back to the picnic area parking lot below the summit.

Visitors to the High Country can still see evidence of the once-abundant American chestnut in the building materials of area homes and rustic lodges that predate the 1920 blight that devastated the species. And on Mount Jefferson you can see American chestnut seedlings that continue to sprout in profusion. Red maple, basswood, tulip trees, and yellow birch also fill these woods, and you can spot a stand of big-toothed aspen below Luther Rock on the northern slopes of Mount Jefferson (only one other North Carolina county, Haywood, in the central mountain region, has these aspen trees).

Picnicking is popular at Mount Jefferson, which has a tree-shaded area with 32 tables and nine grills near the summit. Restrooms and drinking water are available nearby. There is no camping available here. Canoe-in and walk-in camping is available at nearby New River State Park.

Park hours are 9 a.m. to 5 p.m. Nov to Feb; 9 a.m. to 6 p.m. in Mar and Oct; 9 a.m. to 7 p.m. Apr, May, and Sept; and 9 a.m. to 8 p.m. June through Aug.

Rangers urge you to call ahead before visiting Mount Jefferson during the winter. The weather in these northern mountains is often unpredictable, and roads can quickly become impassable.

## MOUNT MITCHELL STATE PARK
**Hwy. 128, off the Blue Ridge Parkway, Mile 355.4**
**(828) 675-4611**

At 6,684 feet Mount Mitchell is the highest peak in the eastern United States, and it also carries the distinction of being the site of North Carolina's first state park. The park covers part of the rugged Black Mountains, which were formed more than a billion years ago and soar higher than the nearby Blue Ridge range or the Great Smokies of Tennessee. This extreme elevation creates a climate more like that of Canada's, and many of the plants and animals found here are also more akin to their northern cousins than their neighbors down the hill.

Mount Mitchell State Park was formed in 1915, a reaction mainly to the effects of overcutting by the logging industry that had come into prominence at the turn of the 20th century in North Carolina. The disappearance of much of the forests in the Black Mountains prompted Gov. Locke Craig, backed by concerned citizens, to preserve the last vestige of natural lands in this range.

Mount Mitchell is named in honor of University of North Carolina science professor Elisha Mitchell who, in 1835, made the rugged trek into the Black Mountain Range to verify his conclusions that peaks here were indeed higher than Grandfather Mountain. Grandfather had long been thought to be the most prominent peak in the region. Mitchell, on a subsequent trip to the Black Mountain Range in 1857 to verify his measurements, which had again come under dispute,

# Close-up

## The Cradle Keeps Rocking

On a sun-filled day legendary Congressman Roy Taylor spoke at a celebration of the Cradle of Forestry.

With his unique mountain humor, Congressman Taylor chided the organizers for putting him on a shaded stand with the participants standing in the blazing sun. "By now you'd think that reason, mountain logic, and just plain common sense would tell you to put the speaker in the sun and the congregation in the shade if you desire a short oration and to the point." Being acutely aware of his constituency, even though retired, his comments *were* emphatic and to the point. He next introduced the heir to Biltmore Estate and great grandson of George Vanderbilt, Bill Cecil Jr. The crowd applauded both men for the wisdom they shared as both Roy Taylor and William Amhurst Vanderbilt Cecil Jr. vowed that the creative forestry program begun at the Cradle, which was the foundation upon which the U.S. Forestry Service began, was a legacy that would endure and continue. The Biltmore Forest School of Dr. Albert Carl Schenck, supported by the wealth of George Vanderbilt, had its "campus" and the beginnings of American forestry here.

A devastating fire had destroyed the building of the Cradle and all that was stored in it during the winter months.

This occasion celebrated both the history and the future of the Cradle with its reopening. Still intact were two trails. One could view the historic buildings of America's first foresters by following one trail. The other trail was lush with forest growth, a historic portable sawmill, and the 1915 Climax logging locomotive, whose bell children love to ring.

The Forestry Discovery Center opened as a new and exciting chapter for the Cradle. In April 1997 18 new exhibits opened in the center. One lets you climb a replicated hillside, complete with rocks, trees, wildflowers, and animals, through the different levels of a forest. Below the hill you can crawl through a 30-foot underground tunnel with roots for handholds to observe the creatures living there. A "Water in the Forest" exhibit teaches the dynamics of a watershed, from raindrops to faucet. Interactive computers let you manage a forest ecosystem and show you the consequences of your actions. A "Global Connections" exhibit and video focuses on issues facing forest managers throughout the world.

A highlight is the "Fire-Fighting Helicopter Simulator," a sensory journey using visuals, sound, movement, and smells to replicate a flight into the depths of a wildfire to drop retardant to quench the flames. Even the simulated pilots bob about with the buffeting of the helicopter. And you are there with them.

Here, also, you can view an 18-minute movie that recounts the history of the first forestry school, dine at the Forest Bounty Café, and browse through an excellent gift shop full of charming toys and a fine selection of regional and outdoor books. Outside two separate trails, which you can take with a guide or on your own, lead to some of the old buildings built by both early settlers and Dr. Schenck for his school and forest rangers. Modern-day craftspeople with 19th-century skills can often be found on the Biltmore Campus Trail: You might see a toy maker crafting a Gee Haw whimmy diddle, or a weaver, a basket maker, and a skilled open-hearth cook.

In addition to all this, there are many special programs and events that take place throughout the Cradle's season, which runs from mid-Apr through the end of Nov.

The Cradle is located on US 276, 4 miles south of the Blue Ridge Parkway at milepost 412, or 11 miles from the intersection of US 64 and 276 and Highway 280 at the Brevard entrance to Pisgah National Forest. It's open from 9 a.m. until 5 p.m. and admission is under $10. Gold Age Passports are honored. For more information call (828) 877-3130 or (828) 884-5713; www .cradleofforestry.com.

unfortunately fell from a cliff above a 40-foot waterfall, where he was knocked unconscious and drowned in the pool below.

This park has a marvelous array of 1,677 acres of woodlands, wildlife habitat, majestic views, trail systems, and public camping and picnic areas. Because of the alpinelike climate, the weather here is always cooler, even in summer, than that in other parts of the state. It's a good idea to keep an extra jacket handy. The mists that roll over Mount Mitchell are a constant reminder of the extreme elevation and have historically been a hazard to small aircraft.

Mount Mitchell's summit has great sightseeing possibilities. On a clear day the stone observation tower at the top of the mountain affords a 70-mile view. Dr. Elisha Mitchell is buried at the base of the tower, and a marker honors his work. A small nature museum that once stood halfway up the trail from the parking area to the tower has been closed. In the spring of 2001 the new museum was opened adjacent to the parking area. It is wheelchair accessible. In this rustic structure dioramas and recordings give you a feel for the mountain's special plants and wildlife, and you can easily imagine the extremes of weather often found on lofty Mount Mitchell. You will also be greeted by Big Tom Wilson, the mountain man who found the body of Dr. Mitchell and then petitioned for his body to be removed from Riverside Cemetery in Asheville where he had been buried to the summit of the peak that bears his name. The life-size statue of Big Tom was carved from a tree trunk by his great-great-great grandson, world class wood-carver David Boone of Pensacola, North Carolina. David is also a direct descendant of Daniel Boone. There is also a gift shop in the same building as the museum.

The parking area at the base of the summit is surrounded by a 40-table picnic area with stone grills and drinking water. Two sites have fireplaces under shelter and are often used for group picnics. Hiking trails branch off in several directions from the parking area. Look for the white-tailed deer.

Stop at the ranger station at the entrance to the park for information on hiking, camping, and maps of trail areas both along the ridge and down the mountain. At Mount Mitchell you can camp family style with a rustic ambience at the nine-site campground that's open May 1 through Oct 31. This is tent camping only, no RVs. Restrooms are nearby, but no showers or hot water are available.

For day visitors who crave sustenance at this mile-high peak, try the concession stand at the summit for light snacks. For a more substantial meal and an inspiring view, you can dine at the park's restaurant a half-mile from the ranger's office. The sturdy stone-and-timber, lodgelike restaurant serves breakfast on weekends and holidays and lunch and dinner daily during park hours. Both food service locations have restrooms.

Hours at Mount Mitchell State Park are 8 a.m. to 6 p.m. Nov through Feb; 8 a.m. to 7 p.m. in Mar and Oct; 8 a.m. to 8 p.m. Apr, May, and Sept; and 8 a.m. to 9 p.m. June through Aug.

## NEW RIVER STATE PARK
**Alleghany County access: by river only, near Sparta, SR 1549 and SR 1308**
**Ashe County access: near Jefferson, SR 1590 (Wagoner Road) and US Highway 221 off Highway 88 East**
**(336) 982-2587 (for both counties)**
The New River, around which this state park is framed, is reported to be the oldest river in North America. It cuts a deep, twisting groove from the state boundary with Virginia and flows like a curling satin ribbon through Ashe and Alleghany, the two northernmost counties of Western North Carolina. The beauty of this primeval river was almost lost more than 30 years ago when the Appalachian Power Company applied for a license to dam the New River and build reservoirs along its length. Fortunately citizen opposition gained momentum, and in 1975, after extensive hearings and litigation, the North Carolina General Assembly acted to preserve a 26.5-mile stretch of this historic river—from its confluence with the Dog Creek to the Virginia line—officially naming it a State Scenic River. The next year the secretary of the interior moved to designate

the same stretch as a part of the National Wild and Scenic River System, and Congress followed suit to affirm the action, thereby prohibiting the construction of dams and reservoirs on the river.

Thus the New River State Park was born. The park covers not only a scenic and tranquil waterway, but three designated parkland areas as well. The pastoral fields and forests along the New River also have their own historic interest: Indian activity here has been documented from 10,000 years ago by archaeological excavations that uncovered pottery shards, arrowheads, stone axes, and other artifacts. This area of the New River Valley appeared to have served as a hunting ground for several neighboring tribes, Cherokee, Shawnee, and Creek Indians, on their way north to hunting lands along the Ohio River.

Today, New River State Park is a popular destination for outdoor recreation. You can picnic at the river's access areas and at tables sheltered by a grove of trees or beneath a bona fide roof or camp at the Wagoner Road access off Highway 88. The New River's placid waters are perfect for canoeing, which makes it an extremely popular sport here. In fact the Alleghany County access area near the Virginia border can be reached only by canoe. This remote spot is bordered on one shore by an imposing rock face and on the other by a primitive camping area. Canoeing campers at this site must register at designated boxes or with a park ranger. Canoes may also be launched from the Wagoner Road access, the US 221 access in Ashe County to the south, and from numerous bridges that cross the New River.

You'll probably see more than one fisherman hip-deep in the well-stocked waters of this river. Area natives claim these waters provide some of the best bass fishing in the state. Anglers do need a license and should also be aware of fishing regulations of the North Carolina Wildlife Resources Commission. Check with park rangers for more information (and see our Recreation chapter).

A note of caution: During heavy rains, be aware that the New River is subject to heavy flooding. Park information and maps of the river's course are available at ranger stations. (See the Ranger Stations sidebar in this chapter.)

Park hours are 8 a.m. to 6 p.m. Nov to Feb; 8 a.m. to 7 p.m. in Mar and Oct; 8 a.m. to 8 p.m. during Apr, May, and Sept; and 8 a.m. to 9 p.m. June through Aug.

## STONE MOUNTAIN STATE PARK
**Located in Alleghany and Wilkes County**
**7 miles southwest of Roaring Gap**
**(336) 957-8185**
From U.S. Highway 21 take SR 1002 4.5 miles to Traphill. Turn north on John P. Frank Parkway for 2 miles.

This area is a delight for the rugged outdoor types who scale mountains and face windstorms. Weathering action over eons of time has created a mini-moonscape on this dome-shaped granite mass. Climbers are invited and must register when entering the park. Bring your ropes and use the available bolts, but leave your metal gear at home as it is not permitted to drive new bolts into the rock.

Of the nine hiking trails most are noted as strenuous. They include the 4-mile Stone Mountain Loop, Summit Trail to the top for 0.75 mile, and the 2.5-mile Widow's Creek Trail. And now we find two that are listed as moderate. They are the Self-Guided Nature Trail for 0.5 mile and Middle Falls/Lower Falls Trail at 0.75 mile.

Bikes are not allowed, but horses are. There's a 5-mile Bridle Trail leading into the park. There are many comfort zones in the park as well: 75 picnic tables each with a grill, 3 picnic shelters with Chestnut and Dogwood each having 8 tables and Hemlock with 12 tables. Pig cookers and portable grills are also permitted at the shelters, but in the grassy areas only. Some group camping is allowed through prearrangement. Toilet facilities are available, and drinking water can be obtained from the forest ranger. Backpack camping is permitted, and you can even roll your RV into the tent/trailer area, but no water or electric hookups are available. Clear flowing streams lure the angler, who must possess a current fishing license and trail stamp. "Fish for Fun" is offered at Bull Head Creek. It is a catch-and-release area. A fly rod, reel, barbless hook, and a net are required.

**Close-up**

## Boojum and Hootin' Annie

The folks at Haywood County's Lake Logan know for certain that the Boojum walk these mountains. There's an inscription in a cave at that site that tells the story.

This large creature has roamed these mountains since time began. The Boojum was apparently on friendly terms with the giant folks of the Cherokee. (They are buried in the Indian mound in Franklin, North Carolina, but that's another story.) As folks began to settle these parts, the Boojum was curious and watched their every move. With the arrival of newborn babies and livestock, the Boojum danced around the mountains with great delight. Some folks mistook the dancing for thunder.

The Boojum was misunderstood. He didn't mean to cause trouble, but being a big old ramblin' sort, he just kind of messed things up. Without meaning to, he'd trample crops, especially after a hailstorm, for example. So folks began to chase him away. This made him terribly distraught, and he formed lots of mountain streams with his big sad tears.

One day a sweet mountain girl named Annie happened upon the Boojum while he was sleeping. His great snoring was creating an infernal roar in the mountains, and his wheezing after each snore stirred up the biggest wind ever. Annie loved everyone and everything, so she had nary a fear of the big fellow.

"Howdy!" she said. The Boojum was used to folks throwing stones and sticks, so he tried to hide himself. This young gal wouldn't stand for that, however, and ran after him. Finally, possessing one of the best sets of lungs ever having come from Spivey,* Annie set up the sweetest hooting, which melted the heart of the Boojum. He slowly peeked out to see what it was all about.

The Big Boojum and sweet Hootin' Annie became the closest of friends that any two critters could be. Every day Annie would hoot for the Boojum. Every day he would come to her, and the two of them would dance from one mountain top to another. They'd start off at the Pisgahs, and the Boojum would whirl and jig until they got to the Balsams. They'd circle their partner and find their way to the Black Mountains. One day they even got as far as one could go dancing from the Grandfather all the way to the Great Smoky Mountains.

When they danced, the Boojum would roar with laughter. Annie would hoot with joy, and her clogging shoe taps would shoot sparks off the flint of the mountain. Not knowing any better, the folks in the valley thought they were besieged with thunder and lightning.

This tale saddened quickly when more folks moved into the mountains. Trains came through, big roads were built, and then everyone came. The Boojum went deeper into the mountains to escape all this. Annie would commence hootin' while looking for him. More and more she had to hoot longer and louder . . . until one day the Boojum didn't answer her. So she went deeper into the mountains on her search and she was never seen again.

Some folks claim that you can still hear them dancing, hootin', and roarin' with Annie's taps striking off the flint.

One other thing. Folks are strange. Even though they drove off the Boojum and Annie, whenever they get together for a good time in these parts, they fill tables with mountains of mouthwatering food, they fiddle and strum, and dance and sing . . . and they call it a "Hootin' Annie." Now doesn't that beat all!

*Spivey is for Spivey Corners located in the eastern part of North Carolina, where a "Hollerin" contest is held annually.

The park is open year-round with seasonal adjustments for openings and closings. Give the ranger a call for more details and to register for the many opportunities.

# STATE FORESTS AND GAME LANDS

### DUPONT STATE FOREST
**Sky Valley Road, Hendersonville**
**(828) 251-6509**

This is Western North Carolina's newest state forest. Its 7,600 acres in Henderson and Transylvania counties were purchased in 1996 and 1997 from DuPont after the company sold its industrial operation and 2,700 acres of surrounding land holdings to Sterling Diagnostic Imaging. An acquisition in 2000 enlarged the forest to 10,300 acres. The forest is situated in an upland plateau of the Little River Valley with elevations that range from 2,300 to 3,600 feet. Its gently rolling land is bordered by moderately steep hills and mountains that are topped by exposed granite slabs and domes.

Most of the forest trails are open for horseback riding and mountain biking. Registered as North Carolina gameland, hunting in season is by lottery only, and no hunting is allowed on Sun. For fishing, streams here are classified as "wild." (Contact the North Carolina Wildlife Resources Commission, 512 North Salisbury St., Raleigh, 27604-1188, 919-733-3391, for more details on both hunting and fishing in this forest.) ATVs are forbidden in the forest.

At present the land is also open for hiking, and the forest has more than 80 miles of trail, ranging from easy to strenuous. (A detailed, hand-marked color map is available at the Henderson County Travel and Tourism office, 201 South Main St., Hendersonville, for $7.) For a short hike to 13-foot Hooker Falls, the site of a former gristmill, take DuPont Road (off Crab Creek Road) for about 3 miles until you see the Little River bridge at the bottom of a long hill. Park near the gated Hooker Falls Road on the right just before the bridge. Walk around the gate and along the dirt road, bearing left at the fork, and continuing parallel to the river. In a few minutes you will approach the top of Hooker Falls. Continue straight on the path to a good viewing location at the pool below. You won't want to miss the other three waterfalls: Triple Falls, High Falls, and Bridal Veil Falls.

If it's a hot day and you'd like to cool off, continue on up DuPont Road for another 2.6 miles until it dead ends into Cascade Lake Road (Buck Forest Road on some maps). Drive almost a mile to a wide parking spot on the right. Walk across the road and go around the gate on the marked Corn's Mill Road and continue on the road. Walk past the intersection of Big Rock Trail to a crossing over Tom's Creek. Continue on the graded road to a fork. Take the right fork, and after a short distance, take the left fork (you'll still be on Corn's Mill Road) until you reach a gentle waterslide and popular ford on the Little River where local residents have enjoyed swimming for years.

There are multiple ways to get to this mecca of land and forest, so ring up the forester to obtain directions that suit you.

### GREEN RIVER GAME LANDS
**Big Hungry Road, SR 1802, Hendersonville**
**(919) 733-3391**

Over 10,000 rugged acres in Henderson and Polk counties make up these state-owned gamelands. There are 15 miles of beautiful trails here ranging from easy to strenuous, but because of the nature of the terrain, it's recommended that you don't hike here alone. It's also wise to avoid the area during hunting seasons. Some of the trails offer great views of Tryon Peak and the Green River Gorge to the south. Others take you on a ridgeline next to the steep and dangerous Loobie Cliffs or for a view from Pace Cliffs. No vehicles or horses are allowed here. A brochure with a map and descriptions of the trails can be found at visitor centers in the area, or contact the North Carolina Wildlife Resources Commission, 512 North Salisbury St., Raleigh 27604-1188, (919) 733-3391. It is also your source for information on hunting here.

**Close-up**

## Big Tom Wilson

In 1835, University of North Carolina Professor Dr. Elisha Mitchell announced that his baro-metric measurements indicated that a mountain (which in time would bear his name) was the highest peak in the Appalachian chain. The measurement of 6,674 feet stood until 1857, when Thomas Clingman claimed that he had found a higher peak. Clingman and his team measured the peak, which stands on the North Carolina and Tennessee line. The summit is in Tennessee and is known as Clingmans Dome. But it proved to be at least 40 feet lower than Mount Mitchell.

Eventually Mount Mitchell was found to be even higher than Dr. Mitchell thought. Officially it stands at 6,684 feet. It is the highest point in the entire Eastern United States.

In response to Clingman's claim, Dr. Mitchell ascended the mountain alone to measure it. He did not return to his base camp at Black Mountain on schedule. After a search party failed to find any trace of Dr. Mitchell, they called upon Big Tom Wilson. Tom was known for his skill, knowledge, and prowess in the mountains. He was already legendary as a young man who had killed more than 100 black bears, which were a main staple in the life of the mountaineers.

Big Tom conducted the search with the help of a young lad of about 14 who carried a huge rope. As they ascended, the "smoke" of the Smokies, which some people might call fog, crowded in on them. Big Tom never faltered. Big Tom pointed out footprints of Dr. Mitchell that seemed to be going steadily up the mountain.

Approaching the summit and nearing the top of the waterfalls, Big Tom pointed out where Mitchell had misstepped. His footprints showed that he had stumbled on a rock or slipped off a log, evidenced by moss scraped off a rock, where Dr. Mitchell apparently tried to steady himself.

Reaching the top of the waterfall, the searchers saw brambles and brushes at the foot of the falls with a large, dark object floating underneath the mass. Big Tom lowered the boy with a rope, and the lad called up that indeed there was a body. He secured the rope to the body, and Big Tom pulled Dr. Mitchell from the pool and carried his body down off the mountain.

Mitchell is now buried at the summit of Mount Mitchell.

Big Tom has been immortalized by his great-great-great grandson, world class wood-carver David Boone. Standing in the museum at the parking lot on Mount Mitchell is the 6-foot 4-inch wood carving created by Boone.

---

### HOLMES EDUCATIONAL STATE FOREST
**Crab Creek Road, Hendersonville**
**(828) 692-0100**

Well-tended trails loop through 235 acres of mountain forests at this pretty state forest. One of the most delightful, and educational, things about it is the Talking Trees Trail, which features different hardwood trees that, at the touch of a button, tell stories about themselves, their sites, and the forest history. Two other trails include the Soil and Water Trail, featuring a 300-foot boardwalk over a wetland area, and Crab Creek Trail, spotlighting firefighting equipment displays and a walk through a pine stand. (Crab Creek Trail was built with wheelchairs in mind.) There is also a Forest Demonstration Trail that teaches actual forest practices. The Forestry Center houses audiovisual exhibits, and a natural amphitheater is available for special sessions or groups.

Holmes also has picnic tables and a group picnic shelter with a massive stone fireplace. For the hardy there are walk-in tent sites in the forest that can be reserved with a phone call. This pleasant state forest is open from mid-Mar through mid-Nov. It is 8.5 miles from Hendersonville on Crab Creek Road (SR 1127).

# ATTRACTIONS

Most of the "attractions" in these mountains are the mountains themselves. There's not much of a need for artificial diversion, what with the natural activities inherent to this area. But if you tire of hiking, tubing down mountain streams, fly-fishing, mountain biking, kayaking, antiquing, and scouring the farmers' market for homemade preserves and string beans, then head over to these more organized attractions of the mountains.

It doesn't matter if rain is pouring through the treetops or sunshine is bursting over the rugged terrain, you'll always find something to do in North Carolina's mountains. We've included attractions in this chapter that can keep a whole family busy without costing a bundle—some are even free. One of the most alluring attractions in our mountains is the palatial Biltmore Estate in Asheville, to which we've dedicated an entire chapter. Other popular destinations, such as the Carl Sandburg Home in Flat Rock, have been included in other chapters. Details on the famous poet's lovely Connemara farm, where he spent the final 22 years of his life, can be found in the Arts and Culture chapter. The Annual Festivals and Events chapter is a good source of ideas for pleasurable outings, as are the Resorts, Rockhounding, and Waterfalls chapters. So pick your pleasure. But remember, these are only a few of the spontaneous, special ways to enjoy a ramble through the North Carolina highlands. Prices and times of operation are always subject to change, so do give a call before you head out.

## NORTHERN MOUNTAINS

### Ashe County

**ASHE COUNTY CHEESE FACTORY**
106 East Main St., West Jefferson
(336) 246-2501, (800) 445-1378
www.ashecountycheese.com
Did you know that it takes 10 gallons of milk to make one pound of cheese? That's one of the facts you'll learn as you watch cheese being made in this factory founded in 1930. The factory's varieties include cheddar, Colby, and Monterey Jack. Guides escort groups through a viewing room, explain the process, and answer questions. Sample your favorites and take a few home from the company cheese shop across the street from the factory. The plant is open 8:30 a.m. to 5 p.m. Mon through Sat. Admission is free.

**CHURCHES OF THE FRESCOES**
St. Mary's, 400 Beaver Creek Rd.,
West Jefferson
Holy Trinity, 120 Glendale School Rd.,
Glendale Springs
(336) 982-3076
Ben Long painted three frescoes at St. Mary's: "Mary Great with Child" in 1974; "John the Baptist" in 1975; and "The Mystery of Faith" in 1977. In the summer of 1980 he painted the frescoes of "The Last Supper" at Holy Trinity. Visitors are welcome.

### Avery County

**GRANDFATHER MOUNTAIN**
US Hwy. 221, outside Linville, Mile 305
1 mile off the Blue Ridge Parkway
(828) 733-2013, (800) 468-7325
www.grandfather.com
The rugged outline of this ridge that takes on the appearance of a bearded face—the "grandfather"—gives this mountain its name. Grandfather

Mountain is the highest in the Blue Ridge chain. It is part of the International Network of Biosphere Reserves, "a special place where man and nature thrive in harmony." Of the 324 existing Biosphere Reserves, Grandfather is the only one privately owned. This wonderful oasis allows you to come close to the natural wildlife habitats of black bears, cougars, deer, eagles, and river otter.

The nature museum offers valuable information. If you have no fear of heights, you might attempt the exhilaration of the famous Mile High Swinging Bridge (keep remembering to look at the view).

Work off those wobbly knees with 12 miles of hiking trails. The Grandfather Trail is a favorite, a rugged but beautiful trail traversing 2.3 miles. The mountain also offers meandering footpaths and scenic walks for novice hikers. Once you've relaxed, spread a picnic and enjoy this majestic place, a reminder of the fragility of our relationship with this earth. The site is open daily except Thanksgiving and Christmas from 8 a.m. to 5 p.m. in winter, 8 a.m. to 6 p.m. in spring and fall, and 8 a.m. to 7 p.m. in summer. Ticket sales stop at 6 p.m. A gift shop and restaurant are on the site. Children younger than four are admitted free.

**i** To see how Grandfather Mountain got its name, head south on Highway 105 from Boone. In the heart of Foscoe, look toward the mountain on your left, and lo and behold, there he is, sleeping on his back. You can almost hear him snore!

## Madison County

**HOT SPRINGS SPA**
**315 Bridge St., Hot Springs**
**(828) 622-7676, (800) 462-0933**
**www.nchotsprings.com**
Historically the mineral springs of Hot Springs, North Carolina, maintaining a natural 100-degree temperature year-round, have provided relief for visitors as early as the turn of the 20th century. That was the heyday of this once-fashionable health resort. With the passage of time and a changing world, the springs fell into disuse, and

the population dwindled away. But in 1990 the famous hot springs came into new ownership and are now back in business, offering a modern version of "taking the waters."

Jacuzzis filled with the curative waters are available for hourly rates, determined by the number of people in your party. Fees run under $20 per person. Several resident massage therapists are available by appointment.

The friendly employees at the spa make you feel like a long lost relative. The word *spa* may be a misnomer, though. This is a very casual place—don't expect luxury—but do expect to commune successfully with nature (leafy trees and the sky are your canopy), while some tubs have plastic "bubbles" so they can be used in inclement weather. Tubs are set alongside the rushing French Broad River and Spring Creek. A log fire in the central yard is perfect for lounging and communing with friends.

The Hot Springs Spa is open year-round. Rates increase for evening sessions (after 7 p.m.). Lodging facilities are available in the RV park and campground, for which options include electric, water, and sewer hookups and tent sites. There is also a facility for hot showers. Primitive camping cabins are also available, as is one fully furnished log cabin with a Jacuzzi on the back porch, fed from the natural spring. When camping, children six or younger stay free. Special discounts and group rates are also available for the campground.

**i** Bring your own empty water bottles to fill with mineral water from the underground hot springs at Hot Springs Spa. A sculptural fountain in front allows you to gather it for free.

## McDowell County

**LINVILLE CAVERNS**
**US 221, between Linville and Marion**
**4 miles south of the Blue Ridge Parkway**
**(828) 756-4171, (800) 419-0540**
**www.linvillecaverns.com**
These limestone caverns with marvelous stalactite and stalagmite formations were first explored

in the late 1880s by H. E. Colton and his local guide Dave Franklin. However the Indians had known about the caverns since 1822. Found deep inside Humpback Mountain, these caverns were also hideouts for army deserters from both sides during the Civil War.

Today, in the company of experienced guides, you can take a path that leads along an underground stream filled with trout whose life in perpetual darkness has resulted in blindness. The limestone formations, suspended like jewels, have developed over eons into interesting shapes, such as the Frozen Waterfall, Natural Bridge, and Franciscan Monk. Did you ever wonder what absolute darkness looks like? You'll get your chance deep in these caverns.

This must be the guides' favorite part—switching off those lights! You literally can't see your hand in front of your face. The temperature underground is a constantly cool 52 degrees, so come prepared with a sweater or jacket. A gift shop is well stocked, and items are reasonably priced. Admission is under $10.

## Mitchell County

### THE ORCHARD AT ALTAPASS
**Mile 328.4, Blue Ridge Parkway, near Little Switzerland**
**(828) 765-9531, (888) 765-9531**
**www.altapassorchard.com**
This historic orchard features fresh apples and peaches from May to Nov and is open only during these months. You can pick your own or just buy the already-picked baskets and brown-paper bags of juicy fruits. Tours of the orchard are free. Come enjoy music, stories, and hayrides on Sat. The Orchard is open seven days a week.

> **i** There are more than 16,000 southern varieties of heirloom apples. The Orchard at Altapass provides hayrides and stories while you ride among some of these heirlooms. You might have the opportunity to taste a Grimes Golden, a Sheepsnose, or a Limbertwig. You might even be able to pick your own.

## Watauga County

### THE BLOWING ROCK
**Off U.S. Hwy. 321, Blowing Rock**
**(828) 295-7111**
**www.theblowingrock.com**
Fanciful tales about this beautiful spot are as interesting as the facts. This rocky granite outcrop is swept by a constant updraft from Johns River Gorge 3,000 feet below. Those are the facts.

The most familiar romantic legend of the Blowing Rock is that a beautiful Indian maiden was taken from the plains to Blowing Rock by her father, a Chickasaw chieftain who was fearful of a white man's adoration of his daughter. The daughter met an Indian brave wandering below the Blowing Rock and shot an arrow in his direction to capture his attention. They fell in love, but a reddening of the sky brought them back to the rock. It was a sign of trouble to the brave, commanding his return to his tribe on the plains. With the maiden's entreaties not to leave her, the brave, torn by conflict of duty and heart, leapt from the rock. The maiden prayed to the Great Spirit every day until one evening, a gust of wind blew her lover back onto the rock and into her arms.

The Blowing Rock claims a panoramic view of Mount Mitchell, Hawksbill, Grandfather, and Table Rock mountains in the distance. Blowing Rock is just outside the town of the same name and is open daily from Mar through Nov; it's open weekends in winter months, weather permitting. Hours are 9 a.m. to 5 p.m. Mar, Apr, and Nov; 9 a.m. to 6 p.m. May through Aug; and 8 a.m. to 7 p.m. Sept through Oct. Admission fees are $4 for adults, $1 for children ages 6 to 11, and $3 for seniors and groups of 20 or more.

### DANIEL BOONE NATIVE GARDENS
**651 Horn in the West Dr.**
**Off Hwy. 105 and US 321/421, Boone**
**(828) 264-6390**
The stone gatehouse bids you welcome as you enter the gardens through the handsome wrought iron gate, a gift made by Daniel Boone VI, a direct descendant of the great pioneer. Adjacent to *Horn in the West*, these beautiful

gardens include an extensive collection of native plants covering six acres, informally landscaped with trails, split-rail fences, and a reflection pool at the Squire Boone Cabin. Many plants, such as bloodroot, dogtooth violet, yellow lady slippers, and maidenhair fern, are marked. A spring trickles through the enormous boulders of the Rockery, while a statue of St. Francis stands in the center of the secluded prayer retreat. There's even a meditation sanctuary that lets you pause and give thanks for such beauty. The gardens are open daily May through Aug and weekends in Oct 10 a.m. to 6 p.m. (until 8 p.m. when *Horn in the West* is running). A small admission is charged, but those under 16 are admitted free.

**i** Jan Karon, author of the best-selling Mitford series of books, based her novels on the village of Blowing Rock.

**HICKORY RIDGE HOMESTEAD**
**591 Horn in the West Dr.**
**Off Hwy. 105 and US 321/421, Boone**
**(828) 264-9089, (828) 264-2120**
You'll swear you just saw Daniel Boone, but it was one of the costumed interpreters at Hickory Ridge Homestead on the grounds of *Horn in the West*. This living museum offers a glimpse into 18th-century mountain life and culture through a variety of activities, including regular demonstrations in weaving and candle making, as well as presentations of other crafts. Try your hand at weaving on a 180-year-old loom, spinning wool, or participating in other hands-on activities. A nominal admission helps support the museum and its projects. Hours vary with the seasons, so call ahead. And while you're at it, ask about the intensive living history weekends and workshops.

**HORN IN THE WEST**
**591 Horn in the West Dr.**
**Off Hwy. 105 and US 321/421, Boone**
**(828) 264-9089, (828) 264-2120**
**www.horninthewest.com**
This outdoor drama, one of several in this region, depicts the lives of North Carolina's early settlers—Daniel Boone among them—and their struggle for independence from Britain. This production, set in pre-Revolutionary 1771, lasts about two hours and is a one-of-a-kind experience: history and excitement all rolled into one. Remember, this is an outdoor production. Summer evenings can be cool, especially at this elevation, so bring a light jacket just in case. The season is mid-June to mid-Aug, and the drama begins each evening at 8, with reserved seating. There are no performances on Mon. Admission is $12 for adults and $6 for children 12 and younger.

**i** The movie *The Green Mile* was partially filmed at Moses Cone Manor on the Parkway in Blowing Rock. The manor portrayed the character's retirement home.

# CENTRAL MOUNTAINS

## Buncombe County

### ASHEVILLE TOURISTS BASEBALL
**30 Buchanan Place, McCormick Field, off Biltmore Ave., Asheville**
**(828) 258-0428**
Professional baseball at McCormick Field has been a fixture in Asheville since 1924. Many of the all-time greats of the game, such as Babe Ruth, Ty Cobb, Jackie Robinson, Pete Rose, and Nolan Ryan, played here en route to the majors.

The new McCormick Field, a much-improved facility, was completed in 1992. The old McCormick Field, with all its well-worn charm, was actually famous for a bit part as background in some of the final scenes for the popular baseball movie *Bull Durham* with Kevin Costner. The new stadium is grand, but it's Asheville's baseball tradition that keeps folks coming to McCormick Field to cheer on the Tourists.

The Tourists baseball season begins in Apr and runs through the first week in Sept. The Asheville team, a member of the South Atlantic League, plays about 72 home games.

### THE ASHEVILLE URBAN TRAIL
**Locations in downtown Asheville**
**(828) 259-5800, ext. 4000**

Asheville's formative period, the boom time from 1880 to 1930, left an indelible imprint on the character of the city. This was the era of George Vanderbilt (Biltmore Estate), E. W. Grove (Grove Park Inn), and George Willis Pack (Pack Square), men whose taste for elegance produced a stunning blend of architectural styles that remains today.

To highlight and pay homage to this remarkable period in Asheville's history, the city has commissioned the development of the Urban Trail. This series of 30 stations is marked by plaques, sculptures, mosaics, murals, and other interpretive visuals created by world-class artists from Russia, Italy, and the United States that bring the area's history to life. The open-air museum runs 1.7 miles around downtown through five themed paths. The walking benefits of the trail are free, along with the pleasure of the path. Regularly scheduled guided tours of the Urban Trail are run from Apr to Nov, the second Fri of each month at 4 p.m., the third Sun of each month at 3 p.m., and other special group tours as requested. The two-hour tour meets in front of Pack Place at the marquee sign, on the southeast corner of Pack Square in downtown Asheville. Tours will be on schedule except in extreme weather conditions. A $5 donation per person is suggested (no charge for children under 12 accompanied by an adult).

**i** Touring the Asheville Urban Trail on your own is made easy with the aid of "Artful Asheville—Along the Urban Trail," a comprehensive take-along guide with maps and informative history about each of the 30 stations (sculptures and plaques) around the city. The booklet is available at bookstores, the Asheville Area Arts Council, and the Asheville Convention and Visitors Bureau.

### THE BOTANICAL GARDENS
**151 W. T. Weaver Blvd., Asheville**
**(828) 252-5190**
**www.ashevillebotanicalgardens.com**
This wonderful 10-acre garden oasis in the middle of bustling north Asheville is adjacent to the campus of the University of North Carolina at Asheville. The gardens were begun in 1960 by the Asheville Garden Club and designed by Doan Ogden, a noted landscape architect, to preserve the heritage of native mountain plants and flowers. Today this mature garden has a wealth of beauty around every bend in the path and within every leafy bower. A bonus is the proliferation of birds and other small wildlife that have made this wonderful garden their home. You may spot a few rabbits at dusk; squirrels and chipmunks abound in the daylight hours. A meadow for sunning, a gazebo for lounging, and a cool creek make this an oasis close to the city, perfect for those after-dinner walks. Many of the trees and other flora are marked with small tags for identification. This site receives support from volunteers, donations, and memberships. A botany center offers nature-related gift items. Admission is free. No pets are allowed.

### FOLK ART CENTER
**Mile 382, Blue Ridge Parkway, Asheville**
**(828) 298-7928**
**www.southernhighlandguild.org**
The Folk Art Center is home to the Southern Highland Craft Guild, an educational nonprofit organization founded in 1930 to give economic support and development to the craftspeople of the Appalachian region. The guild serves nine states and has a membership of more than 700 craftspeople who work to preserve and perpetuate the Appalachian heritage as well as develop the contemporary face of craftsmanship.

The center's century-old Allanstand Craft Shop offers for sale the work of guild members throughout the nine-state region. There is also a fine crafts gallery on the upper level and a 250-seat auditorium that is the scene of workshops, programs, and lectures by the guild and National Park Service. Craft demonstrations are held Apr through Dec in the foyer of the center. Clay Day and Fiber Day are two of the special events also sponsored by the guild at the Folk Art Center each year (see our Annual Festivals and Events and Mountain Crafts chapters for more information on the guild). Admission is free.

## NORTH CAROLINA ARBORETUM
**100 Frederick Law Olmsted Way, Asheville**
**(828) 665-2492**
**www.ncarboretum.org**
This 426-acre facility boasts a 25,500-square-foot Visitor Education Center, the Horticultural Support Facilities and Greenhouses, the Plants of Promise Garden, and the mile-long Natural Garden Trail, all of which are open to the public. The Core Area Gardens include the Stream Garden, Spring Garden, Outdoor Events Garden, Appalachian Quilt Garden, Blue Ridge Court, and Grand Promenade. Numerous woodland trails lace the forested areas and follow the path of Bent Creek. Guided tours are available for groups if you call ahead. Educational lectures, tours, and workshops are scheduled throughout the year. A cafe and plant retail shop are also on the premises.

A per-vehicle car fee is required at the gate. Nominal fees apply for educational programs. The outdoor areas are open seven days a week from 7 a.m. to 7 p.m. The greenhouse is open 8 a.m. to 4 p.m. Mon through Fri.

Turn off U.S. Highway 191 to the Blue Ridge Parkway. The arboretum entrance is directly before you enter the parkway.

## RIVERSIDE CEMETERY
**51 Birch St., Asheville**
**(828) 350-2066**
Sitting high on a hill overlooking part of downtown Asheville is the Riverside Cemetery in the historic Montford district. Among the notables laid to rest here are Sidney Porter (O. Henry); Zebulon Baird Vance, North Carolina's Civil War governor and U.S. congressman; and two detachments of World War I German mariners who had been captured off the coast of the Carolinas.

You can trace writer Thomas Wolfe's life to Riverside, from his birthplace on Woodfin Street to Old Kentucky Home, his mother's boarding house, to First Presbyterian Church on Church Street, where his memorial service was held, and to his final resting place.

The cemetery gate is locked during daylight savings by 8 p.m. Thereafter, from fall to spring, it is locked at 6 p.m. It's a lovely place for strolling,

but please leave your dogs behind; they are not welcome here.

## WESTERN NORTH CAROLINA FARMERS MARKET
**570 Brevard Rd., Asheville**
**(828) 253-1691**
It's been described as shopping at a 36-acre roadside stand. The WNC Farmers Market, southeast of Asheville, offers a bounty of fresh produce and quality plants, shrubs, trees, and garden supplies. The retail area is reminiscent of an old market square with wooden tables overflowing with goods, fresh vegetables, crafts, and other gifts from the farm. The garden center is operated by several generations of garden specialists, Jesse Israel & Sons, supplying every gardening need.

The restaurant, the Moose Cafe, is on US 191 just south of the main entrance and serves good, basic home cooking. The truck stands are a feast for the eye and food for the soul, too. The conversation from the back of the truck gives as much pleasure as the brown-paper sack of Red Delicious apples you carry home with you.

---

## Moose Cafe

Before shopping at the Farmers Market outside of Asheville, try the Moose Cafe, just above the market's entrance, for a hearty country breakfast. Steaming hot biscuits grace your table before you even order and can be slathered with the honey, molasses, or homemade apple butter already provided. Lunches and dinners are traditional Southern fare; the menu includes a daily special and a four-vegetable plate. Prices are reasonable. Soak in the local atmosphere, try a piece of deep-dish pie, and buy a jar of apple butter to take with you.

Sections of the market are open 24 hours daily, and the retail buildings are open from 8 a.m. to 6 p.m. daily in summer and 8 a.m. to 5 p.m. in winter.

## WESTERN NORTH CAROLINA NATURE CENTER
**75 Gashes Creek Rd., Asheville**
**(828) 298-5600**
**www.wildwnc.org**
From the moment you step through the door and a three-dimensional, full-size diorama of woodland creatures greets you, you know you are indeed crossing that bridge to the natural world. Exhibits such as weather forecasting, animal identification, a real working beehive, archaeological displays, and zoological collections of live reptiles and amphibians make this a special stop. (See our Kidstuff chapter for more.)

## ZEBULON B. VANCE BIRTHPLACE
**911 Reems Creek Rd., off Old US Hwys. 19/23, Weaverville**
**(828) 645-6706**
This charming mountain homestead was home to one of North Carolina's most prominent political figures. Zeb Vance began his career as a lawyer, assuming public office by the young age of 24. He was elected governor of North Carolina three times, most notably during the Civil War. He served three terms as senator from North Carolina. At his death in 1894, this most capable public servant was admired by colleagues and beloved by his constituency. His life and career are profiled in an exhibit in the adjoining visitor center. But better yet is the opportunity to see a period mountain home replete with old utensils, kitchenry, rope-spring beds, and other objects whose uses are explained in the informative and free guided tours.

The two-story cabin and outbuildings are reconstructions, built from hewn yellow pine logs around the original chimney with its two massive fireplaces. The furnishings and household items depict the period from 1790 to 1840 and include a few pieces original to the Vance family.

Pioneer Living Days are celebrated here each spring and fall. Costumed staff members demonstrate skills and occupations of earlier days. Military encampments and battle reenactments are frequently part of the events. The homestead is open Mon through Sat 9 a.m. to 5 p.m., Sun 1 to 5 p.m., and admission is free.

# Henderson County
Information about some of Henderson County's attractions, including the Carl Sandburg Home, the Historic Hendersonville Depot and Model Railroad, the Historic Johnson Farm, and the Western North Carolina Air Museum, can be found in the Arts and Culture chapter.

## ST. JOHN IN THE WILDERNESS
**1905 Greenville Hwy., US Hwy. 25 South, Flat Rock**
**(828) 693-9783**
This charming chapel has an interesting background. In 1837 English-born Charles Baring, in search of a healthier summer climate, brought his beloved wife Susan, the former widow of a wealthy Charleston rice planter, to an area between the Watauga settlements in what is now Watauga County and Greenville, South Carolina, known simply as "the Wilderness." Thus began a migration of wealthy families from the coast that turned Flat Rock into "the little Charleston of the mountains." Baring bought hundreds of acres in the area and built a grand home called Mountain Lodge, developed on the order of an English country estate, complete with a gatekeeper's cottage, a billiard house, and a deer park. The hilltop private residence, hidden by tall pines on Rutledge Drive, is one of many grand old homes from this period still in the area.

Most of these homes are private dwellings, not open to the public. However the Barings also built a private chapel that they donated to the Episcopal Diocese of North Carolina in 1836. Here many of the cream of Southern gentry worshipped together with their slaves and were buried together in the same cemetery. The chapel, partially built of now-yellowed bricks thought to have been made by Barings' slaves, was doubled in size in 1852. The beautiful structure is 2.25 miles south of Hendersonville on the west side of US 25. The site has a marker and can be easily seen from the road. Both the graveyard and the church are open to visitors daily from 9 a.m. to 4 p.m.

Charles Baring's decision to move his family to this gentle mountain climate each summer must have been the right one, because Susan lived to be 83, and he died at age 92. They are buried in a vault inside the church under the spot where their pew used to sit.

### WOLFE'S ANGEL
### Oakdale Cemetery, US Hwy. 64 West, Hendersonville

Just a short distance from downtown Hendersonville on US 64 West, the cemetery plot of a local family, the Johnsons, is marked by an angel. She holds a stone lily in her left hand and extends her right hand upward. This statue, imported from Italy and sold to the Johnson family by novelist Thomas Wolfe's father, W. O. Wolfe, is prominently featured in the author's first novel, *Look Homeward, Angel*. Today an iron fence protects the famous angel, and a historical marker on the highway next to the cemetery notes its importance. You can enter the cemetery for a close-up look.

## Polk County
### FOOTHILLS EQUESTRIAN NATURE CENTER
### 3381 Hunting Country Rd., Tryon
### (828) 859-9021

Foothills Equestrian Nature Center—FENCE, as it is commonly called—is a 300-acre nature sanctuary dedicated to education, recreation, and preservation. The state-of-the-art equestrian facility hosts more than 18 events each season, including two steeplechases, hunter/jumper and dressage shows, and driving rallies. The facility is home to the Carolina Carriage Club (see our Recreation chapter). It also has bridle trails.

Even if you aren't a horse person, FENCE has great hiking trails that are open to the public free of charge from dawn until dusk all year long. It also offers on- and off-site programs for school

classes as well as adult classes in wildflowers and other nature subjects. Its Bird Center activities are outstanding. In addition to lectures and slide shows, there are frequent bird-watching outings. These include regular Thurs morning bird walks at FENCE or at nearby good birding sites in the spring and fall, as well as local, regional, and international birding "ventures" throughout the year.

### ROCKHOUSE VINEYARDS
### 1525 Turner Rd., Tryon
### (828) 863-2764
### www.rockhousevineyards.com

Marsha Cassedy and Lee Griffin have led the way in reactivating vineyards in Polk County. Planting of the vineyards began in 1991. Visitors are welcome to bring a picnic to enjoy on the grounds overlooking the vine-covered hills. Be sure to visit the tasting room before buying.

## Rutherford County
### CHIMNEY ROCK PARK
### US Hwys. 64/74-A in Chimney Rock
### (828) 625-9611, (800) 277-9611
### www.chimneyrockpark.com

Chimney Rock Park, in Hickory Nut Gorge, has been a favorite in the Southeast. Its unusual rock formations, spectacular Hickory Nut Falls dropping 404 feet to the gorge below, winding mountainside trails, and delicate wildflowers draw a steady stream of visitors annually. From the parking area, take a 26-story elevator ride to the Sky Lounge, the park's snack and gift shop area. From the deck just outside, you have a wonderful view of the park's landmark and namesake, Chimney Rock. Or try the steps to the Chimney— the rock formations and spectacular views along the way are well worth it.

This prominent rocky pedestal gives visitors a spectacular 180-degree view of the Hickory Nut Gorge area and beautiful Lake Lure. Make your way down a stairway from the chimney and choose one of several beautiful trails threading through the rocky outcrops, cliffs, and mountainside. The Skyline Trail winds upward through the woods, leveling out after about a quarter-mile

# Close-up

## The Bride and Groom of Pisgah

Many years ago 17-year-old Jim Stratton fell in love with Mary Robinson, the 15-year-old daughter of "Old Man" Robinson. Mary lived with her father at Frying Pan Gap, while Jim Stratton lived across the ridge at Bald Mountain.

Old Man Robinson told Jim to leave his daughter alone and not to come around Frying Pan Gap. Jim, however, didn't pay much attention to the warning, because he and Mary were in love. Just about everyone had a still in the mountains in those days, and Old Man Robinson knew that one sure way to get Jim Stratton's attention was to do something grandiose to let Jim know that he meant business.

One late fall day Jim Stratton was stirring the mash at his still, which was hidden high above a clearing of an old trail on the face of Bald Mountain. Suddenly all the animals and insects of the forest fell silent. Jim took up his long rifle and hid amongst the trees as he watched his mash boiling and bubbling. Soon he saw a fellow appear, cautiously at first, then stepping confidently over to the mash bucket. He was a "federal man," one of many, and Jim knew right away that Old Man Robinson had told them where to find his still.

More than a half-dozen federal officers stepped into the clearing. They proceeded to smash the catching bucket and spill all the good "squeezins" onto the ground. With large axes they crushed the mash vat. It was only when the first federal agent held the still's copper worm in the air like some trophy that Jim was seized by anger and lost all control. With a squeeze of the trigger, the bullet entered the left eye of the federal officer, exiting the back of his skull. The other officers ran back into the woods and down the mountain.

Jim leaped into the clearing and scooped up the brass worm and took off up the mountain. He knew that he had a great deal to do before the feds came looking for him for what he had just done. He headed to Frying Pan Gap, planning to even the score with Old Man Robinson. Crossing the Pisgahs he stopped off at the Widow Peggy Higgins's cabin. He had helped her when she lost her husband. He told her he did wrong, and he had to go higher in the mountains. But there were two things he had yet to do: The first was to even the score, and the second was to get Mary to go away with him. The widow said she'd fetch Preacher Ball and that Jim should return with Mary so they could be properly joined.

Jim got to Frying Pan Gap, and he looked for Old Man Robinson. He was actually relieved when Mary said that her daddy left for town that morning and would be gone into the late evening. Mary said that she'd go anywhere with Jim and that she'd be with him forever.

and proceeding along a flat path to the top of beautiful Hickory Nut Falls. A children's trail has playful wildlife sculptures.

The park is full of fascinating rocks, ledges, and natural wildlife. You can squeeze through the crevice known as the Needle's Eye; visit the Grotto, the Rock Pile, and the Moon-Shiner's Cave (with a replica of an old moonshine still); and journey up to the magnificent heights of Inspiration Point. If you get a little weak in the knees at the thought of high places, don't worry. Chimney Rock Park's Forest Stroll Trail, leading from the

parking area, is a leisurely 0.75-mile walk to the base of Hickory Nut Falls. There is a viewing deck with a few picnic tables for your convenience.

Owned by the Morse family since 1902, the park was purchased by the state in 2007. One of the most popular of the special events offered throughout the year is the traditional Easter sunrise service. The park is open year-round and offers a number of annual and ongoing activities. A resident botanist and ornithologist offer several workshops and nature walks throughout the year. There are now five hiking trails.

When the two of them got back to the Widow Higgins's cabin, Preacher Ball was there and ready to perform the wedding ceremony. However, the bride didn't have a proper wedding gown, and they didn't have a wedding ring. Peggy Higgins resolved that right away. She pulled an old trunk from the foot of the bed, and digging down deep, she pulled out a dusty bridal veil, yellowed from age. It was the one she had worn more than 40 years ago. She shook out the dust and smoothed out the wrinkles. Next Peggy Higgins worked the old wedding band off her hand and offered it to the new bride.

When all the right things had been said, the "I dos" and the "I promise," Preacher Ball called down a blessing on them—and it was then they could hear, off in the distance, the braying of the bloodhounds.

The couple went out the back of the cabin and followed the trails that led high up in the Pisgahs. They could hear the hounds coming closer. They climbed higher and ran faster. Soon they could hear the shouts and calling of the men.

Now it's not unusual to see snowfall in the higher elevations in late fall. The snow melts by day and refreezes by night forming rime ice. And that very night a soft snow did begin to fall. As their feet carried them higher and higher, the snow fell faster and faster. The little flakes turned into big flakes. Soon their footprints began to be covered by more snow, and the dogs couldn't follow their scent any longer. The snow got up to their ankles. As they went higher and deeper into the woods the snow reached up to their knees, and when they broke into the clearing on the east face of Pisgah, they were waist deep in the snow.

It was then that winter really set in to the mountains, and it wasn't until the next spring that the federal officers resumed their search. The couple was never found. What was found was a rusted out old long rifle and an old copper worm from a still.

Some say that they got away on that snowy night, over many ridges and through many mountain ranges until they found a place where no one knew them, and where no one ever questioned strangers.

Others know that they are still up on the east face of Pisgah. In fact whenever there is a very hard snowfall, and when it melts and refreezes, you can see Mary standing with her bridal veil down her back, Jim Stratton kneeling beside her with his head bowed. Just stand in Asheville on such a day facing Pisgah, and you'll see them, too.

The Sky Lounge snack and gift shop offers light lunch sandwiches and features a costume exhibit from *The Last of the Mohicans* film as well as theme-related gift items. A nature center on the meadows about halfway up the drive to the top of the park is a pleasant stop. Picnic areas, grills, restrooms, and play areas are nearby.

An annual pass to Chimney Rock Park is a tremendous savings at less than the cost of two visits. Children under 4 are admitted free. Special group rates are available for groups of 20 or more. The ticket office of Chimney Rock Park is open from 8:30 a.m. to 5:30 p.m. (daylight saving time) and 8:30 a.m. to 4:30 p.m. (eastern standard time). The Park closes at 7 p.m. in the summer and one hour and a half after the ticket office closes in the winter.

**LAKE LURE TOURS**
**Lake Lure Marina**
**US 64/74-A in Lake Lure**
**(828) 625-0077**
**www.lakelure.com**

Tour the lake *National Geographic* called "one of the 10 most spectacular man-made lakes in the world." A fleet of modern boats offers deluxe seats, full-length canopies, and clear enclosures to keep you comfortable whatever the weather. Tours take 60 minutes, departing every hour from the Town Marina. Be sure to arrive early enough to enjoy the surroundings. Before hopping on board, stroll the wooden boardwalk along the lake or the mile-long walking trail to the gazebo and picnic area with swings for the kids. Even parking your car is a delight here—the rocky-faced mountains are exquisite (especially when the dogwoods are in blossom in the spring). Tickets cost around $6 for children 4 to 12 and $12 for adults. Tours operate Mar through Nov from 10 a.m. to 8 p.m. Visit the Web site for details about various lunch and dinner cruises. Private charters are also available for all occasions.

**i** Look out! Heading southeast on Highway 74 just as you come into Chimney Rock is a view so beautiful that you might miss a curve on this windy mountain road. Just take it slow and look to your right at the mountains above with shimmering rock faces and the Rocky Broad River with its swift current tumbling and cascading below.

## Transylvania County

### ENGLISH CHAPEL

**US 276, Pisgah National Forest**

This Methodist church just a few miles from the entrance to Pisgah Forest is a simple structure. It is worth a historical exploration and the setting by the Davidson River is lovely. The Rev. A. F. English bought the land for $5 and founded the church in 1860. It was built by local folks and continues to serve the community and forest visitors. It is usually locked except for Sun 9:30 a.m. services. An exercise trail that borders the river's rushing, clear waters leads from the church to the Davidson River Campground. Unlike many trails in the forest, this one is wide and level, making for a relaxed stroll.

### PISGAH CENTER FOR WILDLIFE EDUCATION

**1401 Fish Hatchery Rd., , Pisgah National Forest**

**(828) 877-4423**

**www.ncwildlife.org**

Situated adjacent to the Pisgah Forest Fish Hatchery (see the following entry), this educational facility, operated by the North Carolina Wildlife Resources Commission, has exhibits and programs that explain how human activities affect and are affected by wildlife and the natural environment. The center includes a paved walkway to outdoor exhibits focusing on wildlife and fish management, law enforcement, and conservation education. Indoor exhibits feature aquariums containing coastal, Piedmont, and mountain aquatic species and an auditorium. Wildlife educational programs are offered at the center throughout the year.

The center is open daily from 8 a.m. until 5 p.m. except Thanksgiving Day, Christmas Day, and New Year's Day. Admission to both the center and its courses is free.

### PISGAH FOREST FISH HATCHERY

**1401 Fish Hatchery Rd., Pisgah National Forest**

**(828) 877-3121**

First it was a logging camp, then a camp for the Civilian Conservation Corps during the Great Depression. Today the Pisgah Forest Fish Hatchery, just off US 276 and at the base of John Rock, is operated by the North Carolina Wildlife Resources Commission. It raises thousands of trout that are released in area streams. Children really like this place. They particularly delight in the wild frenzies when the fish, which come in all sizes, are fed. Even more, they like to feed the fish themselves.

To get to the hatchery, drive several miles up US 276 from the Brevard entrance to Pisgah Forest and turn off on FR 475, which is well marked and paved. The hatchery is less than a mile down this road. There are also a number of nice hiking trails in the area.

# SOUTHERN MOUNTAINS

## Cherokee County

### THE EPISCOPAL CHURCH OF THE MESSIAH
Peachtree Street, Murphy
(828) 837-2021
Murphy's "little church around the corner" was organized in 1855, when there were only two Episcopal families in the town. Much of the money to build the church was raised, in 25 cent contributions, by the mother of Lucy Morgan, who is herself renowned for her work at Penland School (see our chapter on Mountain Crafts). The cornerstone of the church dates back to 1896. It is across the street from the blue-marble county courthouse. Its stained-glass windows executed by Tiffany's of New York, its handmade altar, and the herringbone pattern of its heart-pine paneling make this church, which is open to the public, a small work of art.

### FIELD OF THE WOODS
US Hwy. 294, Murphy
(828) 494-7855
Field of the Woods is unique in the world. Stretched over 200 acres, this Christian theme park is made up of symbols and words taken from the Bible, often presented in a majestic form. One of the most spectacular displays is a 300-foot-wide marker listing the Old Testament's Ten Commandments in letters 5 feet high and 4 feet wide. Another is the representation of a huge open Bible that takes its text from Matthew 22:37–40, with the words painted in bold, black lettering that can be read from a great distance.

A 150-foot cross lies atop All Nations Mountain, surrounded by the flags of all the countries where the Church of God of Prophecy, the park's owners, are active. There is a tomb constructed in the likeness of the one in Jerusalem where many believe that Jesus' body was taken after his crucifixion. You'll also find a cafe, gift shop, and Christian bookstore. The cafe is closed on Mon.

The park is open year-round from sunrise to sunset. Admission is free.

### HARRAH'S CHEROKEE CASINO
777 Casino Dr., Cherokee
(828) 497-7777, (800) HARRAHS
www.harrahs.com
The casino, three football fields in size, is open 24 hours a day. Here you'll find 2,300 video gaming machines, including video blackjack, video poker, and video craps, plus many other games. When you've gambled up an appetite, you can satisfy it at three restaurants: the 125-seat Range Steakhouse, open nightly and specializing in steaks, seafood, and chicken dishes; the 400-seat Fresh Market Square Buffet, open daily, featuring a wide array of cuisine and fresh bakery items; and the 60-seat Winning Streaks Grill, open daily, a quick and easy stop for sandwiches, appetizers, and such. Tribal Bingo, run by the Eastern Band of Cherokee Indians, takes place at Harrah's also.

Harrah's also contains a gift shop and a 1,500-seat multipurpose entertainment center that offers big-time shows with big-name stars. And while you shoot for that new pair of shoes, a large, professional, culturally themed child care center will keep your young ones entertained.

## Graham County

### CHIEF JUNALUSKA'S GRAVE
Off Main Street, Robbinsville
In 1814 a Cherokee leader joined the U.S. Army in a fight against the Creek Indians, vowing that he would kill all the Creeks. During the Battle of Horseshoe Bend, he saved General Andrew Jackson's life but had to admit he left some of the enemy alive. It was then that he was given the nickname of Junaluska, which means "he tried repeatedly but failed." Despite his service to Jackson, who became a U.S. president, he also failed to stop the forced removal of his fellow Cherokee and himself to Oklahoma on the infamous Trail of Tears. The chieftain reportedly remarked at the time that had he known what the future would bring, he would have killed Jackson himself at Horseshoe Bend. Later Junaluska walked from Oklahoma all the way back to the North Carolina, where he continued to struggle to keep the remaining Cherokee in their mountain home.

On Jan. 2, 1847, the state legislature made him a North Carolina citizen and gave him a tract of land. When he died on Nov 8, 1858, he was more than 100 years old. His grave and that of Nicie, his wife, are on a hilltop outside Robbinsville. To reach it, drive past the courthouse on Main Street and turn right toward the Stanley Furniture plant. The gravesite is on the left, marked by a sign. A trail leads up to the two boulders that mark the graves, which are surrounded by an iron fence. It's said that it took eight yoke of oxen a half-day to pull Junaluska's gravestone up the hill. There is also a museum near the site devoted to Junaluska.

### FONTANA DAM
**Highway 28, Fontana Dam**
You can drive across this 480-foot-high dam, the highest east of the Rockies, but don't be satisfied with that. Stop at the visitor center for a breathtaking view and make use of the picnic tables there. Inside the center you can take in a short video and other exhibits to learn about the dam's construction and history. After that spend a dollar for a ride in the stainless-steel tram to the dam's base for a look inside the plant itself, where you'll get a lesson on hydroelectric power. This 2,365-foot-wide structure began providing power in 1942 to produce goods during World War II, and it closed in 1944. Today it impounds the 10,600 acres of water that form 29-mile-long Fontana Lake. Historic Fontana Village, now a resort community, was built to house the workers who constructed the dam. The visitor center is open from 9 a.m. until 8 p.m. and is staffed by volunteers who are former TVA employees.

## Haywood County
### CAROLINA NIGHTS MUSIC COMEDY SHOW
**3732 Soco Rd., US 19, Maggie Valley**
**(828) 926-8822, (888) 622-7469**
A cast of locals and entertainers from elsewhere offer dinner theater with a twist. You can stomp your feet to mountain music and shed a tear with the "Grand Old Flag" and patriotic songs. The grand finale pulls out all the stops with a good dose of patriotism and nostalgia in song and dance, complete with a backdrop of the Statue of Liberty, Old Glory, and symbols of "old-time religion." It's hokey, but fun family entertainment. Bus groups are welcome with advance arrangements.

### STOMPIN' GROUND
**3116 Soco Rd., US 19, Maggie Valley**
**(828) 926-1288**
The folks in Maggie claim that this is the "Clogging Capital of the World." It features some of the area's best mountain clogging teams from May to Oct on Fri and Sat from early evening to late. (The opening event for Folkmoot USA is always held at the Stompin' Ground. It takes place the last week in July. See our Annual Festivals and Events chapter.)

## Jackson County
### GREAT SMOKY MOUNTAINS RAILROAD
**119 Front St., Dillsboro**
**(828) 586-8811, (800) 872-4681**
**www.gsmr.com**
There are few attractions more popular in Western North Carolina than this railway, and there's no better way to watch some of our area's great scenery glide by than from one of its passenger cars. When you catch a ride on the Great Smoky Mountains Railroad, you have your choice of diesel, electric, or steam locomotives, with seating in heated and air-conditioned coaches and open-sided cars. Some seating options at a small additional charge are the Club Car (for adults only) and the Crown Coach. Several different excursion options are offered: the Tuckaseigee River Excursion, the Nantahala Gorge Excursion, the Red Marble Gap Excursion, Raft 'n' Rail Excursion, and Twilight Dinner Train.

- **The Tuckaseigee River Excursion:** This is a 34-mile-long, three-hour Dillsboro–Bryson City round-trip that follows the Tuckaseigee River past the spot where the train wreck in *The Fugitive* was filmed. It also takes you through the 836-foot-long Cowee Tunnel and over many trestles before reaching Bryson City, where you'll have a 45-minute layover for shopping, browsing, and eating.

- **The Nantahala Gorge Excursion:** From Bryson City you can take a 44-mile, four-hour round-trip tour that brings you through the Nantahala Gorge, created by a river that's become one of North Carolina's prime spots for canoeing, kayaking, and white-water rafting. En route you'll cross a portion of Fontana Lake on a trestle that is 791 feet long, on piers that are 180 feet tall. There's an hour layover in the gorge for eating and viewing the white-water activity.
- **The Red Marble Gap Excursion:** This 38-mile, four-hour trip departs from Andrews and climbs east toward Red Marble Mountain. It passes through the hand-dug Will Sandlin Tunnel, crosses the 400-foot-long Hawksnest Trestle, and descends a 4-plus percent grade from Topton down to Nantahala. Here, too, you have an hour for white-water viewing and lunch. The mountain scenery on this excursion is particularly spectacular. There are no steam trains from Andrews.
- **Raft 'n' Rail Excursion:** This seven-hour trip offers a 22-mile train ride, an 8-mile guided raft trip, a picnic lunch, and a return by bus.
- **Twilight Dinner Train:** The Twilight Dinner Train departs from the Dillsboro Depot for a luxurious, leisurely two-hour round-trip that follows the Tuckaseigee River through the historic Cowee Tunnel to Whittier and back. A gourmet four-course dinner, elegant ambience—candlelight, china, and white linen—and old-fashioned attentive service are presented in the beautifully restored dining cars. You can select from four seasonal entrees at the time you make your reservations; cocktails and a selection of premium wines are available from the bar. The Dinner Train operates every Sat evening from Apr through Dec and selected Fri evenings from July through Oct.

## JUDACULLA ROCK
**Off Hwy. 107**

Judaculla (a name corrupted from the Indian *tsulkalu*, meaning "slant eyes") was a fearful giant of Cherokee lore whose farm was on Tanasee Bald at a point where Jackson, Haywood, and Transylvania counties converge. One day, it's said, he jumped from his mountaintop home to a valley near what is now Caney Fork Creek, leaving the marks of his landing on a large, exposed piece of soapstone. These marks—pictographic writing on the rock—long predate the Cherokee. There are many theories as to their meanings. Is the rock a boundary marker? A battle commemoration? A peace treaty among unknown tribes? Or is it just ancient graffiti?

Judaculla Rock, well marked by signs, is off Highway 107 between Cashiers and Cullowhee on Caney Fork Road (SR 1737). A lovely 3-mile drive through a bucolic valley of scattered two-story, white frame farmhouses will bring you to the rock, which sits under an open-sided shed next to a cow pasture.

## Macon County

### HIGHLANDS NATURE CENTER AND BOTANICAL GARDENS
**930 Horse Cove Rd., US Hwy. 28 South, Highlands**
**(828) 526-2623**

Drive a short distance out of Highlands on East Main Street, and you'll come to this interesting place. The Highlands Biological Station, one of the oldest research facilities in the country, operates both the center and the gardens. The center is a showcase for the animals and plants found on the Highlands Plateau, a unique ecosystem that attracts top researchers from around the world. Here you'll find user-friendly exhibits, American Indian artifacts, mineral and rock specimens, snakes, salamanders, and mounted specimens of area mammals and birds. In the Botanical Gardens, the trails, with their excellently identified plants and trees, will take you around Lake Ravenel, along a creek, and up to a small waterfall.

The center is open from 10 a.m. to 5 p.m. Mon through Sat from Memorial Day to Labor Day. Admission is free. The gardens are there for you to enjoy anytime. Even in winter thick growths of rhododendron, galax, and doghobble make it a deep-green little paradise.

## JOHN WASILIK MEMORIAL POPLAR TRAIL
**Nantahala National Forest, near
Rainbow Springs**

To see the United States' second-largest yellow poplar, named for a former Wayah district ranger, drive west out of Franklin on US 64 and turn on FR 67 toward the Standing Indian Campground. Park a little more than a mile down the road at the Rock Gap sign before reaching the campground. It's a 1.5-mile, easy-to-moderate, round-trip hike on the Wasilik Poplar Trail, which is lined with second-growth trees up to 8 feet in diameter. The giant memorial tree is 25 feet in circumference, and until a storm blew off its top, it was 125 feet tall. The Ritter Lumber Company took the rest of the virgin timber out of this area in the early 1930s. They even cut down another yellow poplar of the same size. However the oxen had such a hard time hauling it away that the lumbermen decided not to bother with this now-famous tree.

## MUSEUM OF AMERICAN CUT AND ENGRAVED GLASS
**472 Chestnut St., Highlands
(828) 526-3427**

This is a rare museum in many ways. Its collection is one of the most eclectic anywhere in the world of American cut glass. It was opened as a not-for-profit corporation, exclusively for charitable and educational purposes. The exquisite contents are basically the collection of Bonnie and George Siek. They continue to operate the museum without charge and support it philanthropically with 100 percent donations and income from the sale of cut and engraved glass.

There are more than 400 pieces of glass on display. Another 250 pieces are in storage, affording a rotational display. Throughout the exhibition refracted light sparkles off each individual cut with diamond clarity. You'll find other objects in shades of green, cranberry, blue, gold, and turquoise. Names of grandeur and tradition abound, such as Royal, Trellis, North Star, Wedgemere, and Arbaresque. Pueblo and Nautilus by Hawkes are examples of the world-class objects here.

This museum is worth a stop and can open a new world of beauty. Don't be surprised by the log cabin structure that houses this priceless collection. The final rarity is that George Siek insists that you call him on his home phone, listed above, if the museum is closed. He'll make every effort to host you personally. The museum is open Tues, Thurs, and Sat from 1 to 4 p.m., May through Oct.

## PERRY'S WATER GARDEN
**136 Givson Aquatic Farm Rd., Franklin
(828) 524-3264
www.perryswatergarden.net**

Even if you never intend to have a water garden, this 12-acre aquatic plant nursery—with its hundreds of lotuses, water lilies, blue-flag irises, and other old and new water- and bog-loving plants—might change your mind. Claiming to be the largest such nursery in the country, it offers a tropical greenhouse, exotic koi and goldfish, old-fashioned antique rose beds, picnic tables, and walking trails. Perry's is open from 9 a.m. to noon and 1 to 5 p.m. Mon through Sat and 1 until 5 p.m. on Sun from Mar through Sept.

## Swain County

### DARNELL CORN MAZE
**US 74, Bryson City
(828) 488-2376
www.cornfieldmaze.com**

Corn maze season runs July to the end of Oct. The Great Smoky Mountain Corn Maze at Darnell Farms has more than five acres of corn that have been carved in the shape of "Teddy Roosevelt and the Rough Riders." It's a real farm with 20 acres of pumpkins, 17 acres of tomatoes, and 20 acres of sweet corn, ornamental gourds, beans, peppers, and squash. There's entertainment on Sat nights, and in Sept, this is the site for the Old-time and Bluegrass Fiddlers' Convention. There is a small admission charge for the maze.

# KIDSTUFF

North Carolina's mountains are even more fun with kids in hand. Try to view the world the way they do. They can see Daniel Boone behind every log cabin and wood nymphs playing in the shelter of rhododendron thickets. See Santa Claus in the summertime (although there's a logical explanation for that one . . . read on).

Hiking is popular with families. Take the kids hiking on many of the numerous trails appropriate for younger ages and abilities. Stop for a picnic along a mountain stream and watch your kids turn rocks and water into adventures only their uninhibited imaginations can know. Or teach them to ski before adult-size fear paralyzes their sense of adventure.

Organizations throughout the region offer exciting programs for little people. Libraries are always a rich source of activities, storytelling, and, of course, books and tapes. Area arts councils provide opportunities for kids to explore their nascent creativity, setting it free with paints and clay, paper and yarn. Art exhibitions of their work are scheduled throughout the year.

Parks and attractions in the mountains welcome pint-size visitors. Trains, Ferris wheels, swimming pools, natural wonders, clowns, and festivals all beckon, as do seasonal activities, such as Easter egg hunts, jack-o'-lantern carvings, and Christmas decoration classes.

## NORTHERN MOUNTAINS

### Watauga County

**MAGIC MOUNTAIN MINI GOLF & GEM MINE**
**1675 Hwy. 105, Boone**
**(828) 265-GEMS, (828) 265-GOLF**
The kids simply won't get bored here. Open Mon, Tues, and Wed 10 a.m. to 6 p.m.; Thurs, Fri, and Sat 9 a.m. to 9 p.m., spring through fall, Magic Mountain is a kiddie paradise. Adults probably won't mind sifting through the enriched ore either, because there's a chance of finding a ruby, citrine, garnet, amethyst, aquamarine, sapphire, emerald, or other such rocks.

A sandwich and ice-cream parlor provide indoor or patio dining, and a video game room provides entertainment for those members of the family who just don't want to get their hands dirty. The minigolf course is set on a mountainside amidst foliage and waterfalls.

**MYSTERY HILL**
**129 Mystery Hill Ln., between Boone and Blowing Rock**
**(828) 264-2792**
**www.mysteryhill-nc.com**
This is the place to go for interactive fun with your family or group of friends. Celebrating more than 50 years in business, Mystery Hill explores the relationships of science, optical illusion, and natural phenomena in a hands-on entertainment center. Defy gravity in the Mystery House, where the ball rolls up hill, or leave your shadow on the wall. (Just try getting the kids out of this one.) The Appalachian Heritage Museum and the Native American Artifacts Museum are included in the tour for one low price.

Open seven days a week, year-round, Mystery Hill is open 8 a.m. to 8 p.m. June through Aug, and 9 a.m. to 5 p.m. Sept through May. There is an admission charge.

## TWEETSIE RAILROAD
**U.S. Hwy. 321, between Boone and
Blowing Rock
(828) 264-9061, (800) 526-5740
www.tweetsie.com**

Long before there was a Carowinds or Six Flags, there was Tweetsie Railroad. A charming theme park, now more than 30 years old, Tweetsie brings out the little kid in all of us. Not as overwhelming as those other parks, this one maintains a 1914 Tweetsie locomotive that still runs, simple rides, a petting farm with deer, Mouse Mine No. 9, homemade fudge, caramel apples, a Ferris wheel, and souvenir shops. The amusement park also holds special events for certain holidays, such as Halloween, July 4, and others.

Tweetsie Railroad is open daily from 9 a.m. to 6 p.m. from May through Aug. Late Aug through Oct weekend hours (Fri through Sun) are 9 a.m. to 6 p.m. Tweetsie Railroad is also open some evenings in Oct for the Ghost Train Halloween Festival. Admission is $30 for adults, $22 for children. If you enter after 3 p.m., the next day is free. Group rates and discounts are available, and check out the Golden Rail Season Pass.

# CENTRAL MOUNTAINS

## Buncombe County

### ODYSSEY CENTER FOR THE CERAMIC ARTS
**236 Clingman Ave., Asheville
(828) 285-0210
www.highwaterclays.com**

This recreational craft center offers some very special programs for children. Odyssey's kids' classes have been filling up quickly with eager faces and curious hands. Nine-week classes are offered for after-school kids and home-schoolers. Kids of all ages learn basic skills in wheel throwing and hand building, making anything from animals and castles to cups and bowls. Call for a detailed course schedule. (For more information on general classes, see our Mountain Crafts chapter.)

## PACK PLACE EDUCATION ARTS AND SCIENCE CENTER
**2 South Pack Sq., Asheville
(828) 257-4500
www.packplace.org**

Four museums and a performing arts theater make this a must-see with kids, especially if the weather isn't cooperating. The Asheville Art Museum, Health Adventure, Colburn Gem & Mineral Museum, YMI Cultural Center, and Diana Wortham Theatre all offer special programs for children.

Health Adventure (meant to be enjoyed by the whole family), especially, is a blast for kids. Learn how the body works with a life-size torso—you put in the organs like solving a puzzle! Learn how the ear works. Learn about nutrition while "shopping." Learn mechanics and engineering with fun and games you can try. Check your eyesight; look at a bug, a hair, and other objects through a microscope. The ultraviolet light room will make your whites glow and your teeth green! Two floors of tactile fun can keep kids busy and entertained for hours. (See our Arts and Culture chapter for more information.)

## WESTERN NORTH CAROLINA NATURE CENTER
**75 Gashes Creek Rd., Asheville
(828) 298-5600
www.wildwnc.org**

The Western North Carolina Nature Center offers a remarkable blend of services to the area. Officially it's "an environmental educational resource, exhibiting and interpreting plants and animals native to the Southern Appalachian Mountains." But it is much more than that. From the moment you step through the door and a three-dimensional, full-size diorama of woodland creatures greets you, you know you are crossing that bridge to the natural world.

Well-planned exhibits in the educational facility offer a hands-on approach to everything from weather forecasting and animal identification to a real working beehive! In the next building are archaeological displays and zoological exhibits of live reptiles and amphibians.

In another area a special darkened room allows visitors to observe owls, bats, and other nocturnal creatures.

Outside there's more: bobcats, raccoons, cougars, otters, foxes, bears, hawks, eagles, sheep, goats, chickens, peacocks, and even wolves. Make sure you walk along the boardwalk in the treetops; it takes you back to those days of childhood tree houses.

The Nature Center is open 10 a.m. to 5 p.m. seven days a week.

## Rutherford County

**CHIMNEY ROCK PARK**
**Entrance on Main Street, US Hwys. 64/74A, Chimney Rock**
**(828) 625-9611, (800) 277-9611**
**www.chimneyrockpark.com**
Families can picnic in the meadows and elsewhere throughout the park. Self-guided trails are available for explorations, or schedule a time with the naturalists for more exciting adventures. Ride the elevator within the mountain itself, going up 30 stories to the Sky Lounge. More adventure lies ahead in exploring the upper trails. One trail especially for kids mixes learning with fun, replete with giant "critter" sculptures and interactive displays.

**LAKE LURE FUN CENTER**
**US 64/74A, the Beach at Lake Lure, Lake Lure**
**(828) FUN-4-ALL, (828) 625-0077**
All ages can enjoy trampoline games, minigolf, foosball, Ping Pong, bungee jumping, scooters, the children's inflatable play area, motorized Jeeps, and more at the Lake Lure Fun Center. Swimming is another obvious attraction with ever-watchful certified lifeguards. Boat tours of the lake are offered at the marina, and self-propelled boats can be rented as well.

## Transylvania County

**CRADLE OF FORESTRY**
**US Hwy. 276, Pisgah National Forest**
**(828) 877-3130**
**www.cradleofforestry.com**

Children of all ages love the Forest Discovery Center at the Cradle of Forestry. They can see a short movie about the first forestry school in America, which was situated here—and that's only the beginning. There are 15 educational exhibits on the workings of the forest ecosystem and what it takes to manage an ecosystem. For example, there is a replicated hillside, complete with a forest summit. Below, a 30-foot tunnel lets kids crawl underground through "The Great Tree and Burrow" exhibit, complete with all the animals that live there. Another exhibit explains the dynamics of a watershed, all the way to the household faucet.

Outside the building there are two beautiful, mile-long paved trails, each with guided tours that will tell you of the Cradle's history and teach you a lot about the plants and trees along the way. The Forest Festival Trail has many forest demonstration projects, an old sawmill, the first little fish hatchery in Pisgah, and an old Climax logging train. Children love to climb into the cab and ring the bell. The Biltmore Campus Trail winds through the school's old campus of original and reconstructed buildings.

On Sat and Sun afternoons craftspeople in period dress demonstrate crafts such as weaving, spinning, quilting, basketry, and toy making, and life at the turn of the 20th century. There are also a number of special events happening throughout the year, such as Fiber Arts Week and the huge Forest Festival Day held in Oct.

The Cradle, open seven days a week from 9 a.m. to 5 p.m., is located on US 276, 11 miles from the intersection of U.S. Highways 64, 276, and 280 at Pisgah Forest, or 4 miles south of the Blue Ridge Parkway at milepost 412. Fees are under $10. (See the Cradle Keeps Rocking Close-up in the Forests and Parks chapter.)

**SLIDING ROCK**
**US 276, Pisgah National Forest**
Sliding Rock is just 7.6 miles from the junction of US 276 and US 64 outside Brevard. Here you're invited to "take the plunge" down a 60-foot slippery cascade into the 55- to 60-degree, 6-foot-deep pool below. If you don't care to make the

slide, it's fun to watch the action from paved viewing areas at the top or bottom of this natural, exhilarating ride that's fueled by 11,000 gallons of water a minute.

There's a large parking lot adjacent to Sliding Rock (the parking fee is $3) as well as a bathhouse. Lifeguards are on duty from 10 a.m. to 6 p.m. from Memorial Day through Labor Day. The rock, while slick, can take the bottom out of an ordinary bathing suit, so old jeans or cutoffs are best for this fast ride. Also, be careful while getting in and out of the water. The surface of the rock, even where the water isn't flowing, can be slick and accounts for some hard tumbles.

# SOUTHERN MOUNTAINS

## Cherokee County

### JOHN C. CAMPBELL FOLK SCHOOL
1 Folk School Rd., Brasstown
(828) 837-2775, (800) FOLK-SCH
www.folkschool.org

Opened in 1925, this fine craft school offers Little/Middle Folk School each June for one week for youngsters ages 7 to 17. The week is full of crafts, games, and lots of fun. Classes fill quickly so early registration is essential.

Contact the Folk School to be included in a separate mailing for this program. (See our Mountain Crafts chapter for more information on the school's other offerings).

## Cherokee Indian Reservation

For more information on the reservation and other attractions here, see our chapters on Attractions and the Eastern Band of the Cherokee Nation.

### CHEROKEE FUN PARK
US Hwy. 441 North
(828) 497-5877
www.cherokeefunpark.com

This is a great place to drop off teenagers for a couple of hours while you pursue your own pleasures. The four-acre park contains, among other things, two challenging miniature golf courses, a go-kart track, bumper boats, a large arcade, and rides designed for young children.

It opens daily at 11 a.m. on weekdays and 10 a.m. on weekends from May through Oct. Closing time is around 11 p.m. in midsummer and 8:30 or 9 p.m. in the spring and fall. Admission is free, but there is a charge for boats, go-karts, and golf (play all day). Kiddie rides are $2 each.

### SANTA'S LAND FUN PARK AND ZOO
US Hwy. 19
(828) 497-9191
www.santaslandnc.com

Christmas comes alive in the summertime in this theme park. We expect that young children will refuse to miss its Rudi-Coaster ride, Santa's Overland Express train and, of course, Santa. The family can also paddle boats around Monkey Islands in the lake, view Cherokee from the top of a Ferris wheel, and visit a wealth of shops.

In the zoo kids will enjoy petting baby bears and feeding deer and trout. A visit to the gristmill will show them how cornmeal is made, and they can watch pork rinds being cooked. You'll also find a picnic and playground area in the park. It's open from early May until the first weekend in Nov.

Admission is under $20. Children younger than 2 get in free. Prices are, however, subject to change.

## Haywood County

### SOCO GARDENS ZOO
3578 Soco Rd., US 19, Maggie Valley
(828) 926-1746
www.socogardenszoo.com

In addition to many of the usual wild animals, this zoo allows touching and feeding in its petting section. There are guided tours, two snake shows (one venomous and the other nonpoisonous; in the latter visitors can touch or hold the performers), and a gift shop made for animal lovers.

Hours change with the season: 10 a.m. to 5 p.m. in May, Sept, and Oct; 9 a.m. to dark in June, July, and Aug. It is closed in the winter. Admission is under $10.

## Macon County

**HIGHLANDS CHAMBER OF COMMERCE**
**396 Oak St., Highlands**
**(828) 526-2112**
**www.highlandschamber.org**
Check with the chamber for great kid-themed things to do. Nov and Dec are months especially geared to kids and the family. During the week of Thanksgiving, the Tree Lighting Ceremony is held at the Gazebo on Pine Street. The Highlands Olde Mountain Christmas Parade is held on the first Sat in Dec at 11 a.m. It goes down Main Street and the town is dressed for the holidays. (See our Annual Festivals and Events chapter.)

The Highlands Ranger District has a visitor center in downtown Highlands just off Main Street, directly beside the restaurant Wolfgang's on Main. Trail maps and other information for outdoor activities are available at the center.

The Kelsey & Hutchinson Lodge is a "welcome center" for adults who want solitude and comfort, as well as for families traveling with pets. An entire area of the lodge provides a separate, disconnected section to accommodate these lodgers.

The Adventure Depot provides llama trekking and camping experiences.

# SUMMER CAMPS

For generations children and young people have delighted in the many summer camps that thrive in the Western North Carolina mountains. They often attend the same camps that their grandparents enjoyed.

There are 24 camps in Henderson County alone and another 17 in neighboring Transylvania County, plus a number of others in surrounding counties. Some camps are coed, others single sex.

Although summer camps can vary in size, price, duration, and age ranges of the campers, most include such activities as hiking, camping, canoeing, swimming, archery, mountain biking, horseback riding, tennis, golf, team sports, and nature studies—thanks in part to the vast recreational opportunities offered by the nearby public lands (see our Forests and Parks chapter).

As the late Frank "Chief" Bell Sr., founder of Mondamin Camp, put it, "The wilderness can be a magnificent playground and a great university." The cultural heritage of the area's arts and crafts, such as drama, blacksmithing, and pottery, plays a big role in summer activities.

Although most camps draw the majority of their participants from the Southeast, many come from as far away as Alaska, Hawaii, and South America for this mountain experience. Campers have been known to spend every summer for 5 to 15 years at the same camp. Many have come back as camp counselors.

## Central Mountains

**CAMP ARROWHEAD FOR BOYS**
**1415 Cabin Creek Rd., Zirconia**
**(828) 692-1123**
**www.camparrowhead.org**

**CAMP GLEN ARDEN FOR GIRLS**
**Off Green River Road, Tuxedo**
**(828) 692-8362**
**www.campglenarden.com**
Arrowhead is a Christian camp for boys 7 to 15 years old. Set along sparkling Rock Creek, a tributary of the Green River, it has more than 1,000 acres of woodland, streams, meadows, and trails that offer endless opportunities for playing, exploring, camping, and riding. J. O. Bell Jr. started the camp in 1937, and it's been owned and directed by the Bell family ever since. In 1951 its sister camp, Camp Glen Arden for Girls, joined it. The vast grounds contain two lakes, a swimming pool, archery fields, tennis courts, a gym, stables, a woodworking shop, a blacksmith shop, and a great variety of other facilities and cabins. Just inside the Glen Arden gate, a towering 300-foot waterfall greets campers. Both camps offer almost all the activities found at the other camps mentioned in this chapter.

**CAMP CAROLINA FOR BOYS**
**Lamb's Creek Road, Brevard**
**(828) 884-2414, (800) 551-9136**
**www.campcarolina.com**

Though Camp Carolina is only 2.5 miles from Brevard, its 22 acres feel far from town life. It's bordered by mountain ridges and on two sides by the Pisgah National Forest, and it's only a half-mile from the forest's entrance. The camp, established in 1924, has three streams and a four-acre lake for swimming, canoeing, kayaking, and fishing for mountain trout. Both group and individual tennis instruction is provided on six tennis courts. Other activities include riflery, archery, soccer, table tennis, basketball, football, baseball, lacrosse, hang gliding, mountain biking, skateboarding, weightlifting, and arts and crafts. Horseback riding in Western and English saddles, forward seat, and jumping are taught, and campers take day and overnight rides in Pisgah Forest. Wilderness classes are also beginning.

Carolina's nature program involves collecting and identifying area plants and animals; pioneering projects include using hand tools to build tree houses, forts, dams, bridges, and cabins.

The camp, which is open to boys ages 7 to 17, has a capacity of 200.

**i** Before choosing a camp consider some questions: Does the camp carry liability insurance? Does the camp supply references from past campers' families? What is the camp's philosophy?

### CAMP GWYNN VALLEY
**1080 Island Ford Rd., Brevard**
**(828) 885-2900**
**www.gwynnvalley.com**
Camp Gwynn Valley provides a special, sheltered environment for younger children, ages 5 to 12. Mary Gwynn established the camp in 1935, and it has been in continuous operation ever since, attaining an international reputation for dealing with the needs and interests of the younger child. Camp Gwynn Valley, altitude 2,240 feet, sits in a secluded cove that opens onto a sunlit valley with a view of the Pisgah Range.

The camp's 300 acres comprise 250 acres of woods and a 50-acre working farm, where children can take turns feeding the animals, weeding and hoeing the garden, and milking the cow and

goats. Cabin cookouts often begin with a trip to the farm to gather fresh eggs and pick vegetables in season. Baby animals—lambs, rabbits, calves, piglets, and kittens—are favorite members of the camp's "family."

### CAMP HOLLYMONT FOR GIRLS
**475 Lake Eden Rd., Black Mountain**
**(828) 686-5343 (winter)**
**(828) 252-2123 (summer)**
**www.hollymont.com**
Founded by George W. Pickering, who has served in this Christian camp's ministry since 1946, Camp Hollymont's tradition is continued by the McKibbens family. Located on the 300-acre campus of the private Asheville School, Camp Hollymont provides for a fun-filled summer for girls from age 6 to 15 in refined living conditions. Acres of rolling hills and lush green forests provide the perfect summer setting for sports, fun and games, and learning crafts and skills. Girls live in the lodges, in clusters divided by age and grade. A cluster consists of four rooms, with one of the four for the counselor. There are 120 campers per session.

Because it is a Christian camp, Hollymont closes each day with evening devotions—quiet, sharing moments, inspirational stories, and prayer.

### CAMP ILLAHEE
**Illahee Road, Brevard**
**(828) 883-2181**
**www.campillahee.com**
Illahee means "heavenly world" in the Cherokee language, and this camp for girls ages 6 to 16, which was established in 1921, abounds with natural beauty and high spirits. The grounds are beautifully landscaped. They contain 30 cabins, a dining hall, a new recreation lodge that includes a stage and gymnastics area, an infirmary, a crafts shop, a barn, a canoe lake, tennis courts, an open-air woodland chapel, riding rings, rifle range, two climbing walls, and many other facilities.

Each camper sets her own schedule, which can include such activities as riflery, team sports, archery, dance, drama, gymnastics, aerobics, painting, drawing, weaving, stitchery, ceramics, printing, woodworking, synchronized swimming and diving, tennis, horseback riding, hiking, white-water canoeing, rappelling, backpacking, and kayaking.

## CAMP JOY
**Bonclarken Conference Center, Flat Rock**
**(828) 692-2223**
**www.bonclarken.com**
This is a special camp for exceptional children. An opportunity is provided for youngsters who are mentally and physically challenged to experience a wonderful life adventure.

**i** To prevent bugs in cabins, most summer camps now have policies that ask friends and families not to send care packages containing food. You might instead order a "Camp Pack" from Main Street Ltd., 22 East Main St., Brevard; (828) 884-4974, (800) 248-CAMP. It'll custom-make a gift pack and deliver it locally or ship it nationally. (See our Shopping chapter for more information on Main Street Ltd.)

## CAMP MERRI-MAC FOR GIRLS
**1229 Montreat Rd., Black Mountain**
**(828) 669-8766**
**www.merri-mac.com**
Set in the lush Black Mountain area, Camp Merri-Mac offers two four-week sessions for girls aged 6 to 16. Since 1978 Spencer and Dorothy Boyd, parents of six children themselves, have operated Camp Merri-Mac. They have some 40 years of professional camp experience. The camp is located on a 150-acre tract of land in the Blue Ridge Mountains, at an elevation of 2,800 feet. Campers are divided by age groups into Junior, Intermediate, and Senior camps and are housed in 13 screened and shuttered cabins with adjoining baths. The front porches make for great gatherings at dusk. The dining hall, infirmary, laundry, and camp offices are located in the Big House, a former private home. Between mealtimes, campers may purchase a limited amount of snacks and drinks. The Mike, or the gym, is a central place

for recreation, including indoor volleyball and basketball, as well as musical and drama productions. Three tennis courts, volleyball courts, and sports fields assure physical fitness is a large part of the program.

## CAMP MONDAMIN FOR BOYS
**Lake Summit, Tuxedo**
**(828) 693-7446, (800) 688-5789 (information)**
**www.mondamin.com**

## CAMP GREEN COVE FOR GIRLS
**Lake Summit, Tuxedo**
**(828) 692-6355, (800) 688-5789 (information)**
**www.greencove.com**
In 1922 Camp Mondamin, for boys ages 7 to 17, was established by the late Frank "Chief" Bell Sr. on the then-new 350-acre Lake Summit. It has been owned and operated by the Bell family ever since. The lake and surrounding 800 acres of private woodlands make sailing and nature studies a large part of the curriculum. The camp also includes five tennis courts, a crafts shop, an indoor rifle range, a gymnasium, a barn, and three riding rings.

Camp Green Cove, for girls ages 8 to 17, was founded by the Bells in 1945 at Rockbrook Camp in Brevard. In 1949 the Bells moved the camp to the upper end of Lake Summit. The buildings surround a beautiful cove where a dammed-off stream forms a smaller, private lake for swimming and canoeing. The main building houses the dining room, lounges, offices, and craft shops where such subjects as weaving, pottery, macramé, copper enameling, silk-screen printing, and drawing are taught. This building and the camp cabins are on one side of the lake. On the other side are four tennis courts, an archery field, a ball field, a barn, and five riding rings, including a jumping course.

Each of these adjoining camps has its own infirmary with two nurses on staff; one physician in residence serves both camps.

The Bells' philosophy that it is not necessary to inflict a defeat in order to win a victory guides the camps' noncompetitive programs—an advantage for participants who aren't the best athletes. Programs are structured but unregimented to encourage self-direction and initiative.

Each camp has a combined capacity of 180. The camper-to-counselor ratio is 4 to 1.

## CAMP ROCKMONT FOR BOYS
**375 Lake Eden Rd., Black Mountain**
**(828) 686-3885**
**www.rockmont.com**

Driving up a tree-shaded lane, you approach Camp Rockmont at the same time you cast your first glance over Lake Eden and the Black Mountains in the distance. The lake's central position on the 600 acres of the camp's secluded property is a telling symbol of days by the water to come. Only 15 miles east of Asheville, near the town of Black Mountain, Camp Rockmont welcomes boys ages 6 to 17.

Under Christian leadership, the camp carries a prestigious reputation with it, serving more than 1,200 boys in the Blue Ridge Mountains each summer. Ranging from 13-day to 20-day sessions, the camp is divided into Junior Camp, Intermediate Camp, and Senior Camp; campers range in age from 7 to 16.

Rockmont places a spiritual emphasis on the whole camp experience. Counselors enjoy devotional times with their cabins, and a Morning Watch and Sunday services are times set aside for worship through singing, learning, and sharing. Every Sun evening each camp gathers at a Council Ring site on the mountainside to reflect on the prior week. Boys are recognized according to personal performance as it applies to attitude, enthusiasm, and cooperation.

## CAMP TIMBERLAKE FOR BOYS
**1229 Montreat Rd., Black Mountain**
**(828) 669-8766**
**www.camptimberlake.com**

Due to the popularity of Camp Merri-Mac for Girls, the Boyd family founded Camp Timberlake for Boys in 1983. Providing a challenging adventure for boys ages 6 through 16, Timberlake operates on the same campground as Merri-Mac but has a separate program run by its own staff of skilled young men. The two four-week sessions and a smaller two-week session allow boys to familiarize themselves with the outdoors and with a variety of sports they may not have access to in school.

## EAGLE'S NEST CAMP
**43 Hart Rd., Pisgah Forest**
**(828) 877-4349**
**www.enf.org**

The staff of Eagle's Nest Camp believes that the big missing ingredient for American children is membership in a tribe, a village, and a nature-based homeland. This sense of "belonging" is one of the missing links that they strive to create for their campers. One way they achieve the goal is through the joy children gain in knowing that they are, according to the camp's brochure, "responsible and viable parts of a greater idealized whole."

This coed camp, now in business for more than 75 years, is designed for children age 6 through high school and offers three three-week sessions. It has a camper-to-counselor ratio of 4 to 1.

Eagle's Nest also offers expanded wilderness adventures to teenagers, such as 100-mile hikes on the Appalachian Trail.

**i** Provide your children with a variety of fun stationery for letter writing. Should they get homesick, they may feel better writing to you or friends on stationery that you picked out together expressly for this purpose.

## FALLING CREEK CAMP
**Off Falling Creek Road, Tuxedo**
**(828) 692-0262**
**www.fallingcreek.com**

Though conveniently close to I-26 and the Asheville airport, Falling Creek's home in a hidden cove deep in the mountains seems incredibly remote. Its campus spreads over 1,000 acres. The main section surrounds two lakes with many miles of trails and outpost cabins between its mountaintop and the river pastures in the Green River Valley.

This camp for boys offers many competitive activities while realizing it's more important for a boy to work and cooperate with others than to consistently try to outrank his peers.

The camp also has its own camp doctor and dietitian and is the brother camp to Camp Greystone for Girls, about 7 miles away on Lake Summit.

### ROCKBROOK CAMP FOR GIRLS
### US 276, Brevard
### (828) 884-6151
### www.rockbrookcamp.com

Rockbrook Camp, which serves girls ages 6 to 16, has been in existence since 1921. The 200-acre site, 4 miles from Brevard on the French Broad River, is replete with beautiful forests and waterfalls, all of which are accessible by numerous hiking trails. It is also just minutes away from Pisgah National Forest, which is used for day hikes, overnight backpacking trips, and rock-climbing trips. Rockbrook has excellent in-camp rock-climbing facilities as well. These include a 70-foot climbing tower, an indoor climbing wall, and rock faces.

## Southern Mountains

### CAMP MERRIE-WOODE
### 100 Merrie-Woode Rd., Sapphire
### (828) 743-3300
### www.merriewoode.com

Camp Merrie-Woode was founded in 1919 by Mrs. Jonathan C. "Dammie" Day, born of English parents, who founded the camp on "English traditions and Christian principles" as a place where girls could come for adventure and discover the strength in themselves. Since 1978, when former campers bought the operation, Merrie-Woode has been run as a nonprofit foundation.

Though only a mile off US 64, the camp, nestled at the foot of Old Bald Mountain and overlooking the headwaters of Lake Fairfield, sits secluded at 3,300 feet among rhododendron, hemlock, and hardwood forests.

Many camp traditions have developed over the years, not the least of which is the camp uniform. The gray "middy" and green ties and shorts are the same as uniforms used in the past that link present campers to generations before them.

# BILTMORE ESTATE

Touted as "Legacy of the Land," Biltmore Estate attracts close to a million guests each year. George Washington Vanderbilt brought his legendary status of grandson of the Commodore, Cornelius Vanderbilt, to the mountains. This historic family arrived in America in the 17th century, part of the Dutch migration. In the early 1800s, at age 14, the Commodore began his work in opening the frontiers of America through transportation. Eventually he would found the New York Central Railroad.

The Commodore gave this nation another gift in the form of funding Vanderbilt University in Nashville, Tennessee. George Vanderbilt's father, William Henry Vanderbilt, then increased the family's fortunes and founded the Metropolitan Opera Company. While still a bachelor, George Vanderbilt arrived in Asheville with his widowed mother. The railroad had just arrived in this small mountain town, as tunnels through Old Fort Mountain had made easy access possible.

The time was ripe for the legend of the Vanderbilts to take root in Western North Carolina. As the 25-year-old millionaire beheld the beauty of the mountains, he claimed that he would build his private residence in this location. His agents began purchasing land until he amassed 125,000 acres. He then brought the best builders to Asheville. In 1890 America's leading architect, Richard Morris Hunt, began the five-year project that would become known as the country's largest privately owned home. English architect Richard Sharp Smith supervised the building project. Raphael Gustavino came from Barcelona, Spain, to grace the walls and ceilings with his magnificent tile work. Frederick Law Olmsted, who was most renowned for developing Central Park in New York City, came to Biltmore to begin work on the 250 acres of gardens and roadways throughout the estate.

On Christmas Eve, 1895, George Vanderbilt and his mother opened their magnificent home, which was inspired by the 16th-century chateaux of the Loire Valley in France. Family members gathered to celebrate the opening of the house and the season. Eighty-five servants provided service to the guests. Also at this time a multitude of farmers began preparing the earth for spring planting. Thus Biltmore House opened as a residence.

The estate boasted outstanding floral gardens; meanwhile the land produced goods for the table and the local markets. A dairy herd, eventually known as the finest in the Southeast, was begun in 1897; and Gifford Pinchot, who would eventually found the U.S. Forestry Service, began a timber industry and "rotation of the tree crops" in the mountains. Dr. Carl Schenck of Darmstadt, Germany, later took over Pinchot's work. Not only would Schenck continue the work for which he was noted in Europe, but he also founded what has become known as the Cradle of Forestry in America. The Biltmore School of Forestry was the first school of its kind in this nation.

Upon George Vanderbilt's death in 1914, his widow, Edith Stuyvesant Dresser Vanderbilt, began deeding his mountain holdings to the U.S. government. They have since become the nucleus of Pisgah National Forest. On Mar. 6, 1924, the Vanderbilts' only child, Cornelia, married the honorable John Francis Amherst Cecil of England. Together they had two sons.

Eventually the estate was opened to the public in concert with the Asheville Chamber of

Commerce offering an added inducement for travelers to visit Asheville. This was during the last days of the Great Depression in 1930.

In due course, the elder grandson of George Vanderbilt, George Henry Vanderbilt Cecil, continued the operation of the Biltmore Farms and Dairy and allowed public access to Biltmore Estate. In 1960 his younger brother, William Amherst Vanderbilt Cecil, returned to Biltmore and began expanding its enterprise. In the early 1980s the two grandsons of George Vanderbilt divided their inheritance, with William assuming operation and ownership of the Biltmore Company, of which Biltmore Estate is the main component.

The legacy moves forward today, with William A. V. Cecil Jr. as chief officer of Biltmore Estate, watching over 8,000 acres of the estate, which include Biltmore House, Biltmore Gardens, Biltmore Winery, Biltmore Equestrian and Outdoor Center, the Inn on Biltmore Estate, and a farming and beef cattle industry. It remains a Cecil family private enterprise.

While you can tour Biltmore at your own pace, we recommend a "tour by tape," which you can rent for a few dollars. Upon entering the Winter Garden, Coco squawks a greeting and the Karl Bitter fountain, "Boy with Geese," begins gurgling. Once inside, only those with the headsets will hear other sounds of the past, such as servants' footsteps echoing through the corridors of this 250-room house or the great organ resounding in the Banquet Hall.

This great hall features a huge Christmas tree from early Nov through the first week in Jan. Candlelight tours during the Christmas season have become a tradition since the 1980s, when for the first time Biltmore remained open beyond the fall color season. Today Biltmore only closes two days a year—Thanksgiving and Christmas.

The treasures at the Biltmore House were collected by George Vanderbilt. Artworks from the Smithsonian were secreted here for protection during World War II, but have all been returned. The mind-boggling collection of the Biltmore includes paintings by Boldini, Whistler, Renoir,

Gerhardt, and more. The Pellegrini ceiling dominates the Library. Statuary is found throughout the grounds—these friezes are reproductions from the Temple of Athena in Athens. Twenty-five thousand books are in the private collection. The house is a virtual art museum, yet still maintained as George Vanderbilt's palatial residence.

Visiting the four-and-a-half-story house is an adventure in itself. Yet there is even more. Special guided tours are offered at additional fees that provide an "insider's" look at the house. One such tour is Behind the Scenes; another is the Roof Top Tour. The Legacy of the Land tour takes visitors beyond the house and into the gardens and surrounding acres.

Adjacent to the Library Terrace, a pathway leads through the Ramble to the four-acre Walled Garden and the Conservatory just beyond. Paths lead through the estate to the Bass Pond, through the Azalea Garden, with additional hiking trails providing even more adventure. You can pick up a tasty treat at the Ice Cream Parlor, Bakery, or various food stands, and then relax in the courtyard adjacent to the Porte Cochère. A myriad of shops are in the Carriage House and Tack Rooms, including the Chocolate Shop, Book Store, Christmas Shop, and Toy Shop. Should you wish a finer meal, enter the former horse barn known as the Stable Café, where you enjoy the rather unusual experience of dining in the same stalls where the pampered steeds of George Vanderbilt once dined. The fare is quite different from oats and hay, as the kitchen uses the finest produce from the Biltmore vegetable gardens, succulent offerings from the farm, and Biltmore Wine and raspberry lemonade. Top chefs oversee the cuisine prepared and served at all the restaurants on the estate.

As you head back to the parking lot, wind your way through the English Walled Garden, and include a stop at the Conservatory or the Gardener's Shop, situated directly behind the Conservatory, where you can purchase a plant or two as seen growing at Biltmore.

In the summer of 2010 Antler Village, a commons of shops, a bandstand, and entertainment areas, debuted near the River Bend Barn on

# Close-up

## Stone Roberts and the Family Portrait

At age five, Stone Roberts discovered his interest in painting when he pulled art books from his parents' bookshelves in Asheville, North Carolina. He attended the private Gibbons Hall for Boys in Asheville with classmate Donald Sultan, later a venerable New York artist. After receiving a degree from Yale, Roberts returned to Asheville and studied art with Tucker Cooke of UNCA. Roberts's first major piece, "Janet," evocative of Vermeer, is now in the permanent collection of the Metropolitan Museum of Art. Stone Roberts is now a New York resident artist at the top of his profession.

In 1990, William Cecil, owner of Biltmore House, commissioned Roberts to paint a group portrait of the Cecil family for the centennial of the estate. Titled "The William A. V. Cecil Family," the oil-on-canvas work hangs in the second floor Living Hall of the Biltmore House. In the background, Roberts has depicted a painting by the 19th-century American artist Seymour Guy of the last formal portrait of the Vanderbilts, executed in 1873. The position of the Guy painting is depicted as it was for many years until replaced with the current work. The 1873 family portrait is mounted at the opposite end of the Sitting Room.

---

the Estate. For more information on the estate, gardens, or winery, call (828) 225-1333 or (800) 543-2961. These numbers will connect with all facilities at Biltmore. The estate's Web site is www .biltmore.com.

**i** Plan a full day's visit to Biltmore Estate. You're welcome to drive along the meandering estate roads, walk the estate trails, stop off in the many gardens and meadows, have a rest by the lagoons and fishponds . . . take full advantage.

## DINING AT THE ESTATE

### Price Code

Our price code is based on a two-person dinner, excluding drinks, dessert, and tip. Please note that prices vary in all restaurants depending on the season and the time of day (i.e., lunch or dinner). All the restaurants mentioned accept credit cards. (For more dining facilities in the area, see our Restaurants chapter.)

| | |
|---|---|
| $ | Less than $20 |
| $$ | $20 to $35 |
| $$$ | $36 to $50 |
| $$$$ | More than $50 |

You will certainly want to include dining as part of your Biltmore Estate experience. Deerpark Restaurant, the Stable Café, and the Bistro offer creative menus that take advantage of the freshest and finest ingredients. Dining at all of the estate's restaurants is presently open to touring guests only.

### BAKERY

Croissants, danish, muffins, cookies, and other delicacies are offered. Fresh coffee, hot tea, and soft drinks are also sold here.

### THE BISTRO $$–$$$
(828) 225-6231

The Bistro is adjacent to the Biltmore Estate Winery. Its creative interior provides the opportunity to see the chefs in action. This upscale dining facility continues serving throughout the evening. Call for reservations.

### COURTYARD AT BILTMORE HOUSE $

Hot dogs, Polish sausage, and other short-order items are available at the various carts in the courtyard.

### DEERPARK RESTAURANT $$–$$$

Formerly serving as the calving barn, this facility was the first to open as a restaurant on the estate.

It features exquisite buffet dining. The salad bar is staffed to provide you with on-the-spot fresh salad, or you may prepare your own. Two soups are offered. The steam tables are always full of items such as crabcakes, trout, pork, beef, fresh vegetables, vegetable casseroles, potatoes, and all the trimmings. The dessert table truly fulfills the adage, "Life is so short; eat dessert first." The facility is available for weddings and corporate functions in the evenings.

**i** Try one—or more—of the restaurants after your stroll through the Biltmore House. These are not your standard bland and generic tourist stops. Deerpark chefs have won awards, and the restaurant is often host to lavish wedding receptions. The Bistro is exceptional in flavor and freshness of the food. The atmosphere is comfortable and intimate. Don't forget to visit the eclectic shops as well.

### ICE CREAM PARLOR
The original Biltmore Estate dairy formula provides these specially made ice creams at the Ice Cream Parlor. The huge scoops are piled onto a waffle cone or into a dish. Sundaes, brownie-based treats, a small assortment of muffins, and beverages are available also.

### LIONS CREST
A touch of Biltmore magic has transformed the former barn across from the Deerpark Restaurant into an upscale facility for private parties. The tasteful design provides privacy for at least three separate concurrent events. A wedding group could be accommodated in the outside patio and sunken garden. A corporate conference could be ongoing among the rafters with dining space for more than 100. The Chestnut Room easily accommodates a group of 70 or so.

### THE STABLE CAFÉ     $–$$$
The Stable Café is open for lunch throughout the year and in the evenings during special events. Dining is in horse stall booths or tables in the center.  Menu items include rotisserie chicken,

soups, salads, hamburgers, and desserts. Biltmore wine and other beverages are also served. Group reservations can be made for the Loft at the Stable Café.

## BILTMORE ESTATE WINERY
Omar Khayyam touted the romance of "a jug of wine, a loaf of bread, and thou" in the *Rubaiyat*. Biltmore takes it to the next level. Wine is fermenting and bread is baking as one tours the state-of-the-art wine cellar and sits in on a cooking demonstration.

This former milking barn is another dazzling Biltmore transformation. The underground wine cellar opens another world of ambience. The tasting room is bedecked with heraldry of the great Lord Burley. The various family coats of arms have been made into one. This process, in heraldry terms, is called "impaling." At the end of the self-guided tour, a tasting of Biltmore wines is offered. Buy a bottle to take home in the adjacent sales room. Multiple activities surround a visit to the winery, such as an annual jazz weekend. The Champagne Cellar is available for private parties of up to 30.

**i** Biltmore Estate is located across from Biltmore Village in Asheville, North Carolina. Contact for all Biltmore facilities, except where specific phone numbers are provided, is (828) 225-1333 or (800) 543-2961; www.biltmore.com.

## FARM VILLAGE AND OUTDOOR CENTER
Options at Biltmore are so numerous that a visit of two or three days would still be limiting. The Farm Village, located behind the Winery, takes one back to another era. Original farm equipment from the first days of farming at Biltmore is on display. The large barn space is used for a range of events—it could be a bluegrass group, or perhaps a historical overview of farming and gardening at Biltmore. If you walk around the perimeter, you will find the Creamery, where ice

# Close-up

## Fruit of the Tarheel Vine

Prior to passage of Prohibition, North Carolina was legendary for its vineyards and wine production. When America went "dry," only a limited amount of wine could be produced, and for medicinal and religious purposes.

In the case of the Waldensian Winery in Valdese, the huge redwood tankards were sunk—empty—into the mountain lakes. It wasn't until the 1980s that they were retrieved and the Waldensian Vineyards was reactivated.

In 1972 the Fussen family of Rose Hill, North Carolina, in concert with North Carolina State University, explored the idea of making North Carolina a wine-producing state. Using the Muscadine and Scuppernong grapes of eastern North Carolina, they opened the Duplin Winery. Their wine was as sweet as the fresh pressed grapes, and the industry reemerged. Their first fermentation tanks were bought from a dairy; thus milk was turned into wine . . . in a sense.

Other experimental wineries opened, and in the 1970s Biltmore Estate planted its first grapes. By 1982, third-generation wine maker Philippe Jourdain of Carcasson, France, had arrived in North Carolina and applied his techniques in developing the Biltmore Estate Winery. In 1985 the owner of Biltmore Estate, William Amhurst Vanderbilt Cecil, renovated the dairy barn of 1890s vintage, reopening it as the home of Biltmore Estate Winery.

Other wineries followed and are continuing to open, particularly in the northern mountains, where the soil is rich and the climate just right. Of the 26 wineries currently operating in North Carolina, nine are found in the western mountains. The remainder stretch out across the state all the way to Knotts Island, accessible only by ferry. As you tour the Tar Heel state, you have many options to "taste the wine where the grape was grown."

cream is dipped in the Biltmore style, and the General Store, whose shelves are stocked with unique mountain items. You may find a blacksmith working at his forge and other artisans of yesteryear, such as basketmakers and chair caners, demonstrating their trade. In the fields beyond you will see draft horses and other farm animals at pasture.

The Outdoor Center is in this same complex. This is where you can arrange horseback riding and biking on the estate, floating trips on the French Broad River, which flows through Biltmore Estate, a Land Rover drive along a special track, and more.

Vanderbilt views and comfortable opulence at the Inn on Biltmore make an extended stay on the estate a reality dream trip. The mountain views experienced by George Vanderbilt are yours from every vantage point in this 213-room inn. High tea is served in the library with a spectacular view. Award-winning chefs and stylish waitstaff make dining another extraordinary experience. Upon arrival at the inn, secure your vehicle with the valet and rely upon local transport. After a day on the Biltmore trails or a trip on the French Broad River, relax in the hot tub or the outdoor pool. Stop at the lobby bar and then see what other estate experiences await you.

**INN ON BILTMORE**
**(828) 225-1333, (800) 922-0084**
**www.biltmore.com**

# EASTERN BAND OF THE CHEROKEE NATION

As a nation within a nation, the Eastern Band of the Cherokee continues to maintain part of its ancient culture, even in today's modern world. In fact, the Qualla Boundary utilizes much of the latest technology to keep the past accessible to visitors today. Four-lane highways have opened this mountain-locked nation of 60,000 acres.

Cherokee influences can be felt throughout the area. Cherokee words form the basis for many names given to the local towns, rivers, and mountains. Craft techniques, natural dyes, and much more derived from the land and handed down through generations shape our hand-made heritage.

The Oconaluftee Village is a magnificent example of preserved culture. Stepping back into the 1750s, your Cherokee guide leads the way to ladies crafting belts from beads, men demonstrating blow guns for hunting, and others burning out logs for canoes. Pottery-making and food preparation are a part of everyday life in this village from another time. Here you get a real sense of being in Cherokee time.

To achieve the total experience, you must visit the Museum of the Cherokee Indian, which brings the thousand-year-history of this ancient culture into this century. Take time to learn about the ancient Cherokee creation stories. Tune your ear to the 86 symbols that constitute the Cherokee alphabet, whose development established the Cherokee as the first Native Americans to have a written language. Join the Cherokee as DeSoto and his Spanish Conquistadors entered this land in 1540, and note the amazement the Cherokee chiefs caused as they visited the courts of England. Walk slowly with the Cherokee as they began their trek across the nation in the removal to the Oklahoma Territory, now known as "The Trail of Tears."

In the evening, in season, return to the amphitheater for the outdoor production of *Unto These Hills*. This moving presentation begins with a carefree pastoral community before the arrival of the Spanish Conquistadors. Upon their arrival, life changes from innocence to the reality of man's lust for riches. The drama marches across the centuries, illustrating the westward movement of a frontier that unseats the native inhabitants, resulting in the movement of the Cherokee to the Oklahoma Territory.

A visit to Cherokee, North Carolina, is worth at least two nights. Upscale lodging is available at the hotel at Harrah's Casino. (There is an abundance of other lodging and RV parking in the area.) This Cherokee-operated casino and hotel has greatly benefited the 13,000 registered members of the nation, as all tribal members receive a bi-annual stipend from casino profits. For babies, this means that the interest-bearing escrow account will be waiting for them upon high school graduation—the funds are not available until age 25 if the student drops out of school. The education system and medical facilities were major beneficiaries of the casino profits. Full scholarships to any institute in the world are offered to all qualifying students, and social services, hospitals, and medical research facilities have been expanded.

**Close-up**

## From the Paleo People to Qualla

Archeologists have placed the arrival of the Paleo People into Western North Carolina at about 12,000 years ago. The Cherokee are descendants who have been classified in early records as Upper Valley People, Middle Valley People, Hiawassee People, and Dallas People. These early people populated the land from the Great Lakes in the North, down through the Ohio Valley and into seven of the southeastern states.

The major capital of the early Cherokee was located in Georgia along the Little Tennessee and Tellico Rivers. The area was known as Over Hill Towns, Echota, and regarded as a sacred city of refuge. The towns were along the Tuckasegee and the Hiawassee Valley Rivers. The subcapital was Nikwasi, built on the site of what is now Franklin, North Carolina. The Lower Towns were in South Carolina.

Town councils elected their own chiefs. One presided over tribal affairs and the other was in charge of military matters. Women had the vote on war and peace; these women were known as War Women or Pretty Women. They also decided the punishment of captives, torture, death, pardons, and adoptions. Seven matriarchal clans were under this central structure. Children belonged to the clan of the mother.

Although they referred to themselves as "The Principal People," it was the Spanish who first dubbed them *Chalaque*. This was a designation given to them by opposing tribes, more or less meaning "Mole People," because they lived in caves, huts, and eventually cabins. One hundred years after the Spanish, the French called them *Cheraqui*, which the British interpreted as "Cherokee."

During the War of 1812 Junaluska and his Cherokee followers fought alongside Gen. Andrew Jackson, playing a huge role in the defeat of the British at the Battle of Horse Shoe Bend. In fact, history connotes that it was through the efforts of the Cherokee that the life of the general was saved and the British fort fell. Thus in 1835 Junaluska, Sequoyah, and other Cherokee leaders met with then President Andrew Jackson requesting that the Cherokee not be removed from their ancestral land to the Oklahoma Territory. This was to no avail. Thus entered a dark period in the forming of this nation when the Cherokee were forced to leave their land and begin the march that has become known as "The Trail of Tears." More than 5,000 Cherokee died in this forced march.

Junaluska returned from Oklahoma to the North Carolina mountains, providing leadership to the clan of Chief Tsali along with scattered remnants of the other clans who had defied the marching orders and hidden out in these mountains. Will Thomas, a non-Cherokee, was appointed federal agent to the Eastern Band. He was fluent in the language and customs and soon became a champion of their cause to re-establish their community. Thomas was able to purchase 57,000 acres to form the present village of Cherokee and a smaller tract near Robbinsville known as the Snowbird Reservation. This acreage has become known as the Qualla Boundary.

## OTHER CHEROKEE SITES IN WESTERN NORTH CAROLINA

### CHEROKEE HERITAGE MUSEUM & GALLERY

Saunooke Village, US 441 North

Cherokee

(828) 497-3211

This museum and gallery will be a particularly nice stop for those who appreciate the very best in contemporary Cherokee art. The theme here is discovering the past through the present. It offers displays of art and cultural items such as masks, crystals, the *uketena*, and more. The gallery presents a new exhibit each month. Cherokee

Heritage also features educational taped tours, books, and craft demonstrations. It is open daily from Apr through Nov. There is a small admission charge.

**i** When visiting the Cherokee Indian Reservation, your first stop should be at the Cherokee Visitor Center across U.S. Highway 441, facing the Museum of the Cherokee Indian (828-497-9195 or 800-438-1601). Here you'll find brochures and information on all Cherokee and area attractions, local restaurants, and sightseeing. It's open daily from 8 a.m. to 9 p.m. from mid-June through late Aug, 8 a.m. to 6 p.m. from late Aug through Oct, and 8 a.m. to 4:30 p.m. from Nov through mid-June.

## JUNALUSKA MEMORIAL SITE AND MUSEUM
1 Junaluska Dr., Robbinsville
(828) 479-4727
www.grahamcountytravel.com
This small museum is located just off Main Street near downtown Robbinsville. It blends the history of the community as it relates to Cherokee history. The Tatham Gap Trail, which was traveled by the Cherokees in their removal in 1838, stretched 25 miles from Robbinsville to Andrews. Six miles of it into Andrews can still be hiked. The museum has been recognized as an interpretive site along the Trail of Tears National Historic Trail. The grave of Junaluska and his wife, Nicie, is in Robbinsville.

**i** In the early 1800s, Sequoyah (George Gist), an illiterate, non-English-speaking child of a Cherokee mother and an absent white father, invented the Cherokee alphabet, making the Cherokee the first Native Americans to have a written language. In 1828 the first Cherokee-language newspaper came off the press—the *Chero-kee Phoenix*. Sequoyah has been honored, with a spelling change, by having Sequoia National Park and the sequoia tree named for him. Both are in California.

## THE MUSEUM OF THE CHEROKEE INDIAN
589 Tsali Blvd., Cherokee
(828) 497-3481, (888) 665-7249
www.cherokeemuseum.org
Plan to spend at least two hours at this museum, which has been called "a cutting-edge" example of "how all museums should be." Outside the building is a 20-foot wooden sculpture of Sequoyah (the Cherokee genius who is—as far as we know—the only human to create a written form of language all alone), and inside you can literally walk through Cherokee history. Interactive displays and multisensory exhibits allow you to experience the past. You can listen to storytellers, play the ancient butter bean game, travel the infamous Trail of Tears, and much more.

The fine gift shop is loaded with a large selection of books, crafts, artwork, and other Cherokee or Native American items. The museum is open year-round except on Thanksgiving, Christmas, and New Year's Day. Hours are 9 a.m. to 5 p.m. Sept through May and 9 a.m. to 8 p.m. June through Aug. Admission is under $10.

## OCONALUFTEE INDIAN VILLAGE
Drama Road off US 441 North, Cherokee
(828) 497-2315, (828) 497-2111
www.oconalufteevillage.com
Get ready to step back more than two centuries in time when you visit this re-created 1750s Cherokee village. Indian guides in native costumes will take you through the village, while others demonstrate such life skills as weaving, pottery, beadwork, food preparation, canoe construction, and arrow-making and hunting techniques. You will see Cherokee homes, a sweat lodge, and the important seven-sided council house. Cherokee history, culture, and social customs will be explained, and you'll have ample opportunity to ask questions. Afterward go back to the areas that interested you and spend as much time as you like exploring further. The village is open from 9 a.m. to 5:30 p.m. daily May 15 through Oct 25. Admission is under $20.

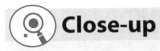

# Close-up

## The Invisible Warriors

The town of Franklin was built where the Cherokee settlement of Nikwasi once stood. Nikwasi was one of the oldest Cherokee towns and an important ceremonial center. In the old days Indians built their town lodges on large manmade mounds, and Nikwasi's was one of the few that possessed the "everlasting fire," or spiritual connection; hence the lodge was used in religious ceremonies.

Once, long ago, a powerful, unknown tribe invaded the land, destroying the villages and killing the people. One morning at dawn the intruders were seen approaching Nikwasi. The villagers rushed to defend their town but were eventually forced to retreat.

Suddenly a stranger appeared. He spoke and dressed like a chief from the Overhills settlements. The villagers thought he had come to their aid with reinforcements. He shouted to the Nikwasi chief to call off his men—he would defeat the enemy. As the Nikwasi villagers fell back toward the lodge, they saw hundreds of warriors, armed and painted for battle, streaming out of an open doorway in the side of the mound where no doorway had existed before. It was then the villagers recognized the warriors as *nunnehi*—"immortals," or the "people who live anywhere."

Theirs was a race of spirit people, fond of music and dancing, who lived in the highlands and had a great many town lodges, especially on mountain balds. As soon as the *nunnehi* got a short distance from the mound, they became invisible. The invaders could see the weapons but could not see who wielded them; frightened, they began to flee. They tried to hide behind large rocks as they retreated, but the *nunnehis'* arrows flew around the boulders and killed them. When only six or so of the invaders were left alive, they were so upset they just sat down and cried. Since that day the Cherokee have called that spot at the head of the Tuckasegee River *dayulsunyi*, "where they cried."

It was Indian custom to spare a few warriors to return home and tell of their defeat. Thus the invaders went home to the north and the *nunnehi* returned to the mound.

There are countless Cherokee stories involving this spirit race who, when they chose to show themselves, looked like ordinary people. They also appeared to whites during the Civil War. It's said that a large troop of Union soldiers came to Franklin to surprise a small number of Confederates posted there but, upon seeing so many soldiers guarding the town, they turned away.

**QUALLA ARTS AND CRAFTS MUTUAL, INC.**
**US 441 and Drama Road, Cherokee**
**(828) 497-3103**

Just across the street from the Museum of the Cherokee Indian, you'll find a cooperative that displays the works of 300 Cherokee craftspeople and a section of American Indian crafts from other areas of the country. The store also has a large section of historical baskets, masks, pottery, finger weaving, wood carving, and the like. It's open 8 a.m. to 8 p.m. June through Aug, 8 a.m. to 6 p.m. Sept through Oct, and 9 a.m. to 4:30 p.m. Nov through May. Admission is free.

In 1767 Josiah Wedgwood imported "Cherokee Clay" from Franklin, North Carolina, and used it as the basis for the world-renowned English Jasperware.

*UNTO THESE HILLS*
**Drama Road and US 441 North, Cherokee**
**(828) 497-2111, (800) 554-4557**
**www.untothesehills.com**

Every summer from mid-June through late Aug, one of the world's longest-running outdoor dramas takes the stage in the 2,800-seat Mountainside Theater just outside the town of Cherokee. In the half-century since the play opened in 1950,

## Cherokee Lands

Historically the land of the Cherokees encompassed parts of the following states: Kentucky, Tennessee, Alabama, Georgia, South Carolina, North Carolina, Virginia, and West Virginia. Today the nation of the Eastern Band of the Cherokee encompasses less than 60,000 acres in Western North Carolina.

The 1838 removal of the Cherokee has become known as "The Trail of Tears" for the thousands who died en route to the Oklahoma Territory. Each Cherokee was allotted 110 acres in the Northeast corner at Thalequah, Oklahoma. Unscrupulous "land grabbers" were able to reduce acreage significantly.

millions of visitors have watched the rich pageant of Cherokee legends, rituals, dances, and history unfold before them. Even if you've seen this outdoor drama in years past, a recomposed musical score makes a return trip a new experience.

June and July performances, which run two hours and 15 minutes, start at 8:45 p.m., with preshow musical entertainment beginning at 8:10 p.m. In Aug shows begin at 8:30 p.m. and preshow entertainment at 7:50 p.m. Reserved seating is available in the front half of the theater; general admission is available all season. Group rates are available for 20 or more people. Tickets may be purchased at the box office at the intersection of US 441 and Drama Road from 9 a.m. to 6:30 p.m. Mon through Sat. After 6:30 p.m. you can buy them at the Mountainside Theater for that evening's performance. You can also order reserve tickets by calling (828) 497-2111 or (800) 554-4557. Both the theater and the box office are closed on Sun.

# WATERFALLS

Whether it's the roar of a great cataract forming rainbows in its drenching spray or a slender, misty stream of water musically splashing in a shallow pool, there are few places where the call of the falls can be so fulfilled as in Western North Carolina. There are literally hundreds of waterfalls in these mountains, more than 250 in Transylvania County alone.

Nature and time have provided waterfalls throughout the mountains. Some are on private property, and others can only be reached by long and strenuous hikes though rugged country. Most of the ones we've chosen are just a short jaunt from a roadway, and some of these falls can be viewed simply by parking your car and taking a look. We have listed several worth the extra effort required to reach them, even though it sometimes means traveling on a narrow, curvy, graveled secondary road (SR) or Forest Service road (FR).

A few words of caution are in order: Water-drenched rocks are extremely treacherous, and a number of serious accidents and deaths occur each year to people who slip and fall from the tops of these falls or from the spray- and moss-slick rocks, steps, and trails nearby. (Even when fording mountain streams, extreme care is needed.) Use common sense and caution. Keep a sharp eye on children. Stay well away from the tops of falls and never try to climb or walk across them. Avoid tragedies.

Areas where nominal fees are collected include Sliding Rock, Dry Falls, and Whitewater Falls. A season pass costs under $20. However one pass is needed for Sliding Rock and another is required for and provides access to Dry Falls and Whitewater Falls, as well as nearby Whiteside Mountain.

## NORTHERN MOUNTAINS

### Avery County

**ELK FALLS**
**Off U.S. Hwy. 19 East**
Sixty-five-foot Elk Falls, just inside the Tennessee–North Carolina border, is one of the most beautiful waterfalls in the mountains. Its lovely pool, one of the largest and deepest around, makes this a superpopular swimming hole, but beware of the fast water here.

Elk Falls is easily accessible; just go north on US 19 East to the town of Elk Park. A short distance up Main Street (SR 1303), turn right on Elk River Road (SR 1305), a residential street. Travel just over 4 miles to a parking area beside the Elk River. Here a short trail leads to the top and on down to the base of the falls.

### Burke County

**LINVILLE FALLS**
**Mile 316.5, Blue Ridge Parkway**
Well-known Linville Falls, at the head of Linville Gorge, pours downward in several stages into one of the deepest gorges in the eastern United States. You can reach the falls by hiking from the Linville Falls Visitors Center at milepost 316.5 on the Blue Ridge Parkway. For specific directions check the maps posted at the center. The trails to various overlooks of the falls range from easy to difficult.

**i** Famous Linville Gorge and Linville Falls were named for William Linville and his son, John, who were killed by Indians in 1766. The Cherokee called the river "eeseeoh" or "river of many cliffs."

## UPPER CREEK FALLS
**Off Hwy. 181**
The main part of this cascade tumbles some 100 feet into a pool of thrashing water. This and the fact that it's moderately easy to get to make Upper Creek Falls a popular swimming and sunbathing area. To reach it take Highway 181 south from the Blue Ridge Parkway for just more than 5.5 miles to a parking area on the left. A nearly mile-long, steep switchback trail descends through the woods to the falls.

## Yancey County
### CRABTREE FALLS
**Mile 339.5, Blue Ridge Parkway**
This 70-foot waterfall, considered to be one of the most photogenic in the state, is in the Crabtree Meadows Recreation Area (elevation 3,700 feet) on the Blue Ridge Parkway, 8.4 miles south of the junction of Highway 226 at milepost 339.5. The steep, rocky trail makes for a moderately difficult hike from the parking lot in the Crabtree Meadows camping area (you can pick up a trail guide at the campground's entrance during the summer months). In winter, when the campgrounds are closed, you'll have to park outside the gate and walk in. A loop trail, lined with birch and hemlock and, in spring and summer, a great variety of wildflowers, leads to this beautiful 70-foot falls. To get to the falls by the shortest route, nearly a mile, descend the trail to the right. You can come back the same way for a trip of slightly less than 2 miles or continue on the 2.5-mile loop. If you do the latter, bear to the left to avoid trails leading into the campground.

### SETROCK CREEK AND ROARING FORK FALLS
**3 miles off Hwy. 80 North**
From the Blue Ridge Parkway, exit onto Highway 80 North (at milepost 344) and go approximately 2 miles north to Forest Service Road 472. Make a left onto FR 472 and drive 4.7 miles to the Black Mountain Campground. Inside the campground you'll see a sign leading to the Briar Bottom group camp. Drive the short distance to a sign on the right that marks the way to this 75-foot

cascade. When the trail forks, bear right. This is a round-trip excursion of a little more than a 0.5 mile.

When you return to your car, continue your journey another 3.9 miles down FR 472 (when the road changes from gravel to pavement, it becomes SR 1205). At the BUSICK WORK CENTER sign, turn right and park at the gate. The trail, an old logging road to the right of the gate, will take you to Roaring Fork River. Turn right on a path at the river. You'll find the falls, which drop in beautiful 5-foot cascades, about a mile away.

The mossy rocks and leaves form alcoves worthy of the Garden of Eden! A trail running up the forested right side of the falls let you into a small pool at the top. Be very careful and use only the trail to get to the top.

### WATERFALL ON BIG CREEK
**Off US 19 West**
This gushing waterfall, which can be viewed from the road, is reached by taking US 19 East west out of Burnsville and then turning right on US 19 West toward the Tennessee border. Drive 17.5 miles to a marked pull-off on the left for a view of the 25-foot falls.

# CENTRAL MOUNTAINS

## Buncombe County
### DOUGLAS (OR CARTER CREEK) AND WALKER FALLS
**5 miles south of Hwy. 197**
A journey into Pisgah's Craggy Mountain Scenic Area to view Douglas Falls offers an added attraction: The falls are surrounded by a stand of rare virgin hemlock. To reach the area take U.S. Highways 19/23 North out of Asheville for 13.5 miles and then go east on Highway 197 to Barnardsville. Turn south on Dillingham Road (SR 2173) about a half-block past the post office. About 4 miles down this winding road, veer to the left and continue until it becomes graveled FR 74; stop for a view of two-tier, 50-foot Walker Falls on the left.

Continue on another 5 miles or so until you dead-end at the Craggy Mountain Scenic Area parking area. Take the trail on the south end (right side) of the parking lot. It's a little more than 0.5 mile to a viewing area at the base of 70-foot Douglas Falls, named in honor of Supreme Court Justice William O. Douglas. Unless you are an experienced hiker armed with a good topographical map and compass, return the way you came. Most trail maps of this area are outdated and confusing. For the best viewing, visit both these falls after heavy rains.

## GLASSMINE FALLS
### Mile 361.1, Blue Ridge Parkway

This waterfall is on private land, and its water flow can be thin when rain is scarce. (It's been known to dry up completely.) However after heavy rains, Glassmine Falls, with its immense slide downward, can be impressive. You can view the falls from Glassmine Falls Overlook at milepost 361.1 on the Blue Ridge Parkway. This overlook is about 200 feet from the parking area, which is 5.7 miles south of Highway 128, the road that leads to Mount Mitchell's summit. It will be on the left when driving south from Mount Mitchell and on the right when driving north. Look east to locate the fall's steep rock face (estimated at 800 feet), framed by stark skeletons of red spruce that have died from air pollution.

## Polk County
### PEARSON FALLS
### Off Pearson Falls Road (SR 1102)

There is a small fee for adults and 50 cents for children 6 to 12 (children younger than 6 are admitted free) to Pearson Falls Park, which is owned and maintained by the Tryon Garden Club, and it's well worth the price. Take U.S. Highway 176 South out of Saluda or north out of Tryon. Watch for a small sign on the Pacolet River side of the road that marks Pearson Falls Road (SR 1102). The entrance to the 250-acre park is slightly less than a mile down this road. This biologically rich glen with its profusion of wildflowers was purchased in 1931 and is now a North Carolina Natural Heritage Area. It's a great place for hiking, bird-watching, and picnicking.

The park is open from 10 a.m. to 6 p.m. daily in the summer. From Nov 1 to Mar 1, it's closed on Mon and Tues and is only open from 10 a.m. to 5 p.m. the rest of the week.

## SHUNKAWAUKEN FALLS
### White Oak Mountain Road, SR 1136

This cascade begins its tumbles practically from the summit of 3,102-foot White Oak Mountain, with the main portion measuring around 150 feet high. Though it's on private land, it can be viewed right from the roadside. From I-26 drive east on Highway 108 for just less than a half-mile and turn left on Houston Road (SR 1137). After another half-mile, take the fork to the left onto White Oak Mountain Road (SR 1136). You'll come to the waterfall in another 2 miles. There is a pull-off on the left just beyond it. If you continue on down the road for just a little more than 0.5 mile, you'll reach an overlook with a great view of Columbus and the surrounding area.

> **i** National Forest Service visitor centers often carry maps to waterfalls in the area.

## Rutherford County
### HICKORY NUT FALLS
### Inside Chimney Rock Park off
### US Hwy. 64 East

This waterfall spilling 404 feet over a granite face is just over the Henderson County line at Lake Lure and can be seen from quite a distance. Hickory Nut Falls are located in the privately owned Chimney RockPark (see our Attractions chapter). Admission ($14 for adults and $6 for children 6 to 15; children under 6 are free) includes a 26-story elevator ride up through solid rock and access to nature trails offering unparalleled views of the falls (the best is from Inspiration Point). It also offers a smashing view of Lake Lure, craggy-faced Rumbling Bald Mountain, and the surrounding countryside. For a preview of the falls, you may want to rent the 1992 movie *The Last of the Mohicans*, which featured the majestic falls prominently. To reach the park take US 64 East off I-26 and drive approximately 15 miles through Bat Cave to the park.

## Transylvania County

### COURTHOUSE FALLS
**Off Hwy. 215**

You'll have to walk a short distance to reach this waterfall, but it's one of our favorites and one of the most beautiful in the mountains. Take Highway 215 for 10.4 miles into Pisgah Forest from its junction with US 64 near Rosman. Turn right on FR 140 and drive approximately 3 miles to a small bridge that crosses a creek; you can park on the far side, on the right. Take the trail on the right for a few hundred yards to a narrow trail that bears left. This 300-foot, short, steep trail leads to the beautiful pool at the base of the falls.

### DANIEL RIDGE FALLS
**FR 475**

Two other fine cascades—Cove Creek and Shuck Ridge Creek Falls—are in this general area, but Daniel Ridge, also known as Toms Spring Falls, is the largest and easiest to find. Drive 5.2 miles up U.S. Highway 276 to FR 475 and go 3.9 miles to a parking area on the right. From there follow the logging road for less than a mile. You'll see the 150-foot falls on the left.

### THE HORSEPASTURE RIVER FALLS
**Off Hwy. 281 South**

The series of waterfalls here are some of the most awe inspiring in the region. To reach the falls from the intersection of US 64 and Highway 281 in Sapphire, turn south on Highway 281 and drive 1.8 miles to the Horsepasture River, 4.2 miles of which have been designated as part of the National Wild and Scenic River System. Find a parking spot along the guardrails near the bridge. Drift Falls, known to locals as "Bust Your Butt Falls," can be seen just downriver. It is privately owned and is not open to the public. The falls can still be viewed from the parking area. There's a pull-off on the right for about three or four cars next to the trailhead, marked by a small green sign on the guardrail. (Make sure your vehicle is completely off the road, or you may get ticketed.) From the trailhead descend the trail for 100 yards until it joins the trail paralleling the river. Privately owned Drift Falls will be to your right. Drop Off/Turtleback Falls, named for its domelike rock, is a few hundred feet farther on your left. Though it looks like a great place for some slide-and-swim fun, don't attempt it; the currents in this pool have caused a number of drownings, and it's dangerously close to the top of Rainbow Falls.

Viewing the other beautiful falls along this wide, deep gorge will require a 1.5-mile steep descent on a sometimes-strenuous trail with precipitous ledges.

Continue down the gorge to the top of roaring, 200-foot Rainbow Falls, where you can often see rainbows in the thunderous spray. Again, stay away from the brink of this waterfall! Instead take the trail to an upper overlook or descend to the lower overlook (if you don't mind a drenching) for a picnic or swim. Avoid these falls in winter; the spray freezes and it makes walking dangerous.

It's another fairly difficult half-mile trek to the base of Stairstep Falls, where the river tumbles down seven 10-foot-tall, river-wide steps. Only the most experienced and intrepid should continue down the strenuous and dangerous 1.3-mile trail to Windy Falls. That series of nine violent cascades plunges 700 feet so mightily that they create their own wind through the narrowing gorge. We definitely advise not attempting this one. There isn't even a viewing place to see all of Windy Falls. A final word of caution: When visiting this wild river gorge, one of the most beautiful and spectacular in the mountains, remember that accidents in the area have kept the local rescue squad busy through the years, and deaths have been a common occurrence.

### LOOKING GLASS FALLS
**US 276**

You barely have to get out of your vehicle to enjoy the most visited of Transylvania County's many waterfalls. This rushing 30-foot-wide, 60-foot-high cascade is set alongside US 276, 5.5 miles into Pisgah Forest from its junction with US 64. A short flight of stone steps leads down to the base of the falls from a paved pull-off area right beside Looking Glass Creek.

## MOORE'S COVE FALLS
### 0.7 miles off US 276

One mile north of Looking Glass Falls on US 276, keep a sharp eye out for the first bridge ahead and pull off in the wide, unpaved area just before reaching the bridge. (When driving south, it's 1.6 miles from Sliding Rock.) A wooden pedestrian bridge will take you across Looking Glass Creek to the lovely, easy 0.7-mile-long Moore's Cove Trail, which is steep only for the first few hundred yards. At its end a small stream tumbles over a deeply recessed ledge that allows you to walk behind the free-falling, 50-foot falls. Avoid the steep path to the top of the ledge; it can be dangerous.

**i** Due to the glare of sunshine on water, waterfall photos usually come out best if shot in the early morning, late evening, or on a cloudy day. If you can keep your camera lens dry, try shooting during light rain or fog for wonderful effects.

## SLICK ROCK FALLS
### FR 475B

To reach this watery attraction just a short distance up the road from Looking Glass Falls, follow the sign to the Pisgah Fish Hatchery (FR 475) on the left. Drive 1.6 miles and turn right on FR 475B. After 1.1 miles you'll come to a sharp bend in the road. Park at the small pull-off on the right, where a trailhead leads up to the summit of Looking Glass Rock. The small but pretty 30-foot-tall Slick Rock Falls, some 50 yards away, spills over a rocky ledge of this rugged mountain. This waterfall well deserves its name "slick," so please don't try to climb it or any other falls.

## SLIDING ROCK
### US 276

Just 1.6 miles farther up US 276 (or 7.6 miles from its junction with US 64) is Sliding Rock, one place where you're invited to "take the plunge" down a 60-foot slippery cascade into the 50- to

60-degree, 6-foot-deep pool below. If you don't care to make the slide, it's fun simply to watch the action from paved viewing areas at the top or bottom of this natural, exhilarating ride that's fueled by 11,000 gallons of water a minute. There's now a $3 per vehicle parking fee that helps pay for lifeguards, who are on duty from 10 a.m. to 6 p.m. from Memorial Day through Labor Day; the parking fee includes the use of a bathhouse.

The rock, while slick, can take the bottom out of an ordinary bathing suit, so old jeans or cutoffs are best for this fast ride. Also be careful while getting in and out of the water. The surface of the rock, even where the water isn't flowing, can be slick and accounts for some hard tumbles.

## TOXAWAY FALLS
### Off US 64

In 1916 the first Lake Toxaway dam burst after a flooding downpour. The water from the lake washed away huge amounts of vegetation and soil and exposed a huge granite dome. As you drive over this dome on a bridge, you can see the once-mighty falls, just a small stream these days.

## TWIN FALLS ON HENRY BRANCH
### 2.2 miles off FR 477

Since we sometimes are able to take this lovely hike to Twin Falls without meeting anyone else along the trail, we almost hesitate to risk jeopardizing such solitude by writing about it. Note that at 4.4 miles for the round trip, this is the longest trek in this list. While it's not a particularly difficult trail, it does involve negotiating a number of log bridges, so we always equip ourselves with a long, sturdy walking stick to help keep our balance, a good idea almost anytime you're walking forest trails that often have slippery and eroded sections.

To reach these two 100-foot waterfalls, drive 2.2 miles north on US 276 from its junction with US 64. Turn right on FR 477 and travel just more than 2.5 miles to a small parking area on the right side at the sign to Avery Creek Trail. Take this yellow-and-blue-blazed path for slightly more than a mile, until Avery Creek Trail crosses orange-blazed Buckhorn Gap Trail, which you should take to the right. In a little more than a half-mile, you'll come to a Trail Falls Loop sign. It's just a short distance in either direction of the loop to Twin Falls (the left loop is usually less overgrown), which are formed by two separate streams. There is no trail to the very base of the falls. Don't try to make one. You'll only disturb the wonderful plants that live here.

### WHITEWATER FALLS AND LAUREL FALLS
#### Off Highway 281

At 411 feet, Whitewater Falls lays claim to being the highest unbroken falls in the Southeast. To reach it take US 64 to Highway 281 and travel south for approximately 9.5 miles. Turn left at the Whitewater Falls Scenic Area for the short drive to the parking area, where there is a $2 per vehicle fee. From there a 0.2-mile trail leads to the upper overlook. Be extremely careful when negotiating the steep trip down to a lower overlook for an even better view. An old roadbed leads to the top of the falls, but we don't recommend any close-up viewing, as a number of deaths occur in the area almost every year.

If you're in excellent shape, you can turn right on the trail that brings you to the middle overlook, and it will take you on a very strenuous hike of just less than a mile down to Laurel Falls, also known as Corbin Creek Falls. When the trees have shed their leaves, you can view this waterfall from Whitewater. It's made up of a series of broken cascades that tumble about the same distance as Whitewater, but only the lowest one, which drops approximately 75 feet, can be easily seen. It's much too dangerous to try to get a close-up view of the others.

## SOUTHERN MOUNTAINS

### Clay County

#### LEATHERWOOD FALLS
#### FR 340

Compared with some falls, 25-foot Leatherwood is not particularly grand, but Fires Creek, which rushes past the falls' base, is great for swimming and fishing. To find it go west out of Hayesville on US 64 for just short of 5 miles and turn right on SR 1302. After 3.7 miles turn left on SR 1344, which will become FR 340 as it enters the Nantahala National Forest. Drive 1.9 miles to the Leatherwood Falls parking and picnic area. You can view the falls from here or wade into the creek (it can be rushing and dangerous after heavy rains), or you can cross the bridge upstream and work your way back to the foot of the falls. Don't, however, be tempted to climb the cascade. It may not look dangerous, but it is. From the picnic area, paved trails provide access for fly-fishing from wheelchairs.

### Haywood County

#### THE GRAVEYARD FIELDS FALLS
#### Mile 418.8, Blue Ridge Parkway

Three waterfalls, Upper Falls, Second Falls, and Yellowstone Falls (the largest of the three), are in Graveyard Fields, a vast area left nearly treeless by a devastating forest fire in 1925. Second Falls can be seen from the parking area at milepost 418.8 on the Blue Ridge Parkway, but most people prefer a closer look and walk to the Graveyard Fields Loop Trail. The parking area is very crowded on weekends. Some parts of the trail are badly eroded, as are many side trails. Check the information board at the parking area for the most direct routes to the falls and be careful at the overlook at Yellowstone Falls, which can be treacherous (see our chapter on the Blue Ridge Parkway). As with all falls, stay out of the water at the top of the falls and stay on the trails.

#### MIDNIGHT HOLE AND MOUSE CREEK FALLS
#### 1.5 and 2 miles off Waterville Road

Seeing these falls requires a 4-mile round-trip hike, but it's an easy walk on a graded road that runs along beautiful Big Creek. To reach Big Creek drive west on I-40 to the Waterville exit (just before you reach the Tennessee border). Turn left on Waterville Road, which will enter the Great Smoky Mountains National Park. After approximately 3 miles, 0.8 mile past the ranger station, the road will end at a parking area of the

Big Creek Campground. (In winter the gate is closed at the ranger station, so you'll have to walk from there, adding 1.6 miles round-trip.) Take the road (Big Creek Trail) just a few feet back from the parking area. A little less than 1.5 miles along this easy route, an obvious path will lead to Midnight Hole, where small (7-foot) but gorgeous twin falls flow into a fantastic 80-foot-wide, 15-foot-deep swimming hole. Back on the road/trail, continue on slightly over another half-mile, and you'll see Mouse Creek Falls, which drop a total of 50 feet, rushing into the creek.

For those with the energy, there is another series of waterfalls called Gunter Fork Cascades. The longest one drops 100 feet, making it one of the tallest waterfalls in the park. They're 8.2 difficult miles from the parking area and are reached by a wonderful route that runs mostly along this beautiful creek then just over 2 miles up Gunter Fork Trail. That, however, is a hard 16.4-mile round-trip, and you'll have to make a number of wet-stream crossings. You should get a trail map and specific directions if you want to see these falls.

**i** A self-guided, 1.5-mile loop trail will take you over the highest mountain in the Great Balsam Mountains, 6,410-foot Richland Balsam, and through a remnant of a spruce fir forest. Drive to the Haywood-Jackson County Overlook at milepost 431, just north of the highest point on the Blue Ridge Parkway. The trail begins at the upper end of the parking lot and is paved at its start.

## Jackson County

### HURRICANE FALLS AND GLASSY CREEK FALLS
#### Hwy. 107 and Norton Road (SR 1145)
Hurricane and Glassy Creek Falls are both on private property, but they can be viewed from the roadside on the same trip. To reach Hurricane Falls drive north out of Cashiers on Highway 107 for 1.8 miles and turn left on Norton Road (SR 1145). It's just more than 0.5 mile to a pull-off where you can see the waterfall, which has an average height of 40 feet that varies according to the height of Lake Thorpe, into which it flows.

For Glassy Creek Falls return to Highway 107 and continue north for 8.6 miles to a pull-off on the left (because of the sharp curve at this location, pass the pull-off, turn around farther up the road, and come back to park). The 100-foot curling falls is formed by the Little River Creek. The river in front of the falls is the West Fork of the Tuckasegee.

### SILVER RUN FALLS
#### Hwy. 107
Would you like a waterfall-fed pool to cool off in on a hot day? Then, from Cashiers drive south on Highway 107 for just more than 4 miles and park at a graveled pull-off on the left with a utility pole at its corner. Follow the short path over a fallen log that bridges the creek or wade the water to this picturesque 20-foot waterfall. Its lovely, sandy beach and pretty pool make it a relatively safe and popular swimming area.

## Macon County

### BIG LAUREL FALLS AND MOONEY FALLS
#### FR 67
Big Laurel Falls is a small but beautiful waterfall that plunges 30 feet in two stages into a tempting pool deep in the Southern Nantahala Wilderness Area. To get there take US 64 West out of Franklin for about 12 miles and turn left onto Old US 64. In slightly less than 2 miles, turn right on FR 67, which is only partly paved, and drive for just short of 7 miles to a marked parking area. Take the easy trail (it's less than a half-mile) to the falls, bearing to the right each time the trail forks. Mooney Falls, actually a series of falls, is just more than a half-mile farther up the road on FR 67. Park at the Mooney Falls sign and take the short trail for several different views of the falls. None of the cascades is more than 15 feet high, but the overall effect is exceedingly breathtaking.

### BRIDAL VEIL FALLS
#### Off US 64
Only a few dozen feet from US 64, 2.5 miles west of Highlands, you can see this 120-foot, ethereal

cascade right from your car. US 64 used to run right behind the falls, but there was a problem with ice on the highway in winter, so the highway was moved. You can still use an old piece of the original highway to detour behind the falls. For a more leisurely view or to take a photograph, there's a pull-off just beyond the falls.

## CULLASAJA FALLS
### US 64

The 250-foot Cullasaja Falls is one of the more majestic of the many cascades in the Cullasaja River Gorge, so it's unfortunate that US 64 is so busy, narrow, and dangerous at this point 8.8 miles west of Highlands, making more than a drive-by glimpse difficult. To get a good look, find a parking place in one of the narrow, frequently crowded, unmarked pull-offs on the highway's precipitous shoulder, keeping a careful eye on traffic when getting in and out of the car. Then be satisfied with a view and photo from the road. The primitive paths down to the base of the falls are much too dangerous to attempt.

## DRY FALLS
### US 64

Less than a mile from Bridal Veil Falls, Dry Falls drops 80 feet; 40 feet of that distance is free fall. The neat thing about this falls is that an easy, paved path leads down from the parking lot, taking you inside the recessed ledge behind the roaring and sometimes-drenching waters for a view from the other side. There is a $2 per vehicle fee.

## GLEN FALLS
### SR 1618

There are several beautiful falls and accompanying cascades here that drop 640 feet in only a half-mile. So, though the well-maintained trail to the 70-, 60-, and 15-foot waterfalls in the Glen Falls Scenic Area is less than a mile long, it is steep and tough to hike back up. But it's worth it! In addition there are marvelous views of the Blue Valley as well as great picnic spots along the route. To reach the area take Highway 106 just south of Highlands for less than 2 miles until you see the Glen Falls Scenic Area sign

on the left and take SR 1618 immediately on the right. From there it's a mile to the trail that leads from a parking area.

### Macon County: Slick Rock

Slick Rock is a granite rock outcrop on an eastward facing slope, the summit of which offers an impressive view of far-off mountains. From Highlands take Horse Cove Road to the end of the pavement, then take the right fork onto Bull Pen Road and drive about 1.5 miles. When you reach a sharp left curve, look for a pull-off and a steep, unmarked path on the right (if you pass a road that intersects Bull Pen on the right at a 45-degree angle, you've gone too far; turn around and go back). This timber sale road runs right beneath Slick Rock. The hike to the top is less than a quarter-mile, and it's a great place to watch a sunrise.

## UPPER AND LOWER SATULAH FALLS
### Off Hwy. 28

Upper Satulah Falls, which looks like a steep waterslide, is on private property, but you can see it easily from the road. From Highlands drive south on Highway 28 for 2.3 miles and look to your left at the foot of the vast rock face of 4,543-foot Satulah Mountain. Park at the overlook a short distance farther on the right side of the road. Continue on Highway 28 for just more than a mile to view the high, narrow Lower Satulah Falls (also known as Clear Creek Falls). It's across the valley from a wide pull-off that also overlooks the Piedmont, including the Blue Valley, Rabun Bald, and Scaly Mountain. This 100-foot, lower waterfall is best seen in the winter when the foliage is off the trees.

## Swain County
### JUNEYWHANK FALLS, TOMS BRANCH FALLS, AND INDIAN CREEK FALLS
#### Off Deep Creek Road

All three of these popular falls in the Great Smoky Mountains National Park can be found by going out Deep Creek Road just outside Bryson City. However, you'll have to jog around several different streets as you pass through town to find this road, so the simplest thing is to go to Bryson City and ask directions to Deep Creek Road. You'll travel 2.2 miles up this road before you enter the actual park. From that boundary it's a little more than a half-mile to the parking area at the end of the road. The quarter-mile trail to 80-foot Juneywhank Falls begins about 100 yards from the picnic area.

To get to another 80-foot-drop cascade, Toms Branch Falls, go past the gate and take the gravel road (part of the park's popular Deep Creek Trail) a quarter-mile to the falls on the right. A half-mile upstream is the well-used tubing launch site, so expect to see hordes of tubers floating by in the summer. Actually you can see the falls much better in the winter when the surrounding trees and bushes have lost their foliage.

Continuing on the Deep Creek Trail for less than a mile will bring you to Indian Creek Trail. The wide 25-foot waterfall known as Indian Creek Falls is just a few hundred yards down this path, where a side trail will take you to the base of the falls.

**i** Some of the waterfalls listed here are deep in the area's forests, so be sure to take food and drink along with you and always wear comfortable shoes with nonskid soles. Packing a towel, a bathing suit, and a change of clothing also isn't a bad idea, but be warned: The water in any mountain pool will be chilly, to say the least. Make sure, too, that the pool you choose to swim in is absolutely safe. Currents near waterfalls can be treacherous. And as we've noted numerous times, never, ever wade above a waterfall, where a slip can be fatal.

### MINGO FALLS
#### Off Big Cove Road

Mingo, on the Cherokee Indian Reservation, is one of the most fabulous falls in the whole Smoky Mountains area, though the landscape around it has been somewhat marred in the past few years by storm damage. To reach it take U.S. Highway 441 out of Cherokee, where it becomes Newfound Gap Road once it enters the Great Smoky Mountains National Park. Just short of a mile after the junction with the Blue Ridge Parkway, turn right at the Jobs Corps Center sign. The road will end after a half-mile at Big Cove Road. Turn left and drive 3.3 miles to the Mingo Cove Campground and park. The trail is only a quarter-mile long, but the first part of it is very steep.

# BLUE RIDGE PARKWAY

In 1935 the first mules and workmen began carving a ribbon of road that would span from Virginia through North Carolina and complete its journey in the Great Smoky Mountains in Tennessee. This scenic highway was born in the 1930s out of a need to provide work for people forced from their jobs by the Great Depression. The parkway was conceived as a link between the Shenandoah National Park in Virginia and the Great Smoky Mountains National Park in North Carolina and Tennessee. After the political wranglings ended and financing was ironed out, the project employed thousands of workers and engineers. The inspiration of a particularly gifted young landscape architect, Stanley Abbott, and northern Italian stonemasons contributed to the parkway's beauty and grace.

The designers' goals were as lofty as the parkway itself: to create for the traveler a sense of connection to the land and its history and to inspire future generations to preserve this connection. They succeeded. As you travel along the 250 miles of the parkway in North Carolina, you pass sights that fill your soul and summon you to be part of this beautiful place. Scores of overlooks, designed for their grand vistas, invite you to pull over and stop. More often than not, a hiking trail will tempt you up the hill where wildflowers with colorful names such as pink lady's slipper, skunk cabbage, and joe-pye weed grow in abundance from Apr through Oct. Several endangered species live on parkway lands, including wildflowers such as Gray's lily, Heller's blazing star, and small-whorled Pogonia and animal species such as bog turtles, flying squirrels, salamanders, and bats. More than 100 bird species can be seen during the spring migration season. Picnic tables scattered along the parkway make the slightest stopover a special occasion. Visitor centers and roadside historical markers bring to life the story of the mountains and regions, their people, and natural beauty.

When the parkway flows into North Carolina from Virginia at milepost 216.9, you find yourself in the rolling pasture land of Alleghany and Ashe Counties. Those cows grazing in the northern meadows, the pioneer cabins just off the road, and the lichen-covered split-rail fences are part of the parkway by design. These farms in the northern stretches of the parkway were welcomed, their owners encouraged to stay and work in harmony with the National Park Service to preserve the look of a simpler time. It's as if you turned down a country road with no particular destination in mind and found yourself in a tranquil yesteryear.

As you get closer to Watauga, Avery, and Mitchell Counties, the mountains grow taller, the mountaintops stretch higher, and the horizon spreads farther. (Elevations on the parkway range from 649 to 6,047 feet.) The section of the parkway known as the Linn Cove Viaduct, near Grandfather Mountain at milepost 304, is an engineering marvel. This section swings 1,243 feet around the curve of the rugged mountain. Borrowing construction techniques developed in Switzerland, the viaduct was designed and built "from the top down" to create the least impact on delicate Grandfather Mountain. The structure was built of 153 precast concrete sections, no two exactly alike, and was completed in the 1980s.

**i** A display depicting the building of the parkway is located at the Big Ivy Historical Park in Dillingham, North Carolina.

Milepost 355.4 marks the entrance to Mount Mitchell State Park, where the highest peak in the eastern United States rises up to 6,684 feet. The mountainside becomes more rugged, the terrain more imposing, and views even more panoramic. Misty blue mountains in the distance cradle the small towns in the valleys below.

The parkway changes again as it approaches Asheville and Buncombe County from the north. Many overlooks provide the opportunity to scan the communities down below. Asheville, the largest metropolitan area in the mountains, is a thriving small city with a unique mix of cosmopolitan and mountain flavors.

Heading south, panoramas widen into vistas that surely must extend to the edge of the world. Many of the parkway's 27 tunnels are in this section. Above Pisgah National Forest near Transylvania County stands the prominent peak of Mount Pisgah, milepost 408.6, at an elevation of 5,721 feet, taking its name from the Biblical mountain from which Moses first viewed the Promised Land.

Past Pisgah the road winds around more incredible peaks and spectacular sights, such as Looking Glass Rock, elevation 4,493 feet. This massive sculpted mountain of rock sits majestically in the valley near the Pink Beds (pink with flowers in May) of Pisgah National Forest below. As the parkway leads south, the names of the land take on a wilder, more mythical flavor: Graveyard Fields, Devil's Courthouse, Shining Rock, Big Witch. Many were derived from Indian legend and pioneer folklore. The road climbs to its highest point at Richland Balsam, elevation 6,047 feet, milepost 431, before beginning its descent to the terminus at milepost 469.1, near the entrance to the reservation of the Eastern Band of the Cherokee Nation and the gateway to Great Smoky Mountains National Park.

There are so many places to stop, by whim or design, it's no wonder that the parkway, with 25 million visitors annually, is the most visited of all the 367 territories in the National Park System. Visitor centers are equipped with amenities to make your trip easier, and you'll find accommodations, rustic inns, and restaurants off many parkway exits. Most are within easy driving distance from the parkway. Two outstanding choices right on the parkway are Bluffs Lodge, (336) 372-4499, at milepost 241, and the Pisgah Inn, (828) 235-8228, at milepost 408.6. Both are highlighted in our Hotels and Motels chapter. Just across the parkway from Bluffs Lodge is the Bluffs Lodge Coffee Shop (336-372-4744), where you can sip coffee and soak in the incredibly breathtaking vistas. (See our Restaurants chapter for more eateries in the area.)

Plan on taking some extra time if you're traveling the parkway—this is far removed from interstate driving. The speed limit on the parkway is always 45 mph, though between the sharp mountain twists and turns and the plodding recreational vehicles, you'll often find yourself driving much slower than that. Just relax and enjoy the scenery of one of the most beautiful drives in the country. As a courtesy of the road use the pull-off areas along the drive so that you can enjoy driving at your own pace without holding up others. You'll be glad you did.

**i** If you love the Parkway and would like to spend more time there than just a drive, consider volunteering with the Friends of the Blue Ridge Parkway's Volunteer in Parks Program (see www.blueridgefriends.org). You may find yourself clearing one of the beautiful trails or doing other beautifying, healthy work in your spare time.

## STOPS ALONG THE WAY

In the pages that follow, we've described some of our favorite stops along the Blue Ridge Parkway in North Carolina, beginning at the state line at milepost 216.9 in Alleghany County and traveling south to the parkway's southern terminus at milepost 469.1 at the Oconaluftee Visitor Center. Mileposts are markers that stretch the length of the parkway, each posted a mile apart. Overlooks and other sites of merit are also noted by milepost numbers. This list is by no means exhaustive—there are literally hundreds of overlooks and other stops along the parkway, and all have merit. But these are some of our favorites.

## Friends of the Blue Ridge Parkway

Friends of the Blue Ridge Parkway is a nonprofit organization that started in 1989. The group's mission is to preserve and protect this national treasure through a series of initiatives focusing on the historical heritage of the parkway and the region and by developing a wider environmental awareness and public education on the issues. The organization works to preserve historic sites and structures along the parkway and lobbies Congress for the protection of scenic vistas and natural habitats.

Contact the office by calling (828) 687-8722 or (800) 228-7275, accessing www.blueridgefriends.org, or writing Friends of the Blue Ridge Parkway, 2301 Hendersonville Rd., Arden 28776.

## CUMBERLAND KNOB
### Mile 217.5
Cumberland Knob, elevation 2,885 feet, was the first recreational area completed on the Blue Ridge Parkway back in 1937. The Civilian Conservation Corps, a government-authorized jobs program during the Great Depression, built the structures at this site and many like it along the parkway and in surrounding areas. On the 1,000 acres at Cumberland Knob, you can picnic, hike, listen to lectures by rangers, or simply marvel at the view. A pleasant 20-minute loop trail starts at the visitor center and passes by Cumberland Knob. For the hardier hiker try the two-hour loop trail from the center of the knob into Gulley Creek

Gorge. Drinking water, restrooms, a book shop, and a public telephone are also available.

## LITTLE GLADE MILL POND
### Mile 230.1
This scenic stop overlooks a delightful pond near an old turbine-type mill. The water is smooth as glass, and a picnic area makes this a restful stop.

## AIR BELLOWS GAP
### Mile 237.1
Air Bellows Gap, elevation 3,729 feet, is designated as the Crest of the Blue Ridge. The spectacular vista includes a 180-degree view into the valley below, which is chock-full of Christmas trees. The rich green of the tree farms stands out in a patchwork of patterns. Hawks soar on the updrafts of this windy gap, and rich autumn colors turn this into a leaf looker's paradise!

## DOUGHTON PARK
### Miles 234.8 to 238.6
This 6,000-acre park has picnic areas (milepost 241), a campground (milepost 239), trailer sites, comfort stations, and drinking water. The park has 30 miles of trails over bluegrass bluffs (see our Autumn in the Mountains Close-up).

## BRINEGAR CABIN
### Mile 238.5
The Brinegar Cabin, an authentic mountain homestead covered in hand-hewn shake shingles, stands as testament to the harsh, isolated, self-sufficient life of mountaineers that lasted even into the 20th century. This tiny cabin was home to Martin (1856–1925) and Caroline (1863–1943) Brinegar. The toll that mountain life takes can be seen in a simple photo portrait of Caroline at her mother's loom inside the cabin. The springhouse is still down a steep rocky path, and the garden patch that once yielded the necessities of life is now overgrown and barely discernible. The couple is buried nearby. (Admission to the cabin is free.)

The Cedar Ridge Trail (4.3 miles) and the Bluff Mountain Trail (7.5 miles) take off from points that begin at the end of the parking area.

## WILDCAT ROCKS
### Mile 241.1
This is the Caudill family homestead, where visitors can get a glimpse into the rugged mountain life.

## NORTHWEST TRADING POST
### Mile 259
### (336) 982-2543
Near Glendale Springs, this delightfully rustic craft shop of knotty pine with a genuine rock fireplace sells all kinds of items made by North Carolina residents in 11 neighboring counties. Home-baked goodies, handmade baskets, bowls, old-time wooden toys, quilts, and jewelry made from antique buttons are just some of the wares offered by this nonprofit group that donates all profits to local charities. The trading post is open from Apr 15 to Oct 31, 9 a.m. to 5:30 p.m. Restrooms (wheelchair accessible) are also available.

i During that intense tourist trek in Oct, Blue Ridge Parkway rangers suggest that you can get maximum enjoyment and avoid the crowds by making your trip here Mon through Fri, when traffic is less heavy. The weekends in Oct can quickly become a bumper-to-bumper snail's pace of leaf lookers, especially on Sunday afternoons.

## BOONE'S TRACE
### Mile 285.1
Daniel Boone passed by this site on his trek westward. An information marker provides details about his blaze to the West.

## MOSES H. CONE MEMORIAL AND VISITORS CENTER
### Mile 293
### (828) 295-3782
Near the town of Blowing Rock, this former 3,600-acre estate of textile giant Moses Cone was donated to the National Park Service in the 1950s. Today the rambling white manor house is home to a craft shop that displays the work of the Southern Highland Craft Guild. The mansion faces a picturesque lake, and the grounds are threaded with miles of hiking trails and include two trout ponds (check at the center for fishing information).

## JULIAN PRICE MEMORIAL PARK
### Mile 295
### (828) 963-5911
This popular park of 4,344 acres includes a lake, campground, hiking trails, picnic area, and limited boating. There's an easy 2.5-mile loop trail around the lakeside.

## LINN COVE VIADUCT
### Mile 304
Built around environmentally fragile Grandfather Mountain, this incredible bridge is a marvel of engineering and gives you the sense of flying over the valley below—breathtaking! There's a visitor center and trails underneath the viaduct. Walking is not allowed on the bridge.

## LINVILLE FALLS AND GORGE
### Mile 316.5
An easy-to-moderate lower trail leads to the falls. A spectacular example of nature's power, these waterfalls were carved from massive quartzite rock millions of years ago. An upper trail with a steeper incline gives you quite a different view (see our Waterfalls chapter).

## CHESTOA VIEW
### Mile 320.7
*Chestoa* is derived from the Cherokee word for *rabbit*. From this spot you can enjoy a scenic view of granite-faced Table Rock.

## MUSEUM OF NORTH CAROLINA MINERALS
### Mile 331
### (828) 765-9483
Informative geology exhibits, rock and mineral displays, parkway information, a book shop, gifts,

and restrooms make the museum a pleasant diversion for children and rock hounds of all ages (see our chapter on Rockhounding).

ℹ️ The intensity of the color season is determined by a number of weather variables. The more vivid leaf color is preceded by long dry spells in summer and cool, moist days in fall. When this happens, and the sunlight diminishes, the trees are "tricked" into quicker cessation of the process of photosynthesis. No sugar is produced to keep the lush green of the chlorophyll, so the underlying pigments emerge.

## CRABTREE MEADOWS COFFEE SHOP
### Mile 339.5
### (828) 675-4236

You can get a good lunch here, as well as parkway guidebooks, maps, and the *Asheville Citizen-Times* newspaper. Facilities also include restrooms, a service station, and a craft shop near Little Switzerland, a community on the edge of the mountain, that are open May 1 through Nov 1. The coffee shop is open from 10 a.m. to 6 p.m.; the craft shop until 7:30 p.m.

## CRABTREE MEADOWS RECREATION CENTER
### Miles 339.5 to 340.3 (ranger kiosk)
### (828) 675-5444

This 250-acre site includes a picnic area, numerous hiking trails, and a campground. Primitive camping is available for tent and RV campers for approximately $10 per night for two adults; add about $2 for each additional adult. Children 18 and younger stay free. Comfort stations are also located here. The 40-minute trek to Crabtree Falls rewards you with a beautiful 125-foot waterfall (see our Waterfalls chapter). Look for wildflowers in spring.

## MOUNT MITCHELL STATE PARK
### Mile 355.4
### (828) 675-4611

Take Highway 128 to the summit of Mount Mitchell, the highest peak in the eastern United States. Hiking trails, a memorial to Elisha Mitchell (for whom the peak is named), a small natural history museum, comfort stations, a snack shop, and a picnic area make this a pleasant stop. In June 2001 a new museum opened at Mitchell State Park. This is an amazing facility that is user-friendly. A life-size wood carving of Big Tom Wilson, the mountaineer whose legend is connected with the mountain, stands on his front porch—a facade within the museum—and greets the visitor with a touch of a button. His great-great-great grandson, David Boone, world-class carver, was commissioned for this sculpture. Pictorials and stuffed animals of the mountains are showcased. The highest peaks in the Appalachia chain are rendered in a stair-step manner for easy comparison. Interactive displays permit the viewer to cause a miniature movement of the earth to form a mountain. The entire museum is of interest to children and adults.

Unfortunately you can see the dramatic evidence of acid rain on Mitchell's slopes from several vantage points. On a brighter note keep your eyes peeled for the deer that dart through these woods. Bring a jacket because the weather is windy and cool up here, even in summer.

The massive stone-and-frame restaurant in the park is about two-thirds of the way up Highway 128 leading to the summit, which makes it the highest restaurant in the eastern United States. Open from May 1 through Oct 31, the restaurant serves lunch and dinner daily and breakfast on weekends and holidays. It closes one hour prior to park closing, which varies seasonally. Call (828) 675-9545 for more information on the restaurant.

**Close-up**

## Autumn in the Mountains

Sometimes gradually, sometimes overnight, the verdant peaks and valleys do a slow burlesque, teasing with a hint of color here, a little more there, each stage more exciting until the grandest week of all when the mix of red and gold, green and yellow present their breathtaking finale. Somehow Mother Nature can wear colors you'd never put together—chartreuse and red, orange and green—and still look stunning. And even when the inevitable happens and the autumn color leaves us, usually no later than mid-Nov, something special is left behind. Like colorful wrapping paper torn away, the fallen foliage exposes a precious gift—the mountains themselves. Breathtaking vistas, obscured much of the year by the lush vegetation that flourishes in our diverse ecosystem, are revealed until spring works its way north again.

The kaleidoscope of colored trees is more than a treat to the eye. It gives those of us who have forgotten our high school botany a break. We can easily identify hickories and poplars glowing their bright yellow against a Carolina-blue sky, or mountain favorites such as dogwood, sourwood, black gum, and maple turning deep red, sassafras a vivid orange. The various oaks turn russet and maroon, while some trees can't decide which color to turn, offering a rainbow mix on the same tree.

It seems no one wants to stay indoors this time of year. In celebration of the fine weather and natural beauty, festivals and craft fairs abound. Harvest dances, apple cider pressings, mountain music and dances, special tours, and steam-driven trains forging through the red and gold are scheduled throughout the season.

A special breed of wildflowers blooms late in the year. Joe-pye weed nods its foot-wide head high above the rest. Purple-blooming blazing star and ironweed, golden sneezeweed, and lilac aster bloom throughout the fall.

As you travel down the highways and byways, you'll pass fanciful Mr. and Mrs. Scarecrows, dressed in flannel shirts and jeans, hay for their bodies and jack-o'-lanterns for their heads. They sit in welcome at roadside stands selling pumpkins, gourds, honey, sorghum, and cider. Take home colorful gourds and doll-size Indian corn for Thanksgiving table decorations. Many stands sell jams and relishes, dried apples and apple butter, pumpkin bread, and pies in anticipation of the coming holidays.

Every year thousands upon thousands of nature's admirers return to North Carolina's mountains to drink in the beauty. Touring the Blue Ridge Parkway is the most favored way of taking in this long sweep of fall color. From Boone and Blowing Rock to Asheville and Cherokee, each turn of the road offers a new horizon, a new definition of beautiful. The ever-popular Mount Mitchell State Park area, just off the Blue Ridge Parkway, as well as the communities of Spruce Pine, Linville Falls, and Little Switzerland and the North Carolina Minerals Museum, are other popular leaf-looking sites along the parkway.

**CRAGGY GARDENS VISITORS CENTER**
**Mile 364.4**

This popular stop offers nature exhibits, comfort stations, and parkway and national forest information. The center is open from May through Oct. At the rear of the visitor center, a narrative directs your view to the village of Dillingham, which is at the foot of Craggy. It states that the flora from that village at 2,000 feet up to the mountaintop of Craggy contains all the varieties found from Georgia to Maine. (See our Autumn in the Mountains Close-up.)

**BULL CREEK VALLEY OVERLOOK**
**Mile 373.8**

This scenic stop-off point overlooks what was once the home of the great bull buffalo.

The fall foliage season generally reaches its peak in mid-Oct, but the degree and intensity of color and peak for each area are determined by elevation. At 6,684 feet, Mount Mitchell, the highest peak in the eastern United States, enjoys the distinction of having the early jump on fall leaf color. The peaks of the High Country of the Boone area are next, about mid-Oct. And the Asheville area and southern stretches near Cherokee along the parkway peak around the third and fourth weeks in Oct. But if you choose the Blue Ridge Parkway as your vantage point for viewing fall color, you can pick any time in Oct. From parkway overlooks high above, you can scan the valleys below to see autumn's transformation at many different elevations.

Alternative routes include the major connecting highways to the parkway or maybe a less-traveled two-laner just outside the major towns and cities. The state of North Carolina publishes a 90-page guide, *North Carolina Scenic Byways*, featuring 11 mountain roads (31 statewide) that give visitors and residents a chance to experience the diverse beauty and culture of the Tar Heel State. Routes are clearly marked with signs stating NC SCENIC BYWAY surrounded by green-mountain and blue-sea motifs. For more information contact the North Carolina Department of Transportation, P.O. Box 25201, Raleigh 27611; (919) 733-2520.

U.S. Highway 194 is a good example of a scenic byway. This winding back road passes near Valle Crucis on its way to Boone, then on to picturesque hilltop ridges near Todd in rural Ashe County. Another gorgeous option is U.S. Highway 321 from Boone to the rocky hills of west Watauga County and the charming country crossroad communities of Sugar Grove and Vilas on the way to the Tennessee state line. Schulls Mill Road off Highway 105 at Foscoe, outside Boone, is a locally used shortcut to Blowing Rock along a beautiful but very winding two-lane road. Cruising along U.S. Highway 221 from Boone through Linville and the Christmas tree country of Linville Falls before heading down the mountain to the beautiful fields of the North Cove Valley area near Marion is a lovely way to spend an Oct afternoon.

Farther south take the Barnardsville exit off U.S. Highways 19/23 North in Asheville for another quiet back road lined with rural farms and old homesteads, or you could take Highway 151 up to the parkway from the pleasant little farm community of Hominy Valley, west of Asheville. U.S. Highway 276 from the parkway down to Brevard is a very popular road in leaf season. It winds down past tumbling creeks and waterways, waterfalls and picnic areas, and the well-known Cradle of Forestry area. The scenic winding roads around Highlands and Cashiers have always been noted for their breathtaking fall beauty. And the exquisite forests and country roads around Fontana Lake and Robbinsville are just being discovered by visitors to the North Carolina mountains.

Some veteran leaf lookers book as much as a year in advance for their favorite bed-and-breakfast inns or family hotels. If you're a spontaneous traveler and miss out on those hoped-for accommodations, check with local chambers of commerce for possible alternative accommodations that spring up during this busy tourism month. (The numbers for local chambers are listed in our Area Overview chapter.)

## FOLK ART CENTER
**Mile 382**
**(828) 298-7928**

Home of the renowned Southern Highland Craft Guild, this 30,000-square-foot contemporary structure of rock, timber, and glass is an attractive complement to the natural woodland surroundings.

Visit Allanstand Craft Shop, America's oldest craft shop, on the main level for exquisitely crafted handblown glassware, functional pottery, handmade toys, handcrafted jewelry, and handwoven coverlets and rugs. The Blue Ridge Parkway also maintains a bookstore and staffs an information center here. Up the sweeping ramp, the second-floor gallery houses the guild's permanent collection as well as changing exhibits by some of its 700-plus members. A library of handcraft and its history is also on the upper level. Craft demonstrations, interpretive talks, and special events keep the Folk Art Center a vital and continuously interesting place for area visitors.

The center is open daily 9 a.m. to 6 p.m. Apr through Dec and 9 a.m. to 5 p.m. Jan through Mar. It's closed for Thanksgiving, Christmas, and New Year's Day. The bustling city of Asheville is just off the next exit (see our Mountain Crafts, Attractions, and Annual Festivals and Events chapters).

**i** Although the Blue Ridge Parkway was designed for motor travel, bicyclists can enjoy the drive as well. Have reflectors and wear high visibility clothing and helmets, and avoid the parkway during fog and periods of low visibility. Also, bring plenty of water and energy bars for those stringent uphill climbs.

## BLUE RIDGE PARKWAY VISITOR CENTER
### Mile 384.7
The Park Service and the Blue Ridge National Heritage Area opened the Blue Ridge Parkway Visitor Center at the end of 2007. The center's exhibits highlight the natural and cultural diversity, economic traditions, and recreational opportunities found in western North Carolina and along the Blue Ridge Parkway. The center also houses a 70-seat theater for a 24-minute film about the famous drive, an information desk, and book sales area.

## FRENCH BROAD RIVER OVERLOOK
### Mile 393.8
One of the few north-flowing rivers in the United States, the French Broad River figures prominently in the history and development of the Asheville/Buncombe County area and all of Western North Carolina. This overlook at milepost 393.8 is an especially good place to get a view of the river. It is from here that you can exit just a few feet to the North Carolina Arboretum. More than a thousand world-class botanists gathered here for their first international conference in the year 2000.

**i** Definitely stop at the parkway information stations. They maintain an excellent supply of books and newspapers devoted to hiking, camping, waterfalls, and nature along the parkway. The staffers are always well informed on a plethora of parkway information and lore.

## HOMINY VALLEY OVERLOOK
### Mile 404.2
This pull-off from the parkway is a scenic view of the pastoral mountain valley farm community west of Asheville.

## MOUNT PISGAH
### Mile 408.6
At 5,721 feet Mount Pisgah is visible for miles around, holding court over the vast land once owned by George Vanderbilt that is now part of Pisgah National Forest. The summit can be reached by a moderate-to-strenuous winding trail from the parking area below. The junction of US 276 and the Blue Ridge Parkway is just south of Mount Pisgah. Traveling down this winding and scenic road to Brevard in Transylvania County, you'll pass the Cradle of Forestry, the site of the first forestry school in America, once a part of the Biltmore Estate. Following US 276 toward Waynesville, you'll come to Cold Mountain, the site and title of Charles Frazier's award-winning book. The parking area just past this road intersection is Wagon Road Gap. It is here that the monarch butterflies pass in Sept as they migrate to South America. They return in the spring. (See the Close-up Finding Cold Mountain in the Recreation chapter.)

## LOOKING GLASS ROCK
### Mile 417
This spectacularly sculpted monolith in the valley below is one of the largest masses of granite in the eastern United States. Its name comes from the shimmering effects of sunlight on its surface when wet. Elevation is 4,493 feet. Though you can't get to Looking Glass from this stop, the view is fantastic. (A trail that leads to the top is off the road to the Pisgah Fish Hatchery, off US 276, just past Looking Glass Rock.)

### GRAVEYARD FIELDS
**Mile 418.8**

These flats were once overgrown with mounds of moss that inspired the name Graveyard Fields, but a fire destroyed the moss mounds in 1925. (See our Autumn in the Mountains Close-up.)

### DEVIL'S COURTHOUSE
**Mile 422.4**

The top of this rocky, rugged cliff can be reached by a steeply ascending, well-worn trail from a parking area below. Legend has it there is a cave inside the mountain where the devil still holds court. Due to the nesting of the peregrine falcon, the rock face is closed to climbers.

### HAYWOOD/JACKSON OVERLOOK
**Mile 431.0**

This self-guided loop trail climbs with moderate difficulty 1.5 miles to the summit of Richland Balsam.

### WATERROCK KNOB
**Mile 451**

Adjoining this parking area is a short trail that leads to an incredible four-state view (North Carolina, Tennessee, South Carolina, and Georgia) with a panorama of the Great Smoky Mountains

just ahead. Information and a comfort station are available here.

### PLOTT'S BALSAM RANGE OVERLOOK
**Mile 457.9**

Yet another beautiful overlook, here you'll see the mountain range that's named for the German immigrant who settled here in the early 1800s. The Plott hound, a legendary dog used for bear hunting, and the state dog of North Carolina, was brought from Hannover, Germany, by these settlers.

### BIG WITCH OVERLOOK
**Mile 461.6**

The interesting name honors one of the last of the great Cherokee medicine men. An exhibit tells of the early Cherokee eagle killers.

### OCONALUFTEE VISITOR CENTER
**Mile 469.1**
**(828) 497-1900**

This milepost marks the terminus of the Blue Ridge Parkway, or its starting point if you are traveling north. The popular visitor center, a half-mile north on U.S. Highway 441, hosts several events during summer, including Women's Day and the Mountain Life Festival, which celebrate the heri-

# Close-up

## Origins of the Southern Highland Craft Guild

Along the Blue Ridge Parkway and throughout Appalachia you'll find signs of the Southern Highland Craft Guild. This group was one of the earliest of its type in the country. It all began at Penland School of Crafts in North Carolina in 1928, when craftsmen from the mountains of North Carolina, Tennessee, and Kentucky met in the weaving cabin on the Penland campus to discuss ways of marketing their work. The Penland Weavers led the dialog and were soon joined by Allanstand Cottage Industries of Asheville, Berea College Churchill Weavers from Kentucky, Brasstown Handicraft Association from North Carolina, Cedar Creek Community Center from Tennessee, Crossnore School of North Carolina, and the Spinning Wheel of Asheville. As the organization took form, Cherokee crafters also joined.

Today the exquisite craft work is produced by 930 members from Alabama, Georgia, Kentucky, Maryland, North Carolina, South Carolina, Tennessee, Virginia, and West Virginia. Items produced by members of the guild range from simple Geehaw whimmy diddles to paintings, sculptures, carvings, jewelry, quilts, fiber craft, and more.

tage of these mountains. Park information and restrooms are available. The center is open daily year-round (except major holidays). Hours vary with the season.

Do be sure to visit Mountain Farm Museum, an open-air museum featuring historic farm buildings brought here from the surrounding area. The old cabin belonged to the John Davis family and was built in 1901. It is a good place for children to see how things used to be. Watch out for the chickens, ducks, and other farm animals strutting around the barns filled with antique farm implements. It feels as though the Davises have just gone down the road for a bit and asked you to set a spell and make yourself at home 'til they return.

Just ahead lies the Cherokee Indian Reservation and the Great Smoky Mountains National Park. For park information call (423) 436-1200.

# CAMPING

Camping is allowed along the Blue Ridge Parkway from May 1 through Oct 31. Designated camping sites require a daily fee of approximately $10 (subject to change) for adults, $5 for Golden Age Passport holders, free for youths younger than 18. Golden Age Passports (62 or older) and Golden Access Passports (visually handicapped or permanently disabled) can be obtained at any visitor center or campground along the parkway. Each of these campgrounds has only primitive facilities, including a fireplace and table. Other amenities may include access to public telephones, water, picnic sites, gasoline, camping supplies, and sanitary dumping stations. There are no electrical hookups. If you are a hardy soul, you can camp in winter, weather permitting. One of the campgrounds is open year-round, at the park's discretion. (The open campground rotates from year to year, so call to find out which one will be open this year.) No fee is required in the winter, but facilities are limited, so you'll need to call in advance. For general parkway and campground information, call (828) 298-0398.

Campground regulations are posted at campsites; additional copies are available at park-

way visitor centers. In case of emergencies, call (800) PARKWATCH. (See our Recreation chapter for additional campground listings.)

ℹ️ In summer views from the parkway can be obscured by haze—partly natural and partly pollution. At those times it's often best to visit the parkway in the morning, before the day heats up and when the air is cleaner. This time of day provides the added beauty of ground fog curling up out of the valleys.

## Campgrounds

None of the campgrounds along the Blue Ridge takes reservations. All are filled on a first-come, first-served basis. Again, the cost is approximately $10 per adult, $5 for Golden Age Passport holders, youths younger than 18 free.

### DOUGHTON PARK
**Mile 239.0**

One hundred and ten tent sites, including tent pads, picnic tables, grills, and lantern posts, are scattered in wooded areas and around a grassy hillside. A smaller area with 25 RV sites lies across the road, though none of the sites have hookups. Restrooms and water spigots are available at this park but no showers. This is camping as it was meant to be! The park itself covers approximately 6,000 acres in Alleghany and Wilkes Counties, and is the largest park on the parkway. It was named after Robert Lee Doughton, a U.S. representative who served from 1911 to 1953 and who was an advocate for the construction of the parkway.

### JULIAN PRICE
**Mile 297.0**
**(828) 963-5911**

This campground sprawls across both sides of the parkway near Price Lake. One hundred and twenty-nine tent sites lie fairly close together, divided by blossoming rhododendron bushes. Sixty-eight RV sites are also available, though with no plug-ins. Tent pads, picnic tables, grills, and spigots provide adequate comforts. There are restrooms but no showers, and firewood may be purchased nearby. The park is marked by mild terrain, covered by a dense hardwood forest. Poplars, chestnut trees, and maples make a pleasant canopy for hikers and campers. Canoes may be rented at the lake, and hiking trails nearby lead to two smaller lakes and creeks.

## LINVILLE FALLS
### Mile 316.3
### (828) 765-7818

There are 55 tent sites and 20 RV sites available in the campground of this 440-acre wooded park. Tent site 15 is the most secluded. The surrounding forest seems almost primordial with moss-covered trees and waterfalls plunging through the granite walls of Linville Gorge. Fishing in the nearby Linville River is allowed, and a visitor center and bookstore provide campers with plenty of area information.

## CRABTREE MEADOWS
### Mile 339.5
### (828) 675-5444

The 71 tent sites and 22 RV sites of Crabtree Meadows lie close to large grassy clearings. The lawn of wildflowers runs up to the forest edge, with mountains visible in the distance. The campground is rarely full and offers the requisite picnic tables, grills, and tent pads but no showers. Water fountains and hand water pumps are centrally located. It is a quiet, peaceful area, awash with rhododendrons and hardwood trees. This is a good base camp for hiking in the Pisgah National Forest; trails lead to scenic falls on Crabtree Creek. Crabtree Falls Trail, a strenuous 2.5-mile loop, begins near the campground entrance. A camp store, gas station, and restaurant/gift shop are also nearby.

## MOUNT PISGAH
### Mile 408.6
### (828) 235-9109

The entrance to Mount Pisgah Campground with its 70 tent sites and 70 RV sites lies directly across from Pisgah Inn on the parkway. The small sites, close together, are arranged in three landscaped loops. A dense forest adds privacy. There are no showers, but central hand water pumps and individual picnic tables, grills, and lantern posts are provided. Maps of the area, including hiking trails, are available at the camp. A picnic area lies in a meadow bordered by rhododendron.

**i** The Weather Channel (www.weather .com) provides an extensive "Fall Foliage Forecast," helpful in planning your trip on the parkway.

# HIKING

Towering trees, awe-inspiring vistas, gurgling mountain streams, colorful birds on the wing, flaming and delicate wildflowers, and the comfort of a well-trod path mark hiking trails on the parkway. This is all free for the taking when you leave the car behind and take advantage of the thousands of miles of trails winding in and around the parkway. Hiking is an easy, inexpensive way to enjoy the outdoors: You don't need much gear, and the rewards are priceless. Just follow basic hiking rules to keep it safe and fun (for additional hiking possibilities see our Recreation chapter).

## Northern Mountains
### CUMBERLAND KNOB

The relatively easy trails of Cumberland Knob (mi. 217.5) allow you to walk where the Blue Ridge Parkway began back in 1935. Cumberland Knob Trail, an easy, paved 0.5-mile walk, starts at the visitor center, swings through a picnic area, and continues up to the Cumberland Knob overlook shelter. This is a good leg-stretching trail, especially if you've been riding the parkway for a while without a stop. It's a good one for kids, too. Gully Creek Trail here is a more strenuous two-hour hike along a mountain stream. Bring your wildflower field guides—these mountain springs give life to some amazing plants.

### TANAWA TRAIL

This 13.5-mile course, which runs more or less parallel to the Blue Ridge Parkway and Grandfather Mountain from Beacon Heights (mi. 305.5) to Julian Price Park (mi. 297.1), deserves special mention. The trail offers a great deal of variety and plenty of access points along the parkway as it winds along the ridge. One particularly popular section, noted for its breathtaking views, is the access just below the Linn Cove Viaduct (mi. 304.4). The Linn Cove information station and access spot are south of the viaduct. The trail passes directly under this bridgelike span and rises steeply up stone steps, then past a massive wall of rock. Next the trail levels and leads into a shady stand of birch and beech trees, then traverses Wilson Creek to a clearing scattered with so many flat rocks that the trail seems more like a flagstone path. The sharp rise to Rough Ridge is followed by the surprise of a 200-foot-long boardwalk. From this point the view of the Piedmont below, which encompasses Linn Cove Viaduct, Table Mountain, and Hawks Bill, is breathtaking.

## Emergency Contacts

The Blue Ridge Parkway emergency number is (800) 727-5928 (PARK-WATCH). For general parkway information call (828) 298-0398, which is a recorded message that updates parkway travelers on road and weather information, park facility closings, and general visitor services, such as campgrounds and lodging.

### CRAGGY DOME TRAIL
The parking area just through the tunnel to the north of the visitor center (mi. 364.4) is the begin-

ning of the trail leading to Craggy Dome. This well-marked path winds through beautiful rhododendron thickets and ascends to the breathtaking summit of Craggy Dome, a 360-degree sight to behold. The trail isn't strenuous, but it does have a continuously rising grade, so allow yourself plenty of time. Besides, seeing the unique wildflowers, velvety mosses, and gnarled, lichen-covered trunks of the rhododendron is worth the extra time. Look for the colorless white stalks of the Indian pipes under cover of the rhododendron.

## Central and Southern Mountains
### GRAVEYARD FIELDS
Take the hiking trails to Upper and Lower Falls (see our Waterfalls chapter), just off the parking area at milepost 418.8. This is a popular area for backpack camping and blueberry picking (which accounts for some of the many side trails) and includes Shining Rock Wilderness, just over the ridge to the southeast.

> **i** Many deli-style shops in our mountain towns will create a splendid picnic basket for taking on the parkway.

### PISGAH NATIONAL FOREST
Pisgah National Forest is a hiker's delight with its varying terrain: the steep slopes of Mount Pisgah, granite monoliths such as Looking Glass Rock, and the level flats of the Pink Beds. There are also a number of relatively easy roadside jaunts along US 276 to Brevard from the parkway junction south of Mount Pisgah. This highway cuts a twisting path down the mountain along a creek bed leading to Looking Glass Falls. Many smaller trail spurs shoot off from the overlooks, and parking turnouts are always worth a look for different views and angles of the falls.

# ROCKHOUNDING

We've all heard of fantasy cities with streets paved with gold and the Emerald City of Oz, but what about real highways paved with rubies? That's occasionally the case in Western North Carolina, where, if you look closely enough, you can see ruby-flecked gravel along the roadsides. That should give some idea of the copious amounts of gemstones in many sections of these mountains.

Important gems you might find are beryl (aquamarine, blue, golden, and green), corundum (bronze sapphire, pink, ruby, and sapphire), feldspar (moonstone), garnet (general, almandite, and rhodolite), olivine, opal, quartz (agate, amethyst, chrysoprase, jasper, and others), spinel, tourmaline, turquoise, and zircon. Rock hounds collect at least 37 other minerals, some of which can occasionally be classified as gem quality. In the late 1800s even a few diamonds supposedly turned up, but we know of none that have been found for more than 100 years.

It's rather ironic that in 1540 Hernando de Soto visited the Cherokee village of Nikwasi (now known as Franklin, the county seat of Macon County) in search of gold, never realizing he was passing through an area awash in precious and semiprecious stones. Admittedly most of the gems and semiprecious stones found in the mountains have no great commercial value, but many are attractive enough to be custom set and taken home as special souvenirs of an exciting and rewarding afternoon of sluicing through buckets of rock and dirt.

Gem mining can be wet and messy, so make sure you approach this exciting search in old clothes. Because you'll be standing at the flumes for a considerable length of time, a comfortable pair of shoes is a must. So is sunscreen. Although many mines offer some shade in the form of shelters, tents, or big, beach-type umbrellas, the sun reflecting off the water can give you an unexpected burn.

## GEM MINES

Although the heaviest concentration of gem mines by far is in the jewel-rich Cowee Valley of Macon County, there are other places scattered throughout the mountains where you can try your luck at finding a jewel or two.

The following list includes several gem-mining operations that are open to the public.

### Northern Mountains
#### Mitchell County
**BLUE RIDGE GEMSTONE MINE & CAMPGROUND**
626 McKinny Mine Rd., Little Switzerland
(828) 765-5264
Established in 1984, this family-owned and -operated mine maintains a 320-foot flume line. It is

enclosed and heated in the spring and fall, so you can comfortably sift through buckets of dirt any time, May through Dec. It is open seven days a week. Inspect the rock and gift shop, and bring a lunch for the picnic area overlooking the mountains. Or, if you would like to camp, full hookups, water, and electricity are provided. For a small fee Blue Ridge Gemstone will cut, grind, and polish the stones you find. You can also have them set into handcrafted jewelry. This mine is closed Dec through Apr.

**EMERALD VILLAGE**
McKinney Mine and Crabtree Creek Roads
Little Switzerland
(828) 765-6463
www.emeraldvillage.com

This mining attraction just 2.5 miles off the Blue Ridge Parkway in Mitchell County not only provides a guaranteed gem find at the Gemstone Mine but also has a mining museum underground in a genuine mine. The unusual antique displays are worth a look. A gift shop is filled with lapidary supplies and souvenirs, and attendants in the shop will answer your gemstone questions. This was the site of the Bon Ami Mine, developed by a French company that produced a soap product used in home cleaning.

**i** Some Western North Carolina colleges and universities have regular and continuing education classes that will help you identify and prospect for gems and other minerals. Often these classes include field trips.

## GEM MOUNTAIN
137 Hwy. 226 South, Spruce Pine
(828) 765-6130
www.gemmountain.com

Open seven days a week from 9 a.m. to 5 p.m. Mar through Dec, and 9 a.m. to 7 p.m. June through Aug, this gemstone mine maintains modern gem-washing facilities and covered flumes. A picnic area by a nearby stream completes the outdoor hounding experience, or you can rest easy and dine in the Gem Mountain restaurant. There are ice-cream cones for the kids, and a gift and jewelry shop—fun for the adults in the group. Gem Mountain will cater birthday parties or special events celebrations and offers discounts on mining and lunches for these catered affairs. Call for details.

## RIO DOCE GEM MINE
14622 Hwy. 226, Little Switzerland
(828) 765-2099
www.riodoce.com

Open mid-Apr (or May 1, depending on the weather) to Halloween from 9 a.m. to 5 p.m., seven days a week, the Rio Doce mine is owned by the Jerry Call family. Jerry Call, a gemologist who worked in Brazil's Vale Rio Doce (Sweet River Valley) for over 20 years, is currently involved in large-scale mining in the Brazilian valley. Some of the fine gem exports from the Brazilian valley end up in Spruce Pine's Rio Doce flumes. Rock hounds may be unearthing Mitchell County gems or Brazilian stones! Jerry Call and his family are master gem cutters and offer a complete gemological laboratory and appraisal services. The adjacent gem and gift shop offers 14k gold, sterling silver, and mineral specimens and provides gem cutting, and rough and cut gems. There is also a picnic area. Rio Doce offers group rates. The mine is located a half-mile north of the Blue Ridge Parkway and the Museum of North Carolina Minerals.

## Watauga County
### MAGIC MOUNTAIN MINI GOLF & GEM MINE
1675 Hwy. 105, Boone
(828) 265-GEMS, (828) 265-GOLF

The kids simply won't get bored here. Open seven days a week, 9 a.m. to 11 p.m., Magic Mountain is kiddie paradise. Adults won't mind sifting through the enriched ore either, because there's a chance of finding a ruby, citrine, garnet, amethyst, aquamarine, sapphire, emerald, or other such rock. The minigolf course is set on a mountainside amidst foliage and waterfalls. (See our Kidstuff chapter for more on Magic Mountain.)

## Central Mountains
## Haywood County
### OLD PRESSLEY SAPPHIRE MINES
286 Pressley Mine Rd., Canton
(828) 648-6320

Some of the world's largest sapphires, including the 1,445-carat "Star of the Carolinas," have been found in this Haywood County mine. In addition to the opportunity to flume for sapphires and other gems, Old Pressley has picnic tables and a rock shop. Better yet, it's open all year, weather permitting, seven days a week from 9 a.m. to 6 p.m. The flume is shut down during freezing weather, but people still can come here to prospect. There is a $5 entrance fee and a charge of $1 for each 10-quart bucket of ore. Premade buckets range from $10 to $45.

In 1989 a Cherokee rock hound found a 10.5 pound (18,000-carat) sapphire—9,719-carat star sapphire worth several million dollars once cut and polished. Other sizable gems of value have been found in Macon and Haywood counties.

## Southern Mountains

### Macon County

This is the heart of gem mining in Western North Carolina. In Macon County's famous Cowee Valley, you can go to more than a dozen gem mines where the entrance fees are usually under $10. There is an additional charge for buckets or bags of gem-bearing gravel that you can sluice in search of that "find of the century," but it's not much. However prices vary with the size of the buckets from mine to mine. Some in Macon County, as well as those in other counties, offer ore "enriched" or "seeded" with minerals not native to this locale; others offer strictly North Carolina stones.

Most gem mines, especially during the busy midsummer season, are open seven days a week

---

### Big Find

In 1999 Jamie Hill of Hiddenite discovered what is now called the Empress Carolina 858-carat emerald. Hill has found 3,000 carats of emeralds in his backyard, which is now known as the North American Emerald Mines. It is located in the Brushy Mountains 50 miles northwest of Charlotte. Local papers note the Empress Carolina weighing in at about three pounds. The emerald is in two pieces, with one a 558-carat crown. The other is a 300-carat base. A consortium of jewelers, six of them from North Carolina, now owns the precious stone.

---

from Apr 1 until Oct 31, and many are open from 8 a.m. until sunset, but times can vary. It's always a good idea to call before heading out to the mines; some closing times may vary according to the numbers of visitors and the weather during the season that you visit. Contact the Franklin Area Chamber of Commerce, 180 Porter St., Franklin, (828) 524-3161 for a listing of the county's many gem mines.

### Swain County

**NANTAHALA GORGE RUBY MINE**
**11900 US Hwy. 19 West, Bryson City**
**(828) 488-3854**

This Swain County mine, which uses enriched and native ore, has been known to produce rubies of good color and clarity. It's open from mid-Mar or mid-Apr through the end of Oct or on into Nov, depending on the weather. Ruby, emerald, and sapphire ore are sold by the bag. More heavily enriched bags of ore (called "super-ruby," "super-emerald," and "super-sapphire" bags) cost a bit more. There is no entrance fee.

Gem mining on your own can be wet and messy—dress appropriately for that venture. No need to worry if sluicing at a commercial dig. Pay for your bucket of fortune, sit on a bench, pick up your sieve, let the water rush down the trough, and let the good times roll.

**SMOKY MOUNTAIN GOLD AND RUBY MINE**
**US Hwy. 441 North, Cherokee**
**(828) 497-6574**

In addition to all the other attractions on the Qualla Boundary or Cherokee Indian Reservation, you can come here to search for such gems as amethysts, garnets, sapphires, rubies, citrine, topaz, and smoky quartz. Fifty dollars will get a mixed gem bucket with a cut gem somewhere in the mix. Other buckets cost between $4 and $10. Next to the shaded and covered water flumes is a gem shop that will also cut and mount your finds. The mine opens at 9 a.m. seven days a week from early spring through Nov.

# GEM MUSEUMS

Aside from small museums associated with some gem mines, there are some outstanding gem museums in the region. At these you can get the scoop on the history of rockhounding in North Carolina and a general education on gems and geology.

## Northern Mountains

### MUSEUM OF NORTH CAROLINA MINERALS
**Off Blue Ridge Parkway at Mile 331**
**(828) 765-2761**
This museum is a great side trip off the parkway. It displays a fascinating collection of minerals in various forms, from raw materials to the cut and polished items we know best. Spruce Pine, just down the road, and Little Switzerland, nearby, are both well known as sources of one of the highest and most varied concentrations of minerals in the United States. A gift shop offers a good variety of rock collections for any young rock hounds and enough material to keep them occupied quite a few miles down the road. The museum is open seven days a week in the summer season. Admission is free. The Mitchell County Chamber of Commerce (828-765-9483) is in the same building.

**i** For over three decades one of the biggest gem shows in the area, called Gemboree, has been held at the Macon County Community Building (U.S. Highway 441 South) in Franklin each July and Oct. Call the Franklin County Chamber of Commerce at (800) 336-7829 for more information.

## Central Mountains

### THE COLBURN EARTH SCIENCE MUSEUM
**2 South Pack Sq., Asheville**
**(828) 254-7162, (828) 257-4500**
**www.colburnmuseum.org**
This gem and mineral museum in the Pack Place Education Arts and Science Center dazzles the eyes. The museum was founded in 1960 and high-

lights gems and minerals of all shapes and sizes from around the world. North Carolina–specific garnets, rubies, emeralds, and gold deposits also feature heavily. Admission is $4 for adults; children ages 4 to 15 and senior citizens receive a discount.

**i** The annual Original North Carolina Mineral and Gem Festival at Spruce Pine takes place during the first weekend in Aug. Demonstrations, loose stone and mineral fossil displays, and the sale of lapidary supplies make this an entertaining event for everyone. Call the Mitchell Area Chamber of Commerce for more information at (800) 227-3912.

## Southern Mountains

### FRANKLIN GEM AND MINERAL MUSEUM
**25 Phillips St., Franklin**
**(828) 369-7831**
**www.fgmm.org**
The museum building, with its barred windows, is interesting in itself. It's the old county jail, located between Palmer and Main Streets, which was built in the 1850s and used as a jail until 1972. Now converted to displays, the North Carolina Room contains a huge sapphire, a 49-pound corundum crystal, and a baseball-size ruby crystal, all found at Corundum Hill Mine in Macon County, along with a rock collection, cut and faceted gems, an exhibit of mica types, and so on.

The Fluorescent Room, a one-time solitary confinement cell, displays the phenomenon of fluorescence and phosphorescence—what the narrative tape calls "nature's hidden rainbows."

The States Room contains specimens from each of the 50 states, including large specimens of fluorite that you can touch. There is also an Indian Artifacts Room with articles, many of which are centuries old, on loan from members and friends of the Gem and Mineral Society of Franklin.

A former high-security lockup known as the Slammer holds a display on rocks used in the manufacture of glass. The museum also has a nice collection of fossils and corals as well as beautiful minerals from more than 30 nations.

In addition to all this, there is a fine library full of gem and mineral books and a special Writings in Stone exhibit. The small gift shop helps support the museum. Admission is free.

ℹ️ Franklin's gem mines are too numerous to detail in this chapter. Do make a stop at the Franklin County Chamber of Commerce at 425 Porter St. or call (866) 372-5546 to get maps and brochures of the many mines in this area. The Web site www.franklin-chamber.com also has a page about gem mining.

**RUBY CITY GEMS AND MINERALS**
**130 East Main St., Franklin**
**(828) 524-3967**
**www.rubycity.com**

There are several "rock shops" in and around the Franklin area, but this establishment also has a great museum section, the result of more than 40 years of collecting specimens, artifacts, ivory carvings, and rare gems. Here you'll find a 385-pound sapphire and a 162-carat gem-quality ruby. The shop carries jewelry, lapidary equipment, and many rough stones. Other treasures found here include arrowheads and old tools, plus pre-Columbian Aztec and Inca vases and statues. This shop is open Apr through Dec.

# MOUNTAIN CRAFTS

All areas of the United States have their talented craftspeople, but few places have the fabulous hand-wrought heritage found in the southern Appalachians. Tucked away in our coves or working in downtown studios, there are cadres of citizens to whom "handmade" is a large part of both life and livelihood.

Many of these crafts flourished in the isolation caused by the lack of good transportation to and from the remote mountain regions. With the advent of good roads in the middle of the 20th century, the crafts of "makin' do" were transformed into beautiful art forms. The Cherokee Indians who occupied the area for countless generations influenced handcrafts, as did the Old World settlers, passing down skills that eventually evolved into the region's style. And there's no doubt that many crafts were inspired by the wealth of natural resources. There were honeysuckle, river cane, and white oak for baskets; willows for furniture; silver bell and rhododendron for making canes; and the country's largest variety of wood for carving bowls, spoons, and statues.

Natural dyes were derived from wild pokeberries, blueberries, black walnuts, yellow root, and any number of other plants. Skilled hands transformed pinecones and weeds of the fields and roadsides into wreaths and stunning dried-flower arrangements. Corn shucks became dolls, flowers, and fans. Handmade toys that amused our great-grandparents still delight our children today. Clay for pottery was there for the digging, and some of this malleable earth was of such high quality that it ended up as table settings for royalty.

To fend off cold mountain winters, craftswomen turned scraps of old clothing into quilts; many of these works of art can be found in national museums. While spinners and weavers kept old skills alive out of necessity, today's fabric artists delight in introducing new and beautiful creations for the sheer joy of it.

The abundance of hardwoods and the need to create entertainment spawned some of the finest instrument makers around. Their delicate fiddles and sturdy dulcimers have inspired a wealth of accomplished musicians, unique songs, and joyous dances, a tradition that also continues.

Three of the country's best craft schools are found in the region, attracting hundreds of craftspeople to settle in places such as Brasstown, Asheville, and Penland. In addition to large and highly influential guilds, such as the Southern Highland Craft Guild, there are also numerous small local guilds for weavers, spinners, quilters, and other crafters that meet in members' homes. And, thanks to the efforts of HandMade in America, many artists' studios are open to visitors for the first time (see our HandMade in America Close-up).

## NORTHERN MOUNTAINS

### BEA HENSLEY & SON BLACKSMITHS
**Route 1, off Mile 331, Spruce Pine**
There aren't many working blacksmiths around, especially in this country. That's what makes this three-generation blacksmithing studio so special. Bea Hensley, winner of the National Endowment of the Arts Heritage Award in 1995, maintains this successful forge with his son Mike. Grandson Luke has also learned bits of the trade. Schooled in the apprenticeship style, which has not changed much from the 1600s, Mike Hensley

does major smithing in wrought iron, fashioning elaborate made-to-order gates and other home ornamentation in this shop.

The sheer power and stamina of these men is staggering. Beefy forearms, callused hands, and thick back musculature are the results of years of working at the anvil. When the blacksmiths make the anvil "sing" while forging a particular piece of iron, smithing is especially transfixing. The "teacher" moves his smaller hammer over the anvil and hot iron, beating out a rhythm and directions that the "apprentice" must follow with the powerful blows of a heavy mallet. Though both Bea and Mike Hensley are past the apprenticing stage, they still make the anvil sing for visitors at times or while working on a particularly intricate project that needs the both of them. This trade is fascinating and rare in this modern world.

## BOLICK POTTERY
**Blackberry Road off US Hwy. 321, Blowing Rock**
**(828) 295-3862**

You'll want to make the special trip to Bolick Pottery on Blackberry Road, just minutes south of Blowing Rock. Here you'll find a family tradition at work. The Bolick family pottery was begun in 1973 by Lula Owens Bolick and her husband, Glenn. Before locating near Boone, the Bolicks worked with Lula's potter father, M. L. Owens, near Seagrove, North Carolina, a place steeped in the pottery tradition.

These fifth-generation potters continue to fashion traditional pieces, candleholders, mugs, bowls, pitchers, and miniature tea sets in the old-time colors of oatmeal, gray, and cobalt blue. All pieces produced by the Bolicks are microwave and dishwasher safe.

**i** Many mountain crafters who don't have other outlets for their wares sell them exclusively at the numerous annual street fairs and celebrations held throughout the year. (See our Annual Festivals and Events chapter for detailed descriptions.)

## CARLTON GALLERY AT CREEKSIDE
**10360 NC Hwy. 105 South, Banner Elk**
**(828) 963-4288**

The Carlton Gallery maintains fine woven works and contemporary art. The fine crafts come from local and regional artisans.

## J & S BEAUMONT POTTERY
**Hwy. 194, Valle Crucis**
**(828) 963-6399**

Located in the Red School House behind the Mast General Store, this pottery studio and gallery makes for wonderful browsing and picking up those little hand-crafted gifts to take back home.

Visitors can view turning, glazing, and decorating processes from a special area just a few feet away from the work area. We spent a good two hours mesmerized by the spin of the potter's wheel and the scent of fresh clay being manipulated.

Adjacent to the airy manufacturing hall is the retail store. Here you'll find handmade and hand-painted dinnerware and other functional pieces for the home. The rich patterns are influenced by European and American art pottery styles. We found the soap dish and water cup combos especially charming. The colors and patterns on display could match just about any bathroom decor. Wonderful urns, pitchers, and salad bowls also tickled our fancy. A special shelf for "seconds" offers some perfectly gorgeous pieces with only slight flaws at reduced prices.

## PENLAND SCHOOL OF CRAFTS
**67 Dora's Trail, Penland**
**(828) 765-2359**
**www.penland.org**

Resting on the crest of a remote mountaintop in Mitchell County, the Penland School is one of the country's finest institutions devoted entirely to the study of crafts. It was founded by Miss Lucy Morgan in 1929 after an inspirational sojourn to the craft haven of Berea, Kentucky, where she spent a summer learning to weave. On her return Miss Lucy set forth with a twofold purpose: to revive the mountain tradition of weaving here at

# Close-up

## HandMade in America

Long before the first tourists came to Western North Carolina, quilts, baskets, tools, and furniture were being crafted as necessities of life. Although they were rarely seen by anyone but family members, these handcrafts were created with an integrity that speaks volumes about the people who made them. Today thousands come each year to see the woodworking, pottery, blacksmithing, and weaving that are now considered treasured keepsakes. They come, too, to reconnect with that part of themselves that longs to create.

The formal development of HandMade began with a three-year grant received from the Pew Partnership for Civic Change in December 1993. More than 360 people participated in a six-month regional planning process that shaped and defined its mission.

Working with three tourism-related organizations, HandMade is guiding the development of a craft "heritage corridor" across 22 Western North Carolina counties. The Blue Ridge Parkway serves as the main link by which visitors can access a series of loop trails that take them to historic craft locations, scenic byways, and other attractions. Two guide books, *The Craft Heritage Trails of Western North Carolina* and *The Farms, Gardens & Countryside Trails*, take you on numerous exciting trails carefully designed to traverse 400 of the region's most fascinating and historical shops, inns, restaurants, galleries, and historical sites. Many were not open to the public before, but HandMade's careful planning and negotiations have created new opportunities. And training sessions for all participating sites mean that you are greeted by people knowledgeable not just about their specialty but all the stops along the way.

Many of the sites in our book are included on HandMade's self-guided trails.

HandMade is also involved in programs to provide craftspeople with some of the advantages that employees of large corporations enjoy, as well as an innovative program called EnergyXChange—America's first landfill conversion using methane to power craft (glass, clay) studios.

Contact HandMade in America at www.handmadeinamerica.org to purchase a copy of *The Craft Heritage Trails of Western North Carolina* and their other publications.

home and to help the economically distressed women add to their livelihood. Word spread; students wanted to learn to weave. Soon new crafts were added, and suddenly Miss Lucy found her project becoming a school.

Today the school has a 450-acre campus and boasts a broad curriculum that includes book arts, glass, photography, printmaking, wood, surface design, metals, iron, drawing, clay, and fibers. The Penland community includes staff, resident artists, and students, who are composed of a mix of college students and graduates, professionals looking for a different career, and retirees who seek the arts as an avocation. This diversity of life

experience only adds to the flow of creativity and the quality of Penland.

Many of the light-filled classrooms overlook a grass-covered bald and ridge upon ridge in the gloaming. Guest teachers, like master Venetian glassblowers, fiber artists from Australia, and many others, conduct two-week workshops. A cozy dining room serves buffet-style meals—the menu changes each day to include wholesome preservative-free organic meals.

To receive information on classes, tuition, or any other aspect of the school, write to the Penland School of Crafts, Penland 28765, or call (828) 765-2359.

## THE WEAVING ROOM/CROSSNORE SCHOOL
**205 Johnson Lane, Hwy. 221, Crossnore**
**(828) 733-4660, (800) 374-4660**
**www.crossnoreschool.org**
The Weaving Room is a self-help project of Crossnore School. All proceeds benefit the boys and girls of Crossnore School, children from the Carolina mountains and foothills. These children from families in crisis find a stable environment on the school's 72-acre campus.

At the Crossnore School watch weavers at their looms, creating traditional patterns and contemporary wares. Since 1920 the school has kept alive the almost forgotten art of producing handwoven clothing and home furnishings in patterns used by the early settlers of the Appalachians. In the Weaving Room, you will find throw rugs in the Lee's Surrender pattern, capes and stoles in a Honeysuckle pattern, and table runners and baby blankets in the Bronson Lace pattern. The weavers use all natural cotton, wool, and linen, as well as some easy-care materials like rayon, orlon, and synthetics.

**i** Pick up a copy of *Rapid River Entertainment Digest*, a free monthly newspaper with literary reviews, artists' showcases, and art gallery listings in the Asheville area. You'll find stacks of the *Digest* in any gallery or cafe.

## WOODY'S CHAIR SHOP
**110 Dale Rd., Spruce Pine**
**(828) 765-9277**
All-in-the-family trade has spanned three generations at Woody's Chair Shop. Rocking chairs, made by hand and by special machinery constructed and designed solely by Woody, are the specialty here. The front shop sells fabulous wooden doodads, from smoothly fashioned business card holders to gravity-defying wine bottle holders, old mountain children's games and adult chess sets, humidors, and grand mirrors.

Woody's chairs are his pride, though, and are sought the world over. Special deliveries are sent to Europe yearly. Ask Woody or his wife for a quick peek into the workshop and he might just oblige. Expect lots of sawdust, some fascinating machinery, and workers in deep concentration.

### Kaolin

In 1767 an English tableware manufacturer, Josiah Wedgwood, sent a South Carolina planter, Thomas Griffith, to make an arrangement with the Cherokee to export the high-quality clay known as "kaolin" that was found in the region. Huge amounts of kaolin were shipped to Wedgwood and transformed into the famous Queensware. A Wedgwood dinner service of Macon County clay graced the table of Catherine the Great.

# CENTRAL MOUNTAINS

## APPALACHIAN CRAFT CENTER
**10 North Spruce St., Asheville**
**(828) 253-8499**
This nondescript storefront on a side street houses an array of mountain crafts, from handmade brooms to turned wood bowls, pottery, quilts, ornaments, and much more. It is located in downtown Asheville between the Renaissance Hotel and College Street. Their pricing of these crafts is customer-favorable.

## ARIEL GALLERY
**19 Biltmore Ave., Asheville**
**(828) 236-2660**
**www.arielcraftgallery.com**
This cooperative arts and craft gallery features the crème-de-la-crème of local artisans. With everything from modern textiles to pottery, jewelry, furniture in wood, glass and metal, numerous decorative items, and wearable art, this is a trea-

sure trove of the region's handcrafted works. The artists themselves man the store, so you may be striking up a conversation with the person who created your find.

## BLACK MOUNTAIN GALLERY
**114 Cherry St., Black Mountain**
**(828) 669-2450**
This downtown gallery is the only one in the area primarily dedicated to lathing turned wooden bowls, both artistic and functional. In a workshop adjacent to the gallery, father and son artists Eddie and Marshall Hollifield transform Mother Nature's abnormalities—the knots of a tree or dome-shaped growths in tree trunks, known as "burls"—into works of art. Feel free to watch this fascinating process. The gallery also features the works of other local artists.

## FOLK ART CENTER
**Mile 382, Blue Ridge Parkway, Asheville**
**(828) 298-7928**
**www.southernhighlandguild.org**
The Folk Art Center is the grand showcase for the work of the more than 700 members of the Southern Highland Craft Guild. The guild was founded in 1930 as an educational, nonprofit organization to provide economic support to the many fine craftspeople of the southern Appalachian region. Guild members come from a nine-state region and produce some of the finest traditional mountain crafts as well as outstanding contemporary craft work being done today.

The Folk Art Center, Asheville's gateway to the Blue Ridge Parkway off U.S. Highway 70, welcomes 350,000 visitors annually from all over the country and the world. They come to see the fine traditional mountain heritage on display in the permanent collection and the traditional and contemporary crafts in the ever-changing exhibitions. Allanstand Craft Shop, America's oldest craft shop, is a feast for the eyes with its displays of glassware, blankets, dishware, wooden toys, exquisitely crafted jewelry, prints, brooms, and baskets.

The main level houses a 250-seat auditorium that serves the guild's educational purposes and is also used by the National Park Service. Here, as well as in the foyer, demonstrations are produced throughout Apr through Dec. Special events, such as Clay Day and Fiber Day, involve the public with hands-on participation projects and provide fun for the entire family. (Call to find out about the special events.)

The essence of the guild and the Folk Art Center is described by a lifetime member, woodcarver and dulcimer maker Edsel Martin of Old Fort, who in 1970 wrote: "The Southern Highland Handicraft Guild is not just a business . . . it is people. People who are proud, who live close to the earth, and who live with an independence and dignity that money can't buy. The Guild is not people who stand behind or in front of each other; it is people standing side by side."

The Folk Art Center is open Apr through Dec from 9 a.m. to 6 p.m. daily except Thanksgiving, Christmas, and New Year's; 9 a.m. to 5 p.m. Jan through Mar. Admission is free.

## GROVEWOOD GALLERY
**111 Grovewood Rd., Asheville**
**(828) 253-7651**
**www.grovewood.com**
This fine gallery is in the former home of the Biltmore Industries woolen homespun operation. The interior of this interesting English-style cottage adjacent to the Grove Park Inn has been wonderfully renovated as gallery and shop space without sacrificing the integrity of its origin. The Grovewood Studios, in the next cottage, houses 11 artists, specializing in wood work, blown glass, stone carving, jewelry, and furniture. Their work, along with the work of other area craftspeople, is represented by the Grovewood Gallery. The furniture gallery upstairs has expanded and features fabulous designs from the Southeast.

## ODYSSEY CENTER FOR THE CERAMIC ARTS
**236 Clingman Ave., Asheville**
**(828) 285-0210**
**www.highwaterclays.com**
This is another studio that has found a home in Asheville's Historic River District. Close to the train tracks and the banks of the French Broad River, this large pottery center offers courses in

## Artisans in Residence at Asheville's River District Studios

Asheville's River District Studios, located along the French Broad River in the city's old industrial area close to downtown, is home to no less than 60 working studios. Over 90 artists and artisans work here. Some buildings include galleries, and many studios have regular hours to welcome visitors, provided a phone call precedes the visit. Ceramics, printmaking, painting, woodworking, sculpting, garden art, photography, welding, candle making, and many other crafts can be found here. Twice a year the River District Studios host a "sunset stroll" through studios and courtyards. Feel free to wander and watch and make a purchase or two. You'll be sure to run into a bevy of local supporters. Strolls take place on a weekend once in the fall and once in summer. The Cotton Mill Studios offer tours of certain studios year-round. For more information call (828) 252-9122.

The River District Studios are concentrated on Riverside Drive, Clingman Avenue, and Lyman and Roberts streets. Check local listings for the dates and times of the Studio Strolls.

internationally known ceramic artists. An independent study program gives returning students the opportunity to use the facility during open studio hours and work independently. The Odyssey Gallery markets and exhibits ceramic works from local and national artists and serves as an educational tool for students as well as the public. Call for a detailed course brochure and workshop schedule.

## SOUTHERN MOUNTAINS

### BURR STUDIO AND GALLERY
136 North Main St., Waynesville
(828) 456-7400
www.burrstudio.com
This gallery showcases the pottery and sculpture of the Burrs, much of it utilitarian in nature, like clay herb markers and decorative terra-cotta wall pockets.

### DOGWOOD CRAFTERS
90 Webster St., Dillsboro
(828) 586-2248
Housed in a large, renovated log building around the corner from Front Street, this is one of Dillsboro's most charming stores. We are particularly taken with the lovely, artistic cornhusk dolls here, but there also are hundreds of contemporary and traditional handicrafts on display, including pottery, pillows, art, and toys.

### HAYWOOD COMMUNITY COLLEGE CRAFT PRODUCTION PROGRAM
1 Freelander Dr., Clyde
(828) 627-4670
This two-year program in jewelry, pottery, weaving, and woodworking is considered one of the finest in the nation. In addition to teaching technique and design, the school is noted for its marketing courses that help turn aspiration into economic reality for the craft artists. Students design their own graduation show at the completion of their chosen program. (See our chapter on Education for more information about Haywood Community College.)

clay crafts for beginners and advanced students. Nine-week classes are offered in pottery, hand building, and figurative sculpture, as well as kids' classes for after school and home schoolers. (Read more about these in our Kidstuff chapter.)

Weekend and weeklong workshops, along with frequent lectures, feature nationally and

# Close-up

## The Swannanoa Gathering

In the heart of the summer, about the time the katydids crank up, folks from all over the country converge upon the Asheville area for the Swannanoa Gathering at Warren Wilson College (see our Education chapter). These five weeks of music workshops run through July and into mid-Aug. The schedule is full of special weeks that focus on specific styles and disciplines, including Celtic Week, Performance Lab, Dulcimer Week, Dance Week, Old-Time Music & Dance Week, Contemporary Folk Week, Guitar Week, and Fiddle Week. Some years include Blues Week as well. With an advisory board that reads like a Who's Who in Folk Music—David Holt, John McCutcheon, Fiona Ritchie, Billy Edd Wheeler, and Asheville's own David Wilcox—it's no wonder the programming and attendance are stellar every year.

The workshops convene at various sites around the Warren Wilson campus. Classes are open to everyone, and many are structured for beginners. Students are free to create their own curriculum for each week (with the exception of some restrictions by individual teachers), although participants are urged to concentrate on one or two classes.

Certain weeks include programs for children ages 6 to 12. Classes in crafts, field trips to local attractions such as Pack Place and the Nature Center, and swimming activities are scheduled during the daytime class sessions.

A typical week begins with supper, an orientation session, and socializing on the Sunday before the courses begin in earnest. Most classes meet for morning or afternoon sessions Mon through Fri. Some may meet in the evenings for performance critiques, rehearsals, or jam sessions. Other evening activities include concerts by staff instructors, dances, song swaps, and impromptu happenings, such as picking sessions and slow jams (tune-learning sessions).

For sports and recreation, the college's facilities include a gymnasium, weight room, aquatic center, and tennis courts, as well as a pond, nature trails, a working farm, and a kayak run on the nearby Swannanoa River.

The musical traditions of Scotland and Ireland, possessing separate and distinctive personalities, nonetheless share a common heritage. **Celtic Week** acknowledges this dual heritage with

---

### JOHN C. CAMPBELL FOLK SCHOOL
1 Folk School Rd., Brasstown
(828) 837-2775, (800) FOLK-SCH
www.folkschool.org

The John C. Campbell Folk School has been a mountain institution for more than 80 years, and there's really no other place like it. Though Brasstown is only two hours from Atlanta, Chattanooga, and Asheville, the school—set in a mountain-rimmed farming valley—seems to be from another century. Actually it began in the 20th, when Indiana-born educator John C. Campbell took his new bride, Olive Dame, on a fact-finding survey throughout the Appalachian Mountains. While he investigated the agricultural practices, she studied the music and handicrafts.

After John's death in 1919, Olive Campbell and friend Marguerite Butler went to Scandinavia to study hands-on schools without credits, degrees, grades, or competition. They returned to the mountains to see if such a school would be welcomed in the region. More than 200 enthusiastic people showed up at an organizational meeting at a Brasstown church. Fred O. Scroggs, the local storekeeper, donated 75 acres of land, and the people pledged labor, building materials, and most importantly, their heartfelt support.

Today the 372-acre campus contains 27 buildings, some designed by Belgian architect Leon Deschamps in a romantic European style, while others are more typical of Appalachian farm houses. It has fully equipped craft studios, a sawmill, meeting rooms, a covered outdoor a program featuring the best from each tradition. Irish flute, Irish step dancing, uilleann pipes, Celtic harp, tin whistle, Scottish fiddle, hammered dulcimer, bodhran (traditional Irish frame drum), Celtic guitar, and bouzouki (like a large, long-necked mandolin) are just some of the courses offered.

**Performance Lab Week** is designed for those who have a serious interest in moving to a higher level in their performing activities. The first three class days are spent on the campus, working on performance skills in a lab setting. Then the acts hit the road to perform three concerts in the region, presented as a revue, with each act doing a short set as a part of each show.

**Old-Time Music & Dance Week** explores the rich music, dance, singing, and storytelling traditions of the southern Appalachian region. Old-time fiddle is a popular course, as are old-time banjo, old-time guitar, and autoharp. Shape-note singing, a fascinating musical tradition stretching back to the 16th century, is also offered.

**Dulcimer Week** includes instruction in both the mountain dulcimer and one of the most appealing and accessible of folk instruments, the hammered dulcimer.

**Contemporary Folk Week** is a unique program of workshops covering a variety of related topics: songwriting, performance, sound reinforcement and recording, and vocal coaching.

**Guitar Week** features contemporary fingerstyle guitar, flatpicking, blues, and guitar accompaniment.

**Fiddle Week** offers instruction in swing, Irish, old-time, and bluegrass fiddle.

Whether you are a musician or not, there's a magic in the air at the Swannanoa Gathering. A series of concerts showcasing workshop staff is scheduled at the end of each week and is open to the public.

For more information contact the Swannanoa Gathering at (828) 298-3434 or www.swan gathering.org.

dance pavilion, a nature trail, a craft shop, a vegetable garden, rustic lodgings, and the Community Room, which has one of the best dance floors in America. The National Register of Historic Places has declared the campus a Historical District.

Over the years the school's role in the community has changed as many of the needs it served (such as health care and job training) have been taken over by public programs. It continues, however, to enrich and serve the local community. Its craft shop, for example, sells the work of more than 200 mountain craftspeople, including the famous Brasstown Carvers, whose delicately carved animals are all-time favorites.

Most of today's 3,000 annual Folk School students come from all over the United States for a week or two to learn a craft, pick up an instrument, or learn to dance.

Regularly scheduled concerts of traditional music, along with dances, are open to the public. For those who want to learn a new skill or improve an old one, there are hundreds of weekend and one- or two-week-long courses offered year-round in basketry, beadwork, blacksmithing, book arts, broom making, calligraphy, chair seats, clay, crochet, dance, dolls, drawing, dyeing, embroidery, enameling, felting, food, genealogy, glass, jewelry, kaleidoscopes, knitting, lace, leather, marbling, metalwork, music, nature studies, painting, paper art, photography, printmaking, quilting, recreation, rugs, spinning, stone carving, storytelling, thread art, tinsmithing, weaving, wood carving, wood turning, wood-working, and writing.

Three family-style meals are included with tuition. Lodging (meals included) is provided in a number of on-campus buildings. Costs vary.

There are 12 campsites with full hookups and modest bathroom facilities on campus. Campsites are available for a cost.

To receive a catalog call one of the numbers above or write to the John C. Campbell Folk School, 1 Folk School Rd., Brasstown 28902.

**i** If you are planning to attend one of John C. Campbell's regular concerts, why not enjoy a meal at the school's table beforehand? Make reservations at least one day in advance by calling (800) FOLK-SCH or (828) 837-2775. Then prepare yourself for a tasty repast!

### THE MUSEUM OF NORTH CAROLINA HANDICRAFTS
**307 Shelton St., Waynesville**
**(828) 452-1551**

The white-framed Shelton House, built in 1875 and listed on the National Register of Historic Places, is as interesting as the museum and offers a perfect setting for the comprehensive exhibits of 19th-century crafts.

Just a short walk from Waynesville's charming Main Street, the museum contains examples of furniture from the 19th century, a Victorian bed and shaving stand, a dining table, handcrafted cupboard, toys (including a handmade miniature farmstead), and a working pioneer village.

It also features an exhibit of handicrafts made by artisans who have participated in the edu-

## Potters of the Roan

Potters of the Roan is a guild of professional potters living and working in the Bakersville area of the mountains of Western North Carolina in Mitchell County. Roan Mountain dominates the views of the area with extensive balds and huge natural rhododendron gardens. Potters of the Roan can be recognized throughout Mitchell County by red signs with white interior ovals. Inside the ovals are the individual names of their studios. (For information contact Fork Mountain Pottery, 1782 Fork Mountain Rd., Bakersville; 828-688-9297; www.forkmountainpottery.com.)

cational demonstration of heritage crafts in the North Carolina State Fair's Village of Yesteryear since 1951. You'll see such once-necessary tools as Saxony spinning wheels and walking spinning wheels. There is also a fine collection of Cherokee Indian artifacts, as well as the Will Shelton collection of Navajo rugs, pottery, jewelry, and baskets.

A small gift shop carries pottery, braided rugs, hand-carved birds, and other handcrafted items and a selection of regional craft books.

The museum is open from 10 a.m. to 4 p.m. Tues through Frid, May through Oct. There is an admission charge.

# ANNUAL FESTIVALS AND EVENTS

Our North Carolina Mountains are a celebration in and of themselves, and just living here seems to give rise to all manner of joyous, lively, enlightening, wondrous festivals. Here's a month-to-month sampling, broken down under the geographic regions of the Northern, Central, and Southern Mountains. The events are free unless we've noted an entry fee. Please note: While we update these events with each new edition, it's still best to check with the chambers of commerce in each county to make sure events planned far ahead of time are still scheduled.

Get set to find a bit of everything: woolly worms, dogwood blossoms, gospel music, Scottish clans, Grandma's finest quilt, and even "whimmy diddles" (Appalachian wooden toys) and washtub race cars. Have fun!

## JANUARY

### Northern Mountains

**WINTERFEST**
**Ski Beech**
**Beech Mountain**
**(828) 387-2011**
This town festival on Beech Mountain in the first week of Jan features an ice show, beauty contest, and tube and box races. Nominal entrance fees are charged for the various events.

**OLD CHRISTMAS HICKORY RIDGE**
**HOMESTEAD**
**591 Horn in the West Dr., Boone**
**(828) 264-2120**
A traditional Christmas celebration held annually on Jan 6, this community event is free and welcomes everyone to take part. A roaring bonfire (it's cold up here this time of year!) is built from the holiday trees and branches brought by the community as a good-luck gesture for the new year. And the good luck begins when delicious food and beverages are provided at the event.

### Central Mountains

**ANNUAL ALL THAT JAZZ WEEKEND AT THE**
**GROVE PARK INN**
**290 Macon Ave., Asheville**
**(828) 252-2711, (800) 438-5800**

Hot jazz warms up a cold January weekend. This annual event features two evening concerts, Sat afternoon jazz, and legendary talents on Sat night. Admission is charged for concerts.

**MARTIN LUTHER KING JR. ANNUAL**
**BIRTHDAY CELEBRATION**
**Various locations, Asheville**
**(828) 259-5800, (828) 253-3714**
A variety of events in a five-day celebration at various locations around town honor the birth and contributions of the famed civil rights leader. It all begins the third Mon of the month. Events include a peace march through town, singing, poetry readings, lectures, and music. The event is cosponsored by the city of Asheville.

## FEBRUARY

### Central Mountains

**BIG BAND DANCE WEEKEND AT THE GROVE**
**PARK INN**
**290 Macon Ave., Asheville**
**(828) 252-2711, (800) 438-5800**
It's swing time at the famed Grove Park Inn. This annual event, on the first weekend in Feb, draws lovers of the Big Band sound of the 1940s and dancers from all over the country. The professional instruction and exhibitions—dancers sweeping across the ballroom in amazingly synchronized steps—are a special treat.

### WINTERFEST ARTS AND CRAFTS SHOW
**3 South Tunnel Rd., Asheville**
**(828) 252-3880**
This annual regional crafts display fills the corridors of the Asheville Mall and offers a pleasant diversion from winter's chill for three days in early Feb. This show is sponsored by the High Country Craft Guild and features traditional mountain crafts, such as quilts, ceramics, dolls, and other items.

### ARTS AND CRAFTS CONFERENCE AT THE GROVE PARK INN
**290 Macon Ave., Asheville**
**(828) 252-2711, (800) 438-5800**
This annual professional conference in praise of the Arts and Crafts Movement of Gustav Stickley and his contemporaries working in furniture, pottery, and metalware could have no better surroundings than the Grove Park Inn, a veritable shrine to the movement. The richness of the red-shingled stone resort and its fine collection of arts and crafts pieces exemplify the natural elements and clean lines of this radical design movement, which set the Victorians on their ears at the turn of the last century. The conference is usually held the third week in Feb.

**i** Don't underestimate the popularity of the festivals and events in these mountains. Most attract hundreds, if not thousands, of visitors. Therefore calling ahead to inquire about the best place to find parking is a wise idea. It can save time that'll be better spent enjoying a festival.

### BLACK MOUNTAIN TO MOUNT MITCHELL MARATHON CHALLENGE
**Black Mountain**
**(828) 669-2300**
This is a 26-mile and a 40-mile foot race on the extreme sports level as it changes elevations drastically and takes place in the middle of winter.

### CLUB DAY AT THE BLUE RIDGE MALL
**1800 Seasons Blvd., Hendersonville**
**(828) 697-1745**
During the last week in Feb, local clubs and organizations set up booths to show the community what's offered within the groups.

### CHILI COOK-OFF
**Kelsey and Hutchinson Lodge, Highlands**
**(828) 526-2112, (888) 245-9058**
One great way to shake off the chills of winter is to warm up by the fireplaces at this upscale and inviting lodge. Another way is to participate in the Chili Cook-off. This fiery potion will stir the gentlest of souls and turn boys into men. Forget winter and welcome spring. The event is cosponsored by the Highlands Chamber of Commerce.

# MARCH

## Central Mountains

### COMEDY CLASSIC
**Grove Park Inn, 290 Macon Ave.**
**Asheville**
**(828) 252-2711, (800) 438-5800**
Always a sellout, this popular weekend features an exciting lineup of top professional talent. It is always scheduled for the first weekend in Mar.

### SAINT PATRICK'S DAY CELEBRATION
**Various locations, Asheville**
Asheville's cobblestoned Market Street is the starting point for this lively celebration of the wearing of the green. Crafts, entertainment, food, and an energetic parade complete the festivities for those with a bit of Irish in their souls.

### WESTERN CAROLINA HOME SHOW
**87 Haywood St., Asheville**
**(828) 259-5544**
Always popular, this annual event fills the Asheville Civic Center with streams of visitors, merchants, and an eye-popping array of the hottest items for the modern homeowner. It's fun to go, even if your dream house is still a dream. Parking is available in the municipal parking garage next door, just behind the public library. There's a small charge for admission.

## HORSE SHOWS
### Western North Carolina Agricultural Center
### Hwy. 280, Fletcher
### (828) 687-1414

Throughout the month, the WNC Agricultural Center hosts the Western North Carolina Quarter Horse Show, the Roping Horse Show, and the Carolina Mountain Arabian Horse Show. Call for exact dates.

Other horses such as palominos, saddlebreds, and racking and walking horses are on parade throughout the year from Mar to Nov. (See our Recreation chapter for more information.)

## SPRING CRAFT SHOW
### 1800 Four Seasons Blvd., Hendersonville
### (828) 697-1745

The Henderson County Crafters Association brings handicrafts to the Blue Ridge Mall on Four Seasons Boulevard toward the middle of this month. Dolls, jewelry, pottery, homemade greeting cards, and brooms are only part of what you'll see.

## SUPER SATURDAY
### Various locations, Tryon
### (828) 894-3051

Downtown is transformed into a children's festival with puppet shows, theater performances, jugglers, magicians, and arts and craft activities. The city of Tryon sponsors the event.

# APRIL

## Central Mountains

### BILTMORE ESTATE'S FESTIVAL OF FLOWERS
### 1 Approach Rd., Asheville
### (828) 225-1333, (800) 624-1575

Not only is Mr. Vanderbilt's 250-room mansion a magnificent sight, but the grounds and gardens, designed by noted landscape architect Frederick Law Olmsted, are just as breathtaking. This month-long festival celebrates the exquisite beauty of the estate's wildflowers, formal plantings, and exotic blooms of the gardens. The mansion itself is arrayed in Victorian floral design, while live music serenades you in the house and gardens. The house is also open for Festival of Flowers Evenings by reservations on Fri and Sat during the event. The festival lasts from mid-Apr to mid-May, and the price is admission to Biltmore Estate. (See our Biltmore Estate chapter.)

## OLD DEPOT ASSOCIATION ART & CRAFTS SHOW
### Old Depot, Black Mountain
### (828) 669-2300

This is a juried art show held at the historic train station in downtown Black Mountain.

## OLDE TYME MUSIC FESTIVAL
### Downtown Hendersonville

On the second Sat in Apr, acoustic musicians will entertain you from 10 a.m. until 5 p.m. on Appalachian and hammered dulcimers, fiddles, guitars, autoharps, and banjos.

## EARTH DAY CELEBRATION
### Chimney Rock Park
### US Highways 64/74-A, Chimney Rock
### (828) 625-9611, (800) 277-9611

Join environmental speakers and guided nature walks in celebration of Mother Nature. Programs, demonstrations, and hands-on displays including animals, dulcimer music, and magic shows compose this celebration.

## THE BLOCK HOUSE STEEPLECHASE
### Foothills Equestrian Nature Center
### 3381 Hunting Country Rd., Tryon
### (828) 859-6109, (800) 438-3681

This free mid-month event, one of the region's most famous and well attended, marks over 60 years of running the horses. It takes place at the Foothills Equestrian Nature Center (FENCE). Gates open at 10 a.m.

## EASTER EGG HUNT
### Jackson Park, Hendersonville

Just before Easter you can bring the young and young-at-heart for an old-fashioned egg hunt in the area's largest park. This free springtime event, when more than 11,000 eggs are hidden in the park for children to find, starts at 11 a.m.

### ANNUAL EASTER SUNRISE SERVICE
Chimney Rock Park
US 64/74-A, Chimney Rock
(828) 625-9611, (800) 277-9611
Deep valleys and craggy ridges are an inspiring backdrop for this service conducted by a guest minister, a free, ongoing tradition for more than 40 years.

### HICKORY NUT GORGE DOGWOOD FESTIVAL
Lake Lure
(828) 625-0204
Lake Lure shimmers, and a cascade of white petals dots the mountains of the gorge, providing inspiration for this festival in honor of the return of spring. Food, entertainment, tournaments, and crafts abound. Sat includes a parade and a 5K run. The festival, usually held the third weekend in Apr, runs from 10 a.m. to 7 p.m., with entertainment going well into the evening.

### PIONEER LIVING DAY
Zebulon B. Vance Birthplace
911 Reems Creek Rd., Weaverville
(828) 645-6706
Walk into the North Carolina mountains of yesteryear at the Zebulon B. Vance Birthplace. Pioneer Living Day at this state historic site is a fascinating event for the whole family, who can all become involved in demonstrations of the day-to-day life of early mountaineers at this country homestead, surrounded by meadows and mountains. Cooking, candle making, and spinning are just a few of the delights. This event occurs the third Sun in Apr.

### HISTORIC JOHNSON FARM FESTIVAL
3346 Haywood Rd., Hwy. 191, Hendersonville
(828) 891-6585
At the end of Apr, there are tours, an auction, demonstrations, arts and crafts, and food at this old tobacco farm, a heritage education center and farm museum now owned by the Henderson County Public Schools. It's 4 miles north of

Hendersonville on Highway 191. The festival runs from 10 a.m. until 4 p.m.

### APPALACHIAN SPRING CELEBRATION
Cradle of Forestry
Pisgah National Forest
US Hwy. 276
(828) 877-3130
Starting the last week in Apr and running for a full month, the Cradle of Forestry celebrates our mountains' diversity of birds, wildflowers, and waterfalls with a variety of programs for children and adults, including guided bird and wildflower walks and a wildflower photography contest. There is an entrance fee of $4 for adults and $2 for students.

### REVOLUTIONARY WAR ENCAMPMENT AT FENCE
Foothills Equestrian Nature Center
3381 Hunting Country Rd., Tryon
(828) 859-9021
Experience Revolutionary times with South Carolina's Second Regiment at the Foothills Equestrian Nature Center (FENCE). See demonstrations of period crafts, cooking, musket shooting, and an authentic campsite. This free event is held near the end of Apr.

## Southern Mountains

### RAZZLE DAZZLE SATURDAY
Various locations, Waynesville
(828) 452-0593, (800) 334-9036
Even the name sounds like fun. On the second Sat in Apr, children of all ages enjoy a downtown, daylong celebration of arts and entertainment. There are live performances and hands-on art, food, face painting, and fun.

### RAMP FESTIVAL
Various locations, Robbinsville
(828) 479-3790
On the last Sun in Apr, the whole town celebrates the pungent ramp. This wild cousin of the onion is the star of this occasion sponsored by the local rescue squad. The day's activities feature a duck

race, dinner with ramp-flavored dishes, and a craft fair.

# MAY

## Northern Mountains

### SPRING STUDIO AND GARDEN TOUR
**Various locations, Spruce Pine**
**(828) 765-9483, (800) 227-3912**
The first Fri and Sat in May, the artists and garden businesses of Yancey and Mitchell Counties open their studios and garden spots for informal viewing just before Mother's Day. Fine handcrafted works and garden accoutrements make for a delightful shopping mixture. The tour runs from 10 a.m. to 5 p.m. and is sponsored by the Toe River Arts Council. Pick up a map of studios on the tour at the Mitchell County Chamber of Commerce at the North Carolina Museum of Minerals or at the Mitchell News Journal in downtown Spruce Pine.

### SPRING ARTS FESTIVAL
**Town Square, Burnsville**
**(828) 682-7413, (800) 948-1632**
This festival at the end of May is usually held on a Sat from 10 a.m. to 4 p.m. in the town square. Meet the artists and see their works. Browse the booths for some creative gifts and fine art, while the children paint and draw to their hearts' content on the Expression Wall. Sponsored by the Toe River Arts Council and the Business Owners Association, this event is free.

## Central Mountains

### SPRING HERB FESTIVAL
**Western North Carolina Farmers Market**
**Off I-26, Brevard exit, Asheville**
**(828) 689-5974**
This event on the first weekend in May offers educational gardening programs as well as an opportunity to speak to herbalists and master gardeners. This festival is free, so you can save your money to buy herbs, books, and herbal products.

### SUNDAY MELODIES IN THE PARK
**Jackson Park Amphitheater**
**Hendersonville**
**(828) 697-1745, (800) 828-4344**
A free summer concert series begins the second Sun of the month. The concerts range from beach music, soft rock and "Tuxedo Junction" tunes of the 40's to the 90's.
Call for more information.

### FOLK ART CENTER FIBER DAY
**Mile 382, Asheville**
**(828) 298-7928**
The Folk Art Center, east of the city on the Blue Ridge Parkway, hosts a special day in the middle of the month to celebrate the fiber arts. The professional demonstrations attract large crowds, who get to watch how these folks spin thread and weave cloth out of the wool from sheep. This demonstration usually includes all the stages, from watching the sheep being shorn to the weaving on the loom.

### LAKE EDEN ARTS FESTIVAL
**Camp Rockmont**
**375 Lake Eden Rd., Black Mountain**
**(828) 686-8742**
**www.theleaf.com**
Lake Eden Arts Festival is an event celebrating the world of folk arts. On the sprawling grounds of a boys' summer camp, this fest features dancing and music, drumming and handicrafts, poetry and storytelling over the three-day Memorial Day weekend in May, then again in Oct. There are also spiritual and healing workshops, a farmers' market, ethnic food booths, massage and aromatherapy, and a vast and funky mixture of world music, folk, and country sounds, all running concurrently on four different stages. This is one very hip festival—call for a brochure with pricing. Camping during the festival is available.

### CARL SANDBURG FOLK AND POETRY FESTIVAL
**Connemara**
**1928 Little River Rd., Flat Rock**
**(828) 693-4178**

One of the mountains' favorite people is the namesake and inspiration for this free entertainment. Carl Sandburg loved to sing, and music still graces Connemara, his farm, now a National Historic Site just outside Hendersonville. The last weekend in May, professional musicians and actors perform songs and poems from Sandburg's works from 10 a.m. until 5 p.m.

### FLAT ROCK PLAYHOUSE
**2661 Greenville Hwy, Flat Rock**
**(828) 693-0731, (828) 693-0403**
North Carolina's official state theater presents comedy, American classics, whodunits, musicals, and farces. (See our write-up in the Arts and Culture chapter for more information.)

### ANNUAL MAIN STREET ANTIQUE SHOW
**Main Street, Hendersonville**
**(828) 692-9057**
Seventy-five antiques dealers show their wares on Main Street from 9 a.m. until 5 p.m. This generally occurs the last of the month or in early June.

### GARDEN JUBILEE
**Visitors Information Center**
**201 South Main St., Hendersonville**
**(828) 693-9708, (800) 828-4244**
The last week in May brings arts and crafts, a plant sale, garden talks, food, and more to the Visitors Information Center. The event is sponsored by downtown merchants, who hold sidewalk sales, treasure hunts, and a free flower drawing and bring in live music that day.

### MONTREAT KIRKIN' O' THE TARTANS
**Montreat Scottish Society, Montreat**
**(828) 669-8011**
Memorial Day Sunday is when the 100 clans of the Scots at Montreat gather. At 10:30 a.m. the Montreat Pipe Band brings the tunes of Scotland to the mountains of Appalachia in front of the great stone building of Anderson Auditorium on the grounds of the Montreat Conference Center and Montreat College. At 11 on the hour, the pipers lead the standard bearers, 100 strong, into Anderson Auditorium for the traditional worship service and blessing of the tartans. Among the illustrious preachers has been Montreat's own resident, the Rev. Dr. Billy Graham.

The idea of Kirkin' in the United States began with the Scottish preacher, Peter Marshall. He was pastor of the Pennsylvania Avenue Presbyterian Church in Washington, D.C., and chaplain of the U.S. Senate. It was during World War II that he initiated the practice, which included gift bearing of goods to send overseas during those times of scarcity in war-torn countries.

## Southern Mountains

### TASTE OF HIGHLANDS
**Highlands Plaza, Highlands**
**(828) 526-2112**
The plaza is bedecked by a festive tent with chefs of the area, wineries and breweries from everywhere, and a lively band exuding sound and excitement. The event begins in the early evening on the first Thurs in May. Admission is charged.

### RAMP CONVENTION
**Various locations, Waynesville**
**(828) 456-3021, (800) 334-9036**
Early May brings a genuine mountain hoedown to again honor the ramp—a rare, wild onionlike plant—in downtown Waynesville. It adds zest to all the day's dishes. There'll be country and bluegrass music, square dancing, and clogging, too. But beware—it's been known to inspire a politician or two to make a speech.

### GREAT SMOKY MOUNTAIN TROUT FESTIVAL
**Recreation Park, Waynesville**
**(828) 456-3021, (800) 334-9036**
This Memorial Day event held in Recreation Park honors the greatest catch in the mountains with exhibitions, contests, crafts, food, and entertainment. The Haywood County Chamber of Commerce sponsors this free event.

# JUNE

## Northern Mountains

### YANCEY COUNTY CLOGGING–
### ART & CRAFT SHOW
Town Square, Burnsville
(828) 682-7413, (800) 948-1632
This dance festival runs for two days in mid-June. Burnsville's town square hosts a pig-pickin' the first night of the fest, serving succulent barbecue, while cloggers dance the traditional mountain jigs handed down through the generations. The first evening culminates in a street dance. Sat includes more clogging and arts and crafts booths.

### NORTH CAROLINA RHODODENDRON
### FESTIVAL
Mitchell Avenue, Bakersville
(828) 765-9483, (800) 227-3912
For more than a half-century this festival has coincided with the blooming of the 600-acre Rhododendron Gardens atop Roan Mountain. A 10K road race, golf tournament, two pageants, historic tours, a car show, and a street dance round out the three-day weekend in the third week of June. These events are free.

### BLUE RIDGE MOUNTAIN FAIR
### CRAFT FESTIVAL
Crouse Park, Sparta
(910) 372-5473, (800) 372-5473
Crouse Park in Sparta is the setting for an old-time mountain fair of food, fun, crafts, and music held the last Sat of the month.

### SINGING ON THE MOUNTAIN AT
### GRANDFATHER MOUNTAIN
Off Hwy. 221 (entrance of Grandfather Mountain)
McRae Meadows, Linville
(828) 733-4337
This traditional Southern gospel sing at magnificent McRae Meadows has been going strong since 1924. Drawing crowds in the tens of thousands, this event hearkens back to old-time preachin', when the message was delivered outdoors under the heavens and voices were lifted up to the skies. Lively gospel singing, entertainers, picnic lunches, preaching by well-known speakers, and wide-open vistas create a joyful good time for the entire family. This event, which takes place on the fourth Sun in June, is free.

## Central Mountains

### BREVARD MUSIC CENTER
349 Andante Lane, Brevard
(828) 884-2011, (888) 384-8682
The renowned music center opens the 2010 season June 25 at 7:30 p.m. for its summer run of more than 80 concerts. Renowned director of the Boston Pops, Keith Lockhart, conducts on opening night. He was a former student of the Brevard Music Center and is now its director. The season continues through its final concert on Aug 8. Throughout the season the offerings are opera, symphony orchestra, symphonic band and sinfonia.

Often a "Bach"s Lunch" concert is offered at noon for picnickers at no charge. Other concerts begin in the afternoon with featured attractions at 7:30 p.m. The grounds are open for early arrivals to share tables in the picnic area. You can bring your own or order from special menus prepared by local restaurants.

### ICE-CREAM SOCIAL/SPRING KICKOFF
Silvermont Mansion
Main Street, Brevard
(828) 884-5255
This early June benefit for the Brevard Little Theatre, held at the Silvermont Mansion on Main Street, gives participants a preview of the community theater's coming season. Admission is free.

### ANNUAL TRYON HORSE SHOW
Foothills Equestrian Nature Center
3381 Hunting Country Rd., Tryon
(828) 859-9021, (800) 4-EVENT-1
Sponsored by the Tryon Riding and Hunt Club at the Foothills Equestrian Nature Center (FENCE)

early in June, this is a free, can't-miss event for horse lovers. Events include dressage, cross-country, and jumping.

### FRENCH BROAD RIVER MONTH
**Various locations in Buncombe, Henderson, Madison, and Transylvania Counties**
**(828) 252-8474**
June is French Broad River Month. This menagerie of events along the riverfront of the French Broad is sponsored by RiverLink, a nonprofit group devoted to improving the river and its banks. Boat races, a Bridge Party and Triathalon, white-water raft trips, biking, and rock climbing are all a part of this outdoors celebration. Activity charges vary, so call ahead.

### THE BLUE RIDGE BARBECUE FESTIVAL AND NORTH CAROLINA STATE BARBECUE CHAMPIONSHIP
**Harmon Field, Tryon**
**(828) 859-6236**
On a weekend in mid-June, the North Carolina state championship barbecue cook-off is held at Harmon Field, attracting even out-of-state barbecue specialists. There's nonstop bluegrass, Piedmont blues, rock and country music, crafts, and children's activities. There is an admission fee.

### RIVER DISTRICT SPRING STUDIO STROLL
**River District, Asheville**
**www.riverdistrictartists.com**
Held the second full weekend in June (and Nov) from 10 a.m. to 4 p.m., the Studio Stroll is a chance to tour over 40 studios, meet with the artists, and purchase artwork.

### SUMMER NIGHTS AT FENCE SCHOOLING SHOW
**Foothills Equestrian Nature Center**
**3381 Hunting Country Rd., Tryon**
**(828) 859-9021, (800) 4-EVENT-1**
From late June through the middle of Aug, a series of horse shows designed for family fun and friendly competition are held at the Foothills Equestrian Nature Center.

## Southern Mountains
### DILLSBORO HERITAGE FESTIVAL
**Various downtown locations, Dillsboro**
**(828) 586-3943**
On the second Sat in June, Dillsboro, one of the mountains' most craft-filled towns, closes off its main shopping street for a festival full of food, arts, crafts, and demonstrations.

### INNKEEPERS TOUR
**Throughout the area, Highlands**
**(828) 526-2112**
The innkeepers of Highlands open their doors and hospitality the second Tues and Wed in June. Chat with the innkeepers, peek behind the scenes, and select the room of your choice for your overnight stay, either then or later. Nibble a cookie here, sip a cup of tea or even a refreshing glass of lemonade there. The inns' adornments range from antiques-filled rooms to extraordinary gardens. Many have wraparound porches, while others offer decks. When you spend a night or two, the innkeepers will be certain to guide you to some of the finest restaurants in the mountains. The Highlands Chamber of Commerce has a map of the inns so you won't have any trouble finding your way around.

### BLUEGRASS FESTIVAL
**Happy Holiday Campground**
**US Hwy. 19 North, Cherokee**
**(828) 864-7203, (800) 438-1601**
You can join in the foot-stompin' that goes on during this three-day, late-June event at the Happy Holiday Campground.

### TASTE OF SCOTLAND
**Square and grounds of Burrell Building, Franklin**
**(828) 524-7472**
Since 1996, the town of Franklin has looked a great deal like "yon, bon bonnie banks of Scotland" on the Sat before Father's Day. This celebration of Scottish heritage is a joint venture of the Scottish Tartan Museum and the Franklin Chamber of Commerce. The day begins with a parade of bag-

pipe bands, followed by dancing, children's games and activities, a display of crafts, and food to please an eclectic taste—if it is Scottish.

# JULY

## Northern Mountains

### OLD-FASHIONED JULY 4TH CELEBRATION ON THE SQUARE
Town Square, Burnsville
(828) 682-7413, (800) 948-1632

The picturesque Town Square is the scene of a Fourth of July like our grandparents enjoyed. Don't miss the wagon train parade, crafts, food, and mountain music. When twilight falls, you would swear it's still 1900.

### GRANDFATHER MOUNTAIN HIGHLAND GAMES AND GATHERING OF THE SCOTTISH CLANS
McRae Meadows, Linville
(828) 733-1333

Expansive McRae Meadows on Grandfather Mountain is the gorgeous venue for a sea of kilts and tartans during the second full weekend in July. For more than 50 years, this gathering has brought Scottish hearts together for ancient games, traditional food, and bagpipes galore.

Don't miss the spectacular Torchlight Opening Ceremony on Thurs evening, invoking the "spirit of the clans" upon the games. This stirring parade of torchbearers and traditional highland bagpipes and drums makes the centuries seem to fall away. A 5-mile foot race from the town of Linville to the top of Grandfather Mountain is also part of the opening night festivities. Evening activities continue throughout the weekend. Charges vary, so call for an informational brochure and for information about parking and the shuttle bus.

### CHRISTMAS IN JULY FESTIVAL
West Jefferson
(336) 246-9550

This festival, which is held in mid-July, is heralded as a celebration of Ashe County's thriving Christmas tree industry. What better fun than to pretend it's Christmas in the heat of midsummer! Christmas crafts, from roping and wreaths to decorated trees, are on display along with traditional mountain crafts. Music to suit just about everyone's tastes, including bluegrass, gospel, and classic rock, fills the air. Helicopter rides, children's activities, and all kinds of mouthwatering food round out the fun. (The exact date of the festival varies from year to year, so call ahead of time.)

## Central Mountains

### OLD-FASHIONED GROVE PARK INN FAMILY 4TH OF JULY
290 Macon Ave., Asheville
(828) 252-2711, (800) 438-5800

Strolling music and sing-alongs, musical fireworks, a bingo scavenger hunt, and tennis and golf clinics at this historic inn help celebrate our national birthday.

### 4TH OF JULY GALA
Various downtown locations, Asheville

A spectacular shower of fireworks illuminates the skyline of historic City/County Plaza in downtown Asheville. Get there early for the food, music, and fun. A variety of food booths, including Greek, Italian, German, Scottish, and all the usual fair fare, line the plaza. Funky tunes from zydeco to rockabilly to country set the stage for inspirational street dancing.

### COON DOG DAY
Various locations, Saluda

This downtown celebration of the coon dog on the Fourth of July weekend is one of the more popular festivals in the region. It is a great day for both dogs and their people, with contests and judging for the dogs and crafts, live music, and a street dance for the people. "Coon" dog is the local term referring to dogs used for hunting raccoons. They range from Beagles to Fox Hounds, Blue Tick Hounds, Red Bones and more.

### FABULOUS FOURTH METRIC CENTURY BICYCLE TOUR
Tryon
(828) 859-6042, (800) 440-7848

As many as 300 participants and many visitors come from throughout the South to enjoy this 63-mile Independence Day tour that begins in Harmon Field in Tryon. The challenging course has ascents to almost 5,500 feet. After cheering the bicyclists on, visitors can go "next door" to Columbus and enjoy that town's Fourth of July festival, an all-day affair that offers food, crafts, a street dance, and evening fireworks.

## HARAMBEE
### Historic Depot and Seventh Avenue District, Hendersonville
### (828) 884-3278
This multicultural festival takes place on the first Sat in July. Here you'll find arts and crafts, entertainment, food, and more.

## SHINDIG-ON-THE-GREEN
### City/County Plaza, Asheville
Every Saturday night in summer, starting the first weekend in July, old-fashioned mountain music thrives in the modern world on Asheville's central City/County Plaza. The Shindig-on-the-Green, now in its 42nd year, is the best free entertainment in the region, drawn from the area's many talented musicians, singers, and dancers. The program, cosponsored by the City of Asheville Parks and Recreation Department and the Asheville Area Chamber of Commerce, began with the simple desire of a few dedicated area musicians to preserve our region's musical heritage. The first stage was set up on the steps of City Hall.

The traditional method of passing down mountain music is by playing it—here, banjo pickers, buck dancers, ballad singers, cloggers, and fans fill the audience and the stage for this celebration of musical heritage. The City/County Plaza swells with a sea of mountain music lovers and spontaneous dancers who begin gathering at 6 p.m. The fun usually goes on until 10 p.m., or until the last banjo picker or guitar player goes home. A house band usually starts the action, followed by an invited team of cloggers or "smooth dance" square dancers. Musicians come from all over the area to be a part of the evening's entertainment. What began modestly

more than four decades ago as a simple desire to keep the ancient strains of mountain music alive has become a living, breathing perpetuation of a unique cultural heritage.

## SUMMERTIME SATURDAY
### Various downtown locations, Brevard
On Sat afternoons throughout July, Brevard's musicians and others from the area perform in the downtown shopping district.

## THE ASHEVILLE POETRY ALIVE FESTIVAL
### University of North Carolina at Asheville, Asheville
### (828) 298-4927
This event is a treat. Poetry workshops and events, many featuring Pulitzer Prize winners, are held in Asheville the second weekend in July. Readings, lectures, and seminars devoted to the written word are open to amateurs, professionals, and the general public. Come watch a "slam," write your own poems, listen to the masters . . . experiment. Admission is charged and varies for the whole event, workshops, or individual days. There is a charge for the weekend pass. Call for event, workshop, or day rates.

## CARNIVAL!
### South Broad Park
### South Broad Street, Brevard
### (828) 877-4777
For four days in mid-July, carnival rides, pony rides, clowns, jugglers, food, prizes, a white elephant sale, dance lessons, and free health screenings are offered, all to benefit the Transylvania Community Hospital. Admission is free, but there is a charge for the rides and some of the games.

## GUILD FAIR
### Asheville Civic Center
### 87 Haywood St., Asheville
### (828) 298-7928
One of the most popular of the annual mountain crafts fairs, Guild Fair is sponsored by the Southern Highland Craft Guild. A juried craft exhibition, professional demonstrations, and fine traditional mountain music set this fair apart from the rest.

Artisans from nine different states in the Appalachians descend on the downtown civic center on the third weekends in July and Oct, offering every kind of craft from wood furniture to glassware to calico dolls and sofa cushions. Here you can get a taste of both the traditional, simple craft and high-end, one-of-a-kind pieces. It's not just a place to observe: The Guild Fair also makes for excellent gift shopping for a special piece of craft heritage. There is an admission fee.

### BELE CHERE
**Various downtown locations, Asheville**
**(828) 253-1009**
This tremendously popular annual street festival has grown over three decades to become one of the premier events in the Southeast, attracting upward of 350,000 people over its three-day span. This is Western North Carolina's largest outdoor festival, featuring more than 100 national and regional entertainment acts. At least five different stages grace various key parts of downtown, and canopied booths line the main streets.

Multicultural crafts and food set the tone—the Greek Orthodox Church always sponsors a booth or two with excellent Mediterranean fare, and the fajitas, gyros, Indian samosas, Thai noodles, and many other mouthwatering selections keep festival goers fairly content. Funnel cakes and shaved ice are sold every few steps. Local restaurants join in, often hosting booths in the central Pack Square.

The musical entertainment, as well as poetry and dance, is excellent, ranging from Andean pan flute music, to throw-down gospel, to reggae, rock and roll, Brazilian samba, zydeco, bluegrass, swing, and much, much more. Street dances continue throughout the day and evening.

Vendors offer colorful batiks, jewelry, leather, pottery, and sundry handcrafted items. Special events like face painting, puppet shows, kiddie concerts, and numerous other activities are geared toward children, making this a terrific family outing. Bele Chere is always held the last Fri, Sat, and Sun of the month. Many sophisticated shopping booths mingle with the more carnival-fare type, presenting hand-wrought fur-

niture, clothing, handmade jewelry, and the popular Indian henna temporary tattoo art mehndi. Best of all, it's free!

**i** Some towns won't allow dogs at their outdoor festivals, so be sure to find out the policy before you bring Fido, or he may end up in "doggie jail"—cages in the shade—while you attend the festival.

### SWANNANOA CHAMBER FESTIVAL
**Warren Wilson College,**
**701 Warren Wilson Rd., Swannanoa**
This annual festival of chamber music is a rarity and a delight. From the campus of Warren Wilson College, a visiting contingent of classically trained professional musicians produces a series of five marvelous concerts. Traveling workshops and concert series for the Hendersonville and Waynesville communities are also part of this five-week-long musical celebration. The festival also combines lectures, demonstrations, and a benefit recital with the regularly scheduled program.

## Southern Mountains
### ANDREWS WAGON TRAIN
**Andrews to Franklin**
**(828) 837-6492**
Since the 1960s this wagon train has wound its way through the mountains, leaving Andrews in late June and arriving in Franklin by the July 4th weekend.

### FOURTH OF JULY FREEDOM FEST
**Town Square, Bryson City**
**(828) 488-3681, (800) 867-9246**
Independence Day in Swain County is celebrated with a bevy of live entertainment, food, crafts, and fireworks, of course.

### JULY 4TH HERITAGE FESTIVAL
**Various downtown locations, Robbinsville**
**(828) 499-3790**
Join the downtown parade featuring local bands. The festival features lots of food and crafts, too.

## MOUNTAINEER ANTIQUE AUTO SHOW
**US 276, Maggie Valley**
**(828) 926-1686, (800) 334-9036**
This is one of the largest gatherings of spiffed-up vintage cars you're likely to see. It takes place over the Fourth of July weekend. There have been more than 500 participants in the past.

## CHRISTIAN HARMONY SINGING
**John C. Campbell Folk School**
**1 Folk School Rd., Brasstown**
**(828) 837-2775, (800) FOLK-SCH**
This annual gathering around the second weekend in July draws nearly 80 singers from much of the Southeast. The four-part, unaccompanied shape-note singing takes place from 10:30 a.m. until 3 p.m., broken only by a covered dish dinner from 12:30 to 1:30 p.m.

## ART FEST
**Downtown, Cashiers**
**(828) 743-5050**
On the second weekend of the month, several thousand people come to view and buy the best in local arts and crafts. Box lunches of tasty barbecue are for sale.

## MOUNTAIN HERITAGE DAY
**Hwy. 107, Cullowhee**
**(828) 227-7272**
This most "mountainy" day of the year attracts some 50,000 people. You can watch chain saw demonstrations, ax-throwing contests, and cat and dog shows. There are also mountain arts and crafts and food. Favorites on the day's program are gospel, bluegrass, and country music with lots of clogging, square dancing, and line dancing.

## ANNUAL SNOWBIRD MOUNTAIN GOSPEL SINGING
**Jacob Cornsilk Community Center**
**Robbinsville**
**(828) 479-8984, (828) 479-3926**
This three-day event, which attracts singers from the entire Southeast, is held in the middle of July in the Jacob Cornsilk Community Center. The

singing starts around 7 p.m. on Fri and Sat and at 2 p.m. on Sun.

## FOLKMOOT USA
**Waynesville and other locations**
**(800) 334-9036**
**www.folkmootusa.org**
An international folk festival the last two weeks in July, this event begins with a parade through downtown Waynesville. The mountains become the world's stage, as musicians and dancers from different countries gather in a celebration of music, dance, and culture. (See the Folkmoot USA Close-up.)

## ANNUAL GEMBOREE
**Macon County Community Building**
**US Hwy. 441 South, Franklin**
**(828) 524-3161, (800) 336-7829**
The "Gem Capital of the World" shows off its rough and cut gems, minerals, fine jewelry, and equipment in late July. You can also shop for gem-related books and supplies, attend lectures, and maybe win a door prize. Admission is free.

## MOUNTAIN ARTISANS SUMMER ARTS AND CRAFT SHOW
**Macon County Community Building**
**US 441 South, Franklin**
**(828) 524-3405**
More than 70 exhibitors from six states show off their country and traditional crafts and fine arts at this show in late July.

## KIRKIN' O' THE TARTANS IN JULY
**First Presbyterian Church of Highlands**
**471 Main St., Highlands**
**(828) 526-3175**
The pipes and drums bring a measure of nostalgia, dignity, and majesty to these mountain communities, which were founded by the Scots. Historic First Presbyterian Church of Highlands is only one of many that honors the tradition of Kirkin'. This is the time when the kilts, tartan banners, and the pipes and drums lead the procession into the church in thankfulness and for the traditional blessings. The Ravenel family played an impor-

tant role in the Highlands community in financing this church in its founding days. At one time a good portion of Whiteside Mountain was part of their holdings as they summered in Highlands.

# AUGUST

## Northern Mountains

### MINERAL AND GEM FESTIVAL
**Pine Bridge Coliseum**
**97 Pine Bridge Ave., Spruce Pine**
**(828) 765-9483, (800) 227-3912**
A rock hound's dream come true, this weeklong event draws crowds to its displays and sales booths. More than 50 dealers descend during the first week in Aug.

### MOUNT MITCHELL CRAFTS FAIR
**Town Square, Burnsville**
**(828) 682-7413, (800) 227-3912**
Here's a spectacular slice of Americana on the grassy Town Square in the quaint village of Burnsville. A splendid array of traditional mountain crafts, food, and music make for an enjoyable day in mid-Aug.

### BANNER ELK ART FESTIVAL
**Old Cannon Hospital, Hickory Nut Gap Road,**
**Banner Elk**
**(828) 898-5605, (800) 972-2183**
This juried fine art exhibit and sale is held the fourth weekend in Aug. It's sponsored by the Avery–Banner Elk Chamber of Commerce.

## Central Mountains

### MOUNTAIN DANCE AND FOLK FESTIVAL
**Downtown Asheville**
**(828) 259-6107**
This granddaddy of all U.S. folk music festivals started informally back in 1927 as just "a little pickin' and a-grinnin' and a-steppin'" at the home of Bascom Lamar Lunsford in Turkey Creek in Buncombe County. Today it has evolved into one of the most revered folk music festivals of its kind in the country.

Lunsford, the festival's founder, devoted his life to the perpetuation of our mountain music heritage. He died in 1973, but his festival still retains the naturalness and spontaneity that gave it life 80 years ago on that porch on Turkey Creek. This toe-tapping, knee-slapping event, cosponsored by the city of Asheville, begins in early Aug each year at various downtown locations.

### VILLAGE ART & CRAFT FAIR
**Throughout Historic Biltmore Village**
**Asheville**
**(828) 274-2831**
What a fabulous setting! Historic Biltmore Village and the grounds of the Cathedral of All Souls in south Asheville, opposite the entrance to Biltmore Estate, come alive the first full weekend in Aug for this annual arts festival. The historic shopping district, once the village of Best, was purchased by George Vanderbilt in the 1890s to accommodate the army of crafters, artisans, and laborers necessary to complete the five-year construction of Biltmore House (see our chapter on Shopping). More than 150 artists offer beautiful jewelry and fiber, pottery, and metalworks. Food and beverage sales benefit community charities.

### SUMMER SOCIAL
**Tryon Fine Arts Center**
**Downtown Tryon**
**(828) 859-8322**
The Fine Arts Council holds an all-day, outdoor arts and entertainment festival on the second Sat of the month at the Tryon Fine Arts Center. It includes local and regional art, food, fun, dances, live music, and magic.

### ANNUAL JAZZ IN BREVARD
**Various locations, Brevard**
**(828) 884-2787**
The Transylvania Arts Council sponsors a day of world-class jazz. This mid-Aug event takes place in various locations.

# Close-up

## Folkmoot USA

Dancers in traditional Kazakh headgear and flowing gowns, Turkish sword dancers with fezes, French stilt dancers in lambskin vests, New Zealand Maori in grass skirts, Bavarian oompah bands, and sombrero-wearing Mexican ensembles are only a few of the multicultural treasures you might encounter at Waynesville's Folkmoot USA festival.

For 10 days every July, this small mountain town transforms itself into a miniature United Nations, melding folk music, dance, and culture from around the world in an event much like one you would have to travel abroad to see. Each year 10 premier folk groups representing different parts of the world demonstrate their cultural heritages through colorful authentic and original reproduction costumes, lively dance, and music played on unique instruments that are often handcrafted. Through the years more than 70 countries have sent more than 130 groups to take part.

It's amazing to look back at the humble beginnings of this festival in 1984. America was in the midst of the Cold War, apartheid ruled South Africa, and yet in one mountain village we could speak to our Russian guests one-on-one or have them visit in our houses. Poles, Kazakhs, Turks, Germans, Lithuanians, Kenyans, and so many others joined together in song and dance, music being the common language. Even today the profound sense of "global family" that this festival evokes is hard to mistake.

Folkmoot is patterned after classic European festivals. More than 300 musicians and dancers from around the globe descend on Waynesville and make their home base in a converted old schoolhouse, now known as the Folkmoot Center. From there, they travel to perform in city, college, and school auditoriums around Western North Carolina. During intermission the foyers turn into eastern bazaars, with the foreign visitors offering traditional souvenirs from their homelands.

International Festival Day is another opportunity to find a mélange of international crafts and to watch some inspired street performances. This street fair was added to Folkmoot USA's lineup in 1986 and attracts 20,000 visitors who mingle among the 100 canopied handicraft and ethnic food booths, along with the costumed performers who might just break into an informal sidewalk song and dance. Local artisans and vendors also join in.

The annual Folkmoot festival closes with a poignant all-group candlelight performance at the Lake Junaluska auditorium. Lights flicker on the water, crickets sing, and a light dew descends on the cool night air as foreign friends bid us good-bye.

For more information on Folkmoot, including a performance schedule and admission costs, call (828) 452-2997 or visit www.folkmootusa.org. You can also write to Folkmoot USA, P.O. Box 658, Waynesville 28786.

**GOOMBAY FESTIVAL**
**Eagle Street and South Market Street, Asheville**
**(828) 252-4614**
This spirited weekend festival celebrates African-American culture in exciting African and Caribbean style. Goombay is a West African term meaning rhythm, and this festival is based on a centuries-old celebration filled with music, dance, and the joy of life.

For more than two decades, Goombay has personified joyous multiculturalism at the corner of Eagle and South Market streets in Asheville. Steel drums; jazz and reggae music; traditional African clothing, jewelry, and decorations; and an incredible assortment of delectable food are all part of the fun. More than 50,000 visitors a year from all over the country step to the Goombay beat, many returning year after year. The festival takes place in late Aug.

## SOURWOOD FESTIVAL

**Various locations, Black Mountain**

**(828) 669-2300, (800) 669-2301**

More than 150 art, craft, and food vendors set up in this picturesque town, a 15-minute ride east of Asheville. A music tent, battle of the bands, and carnival for children are just some of the fun in store Tues through Sun on the third week in Aug. Stroll the old-fashioned main street and peek into the numerous galleries and antiques stores. Many of them have special sales in conjunction with the festival. It features a lot of good old Americana—bring out the corndogs, watermelon, and, of course, the sourwood honey.

## Southern Mountains

**ANNUAL ANTIQUE SHOW**

**Blue Ridge School**

**Hwy. 107, Cashiers**

**(828) 743-5191**

Held the first weekend in Aug, this juried show at the Blue Ridge School draws dealers from all over the Southeast. Come early: The place fills quickly, and people do come to buy!

**J. C. CAMPBELL ANNUAL AUGUST AUCTION**

**1 Folk School Rd., Brasstown**

**(828) 837-2775, (800) FOLK-SCH**

Spend the first Sat of the month bidding on outstanding craft items. It's a great way to support this unique craft school.

# SEPTEMBER

## Northern Mountains

**MUSIC IN THE MOUNTAINS FESTIVAL**

**Toe River Campground Park**

**Hwy. 80, Burnsville**

**(828) 682-7413, (828) 682-7215**

**(800) 948-1632**

Mountain folk music and food at the Toe River Campground Park are a magical combination, especially with Mother Nature's beautiful backdrop. Various bluegrass and mountain music bands play at this all-day jamboree in late Sept, often jamming into the night with visitors who

happen to bring along instruments. The small fee is usually under $5.

## OLDE BOONE STREETFEST

**Various locations, Boone**

This country fair on the streets of Boone has the added appeal of the early fall leaf colors as a backdrop for fun. You can munch all day on traditional mountain foods or go for more modern tastes. The arts and crafts are excellent, and music sets a lively mood. The festival is held in late Sept.

**i** Local newspapers print special supplements for larger events. Take these with you. They are excellent sources for information, schedules, and event locations.

## OVERMOUNTAIN VICTORY TRAIL CELEBRATION

**Mile 331, Spruce Pine**

**(828) 765-9483, (800) 227-3912**

Relive the lives of the "overmountain boys," who walked a trail toward history defending our rights and freedoms. Scheduled events are complemented by demonstrations of frontier cooking, leatherwork, beadwork, spinning, and other Revolutionary-era lifestyle skills. The celebration is held on the third weekend of the month at the North Carolina Museum of Minerals.

## Central Mountains

**ANNUAL APPLE FESTIVAL**

**Hendersonville**

**(828) 692-1413, (800) 282-4244**

For more than half a century this has been Henderson County's biggest event. It takes place from Sept's first Fri through Mon and includes a huge street fair, food, crafts, entertainment, and sporting contests. There are 41 individual events and 25 kinds of entertainment taking place all over town, including the Mountain Music Jamboree, Sunday in the Park, a bike tour, a 10K run, Apple Jack and Apple Jill golf tournaments, and the King Apple Parade.

## CELEBRATE FOLK ART DAY
**Folk Art Center**
**Blue Ridge Parkway, Asheville**
**(828) 298-7928**
Head for the Folk Art Center, east of the city on the Blue Ridge Parkway, for a day dedicated to those who carry on our Appalachian craft heritage. The early crafts of the mountains were made by combining local materials with skills brought over from England and Europe. Chairs, dolls, musical instruments, knives, quilts, weavings, and carvings are all part of the show, plus musicians and storytellers.

## GREEK FESTIVAL
**City/County Plaza, Asheville**
**(828) 253-3754**
Asheville's Greek community has contributed richly to the multicultural fabric of the city for more than 100 years. This annual festival is a special treat for young and old alike. Ethnic music and crafts line the City/County Plaza downtown near Pack Square. And the food! Spanakopita, pastitchio, gyros, baklava—try one of everything! A cafe tent features Greek sweets and rich strong demitasses of finely ground Greek coffee; just don't swallow the dregs.

## FALL PIONEER LIVING DAYS AND MILITARY ENCAMPMENT
**Zebulon B. Vance Birthplace**
**911 Reems Creek Rd., Weaverville**
**(828) 645-6706**
The 1800s come alive at the Zebulon B. Vance Birthplace, a state historic site. Here mountain crafts and traditional cooking are demonstrated, and a 19th-century military encampment is reenacted on the grounds.

## Southern Mountains
### FIREMAN'S DAY FESTIVAL
**Town Square, Bryson City**
**(828) 488-9416**
Held on Town Square on the first Sat of the month, this is a day and evening of festivities in the mountain tradition with music, entertainment, and crafts.

## SMOKY MOUNTAIN FOLK FESTIVAL
**Stuart Auditorium, Lake Junaluska**
**(800) 334-9036**
A freewheeling Labor Day celebration of the finest traditional and old-timey music and dance, this mountain festival is held in the cool, open-air Stuart Auditorium and on the surrounding grounds. There's even a separate show where kids can kick up their heels!

## FESTIVAL OF NATIVE PEOPLES
**Cherokee Indian Fairgrounds**
**(800) 438-1601**
**www.cherokee-nc.com**
This annual festival occurs in late Sept. It was inspired by Folkmoot, a festival of international folk groups gathering annually in nearby Waynesville in late July. The Eastern Band of the Cherokee host Native American dancers from across the country. It differs from a powwow, which is also held in Cherokee, in that it is not a competition. The two-day event features Native American tribes in full regalia of colors. In addition to Cherokee, Apache, Zuni, Southwest Plains, Aztec, and Alaskan Native cultures are also represented. Other features of this festival are the opportunity to taste Native American food, demonstrations, arts and crafts, and storytelling. For additional information check out www.sitkatribe.org or www.cherokeepreservationfdn.org.

## HAYWOOD COUNTY FAIR
**Haywood County Fair Ground**
**Lake Junaluska**
**(828) 452-0152, (800) 334-9036**
There are barbecues, cotton candy, gospel singings under the tent, old-fashioned horse and tractor pulls, a man's biscuit-making contest, a petting zoo, food and craft exhibits, and more! The event takes place at the Haywood County Fair Ground in Lake Junaluska.

## HOMECOMING PARADE
**Downtown Robbinsville**
**(828) 479-3330**
Remember the good ol' days? This is an old-fashioned homecoming the last Sat of the month,

complete with a football game at the high school and the crowning of a homecoming queen.

## OCTOBER

### Northern Mountains

#### MADISON COUNTY HERITAGE FESTIVAL
**Various locations, Mars Hill**
**(828) 689-9351, (828) 689-1424**
The first Sat in Oct is set aside for this celebration of the community and family life of the people of "the Mountains of Madison." Traditional mountain crafts such as rug braiding, basketmaking, spinning and weaving, and musical instrument making are among the exhibitions. This delightful, small college town opens up all of Main Street, serving a wonderful assortment of pies, cakes, breads, and home cooking. Forty craft booths, local musicians, clog dancers, storytellers, and shape-note singers add to the festivities.

#### NEW RIVER FESTIVAL
**Various locations, Todd**
**(336) 877-1128, (336) 877-1067**
Todd, a historic village in Ashe County, is the scene of a festival on the ancient New River in early Oct. Once a bustling train town, Todd is now a quiet hamlet frequented by the traveler who wants a different, more leisurely getaway.

This festival offers an old-fashioned gospel sing, checkers play-off, horseshoe toss, arts displays, storytelling, a fishing tournament, and much more. And don't miss the town's main attraction, the Todd General Store. And you thought community socials were a thing of the past. Admission: one smile.

#### VALLE COUNTRY FAIR
**Apple Barn, Hwy. 194, Valle Crucis**
**(828) 264-1299, (800) 852-9506**
When the colors of the autumn leaves set the mountains afire and the air carries a slight nip, you know it's time for the Valle Country Fair. This delightful mountain festival is the premier arts, crafts, and mountain music event in the High Country, drawing upwards of 15,000 visitors annually for an entire weekend in mid-Oct.

Set on the grounds of the old Apple Barn near the Valle Crucis Conference Center in picturesque Valle Crucis, the event takes you back to simpler times when country fairs were the prime social events in the mountains. Every year more than 150 artisans unveil their handcrafted treasures.

The atmosphere is highlighted by the strains of mountain music, and you might even catch of a glimpse of old, buckskin-clad Dan'l Boone himself. It's actually actor Glenn Causey, who, since 1955, has played the venerable frontiersman in *Horn in the West*, the popular outdoor drama staged in nearby Boone (see our Attractions chapter). All proceeds from the fair benefit local High Country charitable organizations. Don't miss this one! Come early and stake out a parking spot.

To find the Apple Barn, take Highway 194 South past the Mast General Store. You'll find the Apple Barn in just under 2 miles.

#### WOOLLY WORM FESTIVAL
**Banner Elk**
**(828) 898-5605, (800) 972-2183**
A fuzzy weather prognosticator? Tradition says it's so. The woolly worm has earned this distinction here in the mountains, and people gather high up in Banner Elk to celebrate the fact every year during the third weekend in Oct, just before the winds blow chill. Stripes on the woolly worm are traditionally inspected by town elders. Depending on the color, the elders can predict what kind of winter it will be. Along with the honored woolly worm, more than 120 craft artists, races, entertainment, and food make the festival a hit for the whole family.

#### FALL CELEBRATION OF THE ARTS
**Downtown Spruce Pine**
**(828) 765-9483, (800) 227-3912**
This annual juried and invitational exhibition that takes place on the third weekend in Oct features traditional and contemporary glass, fiber, ceramics, metal, wood, sculpture, and jewelry by some of the region's finest artists. It's a good place to start a little early Christmas shopping.

### APPLE FESTIVAL
**591 Horn in the West Dr., Boone**
**(828) 264-2225, (800) 852-9506**
High in the Northern Mountains come apples, apples, and more apples late in Oct. This annual festival celebrates the esteemed fruit with a traditional harvest-time good time. Crafts, entertainment, and food, particularly the apples, "round" out the festival.

### MOUNTAIN HERITAGE FESTIVAL
**Various locations, Sparta**
**(336) 372-5473, (800) 372-5473**
Enjoy an old-time celebration of early mountain life in the "unspoiled province" of Alleghany County, tucked up against the Virginia border. This is harvest time as it used to be. Sparta (population 1,957) serves up an energetic good time with all the ingredients for which these events are noted: food, fun, crafts, and crowds.

## Central Mountains
### ANNUAL FOREST FESTIVAL DAY
**Cradle of Forestry, Pisgah National Forest**
**Brevard**
**(828) 877-3130**
The Cradle of Forestry, a National Historic Site, celebrates our past and future forest resources with old-time demonstrations of carding, spinning, natural dyeing, weaving, whittling, basket making, crosscut sawing, fence rail splitting, and trail building. This popular event takes place the first week in Oct. Admission charged. Over 50 craftspeople, exhibitors, and entertainers take part.

### THOMAS WOLFE FESTIVAL
**Various locations, Asheville**
**(828) 253-8304**
The Thomas Wolfe Memorial Welcome Center and downtown Asheville host two days of events on the first weekend of Oct saluting Asheville's most famous writer. Included are readings, discussions, walking tours, a birthday party, music, and theater events. Most events are free.

### TRANSYLVANIA ART GUILD ANNUAL FALL SHOW AND SALE
**Courthouse Lawn, Brevard**
**(828) 884-4366**
Original art in all media including wood carving and batik is for sale on the courthouse lawn on the second weekend in Oct.

### ANNUAL ANY AND ALL DOG SHOW
**Harmon Field, Tryon**
**(828) 859-6109, (800) 4-EVENT-1**
Calling all dogs! Bring your people and join in the fun the second weekend in Oct at 1:30 p.m. Categories include master and dog look-alike, most unusual tail, best trick, and more.

### GUILD FAIR
**Asheville Civic Center, Asheville**
**(828) 298-7928**
One of the most popular of the annual mountain crafts fairs, Guild Fair is sponsored by the Southern Highland Craft Guild and features a juried craft exhibition, professional demonstrations, and fine traditional mountain music. It's held in the downtown civic center on the third weekends in July and Oct.

### FALL QUILT SHOW
**National Guard Armory, Hendersonville**
**(828) 891-5027**
In mid-Oct cozy covers transformed into works of art are on display at the National Guard Armory. The brilliant colors rival Mother Nature's fall display! Admission charged.

### LAKE EDEN ARTS FESTIVAL
**Camp Rockmont, Black Mountain**
**(828) 686-8742**
The Lake Eden Arts Festival is a fun event filled with dancing and music, drumming and handcrafts, poetry and storytelling. There are also spiritual and healing workshops and a farmers' market during the three-day weekend in late Oct and again in May.

## HALLOWEEN FEST
**Transylvania County**
**Various locations, Brevard**
**(828) 883-3700**
What better place for a fun and scary Halloween than in Transylvania. From 10 a.m. until 6 p.m., there are food vendors, crafters, a musical competition, a bicycle rodeo, and a mask-making workshop. In the afternoon participants can sacrifice their blood, not to a vampire, but to the Bloodmobile; join or watch a costume parade; trick-or-treat in the downtown area; compete in a pumpkin-carving contest; enjoy a kids' carnival; and much more.

## SOUTHEASTERN ANIMAL FIBER FAIR
**WNC Agricultural Center**
**1301 Fanning Bridge Rd., Fletcher**
**(828) 891-2810**
The end of Oct brings a fair that features hundreds of fiber animals, including llamas, Angora goats, rabbits, and many breeds of sheep. Demonstrations teach how to harvest and use such fiber "crops."

## FARM CITY DAY
**Jackson Park, Hendersonville**
**(828) 697-4884**
The free, daylong event, held in Jackson Park, includes tractor pulls, sheep herding, and shearing demonstrations. Here you'll find antique and modern farm equipment, square dancing, clogging, arts and crafts, and food booths. The festivities end with a Civil War reenactment. A special children's section features activities such as a greased pig contest.

## Southern Mountains
### ANNUAL ANDREWS ANTIQUE CAR SHOW
**Downtown Andrews**
**(828) 321-4411**
For over two decades 100 to 200 cars and trucks from as far away as Knoxville, Chattanooga, and Atlanta have been put on display at this huge show held the first Sat of the month. There is an entry fee for vehicles; spectators get in free. It's a lively event with all-day 1950s music, car-related booths, and lots of food. In years past entries have included the world's fastest '57 Chevy.

## J. C. CAMPBELL FALL FESTIVAL
**1 Folk School Rd., Brasstown**
**(828) 837-2775, (800) FOLK-SCH**
This is a two-day fair of food, crafts, children's activities, music, dance, and good company held the first weekend of the month.

## CHURCH STREET ART AND CRAFT SHOW
**Main Street, Waynesville**
**(828) 456-3021, (800) 334-9036**
On the second Sat of the month, Main Street is transformed into an arts and crafts marketplace that showcases the region's finest artisans. There are food booths and traditional mountain music. Only original works of art are accepted in this juried show.

## MAROON DEVIL CLASSIC BAND CONTEST
**Graham County High School**
**Lakeview Drive, Bryson City**
**(828) 488-2152**
On the third Sat of the month, country-and-western bands from North Carolina, Tennessee, and Georgia converge on this town, along with appreciative crowds.

## BRYSON CITY CHILI COOKOFF
**Railroad Station**
**Everett Street, Bryson City**
**(828) 488-3681**
Teams of chili cookers compete for trophies, accompanied by live music, on the last Sat of the month.

## PUMPKIN FEST
**Various locations, Franklin**
**(828) 524-3161, (800) 336-3704**
On the last Sat of the month, school children show off their decorated pumpkins and gourds during this town-wide celebration, which also features costume contests, crafts, and food vendors.

# NOVEMBER

## Northern Mountains

### OLD FASHIONED CHRISTMAS
**Various locations, Blowing Rock**

The town of Blowing Rock launches a series of seasonal festivities that continues through the end of Dec. It begins after Thanksgiving and includes a Christmas parade, "Christmas in the Park" with caroling in the town's Memorial Park, Christmas decorations throughout the town, and various day and evening activities in conjunction with the season. Call the Blowing Rock Chamber of Commerce (828-295-7851) for a complete listing of Yuletide activities.

## Central Mountains

### THE ASHEVILLE FILM FESTIVAL
**Asheville Parks and Recreation, Asheville**
**(828) 259-5800**

A start-up festival for films from around the world, the AFF takes place in venues around Asheville.

### RIVER DISTRICT FALL STUDIO STROLL
**River District, Asheville**
**www.riverdistrictartists.com**

Held the second full weekend in Nov (and June) from 10 a.m. to 4 p.m., the Studio Stroll is a chance to tour over 40 studios, meet with the artists, and purchase artwork.

### CHRISTMAS AT BILTMORE ESTATE
**1 Approach Rd., Asheville**
**(828) 274-6333, (800) 289-1895**

This magnificent re-creation of a Victorian Christmas of a century ago begins just before Thanksgiving and continues through Dec. Daytime visits to George Vanderbilt's mansion are wonderful, but make a point to include on your agenda this nighttime delight—the Biltmore House bathed in the glow of candlelight and blazing hearth fires. It's exquisite, but it's by reservation only, so book early. The cost is admission to the estate.

### CHRISTMAS PARADE
**Patton Avenue, Asheville**

This is a vibrant, rousing, rollicking beginning to the fun of the Christmas season. Always held before Thanksgiving, Asheville's Christmas parade is alive with colorful floats, whirling Shriners, energetic marching bands, high-stepping steeds, tiny twirlers, raucous clowns, and ol' St. Nick himself showering the throngs with candy canes and peppermints. This parade is always well attended by young and old and swells downtown to bursting. Get there early to stake out your spot.

### A GROVE PARK INN CHRISTMAS
**Grove Park Inn**
**290 Macon Ave., Asheville**
**(828) 252-2711, (800) 438-5800**

Here is a special place to fill your family with the Christmas spirit. In addition to beautifully decorated trees, there are gingerbread houses made by area artists, storytelling, caroling, and craft demonstrations. The famed Grove Park Inn Staff Chorus performs daily in the Great Hall, with special appearances by the inn's ambassador, Major Bear. Holiday activities continue from late Nov through New Year's Day.

### HOME FOR THE HOLIDAYS
**Various locations, Hendersonville and**
**Flat Rock**
**(828) 693-9708, (800) 828-4244**

Concerts, exhibits, tours, and special holiday events are scheduled beginning the day after Thanksgiving through Christmas. It starts with the mayoral downtown holiday lighting ceremony and includes tours of historic bed-and-breakfast establishments, Christmas carols, open house at the Curb Market, the Kris Kringle Kids Karnival, and much more.

## Southern Mountains

### J. C. CAMPBELL ANNUAL BLACKSMITH AUCTION
**1 Folk School Rd., Brasstown**
**(828) 837-2775, (800) FOLK-SCH**

Taking place on the second Sat of the month, this auction offers pieces by some the nation's greatest masters. Proceeds help keep the craft school's smithy one of the best.

## ANNUAL HARD-CANDY ARTS AND CRAFTS SHOW
**Macon County Community Building**
**Franklin**
**(828) 524-9801, (800) 336-7829**
In the old days, when times were hard, kids might receive only a few hard candies and perhaps a handmade gift for the holidays. This became known as a Hard-Candy Christmas. You get a free stick of peppermint at this popular show, held just after Thanksgiving. The exhibitors are first class: There are apple crafts, a children's section full of dolls and doll houses, a host of angels, and other crafts reflecting the holiday spirit. Bring your Christmas list!

## TOWN LIGHTING
**Highlands Town Hall and Main Street**
**Highlands**
**(828) 526-2112**
Once again the population of Highlands swells with the guests joining the year-round folks for the lighting. It occurs on the Sat following Thanksgiving. This traditional event ushers in the excitement of the holiday season. The shops are adorned with seasonal decorations, subtle, yet beckoning. It's time to experience the holidays in a tasteful manner.

# DECEMBER

## Northern Mountains

### BOONE CHRISTMAS PARADE
**Downtown, Boone**
**(828) 264-2225, (800) 852-9506**
The first Sat in Dec is set aside to herald the holiday season in this picturesque college town. Choose a Fraser fir from the mountains and watch the magic of the holiday season begin at this old-fashioned parade.

## CHOOSE AND CUT WEEKEND
**Ashe County, (336) 246-9550**
**Sparta/Alleghany County, (800) 372-5473**
**Watauga County, (800) 852-9506**
The Northern Mountains region is the land of Christmas trees, and fragrant "groves" of evergreens spread over remote hillsides begin to bustle with activity as Christmas nears. Choose and Cut Weekend provides the ideal opportunity to select the family Christmas tree. All locations offer tree-cutting festivities, including caroling and cider and cookie sampling in early Dec. After you tie the fir to the car roof, go have a mug of hot chocolate and join in the holiday events and festival fun. Christmas card memories!

## NORTH POLE AT BEECH
**Various locations, Beech Mountain**
**(828) 387-9283, (800) 468-5506**
A lively old-fashioned holiday celebration starts at Fred's General Mercantile in this cozy ski village. You can ride on a caroling hayride and bring the little ones to see Santa in a real horse-drawn carriage. Christmas snow in the Northern Mountains comes more often than not.

## Central Mountains

### BLACK MOUNTAIN CHRISTMAS PARADE AND COMMUNITY CANDLE LIGHTING
**Downtown Black Mountain**
**(828) 669-2300, (800) 669-2301**
The unique village of Black Mountain just east of Asheville is the setting for a traditional parade down a picturesque Main Street to Lake Tomahawk, just a few blocks north of downtown. The event begins in late afternoon the first Sat in Dec and is capped by the lighting of candles and carol singing around the rim of luminaria-lit Lake Tomahawk (where Santa has been known to make an appearance).

### TWILIGHT TOUR AND DICKENS ON MAIN
**Various locations, Brevard**
**(828) 884-3278**
During this evening event on the first Sat in Dec, horse-drawn carriages transport revelers through

the twinkling lights and luminaria-lit streets of downtown, past carolers, musicians, and food vendors. Most stores are open and serve free hot cider and cookies. This event, regardless of the weather, is extremely popular with local residents.

## CHRISTMAS WITH THE GUILD
**Folk Art Center**
**Blue Ridge Parkway, Asheville**
**(828) 298-7928**
The Southern Highland Craft Guild displays Christmas decorations and holiday craft exhibits at the grand showcase venue of the Folk Art Center at the Blue Ridge Parkway entrance just east of the city. Free holiday concerts are featured on weekends throughout Dec.

## FESTIVAL OF TREES
**Silvermont Mansion**
**East Main Street, Brevard**
**(828) 883-3692**
You can buy or just enjoy looking at the exquisitely decorated trees, Christmas cakes, candies, cookies, and gifts prepared for this four-day event in early Dec that benefits the Children's Center. A raffle is also held.

## CHRISTMAS PARADE AND KRIS KRINGLE KARNIVAL
**Downtown, Hendersonville**
**(828) 692-1413, (800) 828-4244**
In early Dec, after a traditional Christmas parade down Main Street, enjoy the Kris Kringle Karnival, which features Santa Claus, crafts, carnival games, entertainment, and food.

## SANTA AND MORE
**Chimney Rock Park, Chimney Rock**
**(828) 625-9611, (800) 277-9611**
Enjoy winter scenes of Hickory Nut Gorge, sounds of the season, and visits with Santa throughout the month of Dec.

## FESTIVAL OF LIGHTS
**Jackson Park, Hendersonville**
**(828) 697-4884**
Held on Fri and Sat nights, from 5:30 until 9:30 p.m. on the second weekend of the month, this festival includes the lighting of the Hospice Tree, Santa, hayrides, and refreshments. On Sat evening 2,000 luminarias light up the park.

## CHRISTMAS AT CONNEMARA
**Connemara**
**1928 Little River Rd., Flat Rock**
**(828) 693-4178**
Follow the luminaria-lined path up the hillside to the Carl Sandburg Home and savor a simple time of Christmas past just as the Sandburg family celebrated it. The one-day event, usually held the third week in Dec, costs $3 for adults. Children younger than 16 are admitted free.

## KWANZAA
**YMI Cultural Center**
**39 South Market St., Asheville**
**(828) 252-4614**
The historic YMI Cultural Center (corner of Market and Eagle streets) in downtown Asheville is the setting for this African-American celebration of the holiday season. Kwanzaa is a Swahili word meaning "first" and signifies the first fruits of the harvest—a time when people come together to celebrate and give thanks for their good fortune. In 1966 these basic principles were adopted in America to create this celebration that includes lighting of the ceremonial Kinara candelabrum, traditional music, readings, and a bounty of ethnic foods. The celebration takes place from Dec 26 to Jan 1.

# Southern Mountains
## CHRISTMAS AT THE LAKE
**Lambuth Inn, Lake Junaluska**
**(828) 452-2881, (800) 222-4930**
From Dec 1 to Christmas Eve, enjoy this three-week celebration that includes self-guided tours of the Lambuth Inn's beautiful Christmas trees, gingerbread houses, and nativity scenes.

## HIGHLANDS OLDE MOUNTAIN CHRISTMAS PARADE
**Main Street, Highlands**
**(828) 526-2112**
Jolly Old St. Nick has the key to the city gates and occupies the mayor's chair during this festive time. The parade winds its way through this mountain town on the first Sat in Dec. Bed-and-breakfasts and the restaurants open their doors to guests, offering hospitality and Christmas-theme meals. The surrounding mountains offer the enchantment of the season and sleigh bells can be heard, especially if one listens carefully. Chestnuts are roasting on an open fire, and hot chocolate couldn't taste better. Highlands at the holidays is always special.

## HOLIDAY TOUR OF HISTORIC HOMES
**Various locations, Maggie Valley**
**(828) 926-1686, (800) 334-9036**
This is a feast for the senses in old-fashioned homes decked out in their Christmas best. It takes place the first week in Dec and is free of charge.

## J. C. CAMPBELL FIRESIDE SALE
**1 Folk School Rd., Brasstown**
**(828) 837-2775, (800) FOLK-SCH**
This craft sale extravaganza on the first Sun in Dec is just one of many community events happening around the hearth and the big Christmas tree at the John C. Campbell Folk School.

## LUMINARIA IN DILLSBORO
**Various locations, Dillsboro**
**(828) 586-3943**
The first two weekends in Dec, all shops hold open houses with thousands of luminaria lighting up the streets and Christmas caroling filling the night. Complimentary refreshments are served.

## Appendix

# LIVING HERE

In this section we feature specific information for residents or those planning to relocate here. Topics include real estate, education, health care, and much more.

# RELOCATION

The great stretch of the Appalachian Mountains spreads from Canada to Alabama. The highest peaks in the eastern United States swoop down through North Carolina, across the Asheville plateau swelling up into the Great Smokies. Rich soils deposited here from the receding glaciers of the Ice Age provided these mountains with the seeds of flora ranging from Georgia to Canada. It is in this verdant land of forested mountains, richly silted bottoms, rushing streams, and brilliant waterfalls that villages, towns, and cities have developed.

The largest city in Western North Carolina is Asheville, with a population of over 78,000. But Western North Carolina reaches from the northern mountains of North Carolina to the borders of neighboring Virginia, West Virginia, Tennessee, Georgia, and South Carolina, with large and small towns throughout—each developing at its own speed. You can always be certain of access to interstates, major U.S. highways, and the Blue Ridge Parkway, while maintaining a sense of quiet Southern relaxation.

Even in the towns and cities, one can spot a black bear now and then. One senses the wilderness is never too far away. Deer are abundant as well, while mountain otter splash in the streams and an elk herd has been reintroduced. There are those who swear to having seen a mountain lion, often called a "painter."

Hospitality continues to be one of the mountains' leading industries. But recreation and sports, particularly mountain biking and kayaking, have almost overtaken even hunting and fishing as favorite pastimes. Golf courses lead from flat land to the high mountains. Artisans gather, wooed by the Penland School of Crafts in the northern mountains and John C. Campbell Folk School in the southern mountains.

Agriculture and aquaculture provide world leadership in the Christmas tree industry, forestry, viniculture, and farm produce. Industry and technology abound in the mountains, with various national and international firms embedded in the infrastructure.

The University of North Carolina at Asheville blazed the trail with its College for Seniors. Community colleges throughout the mountains now provide opportunities for seniors to enter new hobbies.

The North Carolina mountains—more particularly Asheville—have been listed as an ideal place to live in magazines such as *Modern Maturity, Southern Living, Money* magazine, and *Places Rated Almanac*. With such national attention, locals and those who now consider themselves locals are keen on not stretching the resources of these mountains too thin. Move here ... and you, too, may eventually find yourselves defending the beauty of the land from overdevelopment by "outsiders"—and wisely so.

## REAL ESTATE

With so many professional real estate companies in all 18 counties of North Carolina's mountains, we provide you with a registry of real estate publications. Also, every town paper in the mountains runs a Sunday real estate section.

*APARTMENT FINDER*
(800) 222-3651
www.livingchoices.com
This complimentary booklet covers Asheville and Hendersonville and provides contacts for rental and for-purchase apartments.

## CENTURY 21 MOUNTAIN LIFESTYLES HOME GUIDE

(866) 812-2100

www.c21mountainlifestyles.com

This free monthly publication showcases 500-plus homes, commercial properties, and land. Find it available at many freestanding displays in restaurants, airports, and on the street.

**i** There's a lot to be said for a house sitting high on a plateau or mountainside with a spectacular mountain view. But while these higher elevation homes are cooler in summer, they are also much colder in winter. Hilltops, too, are often subject to high winds and ice-covered driveways.

## HOMES & LAND OF ASHEVILLE

(800) 277-7800

www.homesandland.com

Look for this free monthly publication throughout Buncombe and Madison Counties. It serves both counties.

## MATURE LIVING CHOICES

(Senior Selections Carolina Mountains & Upstate)

(800) 222-5771

www.maturelivingchoices.com

This complimentary booklet assists seniors in finding enjoyable housing. A questionnaire at the front of the book can be of assistance. A call to the toll-free number will get an issue mailed to you for your relocation consideration.

## REAL ESTATE WEEKLY

Published by Asheville Board of Realtors

209 East Chestnut St., Asheville

(828) 255-8505

Published weekly, this tabloid is available at newsstands throughout the area and provides color photographs and good descriptions of area homes.

# NEWSPAPERS

## Northern Mountains

### THE ALLEGHANY NEWS

Sparta

www.alleghanynews.com

### THE BLOWING ROCKET

Blowing Rock

www.blowingrocket.com

### JEFFERSON POST

West Jefferson

www.jeffersonpost.com

### THE MITCHELL NEWS JOURNAL

Spruce Pine

www.mitchellnews.com

### THE MOUNTAIN TIMES

Boone

www.mountaintimes.com

### WATAUGA DEMOCRAT

Boone

www.wataugademocrat.com

## Central Mountains

### ASHEVILLE CITIZEN-TIMES

Asheville

www.citizen-times.com

### BLACK MOUNTAIN NEWS

Black Mountain

www.blackmountainnews.com

### LA VOZ INDEPENDIENTE

Henderson

www.spanishnc.com

### MOUNTAIN XPRESS

Asheville

www.mountainx.com

*TIMES-NEWS*
Hendersonville
www.hendersonvillenews.com

## Southern Mountains

*THE ANDREWS JOURNAL*
Andrews
www.theandrewsjournal.com

*THE CHEROKEE SCOUT*
Murphy
www.thecherokeescout.com

*THE FRANKLIN PRESS*
Franklin
www.thefranklinpress.com

*THE HIGHLANDER*
Highlands
www.highlandnews.com

*THE MOUNTAINEER*
Waynesville
www.themountaineer.com

*SMOKY MOUNTAIN NEWS*
Waynesville
www.smokymountainnews.com

*TRYON DAILY BULLETIN*
Tryon
www.tryondailybulletin.com

# WORSHIP

Long known as the Bible Belt of America, the South continues its tradition of spiritual offerings. This nomenclature can be attributed to the early settlers who pushed into a wilderness to scratch out a living. They needed to call upon all the help they could get. Some helpers came over the mountains as circuit riders. One of the earliest was Bishop Asbury, who firmly established the Methodist church in these mountains. Many Methodist churches carry his name. Major world religions have representations in North Caro-

lina's mountains. Also, independent religious and philosophical faiths have found root here.

## Churches and Related Conference Centers

### Northern Mountains

**VALLE CRUCIS CONFERENCE CENTER**
146 Skiles Way, Valle Crucis
(828) 963-4453
www.highsouth.com/vallecrucis
This conference center is host to the Labyrinth of the ministry of the Episcopal diocese of Western North Carolina. It is patterned after the ancient labyrinth at Chartre Cathedral in France. This ancient spiritual tool provides a winding, circuitous walk symbolizing a pilgrim's walk with God. The center is open to all who wish to make a reservation.

**WILDACRES RETREAT**
Wildacres Road, Little Switzerland
(828) 756-4573
www.wildacres.org
Wildacres is a conference center offering its facilities to nonprofit groups that conduct educational or cultural programs and seminars. In 1946, it was dedicated by I. D. and Madolyn Blumenthal to the betterment of human relations and interfaith dialogue. It is situated on 1,600 acres at an elevation of 3,300 feet atop a mountain called Pompey's Knob, near the Blue Ridge Parkway in Little Switzerland, North Carolina. It is about halfway between Asheville and Blowing Rock. Among the many groups using the facilities are music and art master classes; religious and interfaith groups; mineral and lapidary societies; and medical, social science, natural sciences, academic, environmental, and senior citizen groups. All groups must be nonprofit and have planned educational programs.

### Central Mountains

**BASILICA OF ST. LAWRENCE**
97 Haywood St., Asheville
(828) 252-6042
The 34th Minor Basilica in the United States of the Roman Catholic Church is the Basilica of St. Law-

rence in Asheville. This downtown church was built by Spanish architect Rafael Guastavino. A remarkable feature of this church is that the architect is buried in an alcove in the Chapel of Mary. In that same chapel is the restored Stanzionni painting "The Visitation," which was discovered to be the missing painting from the set of four he painted for the Vatican.

The Basilica has a sister church of the same design in Wilmington, North Carolina. In Asheville, services are in both English and Spanish to serve its diverse parish. In celebrating its 10th year as a Minor Basilica, a litany written for the opening of the church in 1908 by architect Guastavino was discovered and was used for the first time.

## CATHEDRAL OF ALL SOULS
### 9 Swann St., Biltmore Village
### (828) 274-2681

This Episcopal church was built as part of George W. Vanderbilt's Biltmore Village. It served as an anchor for the many buildings in the village that now house boutique shops, restaurants, and other functioning businesses. The stained-glass windows are especially noteworthy as they were created by LaFarge. The church, as were other original buildings in the village, was designed in a style similar to that of the Yorkshire Moors in England.

## THE COVE/BILLY GRAHAM TRAINING CENTER
### 1 Porters Cove Rd., Swannanoa
### (828) 298-2092, (800) 950-2092
### www.thecove.org

The Billy Graham Training Center at the Cove is situated on a secluded 1,500 acres of solitude with a bubbling stream and winding trails. The four-story Chatlos Memorial Chapel, with its 87-foot steeple and 8-foot cross, is open to visitors.

The Cove property is an idyllic setting, with mountain streams, hiking trails, and open fields. The cove camp is open for ages 9 to 15. In addition, other camps and retreat sites are provided for junior and senior high school students. The Cove Camp includes full-facility cabins, a dining

hall, and recreational sites. Weekend conferences, summer retreats, and other ongoing seminars are offered in Christian leadership training. The 80,000-square-foot training facility can accommodate groups of up to 450 and offers rooms especially designed for teaching, studying, and worship.

## FIRST BAPTIST CHURCH
### 5 Oak St., Asheville
### (828) 252-4781

America's leader in the art deco movement, Douglas Ellington, lived on Chunns Cove Road. After studying architectural design in Europe, he relocated to Asheville from his birthplace in eastern North Carolina. A group of Baptists in Asheville commissioned him to build them as beautiful a church as he could. He recalled being enthralled with the great architectural style of the Duomo in Florence, Italy. Thus he inculcated the concept of that great Roman Catholic edifice into the design of First Baptist Church of Asheville. One result is that many mistakenly believe this to be Asheville's Minor Basilica of St. Lawrence. The Basilica is located across from the Civic Center. Since 1927 both the building and the ministry of First Baptist church have become a widespread ministry that includes a child development center and a family ministries center.

## KANUGA CONFERENCES
### P.O. Box 250, Hendersonville
### (828) 692-9136
### www.kanuga.org

This Episcopal center hosts conferences and retreats for Episcopal groups. Other church groups, nonprofits, and corporate meetings for educational training are welcome when retreats are not taking place. The center accommodates 450 overnight guests. Ropes courses and team building are available.

## LAKE JUNALUSKA CONFERENCE CENTER AND RETREAT
### Lake Junaluska
### (800) 222-4930, ext. 2
### www.lakejunaluska.com

This conference center is the headquarters of the Southeastern Jurisdiction of the United Methodist Church. It is located in Haywood County south of I-40, exit 27, off U.S. Highways 23/74. The center is tucked in among 18 of the peaks that are over 6,000 feet. The 200-acre lake is surrounded by 1,200 acres of rolling hills and valleys.

The center hosts church-related programs, youth conferences, educational seminars, spiritual retreats, vacations, and family reunions.

---

## "Communion of Saints" Fresco at St. Eugene's Parish in Asheville

This 9-by-12-foot fresco is the first in Asheville. It depicts Christ ascendant over St. Francis, St. Paul, Mary Magdalene, and a pair of anonymous followers. The traditional technique of fresco involves mixing water with lime and plaster, then painting directly onto the plaster. This was the method used by Michelangelo in the Sistine Chapel paintings and Leonardo da Vinci's "The Last Supper." For more than six years artist James Daniel studied with fresco master Ben Long of Asheville. He assisted Long with painting the domes of the TransAmerica Building in Charlotte, the Charlotte Law Enforcement Center, the Chapel of the Prodigal in Montreat, and the Statesville Civic Center. The wall in the day chapel at St. Eugene's was built to the artist's (Daniel's) specifications. It is set into a 15-foot freestanding stone wall. St. Eugene's Parish is 1 block north of Merrimon Avenue just off Beaverdam Road. Open daily 7:30 a.m. to 7:30 p.m. For information call (828) 254-5193.

---

Lodging and conference facilities can accommodate up to 2,000 people. Lodging is in private cottages, the majestic Terrace Hotel, and the Lambuth Inn, which jointly have 231 rooms.

Closing ceremonies for Folkmoot USA have been held each summer for more than 20 years at Stuart Auditorium. (See Close-up about Folkmoot USA in our Annual Festivals and Events chapter.)

The center takes its name from the Cherokee Chief Junaluska, who led his warriors in victory with Gen. Andrew Jackson and his federal troops against the British at Horseshoe Bend in the War of 1812.

### MONTREAT CONFERENCE CENTER
**101 Assembly Dr., Montreat**
**(828) 669-2911**
**www.montreat.org**

The Scots brought with them the banner of Calvinism and the Presbyterian church as they explored these mountains. Schools and churches were established. An outgrowth has been a conference retreat center known originally as Mountain Retreat, now known as the town of Montreat. The Presbyterian Scots established a grammar school for boys, which has grown into Warren Wilson College, and their school for girls is now Montreat College. One prominent resident at Montreat is the world-renowned evangelist—a boy who came off a dairy farm in Charlotte, North Carolina—Rev. Dr. Billy Graham.

The books and movie about the chaplain of the U.S. Senate and pastor of the New York Avenue Presbyterian church in Washington, D.C., Peter Marshall, were penned by his wife Catherine, a resident of Montreat. She later wrote about her mother, who was an educational missionary in these mountains. Her book, *Kristy*, became a television series as well. Within this small mountain enclave reside around 300 registered voters. The population swells as summer homes are filled, the Montreat Conference Center conducts business, and Montreat College operates two campuses between Montreat and Black Mountain, with advanced degree programs offered across the state in various centers. With the erection of the Chapel of the Prodigal on the college campus in 1998, the Ben Long fresco "Return of the Prodigal" has been visited by more than 20 million people.

## RIDGECREST CONFERENCE CENTER
**Ridgecrest**
**(828) 669-8022**
**www.ridgecrestconferences.com**
This conference site is owned by the Southern Baptist Convention. Established in 1907, it is situated on 1,300 acres with spectacular views of the mountains and seasonal changes. It offers conferences for Baptist groups and is also available to non-Baptist groups. It operates year-round. The center is 17 miles east of Asheville off I-40.

**i** Meet new people in the area by contacting local hiking, biking, winetasting, or other special interest clubs. Asheville even has a newcomer's club. Find up-to-date contact numbers in the "Organizations" section of the local free weekly newspaper.

## ST. MATTHIAS EPISCOPAL CHURCH
**1 Dundee St., Asheville**
**(828) 285-0033**
Located on Catholic Hill in Asheville is this integrated church that once served the Afro-American Episcopal population of Asheville. It has specific links to the Vanderbilts. In the 1880s segregation was the key word in the South. Freed men were not permitted to worship at All Souls. Vanderbilt donated materials and craftsmen from his estate to build St. Matthias in 1895. Much of the interior is similar to that of Biltmore House. The building is on the National Register of Historic Places. The contracting builder was James Victor Miller. Across the street from the Young Men's Institute (YMI) on South Market Street in Asheville is a station of the Urban Trail honoring James Miller. Today the ministry of the church includes Sunday afternoon

concerts, usually beginning at 3 p.m. There is no admission charge.

## YMCA BLUE RIDGE ASSEMBLY INC.
**84 Blue Ridge Circle, Black Mountain**
**(828) 669-8422**
**www.blueridgeassembly.org**
In 1906 Willis Duke Weatherford Sr. climbed a tree to see whether this site provided an inspirational view. It certainly did, as this is where thousands have come since then to enjoy all aspects of inspiration. It hosts international conferences as well as serving as a day camp in the summer. It is a full-service, year-round conference center and is available to groups and organizations, particularly not-for-profit, religious, educational, government, and social services groups and family reunions. The assembly can accommodate 950 overnight guests. Rope courses and team building programs are offered. Cameras captured this site with Sandra Bullock in the film *28 Days*.

## Synagogues

### BETH HA-TEPHILA CONGREGATION
**43 North Liberty St., Asheville**
**(828) 253-4911**
Beth-ha-Tephila Congregation was founded in 1891. At that time the Conservative congregation met at the Lyceum Hall on Biltmore Avenue. Property for a Jewish cemetery was purchased in 1902 at Riverside. In the same year, a building was purchased at Spruce and Woodfin Streets.

### BETH ISRAEL SYNAGOGUE
**229 Murdock Ave., Asheville**
**(818) 252-8431**
Not only are there Jewish temples and synagogues in the mountains, but Riverside Cemetery in Asheville has incorporated within it a special Jewish cemetery with all stones engraved in Hebrew. A hemlock hedge outlines the area.

# RETIREMENT

North Carolina's mountain towns and cities have been at the top of leading publications' lists of "top places to retire" for some time now. It's no wonder—with cultural offerings in the cities and pastoral tranquility in the countryside—retirees can be as active or as relaxed as they want to be.

When moving to the North Carolina mountains, you won't feel like you are retiring, but rather beginning a second career of healthy recreation, travel, cultural enrichment, culinary arts, entertainment, and the discovery of nature. Whether settling down in the placid seasonal community of Blowing Rock, where fine and unique restaurants line the main street along with quality antiques stores, bakeries, and sweet shops, or the rolling green countryside of Valle Crucis, where your visitors will adore the many bed-and-breakfasts they will encounter in this rural valley, you will not go wrong in choosing to continue your lives here. With all the cultural treats of the area—universities and music schools, museums and galleries, mountain craft schools and studios, unique shops and arrays of excellent restaurants, botanical gardens, and nearby forests and waterfalls—you would be hard pressed to find time to while away the hours sitting in a rocking chair!

A number of counties around North Carolina hold Senior Games competitions, which were founded in 1983 to create a year-round health promotion and educational program for North Carolinians 55 and older. Today over 36,000 seniors participate in 52 local games that serve all 100 counties across the state. For example, in Transylvania County, these qualifying games are sponsored each spring. To participate you must be 55 or older and reside in the county for at least three months out of the year. For more information call North Carolina Senior Games (919-851-5456).

At the same time Transylvania and other counties also sponsor the Silver Arts Competition. Entries must be the original work of the artist, must be work created after the age of 55, and must have been completed within two years of the local games' qualifying date. First-place winners in each visual and heritage arts subcategory are entered in the state finals.

If help is needed, it's available. In counties that have long dealt with seniors' needs—such as Buncombe and Henderson—such services are broad and highly organized. In some of the more rural counties, what may be lacking in highly organized structures is more than made up for in small-town and community caring. (See our Health Care chapter for information on the health services in the area.) Here—aside from the usual government agencies, such as health departments, departments of social services, the public libraries, parks and recreation departments (which coordinate annual Senior Games), and commercial in-home health services that can be located in the Yellow Pages—is just a partial list of places you may call on for support systems, socializing, and just plain fun.

# REGIONAL SERVICES

## Northern Mountains

### AREA AGENCY ON AGING COUNCIL OF GOVERNMENTS
155 Furman Rd., Boone
(828) 265-5434
www.regiond.org
This agency serves senior citizens in the seven northwestern counties of North Carolina. The agency directs a Long-Term Care Ombudsman Program for the region and serves as a funding and information resource for agencies involved in senior care, education, and public awareness in Alleghany, Ashe, Avery, Mitchell, Watauga, and Yancey counties to the north. Senior centers in each of these locations offer a variety of programs that include group meals at the centers as well as home-delivered meals, In-Home Aide, recreational programs, legal services, health screening, and nutrition guidance. Transportation and adult day care are also provided through some locations. They also publish a helpful directory, listing agencies and telephone numbers.

### LEGAL SERVICES OF THE BLUE RIDGE
171 Grand Blvd., Boone
(828) 264-5640, (800) 849-5666
Senior citizens can get advice for problems with Social Security, Medicaid and Medicare, food stamps, housing, institutional care, and consumer issues.

## Alleghany County

### ALLEGHANY COUNCIL ON AGING INC.
Senior Center, Greyson and Whitehead Streets, Sparta
(336) 372-4640
This organization oversees In-Home Aide, group meals, home-delivered meals, health promotion, Senior Games, AARP, recreation, and educational classes.

### AMERICAN ASSOCIATION OF RETIRED PERSONS (AARP)
Senior Center, Greyson and Whitehead Streets, Sparta
(336) 372-4640

This branch of the national organization meets the fourth Tues of each month at 6 p.m. at the Alleghany Senior Center for discussion, support, counseling, and social time.

### BLUE RIDGE OPPORTUNITY COMMISSION
1747 U.S. Hwy. 21 North, Sparta
(336) 372-7284
The BROC provides information and referral, housing weatherization, and repair.

### COOPERATIVE EXTENSION SERVICE
90 South Main St., Sparta
(336) 372-5597
This office provides advice on energy resources conservation, homemaking, and personal financial management counseling for Alleghany County senior citizens.

### DEPARTMENT OF SOCIAL SERVICES
182 Doctors St., Sparta
(336) 372-2411, (336) 372-2414 (food stamps)
The Department of Social Services can help you arrange for health support services, Medicaid, protective services, senior citizens transportation, emergency assistance programs, and nursing home placement. Food stamps are also available through this office.

## Ashe County

### ASHE SERVICES FOR AGING INC.
180 Chatty Rob Lane, West Jefferson
(336) 246-2461
www.asheaging.org
This agency oversees programs for transportation, In-Home Aide II, group and home-delivered meals, and educational classes. Senior Tar Heel discount cards, the Health Insurance Information Program, adult day care, and daily activity programs are some of the benefits available here for Ashe County's older residents.

### BLUE RIDGE OPPORTUNITY COMMISSION
169 Warrensville School Rd., Warrensville
(336) 384-4543

The group offers assistance with weatherization and repair, housing and community action, and crisis intervention regarding fuel and electricity.

## DEPARTMENT OF SOCIAL SERVICES
**303 East Main St., Jefferson**
**(336) 246-1900**
This public agency offers senior citizens resources, information, aid for medical expenses, adult protective services, food stamps, and (home-heating) fuel assistance.

## HEALTH DEPARTMENT, SENIOR COMPANION PROGRAM
**707 Ray Taylor Rd., West Jefferson**
**(336) 246-4898**
Companionship is key to the success of this in-home service that involves active senior citizens working with disabled or less-active senior citizens in the community and provides assistance with light housekeeping, meal preparation, laundry, bookkeeping, bill-paying, and transportation.

## Avery County
### AVERY COUNTY VETERANS OFFICE
**205 Administrative Building, Newland**
**(828) 733-8211**
This local office assists veterans with claims to the Veterans Administration for such things as education, medical care, insurance, and loans.

### AVERY SENIOR SERVICES SENIOR CENTER
**165 Shultz Circle, Newland**
**(828) 733-8220**
Transportation, In-Home Aide I, group and home-delivered meals, and health promotion are a few of the many services Avery provides.

### W.A.M.Y. COMMUNITY ACTION
**260 Eastotoa Ave., Newland**
**(828) 733-0156**
This group provides community center crafts, weatherization and home repair, job training, a garden program, and transportation assistance. (W.A.M.Y. stands for Watauga, Avery, Mitchell, and Yancey counties.)

## Madison County
### MADISON COUNTY DEPARTMENT OF COMMUNITY SERVICES SENIOR CENTER
**462 Long Branch Rd., Marshall**
**(828) 649-2722**
This site is the central location for a network of centers that offers activities, health screening, chore services, nutrition information, and home-delivered meals, as well as congregate meals on site and information on other vital services of interest to Madison County senior citizens.

### MARS HILL COLLEGE PROGRAMS FOR SENIOR CITIZENS
**100 Athletic St., Mars Hill**
**(828) 689-1167**
Mars Hill College participates with Elderhostel, a worldwide continuing education enrichment series for senior citizens. Programs from history and music to science and art are part of this learning opportunity offered 22 weeks each year. The college provides a regular continuing education program linked with the Mars Hill curriculum. The Summer Alternative Vacation Program and the Learning Institute for Elders (LIFE) have learning tours on a variety of subjects.

## Mitchell County
### COOPERATIVE EXTENSION SERVICE
**County Building, Annex East**
**10 South Mitchell Ave., Bakersville**
**(828) 688-4811**
This county extension service provides senior citizens with advice on energy resources conservation, financial management, and homemaking.

### DEPARTMENT OF SOCIAL SERVICES
**271 Crimson Laurel Way, Bakersville**
**(828) 688-2175**
Senior citizens around Bakersville can find resource information, In-Home Aide services, food stamps, energy assistance, health support services, transportation, and home improvement assistance through this agency.

## MITCHELL SENIOR CENTER
**152 Ledger School Rd., Bakersville**
**(828) 688-3019**
Transportation, In-Home Aide I, group and home-delivered meals, and health and nutrition assistance are some of the services provided by this center.

## VETERANS SERVICE OFFICE
**130 Forest Service Dr., Suite C, Bakersville**
**(828) 688-2200**
This local office assists veterans with claims to the Veterans Administration for such things as education, medical care, insurance, and loans.

## W.A.M.Y. COMMUNITY ACTION INC.
**213 Oak Ave., Spruce Pine**
**(828) 766-9150, (828) 765-9151**
Transportation, weatherization and home repair, elderly nutrition, and gardening programs are some of the services provided by this office.

## *Watauga County*
### APPALCART TRANSPORTATION
**274 Winklers Creek Rd., Boone**
**(828) 264-2280, (828) 264-2278**
AppalCART provides county and town transportation service to seniors and the general public. Call for schedules and arrangements.

### COOPERATIVE EXTENSION SERVICE
**971 West King St., Boone**
**(828) 264-3061**
Homemaking and housing information as well as energy resources conservation and financial management counseling are provided through the county extension service.

### DEPARTMENT OF SOCIAL SERVICES
**132 Poplar Grove Connector, Suite C, Boone**
**(828) 265-8100**
Health support services are among the many types of aid available through this department.

### VETERANS SERVICE OFFICE
**Courthouse Annex, Room 100, Boone**
**(828) 265-8065**

This local office assists veterans with claims to the Veterans Administration for such things as education, medical care, insurance, and loans.

## W.A.M.Y. COMMUNITY ACTION PROGRAM
**Main Office**
**152 Southgate Dr., Suite 2, Boone**
**(828) 264-2421**
Watauga County senior citizens benefit from the active participation of this office in the areas of weatherization and home repair, transportation for elderly, and job and gardening programs.

## WATAUGA COUNTY PROJECT ON AGING
**132 Poplar Grove Connector, Suite A, Boone**
**(828) 265-8090**
**www.wataugacounty.org/aging**
Transportation, In-Home Aide I and II, group and home-delivered meals, and health screenings are provided to Watauga County senior citizens.

## *Yancey County*
### COOPERATIVE EXTENSION SERVICE
**10 Orchard St., Burnsville**
**(828) 682-6186**
Financial management counseling, housing information, homemaking services, and information on energy resources conservation, agriculture, and home horticulture are offered by the county extension service.

### DEPARTMENT OF SOCIAL SERVICES
**222 Lincoln Park, Burnsville**
**(828) 682-6148, (828) 682-2470**
Health support services, transportation, and aid for medical expenses and family and veteran support services are some of the services of this department.

### W.A.M.Y. COMMUNITY ACTION PROGRAM
**22 East Bypass, Burnsville**
**(828) 682-2610**
Above Pollard's Drug Store, the W.A.M.Y. program offers limited home repair assistance as well as elderly transportation.

## YANCEY COUNTY COMMITTEE ON AGING
Senior Center
10 Swiss Ave., Burnsville
(828) 682-6011
This lively place offers In-Home Aide I, group and home-delivered meals, transportation, and health promotion like blood pressure and cholesterol checks. Senior Tar Heel Discount cards and the Seniors' Health Insurance Information Program (SHIIP) are also part of the services offered here.

## YANCEY TRANSPORTATION AUTHORITY
Courthouse, 15 East Blvd., Burnsville
(828) 682-6144
Yancey offers senior transportation assistance through a contract with the senior center.

# Central Mountains
## *Buncombe County*
## BUNCOMBE COUNTY COUNCIL ON AGING
Community Services Center
50 South French Broad Ave.,
Suite 141, Asheville
(828) 258-8027, (828) 258-8028
This private, nonprofit corporation, a United Way agency, is composed of senior citizens groups and organizations providing services to Buncombe County senior citizens. Outreach services include friendly visitation, senior companionship, home repair, weatherization, and fan distribution. The agency coordinates various countywide programs that offer nutrition assistance, congregate meals at 17 locations, the Senior Tar Heel discount program, and volunteer opportunities for older citizens and other people.

## BUNCOMBE COUNTY MOUNTAIN MOBILITY
185 Coxe Ave., Asheville
(828) 258-0186
This service provides door-to-door transportation services for the elderly, disabled, and transportation disadvantaged.

## BUNCOMBE COUNTY SHERIFF'S DEPARTMENT REASSURANCE PROGRAM
Sheriff's Department
202 Haywood St., Asheville
(828) 250-4492
This helpful program, staffed by citizen volunteers, provides daily telephone check-in service for a number of Buncombe County's elderly. This program also works in connection with Visiting Health Professionals, Department of Social Services, and the Meals on Wheels program. The Buncombe County Sheriff's Department makes home visits when needed.

## CENTER FOR CREATIVE RETIREMENT
College for Seniors, University of
North Carolina Asheville
1 University Heights, Asheville
(828) 251-6140, (828) 251-6384
www.unca.edu
The University of North Carolina Asheville was one of the first to establish a college for seniors. Through the generosity of the Janirve Foundation the college found a home as the Center for Creative Retirement. This newest building on campus, known as the Reuter Center, is named for the founder of the foundation.

This innovative university program, begun in 1988, offers learning, leadership, and community-service opportunities for older adults. Among these are the College for Seniors, a peer learning and teaching program; Schools and Campus Volunteer Programs, a variety of student/mentor learning experiences; Leadership Asheville Seniors, a series of daylong sessions geared toward community service; and a continuing program of research into issues concerning older adult education.

## LAND OF THE SKY REGIONAL COUNCIL
25 Heritage Dr., Asheville
(828) 251-6622
www.landofsky.org
The following counties comprise Land of the Sky Regional Council: Madison, Buncombe, Henderson, and Transylvania. Its purpose is to provide total services for seniors in all these counties.

Two of the Council's guide books that contain contacts for all services from health services to activity clubs and beyond are *Senior Adult Directory for Buncombe County* and *Madison County Senior Services Directory*.

### Henderson County

#### AMERICAN ASSOCIATION OF RETIRED PERSONS (AARP)
314 Oklawaha Circle, Hendersonville
(828) 697-0187

This organization offers a 55 Alive/Safe Driving Course for senior citizens and tax aid services. A member of the organization coordinates the Seniors' Health Insurance Information Program (SHIIP). It informs and educates seniors regarding relevant issues through speakers and literature and is one of the sponsors of the Widowed Persons Services (see below). It is an advocate for seniors' issues at the state and national level.

#### BLUE RIDGE COMMUNITY COLLEGE
1 College Lane, Flat Rock
(828) 694-1700

BRCC offers a variety of courses, day adventures, and cultural events. Most important for retirees, it operates the Center for Lifelong Learning, which provides adults older than 50 the opportunity to buy a lifetime membership.

#### COUNCIL ON AGING
304 Chadwick Ave., Hendersonville
(828) 692-4203

The council provides a variety of services that help older adults cope with physical, social, or other aging problems. Specific programs include Meals on Wheels, Service Advocates for the Elderly (SAFE), Elder Neighbors, minor home repairs, installation and repair of smoke alarms (Fire Alert), and an Information and Referral Helpline (828-697-4357). Other services include lending out heaters and fans, a hearing-aid bank, a thrift shop (213 South Church St., 828-693-7756), and living wills. The council also offers congregate meals at the Sammy Williams Senior Center located at Third Avenue West and Justice Street (828-692-3320), for those persons wishing to travel to the center.

#### FISH VOLUNTEER MEDICAL TRANSPORTATION
P.O. Box 2411, Hendersonville
(828) 693-5100

FISH provides round-trip transportation within the county and, when medical services are not available, to Asheville for health-related appointments. Although the organization does not provide emergency medical transportation, it will take patients home from the hospital after outpatient surgery.

#### LIFELINE PERSONAL EMERGENCY RESPONSE SYSTEM
Pardee Hospital/Lifeline
2029A Asheville Hwy., Hendersonville
(828) 692-9061

This program offers round-the-clock, professional monitoring of every emergency call for help direct to Pardee Hospital.

#### OPPORTUNITY HOUSE
1411 Asheville Hwy., Hendersonville
(828) 692-0575

This arts, crafts, and cultural center is a nonprofit organization that opened its doors in 1958. Now, as then, it continues to offer fellowship and learning opportunities to individuals of all ages and faiths. Activities include bridge, crafts, dance, golf, ladies club, seminars, and smoke-free bingo. The gift shop on the premises features many handcrafted items and is open to the public. Opportunity House is open Mon through Fri from 9 a.m. to 5 p.m., and visitors are always welcome. There is an annual membership fee.

#### PARDEE PAVILION (ADULT DAY CARE)
104 College Dr., Flat Rock
(828) 696-7070

This adult day-care facility has planned activities to meet an individual's specific needs. It provides educational, recreational, social, diversional, and volunteer programs.

## SENIORS HEALTH INSURANCE
**Pardee Health Education Center**
**1800 Four Seasons Blvd., Hendersonville**
**(828) 692-4600**
Personal insurance counseling provided by the Seniors' Health Insurance Information Program (SHIIP) is available at Pardee Hospital's Health Education Center in the Blue Ridge Mall. The trained SHIIP volunteers provide free counseling to older adults on long-term care insurance, Medicare, and Medicaid Supplement insurance.

## WESTERN CAROLINA COMMUNITY ACTION
**526 Seventh Ave. East, Hendersonville**
**(828) 693-1771**
This organization develops and administers programs of interest to older adults that include weatherization, a heating appliance replacement and repair program (HARRP), FISH medical transportation answering and dispatch, a variety of transportation services, emergency assistance, emergency fuel, plastic for windows, a garden program, a food closet, job placement with supportive services, liquid nutrient supplement (Ensure), and Section 8 Housing Assistance, to name a few.

## YMCA
**810 Sixth Ave. West, Hendersonville**
**(828) 692-5774**
Adult programs include fitness classes, health enhancement programming, swimming classes, volleyball, basketball, special events, and workshops. Specifically for older adults, the Y offers a Water Exercise program, an Arthritis Water Exercise program, a Senior Pep Exercise program, and a Deep Water Aerobic program.

## *Polk County*
### THE MEETING PLACE
**Jervey-Palmer Building**
**330 Carolina Dr., Tryon**
**(828) 859-9707**
This center serves both congregate and in-home lunches Mon through Fri. It also offers classes in exercise, quilting, and sewing, but one of its biggest draws is its ceramics workshop.

The Meeting Place also has a pool room, a television lounge, and frequent games of cards, bingo, and checkers. It has its own library and is visited regularly by a bookmobile. There is also a regular Wed music session. Other services include regularly scheduled transportation for shopping and medical appointments, and special holiday trips are offered. Seniors may also take advantage of nutrition education programs, legal services, and tax services. There are satellite centers with many of the same services in both Saluda and Green Creek.

## *Transylvania County*
### AMERICAN ASSOCIATION OF RETIRED PERSONS (AARP)
**P.O. Box 1336, Brevard**
**(828) 883-8486**
AARP meets at 10 a.m. on the fourth Tues of each month in the Fellowship Hall of the First United Methodist Church in Brevard to hear speakers and participate in other programs of interest to the retirement community.

### BREVARD COLLEGE
### COMMUNITY EDUCATION
**400 North Broad St., Brevard**
**(828) 884-8256**
Reaching beyond the college-aged population, Brevard has a wide variety of continuing education programs for adults. The Office of Community Education currently offers more than 200 courses annually, with an enrollment of nearly 2,000 participants, that include intellectual and academic subjects, cultural experiences, local orientation, hobbies and self-improvement, and health and physical fitness classes. Classes are noncredit. However, CEUs are offered for specific programs. In addition musical performances, dramatic presentations, art gallery exhibits, and lecture series are presented throughout the year and are open to the public.

Computer courses are offered as well as a program that is lauded by the Transylvania newspaper as being one of the finest: the "Inside Transylvania" program. This course is designed for newcomers, but open to all. Participants meet face to face with leaders in Transylvania County. It offers 3.0 CEUs.

The Brevard College library is also an integral part of the intellectual life here. It has over 45,000 books, 200 periodical subscriptions, valuable electronic resources available on CD-ROM, Web access, and access to nearby colleges through the Mountain College Library Network.

## KOALA ADULT DAY CARE
**19 Carolina Ave., Brevard**
**(828) 884-2980**
Caregivers can leave loved ones here while they work or just take time for themselves. It offers its clients crafts, remotivation, reminiscing, fun and games, medication, and a hot lunch. Call for information about the daily fee. Grants are available to those unable to pay the full amount.

**i** College for Seniors and Elderhostel programs are offered through the University of North Carolina at Asheville. Contact the university for more information and turn your vacation into a journey of knowledge.

## LIFELINE: EMERGENCY RESPONSE
**Transylvania Community Hospital**
**Home Care, Hospital Drive, Brevard**
**(828) 883-5254**
Lifeline provides 24-hour access to emergency help when a person is at home alone or with a caregiver who may be unable to provide necessary assistance in an emergency. It links, via telephone and specialized electronic equipment, with continuous emergency assistance at Transylvania Community Hospital.

## MEALS ON WHEELS OF BREVARD
**Transylvania Community Hospital**
**Hospital Drive, Brevard**
**(828) 884-5298**
Like so many other of these helpful programs, MOW provides hot, well-balanced noontime meals, weekdays, to shut-ins without age or income restrictions. Volunteers deliver the meals, and the cost is based on the client's ability to pay.

## TELEPHONE REASSURANCE PROGRAM
**Brevard Police Department, City Hall**
**Brevard**
**(828) 883-2212**
This 24-hour service is for people who live alone. They can leave their name, age, address, doctor's name, and who to call in an emergency. Every morning these people call or are called by the police department to make sure everything is okay. If there is no response or if help is needed, a police officer is sent to the address and proper steps are taken.

## TRANSYLVANIA COUNTY MED-DRIVE TRANSPORTATION
**(828) 884-3203**
Med-Drive volunteers provide transportation to medical appointments for any person over 60 within Transylvania County. Limited out-of-county transportation is available for chemotherapy, radiation, and renal dialysis. Med-Drive doesn't accommodate emergency medical transportation.

## WESTERN CAROLINA COMMUNITY ACTION
**203 East Morgan, Brevard**
**(828) 884-3219**
A branch of the WCCA in Henderson County, Transylvania's office serves congregate lunches Mon through Fri at both Silvermont in Brevard and in Quebec on U.S. Highway 64 West and provides transportation to both sites as well as out-of-county medical transportation. It joins with the AARP in providing trained tax preparers to assist with tax returns and oversees the Seniors' Health Insurance Information Program (SHIIP), job training for those older than 55, a weatherization program for both renters and homeowners with limited incomes, emergency assistance, liquid nutrient supplement (Ensure) program, plastic for windows, spring and fall garden supplies, a heating appliance repair and replacement program, and rental assistance. Program eligibility is based on income.

## Southern Mountains

### Cherokee County

**CHEROKEE COUNTY SENIOR SERVICES**
**69 Alpine St., Murphy**
**(828) 837-2467**

Many activities take place at the Penland Senior Citizens Center, including craft classes and exercise programs conducted by the health department. A Friendly Visitor Program visits homebound seniors for "cheers and chores," and there's a congregate meal program at the center Mon through Fri, as well as a home-delivered meals program. It also offers information and referrals to various community services.

The organization's red vans offer regularly scheduled runs into each section of the county. Out-of-county trips are also scheduled for shopping, recreation, and medical appointments. SHIIP (Seniors' Health Insurance Information Program) is active here with trained counselors helping senior citizens with health insurance information. It also supports annual Senior Games and holds an annual picnic. In the Andrews branch (The Sunshine Club, 19 Business, Andrews; 828-321-4505), there is also a nutrition program, an exercise program, and classes.

### Clay County

**CLAY COUNTY SENIOR CENTER**
**196 Ritter Rd., Hayesville**
**(828) 389-9271**

The center provides a congregate "Meals with Friends" and Meals on Wheels, Mon through Fri. It also holds classes in painting, wood carving, crocheting, and exercise, and has popular Thrusday Morning Music Sessions.

### Graham County

**SENIOR CITIZENS CENTER**
**115 Moose Branch Rd., Robbinsville**
**(828) 479-7977**

A congregate lunch is served at the center five days a week with home-driven meals to homebound seniors. There are also art and carving classes and bingo.

## Haywood County

**CANTON SENIOR CENTER**
**Old Canton Armory**
**1 Pigeon St., Canton**
**(828) 648-8412**

The center promotes wellness in older adults through group socialization, special activities, crafts, speaking, educational opportunities, and organized trips. A meal is offered at 11:45 a.m., Mon through Fri. They also serve as a conduit for Meals on Wheels for the Department of Social Services.

**COUNCIL ON AGING**
**1271 East St., Waynesville**
**(828) 452-2370**

The council provides information and referral, resource directory, advocacy, coordination of services, special programs, and the Senior Games. The council is also the lead agency for CAP/DA, which serves elderly adults needing care in an in-home setting. Faith in Action provides aid to seniors with disabilities in installing railings and ramps and other devices necessary for well-being.

**HAYWOOD COMMUNITY COLLEGE**
**185 Freelander Dr., Clyde**
**(828) 627-4500**

Tuition is free to persons over 65, except for an activity fee and the cost of materials in arts and crafts classes. (See the HCC listing in our Education chapter.)

**INTENTIONAL GROWTH CENTER**
**959 North Lakeshore Dr., Lake Junaluska**
**(828) 452-2881, ext. 721, (800) 482-1442**

The center, an agency of the United Methodist Church, is a nationally accredited provider of continuing education courses and programs of clergy and laity. It also serves as a popular center for the national Elderhostel program and for church-related older adult events, such as Fall Flings and Christmas at Lambuth Inn.

## MEALS ON WHEELS
Department of Social Services
486 East Marshall St., Waynesville
(828) 452-6620, ext. 377
Meals are provided five days a week based on need. Fees are based on income.

## MOUNTAIN PROJECTS, INC.
2251 Old Balsam Rd., Waynesville
(828) 452-1447
This organization is a community action agency serving Haywood and Jackson counties. It operates numerous programs for low-income and disadvantaged persons. These currently include housing rehabilitation, Head Start, a congregate nutrition program, foster grandparents, a retired senior volunteer program, Section 8 rental assistance, Haywood Public Transit, employment and training programs, and in-home chore services for the elderly. The eligibility for program participation is determined by the particular grant funding the program.

## WAYNESVILLE OLD ARMORY RECREATION CENTER
44 Boundary St., Waynesville
(828) 456-9207
Senior citizens meet here for lunch Mon through Fri. The center, which serves the entire community, also offers special activities, crafts, bridge, lectures, and organized trips.

## *Jackson County*
## AMERICAN ASSOCIATION OF RETIRED PERSONS (AARP)
Sylva
(828) 631-0193 (president)
This active chapter holds a monthly meeting. Additionally they support the functions at the Golden Age Club and programs that present topics of interest to senior citizens. On an as-needed basis, they offer a seven-week course teaching personal financial management to women and a 55 Alive driver refresher course.

## CASHIERS SENIOR C.A.F.E.
Cashiers Community Building
Off US 64 West, Cashiers
(828) 743-9215
This center provides congregate meals, home-delivered meals, and social activities for senior citizens in the Cashiers area. Seniors can also use and receive instruction on the center's public access computer with Internet access.

## GOLDEN AGE CLUB
1 Central Ave., Sylva
(828) 586-4944
This is one of the more active senior citizen centers in the mountains. Its 300 members enjoy classes in exercise, beginner and advanced line dancing, square dancing, tai chi exercise, wood carving, basic computer instruction, tennis, hiking, and creative writing. There are coffee klatsches for men and women, organized card games, and co-ed softball games. A philosophy group uses the center for its discussions. Another group is devoted to bowling. There is also a singing group and a line-dancing group that give performances around the area. Other activities include income tax preparation, a walking program, Senior Games, shuffleboard, horseshoes, billiards, fund-raisers, and intergenerational programs. A covered-dish supper is held once a month with dancing afterward.

## JACKSON COUNTY DEPARTMENT ON AGING
30 Central St., Sylva
(828) 586-8562
This active agency provides programs and resources for county seniors. In addition to coordinating services with other agencies and councils, it provides information and referral services on a variety of subjects and health issues, initiates new services, and is a senior advocacy group. It also publishes a monthly newsletter, *Jacksonian*, with information about local senior events and happenings.

## JACKSON COUNTY TRANSPORTATION
**(828) 586-3133**

This organization fills a need that many residents in rural counties encounter. It provides on-call transportation for medical visits and to nutrition sites. One day a week it follows established routes in outlying areas to take people shopping, to banks, and to doctors. It also visits the county's rehabilitation center and offers low-cost, zoned transportation to the general public.

## MOUNTAIN PROJECTS, INC.
**23 Schulman St., Sylva**
**(828) 586-2345**

For information on this agency's services, see our Mountain Projects, Inc. entry in this chapter under Haywood County.

## SOUTHWESTERN COMMUNITY COLLEGE
**Hwy. 107, Sylva**
**(828) 586-4091**

SCC's Continuing Education program—serving Jackson, Macon, Swain, and the Qualla Boundary—offers classes in everything from computers to crafts. You can reach the center nearest you by calling the Sylva campus number above, the Cherokee Center (828-497-7233), the Macon County Center (828-369-7331), or the Swain County Center (828-488-6413).

## SYLVA SENIOR C.A.F.E.
**Community Services Building**
**538 Scots Creek, Sylva**
**(828) 586-6710**

A congregate lunch is served here Mon through Fri, and the Home-Delivered Meals Program delivers hot, nutritious meals daily to Jackson County's homebound elderly seven days a week. This center has a public access computer with Internet connection for seniors in the Sylva area, and instruction is available. It also offers occasional programs, including exercises, bingo, and adventurous outings, but simply socializing is one of the biggest attractions.

## WESTERN CAROLINA UNIVERSITY
**Hwy. 107, Cullowhee**
**(828) 227-7397**

In addition to all the arts and culture found at a large university, this institution offers an outstanding continuing education program. (See the WCU entry in our Education chapter for more information.)

## *Macon County*

## CENTER FOR LIFE ENRICHMENT
**Peggy Cross Center**
**Corner of Fifth and South Streets, Highlands**
**(828) 526-9381**

The center is aligned with four regional institutions of higher education: Western Carolina University, Southwestern Community College, Piedmont College, and Brevard College. Programs are offered for personal enrichment. One such offering is "Cooking with Culinary Herbs," taught by Stewart House bed-and-breakfast owner Barbara Werder. She is an avid gardener who raises spectacular herbs and flowers. Another course entitled "Wine Trends" is taught by restaurateur Steve Pignatiello at his colleagues' restaurant, Wolfgang's On Main. Mindy and Wolfgang Green now list over 280 wines on their menu. Other programs present computer knowledge, art and music, and much more, including resources for everyday living.

## MACON COUNTY DEPARTMENT OF AGING
**125 Hyatt Rd., Franklin**
**(828) 349-2058**

The department is the only full-service agency to serve anyone older than 60 west of Hickory. A sampling of the services provided: congregate meals, home-delivered meals, chores, respite care services, in-home services, an Alzheimer's support group, an Alzheimer's day-care center, overnight respite, case management, information and referral, SHIIP, a lending library on dementia, and medical equipment for loan.

## Swain County

**STATE OF FRANKLIN SERVICES TO SENIOR CITIZENS**
**Courthouse-on-the-Square, Bryson City**
**(828) 488-3047**

The Swain County Senior Center provides an Elderly Nutrition Program for people older than 60 at noon Mon through Fri as well as transportation to the center. Transportation is also provided for medical appointments and shopping. On certain days of the month, there are regularly scheduled trips for out-of-town medical appointments.

Through the National Council of Senior Citizens, a Senior AIDES Program provides an employment service for people older than 55 for 20-hour-week jobs with nonprofit organizations and governmental positions. Other activities include line dancing and classes through Southwestern Community College. Bingo is played on Wed and Fri, and there's a health screening at the center twice a month.

# RETIREMENT COMMUNITIES

Because Western North Carolina is so popular with retirees, it naturally follows that many retirement communities have sprung up here. Although most are concentrated in the Asheville-Hendersonville area, others are sprouting in surrounding areas. They offer everything from an independent living style to total life care. They also offer a wide range of options to fit various retirement needs and budgets: manufactured homes, cluster or attached homes, town houses, condominiums, apartments, and luxurious life-care facilities.

Most counties have low-cost retirement apartments through their departments of social services that are priced according to income levels, though there is often a waiting list for these. Here are a few examples of what is available. For more information contact local chambers of commerce.

## Northern Mountains

**APPALACHIAN/BRIAN ESTATES**
**163 Shadowline Dr., Boone**
**(828) 264-1006, (800) 333-3432**

This 91-residence community for older adults is unique in that it offers both annual and seasonal apartments. Appalachian/Brian Estates is strictly a rental retirement community developed as a cooperative venture between Appalachian State University Foundation and Don Beaver of Beaver Sports Properties.

Modern facilities, including lounges, a club room for parties, exercise facilities, a professional hair salon, library, and sundry store are all on site. A guest suite is provided for visiting family members.

## Central Mountains

**COLLEGE WALK**
**100 N. College Row, Brevard**
**(828) 884-5800, (800) 280-9600**

College Walk borders Brevard College and is convenient to the Brevard Music Center, shopping, and Pisgah National Forest. This community offers two- and three-bedroom cluster homes; studio, one-bedroom, and two-bedroom apartments; and a state-licensed assisted-living facility. Fees include one meal daily, land lease, outside maintenance, security patrol, and use of the clubhouse, library, game room, auditorium, workshop, and other common areas.

**CRESCENT VIEW**
**2533 Hendersonville Rd., Asheville**
**(828) 687-0068**

This Lutheran-sponsored planned community in Buncombe County has a variety of studio, one-bedroom, and two-bedroom apartment homes for retired seniors. Fine dining, housekeeping, and linen services are available here, as well as 24-hour security and transportation. Crescent View also offers assisted-living residences. On the south end of Asheville, it is close to major supermarkets, movie theaters, shopping, and easy access to the Blue Ridge Parkway.

**DEERFIELD**
**1617 Hendersonville Rd., Asheville**
**(828) 274-1531, (800) 284-1531**
**www.deerfieldwnc.org**

This pleasant Episcopal retirement community on Asheville's south end offers apartments and cottages for seniors. The attractively landscaped estate maintains a health center, a central formal dining room with wait service, and a community center with a host of amenities. Deerfield maintains Life Care assisted living and will be expanding over the next few years. Just off a main thoroughfare on Asheville's south side, Deerfield is close to shopping, restaurants, cinemas, and access to the Blue Ridge Parkway.

### GIVENS ESTATE UNITED METHODIST RETIREMENT COMMUNITY
**2360 Sweeten Creek Rd., Asheville**
**(828) 274-4800**
This United Methodist retirement community is spread over 160 wooded acres in south Asheville. The retirement village has residential options that include apartments, duplexes, and individual houses scattered across the campus. Asbury Hall, in the community's center, offers congregate living with dining and recreational facilities. Also within this facility is Sales Health Care Center, designed to provide domiciliary or skilled nursing care to residents who can no longer live alone. A campus nurse and 24-hour emergency call system and housekeeping are additional services.

### HIGHLAND FARMS RETIREMENT COMMUNITY
**200 Tabernacle Rd., Black Mountain**
**(828) 669-6473**
Highland Farms was one of the first retirement communities in Western North Carolina. This beautiful spot, nestled in the mountains in Buncombe County near the village of Black Mountain, has drawn retirees since the 1970s. Cluster homes, condominiums, apartments, individual homes, a residential lodge, a health care center, and a rest home are spread over a lovely campus with the mountains in view.

A library, music area, art and craft studio, and even a vegetable garden keep those at Highland Farms active. Seminars and on-campus workshops foster a close relationship with the surrounding communities of Asheville and Black Mountain.

### LAKE POINTE LANDING
**333 Thompson St., Hendersonville**
**(828) 693-7800, (800) 693-7801**
The 32-acre complex has easy access to I-26 and is less than a mile from Hendersonville's restaurants, shopping, banks, and medical offices. The lush landscaping and one-plus-acre lake make it seem more a "country place."

Lake Pointe is made up of patio homes known as the Villas, where retirees can enjoy 100 percent equity ownership. There are two- and three-bedroom units, each with a second-floor loft to use as a study or for extra storage. Both units come with two baths; a living room; a fully equipped, all-electric kitchen; a fireplace; a screened-in back porch; and an enclosed garage. For more space there are special homes with a lakeside view, retirement center proximity, or seclusion and privacy.

Rental apartments, called the Harbor, are also available. Residents here have biweekly maid service and evening meals in a full-service dining room. All utilities except personal telephone service are included in the rental fee, along with maintenance and a full calendar of activities with scheduled transportation and use of the Club House. Special guest suites are available for family and friends when they come to visit.

In addition there are assisted living apartments at the Inn at Lake Pointe Landing with a choice of alcove and one-bedroom apartments. A licensed staff provides help in monitoring medications, grooming, housekeeping, and access to transportation and other assistance.

Lake Pointe Landing also offers an on-site, long-term-care facility, Life Care Center of Hendersonville. It provides rehabilitation, skilled, and long-term care services.

### PINE PARK RETIREMENT INN
**2601 Hwy. 64 East, Hendersonville**
**(828) 692-1911**
Pine Park is a month-to-month rental retirement center with no "buy in" or long-term lease. There is, however, a processing fee, payable in advance (refundable until the day of occupancy). The center has 110 units: 63 independent-living units

and 47 assisted-living units. Prices for apartments include three meals a day; a social activities program; once-a-week housekeeping, including linens; all utilities and cable television; two-way intercom service; 24-hour attendant services; and transportation to medical services, shopping, and other outside activities.

### RIVERWIND ADULT COMMUNITY
**100 Riverwind Dr., Hendersonville**
**(828) 891-2010, (800) 452-3058**
This community of manufactured homes, created by the Oakwood Homes Corporation, is just off US 64 West in Etowah, between Brevard and Hendersonville. It's also just a mile from two championship golf courses (Etowah Valley Country Club and the Cummings Cove Golf Course; see our Golf chapter for more info) and is convenient to medical facilities and shopping (including groceries). Riverwind offers Freedom, Oakwood, and Virginia homes in two- and three-bedroom, two-bath models with brick/block foundations that contain approximately 1,950 to 3,940 square feet. The prices include the property that the home is on. Its cable, city water, electricity, natural gas, and telephone lines are all underground. Homeowners Association dues are assessed monthly and include sewer service, street and entrance lights, common area maintenance, garbage collection, and use of the clubhouse, swimming pool, and whirlpool spa.

### TRYON ESTATES
**617 Laurell Lake Dr., Columbus**
**(828) 894-3000, (800) 633-2718**
Tryon Estates—owned and operated by ACTS, Inc., a not-for-profit corporation—lies on a 215-acre wooded site in Polk County's thermal belt. It offers one-, two-, and three-bedroom apartments and two- and three-bedroom villas with all buildings connected by covered walkways. Chef-prepared gourmet meals are served each day in an elegant central dining room. There are also private dining rooms. It has a regular activity schedule and a full-time activity director. Other amenities include a theater-style auditorium, library, woodworking shop, billiard room, an activity-craft room, a card room, a beauty/barber shop, a pharmacy, banking and postal services, a gift shop, and an indoor, heated swimming pool. Outside you'll find garden plots, walking and biking paths, a stocked fishing pond, croquet, and shuffleboard. Maid service is available.

Residents are also offered portable emergency-call buttons, home health care, and a state-licensed, Medicare-approved health care center with a medical staff on duty 24 hours a day. This community includes 44 personal-care units (assisted living) and 52 skilled-nursing units. There is a dining room/activity area in the health-care center with three meals served daily.

# HEALTH CARE

Even before the turn of the 20th century, when these mountains became a haven for sufferers of tuberculosis, health care held a prominent position in Western North Carolina. Carriage upon carriage of visitors arrived to "take the air" and enjoy the healthful climate at local spas. Many of these visitors remained as permanent residents. Today the legacy of these early mountain sanitariums forms a strong foundation for the rapidly expanding modern medical facilities found in each county of the region.

Increased national focus on health care and technological advancements is one important reason that the latest medical services are available to residents of even the most remote mountain counties. Innovative pooling of related or crossover medical services is also a growing trend here. Buncombe County's Memorial Mission Hospital and St. Joseph's Hospital, for example, have merged. Asheville and Buncombe County, especially, boast a thriving and continually growing medical community.

Throughout the region services ranging from large, centrally located full-service hospitals, 24-hour emergency treatment centers, and urgent-care and outpatient centers to community hospitals, community medical centers, and special private clinics directed to the needs of the underinsured can be found. Special medical concerns, such as cancer treatment, heart care, women's services, orthopedics, pediatric medicine, psychiatric services, rehabilitative therapy, and veterans' services are a major focus at many of the region's medical facilities. The latest diagnostics services, including ultrasound, mammography, CT scan, and MRI (magnetic resonance imaging) are available at all the region's larger medical facilities. With the increasing accessibility of technology, even some of the smaller community hospitals in the region can offer this level of medical service.

In this chapter we offer you an overview of the region's larger medical facilities, the community hospitals, a number of the community clinics, and their basic and specialized services. To find out more about the many services that each of the health care outlets offer, call the information numbers that we've provided.

If you unfortunately encounter a medical emergency in Western North Carolina, all our counties offer 911 emergency telephone service. For non-emergencies, check the front of the local phone book for other important phone numbers.

## NORTHERN MOUNTAINS

### Alleghany County

**ALLEGHANY MEMORIAL HOSPITAL**
**233 Doctor's St., Hwy 18, Sparta**
**(336) 372-5511**
Just off the intersection of North Carolina Highways 21 and 18 North, in the heart of Sparta, Alleghany Memorial Hospital has served this rural northern county since 1951. Personalized service and quality care are the missions of the 150-member staff at Alleghany Memorial. Comprehensive services are provided 24 hours a day. These include a well-staffed emergency room; radiology services such as CT scanning, mammography, ultrasound, MRI, and fluoroscopic services; rehabilitation services; obstetrics; and restorative, respite, and terminal care. An additional primary care clinic handles specialty services like urology, orthopedics, cataract surgery,

and everyday health problems. An In-Home Aide program, home-care program, and Lifeline provide outreach services to the community.

## Ashe County

**ASHE MEMORIAL HOSPITAL**
**200 Hospital Ave., Jefferson**
**(336) 246-7101**

About 40 minutes from Boone, this small rural hospital maintains a sophisticated level of care for a county population of just 23,000. The hospital, established in 1939, is licensed for 76 beds and has a staff that includes two general surgeons, nine family practitioners, one radiologist, two ophthalmologists, one pediatrician, and one internist. A full-service hospital, Ashe Memorial offers general, laparoscopic, and orthopedic surgery; complete eye care, including cataract treatment and laser surgery; diagnostic imaging; pediatric medicine; cardiopulmonary therapy and testing; nutritional counseling; Lifeline emergency response program; and a 24-hour emergency unit. The hospital also runs the Mountain Hearts Cardiac Rehabilitation Center and Segraves Care Center, a 60-bed skilled nursing home.

## Avery County

**CHARLES A. CANNON, JR., MEMORIAL HOSPITAL**
**434 Hospital Dr., Linville**
**(828) 737-7000**

The Sloop Memorial and Charles A. Cannon Hospitals have merged and operate under the umbrella of the Avery Health Care System, 1955 Newland Hwy.; (828) 733-4410. Both are full-service facilities serving small rural communities. Cannon, with a 79-bed capacity, was founded in 1908 and is in Banner Elk, just 17 miles from Boone. Sloop, with 38 beds and a staff of 15 doctors, was founded in 1929 and is in Crossnore, 25 miles from Boone. Both offer a wide range of modern services, including critical-care units, obstetric services, and radiology departments, featuring CT scanning, nuclear medicine, and MRI services. A 24-hour emergency service is available

in both hospitals. Cannon also houses an inpatient psychiatric unit.

Two community clinics—Foscoe Family Health Center, Highway 105, Sugar Grove, (828) 963-7161; and Newland Family Medical Center, 358 Beech St., Newland, (828) 733-9276—serve as outreach affiliates of the hospitals.

## Madison County

**MARS HILL MEDICAL CENTER**
**119 Mountain View Rd., Mars Hill**
**(828) 689-3507**

Mars Hill Medical Center is in the small college town of Mars Hill, roughly 20 minutes north of Asheville. This private medical group, founded in 1971, serves the primary health care needs of the remote rural communities of Mars Hill, Marshall, Hot Springs, and Laurel in Madison County.

The Mars Hill location is the coordinating site for the various community services encompassed by the Hot Springs Health Program, and caregivers spend a great deal of hands-on time in the community. The 150 health care professionals and support staff of the Hot Springs Health Program all work with a high degree of mobility, providing primary medical care, pharmacy and dental services, home health and hospice care, occupational and physical therapy, and social services.

This group is professionally affiliated with the schools of medicine of the University of North Carolina at Chapel Hill, Duke University, the Mountain Area Health Education Center of Asheville, and Bowman-Gray in Winston-Salem, acting as a teaching site for each. The experience in this rural community offers young medical students a perspective different from the usual city hospital internship.

The Marshall/Walnut Medical Center (828-649-3500) is at 8625 U.S. Highways 25/70. The Hot Springs Medical and Dental Center (828-622-3245) is on US 25/70 close to the BP gas station. The Laurel Medical Center is at 400 Cook Farm Rd. off Highway 208, which leads to Greeneville, Tennessee.

## Close-up

## Veterans' Art and Healing

When the VA Medical Center in Asheville received a new ambulatory wing some years ago, the center's interior designers opted to personalize the space by providing two galleries for art and historical displays close to the entrance. The art featured in the galleries would come from many of the veterans themselves, and even VA Medical Center employees. Beyond that, designers planned for local artists to embellish the design of each atrium floor, to feature historical photography and nature photography, as well as other works.

A copper fountain, fashioned by a local artist, on the bottom floor of the atrium allows visitors and patients to see and hear the calming waters when they approach the balconies within. But the pièce de résistance came with the Veterans' Memorial that was commissioned by the VA Center.

International sculptor Vadim Bora, who lives in Asheville, created an ode to veterans wounded in war with his evocative sculpture *The Wings of Freedom*. A grand eagle stands guard over a wounded soldier, sheltering him from the battle and the elements until help arrives. The sculpture stands just inside the entrance of the ambulatory wing of the Medical Center.

## Mitchell County

### BAKERSVILLE COMMUNITY MEDICAL CLINIC
**86 North Mitchell Ave., Bakersville**
**(828) 688-2104**

The tiny, rural community of Bakersville is served by this private clinic of five family physicians, one chiropractor, and one nurse practitioner. The clinic offers a wide range of primary care services, including obstetrics and gynecology, flexible sigmoidoscopy, orthopedic medicine, drug screening, pediatrics, sports and industrial medicine, geriatrics, and nutrition counseling. The clinic is affiliated with the Spruce Pine Community Hospital.

### SPRUCE PINE COMMUNITY HOSPITAL
**125 Hospital Dr., Spruce Pine**
**(828) 765-4201**

Founded in 1955, this 80-bed community hospital is within the town of Spruce Pine, in the mountains north of Burnsville. The hospital serves Mitchell, Avery, and Yancey counties. Spruce Pine Hospital is also a member of the Mission St. Joseph's Health System. The full-service Spruce Pine facility staffs a 24-hour emergency room. Social workers assist the hospital in arranging nursing home care.

## Watauga County

### BLOWING ROCK HOSPITAL
**416 Chestnut Dr., Blowing Rock**
**(828) 295-3136**

This 100-bed, full-service community hospital is located in the village of Blowing Rock, north of Boone. It is a private, nonprofit hospital, with an adjacent medical office complex. Facilities include acute and long-term care; surgery, X-ray, and lab facilities; on-call physicians; and an emergency room. The hospital and long-term care unit are fully accredited by the Joint Commission of Accreditation of Hospitals.

### WATAUGA MEDICAL CENTER
**336 Deerfield Rd., Boone**
**(828) 262-4391**

Watauga Medical Center started in 1936 as a humble medical clinic on the campus of Appalachian State Teacher's College in Boone. The clinic quickly developed into a regular 50-bed hospital and by 1967 had expanded to an 83-bed facility at its present Deerfield Road site. Watauga almost doubled its capacity by 1979 and by 1985 began an expansion project to house an enlarged imaging department. In the early 1990s the Medical Center also completed an outpatient facility. Today the hospital is licensed as a 147-bed complex. To reflect the expanding services, the hospital changed its name in 1993 to Watauga Medical Center.

Some of the services at Watauga Medical Center include a critical care center; a complete surgical suite covering general and specialized surgery; an imaging unit offering CT scanning, MRI, X-ray, mammography, and ultrasound; a birthing suite featuring relaxed birthing rooms, Cesarean section rooms, two well-baby nurseries, a level II neonatal intensive-care nursery, and an isolation nursery; and a well-equipped, well-staffed pathology department for routine and special procedures, including forensic pathology. A special kidney dialysis unit and a regional cancer center are also part of Watauga Medical Center's comprehensive medical complex. The center has a 24-hour physician-staffed emergency room and has air access via helicopter to Sanger Clinic in Charlotte for heart patients and Baptist Hospital in Winston-Salem for head trauma patients.

## Yancey County

**YANCEY COMMUNITY MEDICAL CENTER**
**320 Pensacola Rd., Burnsville**
**(828) 682-6136**
Serving the Burnsville area, this primary care clinic is open Mon through Fri, 8 a.m. to 5 p.m. with evening hours on Thurs until 8 p.m. X-ray facilities are available, and there's a lab operated by Spruce Pine Community Hospital on the premises. The clinic is affiliated with Mission St. Joseph's Health System. This medical center will see walk-ins with emergencies. After hours, it's best to go to the Spruce Pine Community Hospital (828-765-4201), 125 Hospital Dr.

# CENTRAL MOUNTAINS

## Buncombe County

**THE ASHEVILLE VETERANS AFFAIRS**
**MEDICAL CENTER**
**1100 Tunnel Rd., Asheville**
**(828) 298-7911**
The Asheville VA Medical Center is in the Oteen area, in east Asheville, just minutes from an entrance to the Blue Ridge Parkway. The facility has a 90-year history of service to veterans in the mountains of Western North Carolina, beginning in March 1918 when it became U.S. Army General Hospital No. 19, a cantonlike collection of 104 frame buildings accommodating 1,200 beds. The first patient was admitted in Sept of the same year. Treatment of tuberculosis was the primary focus.

In 1920 administration of the hospital was transferred to the U.S. Public Health Service. It was during this period that the Cherokee Indian term *oteen*, meaning "chief aim," was proposed for use with the hospital as an encouragement to every patient to adopt as his chief aim "to get well."

The mission of the USPHS hospital continued to be the treatment of tuberculosis. More permanent buildings were constructed on site from 1924 to 1936 to help provide better treatment facilities for this disease. Modernization of these structures was completed and capacity expanded during World War II. The 40-year mission as a tuberculosis treatment center was enhanced and the scope of treatment broadened when the hospital was officially designated as a General Medical and Surgical Hospital in 1961.

Asheville's VA Medical Center is recognized as a major general medical and surgical hospital. The center is known for its strong programs in vascular, thoracic, and cardiac surgery. Its successful cardiac surgery program is the longest-running, continuously cost-effective program of its kind in the VA system and serves veterans from Virginia, West Virginia, upstate South Carolina, east Tennessee, and Western North Carolina.

The VA Medical Center provides a number of special programs, including cardiac catheterization, nuclear medicine, respiratory care, audiology and speech pathology, geriatric evaluation and management, mental health programs, a 25-bed substance-abuse program, a residential rehabilitation treatment program, a community nursing program, and a hospital-based primary care program.

A nonprofit research corporation administers an ongoing research program here. It currently consists of nine projects, most of which are clinical trials.

## MISSION HOSPITAL IN ASHEVILLE:
## ST. JOSEPH AND MEMORIAL CAMPUSES
**509 Biltmore Ave., Asheville**
**(828) 213-1111**

This private not-for-profit medical facility began in 1885 as the Asheville Mission Hospital. Today this nearly 500-bed hospital and the staff of 390 physicians and 2,000-member support staff provide medical expertise and high-quality care. Most specialties are represented at Mission, which has expanded over the years to cover virtually an entire hilltop in downtown Asheville. It offers a level of sophistication of medical care found at large university medical centers.

The partnership was the first of its type in North Carolina and one of the first in the nation. Combined, the two large hospitals cover more than 2 million square feet. The 500 physicians—primary care doctors, specialists, and subspecialists—care for patients in the hospitals as well as in the new critical care, heart, genetics, and women's and children's centers. Medical services are organized according to clinical specialty: The Owen Health Center provides for cardiology and heart surgery and a cardiac rehabilitation program. It's also a national leader in minimally invasive and valve replacement surgery. The Ruth and Billy Graham Children's Health Center is an inpatient hospital, pediatric intensive care unit, and neonatal ICU for newborns. Orthopedic care ranks among the top 35 hospitals in the country in the number of joint replacement surgeries done. The Women's Health Center educates and supports women of all ages, including high-risk obstetrics patients. The Fullerton Genetics Center diagnoses and provides laboratory testing and counseling for individuals and families who may be affected by inherited health problems. Services include the Copestone behavioral medicine unit, with geriatric, adolescent, psychiatric, and substance abuse programs.

Surgical services include one-day and laser-assisted surgery and a vascular center. Neuro-sciences, adult medicine, and oncology are, of course, included in the comprehensive hospital program. Emergency trauma services are staffed 24 hours a day and include hospital-operated air and ground transportation services.

## THOMS REHABILITATION HOSPITAL
**68 Sweeten Creek Rd., Asheville**
**(828) 274-2400**

Established as the Asheville Orthopedic Home in 1938 by the Rotary Club and the Junior League of Asheville, Thoms Rehabilitation Hospital was originally a facility for children with disabilities from the remote areas of the mountains of Western North Carolina. Thoms is now a nonprofit regional referral center offering acute care, day treatment, and transitional outpatient rehabilitation services to those with physical, cognitive, and developmental impairments. Traditional and specialized rehabilitation programs are offered for all ages.

The hospital works with brain trauma cases, spinal cord injuries, stroke and developmental disabilities, pain and industrial injuries, and conditions of amputation and neuromuscular disorders.

The staff is composed of physicians, psychologists, nurses, and physical and occupational therapists and speech/language pathologists, among other professionals. Thoms is a founding member of Community CarePartners, a post-acute continuum of care.

## Henderson County
**BLUE RIDGE DENTAL PRACTICE**
**1801 Asheville Hwy., Hendersonville**
**(828) 696-0512**

**BLUE RIDGE HEALTH CENTER**
**US 64 East and Howard Gap Road,**
**Hendersonville**
**(828) 692-4289**

**DRUID HILLS FAMILY PRACTICE**
**1801 Asheville Hwy., Hendersonville**
**(828) 696-0545**

**GEORGE BOND MEMORIAL HEALTH CENTER**
**US Hwy. 74, Bat Cave**
**(828) 625-9141**

**KATE B. REYNOLDS WOMEN'S**
**AND CHILDREN'S CENTER**
**US 64 East and Howard Gap Road,**
**Hendersonville**
**(828) 692-7057**

Blue Ridge Community Health Service is a private, not-for-profit community health center with five locations in Henderson County. A staff of board-certified family practice physicians, internists, and pediatricians, along with physician assistants, family nurse practitioners, and certified nurse-midwives, work as a team to provide personal-ized comprehensive health care for the entire family, from newborns to the elderly. Doctors are on 24-hour call and enjoy staff privileges at Margaret R. Pardee Hospital in Hendersonville.

Maternal Outreach and Child Service Coordi-nation Programs support the obstetrics and gyne-cology services. A nutritionist provides dietetic education and counseling, and home-health nurs-ing services are available for homebound patients.

Board-certified dentists, along with hygien-ists, provide restorative and preventive dental care to children and pregnant women and emer-gency care for established Blue Ridge patients. Blue Ridge Community Health Services leads the way in providing access to health care and dental care—a major concern for many people throughout Western North Carolina. The doors are open to "everyone" without regard to finan-cial status. Their focus is providing quality health care at affordable rates with an emphasis on the medically underserved. Most insurance plans are accepted, including Medicare and Medicaid. A sliding fee schedule is available for those who qualify, and payment plans can be arranged.

All locations can be reached after hours by calling (828) 692-4289.

## MARGARET R. PARDEE
## MEMORIAL HOSPITAL
### 715 Fleming St., Hendersonville
### (828) 696-1000

This hospital was founded in 1953 with the help of a $100,000 donation from Ivor Pardee in memory of his aunt, Margaret R. Pardee. This hos-pital's advanced diagnostic equipment and treat-ment facilities include a sleep disorder lab, MRI, CT scan, echocardiograms, advanced angiogram equipment, nuclear medicine, endoscopy, mam-mography, ultrasound, kidney stone lithotripsy, and bone densitometer.

The Kayden Radiation Oncology Center was built to meet the needs of cancer patients who require radiation therapy five days a week for six weeks or more. The addition of radiation therapy means that all three major treatment modes are available at Pardee: surgery, chemotherapy, and radiation therapy. The American College of Surgeons certified Pardee as a cancer center in 1997. (The certification process takes three years and involves a cancer registry, which records and reports cancers and treatments to the N.C. Cen-tral Cancer Registry. This information becomes part of the national database on cancer care.)

Family-centered, one-room birthing in the Family Way unit allows families to fully appreciate the childbirth experience. Pardee's day-surgery unit, freestanding outpatient radiology depart-ment, and large emergency department make treatment more convenient. Express Care (same address as the hospital) is open evenings, week-ends, and holidays for care of minor emergencies and illnesses without the waiting time that is sometimes seen in the emergency room.

Pardee's Home Care includes OB and pediat-ric nursing, psychiatric nursing, and personal care services. Other services include cardiac and pul-monary rehabilitation, respite care of dependent adults, geriatric evaluations, and adult day care.

Pardee provides health education to the com-munity through a variety of means. The Pardee Health Education Center at the Blue Ridge Mall on Four Seasons Boulevard has served the com-munity in health promotions and wellness since 1989. Free or low-cost screenings, seminars by doctors and health care professionals, support groups, and a wealth of literature and videos on health topics are available at the center. The Hen-derson County Breast Cancer Initiative, sponsored by Pardee, provides education on breast cancer, bringing services such as mobile mammography, breast self-examination education, and a breast cancer awareness speakers bureau to neighbor-hoods, community organizations, and businesses.

Pardee Care Center is a nursing home on land adjacent to Blue Ridge Community College. It shares space with both the college and Four Seasons Hospice.

## PARK RIDGE HOSPITAL
**100 Hospital Dr., Fletcher**
**(828) 684-8501**

First opened in 1910, the Mountain Sanitarium eventually evolved into Fletcher Hospital. Then in 1986 its new 103-bed facility was opened, and this not-for-profit facility, operated by the Seventh-day Adventists, became the Park Ridge Hospital. The facility is a full-service general, acute-care hospital that has a 24-hour emergency department, OB/GYN, and psychiatric services. With 150 physicians and more than 450 employees, it averages about 23,000 patient visits per year, with a focus on "the well-being of the whole person" that includes a vegetarian option for all hospital meals.

Park Ridge offers the latest in health care technology, including a CT scanner, a mobile MRI unit, and nuclear medicine. Specialized spine and orthopedic surgery capabilities are available at Park Ridge. Comprehensive ophthalmology services also are provided. Approximately 750 cataract surgeries are performed every year. Park Ridge also provides a variety of educational and rehabilitative programs that include child and adolescent psychiatry, occupational health, cardiac and pulmonary rehabilitation, wellness, smoking cessation, classes for expectant parents, and HOPE, a women's program that treats eating and psychological disorders.

The emergency department operates 24 hours a day. The Home Health Agency provides skilled nursing care and rehabilitation at home. The hospital also has birthing rooms and a large physical therapy department that's part of its cardiac rehabilitation and occupational health program for area industry. Blending faith and technology, Park Ridge Hospital provides the highest quality health care.

## Polk County
### ST. LUKE'S HOSPITAL
**101 Hospital Dr., Columbus**
**(828) 894-3311**

St. Luke's, founded in 1929, is a private, nonprofit facility serving 34,000 patients annually from Polk,

Spartanburg, and Greenville counties. It offers primary, emergency, and outpatient services, including a geriatric psychiatric unit, a Center of Behavioral Medicine for psychiatric outpatients, a restorative care unit, an ICU, and a 24-hour, physician-staffed emergency department. St. Luke's also offers state-of-the-art diagnostics, including a CT scanner, GE mammography equipment, a heart-monitoring system for both the ER and ICU, nuclear medicine, and a bone densitometer. It also offers physical, occupational, respiratory, and speech therapies.

St. Luke's staff specialties include general, orthopedic, and pain-management surgery, as well as ophthalmology, family practice, gerontology, internal medicine, pathology, psychiatry, urology, and radiology.

## Transylvania County
### TRANSYLVANIA COMMUNITY HOSPITAL
**260 Hospital Drive, Brevard**
**(828) 884-9111**

Transylvania Community Hospital is a 94-bed, not-for-profit community facility. The hospital, formed in 1933, is fully accredited and offers a wide range of services including preventative care, wellness programs, inpatient and outpatient medical/surgical services, a complete physical/occupational/speech therapy department, cardiac and pulmonary disease rehabilitation, and follow-up care. Services include Bridgeway, an inpatient and outpatient alcohol and substance abuse unit; Work Well, an occupational health program that helps injured workers get back to work; and the Living Well with Diabetes program, a comprehensive diabetes management and education service. The Wound Care, Ostomy, and Continence Department offers special care for patients with nonhealing wounds or infections, temporary or permanent ostomies, or incontinence.

The medical staff at TCH includes specialists in emergency medicine, ENT, internal medicine, family practice, pediatrics, sports medicine, ophthalmology, oncology, orthopedics, radiology, and urology, among others.

# SOUTHERN MOUNTAINS

## Cherokee County

**DISTRICT MEMORIAL HOSPITAL**
**415 Whitaker Lane, Andrews**
**(828) 321-1200**
Nationally accredited by the Joint Commission on Accreditation of Healthcare Organizations, DMH is a state-licensed, 60-bed, acute-care facility located in the beautiful valley town of Andrews. Its growing medical staff of more than 20 physicians includes specialists in cardiology, critical care, emergency medicine, family practice, gastroenterology, general surgery, internal medicine, ophthalmology, orthopedics, pathology, pulmonology, radiology, and urology.

District Memorial's 24-hour emergency department is complemented by its 24-hour laboratory, respiratory, and X-ray services. It has a fully equipped intensive care unit and a growing surgical unit for both inpatient and outpatient procedures. DMH also has a Convalescent Unit and offers occupational, physical, and speech therapy.

**MURPHY MEDICAL CENTER**
**4130 Hwy. 64 East, Murphy**
**(828) 837-8161**
Located 5 miles from Murphy on the Hiwassee River, the Murphy Medical Center opened in 1979 and is one of the more modern facilities in the region. A full-service hospital with 50 beds and a 120-bed nursing home, MMC serves the residents of Cherokee, Clay, and Graham counties and adjoining counties in Georgia and Tennessee with a 24-hour emergency room and can respond to most medical needs.

It provides services in the fields of family practice, general surgery, internal medicine, orthopedics, pediatrics, radiology, ophthalmology, urology, obstetrics, gynecology, and oncology. The hospital also provides a personal-response emergency system.

## Haywood County

**HAYWOOD REGIONAL MEDICAL CENTER**
**262 Leroy George Dr., Clyde**
**(828) 456-7311, (800) 834-1729**

Established in 1927, this is the largest hospital west of Asheville serving the westernmost counties as the provider of primary, acute hospital care and numerous medical specialty services.

The medical center offers imaging services, diabetes education, and health and fitness centers. HRMC also houses a state-funded adult psychiatric inpatient program managed by Smoky Mountain Center, a local provider of behavioral health care services. The HRMC Foundation provides charitable giving and administration services.

**HOME HEALTH CARE OF HAYWOOD REGIONAL MEDICAL CENTER**
**262 Leroy George Dr., Clyde**
**(828) 452-8292, (888) 456-0011**
Now serving all the counties included in this book, Haywood County's Home Care Services' certified nursing assistants provide home care under the supervision of a registered nurse. CNAs perform personal care tasks such as bathing, essential housekeeping, and home management, while a team of RNs and pharmacists provide infusion therapy, skilled nursing, rehabilitation services, and medical social work.

Home Care Services also provides hospice services. Haywood Regional Medical Center also has designated beds for hospice respite care and inpatient use. In addition the organization offers many specialized services, including maternal/infant, psychiatric, respiratory, bereavement, and Lifeline programs.

## Jackson County

**SWAIN COUNTY HOSPITAL**
**45 Plateau St., Bryson City**
**(828) 488-2155**

**WESTCARE HEALTH SYSTEM**
**Harris Regional Hospital**
**68 Hospital Rd., Sylva**
**(828) 586-7000**
WestCare Health System was established in 1994 by Harris Regional Hospital to meet the expanding health needs of a growing Western North Carolina population and to enhance the delivery

of health care in the region. Swain County Hospital and its affiliated services joined the system in 1997. WestCare Health System—through Harris Regional Hospital, Swain County Hospital, and affiliated medical resources—offers clinical services, acute-care inpatient services, outpatient services, cardiopulmonary services, emergency departments, an Urgent Care Center, emergency medical services, Home Health and Hospice, imaging services, laboratory services, a medical resource center, nutrition services, wellness services, occupational health management, rehabilitation services, surgical services, and women's and children's services. WestCare Health System and its affiliated hospitals and services and its associated medical staff are widely recognized as a provider of choice in the health care field.

## Macon County

### ANGEL MEDICAL CENTER
120 Riverview St., Franklin
(828) 524-8411
The 25 doctors at this modern, multipurpose 59-bed facility specialize in allergies, orthopedics, family practice, internal medicine, pathology, emergency medicine, urology, ophthalmology, OB/GYN, and pediatrics. Angel provides 24-hour emergency service and outpatient surgeries. The Home Health Agency is fully accredited, and the American College of Radiology certifies its mammography unit.

AMC also offers, among other services, physical therapy, diet/nutrition classes, MRI, CT scanning, nuclear medicine, speech therapy, pathology, chemotherapy, cardiopulmonary services, family services, and an occupational health program for business and industry.

Two additional services are the Urgent Care Center (828-369-4427), at the intersection of U.S. Highways 23 and 441, which treats nonemergency medical problems, and the 24-hour Angel Medical Answer Line (828-369-4455), which is staffed by nurses.

### HIGHLANDS-CASHIERS HOSPITAL
190 Hospital Dr. and US 64 East, Highlands
(828) 526-1200

A private, nonprofit health care provider, Highlands-Cashiers Hospital has served the medical needs of the people of southern Macon and Jackson counties and western Transylvania County for more than half a century. A new hospital and nursing facility opened its doors in 1993. It offers a wide range of diagnostic services, state-of-the-art medical technology, and a board-certified medical staff of nearly 30 physicians, including specialists in cardiology, gastroenterology, general surgery, plastic and reconstructive surgery, urology, rheumatology, orthopedic surgery, ophthalmology, podiatry, and pulmonary medicine. The hospital has a 24-hour emergency room and offers Saturday morning Urgent Care. It's affiliated with both Mission St. Joseph's Health System in Asheville and Emory Healthcare System in Atlanta, Georgia.

The Fidelia Eckerd Nursing Center, a part of the hospital, offers long-term nursing care, respite care, and assisted living.

### MACON COUNTY PUBLIC HEALTH CENTER
1830 Lakeside Dr., Franklin
(828) 349-2081
Opened in 1980, this health center offers a wide range of public health services, including family planning, prenatal, child and adult health screenings, orthopedic, and hypertension services. The health center's laboratory offers support for the public health programs and may file forms for Medicare, Medicaid, and some insurance companies. Routine vaccinations are given free; other services are also free or provided at low cost. While no appointments are necessary, Mon and Thurs are generally considered the center's walk-in days. The Macon County Public Health Center also holds clinics in Highlands and Nantahala on a regular schedule.

The center also provides environmental health services, such as water testing, issuing septic system permits, and food and lodging inspections.

# EDUCATION

Formal education came to the mountains in 1793, only 10 years after the first settlers moved west of the Blue Ridge. Presbyterians established the first school here, an academy called Union Hill in what is now the city of Asheville. Only two years later the University of North Carolina, the oldest state university in the nation, opened its doors in Chapel Hill.

Father of the geodesic design, forerunner of today's domed stadiums, was Buckminster Fuller, one of the leaders of the formation of Black Mountain College. Now defunct, the college was home to creative minds like John Cage and Robert Rauschenberg.

Today the University of North Carolina, as well as a number of other colleges and prep schools, offers a wide range of educational and cultural options. They provide a wealth of affordable continuing education courses that draw on the skills of the area's large number of talented retirees.

In addition the mountains are home to renowned craft and music schools. The Penland School of Crafts is the oldest and largest school for high-quality mixed-media arts and crafts in North America. For more than 80 years the John C. Campbell Folk School has offered outstanding courses in traditional crafts, music, and dance (see our Mountain Crafts chapter). At the Brevard Music Center, approximately 300 gifted students from across the nation have the opportunity to join teaching professionals and famous guests in the performance of 50 summer concerts (see our Arts and Culture chapter).

## NORTHERN MOUNTAINS
### Universities

**APPALACHIAN STATE UNIVERSITY**
**287 River St., Boone**
**(828) 262-2000**
**www.appstate.edu**
From its beginnings as a teachers academy, Appalachian State University has grown into one of the top comprehensive universities in the South. Today students major in a variety of fields, including graphic arts, business, exercise science, criminal justice, and teacher education. University programs, such as Freshman Seminar, have received national recognition. Innovative partnerships with public schools, community colleges, business and industry, retirement centers, and others provide students opportunities to translate classroom learning into real-world experience. Off-campus properties in Washington, D.C., and New York City provide opportunities for special learning experiences.

Appalachian offers approximately 100 undergraduate majors, more than 75 graduate majors, and a doctorate in educational leadership. The university consistently has ranked among the top 15 comprehensive regional universities in the South since *U.S. News & World Report* began ranking colleges and universities in 1986.

Appalachian's enrollment is approximately 12,300 students. Beautifully set in the rugged Watauga County mountains, Appalachian attracts students from the state's larger cities as well as its hometown of Boone.

### Four-Year Colleges

**LEES-MCRAE COLLEGE**
**375 College Dr., Banner Elk**
**(828) 898-8780, (828) 898-5241**
**www.lmc.edu**
Lees-McRae College is a coeducational liberal arts institution that, at 4,000 feet above sea level, boasts the highest elevation of any college east of the Mississippi River.

This private college is affiliated with the Presbyterian Church (U.S.A.). Its beginnings go back to 1900 and the Rev. Edgar Tufts, who founded what was then a high school as an outgrowth of his ministry in the Appalachian Mountains. Elizabeth A. McRae was the teacher for the first class of 14 girls. In the ensuing years the school grew, thanks in great measure to the generosity of the school's benefactor Mrs. S. P. Lees. The efforts of these two women were not forgotten when the school was chartered in 1907 as the Lees-McRae Institute. It was renamed Lees-McRae College in 1931 when it gained accreditation as a coeducational junior college.

The college attained senior college status in 1990. The attractive campus has 30 buildings, many built of native stone. There are 13 residence halls, 2 classroom buildings, an 89,000-volume library, an auditorium, a student center, and a physical education center. The 32-member faculty reflects a variety of religious, ethnic, and national origins. Enrollment is 470, and the student-faculty ratio is 15 to 1. Scholarships are also available in academics, athletics, and performing arts.

Lees-McRae offers both bachelor of arts and bachelor of science degrees as well as course work in a number of pre-professional areas. The school also maintains study-abroad and community service programs as well as an honors curriculum.

## MARS HILL COLLEGE
**100 Athletic St., Mars Hill**
**(828) 689-1201, (800) 543-1514**
**www.mhc.edu**

Mars Hill College is tucked away on a ridge in rural Madison County, just over the mountain from Tennessee. This four-year, private coeducational college has the distinction of being the oldest educational institution in Western North Carolina. It was founded in 1856 as the French Broad Baptist Academy by a group of citizens descended from the original settlers of the area. The school was chartered officially as Mars Hill College in 1859 by the North Carolina General Assembly.

The Civil War brought hard times to the South, and Mars Hill College felt its share. Struggling with the deprivations of war, the college was able to stay in operation for the first two years of the war but was forced to close from 1863 to 1865. For much of its history, the school operated as an academy or boarding school, one that provided some college-level courses. In 1921 Mars Hill was reorganized as a junior college and became a pioneer in that field of education. This Baptist-affiliated college subsequently became a four-year institution, awarding the first baccalaureate degrees in May 1964.

The campus lies on 194 acres of rolling hills with a panoramic view of Mount Pisgah, Clingman's Peak, and the Craggies. It's hard to tell where the campus ends and the town of Mars Hill begins, so closely are they linked in every way. The pace is a little slower here, more conducive to inspiration. And when the need for city life arises, Asheville is just 18 miles south.

For all its bucolic charm, Mars Hill College is recognized today as educationally progressive in the fields of innovative curriculum development, continuing education, regional cultural studies, the arts, and international education. The campus houses the Rural Life Museum, which facilitates the collection, preservation, exhibition, and interpretation of rural life artifacts in the southern Appalachian region.

With an average enrollment of about 1,300 students, Mars Hill College offers a 16-to-1 student-teacher ratio. The college offers five degrees in 31 majors in its curriculum. Approximately 50 international students come to the campus each year, and out-of-state students comprise 40 percent of the student body. Mars Hill's athletic program includes 18 NCAA Division II sports.

## Two-Year Colleges

## MAYLAND COMMUNITY COLLEGE
**200 Mayland Dr., Spruce Pine**
**(828) 765-7351, (800) 4-MAYLAND**
**www.mayland.edu**

This small community college offers a unique family atmosphere in a natural mountain set-

## Black Mountain College

Founder John Edward Rice brought renown to Black Mountain College with an open curriculum based on the theories of Plato and Aristotle. Professors came from Harvard, University of Chicago, and the University of North Carolina, just to name a few. Some of its most famous faculty members included Buckminster Fuller and Albert Einstein. Started in the Swannanoa Valley in 1933, the college closed its doors in 1965, then experienced a brief revival in the 1980s to 1990s but was eventually closed again due to financial problems. Even though it had a brief history, it brought a brilliance to the mountains and continues to serve the community by bringing art, philosophy, and learning into the valley in its current museum posture.

A Black Mountain College Museum and Art Center, located on Broadway Street in downtown Asheville, features works of the college's graduates and teachers, as well as multimedia shows about the history of the institution itself.

Colleges of the Southern Association of Colleges and Schools to award the associate in arts degree, diplomas, and certificates.

In addition to curriculum programs, Mayland also provides a wide variety of classes under the umbrella of continuing education. Included in this division are classes in occupational extension, community service, Small Business Center, and Human Resources Development.

The Basic Skills Program offers adults opportunities to develop basic and computational skills necessary to function in employment in the community. Two outreach facilities, the Avery Learning Center in Newland and the Yancey Learning Center in Burnsville, complete the campus of Mayland Community College.

**i** Check in with the local colleges and universities where you are vacationing. They vary in offering summer accommodations in empty dorms and serve meals throughout the year, all at a great savings.

**WATAUGA CAMPUS OF CALDWELL COMMUNITY COLLEGE AND TECHNICAL INSTITUTE**
**Community College Drive, Boone**
**(828) 297-2185**
**www.caldwell.cc.nc.us**
This satellite college of nearby Caldwell Community College and Technical Institute provides quality continuing education opportunities for residents of Watauga County. Both two-year degrees and one-year diploma programs are available. Occupational programs offer one or two years of training in vocational and technical subjects. College parallel programs provide freshman and sophomore courses for students who may wish to transfer to four-year institutions.

Established in 1973, the CCC&TI offers instruction leading to completion of certificates, diplomas, and degrees, as well as continuing education courses. A permanent Watauga campus was established in 1998 with the addition of a 23,000-square-foot instructional facility. In addition to this 39-acre site, classes are also taught at four other locations in the county.

ting in the Blue Ridge Mountains on 41 acres just east of the town of Spruce Pine. Nearby is Mount Mitchell, the highest mountain east of the Mississippi. A little to the north is world-famous Grandfather Mountain. The Blue Ridge Parkway also winds its way through this scenic area.

The college, established in 1971, takes its name from the initials of the tri-county area it serves: Mitchell, Avery, and Yancey. With an enrollment of around 800, this coeducational institution can provide personal student-instructor interaction. Mayland is accredited by the Commission on

# CENTRAL MOUNTAINS

## Universities

**THE UNIVERSITY OF NORTH CAROLINA ASHEVILLE**
**One University Heights, Asheville**
**(828) 251-6600**
**www.unca.edu**
The University of North Carolina Asheville is the designated public liberal arts university of the 16-campus University of North Carolina system. The university sits on a wooded 265-acre site a mile north of downtown Asheville. UNCA opened in 1927 as Buncombe County Junior College, and through an ongoing community commitment has evolved into a small, distinguished public liberal arts university.

UNCA has been named a "best buy" by the *Fiske Guide to Colleges* and the school offers four-year undergraduate degree programs in the arts and humanities, the natural and social sciences, and selected pre-professional and professional programs. UNCA also offers an undergraduate "2-plus-2" program in engineering with North Carolina State University in Raleigh. Undergraduates spend two years at UNCA and two years at NCSU. The Asheville Graduate Center offers graduate degree programs from NC State, UNC–Chapel Hill, UNC-Greensboro, and Western Carolina University, as well as UNCA's Master of Liberal Arts program.

UNCA is the home of the North Carolina Center for Creative Retirement, including its College for Seniors, an additional avenue for continuing education.

The D. Hiden Ramsay Library is the cultural and architectural heart of the campus. It houses nearly 318,000 volumes on open shelves, approximately 50,000 government documents, and several hundred audio- and videotapes. A computerized, one-day library network with sister universities extends the collection to more than a million volumes.

The arts figure prominently in UNCA campus life. The proximity of cosmopolitan Asheville is a definite influence, and the two frequently intertwine. Access to the university is of prime benefit to the citizens of Asheville. The university's theater programs, concerts, dance performances, arts exhibits, and lecture series enrich the community.

Ongoing construction at UNCA provides for the growth of this increasingly popular campus. UNCA has about 3,500 students and an average class size of 21.

## Four-Year Colleges

**BREVARD COLLEGE**
**400 North Broad St., Brevard**
**(828) 884-8300, (800) 527-9090**
**www.brevard.edu**
Brevard College offers an innovative, interdisciplinary course of study culminating in a four-year degree. Located on a beautiful mountain campus, the college has a faculty to student ratio of 8 to 1. Environmental studies, wilderness leadership and experiential education, ecology, music, art, theater, and organizational studies (business) are just some of the majors offered here. A strong affiliation with the United Methodist Church dates back to 1853 when the college was established as the first institution of higher learning in Western North Carolina. A small liberal arts residential college, Brevard has approximately 670 students representing 30 states and 15 foreign countries.

Long recognized for its outstanding tradition in music, the college now features the Paul Porter Center for Performing Arts with the acoustically impressive concert hall, Blackbox Theater, and Institute of Sacred Music. Opened in the fall of 1998, the Porter Center provides excellent venues for nationally known performers as well as BC's own student ensembles, choirs, and thespians.

With numerous national championships from competition in the NJCAA, the college's male and female athletes now compete in the NAIA in such sports as soccer, baseball, softball, volleyball, cross-country, track and field, and more. Intramural sports are available, and adventure-based sports such as kayaking, climbing, rappelling, and mountain biking are offered through the college's wilderness leadership program. The college runs a variety of "immersion" educational experiences for academic credit, including the 1997 Voice of the Rivers Expedition—a 2,000-mile kayaking experience on the French Broad, Tennessee, Ohio, and Mississippi Rivers to the Gulf of Mexico, where participants have taught some 6,000 students along the way about environmental issues.

The philosophy of Brevard College is that service be a vital part of the classroom experience, so the Center for Service Learning coordinates service activities in the surrounding community.

## MONTREAT COLLEGE
**310 Gaither Circle, Montreat**
**(828) 669-8011**
**www.montreat.edu**
Seeming to emerge from the woods, Montreat College is a unique, four-year liberal arts college affiliated with the Presbyterian Church (U.S.A.). This lovely, small college has a heritage of quality education founded on Christian beliefs.

In 1916 the Montreat Normal School for women was founded. In 1934, during Dr. Robert C. Anderson's tenure as president, Montreat Normal School was renamed simply Montreat College. The college grew as its academic program expanded. It began a four-year degree program in 1945. After 14 years as a four-year women's college, the college was restructured in 1959 as a coeducational junior college and was given a new name, Montreat-Anderson College. In 1985 the college board of trustees realized the demands and changing circumstances in higher education and made the decision to again become a baccalaureate institution, re-creating the dream of Dr. Anderson. The recent name change back to Montreat College returns the school to its original vision and identity.

Students benefit from Montreat's small classes, and they grow through one-on-one interaction with professors and classmates. Studies challenge them to integrate faith and learning while considering subjects in ways never thought possible. Hands-on experiences in the majors (internships, field studies, mission programs,

community service, and independent research) enable students to gain practical career and life preparation.

Montreat College is tucked within the wooded paradise of the community of Montreat, near Black Mountain, 15 miles east of Asheville. The campus follows a tree-lined valley, woven through with numerous streams. This beautiful campus features buildings constructed of native stone whose interiors are uniquely highlighted by wide use of flint, colorful mica, granite, sandstone, and marble. The facilities of the Mountain Retreat Association and the Presbyterian Department of History are also in Montreat.

Montreat College offers majors in American studies, Bible and religion, business administration, English, environmental studies, history, human services, liberal arts, mathematics, and outdoor education. A teaching certification program is available on the secondary school level. The college's School of Professional and Adult Studies offers associate's, bachelor's, and master's degrees for working adults with campus facilities in Charlotte and Asheville.

A significant aspect of Montreat College is the fact that the college provides extensive financial aid to enable any qualified student to get a college education. More than 80 percent of the student body receives some form of financial aid through a variety of federal and state grants. The Chapel of the Prodigal on campus contains a fresco by artist Ben Long.

## WARREN WILSON COLLEGE
**701 Warren Wilson College Rd., Swannanoa**
**(828) 298-3325**
**www.warren-wilson.edu**
Warren Wilson College has always combined academic rewards with a strong work ethic and service to the community. In 1894 the national Presbyterian Board of Missions started the Asheville Farm School to provide education for boys of the Appalachian mountain area. In the early 1940s the college merged with the Dorland-Bell School for Girls in Hot Springs in Madison County. At that time it became Warren Wilson High School, named in honor of a young sociologist

who worked with the school through the auspices of the Presbyterian Church. The year 1942 saw the addition of a junior college division, and in 1966 Warren Wilson finally became a four-year, liberal arts college.

Of the school's 700 students, 25 percent come from North Carolina, 5 percent from outside the United States, and the remainder from 40 other states. The college is known for its unusual curriculum that combines in equal measure strong academics, work for the school, and service to the community. Each student works 15 hours per week on one of 105 essential work crews. These crews range from plumbing and landscaping to farm labor and administrative support. Students also must perform a minimum of 100 hours of community service while they are enrolled. Students generate service projects to fill any needs they see. Projects are also offered through the campus center for service learning.

The 1,100-acre campus sits in the Blue Ridge Mountains just east of Asheville. The campus features a 300-acre working farm, an archaeological site, and 600 acres of forest. Dormitories built of native stone dot the intimate main campus, and 25 miles of hiking trails are available to students right on campus, along with a campus whitewater paddling location.

Ties to the land are evident in the fact that the most popular major at Warren Wilson is environmental studies. A highly touted low-residency program awarding an M.F.A. in creative writing, as well as a widely respected program in traditional Appalachian folk music, are two additional facets of this creative school.

## Two-Year Colleges

### ASHEVILLE-BUNCOMBE TECHNICAL COMMUNITY COLLEGE
340 Victoria Dr., Asheville
(828) 254-1921
www.abtech.edu
A member of the North Carolina Community College System, A-B Tech offers associate degrees, diplomas, or certificates in 48 curriculum programs through four academic divisions: Allied Health and Public Service Education, Arts and Sciences, Business and Hospitality Education, and Engineering and Applied Technology. A fifth division, Continuing Education, offers opportunities for specific job training and retraining, basic skills education, and vocational courses for individual enrichment.

A-B Tech celebrates its 49th anniversary in 2008. Established Sept 1, 1959, the college was originally funded by a bond election and called the Asheville Industrial Education Center. Over the years community support has helped A-B Tech grow and expand its services so that it currently enrolls approximately 20,000 curriculum and continuing education students annually.

The main campus is made up of 144 acres off Victoria Road, and 22 buildings house academic programs and campus services. Included are three historic homes: Sunnicrest, one of George Vanderbilt's villas renovated to house the college's Business and Industry Services; the Smith-McDowell Museum, the oldest brick house in Buncombe County, which is leased to the Western North Carolina Historical Association; and Fernihurst, a circa-1875 mansion A-B Tech renovated. The college operates a campus in Madison County that offers adult education and college credit courses. A campus is now located at the Industrial Complex in western Buncombe County, in coordination with the BASF Company.

### BLUE RIDGE COMMUNITY COLLEGE
### BREVARD CAMPUS
1030 Asheville Hwy. and Osburn Road, Brevard
(828) 883-2520
www.blueridge.edu
In the fall of 1997, BRCC in Transylvania County moved to its new, conveniently located campus on the north side of Brevard. The building, which once housed an elementary school, was renovated to become the college's Transylvania Center and include a student center, a science lab, and computer labs. The space also houses an adult high school program, an industrial maintenance program, and classrooms for curricula programs and continuing education classes.

Regular curricula programs include business administration, health unit coordinator, horticulture, office systems technology, and college transfer. In addition the college offers all prerequisites for any BRCC program, including the Associate Degree Nursing program.

## BLUE RIDGE COMMUNITY COLLEGE
## FLAT ROCK CAMPUS
**181 West Campus Dr., Flat Rock**
**(828) 692-3572**
**www.blueridge.edu**

BRCC was established in 1969 with campuses in both Henderson and Transylvania counties. The college offers academic credit programs leading to associate degrees, vocational diplomas, and vocational certificates as well as a college transfer program. It enrolls approximately 1,600 curriculum students and serves around 12,000 with both job-related and continuing education courses. In 1997 BRCC opened its Allied Health and Human Services Building. This 66,000-square-foot building houses the Associate Degree Nursing, Surgical Technology, Health Unit Coordinator, Certified Nursing Assistant, Emergency Medical Technician, Cosmetology, and Early Childhood Development Center. The Office for Student Services anchors the building.

The college works closely with area businesses to develop special programs needed by new industries, and its Small Business Center holds workshops, seminars, and classes to aid new and existing businesses and professions.

The college also provides the community with various cultural programs. One of the most popular is the Blue Ridge Concert Series, which brings outstanding artists to the college at affordable prices. (For more information on these events, see our Arts and Culture chapter.)

## ISOTHERMAL COMMUNITY COLLEGE
**1255 West Mills St., Columbus**
**(828) 894-3092**
**www.isothermal.cc.nc.us**

This two-year institution, chartered in 1964 to serve the people of Polk and Rutherford counties, offers associate of arts and associate of science degrees in 22 areas of study transferable to four-year colleges and universities. It also serves its communities with technical, vocational, and continuing educational programs, and its libraries are open to the public.

The main 132-acre campus, which serves almost 58,000 students, is at Spindale in Rutherford County. The radio station, WNCW, operates out of the main campus. It is outside the geographic scope of this book, but our coverage does include the 11-acre Polk County satellite campus, located on property adjacent to St. Luke's Hospital in Columbus, which serves some 1,500 students. It offers curriculum classes in business administration, administrative office technology, computers, and liberal arts. There is also a wide range of continuing education classes, which include training for nurses' aids, emergency medical technicians, and fire and rescue personnel. Lifelong learning enrichment courses include art, piano, jazz, languages, genealogy, Appalachian/North Carolina history and folklore, other history-related subjects, investing, fitness, classic films, and English as a second language classes. The college also sponsors periodic special events for the community.

## SHAW UNIVERSITY
**31 College Place, Asheville**
**(828) 252-7635**
**www.shawuniversity.edu**

Shaw University is the oldest historically black university in the South. Its main campus is located in the state capital of Raleigh. The university was founded in 1865. The Asheville campus is located in the former Allen Center, which originally was established as a finishing school for African-American women.

Two colleges, one school, and 10 departments constitute a variety of academic offerings that are geared toward today's employment market. Evening classes are offered to the non-traditional student.

The Center for Alternative Programs of Education (CAPE) allows adult students in nine cities across North Carolina the opportunity to pursue an academic degree through flexible course scheduling and credit for prior learning experiences. Approximately 2,700 students from the United States, the Caribbean, African countries, and the Middle East attend Shaw University.

## SOUTH COLLEGE
**1567 Patton Ave., Asheville**
**(828) 252-2486**
**www.southcollegenc.com**
Until moving to an eight-acre site west of the city in 1977, South College, formerly known as Cecils College, had been a landmark in downtown Asheville. Founded in 1905 by Robert Talmadge Cecil, the college was well known as a business school, primarily providing secretarial training. Mr. Cecil owned the college until his death in 1956. Through the years Cecils College was owned by a succession of out-of-state corporations operating similar small business colleges elsewhere. In 1972 Cecils College finally returned to ownership by a North Carolina-based, family-owned corporation, Executive Schools Inc. On Nov. 1, 1998, the college was acquired by a family member who formed a new ownership corporation, South College of North Carolina.

The college is accredited as a junior college by the Accrediting Council for Independent Colleges and Schools and is licensed by the Board of Governors of the University System of North Carolina to confer the degree of applied science. The associate of applied science degree is awarded to South graduates in the areas of business administration, computer information systems, medical assisting, office administration, accounting, and paralegal studies.

# SOUTHERN MOUNTAINS

## Universities

### WESTERN CAROLINA UNIVERSITY
**Hwy. 107, Cullowhee**
**(828) 227-7211, (800) 928-2369**
**www.wcu.edu**
Founded by Professor Robert Lee Madison in 1889 as a semipublic community school to train teachers, Western Carolina University has grown and evolved over the years to become one of the most technologically advanced campuses in the country. The approximately 6,700 students that make up Western's student body hail from North Carolina's mountains and from other regions of the state, the country, and the world.

Undergraduate students may choose from more than 80 majors in one of the four colleges: Applied Sciences, Arts and Sciences, Business, and Education and Allied Professions. Students interested in careers in engineering, law, medicine, dentistry, optometry, veterinary medicine, and pharmacy may enroll in pre-professional programs. The graduate school offers more than 50 programs leading to a master's degree, educational specialist degree, and the doctor of education degree.

A faculty of 330 leads WCU's rigorous academic program. Classes are small enough that individual effort can be recognized and encouraged. The residential Honors College offers a rare learning environment for gifted students.

Numerous service and research centers at WCU serve Western North Carolina, including the Mountain Resource Center, Highlands Biological Station, and the Mountain Aquaculture Research Center. Western's centers in Asheville and Cherokee extend graduate and undergraduate programs to the region.

The use of nine multimedia electronic classrooms puts WCU at the national forefront in the use of educational technology, leading Cullowhee to be called the "most wired" small town in North Carolina.

Western's 230-acre main campus in Cullowhee sits in a beautiful valley between the Blue Ridge and Smoky Mountains, with world-class outdoor recreation opportunities just minutes away. The 8,000-seat Liston B. Ramsey Regional Activity Center regularly hosts national-caliber sports and entertainment events. The university's Lectures, Concerts and Exhibitions Series brings music, dance, and theatrical productions to campus each year. WCU's own department of communication and theater arts stages its own high-quality plays, and Western's galleries maintain a regular schedule of art exhibitions.

Western's Mountain Heritage Center depicts the natural and cultural heritage of the southern Appalachian region through exhibitions, publications, educational programs, and demonstrations. Mountain Heritage Day, WCU's annual celebration of the mountain spirit, draws more than 30,000 visitors to the campus on the last Sat of each Sept.

## Two-Year Colleges

### HAYWOOD COMMUNITY COLLEGE
**185 Freelander Dr., Clyde**
**(828) 627-4500, (828) 627-2821**
**www.haywood.edu**

Haywood's facilities are impressive. The 83-acre campus features a student center with a 1,100-seat auditorium and the Regional High Technology Center—one of only two in the state. The Learning Resource Center houses more than 25,000 books, 167 serial subscriptions, and 38,000 microfiche, and offers video- and audiotaping services. Computerized searches of indexes and abstracts are available, as well as an online interlibrary loan service. The beautiful campus also includes a horticulture complex with greenhouses, a dwarf conifer garden, a millhouse with a fishpond, a rhododendron garden, an extensive arboretum, a commercial sawmill and dry kiln, and a 320-acre teaching forest.

Programs take from one semester to two years to complete and lead to a certificate, diploma, or an associate degree in such fields as business administration, engineering technologies, natural resources, human services, and professional crafts. (See our Mountain Crafts chapter for more on the crafts program.) Students also learn skilled trades like welding, plumbing, and electrical installation.

Continuing education programs include GED certification, business and industry training courses, crafts, and emergency medical training. The college also offers small business and occupational training courses.

### SOUTHWESTERN COMMUNITY COLLEGE
**477 College Dr., Sylva**
**(828) 586-4091**
**www.southwest.cc.nc.us**

Established in 1964 to serve Swain, Jackson, and Macon counties and the Cherokee Indian Reservation, SCC combines a strong vocational-technical program with general education. Its student body of 1,700 attends classes both on its main 57-acre campus between Webster and Sylva on Highway 116 and at centers in Bryson City, Cashiers, Cherokee, and Franklin.

The centers in Franklin are listed as the Macon Center and the Business Assistance Center. The third center in Macon County is the Public Safety Training Center. It is located between Franklin and Otto at the Macon County Industrial Park.

The programs, courses, and activities, offered in day, evening, and weekend classes, prepare students for the workforce by helping them qualify for jobs in new or existing industries and by providing specific skills training. There are also courses leading to the college's degree programs and transfer courses as well as GED and continuing education classes in such subjects as basic investment, weaving, computers, CPR certification, law enforcement, fire-and-rescue training, and a National Park Service program. In 1999 SCC added programs in speech and language, literacy, pathology assistant, and environmental science technology.

### TRI-COUNTY COMMUNITY COLLEGE
**4600 U.S. Hwy. 64 East, Murphy**
**(828) 837-6810 (Peachtree Campus)**
**(828) 479-9256 (Robbinsville Campus)**
**(828) 321-2300 (Andrews Site)**
**www.tccc.cc.nc.us**

This Murphy-based college was originally an extension of the Asheville-Buncombe Technical College, but in 1967 it became an individual unit called the Tri-County Industrial Educational Center. When the state approved its college-transfer program in 1978, its status was upgraded to the Tri-County Community College.

The college serves students primarily from Cherokee, Clay, and Graham counties at its two campuses in the Peachtree community of Cherokee County and in Robbinsville and offers classes at a site in Andrews. It offers college-transfer and technical and vocational programs, including certificates in real-estate appraisal and horticulture, diplomas in cosmetology and welding, and associate degrees in applied science, accounting, general business, health, nursing, and emergency medical services. The continuing education department offers basic skills programs, occupational extension courses, firefighter training, and community service classes, including cooking classes, craft, and painting courses. A small-business center has opened at the college to help increase the success rate and number of small businesses in the area. Many services and seminars are offered here at little or no cost.

The child care center at the TCCC's Peachtree campus offers model day-care program care for 45 children. It has been rated five stars, the highest rating possible, by the North Carolina Day Care regulatory commission.

## PREPARATORY SCHOOLS

### THE ASHEVILLE SCHOOL
360 Asheville School Rd., Asheville
(828) 254-6345
www.ashevilleschool.org

Set on a commanding hill sheltered by woods, the Asheville School is the personification of tradition. This venerable preparatory school was founded in 1900 on the western edge of Asheville. The campus is dotted with majestic trees and graced with architecture from another era, each building having a distinct history. Stately, rambling structures, known in the early days simply as the "House" and the "School," were the heart of the campus, providing basic student housing and classroom instruction. Anthony Lord, an Asheville native and noted architect, designed three of the most beautiful structures on the campus: the Crawford Music House and the Howard Bement House in 1937 and Memorial Hall in 1947. The newest additions to Asheville School architecture in the 1980s and '90s maintain the artistic integrity of existing structures. The school was named to the National Register of Historic Places in 1996.

The rich heritage of this traditionally male boarding school has seen a number of additions brought on by a changing society. The Asheville School is now coeducational, with an average of 200 students, 60 percent male and 40 percent female. Around 17 states and 13 foreign countries are represented.

### CAROLINA DAY SCHOOL
1345 Hendersonville Rd., Asheville
(828) 274-0757
www.cdschool.org

Carolina Day School, on 28 acres just 15 minutes south of Asheville, is a nonsectarian, coeducational, independent school with approximately 500 students, ranging from prekindergarten to grade 12. The present school, formed by the merger in 1987 of Asheville Country Day School (founded in 1936) and St. Genevieve/Gibbons Hall (founded in 1905) carries on traditions of both schools.

### CHRIST SCHOOL
500 Christ School Rd., Arden
(828) 684-6232
www.christschool.org

This Episcopal prep school for boys in grades 8 through 12 is 9 miles south of Asheville, 12 miles north of Hendersonville, and 20 miles northeast of Brevard. There are 160 boarding students from 15 states and eight foreign countries. With 18 of the 30 faculty members living on campus, Christ School offers a true sense of community.

The school prides itself on the statement that "teachers at Christ School are instructors, advisors, coaches, mentors, and friends." The core campus and faculty homes make up a small part of the beautifully landscaped, 500-acre wooded campus. Chapel bells ring out daily, reminders of the school's strong emphasis on spiritual growth. The extensive campus acreage encourages a variety of team sports and outdoor activities, including cross-country, soccer, and football. Weekend trips to the surrounding mountains include Outward Bound–style rock climbing, backpacking, kayaking, rafting, and mountain biking as part of the regular outdoor program.

The school work program involves every student and fosters a sense of contributing to the community. Each student is responsible for maintaining upkeep of his personal dorm room, for performing a daily 20-minute task, and for joining in the regular Fri total campus cleanup.

The academic program at Christ School is designed to prepare boys for rigorous college programs.

## PUBLIC SCHOOLS

To register a child for school in North Carolina, a parent or legal guardian must present the child's birth certificate, up-to-date immunization record, and previous report cards, if the child was enrolled in another school system.

Western North Carolina public schooling ranges from larger urban schools to small country schoolhouses. Outside of Buncombe County, however, the schools tend to be smaller, and, obviously, more rural. Classes are usually small— 20 students being the average. Each system offers advanced placement courses, honors programs, and classes for the academically gifted. All public schools are fully accredited by the state of North Carolina and the Southern Association of Colleges and Schools.

**i** **The North Carolina Department of Public Instruction can be reached at (919) 715-1246.**

# INDEX

# INSIDERS' GUIDE®

The acclaimed travel series that has sold more than 2 million copies!

## Pointing You in the Right Direction

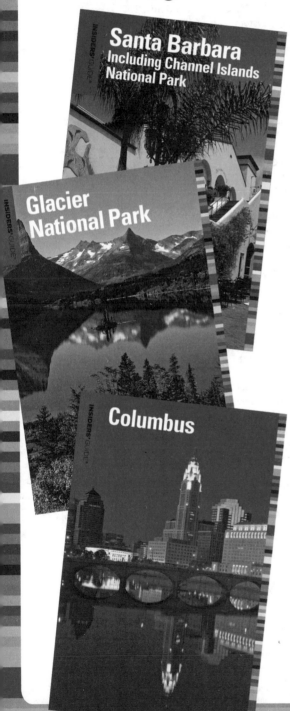

Santa Barbara
Including Channel Islands National Park

Glacier National Park

Columbus

INSIDERS' GUIDE

Columbus

North Carolina's Outer Banks

The Twin Cities

Pittsburgh

Savannah and Hilton Head

### Now with a fresh new look!

Written by locals and true insiders, each guide is packed with information about places to stay, restaurants, shopping, attractions, fun things for the kids, day trips, relocation tips, and local history. For over twenty years, travelers have relied on *Insiders' Guides* for practical and personal travel and relocation information.

To order call **800-243-0495**
or visit www.InsidersGuides.com